MANAGEMENT 97/98

Fifth Edition

Editor

Dr. Fred H. Maidment
Park College

Dr. Fred Maidment is associate professor and department chair of the Department of Business Education at Park College. He received his bachelor's degree from New York University in 1970 and his master's degree from Bernard M. Baruch College of the City University of New York. In 1983 he received his doctorate from the University of South Carolina. His research interests include training and development in industry. He resides in Kansas City, Missouri, with his wife and children.

Annual Editions
A Library of Information from the Public Press
Dushkin/McGraw·Hill
Sluice Dock, Guilford, Connecticut 06437

*Visit us on the Internet—*http://www.dushkin.com

The Annual Editions Series

ANNUAL EDITIONS is a series of over 65 volumes designed to provide the reader with convenient, low-cost access to a wide range of current, carefully selected articles from some of the most important magazines, newspapers, and journals published today. ANNUAL EDITIONS are updated on an annual basis through a continuous monitoring of over 300 periodical sources. All ANNUAL EDITIONS have a number of features that are designed to make them particularly useful, including topic guides, annotated tables of contents, unit overviews, and indexes. For the teacher using ANNUAL EDITIONS in the classroom, an Instructor's Resource Guide with test questions is available for each volume.

VOLUMES AVAILABLE

Abnormal Psychology
Adolescent Psychology
Africa
Aging
American Foreign Policy
American Government
American History, Pre-Civil War
American History, Post-Civil War
American Public Policy
Anthropology
Archaeology
Biopsychology
Business Ethics
Child Growth and Development
China
Comparative Politics
Computers in Education
Computers in Society
Criminal Justice
Criminology
Developing World
Deviant Behavior
Drugs, Society, and Behavior
Dying, Death, and Bereavement

Early Childhood Education
Economics
Educating Exceptional Children
Education
Educational Psychology
Environment
Geography
Global Issues
Health
Human Development
Human Resources
Human Sexuality
India and South Asia
International Business
Japan and the Pacific Rim
Latin America
Life Management
Macroeconomics
Management
Marketing
Marriage and Family
Mass Media
Microeconomics

Middle East and the
  Islamic World
Multicultural Education
Nutrition
Personal Growth and Behavior
Physical Anthropology
Psychology
Public Administration
Race and Ethnic Relations
Russia, the Eurasian Republics,
  and Central/Eastern Europe
Social Problems
Social Psychology
Sociology
State and Local Government
Urban Society
Western Civilization,
  Pre-Reformation
Western Civilization,
  Post-Reformation
Western Europe
World History, Pre-Modern
World History, Modern
World Politics

Cataloging in Publication Data
Main entry under title: Annual Editions: Management. 1997/98.
        1. Management—Periodicals. I. Maidment, Fred, *comp.* II. Title: Management.
    ISBN 0–697–37306–1   658'.05

Fifth Edition

Cover image ©1996 PhotoDisc, Inc.

Printed in the United States of America

Printed on Recycled Paper

Editors/Advisory Board

Members of the Advisory Board are instrumental in the final selection of articles for each edition of ANNUAL EDITIONS. Their review of articles for content, level, currentness, and appropriateness provides critical direction to the editor and staff. We think that you will find their careful consideration well reflected in this volume.

EDITOR

Fred H. Maidment
Park College

ADVISORY BOARD

Staff

Ian A. Nielsen, Publisher

To the Reader

In publishing ANNUAL EDITIONS we recognize the enormous role played by the magazines, newspapers, and journals of the *public press* in providing current, first-rate educational information in a broad spectrum of interest areas. Many of these articles are appropriate for students, researchers, and professionals seeking accurate, current material to help bridge the gap between principles and theories and the real world. These articles, however, become more useful for study when those of lasting value are carefully *collected, organized, indexed,* and *reproduced* in a *low-cost format,* which provides easy and permanent access when the material is needed. That is the role played by ANNUAL EDITIONS. Under the direction of each volume's *academic editor,* who is an expert in the subject area, and with the guidance of an *Advisory Board,* each year we seek to provide in each ANNUAL EDITION a current, well-balanced, carefully selected collection of the best of the public press for your study and enjoyment. We think that you will find this volume useful, and we hope that you will take a moment to let us know what you think.

Management is evolving into a highly exciting and diverse profession. Managers are the people charged with getting things done in today's society—a society that has been molded by the success of the management profession. The world faces many new challenges, and those challenges will be met, at least in part, by managers.

Managers must respond to a changing society by keeping informed on the developments in the field. The articles that have been chosen for *Annual Editions: Management 97/98* comprise a cross-section of the current writing on the subject, with a selected few classics. This collection addresses the various components of management, with emphasis on the functions of planning, organizing, directing, controlling, and staffing. Readings have been chosen from a wide variety of publications, including *The Harvard Business Review, Inc., Vital Speeches,* and *Business Week.*

This publication contains a number of features designed to make it useful for people interested in management. These features include a *Topic Guide* for locating articles on specific subject and a *Table of Contents* with *abstracts* that summarize each article, highlighting key ideas in bold italics. This volume is organized into seven units, each dealing with specific interrelated topics in manage-

ment. Each unit begins with an overview that provides the necessary background information that allows the reader to place the selections in the context of the book. Important topics are emphasized, and *challenge questions* address major themes. Also, at the end of each unit are short classic *cases and exercises* that are designed to easily and effectively implement and expand on the general topic of the unit.

This is the fifth edition of *Annual Editions: Management,* and I hope that it will be one of a long line of books addressing the evolution of management. This collection, I believe, provides the reader with the most complete and current selection of readings available on the subject. We would like to know what you think. Please take a few minutes to complete and return the postage-paid *article rating form* at the back of the volume. Any book can be improved, and we need your help to improve *Annual Editions: Management.*

Fred Maidment
Editor

Contents

UNIT 1

Managers, Performance, and the Environment

The six articles in this section examine some of the dynamics of management in today's business environment.

The concepts in bold italics are developed in the article. For further expansion please refer to the Topic Guide and the Index.

UNIT 2

Planning

Five articles in this section discuss the elements of planning, decision making, support systems, and strategic analysis.

UNIT 3

Organizing

In this section, six selections examine how organization impacts on the job of managing. Topics discussed include elements of organization, job design, and what is needed to fundamentally change a business.

The concepts in bold italics are developed in the article. For further expansion please refer to the Topic Guide and the Index.

UNIT 4

Directing

The seven selections in this
section examine how the
elements of communication,
leadership, motivation, and
performance contribute
to the art of directing a
business organization.

UNIT 5

Controlling

Six articles in this section
consider what makes up
effective control of the
business organization.

UNIT 6

Staffing and Human Resources

This section's six selections examine the elements necessarily considered when a workforce is developed.

The concepts in bold italics are developed in the article. For further expansion please refer to the Topic Guide and the Index.

UNIT 7

Perspectives and Trends

The ten articles in this section examine some of the current and future challenges faced by business. Topics include the multinational enterprise, small business management, social responsibility, and the future of a career in management.

Topic Guide

This topic guide suggests how the selections in this book relate to topics of traditional concern to students and professionals involved with the study of management. It is useful for locating articles that relate to each other for reading and research. The guide is arranged alphabetically according to topic. Articles may, of course, treat topics that do not appear in the topic guide. In turn, entries in the topic guide do not necessarily constitute a comprehensive listing of all the contents of each selection.

TOPIC AREA	TREATED IN	TOPIC AREA	TREATED IN
Business Ethics	4. Denny's Changes Its Spots 10. Dilbert's Management Handbook 17. When Is Virtual Virtuous? 22. Opening Up Books to Employees 28. Spies Like Us 32. Gannett's View on Managing Employees 33. Building a Global Workforce 36. "How Accommodating?" 37. Social Responsibility in Future Worlds 41. What's Your Story? 42. Privacy: Entitlement or Illusion? 43. Ethics for Hire 44. No More Sweetheart Deals	**Decision Making (continued)**	18. Abilene Paradox 19. Overload 21. Bill Gates and Paul Allen Talk 22. Opening Up Books to Employees 23. Failure of Participatory Management 24. Innovate or Evaporate 25. Meaning of Control 29. Why Markets Tolerate Mediocre Manufacturing 30. Business of Business Is People 31. Human Side of Enterprise 36. "How Accommodating?" 38. Pangs of Conscience 39. Leader of the Pack 42. Privacy: Entitlement or Illusion? 45. Taping Your Hidden Assets
Corporate Strategy/ Organization	2. 'Flashes of Genius' 3. Dr. Deming 4. Denny's Changes Its Spots 5. Learning to Change 6. New Millennium Workplace 7. Managerial Decision Making 8. Why Do Employees Resist Change? 9. Have a Ball 10. Dilbert's Management Handbook 11. Global Strategic Management 13. Of Things Fundamental 15. New Workplace 16. Buy-in to Change 17. When Is Virtual Virtuous? 19. Overload 20. Lead, Don't Manage 21. Bill Gates and Paul Allen Talk 23. Failure of Participatory Management 25. Meaning of Control 28. Spies Like Us 29. Why Markets Tolerate Mediocre Manufacturing 30. Business of Business Is People 32. Gannett's View on Managing Employees 33. Building a Global Workforce 36. "How Accommodating?" 38. Pangs of Conscience 39. Leader of the Pack 40. Writing a Winning Business Plan 41. What's Your Story? 44. No More Sweetheart Deals 45. Tapping Your Hidden Assets	**Employee Benefits**	14. Happiest Workers in the World 15. New Workplace 32. Gannett's View on Managing Employees 33. Building a Global Workforce 35. Labor's Last Stand 36. "How Accommodating?" 38. Pangs of Conscience
		Human Resources	3. Dr. Deming 4. Denny's Changes Its Spots 10. Dilbert's Management Handbook 12. Classifying the Elements of Work 14. Happiest Workers in the World 15. New Workplace 17. When Is Virtual Virtuous? 22. Opening Up Books to Employees 28. Spies Like Us 30. Business of Business Is People 31. Human Side of Enterprise 32. Gannett's View on Managing Employees 33. Building a Global Workforce 34. Labor Adversaries Bury the Hatchet 35. Labor's Last Stand 36. "How Accommodating?" 38. Pangs of Conscience 42. Privacy: Entitlement or Illusion? 46. Job Seekers
Decision Making	1. Manager's Job 2. 'Flashes of Genius' 3. Dr. Deming 4. Denny's Changes Its Spots 5. Learning to Change 7. Managerial Decision Making 8. Why Do Employees Resist Change? 9. Have a Ball 10. Dilbert's Management Handbook 13. Of Things Fundamental 16. Buy-in to Change 17. When Is Virtual Virtuous?	**Management Accountability**	1. Manager's Job 2. 'Flashes of Genius' 3. Dr. Deming 4. Denny's Changes Its Spots 5. Learning to Change 6. New Millennium Workplace 9. Have a Ball 10. Dilbert's Management Handbook 13. Of Things Fundamental 16. Buy-in to Change 17. When Is Virtual Virtuous? 18. Abilene Paradox 20. Lead, Don't Manage 21. Bill Gates and Paul Allen Talk

Managers, Performance, and the Environment

- Management Classic (Article 1)
- Managers and Management (Article 2)
- Management Skills, Roles, and Performance (Articles 3 and 4)
- The Environment (Articles 5 and 6)

The need for management has been recognized since the early days of civilization. The concepts of leadership, administration, and management have existed since at least before the time of Plato. Some of the early modern writers in management include Frederick W. Taylor, Elton Mayo, and Mary Parker Follett. These people helped to establish the basis of modern management theory during the first part of the twentieth century.

Management has come a long way since the days of Taylor, Mayo, and Follett. The techniques and theories that they and their successors helped to develop have contributed to the establishment of industrialized countries as major forces in the world. These ideas have helped American culture dominate the better part of this century, and the success of Western concepts is even now being seen in Eastern Europe and the republics of the former Soviet Union. Management—the way people arrange their lives and businesses—is a major part of the success that capitalism is currently enjoying. The failure that the communist system experienced in the former Soviet bloc was not a failure of industrialism; rather, it was a failure of a system that attempted to use that industrial base unsuccessfully. This was not a failure of the machines or the workers that comprised the system, but of the way the system operated and managed its equipment and people. It was a situation that people of those countries would no longer tolerate as they rushed to embrace capitalism, democracy, pluralism, and, finally, management, as a key to their future in the twenty-first century.

As a discipline, management faces new challenges. These challenges are mostly the result of management's success. They include the transformation of the American economy from one based upon industrialization to one based upon knowledge and the challenge of other economies, in particular the Japanese and the other "tigers" of the Pacific Rim, as well as the new integrated Europe. Another challenge is the new role of managers and management, with more women, African Americans, and other minorities, as well as a more demanding group of workers with different expectations entering the workforce.

Management is responding to these challenges in various ways. Many new ideas are constantly being projected in the midst of the chaos that is the legacy of the post–cold war world. Times have, indeed, changed, and the tools necessary to meet those changes are only now being developed, as may be seen in the article "Denny's Changes Its Spots." The new economy and the forms it will support will be very different from the environment of the past. As shown in "Learning to Change," the dominating strength of corporations will be based on brains, not brawn; the economic system will be international, not national, in scope; and competition will be even more fierce, while an organization's competitive advantage in the marketplace will be more fleeting. This is a result of the dependance upon ideas and creativity that is necessary to build and sustain organizations. Future organizations that think, create, and adapt to the changing conditions of an in-

creasingly fluid environment are the ones that will survive and be successful.

America's new economy, and the managers who plan, direct, organize, control, and staff its businesses, must provide new, different, and creative approaches to meet the new competitive global environment. This will require better products and services, produced and marketed with improved, more efficient methods. Organizations no longer compete only domestically, as they did in the 1950s, when General Motors, Ford, and Chrysler dominated an American auto industry that also included such names as Studebaker, Packard, Hudson, DeSoto, and Nash. Today, the same three top U.S. auto firms compete on an international basis with names like Nissan, Toyota, Honda, Volkswagen, and B.M.W. Corporations the world over must meet these new conditions or accept the fate of past organizations and follow Studebaker in its drive to oblivion.

Looking Ahead: Challenge Questions

Management, as a discipline, has evolved significantly during the twentieth century. What do you think will happen in the future?

Managers are learning that different situations require different skills and different approaches. How will this change the job of manager in the future?

Managers cannot change the external environment in which they must operate. In what ways do you think this environment will change during your life?

The Manager's Job: Folklore and Fact

The classical view says that the manager organizes, coordinates, plans, and controls; the facts suggest otherwise.

Henry Mintzberg

Henry Mintzberg is the Bronfman Professor of Management at McGill University. His latest book is Mintzberg on Management: Inside Our Strange World of Organizations *(Free Press, 1989). This article appeared originally in HBR July-August 1975. It won the McKinsey Award for excellence.*

If you ask managers what they do, they will most likely tell you that they plan, organize, coordinate, and control. Then watch what they do. Don't be surprised if you can't relate what you see to these words.

When a manager is told that a factory has just burned down and then advises the caller to see whether temporary arrangements can be made to supply customers through a foreign subsidiary, is that manager planning, organizing, coordinating, or controlling? How about when he or she presents a gold watch to a retiring employee? Or attends a conference to meet people in the trade and returns with an interesting new product idea for employees to consider?

These four words, which have dominated management vocabulary since the French industrialist Henri Fayol first introduced them in 1916, tell us little about what managers actually do. At best, they indicate some vague objectives managers have when they work.

The field of management, so devoted to progress and change, has for more than half a century not seriously addressed *the* basic question: What do managers do? Without a proper answer, how can we teach management? How can we design planning or information systems for managers? How can we improve the practice of management at all?

What do managers do? Even managers themselves don't always know.

Our ignorance of the nature of managerial work shows up in various ways in the modern organization—in boasts by successful managers who never spent a single day in a management training program; in the turnover of corporate planners who never quite understood what it was the manager wanted; in the computer consoles gathering dust in the back room because the managers never used the fancy on-line MIS some analyst thought they needed. Perhaps most important, our ignorance shows up in the inability of our large public organizations to come to grips with some of their most serious policy problems.

Somehow, in the rush to automate production, to use management science in the functional areas of marketing and finance, and to apply the skills of the behavioral scientist to the problem of worker motivation, the manager – the person in charge of the organization or one of its subunits – has been forgotten.

I intend to break the reader away from Fayol's words and introduce a more supportable and useful description of managerial work. This description derives from my review and synthesis of research on how various managers have spent their time.

In some studies, managers were observed intensively; in a number of others, they kept detailed diaries; in a few studies, their records were analyzed. All kinds of managers were studied – foremen, factory supervisors, staff managers, field sales managers, hospital administrators, presidents of companies and nations, and even street gang leaders. These "managers" worked in the United States, Canada, Sweden, and Great Britain.

A synthesis of these findings paints an interesting picture, one as different from Fayol's classical view as a cubist abstract is from a Renaissance painting. In a sense, this picture will be obvious to anyone who has ever spent a day in a manager's office, either in front of the desk or behind it. Yet, at the same time, this picture throws into doubt much of the folklore that we have accepted about the manager's work.

Folklore and Facts About Managerial Work

There are four myths about the manager's job that do not bear up under careful scrutiny of the facts.

Folklore: The manager is a reflective, systematic planner. The evidence on this issue is overwhelming, but not a shred of it supports this statement.

Fact: Study after study has shown that managers work at an unrelenting pace, that their activities are characterized by brevity, variety, and discontinuity, and that they are strongly oriented to action and dislike reflective activities. Consider this evidence:

Half the activities engaged in by the five chief executives of my study lasted less than nine minutes, and only 10% exceeded one hour.[1] A study of 56 U.S. foremen found that they averaged 583 activities per eight-hour shift, an average of 1 every 48 seconds.[2]

How often can you work for a half an hour without interruption?

The work pace for both chief executives and foremen was unrelenting. The chief executives met a steady stream of callers and mail from the moment they arrived in the morning until they left in the evening. Coffee breaks and lunches were inevitably work re-

lated, and ever-present subordinates seemed to usurp any free moment.

A diary study of 160 British middle and top managers found that they worked without interruption for a half hour or more only about once every two days.[3]

Of the verbal contacts the chief executives in my study engaged in, 93% were arranged on an ad hoc basis. Only 1% of the executives' time was spent in open-ended observational tours. Only 1 out of 368 verbal contacts was unrelated to a specific issue and could therefore be called general planning. Another researcher found that "in *not one single case* did a manager report obtaining important external information from a general conversation or other undirected personal communication."[4]

Is this the planner that the classical view describes? Hardly. The manager is simply responding to the pressures of the job. I found that my chief executives terminated many of their own activities, often leaving meetings before the end, and interrupted their desk work to call in subordinates. One president not only placed his desk so that he could look down a long hallway but also left his door open when he was alone – an invitation for subordinates to come in and interrupt him.

Clearly, these managers wanted to encourage the flow of current information. But more significantly, they seemed to be conditioned by their own work loads. They appreciated the opportunity cost of their own time, and they were continually aware of their ever-present obligations – mail to be answered, callers to attend to, and so on. It seems that a manager is always plagued by the possibilities of what might be done and what must be done.

When managers must plan, they seem to do so implicitly in the context of daily actions, not in some abstract process reserved for two weeks in the organization's mountain retreat. The plans of the chief executives I studied seemed to exist only in their heads – as flexible, but often specific, intentions. The traditional literature notwithstanding, the job of managing does not breed reflective planners; managers respond to stimuli, they are conditioned by their jobs to prefer live to delayed action.

Folklore: The effective manager has no regular duties to perform. Managers are constantly being told to spend more time planning and delegating and less time seeing customers and engaging in negotiations. These are not, after all, the true tasks of the manager. To use the popular analogy, the good manager, like the good conductor, carefully orchestrates everything in advance, then sits back, responding occasionally to an unforeseeable exception. But here again the pleasant abstraction just does not seem to hold up.

Fact: Managerial work involves performing a number of regular duties, including ritual and cere-

mony, negotiations, and processing of soft information that links the organization with its environment. Consider some evidence from the research:

A study of the work of the presidents of small
companies found that they engaged in routine activities because their companies could not afford staff
specialists and were so thin on operating personnel
that a single absence often required the president to
substitute.[5]

One study of field sales managers and another of
chief executives suggest that it is a natural part of
both jobs to see important customers, assuming the
managers wish to keep those customers.[6]

Someone, only half in jest, once described the manager as the person who sees visitors so that other people can get their work done. In my study, I found that
certain ceremonial duties – meeting visiting dignitaries, giving out gold watches, presiding at Christ-
mas dinners – were an intrinsic part of the chief
executive's job.

Studies of managers' information flow suggest that
managers play a key role in securing "soft" external
information (much of it available only to them because of their status) and in passing it along to their
subordinates.

*Folklore: The senior manager needs aggregated in-
formation, which a formal management information system best provides.* Not too long ago, the
words *total information system* were everywhere in
the management literature. In keeping with the classical view of the manager as that individual perched
on the apex of a regulated, hierarchical system, the
literature's manager was to receive all important information from a giant, comprehensive MIS.

But lately, these giant MIS systems are not
working – managers are simply not using them. The
enthusiasm has waned. A look at how managers actually process information makes it clear why.

*Fact: Managers strongly favor verbal media, tele-
phone calls and meetings, over documents.* Consider
the following:

In two British studies, managers spent an average
of 66% and 80% of their time in verbal (oral) commu-

Today's gossip may be tomorrow's fact – that's why managers cherish hearsay.

---

nication.[7] In my study of five American chief executives, the figure was 78%.

These five chief executives treated mail processing
as a burden to be dispensed with. One came in Saturday morning to process 142 pieces of mail in just over
three hours, to "get rid of all the stuff." This same

manager looked at the first piece of "hard" mail he
had received all week, a standard cost report, and put
it aside with the comment, "I never look at this."

These same five chief executives responded immediately to 2 of the 40 routine reports they received
during the five weeks of my study and to 4 items in
the 104 periodicals. They skimmed most of these periodicals in seconds, almost ritualistically. In all,
these chief executives of good-sized organizations
initiated on their own – that is, not in response to
something else – a grand total of 25 pieces of mail
during the 25 days I observed them.

An analysis of the mail the executives received reveals an interesting picture – only 13% was of specific and immediate use. So now we have another
piece in the puzzle: not much of the mail provides
live, current information – the action of a competitor,
the mood of a government legislator, or the rating of
last night's television show. Yet this is the information that drove the managers, interrupting their
meetings and rescheduling their workdays.

Consider another interesting finding. Managers
seem to cherish "soft" information, especially gossip, hearsay, and speculation. Why? The reason is its
timeliness; today's gossip may be tomorrow's fact.
The manager who misses the telephone call revealing that the company's biggest customer was seen
golfing with a main competitor may read about a dramatic drop in sales in the next quarterly report. But
then it's too late.

To assess the value of historical, aggregated, "hard"
MIS information, consider two of the manager's
prime uses for information – to identify problems
and opportunities[8] and to build mental models (e.g.,
how the organization's budget system works, how
customers buy products, how changes in the economy affect the organization). The evidence suggests
that the manager identifies decision situations and
builds models not with the aggregated abstractions
an MIS provides but with specific tidbits of data.

Consider the words of Richard Neustadt, who
studied the information-collecting habits of Presidents Roosevelt, Truman, and Eisenhower: "It is not
information of a general sort that helps a President
see personal stakes; not summaries, not surveys, not
the *bland amalgams*. Rather...it is the odds and ends
of *tangible detail* that pieced together in his mind
illuminate the underside of issues put before him.
To help himself he must reach out as widely as he
can for every scrap of fact, opinion, gossip, bearing
on his interests and relationships as President. He
must become his own director of his own central
intelligence."[9]

The manager's emphasis on this verbal media
raises two important points. First, verbal information is stored in the brains of people. Only when people write this information down can it be stored in

the files of the organization—whether in metal cabinets or on magnetic tape—and managers apparently do not write down much of what they hear. Thus the strategic data bank of the organization is not in the memory of its computers but in the minds of its managers.

Second, managers' extensive use of verbal media helps to explain why they are reluctant to delegate tasks. It is not as if they can hand a dossier over to subordinates; they must take the time to "dump memory"—to tell subordinates all about the subject. But this could take so long that managers may find it easier to do the task themselves. Thus they are damned by their own information system to a "dilemma of delegation"—to do too much or to delegate to subordinates with inadequate briefing.

Folklore: Management is, or at least is quickly becoming, a science and a profession. By almost any definition of *science* and *profession*, this statement is false. Brief observation of any manager will quickly lay to rest the notion that managers practice a science. A science involves the enaction of systematic, analytically determined procedures or programs. If we do not even know what procedures managers use, how can we prescribe them by scientific analysis? And how can we call management a profession if we cannot specify what managers are to learn? For after all, a profession involves "knowledge of some department of learning or science" *(Random House Dictionary).*[10]

Fact: The managers' programs—to schedule time, process information, make decisions, and so on—remain locked deep inside their brains. Thus, to describe these programs, we rely on words like *judgment* and *intuition*, seldom stopping to realize that they are merely labels for our ignorance.

I was struck during my study by the fact that the

Research on Managerial Work

In seeking to describe managerial work, I conducted my own research and also scanned the literature to integrate the findings of studies from many diverse sources with my own. These studies focused on two different aspects of managerial work. Some were concerned with the characteristics of work—how long managers work, where, at what pace, with what interruptions, with whom they work, and through what media they communicate. Other studies were concerned with the content of work—what activities the managers actually carry out, and why. Thus, after a meeting, one researcher might note that the manager spent 45 minutes with three government officials in their Washington office, while another might record that the manager presented the company's stand on some proposed legislation in order to change a regulation.

A few of the studies of managerial work are widely known, but most have remained buried as single journal articles or isolated books. Among the more important ones I cite are:

☐ Sune Carlson developed the diary method to study the work characteristics of nine Swedish managing directors. Each kept a detailed log of his activities. Carlson's results are reported in his book *Executive Behaviour.* A number of British researchers, notably Rosemary Stewart, have subsequently used Carlson's method. In *Managers and Their Jobs,* she describes the study of 160 top and middle managers of British companies.

☐ Leonard Sayles's book *Managerial Behavior* is another important reference. Using a method he refers to as "anthropological," Sayles studied the work content of middle and lower level managers in a large U.S. corporation. Sayles moved freely in the company, collecting whatever information struck him as important.

☐ Perhaps the best-known source is *Presidential Power,* in which Richard Neustadt analyzes the power and managerial behavior of Presidents Roosevelt, Truman, and Eisenhower. Neustadt used secondary sources—documents and interviews with other parties.

☐ Robert H. Guest, in *Personnel,* reports on a study of the foreman's working day. Fifty-six U.S. foremen were observed and each of their activities recorded during one eight-hour shift.

☐ Richard C. Hodgson, Daniel J. Levinson, and Abraham Zaleznik studied a team of three top executives of a U.S. hospital. From that study they wrote *The Executive Role Constellation.* They addressed the way in which work and socioemotional roles were divided among the three managers.

☐ William F. Whyte, from his study of a street gang during the Depression, wrote *Street Corner Society.* His findings about the gang's workings and leadership, which George C. Homans analyzed in *The Human Group,* suggest interesting similarities of job content between street gang leaders and corporate managers.

My own study involved five American CEOs of middle- to large-sized organizations—a consulting firm, a technology company, a hospital, a consumer goods company, and a school system. Using a method called "structural observation," during one intensive week of observation for each executive, I recorded various aspects of every piece of mail and every verbal contact. In all, I analyzed 890 pieces of incoming and outgoing mail and 368 verbal contacts.

executives I was observing—all very competent—are fundamentally indistinguishable from their counterparts of a hundred years ago (or a thousand years ago). The information they need differs, but they seek it in the same way—by word of mouth. Their decisions concern modern technology, but the procedures they use to make those decisions are the same as the procedures used by nineteenth century managers. Even the computer, so important for the specialized work of the organization, has apparently had no influence on the work procedures of general managers. In fact, the manager is in a kind of loop, with increasingly heavy work pressures but no aid forthcoming from management science.

Considering the facts about managerial work, we can see that the manager's job is enormously complicated and difficult. Managers are overburdened with obligations yet cannot easily delegate their tasks. As a result, they are driven to overwork and forced to do many tasks superficially. Brevity, fragmentation, and verbal communication characterize their work. Yet these are the very characteristics of managerial work that have impeded scientific attempts to improve it. As a result, management scientists have concentrated on the specialized functions of the organization, where it is easier to analyze the procedures and quantify the relevant information.[11]

But the pressures of a manager's job are becoming worse. Where before managers needed to respond only to owners and directors, now they find that subordinates with democratic norms continually reduce their freedom to issue unexplained orders, and a growing number of outside influences (consumer groups, government agencies, and so on) demand attention. Managers have had nowhere to turn for help. The first step in providing such help is to find out what the manager's job really is.

Back to a Basic Description of Managerial Work

Earlier, I defined the manager as that person in charge of an organization or subunit. Besides CEOs, this definition would include vice presidents, bishops, foremen, hockey coaches, and prime ministers. All these "managers" are vested with formal authority over an organizational unit. From formal authority comes status, which leads to various interpersonal relations, and from these comes access to information. Information, in turn, enables the manager to make decisions and strategies for the unit.

The manager's job can be described in terms of various "roles," or organized sets of behaviors identified with a position. My description, shown in "The Manager's Roles," comprises ten roles. As we shall see, formal authority gives rise to the three interpersonal roles, which in turn give rise to the three informa-

The Manager's Roles

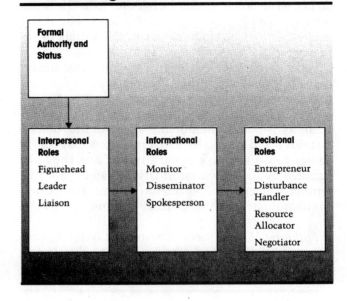

tional roles; these two sets of roles enable the manager to play the four decisional roles.

Interpersonal Roles

Three of the manager's roles arise directly from formal authority and involve basic interpersonal relationships. First is the *figurehead* role. As the head of an organizational unit, every manager must perform some ceremonial duties. The president greets the touring dignitaries. The foreman attends the wedding of a lathe operator. The sales manager takes an important customer to lunch.

The chief executives of my study spent 12% of their contact time on ceremonial duties; 17% of their incoming mail dealt with acknowledgments and requests related to their status. For example, a letter to a company president requested free merchandise for a crippled schoolchild; diplomas that needed to be signed were put on the desk of the school superintendent.

Duties that involve interpersonal roles may sometimes be routine, involving little serious communication and no important decision making. Nevertheless, they are important to the smooth functioning of an organization and cannot be ignored.

Managers are responsible for the work of the people of their unit. Their actions in this regard constitute the *leader* role. Some of these actions involve leadership directly—for example, in most organizations the managers are normally responsible for hiring and training their own staff.

In addition, there is the indirect exercise of the leader role. For example, every manager must moti-

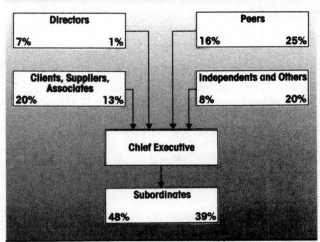

The Chief Executive's Contacts

Directors		Peers	
7%	1%	16%	25%

Clients, Suppliers, Associates		Independents and Others	
20%	13%	8%	20%

Chief Executive

Subordinates

48%   39%

Note: The first figure indicates the proportion of total contact time spent with each group and the second figure, the proportion of mail from each group.

vate and encourage employees, somehow reconciling their individual needs with the goals of the organization. In virtually every contact with the manager, subordinates seeking leadership clues ask: "Does she approve?" "How would she like the report to turn out?" "Is she more interested in market share than high profits?"

The influence of managers is most clearly seen in the leader role. Formal authority vests them with great potential power; leadership determines in large part how much of it they will realize.

The literature of management has always recognized the leader role, particularly those aspects of it related to motivation. In comparison, until recently it has hardly mentioned the *liaison* role, in which the manager makes contacts outside the vertical chain of command. This is remarkable in light of the finding of virtually every study of managerial work that managers spend as much time with peers and other people outside their units as they do with their own subordinates—and, surprisingly, very little time with their own superiors.

In Rosemary Stewart's diary study, the 160 British middle and top managers spent 47% of their time with peers, 41% of their time with people inside their unit, and only 12% of their time with their superiors. For Robert H. Guest's study of U.S. foremen, the figures were 44%, 46%, and 10%. The chief executives of my study averaged 44% of their contact time with people outside their organizations, 48% with subordinates, and 7% with directors and trustees.

The contacts the five CEOs made were with an incredibly wide range of people: subordinates; clients, business associates, and suppliers; and peers—managers of similar organizations, government and trade organization officials, fellow directors on outside boards, and independents with no relevant organizational affiliations. The chief executives' time with and mail from these groups is shown in "The Chief Executive's Contacts." Guest's study of foremen shows, likewise, that their contacts were numerous and wide-ranging, seldom involving fewer than 25 individuals, and often more than 50.

Informational Roles

By virtue of interpersonal contacts, both with subordinates and with a network of contacts, the manager emerges as the nerve center of the organizational unit. The manager may not know everything but typically knows more than subordinates do.

Studies have shown this relationship to hold for all managers, from street gang leaders to U.S. presidents. In *The Human Group*, George C. Homans explains how, because they were at the center of the information flow in their own gangs and were also in close touch with other gang leaders, street gang leaders were better informed than any of their followers.[12] As for presidents, Richard Neustadt observes: "The essence of [Franklin] Roosevelt's technique for information-gathering was competition. 'He would call you in,' one of his aides once told me, 'and he'd ask you to get the story on some complicated business, and you'd come back after a couple of days of hard labor and present the juicy morsel you'd uncovered under a stone somewhere, and *then* you'd find out he knew all about it, along with something else you *didn't* know. Where he got this information from he wouldn't mention, usually, but after he had done this to you once or twice you got damn careful about *your* information.' "[13]

We can see where Roosevelt "got this information" when we consider the relationship between the interpersonal and informational roles. As leader, the manager has formal and easy access to every staff member. In addition, liaison contacts expose the manager to external information to which subordinates often lack access. Many of these contacts are with other managers of equal status, who are themselves nerve centers in their own organization. In this way, the manager develops a powerful database of information.

Processing information is a key part of the manager's job. In my study, the CEOs spent 40% of their contact time on activities devoted exclusively to the transmission of information; 70% of their incoming mail was purely informational (as opposed to requests for action). Managers don't leave meetings or hang up the telephone to get back to work. In large part, communication *is* their work. Three roles describe these informational aspects of managerial work.

As *monitor*, the manager is perpetually scanning

Retrospective Commentary

Henry Mintzberg

Over the years, one reaction has dominated the comments I have received from managers who read "The Manager's Job: Folklore and Fact": "You make me feel so good. I thought all those other managers were planning, organizing, coordinating, and controlling, while I was busy being interrupted, jumping from one issue to another, and trying to keep the lid on the chaos." Yet everything in this article must have been patently obvious to these people. Why such a reaction to reading what they already knew?

Conversely, how to explain the very different reaction of two media people who called to line up interviews after an article based on this one appeared in the *New York Times.* "Are we glad someone finally let managers have it," both said in passing, a comment that still takes me aback. True, they had read only the account in the *Times,* but that no more let managers have it than did this article. Why that reaction?

One explanation grows out of the way I now see this article—as proposing not so much another view of management as another face of it. I like to call it the insightful face, in contrast to the long-dominant professional or cerebral face. One stresses commitment, the other calculation; one sees the world with integrated perspective, the other figures it as the components of a portfolio. The cerebral face operates with the words and numbers of rationality; the insightful face is rooted in the images and feel of a manager's integrity.

Each of these faces implies a different kind of "knowing," and that, I believe, explains many managers' reaction to this article. Rationally, they "knew" what managers did—planned, organized, coordinated, and controlled. But deep down that did not feel quite right. The description in this article may have come closer to what they really "knew." As for those media people, they weren't railing against management as such but against the cerebral form of management, so pervasive, that they saw impersonalizing the world around them.

In practice, management has to be two-faced—there has to be a balance between the cerebral and the insightful. So, for example, I realized originally that managerial communication was largely oral and that the advent of the computer had not changed anything fundamental in the executive suite—a conclusion I continue to hold. (The greatest threat the personal computer poses is that managers will take it seriously and come to believe that they can manage by remaining in their offices and looking at displays of digital characters.) But I also thought that the dilemma of delegating could be dealt with by periodic debriefings—

disseminating words. Now, however, I believe that managers need more ways to convey the images and impressions they carry inside of them. This explains the renewed interest in strategic vision, in culture, and in the roles of intuition and insight in management.

The ten roles I used to describe the manager's job also reflect management's cerebral face, in that they decompose the job more than capture the integration. Indeed, my effort to show a sequence among these roles now seems more consistent with the traditional face of management work than an insightful one. Might we not just as well say that people throughout the organization take actions that inform managers who, by making sense of those actions, develop images and visions that inspire people to subsequent efforts?

Perhaps my greatest disappointment about the research reported here is that it did not stimulate new efforts. In a world so concerned with management, much of the popular literature is superficial and the academic research pedestrian. Certainly, many studies have been carried out over the last 15 years, but the vast majority sought to replicate earlier research. In particular, we remain grossly ignorant about the fundamental content of the manager's job and have barely addressed the major issues and dilemmas in its practice.

But superficiality is not only a problem of the literature. It is also an occupational hazard of the manager's job. Originally, I believed this problem could be dealt with; now I see it as inherent in the job. This is because managing insightfully depends on the direct experience and personal knowledge that come from intimate contact. But in organizations grown larger and more diversified, that becomes difficult to achieve. And so managers turn increasingly to the cerebral face, and the delicate balance between the two faces is lost.

Certainly, some organizations manage to sustain their humanity despite their large size—as Tom Peters and Robert Waterman show in their book *In Search of Excellence.* But that book attained its outstanding success precisely because it is about the exceptions, about the organizations so many of us long to be a part of—not the organizations in which we actually work.

Fifteen years ago, I stated that "No job is more vital to our society than that of the manager. It is the manager who determines whether our social institutions serve us well or whether they squander our talents and resources." Now, more than ever, we must strip away the folklore of the manager's job and begin to face its difficult facts.

the environment for information, interrogating liaison contacts and subordinates, and receiving unsolicited information, much of it as a result of the network of personal contacts. Remember that a good part of the information the manager collects in the monitor role arrives in verbal form, often as gossip, hearsay, and speculation.

In the *disseminator* role, the manager passes some privileged information directly to subordinates, who would otherwise have no access to it. When subordinates lack easy contact with one another, the manager may pass information from one to another.

In the *spokesperson* role, the manager sends some information to people outside the unit—a president makes a speech to lobby for an organization cause, or a foreman suggests a product modification to a supplier. In addition, as a spokesperson, every manager must inform and satisfy the influential people who control the organizational unit. For the foreman, this may simply involve keeping the plant manager informed about the flow of work through the shop.

The president of a large corporation, however, may spend a great amount of time dealing with a host of influences. Directors and shareholders must be advised about finances; consumer groups must be assured that the organization is fulfilling its social responsibilities; and government officials must be satisfied that the organization is abiding by the law.

Decisional Roles

Information is not, of course, an end in itself; it is the basic input to decision making. One thing is clear in the study of managerial work: the manager plays the major role in the unit's decision-making system. As its formal authority, only the manager can commit the unit to important new courses of action; and as its nerve center, only the manager has full and current information to make the set of decisions that determines the unit's strategy. Four roles describe the manager as decision maker.

As *entrepreneur*, the manager seeks to improve the unit, to adapt it to changing conditions in the environment. In the monitor role, a president is constantly on the lookout for new ideas. When a good one appears, he initiates a development project that he may supervise himself or delegate to an employee (perhaps with the stipulation that he must approve the final proposal).

There are two interesting features about these development projects at the CEO level. First, these projects do not involve single decisions or even unified clusters of decisions. Rather, they emerge as a series of small decisions and actions sequenced over time. Apparently, chief executives prolong each project both to fit it into a busy, disjointed schedule, and so that they can comprehend complex issues gradually.

Second, the chief executives I studied supervised as many as 50 of these projects at the same time. Some projects entailed new products or processes; others involved public relations campaigns, improvement of the cash position, reorganization of a weak department, resolution of a morale problem in a foreign division, integration of computer operations, various acquisitions at different stages of development, and so on.

Chief executives appear to maintain a kind of inventory of the development projects in various stages of development. Like jugglers, they keep a number of projects in the air; periodically, one comes down, is given a new burst of energy, and sent back into orbit. At various intervals, they put new projects on-stream and discard old ones.

The scarcest resource managers have to allocate is their own time.

While the entrepreneur role describes the manager as the voluntary initiator of change, the *disturbance handler* role depicts the manager involuntarily responding to pressures. Here change is beyond the manager's control. The pressures of a situation are too severe to be ignored—a strike looms, a major customer has gone bankrupt, or a supplier reneges on a contract—so the manager must act.

Leonard R. Sayles, who has carried out appropriate research on the manager's job, likens the manager to a symphony orchestra conductor who must "maintain a melodious performance,"[14] while handling musicians' problems and other external disturbances. Indeed, every manager must spend a considerable amount of time responding to high-pressure disturbances. No organization can be so well run, so standardized, that it has considered every contingency in the uncertain environment in advance. Disturbances arise not only because poor managers ignore situations until they reach crisis proportions but also because good managers cannot possibly anticipate all the consequences of the actions they take.

The third decisional role is that of *resource allocator*. The manager is responsible for deciding who will get what. Perhaps the most important resource the manager allocates is his or her own time. Access to the manager constitutes exposure to the unit's nerve center and decision maker. The manager is also charged with designing the unit's structure, that pattern of formal relationships that determines how work is to be divided and coordinated.

Also, as resource allocator, the manager authorizes the important decisions of the unit before they are implemented. By retaining this power, the manager can ensure that decisions are interrelated. To fragment this power encourages discontinuous decision making and a disjointed strategy.

There are a number of interesting features about the manager's authorization of others' decisions. First, despite the widespread use of capital budgeting procedures – a means of authorizing various capital expenditures at one time – executives in my study made a great many authorization decisions on an ad hoc basis. Apparently, many projects cannot wait or simply do not have the quantifiable costs and benefits that capital budgeting requires.

Second, I found that the chief executives faced incredibly complex choices. They had to consider the impact of each decision on other decisions and on the organization's strategy. They had to ensure that the decision would be acceptable to those who influence the organization, as well as ensure that resources would not be overextended. They had to understand the various costs and benefits as well as the feasibility of the proposal. They also had to consider questions of timing. All this was necessary for the simple approval of someone else's proposal. At the same time, however, the delay could lose time, while quick approval could be ill-considered and quick rejection might discourage the subordinate who had spent months developing a pet project.

One common solution to approving projects is to pick the person instead of the proposal. That is, the manager authorizes those projects presented by people whose judgment he or she trusts. But the manager cannot always use this simple dodge.

The final decisional role is that of *negotiator*. Managers spend considerable time in negotiations: the president of the football team works out a contract with the holdout superstar; the corporation president leads the company's contingent to negotiate a new strike issue; the foreman argues a grievance problem to its conclusion with the shop steward.

These negotiations are an integral part of the manager's job, for only he or she has the authority to commit organizational resources in "real time" and the nerve-center information that important negotiations require.

The Integrated Job

It should be clear by now that these ten roles are not easily separable. In the terminology of the psychologist, they form a gestalt, an integrated whole. No role can be pulled out of the framework and the job be left intact. For example, a manager without liaison contacts lacks external information. As a result, that manager can neither disseminate the information that employees need nor make decisions that adequately reflect external conditions. (This is a problem for the new person in a managerial position, since he or she has to build up a network of contacts before making effective decisions.)

Here lies a clue to the problems of team management.[15] Two or three people cannot share a single managerial position unless they can act as one entity. This means that they cannot divide up the ten roles unless they can very carefully reintegrate them. The real difficulty lies with the informational roles. Unless there can be full sharing of managerial information – and, as I pointed out earlier, it is primarily verbal – team management breaks down. A single managerial job cannot be arbitrarily split, for example, into internal and external roles, for information from both sources must be brought to bear on the same decisions.

To say that the ten roles form a gestalt is not to say that all managers give equal attention to each role. In fact, I found in my review of the various research studies that sales managers seem to spend relatively more of their time in the interpersonal roles, presumably a reflection of the extrovert nature of the marketing activity. Production managers, on the other hand, give relatively more attention to the decisional roles, presumably a reflection of their concern with efficient work flow. And staff managers spend the most time in the informational roles, since they are experts who manage departments that advise other parts of the organization. Nevertheless, in all cases, the interpersonal, informational, and decisional roles remain inseparable.

Toward More Effective Management

This description of managerial work should prove more important to managers than any prescription they might derive from it. That is to say, *the managers' effectiveness is significantly influenced by their insight into their own work.* Performance depends on how well a manager understands and responds to the pressures and dilemmas of the job. Thus managers who can be introspective about their work are likely to be effective at their jobs. The questions in "Self-Study Questions for Managers" may sound rhetorical; none is meant to be. Even though the questions cannot be answered simply, the manager should address them.

Let us take a look at three specific areas of concern. For the most part, the managerial logjams – the dilemma of delegation, the database centralized in one brain, the problems of working with the management scientist – revolve around the verbal nature of the manager's information. There are great dangers in centralizing the organization's data bank in the minds of its managers. When they leave, they take their memory with them. And when subordinates are out of convenient verbal reach of the manager, they are at an informational disadvantage.

The manager is challenged to find systematic ways to share privileged information. A regular debriefing session with key subordinates, a weekly memory dump on the dictating machine, maintaining a diary for limited circulation, or other similar methods may ease the logjam of work considerably. The time spent disseminating this information will be more than regained when decisions must be made. Of course, some will undoubtedly raise the question of confidentiality. But managers would be well advised to weigh the risks of exposing privileged information against having subordinates who can make effective decisions.

If there is a single theme that runs through this article, it is that the pressures of the job drive the manager to take on too much work, encourage interruption, respond quickly to every stimulus, seek the tangible and avoid the abstract, make decisions in small increments, and do everything abruptly.

Here again, the manager is challenged to deal consciously with the presures of superficiality by giving serious attention to the issues that require it, by stepping back in order to see a broad picture, and by making use of analytical inputs. Although effective managers have to be adept at responding quickly to numerous and varying problems, the danger in managerial work is that they will respond to every issue equally (and that means abruptly) and that they will

Self-Study Questions for Managers

1. Where do I get my information, and how? Can I make greater use of my contacts? Can other people do some of my scanning? In what areas is my knowledge weakest, and how can I get others to provide me with the information I need? Do I have sufficiently powerful mental models of those things I must understand within the organization and in its environment?

2. What information do I disseminate? How important is that information to my subordinates? Do I keep too much information to myself because disseminating it is time consuming or inconvenient? How can I get more information to others so they can make better decisions?

3. Do I tend to act before information is in? Or do I wait so long for all the information that opportunities pass me by?

4. What pace of change am I asking my organization to tolerate? Is this change balanced so that our operations are neither excessively static nor overly disrupted? Have we sufficiently analyzed the impact of this change on the future of our organization?

5. Am I sufficiently well-informed to pass judgment on subordinates' proposals? Can I leave final authorization for more of the proposals with subordinates? Do we have problems of coordination because subordinates already make too many decisions independently?

6. What is my vision for this organization? Are these plans primarily in my own mind in loose form? Should I make them explicit to guide the decisions of others better? Or do I need flexibility to change them at will?

7. How do my subordinates react to my managerial style? Am I sufficiently sensitive to the powerful influence of my actions? Do I fully understand their reactions to my actions? Do I find an appropriate balance between encouragement and pressure? Do I stifle their initiative?

8. What kind of external relationships do I maintain, and how? Do I spend too much of my time maintaining them? Are there certain people whom I should get to know better?

9. Is there any system to my time scheduling, or am I just reacting to the pressures of the moment? Do I find the appropriate mix of activities or concentrate on one particular function or problem just because I find it interesting? Am I more efficient with particular kinds of work, at special times of the day or week? Does my schedule reflect this? Can someone else schedule my time (besides my secretary)?

10. Do I overwork? What effect does my work load have on my efficiency? Should I force myself to take breaks or to reduce the pace of my activity?

11. Am I too superficial in what I do? Can I really shift moods as quickly and frequently as my work requires? Should I decrease the amount of fragmentation and interruption in my work?

12. Do I spend too much time on current, tangible activities? Am I a slave to the action and excitement of my work, so that I am no longer able to concentrate on issues? Do key problems receive the attention they deserve? Should I spend more time reading and probing deeply into certain issues? Could I be more reflective? Should I be?

13. Do I use the different media appropriately? Do I know how to make the most of written communication? Do I rely excessively on face-to-face communication, thereby putting all but a few of my subordinates at an informational disadvantage? Do I schedule enough of my meetings on a regular basis? Do I spend enough time observing activities firsthand, or am I detached from the heart of my organization's activities?

14. How do I blend my personal rights and duties? Do my obligations consume all my time? How can I free myself from obligations to ensure that I am taking this organization where I want it to go? How can I turn my obligations to my advantage?

never work the tangible bits and pieces of information into a comprehensive picture of their world.

To create this comprehensive picture, managers can supplement their own models with those of specialists. Economists describe the functioning of markets, operations researchers simulate financial flow processes, and behavioral scientists explain the needs and goals of people. The best of these models can be searched out and learned.

In dealing with complex issues, the senior manager has much to gain from a close relationship with the organization's own management scientists. They have something important that the manager lacks—time to probe complex issues. An effective working relationship hinges on the resolution of what a colleague and I have called "the planning dilemma."[16] Managers have the information and the authority; analysts have the time and the technology. A successful working relationship between the two will be effected when the manager learns to share information and the analyst learns to adapt to the manager's needs. For the analyst, adaptation means worrying less about the elegance of the method and more about its speed and flexibility.

Analysts can help the top manager schedule time, feed in analytical information, monitor projects, develop models to aid in making choices, design contingency plans for disturbances that can be anticipated, and conduct "quick and dirty" analyses for those that cannot. But there can be no cooperation if the analysts are out of the mainstream of the manager's information flow.

You can't teach swimming or management in a lecture hall.

The manager is challenged to gain control of his or her own time by turning obligations into advantages and by turning those things he or she wishes to do into obligations. The chief executives of my study initiated only 32% of their own contacts (and another 5% by mutual agreement). And yet to a considerable extent they seemed to control their time. There were two key factors that enabled them to do so.

First, managers have to spend so much time discharging obligations that if they were to view them as just that, they would leave no mark on the organization. Unsuccessful managers blame failure on the obligations. Effective managers turn obligations to advantages. A speech is a chance to lobby for a cause; a meeting is a chance to reorganize a weak department; a visit to an important customer is a chance to extract trade information.

Second, the manager frees some time to do the things that he or she—perhaps no one else—thinks important by turning them into obligations. Free time is made, not found. Hoping to leave some time open for contemplation or general planning is tantamount to hoping that the pressures of the job will go away. Managers who want to innovate initiate projects and obligate others to report back to them. Managers who need certain environmental information establish channels that will automatically keep them informed. Managers who have to tour facilities commit themselves publicly.

The Educator's Job

Finally, a word about the training of managers. Our management schools have done an admirable job of training the organization's specialists—management scientists, marketing researchers, accountants, and organizational development specialists. But for the most part, they have not trained managers.[17]

Management schools will begin the serious training of managers when skill training takes a serious place next to cognitive learning. Cognitive learning is detached and informational, like reading a book or listening to a lecture. No doubt much important cognitive material must be assimilated by the manager-to-be. But cognitive learning no more makes a manager than it does a swimmer. The latter will drown the first time she jumps into the water if her coach never takes her out of the lecture hall, gets her wet, and gives her feedback on her performance.

In other words, we are taught a skill through practice plus feedback, whether in a real or a simulated situation. Our management schools need to identify the skills managers use, select students who show potential in these skills, put the students into situations where these skills can be practiced and developed, and then give them systematic feedback on their performance.

My description of managerial work suggests a number of important managerial skills—developing peer relationships, carrying out negotiations, motivating subordinates, resolving conflicts, establishing information networks and subsequently disseminating information, making decisions in conditions of extreme ambiguity, and allocating resources. Above all, the manager needs to be introspective in order to continue to learn on the job.

No job is more vital to our society than that of the manager. The manager determines whether our social institutions will serve us well or whether they will squander our talents and resources. It is time to strip away the folklore about managerial work and study it realistically so that we can begin the difficult task of making significant improvements in its performance.

References

1. All the data from my study can be found in Henry Mintzberg, *The Nature of Managerial Work* (New York: Harper & Row, 1973).

2. Robert H. Guest, "Of Time and the Foreman," *Personnel*, May 1956, p. 478.

3. Rosemary Stewart, *Managers and Their Jobs* (London: Macmillan, 1967); see also Sune Carlson, *Executive Behaviour* (Stockholm: Strombergs, 1951).

4. Francis J. Aguilar, *Scanning the Business Environment* (New York: Macmillan, 1967), p. 102.

5. Unpublished study by Irving Choran, reported in Mintzberg, *The Nature of Managerial Work*.

6. Robert T. Davis, *Performance and Development of Field Sales Managers* (Boston: Division of Research, Harvard Business School, 1957); George H. Copeman, *The Role of the Managing Director* (London: Business Publications, 1963).

7. Stewart, *Managers and Their Jobs*; Tom Burns, "The Directions of Activity and Communication in a Departmental Executive Group," *Human Relations* 7, no. 1 (1954): 73.

8. H. Edward Wrapp, "Good Managers Don't Make Policy Decisions," HBR September-October 1967, p. 91. Wrapp refers to this as spotting opportunities and relationships in the stream of operating problems and decisions; in his article, Wrapp raises a number of excellent points related to this analysis.

9. Richard E. Neustadt, *Presidential Power* (New York: John Wiley, 1960), pp. 153-154; italics added.

10. For a more thorough, though rather different, discussion of this issue, see Kenneth R. Andrews, "Toward Professionalism in Business Management," HBR March-April 1969, p. 49.

11. C. Jackson Grayson, Jr., in "Management Science and Business Practice," HBR July-August 1973, p. 41, explains in similar terms why, as chairman of the Price Commission, he did not use those very techniques that he himself promoted in his earlier career as a management scientist.

12. George C. Homans, *The Human Group* (New York: Harcourt, Brace & World, 1950), based on the study by William F. Whyte entitled *Street Corner Society*, rev. ed. (Chicago: University of Chicago Press, 1955).

13. Neustadt, *Presidential Power*, p. 157.

14. Leonard R. Sayles, *Managerial Behavior* (New York: McGraw-Hill, 1964), p. 162.

15. See Richard C. Hodgson, Daniel J. Levinson, and Abraham Zaleznik, *The Executive Role Constellation* (Boston: Division of Research, Harvard Business School, 1965), for a discussion of the sharing of roles.

16. James S. Hekimian and Henry Mintzberg, "The Planning Dilemma," *The Management Review*, May 1968, p. 4.

17. See J. Sterling Livingston, "Myth of the Well-Educated Manager," HBR January-February 1971, p. 79.

'Flashes of GENIUS'

Peter Drucker on entrepreneurial complacency and delusions . . . and the madness of always thinking you're number one

WHENEVER PETER F. Drucker is introduced, you invariably hear him described as "the seminal thinker on 20th-century business organization." Those illustrious terms actually do Drucker a disservice. They relegate his substantial works to the dubious category of *classics*, tomes revered by many but read by few. And for reasons that continue to baffle me, Drucker continues to be thought of as someone whose thinking is a lot more relevant to people working in large companies than in entrepreneurial ones. Nothing is further from the truth. In fact, Drucker's *Innovation and Entrepreneurship* (Harper & Row, 1985) is still the most authoritative book on the subject.

At 86, Drucker is Clarke Professor of Social Science and Management at Claremont Graduate School, in California. Both the man and his work have been my intellectual compass for the past two decades. He possesses the boundless curiosity of a great reporter but combines it with a refusal to be cynical about the individuals and institutions he observes. His work is concrete, specific, and clear at a time when too much economic and organizational observation is muddled and confused.

A friend who is a lifelong Drucker devotee and I were fishing the San Juan River in New Mexico recently when a violent thunderstorm hit. We stayed on the river until we could feel static electricity building in our fishing poles. Finally we ran for cover. "Remember you were asking what it was like interviewing Peter Drucker?" I asked. "Well, it's a lot like holding a fiberglass fishing pole during a violent storm." If you enjoy a bit of electricity in your life, the interview that follows offers an alternative to standing in a large body of water in the middle of a thunderstorm.

—George Gendron

Inc.: *Do you agree that we in the United States are the best practitioners of entrepreneurship, that we're way ahead of other countries?*
Drucker: Absolutely not! It's a delusion, and a dangerous one. We may have the largest number of new-business starts and new-business failures, but that's all. We're probably not even number two.

Inc.: *Who's number one?*
Drucker: Undoubtedly Korea. Barely 40 years ago, Korea had no industry at all. The Japanese, who had ruled Korea for decades, didn't allow any. They also didn't allow any higher education, so there were practically no educated people in Korea. By the end of the Korean War, South Korea had been destroyed. Today Korea is world class in two dozen industries and the world's leader in shipbuilding and other areas.

Inc.: *If Korea is number one, and we're not number two, who is?*
Drucker: Not too far behind Korea is Taiwan, which like Korea was preindustrial in 1950. Today Taiwan is a world leader in a number of high-tech areas, including microchips. And don't forget the Chinese, who are starting new business after new business on both sides of the Pacific.

Inc.: *Okay, so third is still respectable, no?*
Drucker: The U.S. record is no better than Japan's or Germany's. Japan has a larger proportion of world-class companies that either didn't exist 40 years ago or were mom-and-pop shops: Sony, Honda, Yamaha, Kyocera, Matsushita, for example.

Germany owes its rise from the ashes

From *Inc.*, The State of Small Business, Special Issue, May 21, 1996, pp. 30-32, 34, 36, 38, 40, 43. © 1996 by Goldhirsh Group, Inc., 38 Commercial Wharf, Boston, MA 02110.

of World War II to its present position—the world's third-largest economy and number one in per capita exports of manufactured goods—to an explosion of entrepreneurship that turned hundreds of brand-new or obscure little shops into world-class manufacturers and industry leaders.

One example is Bertelsmann, one of the world's largest multimedia companies, which is active in 40 countries. In 1946, when Reinhard Mohn, the great-grandson of the founder, returned from a prisoner-of-war camp, Bertelsmann was a small-town publisher of religious tracts.

Inc.: You said a moment ago that America's entrepreneurial "delusion" is dangerous. How so?
Drucker: What bothers me more than the fact that the common belief in our entrepreneurial superiority simply isn't true is that it's lulling us into a dangerous complacency—not unlike our complacency about management in the early 1970s. Then we were convinced that American management reigned supreme, just as the Japanese were about to run circles around us in mass production and customer service.

I'm afraid our complacency about our entrepreneurship and innovation is going to have us outflanked again, not only by the Japanese but also by the Koreans.

Inc.: Why do you think this is happening?
Drucker: In this country we by and large still believe that entrepreneurship is having a great idea and that innovation is largely R&D, which is technical. Of course we *know* that entrepreneurship is a discipline, a fairly rigorous one, and that *innovation*—an economic not a technical term—has to be organized to create a new business. That's not news. In fact, it's what made Edison so successful more than a century ago. But American businesses with few exceptions—Merck, Intel, and Citibank come to mind—still seem to think that innovation is a "flash of genius," not a systematic, organized, rigorous discipline.

The Japanese are organizing innovation. So are the Koreans. They've set up small groups of their brightest people to systematically apply the discipline of innovation to identify and develop new businesses.

Inc.: Is there any one key to that discipline?

Drucker: Innovation requires us to systematically identify changes that have already occurred in a business—in demographics, in values, in technology or science—and then to look at them as opportunities. It also requires something that is most difficult for existing companies to do: to abandon rather than defend yesterday.

The Four Entrepreneurial Pitfalls

Inc.: So many new businesses start out with high promise. They do extremely well the first year or two and then suddenly are up to their ears in trouble. If they survive at all, they are forever stunted. Are there typical mistakes entrepreneurs make but could avoid?
Drucker: There are actually four points—I call them *entrepreneurial pitfalls*—where the new and growing business typically gets into trouble. All four are foreseeable and avoidable.

The first comes when the entrepreneur has to face the fact that the new product or service is not successful where he or she thought it would be but is successful in a totally different market. Many businesses disappear because the founder-entrepreneur insists that he or she knows better than the market.

Inc.: So, often the entrepreneur is actually succeeding but doesn't realize it?
Drucker: No, it's worse than that. He or she rejects success. You want examples? There are thousands of them, but one of the best is over 100 years old.

A man by the name of John Wesley Hyatt had invented the roller bearing. He made up his mind that it was just right for the axles of railroad freight cars. Railroads traditionally stuffed the wheels of their cars with rags soaked in oil to handle the friction. The railroads, however, were not ready for radical change; they liked their rags. And Mr. Hyatt went bankrupt trying to persuade them otherwise.

When Alfred Sloan, the man who later built GM, graduated from MIT at the head of his class in the mid-1890s, he asked his father to buy him Hyatt's small bankrupt business. Unlike Hyatt, Sloan was willing to broaden his vision of the product. It turned out that the roller bearing was ideal for the automobile, which was just coming to market. In two years Sloan had a flourishing business; for 20 years Henry Ford was his biggest customer.

Inc.: Good story, but is the rejection of success really all that common?
Drucker: I'd say that the majority of successful new inventions or products don't succeed in the market for which they were originally designed. I've seen it again and again. Novocaine was invented in 1905 by German chemist Alfred Einhorn for use in major surgery, but it wasn't suitable. Dentists immediately wanted the product, but the inventor actually tried to stop them from using it for the "mundane purpose" of drilling teeth. To the end of his days, Einhorn traveled all over the world

---

DRUCKER ON 'INTRAPRENEURSHIP'

'There are companies that are good at improving what they're already doing.... There are companies that are good at extending what they're doing. And finally there are companies that are good at innovation. Every large company has to be able to do all three—*improve, extend, and innovate*—simultaneously. I don't know of any large companies that can do that yet. But they're learning.'

preaching the merits of novocaine as a general anesthetic.

More recently, I know of a company whose founder created a software program that he was absolutely sure was what every hospital needed to operate smoothly. Well, the hospitals told him they weren't organized the way he assumed. He didn't make a single sale to a hospital. By pure accident, though, a small city stumbled over the program and found it was just what it needed. Orders began to come in from medium-size cities around the country. And he refused to fill them.

Inc.: Why do entrepreneurs reject unexpected success?

Drucker: Because it's not what they had planned. Entrepreneurs believe that they are in control. That leads to pitfall number two. *Entrepreneurs believe that profit is what matters most in a new enterprise. But profit is secondary. Cash flow matters most.*

Growing bodies need to be fed, and a business that grows fast devours cash. You have to make constant investments just to keep even with it. This is totally predictable, so getting caught in a cash crunch is totally unnecessary. I have saved more new enterprises than I can remember by simply telling the founder who showed me how beautifully things were going that *now* is the time to provide for your next financing. If you have six months' to a year's time to provide for your next financing, you can be reasonably sure you'll get it and at favorable terms.

Inc.: Why do you think entrepreneurs have such a hard time grasping the concept of cash flow?

Drucker: They're not the only ones. Warren Buffet once said that if he wants to find out how a company is doing, he doesn't listen to security analysts. They talk profit, which is irrelevant. He listens to bank credit analysts; they talk cash flow. I have yet to see one of the stock market newsletters I get talk about liquidity and the financial position of a growing company. They talk about profit margins and profitability.

Inc.: Why is that? Is it a product of our business schools?

Drucker: No. Fundamentally, business-people are financially illiterate.

Inc.: Well, let's say the business pays atten-

tion to cash flow, gets beyond the cash crunch, and grows rapidly, beyond expectations. What's the third pitfall looming on the horizon?*

Drucker: *When the business grows, the person who founded it is incredibly busy. Rapid growth puts an enormous strain on a business. You outgrow your production facilities. You outgrow your management capabilities.*

The entrepreneur begins running around like the proverbial one-armed paperhanger. He sees the sales figures, and he sees profit forecasts. Those make him believe that in another year he can sell out and get $10 million. And he doesn't see that he's outgrowing his management base.

You know, I've worked with entrepreneurs for 50 years and can say that there is a fairly normal curve; 80% fall within it. Even if your business is growing at a normal rate—not tripling in size every six months, but growing at a good, solid, sustainable rate—the management crunch hits you at the end of the fourth year.

Inc.: That's when you outgrow your management base?

Drucker: Yes. Starting out, the typical founder does everything himself. He has helpers, but he doesn't have colleagues. Then suddenly everything goes wrong. The quality falls out of bed. Customers don't pay. Deliveries are missed.

Inc.: But every young business makes mistakes, lots of them. What's the one symptom an entrepreneur cannot afford to ignore when it comes to outgrowing management?

Drucker: I always ask people who come to me how they respond to opportunity. "Suppose a customer says, 'If you make 10,000 of product X, we'll give you a contract.' Do you see this as a burden or an opportunity?" When they say, "Of course it's an opportunity, but I'm worried about it because it's an extra burden," I say, "Look, my friend, you've outgrown your management base."

To avoid a crisis, you should sit down and create a management team. By that time you have maybe 40 people working for you. Look them over to see who shows management ability. You call in those 4 or 5 people (you're not likely to have more), and you say, "I want each of you to sit down alone next weekend and look at the other people here, including me. Don't look at yourself. Look at the

others, and think about what each of them is good at." And then you all sit down together, take a fresh sheet of paper, and list the key activities of the business. Today we call this "establishing our core competencies."

Young entrepreneurs can't pay to bring in a management team. But here's Tom, and Tom is good at customer service, so you might also let him run the office. Give him an extra load for a few months or a few years, or give him an assistant. But Tom's job now is customer service. And here's Jane, your manufacturing person, who's better than anybody else at handling people. So your manufacturing person also becomes your people person.

And you start to meet once a month, maybe on a Saturday, and within a year you have a management team. It takes at least a year, more likely 18 months, to create a team.

Inc.: To really begin to work together as a team?

Drucker: Yes, but also to know that even though Joe's a difficult person to work with, he's exactly the financial person you need. Or to know that Tom is developing into a first-rate sales and marketing manager but is a weak customer-service manager. Tom may have been the best you had, but he ain't good enough.

Inc.: That's a hard decision for an entrepreneur to make, especially if Tom was there at the start.

Drucker: Yes, but if you start to build your team 18 months ahead of time, Tom's going to know that it's time to step aside. You can do it, but you can't wait until everything falls out of bed at the same time.

Inc.: And the fourth pitfall?

Drucker: The fourth pitfall is the most difficult one. *It's when the business is a success, and the entrepreneur begins to put himself before the business.* Here is a person who's worked 18 hours a day for 14 years and has a $60 million business and a management team that works. Now he asks himself, "What do I want to do? What's my role?" Those are the wrong questions. If you start out with them, you invariably end up killing yourself and the business.

Inc.: What should you be asking?

Drucker: You should be asking, "What does the *business* need at this stage?"

The next question is "Do I have those qualities?"

You have to start with what the business needs. That's where an outsider can be very helpful.

Over the years I've had maybe 100 people come to me in that situation. And when I ask them why they've come to me, most say that their wife says that they're not doing a good job anymore, that they're destroying themselves, their family, and the business. Occasionally you have a bright daughter who says it. If the son says it, he's brushed aside by the founder, who's thinking, "Does he want to take over and push me out?" But a wife or a bright daughter can say that.

Sometimes an outside shareholder speaks up, or an accountant or a lawyer. Usually somebody has to kick that entrepreneur hard to get him to face up to the harsh reality that he doesn't enjoy this anymore. He knows he's not concentrating on the right things.

Inc.: Do you think entrepreneurs today are smarter about avoiding the pitfalls you've been describing?
Drucker: No.

Inc.: No? With all the education, with all the MBAs?
Drucker: No. Education gives you neither experience nor wisdom.

Can Large Companies Foster Entrepreneurship?

Inc.: Back in the 1980s we heard a lot about "intrapreneurship," but it all seemed very faddish. Now that the hype has died down, can large companies really foster entrepreneurship?
Drucker: Of course it's possible. Quite a few do it. And many midsize companies are even better at it. But it's different from what most books mean by the term *entrepreneurship*. Most books take their cue from the last great entrepreneurial period in Western history before ours—the 60 years before World War I. All our major institutions, not just our business institutions, were created and shaped in that period.

The period began with the Great Exhibition, in London, in 1851, which ushered in the Second Industrial Revolution. The 1850s saw William Henry Perkin, in England, invent the first aniline dye and with it the modern chemical industry.

That was the decade that saw Werner von Siemens, in Germany, invent the first electric motor and with it the modern electrical industry. That was the decade that saw the triumph of Cyrus McCormick's reaper and with it the invention of mechanized agriculture. That was the decade that brought the first transatlantic cable and the first regular transatlantic steamship service. That was the decade in which Bessemer, in England, invented the steelmaking process, and the brothers Pereire, in France, founded the *Crédit Mobilier* and with it modern finance.

From that point until 1914, we had a major new invention every 14 months or so, each immediately creating a new industry.

Inc.: How was that period of innovation different from today's?
Drucker: *All those new industries moved into a vacuum.* There were no large corporations when the railroad in this country became one. And there was no competition. The railroad didn't displace anybody, didn't cause any dislocation. But now the world is full of organizations. And we're in turmoil because so many of the organizations whose roots go back 100 years or more are not going to survive.

Inc.: What does that mean for entrepreneurship in large companies?
Drucker: The large organization has to learn to innovate, or it won't survive. For some companies that means reinventing themselves. Increasingly, large companies are growing through alliances and joint ventures. Yet very few of the big boys know how to manage an alliance. They're used to giving orders, not to working with a partner, and it's totally different. In an alliance or a joint venture, you have to begin by asking, "What do our partners want? What are our shared values and goals?" Those aren't easy questions for somebody who grew up at GE or Citibank and is now at the top or near the top of a huge worldwide enterprise.

But innovation also means changing your products and services to keep up with markets that are changing faster than anybody has ever seen. Look at what's happening with banks. There are only a few large banks today in this country that make a profit out of doing the things banks traditionally do—commercial loans or deposits, for exam-ple. Banks are making profits out of credit cards, ATM fees, currency trades, and mutual fund sales. To stay in business, the large organization has to innovate.

Inc.: But can large companies foster entrepreneurship?
Drucker: They have to, to compensate for the difficulty they usually have learning how to work in a partnership or alliance. What do they do? They set up a unit internally that behaves quite differently from the rest of the company. The more successful the unit, the more difficult it is to make sure that the large company doesn't put the same expectations on it as it does for the rest of the company.

When it's a new venture, whether it's outside or inside the business, it's a child. And you don't put a 40-pound pack on a 6-year-old's back when you take her hiking.

Inc.: What are some examples of companies that have been successful at internal entrepreneurship?
Drucker: There are companies that are good at improving what they're already doing; the Japanese call this *kaizen*. There are companies that are good at extending what they're doing. And finally there are companies that are good at innovation. Every large company has to be able to do all three—*improve, extend, and innovate*—simultaneously. I don't know of any large companies that can do that yet. But they're learning.

The Rise of Social Entrepreneurship

Inc.: Could you step back and summarize your views about social entrepreneurship?
Drucker: First, it's as important as economic entrepreneurship. More important, perhaps. In the United States, we have a very healthy economy but a very sick society. So perhaps social entrepreneurship is what we need the most—in health care, education, city government, and so on. Fortunately there are enough successes around so that we know it can be done—and also how to do it.

Inc.: For instance?
Drucker: You have to start small—the big cure-alls never work. That was the problem with President Clinton's health care–reform plan. Now we are experimenting in health care all over the lot, and the outline of a new American health-care system is slowly emerging

out of literally hundreds of local experiments. We still talk about big, ambitious, nationwide educational cure-alls, yet in a lot of places *local* schools—public, parochial, *and* private—are having successes based on *local* entrepreneurs. And we know that the American public—especially the young, educated, double-earner family—is ready to support social entrepreneurship, especially as volunteers.

Inc.: You've said that more and more community jobs are being handled by local institutions, for-profits and nonprofits. Why are so many small nonprofits, to use your phrase, "grotesquely mismanaged"?
Drucker: Because they wrongly believe that good intentions move mountains. Bulldozers move mountains. But there are exceptions.

I helped start a foundation for nonprofit management in 1990. We have in our files more than 1,000 stories of small and mostly local institutions that do a job that nobody else can do. We gave our annual innovation award this year to the Rainforest Alliance, which has found a way to save the rain forest while increasing both the crop and the income of the banana farmers, once the greatest enemy of the rain forest. Even the runners-up for the award are social innovators.

These are social entrepreneurs, not business entrepreneurs. The social entrepreneur changes the performance capacity of society. Clearly the need is there, or we wouldn't have founded 800,000 nonprofits over the past 30 years.

Yesterday *charity* meant writing out a check. Today more and more people who are reasonably successful don't feel that's enough. They are looking for a parallel career, not a second career. Very few of them change jobs.

Inc.: You've said that you think we're on the verge of a period of enormous innovation. We've also got enormous numbers of

people in the private sector who want to be involved in social entrepreneurship. Are you arguing that we're now going to see more social innovation than we've seen in a long time?
Drucker: No doubt about it.

Inc.: But so many people in business are leery of nonprofits because they see them as nonprofessional.
Drucker: And they're both right and wrong. They're right because far too many nonprofits are either poorly managed or not managed at all. But they're wrong because nonprofits are not businesses and should be run differently.

Inc.: In what way?
Drucker: They need more not less management, precisely because they don't have a financial bottom line. Both their mission and their "product" have to be clearly defined and continually assessed. And most have to learn how to attract and hold volunteers whose satisfaction is measured in responsibility and accomplishment, not wages.

Inc.: What about innovation and entrepreneurship in government?
Drucker: That's probably our most important challenge. Look, no government in any major developed country really works anymore. The United States, the United Kingdom, Germany, France, Japan—none has a government the citizens respect or trust.

In every country there's a cry for leadership. But it's the wrong cry. When you have a malfunction across the spectrum, you don't have a people problem, you have a systems problem.

Modern government needs innovation. What we have now is roughly 400 years old. The invention of the nation-state and of modern government in the closing years of the 16th century was certainly one of the most successful innovations ever. Within 200 years they conquered the globe.

But it's time for new thinking. The

same holds true for the economic theories that have dominated the past 60 years or so. Government—not businesses or nonprofits—is going to be the most important area of entrepreneurship and innovation over the next 25 years.

Inc.: Do you see any signs of that happening?
Drucker: No one, as far as I can see, is asking the right question. In developed countries the question is not "What *should* government do?" It's "What *can* government do?" Still, there are signs of entrepreneurship and innovation in government.

Inc.: Such as?
Drucker: It doesn't matter whether I approve of his policies or not—and I have grave doubts—but the most visible entrepreneur in this country today is in government. It's Newt Gingrich. If ever I've seen a real entrepreneur, he's one. He is trying to totally change American politics. And if he succeeds—which is by no means certain—he will have created what we have never had, not even during the New Deal: a disciplined party in Congress under a Speaker's control. And he started with that goal 10 or 12 years ago.

Inc.: Hmm, Newt Gingrich. I suppose it depends on one's definition of entrepreneur.
Drucker: There is only one definition. An entrepreneur is someone who gets something *new* done.

Inc.: Well, from that perspective do you think of yourself as an entrepreneur?
Drucker: No, I'm a writer. I could not or would not ever run a business. You know, I don't even have a secretary. And contrary to some of the stereotypes, entrepreneurs are not loners. I am.

George Gendron (george_gendron@inc mag.com) is editor in chief of Inc.

Dr. Deming: 'Management Today Does Not Know What Its Job Is.'

In his last interview, Dr. W. Edwards Deming shared his thoughts on quality, management, innovation, and more.

Tim Stevens

Perhaps no one worked harder or enjoyed his job more than Dr. W. Edwards Deming. Less than two weeks before his death late last month at age 93, he was conducting one of his four-day seminars in Los Angeles. Always learning, Dr. Deming continued to integrate new ideas into his inspiring presentations. On a sunny Saturday morning last Oct. 23, sandwiched between his seminars in Detroit and Richmond, we had a chance to meet for a few hours at his home in Washington. Seated at a small circular table in his modest kitchen, we chatted over his breakfast of Quaker Oats granola with milk and cream, toast, and tea. Though Dr. Deming's legacy will be that of the man who transformed Japan into a formidable business competitor, a sometimes gruff taskmaster who wouldn't visit a company unless he could talk to the man at the top, I was taken by his patience, warmth, and caring nature . . . like the wise great-grandfather he was. While he focused intently on his topic throughout our discussion, afterward we spoke of family and travels and he offered to find time for us in the future. His passing makes our get-together that much more meaningful and his timeless words even more valuable.

IW: *Things are so much different now than when you were formulating your 14 points for transformation of American management. Are you saying anything now that you weren't saying before?*

Dr. Deming: No. The 14 points are good enough for me.

IW: *What can you say to* Industry Week's *readers that they might benefit from and apply to the way they are running their businesses?*

Dr. Deming: Management today does not know what its job is. In other words, [managers] don't understand their responsibilities. They don't know the potential of their positions. And if they did, they don't have the required knowledge or abilities. There's no substitute for knowledge.

IW: *What is their job?*

Dr. Deming: What should be the aim of management? What is their job? Quality is the responsibility of the top people. Its origin is in the boardroom. They are the ones who decide.

Quality means what will sell and do a customer some good—at least try to. The customer is the one who supports us. We have to present to him something that he needs, in a way that he can use it. Study his needs, get ahead of him. The customer invents nothing. The customer does not contribute to design of product or the design of the service. He takes what he gets. Customer expectations? Nonsense. No customer ever asked for the electric light, the pneumatic tire, the VCR, or the CD. All customer expectations are only what you and your competitor have led him to expect. He knows nothing else.

IW: *What then is the source of innovation?*

Dr. Deming: The source of innovation is freedom. All we have—new knowledge, invention—comes from freedom. Somebody responsible only to himself has the heaviest responsibility. "You cannot plan to make a discovery," Irving Langmuir said. Discoveries and new knowledge come from freedom. When somebody is responsible only to himself, [has] only himself to satisfy, then you'll have invention, new thought, new product, new design, new ideas.

"You cannot measure performance. Appraisal of people is ruinous. You cause humiliation, crush out joy of learning, innovation, joy on the job."

IW: *How does a company, a research manager, a manager of people create an environment where there is freedom?*

Dr. Deming: Give people a chance to make use of their diverse abilities, capabilities, family life, education, hopes. Help them to accomplish their aim.

IW: *One of your more controversial ideas is eliminating performance evaluations.*

Dr. Deming: Well, yes, because you cannot measure performance. Appraisal of people is ruinous. You cause humiliation, crush out joy of learning, innovation, joy on the job. Most of what anybody does is governed by the system that he works

Reprinted with permission from *Industry Week*, January 17, 1994, pp. 21, 24, 26, 28. © 1994 by Penton Publishing, Inc., Cleveland, OH.

in. You are not evaluating *him,* you are evaluating the interaction with him and the system, the rules and constraints he works in.

IW: *I like one of your quotes, which is "Reward for good performance may be the same as reward to the weatherman for a nice day."*

Dr. Deming: That's about right.

IW: *What is the alternative?*

Dr. Deming: The alternative is joy on the job. To have it, people must understand what their jobs are, how their work fits in, how they could contribute. Why am I doing this? Whom do I depend on? Who depends on me? Very few people have the privilege to understand those things. Management does not tell them. The boss does not tell them. He does not know what *his* job is. How could he know? It's a sad question. It's a very important question. How could he know? When people understand what their jobs are, then they may take joy in their work. Otherwise, I think they cannot.

IW: *Quoting from you book [The New Economics (1993, MIT Center for Advanced Engineering Study)], you say, "You can learn a lot about ice and know nothing about water." What does that mean?*

Dr. Deming: It means you can understand your present job and understand it very well. But what is the result of hard work and best efforts? What they do is only to dig deeper the pit that we are in. But they will not dig us *out* of the pit, only dig it deeper, make it more difficult to get out of. To get out of the pit we require an outside view. No chance from the inside. A system cannot understand itself. Understanding comes from outside. An outside view provides a lens for examination of our present actions, policies. Outside view is the aim of my chapter four [The New Economics] on profound knowledge. Knowledge from outside is necessary. Knowledge from outside gives us a view of what we're doing, what we might do, a road to improvement, continual improvement.

IW: *Is that view provided by other people?*

Dr. Deming: It's a very good idea. Knowledge will not come from a committee inside. How could a committee produce new knowledge? The view must come from the outside. A committee in a company can hardly stumble onto it. You enlarge the committee, bigger and bigger. That still doesn't do it. Enlarge the committee, make the committee everybody. Popular vote. Will popular vote provide the right answer? Maybe, by accident. How else could it? It's frightening. Popular vote does not solve our problems. Popular vote makes everybody responsible for the results. Let's work on it, do our best, within a framework. We could do that. Far better, more trustworthy, is an outside view. A new way of looking at things. It is only by that outside view that we get ahead, I believe.

IW: *You are referring to your system of profound knowledge.*

Dr. Deming: Yes. By profound knowledge, I mean knowledge from outside.

IW: *Your system of profound knowledge has four components: appreciation for a system, knowledge of variation, theory of knowledge, and psychology. Please elaborate a bit on each of the four components.*

Dr. Deming: Well, the theory of psychology. How could anyone learn about psychology of people, of individuals, without knowledge of variation? What do the variations mean between people, between groups? How can we capitalize on those differences? How can we assist people, because they have those differences? A good manager of people capitalizes on the family background, abilities, capabilities, and hopes of his people. He tries to give everybody a chance to take pride in his work, joy in his work. Why is it that your company is not as good as the people in it? Because the management of the company may not be good at finding the right job for the right people, or because interactions between people are not good. A company could put a top man at every position and be swallowed by a competitor with people only half as good, but who are working together.

IW: *One of the components of your system of profound knowledge is theory of knowledge. Please comment on that.*

Dr. Deming: Any decision that management makes, that anybody makes for himself or for other people, is prediction. The simplest plan is prediction, with a chance to be wrong. How may I get home tonight? I predict that my automobile will start and run, or that the bus will come, or that the train will come. I make plans. Those plans are predictions. Management is prediction; our lives are prediction. We predict what will happen. We try to choose a course of action that will react in favor of us. That's our aim. We predict the consequence of actions.

IW: *Please comment on appreciation for a system, another of the four components of your system of profound knowledge.*

Dr. Deming: Psychology and action. What happens to bearers of bad news? There's a psychology behind this—don't bring me bad news. Bring only good news. Harold F. Dodge of the Bell Telephone Laboratories, around 1934, showed that the number of defective items in a lot depends on the size of the workload that you hand over to the inspector. Give it to him in large doses, he finds some defective. He finds more defective if you present the work in smaller workloads. That the entwinement of psychology with the system results.

IW: *Theory of variation—you touched on it in terms of psychology. A manager must understand that there is a difference between people. But is that what you mean when you cite it as one of the components of profound knowledge? What about statistical variation?*

Dr. Deming: It's extremely important to understand that there are two kinds of variation. The variation that comes from common causes and the variation from something special.

IW: *How do you recognize the difference between the two?*

Dr. Deming: That's a function of the control chart. The control chart is a gift from Dr. Walter A. Shewhart, who invented it while working at the Bell Telephone Laboratories around 1924. What happens within the control limits belongs to the system, a common cause. A point outside the control limits would indicate a special cause. The usual procedure is that when anything happens, [we] suppose that somebody did it. Who did it? Pin a necklace on him. He's our culprit. He's the one who did it. That's wrong, entirely wrong. Chances are good, almost overwhelming, that what happened, happened as a consequence of the system that he works in, not from his own efforts. In other words, performance cannot be measured. You only measure the combined effect of the system and his efforts. You cannot untangle the two. It is very important, I believe, that performance cannot be measured.

IW: *Is confusing special-cause variation with common-cause variation a basic mistake that American industry is making?*

Dr. Deming: Yes. Attributing nonuniformity to a special cause, when actually it came from a common cause, and vice versa. What we want is to make the frequency of both mistakes zero. It can't be done. Our goal must be to minimize the economic loss from both mistakes.

IW: *Two words that are popular today in describing changes in American industry are downsizing and reengineering. What do these words mean to you?*

Dr. Deming: Desperation. Management doesn't know anything else to do. They don't have the knowledge to manage with. All they can do is sack people. Crude. A crude way to do it. You only dig yourself into another pit.

IW: *What is the role of government?*

Dr. Deming: The responsibility of government is equity. If we do not keep equity in the forefront, we will destroy our society. Of the people, by the people, for the people. Sounds great. Doesn't mean a damn thing. The top priority of government is equity. Accused and the accuser both have a right to be heard. This is very inefficient, wasteful, you might say. But we dare not have it any other way.

IW: *How does that apply to government's role and interaction with American business?*

Dr. Deming: The main function of government is equity, and business must work within that framework.

IW: *ISO 9000 seems to be the ticket to participating in the new world economy. Where is ISO 9000 going?*

Dr. Deming: ISO 9000, 9001, 9002 are conformance specifications—conform to requirements. Of course we must conform to requirements. But that's not enough; that won't do it. One must seek the nominal value of anything, what the *best* way is, not just pass the course. To meet specifications, do what is required—that is not enough. You have to do better than that. Achieve uniformity about the nominal value, best value. Shrink, shrink, shrink variation about the nominal value. That is where you get your payoff; that is where you get ahead.

IW: *What about the Malcolm Baldrige National Quality Award and companies striving for the award? Does that equate to being on a mission to improve quality?*

Dr. Deming: No, nothing could be worse. The evil effect of the Baldrige guidelines on American business can never be measured. If you had the Baldrige guidelines in front on you, you would see it asks for data, figures on what cannot be measured. The effect of training, for example. You may spend $20,000 to train six people in a skill. That benefit will come in the future. We'll never be able to measure that benefit. Never. So why do we spend that money for training? Answers are guided by theory. We believe that that training will have its effect on future output. And though we cannot measure that effect, we believe that it is positive. In other words, we govern our actions, our life, by theory. That's good. Without theory, we learn nothing. Theory has temporal spread. That is, the theory that we can hold on to must fit without failure events of the past and predict events of the future.

IW: *Where are American business schools falling short in design of their curriculum, the things they are teaching?*

Dr. Deming: I'm afraid that what they teach is continuance of our present methods of management, which are failures. They teach how to fail, how to continue to fail.

IW: *What should they be teaching?*

Dr. Deming: I think the teaching ought to be on how to improve. Improvement, understanding of people, understanding of product. In other words, it would require what I call profound knowledge, of which I mean a view from the outside.

IW: *Is there anything else that you would like to say to the management of American business?*

Dr. Deming: Yes. Quality. Quality is characteristic of a product or service that helps somebody and which has a market. Without the market, we don't stay in business. Sometimes the market has to be created. But, the market itself is not enough.

For example, today where are the makers of carburetors? Gone. Every engine had a carburetor. How could it run without one? The maker of carburetors made better and better carburetors, lower and lower cost, and went out of business. What happened? Came the fuel injector, which costs more than a

---

MORE WORDS OF WISDOM

• "In the world economy, one of our greatest sources of dollars is service—American movies. Money flows into this country from American movies. A service, a good earner."

• "When a business is not managed as a system, the individual people, teams, divisions, components of various kinds, become independent profit centers, thus destroying the system."

• "Managing by results, assigning reason to every event, is fatal."

• "The president of a huge organization said quality is in the hands of his plant managers. Nonsense. The plant manager can only try to get that stuff out today. He tries to meet his quota—that's his worry. It has nothing to do with quality, nothing to do with the design. All he does is try to get that stuff together and push it out the door."

• "The best for everybody concerned should be the basis for negotiation between persons, competitors, countries. With good management, everyone will be the beneficiary. We want everyone to win. We *have* to have it that way."

carburetor, but does the job of the carburetor and a lot more. The fuel injector came in, carburetors went out. Carburetor manufacturers made a good product, better and better carburetors, lower and lower cost, happy customers. But that is not a sound basis for a continuance. You must take account of possible changes. The function of the carburetor, as everybody knows, is to put a stoichiometric mixture of fuel and air into the combustion chamber. That is its function. Now what is the best way to accomplish that? Maybe by a carburetor, maybe not. Fuel injection provides a better way. Fuel injectors took over the market. Carburetors went out, no matter how good they were. In due time fuel injectors will go out with a new kind of engine. Don't ask me what it might be; I know not. But you must think of function, not particular products.

IW: *You are an amazing person. How do you keep going? What's your secret?*

Dr. Deming: I love my work—continue learning, advancement in presentation, advancement in understanding.

LESSONS FOR MANAGEMENT

Dr. Deming's 14 points for the transformation of management from *Out of the Crisis*
(1982, MIT Center for Advanced Engineering Study):

1. Create constancy of purpose toward improvement of product and service, with the aim to become competitive and to stay in business, and to provide jobs.

2. Adopt the new philosophy. We are in a new economic age. Western management must awaken to the challenge, must learn their responsibilities, and take on leadership for change.

3. Cease dependence on inspection to achieve quality. Eliminate the need for inspection on a mass basis by building quality into the product in the first place.

4. End the practice of awarding business on the basis of price tag. Instead, minimize total cost. Move toward a single supplier for any one item, on a long-term relationship of loyalty and trust.

5. Improve constantly and forever the system of production and service, to improve quality and productivity, and thus constantly decrease cost.

6. Institute training on the job.

7. Institute leadership. The aim of supervision should be to help people and machines and gadgets to do a better job. Supervision of management is in need of overhaul, as well as supervision of production workers.

8. Drive out fear, so that everyone may work effectively for the company.

9. Break down barriers between departments. People in research, design, sales, and production must work as a team, to foresee problems of production and in use that may be encountered with the product or service.

10. Eliminate slogans, exhortations, and targets for the workforce asking for zero defects and new levels of productivity. Such exhortations only create adversarial relationships, as the bulk of the causes of low quality and low productivity belong to the system and thus lie beyond the power of the workforce.

11a. Eliminate work standards (quotas) on the factory floor. Substitute leadership.

11b. Eliminate management by objective. Eliminate management by numbers, numerical goals. Substitute leadership.

12a. Remove barriers that rob the hourly worker of his right to pride of workmanship. The responsibility of supervisors must be changed from sheer numbers to quality.

12b. Remove barriers that rob people in management and in engineering of their right to pride of workmanship. This means, *inter alia*, abolishment of the annual or merit rating and of management by objective.

13. Institute a vigorous program of education and self-improvement.

14. Put everybody in the company to work to accomplish the transformation. The transformation is everybody's job.

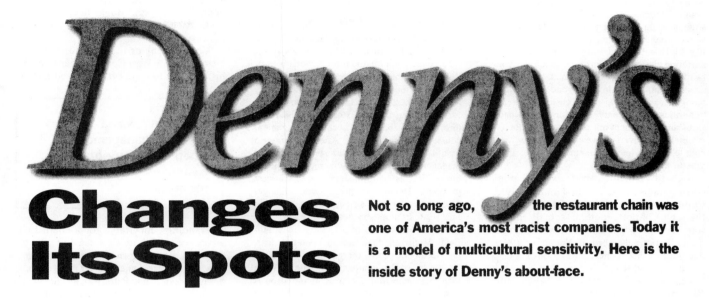

Denny's

Changes Its Spots

Not so long ago, the restaurant chain was one of America's most racist companies. Today it is a model of multicultural sensitivity. Here is the inside story of Denny's about-face.

Faye Rice

ON APRIL 1, 1993, the very same day that Denny's settled a federal suit for discriminating against African American customers in California, six black Secret Service agents at a Denny's restaurant in Annapolis, Maryland, waited nearly an hour for breakfast. While they were ignored, their white colleagues sitting at a nearby table downed second helpings of French toast, bacon, and coffee. When the black agents went public with their treatment, Denny's became, almost overnight, a national symbol of big-business bigotry.

Within months, Ron Petty, former head of Burger King U.S.A., arrived to begin repairing Denny's shattered image. That metamorphosis has been no less dramatic than the restaurant chain's precipitous decline. A company that was once a shameful example of entrenched prejudice is now a model of multicultural sensitivity. The story doesn't stop there. In early 1995, Jim Adamson, another Burger King veteran, was named CEO of Denny's parent company, Flagstar, which is 47% owned by Kohlberg Kravis Roberts. Adamson immediately expanded the re-education efforts beyond Denny's to Flagstar's entire $2.6 billion restaurant empire, including regional chains El Pollo Loco and Quincy's steak houses, plus 593 Hardee's outlets that Flagstar operates as its largest franchisee.

Ron Petty, now Denny's CEO, likes to cite a few numbers to reveal the extent of the about-face. The percentage of minority officers, vice presidents and above, has risen

REPORTER ASSOCIATE *Anne Faircloth*

from zero in 1993 to 11% today. Minorities hold 20% of the jobs directly below vice president, a category called director; there were no nonwhites in 1993. Of Denny's 512 franchisees, 27 are African American, vs. one in 1993; the goal is 65 by the end of 1997. Petty has also slashed three layers of management so he can be close enough to restaurants to head off another mishap. Critics who once excoriated Denny's have changed their tune. "Denny's has jumped out in front and taken a positive approach to solving its problems, unlike most companies that do the minimum required by law," says Terry Demchak, a partner at Saperstein Goldstein Demchak & Baller, the California law firm that represented black customers in one of two class-action suits against the chain.

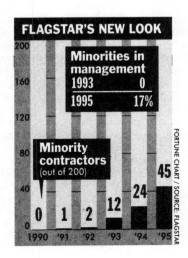

FLAGSTAR'S NEW LOOK

Minorities in management

1993	0
1995	17%

Minority contractors (out of 200)

1990	'91	'92	'93	'94	'95
0	1	2	12	24	45

FORTUNE CHART / SOURCE: FLAGSTAR

HIRING PETTY was a smart decision made out of desperation by Jerry Richardson, Flagstar's former CEO. Now 59, he co-founded the company in 1961 with a single Hardee's hamburger stand. But Richardson, a former wide receiver for the Baltimore Colts, knew he needed bigtime help in 1993 after the black Secret Servicemen filed the third discrimination suit in a year against Denny's. At the time he was negotiating to buy the Carolina Panthers NFL franchise, and the negative press could have blown the deal.

With Petty in place, Richardson moved quickly to resolve the suits. In May 1994, Denny's settled the two class-action suits, one of which was consolidated with the case originally settled in 1993 with the U.S. government. By December 1995, Denny's had paid $54 million to 295,000 aggrieved customers and their lawyers, the largest public accommodations settlement ever. In the consent decree it signed with the plaintiffs, Denny's promised to treat all customers equally in the future. The consent decree also mandated that Denny's publicize its nondiscriminatory policies and train employees in diversity issues. An independent civil rights monitor was appointed to supervise Denny's for seven years and to investigate any further charges of discrimination.

While Petty worked to get Denny's in compliance with federal law, KKR, Flagstar's controlling stockholder, had another problem to deal with. Richardson was struggling as CEO. Flagstar had $2.3 billion of debt and more aliases than a Russian spy, due to a mind-boggling series of restructurings in the late 1980s. Its past incarnations include Spartan Food Systems and TW Services, once a division of Transworld Corp., the parent company of TWA. By whatever name it went, the company, based in Spartanburg, South Carolina, had lost money for five straight years beginning in 1989. Then there was the racial situation. Industry competitors like McDonald's and Burger King had been nurturing ties with minority communities for nearly 20 years. Flagstar, in contrast, was an anachronism stuck in a bygone era. Even though nearly a third of its customers were minorities, it had only two minority-owned firms among its network of some 200 suppliers in 1992. Diversity was a concept as foreign to its all-white management team as foie gras to a Denny's menu.

Richardson relinquished his CEO title when Adamson arrived in January 1995, turning his attention to the Carolina Panthers, his Charlotte football team. Richardson, who will remain on the Flagstar payroll until his contract expires in November 1997, declined to talk to FORTUNE about his departure, as did KKR's Henry Kravis.

Flagstar's real reconstruction began with Richardson's retreat. Jim Adamson made a thunderous entrance as CEO, telling employees at his first meeting that he was "going to do everything possible to provide better jobs for women and minorities. And I will fire you," he warned, "if you discriminate. Anyone who doesn't like the direction this train is moving had better jump off now." Within a few months of the change in management, all but four of the company's top 12 officers left. Among Adamson's replacements were a Hispanic man and an African American woman.

Adamson devised a four-part strategy to put cultural diversity in motion: Loosen up the hierarchical environment; make diversity a performance criterion for all managers; require the entire staff to attend workshops on racial sensitivity; and never miss an opportunity to preach the gospel of diversity. He had been at Flagstar only three months when he got a taste of the bad old days. He declared Martin Luther King Jr.'s birthday a companywide holiday. (The restaurants did not close, but for the first time, office workers were given the day off.) Some employees at headquarters fired off angry E-mail messages opposing his decision and requesting another day off instead. While the messages upset Adamson, he says he is pleased to have "opened up the company enough for employees to disagree. The bad news is that we have more educating to do than we anticipated."

TOGETHER, Adamson and Petty hope to implant diversity as deeply in the new Flagstar/Denny's as racism was in the old. They have created management training programs to give minorities entree to the executive ranks and begun a fast-track program to help them become Denny's franchisees. Applicants enroll in a training program for one to three years, depending on their experience, during which time they must prove that they can successfully operate a restaurant. Every applicant who completes the training can buy a franchise with a loan guaranteed by Denny's.

Jerome Edmondson, 33, got the first spot on the fast-track program six months before it officially began last fall. Denny's ran a credit check on him and interviewed his family and previous employers. Since Edmondson is a former market manager at Kentucky Fried Chicken, where he had responsibility for more than a dozen restaurants, he raced through the basic 13-week management course in eight weeks. After spending a month working as an assistant restaurant manager, he thought he was ready to prove himself. He asked to manage one of the least profitable Denny's in the system. Management was reluctant at first, fearing he might fail. But Edmondson was persistent. Last June, he took charge of a Denny's in Southfield, Michigan, that had an operating loss. By October, profit margins had risen to 17.2%, near the company average. With a loan guarantee from Denny's, Edmondson is now buying the Southfield franchise, the first of 20 he hopes to own. "I was skeptical about Denny's at first," says Edmondson. "But after a few months I knew this company was really committed to helping minorities."

Besides expanding opportunities for people who were shunned in the past, Adamson and Petty are introducing techniques to sort out bad apples. A new computerized interviewing technique called H.R. Easy tries to screen job applicants for racial bias. Prospective employees dial an 800 number to answer a series of questions, including "Have you ever used drugs?" "Do you like dealing with people of different races?" "Do you have a problem working with people of different races?" Explains Norman Hill, Denny's VP of human resources: "There is an average response time for each question. It usually takes longer to tell a lie than to tell the truth. If there is a longer response time to questions about bias, drugs, or theft, we will follow up with face-to-face interviews."

Denny's new approach to racial issues comes after years of active resistance to diversity. In 1990, a year or so before the first bias-related incident made the papers, Jerry Richardson had commissioned Synectics, a Cambridge, Massachusetts, consulting firm, to revamp the financially ailing Flagstar. "The lack of diversity was the first issue we identified," recalls Bill Boggs, a managing partner. "I told the senior managers that Flagstar was in a strategically dangerous position, since their customers are certainly not all white males."

A born-and-bred Southerner like Richardson, Boggs vividly recalls a walk he took with Flagstar's then CEO. "Jerry turned to me and said, 'I'm sure you're right about our being behind on diversity, but I just never thought about it.' " To his credit, Richardson replaced a few of the old-timers in his executive suite. He recruited Flagstar's first female senior executive, Edna Morris, to run the notably neglected human resources department. "But the company was 20 years behind the curve," Boggs declares, "and Richardson didn't move nearly fast enough or deep enough."

When racial problems erupted at a Denny's on the West Coast, Richardson and his team wrote them off as isolated misun-

> **B**lackout" was a term used by management when too many black customers were in the restaurant.

derstandings, inevitable for a chain that serves one million meals a day. But piles of court documents from customers and employees indicated something far more serious was going on. Sandy Patterson, a white waitress who worked at several Denny's in California, stated in her court declaration that use of the N word was "not uncommon," nor were the terms "them," "those people," or "that kind" in referring to blacks. "I was told by management that we did not want to encourage black customers to stay in the restaurant," she said.

Robert Norton, who is also white, says that when he began his new job managing a Denny's in San Jose, he observed staffers "routinely" closing the restaurant when "they were concerned about the number of black customers" entering. Says Norton: " 'Blackout' was used by Denny's management to refer to a situation where too many black customers were in the restaurant." Norton says that when he discontinued the policy, his district manager threatened to fire him.

Flagstar management was nearly as insensitive to minority business people as it was to its customers. Take the topic of minority vendors. Samuel Maw, Flagstar's executive vice president in charge of procurement until he left last year, still insists, "It is extremely difficult to find them, because they aren't out there." But even minority vendors who banged on Flagstar's door were ignored by the company's buyers. Michele Hoskins says it took her a year and a half to land a $3 million contract to supply syrup to Denny's. Explains Hoskins, an African American who has been selling syrup to supermarkets for 12 years, "When I first called Flagstar, someone told me the company couldn't buy from me because it had a deal in the works with Log Cabin. I said, 'You'll have to give me a better excuse than that.' "

Hoskins made daily phone calls and dispatched weekly letters. The standoff ended a month or so after Adamson became CEO. Suddenly Flagstar's purchasing agents were glad to give her the lowdown on the prices and specs she should meet to get an order. "Now everyone is cooperative, and we work as a team," says Hoskins. Magaly Petersen, brought in by Adamson from Michelin Tires to be director of minority business development, emphasizes that she has no problem locating nonwhite vendors for Denny's and its sister chains.

Adamson, the son of a U.S. Army general, was born in Japan and grew up on bases around the world. He remembers being the only white kid on his neighborhood basketball courts in Washington, D.C., and later, as a teenager living in Hawaii, the only "haole"—the islanders' term for nonnative whites—riding the waves at his local beach. "Prejudice is just not part of Jim's personality," says Boake Sells, a venture capitalist who was Adamson's boss during the 1980s at both Dayton Hudson and Revco. Sells says he first noticed Adamson at Dayton Hudson because his team was so devoted to him. That hasn't changed over the years. Approachable and calm, he strolls the halls at Flagstar in his $1,000 Ralph Lauren loafers and slicked-back Jay Gatsby hair, chatting with staffers. He schedules regular lunches with groups of ten and 12 from all levels of the company, and spends 30 minutes a day writing personal notes to employees and stockholders.

Adamson has assembled a dedicated team to help make over the Flagstar culture. One trusted lieutenant is Rachelle "Ray" Hood-Phillips, head of diversity affairs. She worked closely with both Adamson and Petty at Burger King, where she was a vice president. A year ago Adamson lured her to Flagstar, "to fight the battles," he says. Hood-Phillips and her team are currently creating a diversity-training program for 800 staffers in the Spartanburg corporate office. They will be the first group of employees outside the Denny's network to be exposed to sensitivity workshops. Says Hood-Phillips optimistically: "We want to help people communicate and connect across a line of difference. We want to change their hearts, their perspectives, and their behavior."

At Denny's the diversity training reinforces the requirements of the consent decree forbidding discrimination, such as failure to seat blacks as quickly as whites. The legal points are combined with customer-service guidelines, since the best way to avoid complaints is to treat everyone equally. During the customer-service segment, filmed vignettes (much like those on *America's Most Wanted*) dramatize the right and wrong ways to seat and serve customers. Employees must attend the sessions; refusal to do so is considered insubordination. "We have fired people who have resisted the training," says Norm Hill.

Because of confidentiality clauses in the consent decree, Hill cannot disclose any names or even the number of obstinate employees. He does, however, offer a generic example: "Mr. Surly will come to the training with an attitude and say, 'I'm just here to save my job. You guys are caving in to all of this diversity stuff.' Our reaction is immediate," Hill says. "We say you have an opportunity to complete the program, or you can leave the company."

If Mr. Surly wants to keep his job, and the company feels he needs more attention, he will have to participate in advanced sensitivity training, an intense, daylong session conducted by the National Coalition Building Institute in Washington, D.C., which specializes in changing bigoted attitudes. Faking his way through training will only delay the inevitable for Mr. Surly. "He will be caught down the line," Hill promises. "Someone will make a complaint about him, and once we see that he has been trained, he'll be fired." Michael Thrower, a Denny's manager in Dallas, believes the training has been good for everyone, especially "the higher-ups." Thrower, an African American, says, "Before, some of them would belittle you in front of guests, and if you objected they would say, 'Hey, you ought to be glad you have a job.'"

MUCH of the resistance to Denny's training is in small towns. "The mores in these towns dictate the standards in the restaurants there," notes Hill, "and our positive message of equal opportunity and diversity is not always well received." Small-town mores occasionally lead to another problem: disruptive customers. "Some customers come in and say they don't want to be served by Asians, Mexicans, or blacks," Hill says. A pilot program to demonstrate the proper way to handle such customers began earlier this year. Lesson No. 1: Kindly ask them to leave!

Denny's public face has also changed. The consent decree stipulates that newspaper ads and other print promotions depicting customers or employees must feature a minimum of 30% African American or other "identifiably nonwhite" persons. Says Derrell Pierce, a black restaurant manager from San Diego who joined the company 16 months ago: "Denny's is now an organization for all people."

> **D**espite all the progress it has made on issues of diversity, Flagstar's finances are discouraging.

Despite the progress it has made on diversity, Flagstar's finances are discouraging. Debilitated by annual interest payments of $230 million, it lost $55.2 million last year, on revenues of $2.6 billion. The stock has hovered near its all-time low ($2.88) for more than six months. The challenge is to raise profits enough to offset the suffocating debt, not a simple task. To pull it off, Adamson is rethinking everything from menus to advertising and implementing strategic changes for long-term growth. By June he will have divested all of Flagstar's low-margin, nonrestaurant businesses, and he is replacing the company's antiquated information technology systems.

At Denny's, operating income edged up less than 2% last year, after rebounding 35% in 1994; it fell 30% in 1993, the year of the worst racial incidents, and customer traffic declined 4%. Traffic is on the rise again, but revenue growth has been slow. Revenues actually declined slightly in 1995, from $1.55 billion to $1.49 billion, because about 45 company-owned restaurants were sold to franchisees, many of them minorities.

Denny's main problem is that it is caught between two flourishing categories: fast-food giants that have lower prices, and casual dining chains like Chili's and Applebee's that are more expensive but offer liquor and ambiance. To heat up sales, Adamson is lowering prices and improving quality—the same formula he used to revive Burger King. Denny's, famous for its $1.99 Grand Slam breakfast of pancakes, eggs, bacon, and sausage, is dishing up five new morning meals priced under $2. It is also introducing "value" luncheon platters from $2.99 to $4.99 that feature everything from Philly cheese steaks to crispy chicken salad.

Hardee's, Flagstar's second-largest business, needs help too. After years of robust growth, revenues are slumping; same-store sales fell 8.6% in 1995, and revenues declined from $700 million to $660 million. At Adamson's direction, Hardee's customers recently began getting bigger, juicier, cheaper burgers. The price: 79 cents. "When you are hemorrhaging the way we are, you have to get customers back into the restaurants," Adamson says.

Like many good leaders, Adamson is dangling cash to motivate his employees. The twist is that he is using his own money. Last year he donated his entire signing bonus of $500,000 to a pool for Hardee's restaurant managers. During the last four months of 1995, 600 managers competed against their previous eight-month sales numbers. Those who improved sales 1% to 3% received $500; the payout was $1,000 for a 3% to 7% increase, and $2,000 for a sales jump of 7% or more. More than half the managers pocketed bonuses. "Adamson brings a real sense of urgency to a company whose brands are not ideally positioned," says industry analyst Michael Mueller of Montgomery Securities. "He's moving at 90 miles an hour to market them more effectively."

Mueller expects Adamson's turnaround to gather momentum. Flagstar's cash flow, he says, will rise 8% in 1997, and he believes the company could be profitable by 1998. Adamson promised KKR that he will stay at Flagstar until the red ink disappears. Says he: "When I leave, I want it said that I made Flagstar a much more inclusive, user-friendly company." In other words, he wants diversity to really pay.

Learning to Change

Stanley F. Slater

A colleague and I recently examined the "Letters to the Shareholders" from about 50 corporate annual reports to try to understand what is on corporate leaders' minds. What we found is that leaders today are preoccupied with changing the way their organizations do business. Almost all are on a quest for superior quality; many want to speed new product development; others are committed to improving the level of service their firms provide; and reengineering key business processes seems to be a must. We also were curious about how these priorities had developed or evolved, so we studied the letters from several of the same corporations from five years earlier. Somewhat to our surprise, we found many of the same themes running through those letters.

This suggests that, even with the current popularity of books, articles, and consultants on change programs, very few businesses have mastered the ability to transform effectively and continuously. I believe this is because the idea of a "change program" is an oxymoron. As markets fragment, product life cycles shorten, and technology rapidly advances, change must be a philosophy, not a program. A programmatic approach implies a beginning and an end to the change effort. Today there is little time to rest, much less stop, in the pursuit of innovation and continuous improvement. The competency that allows businesses to change fluidly and effectively is the ability to learn continuously.

This article discusses first the nature of change and the role of learning. Second, it focuses on three key organizational features that my research has shown are necessary, in combination, to produce higher-order organizational learning and its associated benefits of new product success, growth, and superior profitability.

THE NATURE OF CHANGE

When I hear managers talk about how their businesses must abandon the status quo and find ways to change the way they operate, I wonder whether they really understand what is going on in those businesses. They speak of change as something a company either does or does not do. In reality, even the stodgiest organizations are changing in many ways at all times. They hire new people, implement new software systems, build or acquire new facilities, and introduce new products or services. Admittedly, many of these changes are subtle and do little to alter the firm's strategic trajectory.

> *Continuous, market-driven learning is the best change strategy for an unpredictable environment.*

Organizational change should be viewed as a continuum that runs from Genesis, where there is little stability and the change effort seeks to create or fundamentally reorient the firm's strategic architecture, to Paralysis, where stability is highly valued and changes are minor and insubstantial. There is a balance point, too—Synthesis—where the firm's leaders seek to match stability and change among the elements of its strategic architecture. At any time in an organization that is able to maintain Synthesis, some elements of its architecture, particularly its core values, will be stable while others will be in transition. The objective is to create and maintain an alignment between the organization and the changing needs of its key external constituencies. **Figure 1** illustrates these stages in terms of a balance between organizational change and stability. Compaq Computer provides an interesting example of a corporation that is already in its second pass through the continuum in just a little more than a decade.

Genesis

If the opposite of stability is change, then the Genesis or creation of an organization must be completely focused on managing major change. Shortly after founding NeXT Computer, Steve

Figure 1
Balancing Change and Stability

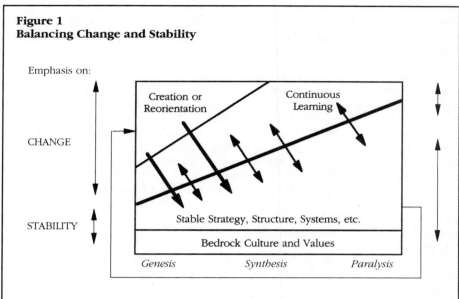

The heavy diagonal line illustrates the shifting balance between organizational change and stability. During Genesis, change is fundamental and substantial.

In Synthesis, the focus on continuous learning creates a healthy balance between change and stability. An organization in Paralysis has created barriers to learning and change. The respective emphases have reversed from Genesis.

you only get one shot at writing on it. Any startup has that advantage. It's just a question of whether you make good use of it" (Gannes 1988).

This carefully orchestrated approach to the genesis of an organization is atypical of entrepreneurial ventures. Although many organizations carefully describe comprehensive, programmed initiatives in "The Business Plan," firms that survive this phase act swiftly to learn about their environment and allow their architecture and strategy to adapt as key players learn from these early experiences in the business. Regardless of whether the result is from careful planning or emergent processes, the emphasis during this stage is on major initiatives that will have a lasting impact on the new company's definition. This is a time when organizations often must "bet the firm" to establish themselves in markets that already are very competitive or in which technological uncertainty creates substantial risk.

Although experimentation and learning by doing are crucial to success, particularly in the development and refinement of the new product or service, developing relationships with learning partners can reduce both financial and product-market risk. From its earliest days, Nike used a network of offshore manufacturers to supply the shoes it designed and marketed. Compaq drew on the knowledge and experience of its distributors in the development of new products. Other computer manufacturers rely heavily on Intel, Motorola, Cyrix, and other microprocessor manufacturers for the development of advanced personal computer technology. The time may have passed when a new company can succeed by performing all of the key business tasks itself. Developing effective relationships with consultants, suppliers, and distributors is essential to creating the proper architecture, minimizing business risk, and increasing the odds of success.

Jobs remarked on how many little things it took to get a new company running. Seemingly trivial things—buying a coffee-maker, setting up a general ledger, ordering furniture—take a lot of time. Of course, the big things, such as articulating a vision, recruiting staff, developing relationships with potential customers and suppliers, and designing the new product, are on an entirely different order of magnitude.

As high historical failure rates point out, this is a period of great risk for the new company. Compaq Computer minimized this risk and grew to become a $1 billion company in less than five years by having an aggressive plan for developing a viable business architecture. By starting with a group of seasoned executives from Texas Instruments, Compaq had the luxury of an experienced and cohesive management team. They differentiated themselves from IBM and other DOS-based system manufacturers by developing the first truly portable computer, achieving sales of more than $100 million in 12 months. Instead of competing with retailers as IBM and Apple did, they offered key dealers exclusive franchises and high margins. They had all of their administrative systems in place before day one; five years later they were using the same accounting system and had not substantially changed their management structure. As John Gribi, senior vice president of finance, said, "You have a clean slate, but

Synthesis

Passing the initial product-market test does not mean a company has found a sustainable formula for success. Consultants estimate that competitors secure detailed information on 70 percent of new products within one year of introduction, and that 60 to 90 percent of all "process learning" is eventually acquired by competitors. The objective during the Synthesis stage is to manage the tension between the need for change and the desire for stability. This is done by developing a sound foundation of core values that guides the changes in strategy, structure, capabilities, and human resources necessary to deliver superior customer value in turbulent and dynamic conditions. A commitment to continuous, market-driven learning provides the context for recognizing when and where change is required to sustain competitive advantage.

Organizational learning is the development of new knowledge or insights that have the potential to influence behavior. Learning organizations continuously acquire, analyze, and disseminate knowledge about markets, products, technologies, and business processes. Information may be acquired through direct experience, from the experiences of others, and from organizational memory. The clearest illustration of acquiring knowledge from experience is seen in the learning curve, or experience curve, which shows the effect of cumulative production and user experience on productivity in manufacturing. Other examples of learning from experience include the use of large-scale demonstration projects and small-scale market experiments. Learning by experience is of particular importance, because commitment to change is most likely to occur when employees see that a new way of doing something leads to improved performance.

Learning from others encompasses such common practices as benchmarking, working with lead customers, forming joint ventures, networks, and strategic alliances, and providing continuous education or training. Effective managers establish multiple credible internal and external sources to obtain objective information about their enterprise and its environment. To avoid tunnel vision, executives who aggressively seek new potential threats or opportunities make sure their networks include people who look at the world quite differently from the dominating culture of the firm. For example, Coca-Cola recently undertook a "secret and unorthodox" study that solicited advice from "ten unconventional thinkers"—including Peter Drucker, Ted Levitt, and Arthur Nielsen—in an attempt to reorient its advertising campaign radically to distinguish itself from Pepsi-Cola.

Once the knowledge has been acquired, managers must balance the importance of further refinements to existing processes with the benefits from continued exploration. Without refinement, the organization will not maximize the potential of the innovation, thereby possibly leaving a substantial opportunity for a competitor to perfect the idea and gain the greatest advantage from it. However, too much reliance on exploitation focuses the company on what it is already doing and may lead it into a competency trap.

Conversely, too much reliance on exploration may lead to too many underdeveloped concepts and ideas, and may be too inefficient and expensive as well.

Through complex communication, coordination, and conflict resolution processes, learning firms reach a shared interpretation of the information that enables them to act swiftly and decisively to exploit opportunities and defuse problems. Learning firms are constantly in motion and constantly improving. Because change is the norm, it rarely seems dramatic. Organizations that are able to sustain synthesis stand out in their ability to anticipate and act on opportunities in turbulent and fragmenting markets.

Paralysis

Roger Martin (1993), a high-tech consultant, describes Paralysis as a situation wherein "corporations have created a world in which managers not only cannot see what is salient in their markets, they have gradually become impervious to learning." An inability to learn and adapt in changing conditions is responsible for the predicaments in which such icons of American industry as GM, IBM, and Sears have recently found themselves. The irony is that many of these companies believe they are making fundamental changes through what I call the "Program du Jour." Under the banners of "total quality," "process reengineering," or "world class service," among others, these programs advance a managerial philosophy and give managers and employees a warm feeling, but have very little impact on the company's capacity for delivering superior customer value. This helps to understand the pervasive dissatisfaction with the results of these programs.

Because of the rapid change in the personal computer industry, Compaq maintained its competitive advantage by constantly focusing on technology. But its mistake was to overlook the emergence of a new type of competitor, such as Dell. As Compaq's head of North American operations said, "We had so much success for so long, it got embedded in our DNA code" (Kirkpatrick 1992). The result was the kind of tunnel vision that left them vulnerable to ambush. Even after sales and earnings began to decline, managers continued to deny that anything was fundamentally wrong.

This is characteristic of the conditions that lead to the necessity for dramatic change. Like so many U.S. companies, Compaq had focused its efforts on maintaining excellence in key functional areas (some call this the silo or chimney mentality), such as R&D or manufacturing, and had focused its programmatic learning efforts in those areas. What was happening, though, was the commoditization of the personal computer, which substantially changed the value equation for both buyers and manufacturers. Thus, the crisis Compaq faced in 1991 was so fundamental to its entire business structure that nothing short of a radical reorientation would be enough to restore the firm to a position as market leader.

The first step was to promote Eckhard Pfeiffer, the head of the company's very successful European operation, to CEO. To increase product availability and combat the service offered by mail order competitors, Compaq added thousands of retailers to its distribution scheme. To become cost competitive, the company reevaluated its traditional practice of assembling every nut and bolt itself and began subcontracting subassembly work. To ensure on-time product delivery to customers, it developed a worldwide integrated logistics system and a built-to-order manufacturing system. All these changes required extensive coordination among Compaq's suppliers, factories, and distribution centers around the world, but the efforts managed to double Compaq's share of the PC market and returned it to profitability.

Two observations emerge from this example. First, the "Program du Jour" philosophy will not produce fundamental learning, change, and performance improvement, and will ultimately require a widespread strategic reorientation. Second, it seems that progression through the stages cannot be reversed. Compaq essentially had to return to the genesis stage, where major change rested on very little stability. Once a firm reaches paralysis, either the threats are too imminent or the organizational routines too entrenched for

transformation to occur in a meaningful and timely way.

CHARACTERISTICS OF LEARNING ORGANIZATIONS

Although it certainly is possible for a company to reinvent itself—as the examples of such companies as Compaq, AT&T, and Ford demonstrate—it is a gut-wrenching experience for employees, managers, and stockholders. How is it that the 3Ms, Johnson & Johnsons, and PepsiCos seem able to avoid the turmoil of paralysis and reinvention? My research in this area, described in **Figure 2**, and my work with several companies on issues of change and learning have demonstrated that there are three essential features of a learning organization: facilitative leadership; a market-driven, entrepreneurial culture; and an open, organic structure. Let's turn now to a discussion of what these terms really mean.

Facilitative Leadership

Facilitative leaders are adept at three critical tasks. First, they articulate a clear and challenging vision for their firm based on their insights into key industry trends that can be the catalyst for redefining the foundation of competition. Second, they focus on developing the people around them, motivating them to want to learn and take greater responsibility. Third, they lead in "unlearning"—the conscious effort to challenge traditional assumptions about the company and its environment.

Why does articulating a vision facilitate organizational learning? The reason is that the vision itself must be the product of a thorough inquiry process. An organizational vision is not the result of the CEO going to the mountaintop and "having a vision." It must be grounded in a thorough understanding of trends in the nature of market composition, customer needs, relevant technologies, and competitive forces.

Just as important, the vision provides focus for the learning efforts taking place in the firm. It is the glue that holds all the change efforts together in such a way that the learning in product development, quality management, and customer service all work together to move the organization forward in a purposeful manner. This is crucial, for it is possible to learn a great deal about things that are not relevant to the organization's future. Xerox has been criticized for failing to capitalize on its many innovations in the "office of the future," which fell outside the corporation's vision of where it wanted to go and what it

Figure 2
Research Description

This study was conducted with 53 independent businesses or strategic business units of larger corporations in three large western cities. We surveyed the general manager, top marketing officer, and human resource manager in each business to obtain information about its competitive environment, strategy, leadership style, culture, planning style, organization, personnel policies, and performance. Each respondent in the business provided information about a unique set of business characteristics to avoid the frequent problem of common respondent bias. Responses were subjected to standard tests to ensure their reliability and validity. Business data were analyzed by step-wise multiple regression analysis with interaction terms to determine the combinations of variables that have the greatest influence on performance. After controlling for competitive environment and such theoretically important business-specific factors as cost and quality position, the key performance indicators of profitability, growth, and new product success appear to be maximized in a business characterized by a facilitative style of leadership; a market-driven, entrepreneurial culture; and a flexible, organic structure.

wanted to be. Though a more insightful vision might have enabled Xerox to take advantage of the knowledge it had developed, pursuing activities outside the corporate vision was a distraction and a waste of shareholders' money.

Because of increasing market, technological, and managerial complexity, the day of the CEO as forceful commander has passed. Jack Welch, CEO of General Electric, has succeeded at empowering his management and executive staff to manage their own businesses, and has handed over substantial power to "process champions." His intention is "to take out the boss element." Raymond Smith, according to Kanter (1991), explains that Bell Atlantic is moving from a leadership style "in which people are handed procedures to follow mindlessly" to one that "helps them make tough choices."

These leaders are able to raise the awareness of colleagues, clients, and others about key issues. They arouse or alter the strength of values that may have been dormant or subverted. They foster a climate in which "inquiry and commitment to the truth are the norm, and where challenging the status quo is expected," says Senge (1990). They motivate their people to do more than what is expected of them. Such a leadership style means abandoning the role of expert, whose job it is to tell subordinates the correct way to do things. Instead, the leader acts as a coach, helping to surface assumptions and see patterns and relationships among people, firms, and events. By understanding the nature of these systematic relationships, subordinates take responsibility for learning and make better decisions with less interference from top management.

A caveat is in order here, though: Empowering subordinates must be done carefully. Increasing responsibility without providing the training or tools to execute it effectively will lead to poor decisions, demoralized employees, and probably a reversion to the old management paradigm of centralized decision making. Grooming and developing a sense of capability before empowering with additional responsibility is critical.

Leaders must also take a key role in "unlearning" traditional but detrimental practices. By surfacing and challenging their own assumptions and mental models, they encourage employees to do the same. Faced with turbulence in traditional markets and an entrenched culture, Ed Artzt, CEO of Procter & Gamble, found himself in the peculiar situation of having to make "rules that give [employees] intellectual permission to make changes" (Saporito 1994). As John Seely Brown (1991), the chief scientist of the Xerox Palo Alto Research Center, explains, "Unlearning is critical in these chaotic times because so many of our hard-earned nuggets of knowledge, intuitions,

and just plain opinions depend on assumptions about the world that are simply no longer true." Encouraging unlearning could be the single most important task of the CEO in sustaining the momentum of continuous learning and to avoid slipping into paralysis.

A Market-Driven, Entrepreneurial Culture

Organizational culture is the set of values and beliefs that provide norms for individual behavior. A market-driven, entrepreneurial culture: (1) places the highest priority on the profitable creation and maintenance of superior customer value while considering the interests of other key stakeholders; (2) encourages the company-wide development of and responsiveness to market intelligence; and (3) empowers people and teams to experiment and take well-conceived risks.

Sinkula (1994) and Slater and Narver (1995), among others, argue that market orientation, as an overall organizational value system, provides strong norms for sharing information and reaching consensus on its meaning. Through its external emphasis on developing information about customers, competitors, and other key market influencers, the market-driven business is well-positioned to anticipate the developing needs of its customers and respond through the addition of innovative new products and services. This gives the market-driven business an advantage in both the speed and effectiveness of its responsiveness to opportunities and threats. Slater and Narver (1994) have demonstrated a strong relationship between the behaviors exhibited by market-oriented businesses and learning-driven performance outcomes, such as superior new product success and sales growth.

A culture that also values entrepreneurship and innovation provides an environment in which learning from exploration and experimentation is most likely to occur. Entrepreneurial cultures value such traits as high tolerance for risk, action, receptivity to innovation, and active resistance to bureaucracy. These traits promote the acquisition of knowledge through exploration—challenging assumptions to create breakthrough opportunities—and the rapid development of new behaviors to leverage learning.

To maximize learning and minimize the risk inherent in entrepreneurial activities, successful innovators frequently work intensively with lead customers, undertake low-cost market experiments, or continuously experiment around the edges through ongoing programs. To ensure understanding of the causes of success or failure, these activities are subjected to systematic analysis, such as the "Five Whys" in Womack, Jones, and Roos (1990) or Deming's "Plan-Do-Check-

Act" process (Garvin 1993). This systematic analysis reduces the chances that the firm will move on too quickly to the next experiment without reaping the benefits of the current exercise. It also increases the likelihood of a shared interpretation of the meaning of the experience, leading to improved prospects for coordinated action to leverage the learning.

As Webster (1994) summarizes, "Management must develop a broader concept of organizational culture that focuses the firm outward—on its customers and competitors—and creates an overwhelming predisposition toward entrepreneurial and innovative responsiveness to a changing market." These core values provide the stable foundation on which variations in strategy, structure, and capabilities may be developed.

An Open, Organic Structure

Learning organizations recognize the substantial opportunity to learn from collaborations with customers, suppliers, universities, and other potential learning partners. Information is most valuable when it is shared because each partner brings additional knowledge and insight to the situation. Business is moving away from Porter's (1980) model, in which the strength of competitive forces dictates strategic choice, toward the recognition that the power of collaborative forces also influences company strategy and performance. As Webster (1992) notes, "New organization forms, including strategic partnerships and networks, are replacing simple market-based transactions." Organizational learning capability is strongly influenced by a willingness to develop and work closely with learning partners.

In complex and dynamic environments, high-performing firms employ an "organic form," an organizational architecture that is decentralized, with fluid and ambiguous job responsibilities and extensive lateral communication processes. Members of these organizations, both internal and external, recognize their interdependence and are willing to cooperate and share information to sustain the firm's effectiveness. The necessity of effective information sharing in the learning organization demands that systematic or structural constraints on information flows be dismantled and that there is high frequency and informality in organizational communication patterns.

An organic structure has both formal and informal features. People are grouped into functional units for housekeeping purposes, but deployed in project teams to accomplish specific tasks. Mutual adjustment within and between the task teams requires that information be shared efficiently and that decisions be made flexibly

and informally to promote innovation and creativity. Because standardization and bureaucratic routines are precluded as coordinating mechanisms, coordination becomes the responsibility of experts rather than people with hierarchical authority. Consequently, the organization must make use of liaison devices, such as cross-unit committees, integrator positions, shared databases, and matrix structures, to encourage informal information sharing and discussion.

The emphasis on information in an organic structure facilitates achievement of consensus on its meaning and its implications for the business. High-performing firms in dynamic and complex markets strive for consensus to assure more effective strategy implementation. However, before achieving consensus, says Dess (1987), "Organizations competing within an industry experiencing high growth may benefit from a relatively high level of disagreement in assessing the relative importance of company objectives and competitive methods." The result of disagreement is a closer inspection of the validity of different assumptions and alternatives. High performance in high-velocity environments requires balancing the need for rapid decision-making with the need to consider carefully the ramifications of alternative action plans through effective conflict resolution processes.

It has often been paraphrased that change is the only constant. It is essential, then, that businesses embrace this philosophy and the corollary that there can be no beginning or end to the transformation process. Rejecting these concepts ensures that a firm will eventually slip into paralysis, where its strategy and structure are no longer appropriate to the demands of the competitive environment. Maintaining synthesis or alignment with the demands of the environment requires a total commitment to the principles of continuous organizational learning.

My research has shown that continuous, innovative learning is most likely to occur in firms characterized by a facilitative, empowering style of leadership; a market-driven, entrepreneurial culture in which challenging the status quo is encouraged; and a structure that has flexible processes for communication, coordination, and conflict resolution among its own members and with its learning partners. Companies that possess all three characteristics achieve superior new product success, sales growth, and profitability. In a dynamic environment, a well-honed learning capability is a necessity for developing and sustaining competitive advantage.

References

C. Argyris and D. Schon, *Organizational Learning: A Theory of Action Perspective* (Reading, MA: Addison-Wesley, 1978).

M. Beer, R.A. Eisenstat, and B. Spector, "Why Change Programs Don't Produce Change," *Harvard Business Review*, November-December 1990, pp. 158-166.

L.J. Bourgeois and K. Eisenhardt, "Strategic Decision Processes in High Velocity Environments: Four Cases in the Microcomputer Industry," *Management Science*, 34 (1988): 816-835.

John Seely Brown, "Research That Reinvents the Corporation," *Harvard Business Review*, January-February 1991, pp. 102-111.

George S. Day, *Market Driven Strategy: Processes for Creating Value* (New York: The Free Press 1990).

Gregory G. Dess, "Consensus on Strategy Formulation and Organizational Performance: Competitors in a Fragmented Industry," *Strategic Management Journal*, May-June 1987, pp. 259-277.

Gregory G. Dess and Nancy K. Origer, "Environment, Structure, and Consensus in Strategy Formulation: A Conceptual Integration," *Academy of Management Review*, April 1987, pp. 313-330.

Jeanie Daniel Duck, "Managing Change: The Art of Balancing," *Harvard Business Review*, November-December 1993, pp. 109-118.

Kathleen M. Eisenhardt, "Making Fast Strategic Decisions in High-Velocity Environments," *Academy of Management Journal*, September 1989, pp. 543-576.

Stuart Gannes, "America's Fastest-Growing Companies," *Fortune*, May 23, 1988, pp. 28-40.

David A. Garvin, "Building a Learning Organization," *Harvard Business Review*, July-August 1993, pp. 78-91.

Pankaj Ghemawat, "Sustainable Advantage," *Harvard Business Review*, September-October 1986, pp. 53-58.

Anil K. Gupta and Vijay Govindarajan, "Knowledge Flows and the Structure of Control Within Multinational Corporations," *Academy of Management Review, 16*, 4 (1991): 768-792.

Gary Hamel and C.K. Prahalad, "Corporate Imagination and Expeditionary Marketing," *Harvard Business Review*, July-August 1991, pp. 81-92.

Rosabeth Moss Kanter, *When Giants Learn to Dance* (New York: Touchstone, 1989).

Rosabeth Moss Kanter, "Championing Change: An Interview with Bell Atlantic's CEO Raymond Smith," *Harvard Business Review*, January-February 1991, pp. 118-130.

David Kirkpatrick, "The Revolution at Compaq Computer," *Fortune*, December 14, 1992, pp. 80-88.

Stephanie Losee, "How Compaq Keeps the Magic Going," *Fortune*, February 21, 1994, pp. 90-92.

James G. March, "Exploration and Exploitation in Organizational Learning," *Organization Science, 2*, 1 (1991): 71-87.

Roger Martin, "Changing the Mind of the Corporation," *Harvard Business Review*, November-December 1993, pp. 81-94.

R.E. Miles and C.C. Snow, "Causes of Failure in Network Organizations," *California Management Review*, Summer 1992, pp. 53-72.

H. Mintzberg, "The Innovative Organization," in H. Mintzberg and James Brian Quinn, eds., *The Strategy Process: Concepts, Contexts, Cases*, 2nd ed. (Englewood Cliffs, NJ: Prentice-Hall, 1991), pp. 731-746.

Ikujiro Nonaka, "The Knowledge-Creating Company," *Harvard Business Review*, November-December 1991, pp. 96-104.

Tom Peters, "Do We Know Anything For Sure?" (Peters on Excellence), *Colorado Springs Business Journal*, July 15, 1994, p. 20.

M.E. Porter, *Competitive Strategy: Techniques for Analyzing Industries and Competitors* (New York: The Free Press, 1980).

James B. Quinn, *Intelligent Enterprise* (New York: The Free Press, 1992).

Bill Saporito, "Behind the Tumult at P&G," *Fortune*, March 7, 1994, pp. 74-82.

Robert Schaffer and Harvey Thomson, "Successful Change Programs Begin with Results," *Harvard Business Review*, January-February 1992, pp. 80-89.

Patricia Sellers, "Do You Need Your Ad Agency?" *Fortune*, November 15, 1993, pp. 147-164.

P.M. Senge, *The Fifth Discipline* (New York: Doubleday, 1990).

James M. Sinkula, "Market Information Processing and Organizational Learning," *Journal of Marketing*, January 1994, pp. 35-45.

Stanley F. Slater and John Narver, "Does a Competitive Environment Moderate the Market Orientation Performance Relationship?" *Journal of Marketing*, January 1994, pp. 46-55.

Stanley F. Slater and John Narver, "Market Orientation and the Learning Organization," *Journal of Marketing*, July 1995, pp. 63-74.

Ray Stata, "Organizational Learning—The Key to Management Innovation," *Sloan Management Review*, Spring 1989, pp. 63-74.

Thomas A. Stewart, "GE Keeps Those Ideas Coming," in R. Kanter, B.A. Stein, and T.D. Jick, eds., *The Challenge of Organizational Change* (New York: The Free Press, 1992): 474-482.

E. Von Hippel, "Lead Users: A Source of Novel Product Concepts," *Management Science*, July 1986, pp. 791-805.

Frederick E. Webster Jr., "The Changing Role of Marketing in the Corporation," *Journal of Marketing*, October 1992, pp. 1-17.

Frederick E. Webster Jr., "Executing the New Marketing Concept," *Marketing Management, 3*, 1 (1994): 9-16.

James P. Womack, Daniel T. Jones, and Daniel Roos, *The Machine That Changed the World: The Story of Lean Production* (New York: Harper Collins Publishers, 1990).

Richard W. Woodman, John E. Sawyer, and Ricky W. Griffin, "Toward a Theory of Organizational Creativity," *Academy of Management Review, 18*, 2 (1993): 293-321.

Stanley F. Slater is an associate professor of strategic management and marketing at the University of Colorado in Colorado Springs. The author gratefully acknowledges the research assistance of Ethan Bronner and the financial support of the UCCS Committee for Research and Creative Works.

THE NEW MILLENNIUM WORKPLACE:

Seven Changes That Will Challenge Managers— And Workers

By Robert Barner

Work provides the food we eat, the clothes we wear, the roof over our heads, and far more. So it behooves us all to better understand the changes surrounding the workplace.

In the years ahead, the workplace will become dramatically different from what it is now, due to such factors as electronically linked work sites, computerized coaching and monitoring equipment, and a more diverse work force.

To obtain firsthand information on the changes occurring in the workplace, during the past year I conducted a detailed literary research of workplace trends, supplemented by five focus-group sessions and individual interviews involving over 200 work professionals, representing such diverse industries as telecommunications, electric utilities, retail sales, and governmental organizations.

What emerged from this research are the following seven trends that I believe will reshape work environments over the next 10 years.

1 The Virtual Organization

We are rapidly moving toward a distributed work force that uses electronic technology to link workers and functions at scattered sites. This change is rapidly altering the nature of work, from the sales representative whose company database allows her to give customers immediate information on new product features, to the shipping employee who can monitor goods in real time.

The growth of the virtual organization will be fueled by three factors:

• The rapid evolution of electronic technologies, which are facilitating the digital, wireless transfer of video, audio, and text information.

• The rapid spread of computer networks, in which the United States now maintains a strong global advantage over many other countries, including Japan.

• The growth of telecommuting, which will enable companies to provide faster response to customers, reduce facility expenses, and help workers meet their child- and elder-care responsibilities.

One implication of this trend is that people will need to develop specialized communication and planning skills to succeed in the virtual-work environment. Traditionally, managers who lacked communication and planning skills often compensated for these skills through iterative face-to-face discussions, requiring team members to come back to them again and again to clarify performance goals or decision-making authority. To capitalize on the flexibility and speed that are possible through distributed, networked teams, managers and team members will have to form clear, upfront agreements regarding: (a) performance expectations; (b) the team's priorities; (c) how communications are to be carried out among members; and (d) the degree of resource support for telecommuters (e.g., dedicated business lines installed in the home or home-based printers).

Another challenge will be information overload—the kind that occurs when a worker finds 60 e-mail messages waiting. Some people are already finding ways to counter this through the use of "bozo filters"—software programs that automatically screen out the messages of certain e-mail senders.

To prevent information overload, communication skills will need to be geared for the virtual organization. An example is the ability to communicate electronically without the subtle, nonverbal cues that we get in face-to-face communications. When these cues are suddenly absent, as they are in e-mail correspondence, the result can be a misunderstanding or misinterpretation of messages that seem extremely blunt or antagonistic.

Electronic networking can redistribute power in organizations. Computer networks make it technically feasible for employees to skip levels in the chain of command, providing senior managers with direct feedback on performance problems and questions regarding organizational issues. Electronic bulletin boards let workers anonymously raise organizational issues, and they provide an effective rumor-control mechanism. But networks can also make employees at remote sites feel as if they are part of the team.

Computer networks require faster decisions from both individuals and groups. Only a few years ago, many people relied on "float"—the gap between when you wrote a check and when the bank actually cashed it—as a safety buffer for ensuring sufficient funds. Computer technology has eliminated that financial float, and it has also eliminated decision float. Workers who are given immediate access to business information and feedback on team performance are under greater pressure to respond faster to organizational demands; those who demonstrate skills in fast-response decision making will find themselves in a strong, competitive position in the networked marketplace.

The virtual organization will also reshape traditional approaches to group decision making. Research done by Lee Sproull and Sara Kiesler, authors of *Connections: New Ways of Working in the Networked Organization* (MIT Press, 1991), suggests that, in contrast to face-to-face discussions, e-mail discussions make low-status individuals less hesitant to participate in discussions and to relinquish their points of view. As a result, e-mail decision-making sessions can take much longer to resolve—a phenomenon that runs counter to current pressures to streamline group decision making. This finding will have serious implications for organizations attempting to support employee empowerment and strengthen team performance.

To meet these challenges, workers will need to develop skills in network-based decision making, including the use of such specialized tools as group-decision-support software. Such tools will help to streamline decision making by enabling each worker to evaluate options without discussing it with the group, then automatically computing the team's overall decision. This approach offers obvious advantages for teams that are trying to coordinate efforts across different time zones or work shifts.

The virtual organization will change recruiting and career development. More headhunting firms and employees are using the Internet to match jobs and candidates. Organizations are using internal databases to profile employees' skills and find the most-qualified job candidates within the organization.

These changes will help employees identify alternative career targets and let cross-functional teams obtain the best possible mix of technical skills. Employee-skill databases will also make it more difficult for managers to hoard talent within their own teams.

2 The Just-in-Time Work Force

In the United States, the number of individuals employed by temporary agencies has increased 240% in the last 10 years. Along with using more just-in-time workers, organizations are also streamlining operations and reducing costs by outsourcing support functions such as information services, security, and human resources.

Finding new ways to motivate temporary employees will become a key issue. When organizations fail to address this issue, problems can occur in performance and morale. A recent *Fortune* article cites Kolmar Laboratories, a New York–based cosmetics firm, which experienced conflicts when the full-time employees tried to pressure temporary workers (almost half of the company's assembly work force) to speed up their production. Full-time workers were already motivated to increase their productivity, since they were being paid according to their production levels. But the temporary workers earned a flat hourly rate and therefore had no incentive to work harder or faster.

This example illustrates the difficulty of motivating just-in-time workers, who lack traditional motivators such as promotions, merit increases, and profit-sharing programs. Just-in-time workers will be encouraged to take a higher degree of ownership in their work by providing them with access to information and training—formerly the prerogative of full-time staff. Another morale-boosting motivator is to solicit input and ideas from just-in-time workers.

In tomorrow's workplace, new just-in-time workers will need to be brought up to speed more quickly on company policies, procedures, and work practices. The issue of new-employee orientation is particularly important for highly paid professional positions such as engineers, computer programmers, and human resources personnel—areas experiencing rapid growth in just-in-time employees. Companies simply won't be able to afford to let such individuals gradually become acquainted with the workings of the organization. Electronic performance-support systems are one way to help increase the effectiveness of company orientation programs, providing just-in-time workers with real-time coaching and automated decision making.

3 The Ascendancy of Knowledge Workers

We are rapidly shifting from a work force that produces products to one that primarily manages information. Perhaps the fastest-growing segment of the knowledge work force is composed of technical specialists, such as medical technologists, paralegals, and computer installers, who have proliferated as a direct result of the growing need for hands-on technical experts who can support new technologies. Another factor has been the need for employers in fields such as law and medicine to reduce labor costs by shifting responsibilities to technical assistants.

The rapid growth of knowledge workers will require organizations to rethink their traditional approaches to directing, coaching, and motivating employees. In addition, as companies continue to downsize, they will be less willing to pay for "managerial purists"—people who do nothing but manage. Instead, managers will be expected to contribute technical expertise to their jobs and to be willing to roll up their sleeves and contribute when necessary.

Given the shrinking half-life for many technical skills, this change will place managers under additional pressure to avoid technical obsolescence. As an example, consider how long current software or engineering managers can afford to lag behind new technical developments

before finding themselves hopelessly outdated. Managers will have to make a strong commitment to life-long learning and skill advancement to achieve job security in the new work environment.

Given an increasingly mobile work force, tomorrow's managers will need to provide their teams with the historical context needed to understand the workings of the organization.

As corporate downsizings force knowledge workers to market themselves to a variety of companies, managers will have to continually educate new employees on corporate culture and values.

Knowledge about what was accomplished with the company's clients two years ago may get lost when the staff reshuffles, so managers will have to become repositories for organizational history. Some companies are beginning to respond to this challenge by factoring in human knowledge as a key component of their asset base and by creating cross-indexed "knowledge bases" that enable workers to shorten learning curves by tapping into each others' experiences.

Organizations will also be challenged to build effective team relationships between two different levels of knowledge workers—professionals and paraprofessionals. There is a growing potential for conflict between broad-based professionals and lower-paid technical specialists who are extremely skilled within a relatively narrow spectrum of their career field.

4 Computerized Coaching And Electronic Monitoring

Over the next 10 years, there will be a dramatic increase in the use of electronic systems to accelerate employee learning, augment decision making, and monitor performance. Proponents of these systems argue that they enable employees to learn their jobs faster, provide workers and managers with immediate performance feedback, and make it easier to pinpoint performance problems in large call-in centers.

The biggest drawback of electronic monitoring systems is that they can make employees feel helpless, manipulated, and exploited. Some employees might feel that their managers are using these tools to peer over their shoulders electronically. This could put many management–employee relationships under great stress. To address these concerns, organizations will need to ensure that managers use electronic monitoring systems appropriately in order to avoid legal challenges of misuse.

As we move toward the virtual organization over the next few years, it will become more difficult to delineate the dividing line between work and home, and to determine when an employee's rights of privacy have been violated. For example, should an e-mail message sent to an employee's home at 9 p.m. be viewed as an inherent feature of the networked job, or does it constitute a personal infringement on an employee's privacy?

Electronic "performance enhancement" systems will also decrease employees' dependence on managers for coaching, training, and performance feedback and help make self-directed learning a reality. While this will free up the manager's time, some managers may feel that these changes will threaten their traditional roles as coaches and advisers.

5 The Growth of Worker Diversity

In the next 10 years, worker diversity will become a critical issue. One reason is that, by the year 2000, 85% of people entering the U.S. job market for the first time will be women and minorities, and just 15% will be white males, according to U.S. Labor Department projections. Another factor is that companies are increasingly setting up manufacturing and assembly plants in other countries, and many smaller companies are expanding into international markets.

As a result, during the next few years many people will have their first experiences with multicultural work groups and will need to adapt to different work expectations and communication styles. Added to these changes is the explosion of computer networks. When we consider the phenomenon of flaming, it becomes easy to understand the types of e-mail based, cross-cultural communication breakdowns that could be generated as a byproduct of increased global interconnectivity.

These factors will encourage organizations to value highly those workers and managers who can operate within diversified employee groups. Sensitivity training will help managers understand the needs and perspectives of different members in work groups, including white male employees who may feel disenfranchised from their former power base. Companies will also need to become more adept at assessing workers' potential for success within long-term, multicultural, high-risk work assignments.

6 The Aging Work Force

By the turn of the century, the median age of U.S. workers will be 45; by 2005, more than 15% of the work force will be over 55. In addition, the trend toward early retirement has begun to reverse itself, as retirees facing rising costs are returning to paid employment.

Many managers assume that older workers are less productive, less flexible, and more expensive. Research shows that many such assumptions aren't true. One consequence of age bias is that managers tend to deny older workers challenging job assignments or technical training, thus creating a self-fulfilling prophecy that older employees are less competent.

Managers often don't even recognize when they are performing in ways that reflect age bias. To combat this, organizations must train managers to detect and combat age bias within themselves and others.

Companies are beginning to see the value of recruiting older employees, who can provide experience and maturity to the organization and who are often more flexible about taking part-time and odd-hour shifts. In addition, older workers better understand the needs of older customers.

The flip side of the age-bias problem occurs when younger managers are asked to direct older, more-experienced employees who have extensive knowledge of the organization's customers and work processes. Younger managers may find themselves threatened when directing the efforts of older, more-experienced workers. In this situation, managers need teamwork and communication skills that can enable them to extract the best efforts from their teams.

7 The Birth of the Dynamic Work Force

Work methods and functions are no longer permanent and immutable structures; they are fluid processes that require workers to adapt continuously. Organizations will be forced to question many of the "stable state" assumptions under which they've traditionally operated, such as who their competitors are and who their potential customers may be. For example, U.S. defense contractors are now shifting from governmental to commercial markets, while companies such as Motorola and Federal Express are recognizing the strong market advantage that can be obtained by meeting the growing customer demand for fast response in product design and delivery.

One impact of these trends is that, over the next few years, managerial performance will be based less on the ability to direct and coordinate work functions and more on improving key work processes.

Within stable-state organizations, a good manager is viewed as someone who consistently maintains solid performance within a team, while company loyalty is synonymous with defending the value of the organization's policies, procedures, and processes. In contrast, the dynamic organization recognizes the need for continuous improvement to meet changing customer requirements and competitor actions. In such organizations, managers will be increasingly judged on their ability to identify and implement improvements and to encourage innovative thinking from team members, while professionals will be judged on their ability to adapt quickly to widely different work environments.

Finally, the dynamic organization will require workers to be able to jump quickly into new ventures and manage temporary, project-focused teams, as more and more of their work responsibilities will lie outside of the traditional "work niche" consisting of a rigid job description and functional organizational "home."

Six Survival Skills For the "Protean" Manager

As these seven changes and implications have shown, the workplace of tomorrow will require managers who are "protean"—that is, flexible and adaptive enough to thrive within an ever-changing environment. The following six skills will prove to be an important part of the protean manager's job survival kit:

Skill 1: Rapid response. Managers will be expected to make fast decisions and respond quickly to changing demands. They'll need to know how to get immediate access to business information and performance feedback. Environmental scanning—tracking and identifying business and technological trends—can also help managers to improve the speed of their response.

Skill 2: Sharp focus. Managers directing just-in-time teams will need to precisely communicate goals, roles, and expectations. This will be especially true when team members are knowledge workers, for whom managers often find it difficult to articulate performance expectations and measures.

Skill 3: Stress busting. A critical skill for the future will be to maintain team performance in turbulent, high-pressure organizations. While tomorrow's managers won't be expected to be therapists, they will be expected to spot the warning signs of impending employee burnout and to help workers deal with high-stress situations.

Skill 4: Strategic empowerment. Tomorrow's managers will be trying to persuade employees to meet tougher performance standards even as companies severely reduce staff, resources, and motivators (e.g., promotional paths, job security, etc.). To meet this challenge, managers will need to both *empower* employees with authority and information, and *enable* them with successful self-management skills.

Skill 5: Staff juggling. The growth of the virtual organization

and the just-in-time work force, as well as the increased pressure to adopt flextime arrangements for core workers, means that managers will have to learn to juggle team assignments. To balance different work demands, managers will have to know how to realign workers quickly to meet performance goals and staff availability.

Skill 6: Team building. The ability to form teams in an environment of organizational diversity and geographically dispersed decision making will become paramount. Managers who are strong team builders will be especially critical in post-downsized work environments, in which teams are often locked in hostile, win–lose battles for limited

project resources and executive support.

About the Author

Robert Barner, a speaker and management consultant, is the Director of Organization and Management Development at Chep, USA. Telephone 407/422-4510.

His last article for THE FUTURIST was "The New Career Strategist: Career Management for the Year 2000 and Beyond" in the September–October 1994 issue.

The survival strategies mentioned in this article are adapted from his most-recent book, *Crossing the Minefield* (AMACOM, 1994). His first book, *Lifeboat Strategies* (AMACOM, 1994), is available from the Futurist Bookstore for $16.95 ($15.50 for Society members), cat. no. B-1788.

Case I: *Robin Hood*

Robin Hood awoke just as the sun was creeping over the crest of the hill in the very middle of Sherwood Forest. He was not the least rested, for he had not slept well that night. He could not get to sleep because of all the problems he was going to have to face today.

Certainly his campaign against the sheriff was going well, perhaps too well. It had all started out as a personal quarrel between the two of them, but now it was much more than just that. There was a price on his head of 1000 pounds, and there was no doubt that he was causing the sheriff a great deal of trouble, as taxes went uncollected or undelivered to the Crown, and rich men could not sleep soundly at night anywhere near Sherwood.

Things had changed since the early days, however. In those days it was just a small band of men, united in their cause against the sheriff, and for that matter, against Prince John, for the sheriff was simply doing John's bidding. But that was no longer the case. The fame of the Merry Men had grown and with it their numbers. He used to know each man as both a friend and companion, but now he didn't even know all of their names. Little John continued to keep discipline among the men as well as maintaining their skills with the bow, while Will Scarlet kept an eye on the sheriff, as well as any rich prospect who was foolish enough to travel Sherwood. Scarlock took care of the loot as he always had, and Much the Miller's Son continued to keep the men fed.

All this success was leading to problems. Game was, frankly, getting scarce as the number of men in the band increased, and the corresponding demand for food grew. Likely targets for the Merry Men were getting hard to find as more and more wealthy travelers were giving Sherwood a wide berth, as they were reluctant to part with their gold. Finally, the Sheriff and his men were getting better. Robin had always had the advantage of knowing Sherwood better than any man alive, but now there were at least several men who knew it almost as well as he, and some of them wore the colors of Prince John.

All this was leading Robin to reconsider his old ways. Perhaps a simple transit tax through Sherwood might be a part of the answer. But that might destroy his support among the people of the forest, and it had been rejected by the Merry Men, who were proud of their motto "Rob from the rich and give to the poor!" Besides, he needed the support of the poor, as they were his main source of information on the movements of the sheriff.

Killing the sheriff was not the answer. He would just be replaced, and, aside from quenching Robin's personal thirst for revenge, the new sheriff might be even more treacherous. Robin hated his enemy, but he had the advantage of knowing the sheriff's strengths and weaknesses. He would not know a new man's talents.

Prince John, on the other hand, was a vicious tyrant, a good part of which stemmed from his very weakness. The Barons were growing more restless every day, and the people simply hated him. They wanted King Richard back from his jail in Austria. Robin had been discreetly approached by several nobles loyal to Richard to join in the effort to free the King with the promise of a full pardon for him and all his men should they succeed. But Robin knew that if they failed, John would burn Sherwood and the rest of England to the ground to reap his vengeance. Theft and unrest in the provinces were one thing, intrigue at court was another.

Robin knew the days of the Merry Men were numbered. Even as they grew stronger, they grew weaker. Time was on the side of the sheriff, who could draw on all the power of the Crown if he had to, and, if Robin became too much of a threat, would surely do so.

Just then the horn blew for the traditional English breakfast of bread and ale. Robin would have breakfast with the Merry Men and then confer with Will Scarlet, Little John, and Scarlock.

Using the Case of *Robin Hood*

Robin Hood is a perfect example of a manager facing the problems of success. Robin's very success has created his problems.

Questions for Discussion

1. What are some of the problems facing Robin and the Merry Men?
2. What are some of the situations in the environment that will have an impact on whatever Robin decides to do?
3. What are some of the alternatives that Robin is considering for dealing with his problems? Can you identify some additional alternatives?
4. What do you think the reaction of Merry Men will be? The sheriff? The people?
5. What do you think Robin should do?

Exercise I: Managerial Development

1. Identify the best manager with whom you personally have interacted within the last seven years:
2. Why did you select that person? I selected him/her because:
   A. s/he:
   B. s/he:
   C. s/he:
3. Of the attributes you listed above, which is the most important for you? A, B, or C?
4. Why do you feel that is the most important attribute of a manager?
5. Identify the best employee with whom you personally have interacted within the past seven years.
6. Why did you select that person? I selected him/her because:
   A. s/he:
   B. s/he:
   C. s/he:
7. Of the attributes you listed above, which is the most important? A, B, or C?
8. Why do you feel that is the most important attribute of an employee?

Using the Exercise for *Managerial Development*

This exercise has been developed to give you the opportunity to establish a role model for managerial and employee behavior. It provides a useful tool for determining your attitude toward what makes a good manager and a good employee.

It might be particularly useful to do the exercise during the first few days of class, discuss it, and then, at the end of the term, redo the exercise to determine if there has been any changes in your perception of the best manager and employee and what they did.

It is recommended that you keep the papers so that they can be used for reference during a class discussion of managerial and employee behavior. The names of the individuals are not important. The ideas, perceptions, and attitudes of those people are what count.

Planning

Managers must plan. Planning must be accomplished before action takes place. The question is, how should managers plan and decide on a course of action?

There are various styles, methods, and techniques a manager can use in planning and decision making. As Victor Vroom demonstrates in his classic essay, "A New Look at Managerial Decision Making," the way the decision is made will be a key factor in the implementation of the plan. People who feel they have some participation in making important decisions that will affect them are far more likely to support the plan enthusiastically than are people who feel the decision is a fiat from the upper reaches of the organization chart. Of course, a manager can make some decisions alone, or in consultation with a few people. The important point is to select the appropriate planning/decision-making style, so that the action will have the greatest chance for success. The way to accomplish this is to involve the people who will be most directly concerned with the implementation of that decision.

It is basic to the function of a manager that he or she must make decisions. It is not possible for the policy manual to cover every situation that can arise. Managers must be able to interpret the goals and objectives of the plans they have devised and make decisions for the good of the organization—not an easy task. Since there is always a degree of uncertainty in an important decision, the organization is also obligated to provide the manager with support and resources so that the decisions will succeed. Support includes not only a recognition and knowledge of the firm and its plans, but an understanding of the organization's internal and external environment.

Planning must consider the internal strengths and weaknesses of the organization, including finance, human resources, manufacturing, distribution, and marketing. Capitalizing on strengths while minimizing the impact of weaknesses is vital to successful planning. Strategic decision making also involves an assessment of the environment as well as an understanding of the corporate culture, as seen in "Global Strategic Management in a New World Order," and humorously expressed by Scott Adams in "Dilbert's Management Handbook." Organizations must interact with their surroundings. Those who manage and plan for organizations must recognize that the only constant is change. Everything is fluid: people, places, and things, and managing the strategic agenda will be a key to success.

Finally, there are many ways to plan and make strategy. The effectiveness of the plans depends on the nature and needs of the business, the styles of the people, and the goals and plans of the firm. The four basic questions in strategic planning are: (1) Where have we been? (2) Where are we now? (3) Where do we want to go? (4) How do we want to get there? These questions must be answered by each firm's management as they plan for the organization in a changing and uncertain world.

Looking Ahead: Challenge Questions

Decision making can vary in approach and style. What styles would you use in certain situations?

The job of the manager is to make decisions. What can organizations do to assist managers in decision making?

Strategic analysis is a big part of the planning process. What factors must managers consider when planning for the firm?

UNIT 2

A NEW LOOK AT MANAGERIAL DECISION MAKING

Victor H. Vroom

Victor H. Vroom, Professor, Yale University

All managers are decision makers. Furthermore, their effectiveness as managers is largely reflected in their track record in making the right decisions. These right decisions in turn largely depend on whether or not the manager has utilized the right person or persons in the right ways in helping him solve the problem.

Our concern in this article is with decision making as a social process. We view the manager's task as determining how the problem is to be solved, not the solution to be adopted. Within that overall framework, we have attempted to answer two broad sets of questions: What decision-making processes should managers use to deal effectively with the problems they encounter in their jobs? What decision-making processes do they use in dealing with these problems and what considerations affect their decisions about how much to share their decision-making power with subordinates?

The reader will recognize the former as a normative or prescriptive question. A rational and analytic answer to it would constitute a normative model of decision making as a social process. The second question is descriptive, since it concerns how managers do, rather than should, behave.

Towards a Normal Model

About four years ago, Philip Yetton, then a graduate student at Carnegie-Mellon University, and I began a major research program in an attempt to answer these normative and descriptive questions.

We began with the normative question: What would be a rational way of deciding on the form and amount of participation in decision making that should be used in different situations? We were tired of debates over the relative merits of Theory X and Theory Y and of the truism that leadership depends upon the situation. We felt that it was time for the behavioral sciences to move beyond such generalities and to attempt to come to grips with the complexities of the phenomena with which they intended to deal.

Our aim was ambitious—to develop a set of ground rules for matching a manager's leadership behavior to the demands of the situation. It was critical that these ground rules be consistent with research evidence concerning the consequences of participation and that the model based on the rules be operational, so that any manager could see it to determine how he should act in any decision-making situation.

Table 1 shows a set of alternative decision processes that we have employed in our research. Each process is represented by a symbol (e.g., AI, CI, GII) that will be used as a convenient method of referring to each process. The first letter in this symbol signifies the basic properties of the process (A stands for autocratic; C for consultative; and G for group). The Roman numerals that follow the first letter constitute variants on that process. Thus, AI represents the first variant on an autocratic process, and AII the second variant.

Conceptual and Empirical Basis of the Model

A model designed to regulate, in some rational way, choices among the decisions processes shown in Table 1 should be based on sound empirical evidence concerning the likely consequences of the styles. The more complete the empirical base of knowledge, the greater the certainty with which we can develop the model and the greater will be its usefulness. To aid in understanding the conceptual basis of the model, it is important to distinguish among three classes of outcomes that bear on the ultimate effectiveness of decisions. These are:

1. The quality or rationality of the decision.
2. The acceptance or commitment on the part of subordinates to execute the decision effectively.
3. The amount of time required to make the decision.

The effects of participation on each of these outcomes or consequences were summed up by the author in *The Handbook of Social Psychology* as follows:

The results suggest that allocating problem solving and decision-making tasks to entire groups requires a greater

TABLE 1

TYPES OF MANAGEMENT DECISION STYLES

AI   You solve the problem or make the decision yourself, using information available to you at that time.

AII   You obtain the necessary information from your subordinate(s), then decide on the solution to the problem yourself. You may or may not tell your subordinates what the problem is in getting the information from them. The role played by your subordinates in making the decision is clearly one of providing the necessary information to you, rather than generating or evaluating alternative solutions.

CI   You share the problem with relevant subordinates individually, getting their ideas and suggestions without bringing them together as a group. Then *you* make the decision that may or may not reflect your subordinates' influence.

CII   You share the problem with your subordinates as a group, collectively obtaining their ideas and suggestions. Then *you* make the decision that may or may not reflect your subordinates' influence.

GII   You share a problem with your subordinates as a group. Together you generate and evaluate alternatives and attempt to reach agreement (consensus) on a solution. Your role is much like that of chairman. You do not try to influence the group to adopt *your* solution and you are willing to accept and implement any solution that has the support of the entire group.

(GI is omitted because it applies only to more comprehensive models outside the scope of this article.)

investment of man hours but produces higher acceptance of decisions and a higher probability that the decision will be executed efficiently. Differences between these two methods in quality of decisions and in elapsed time are inconclusive and probably highly variable. . . . It would be naive to think that group decision making is always more "effective" than autocratic decision making, or vice versa; the relative effectiveness of these two extreme methods depends both on the weights attached to quality, acceptance and time variables and on differences in amounts of these outcomes resulting from these methods, neither of which is invariant from one situation to another. The critics and proponents of participative management would do well to direct their efforts toward identifying the properties of situations in which different decision-making approaches are effective rather than wholesale condemnation or deification of one approach.

We have gone on from there to identify the properties of the situation or problem that will be the basic elements in the model. These problem attributes are of two types: 1) Those that specify the importance for a particular problem of quality and acceptance, and 2) those that, on the basis of available evidence, have a high probability of moderating the effects of participation on each of these outcomes. Table 2 shows the problem attributes used in the present form of the model. For each attribute a question is provided that might be used by a leader in diagnosing a particular problem prior to choosing his leadership style.

In phrasing the questions, we have held technical language

to a minimum. Furthermore, we have phrased the questions in Yes-No form, translating the continuous variables defined above into dichotomous variables. For example, instead of attempting to determine how important the decision quality is to the effectiveness of the decision (attribute A), the leader is asked in the first question to judge whether there is any quality component to the problem. Similarly, the difficult task of specifying exactly how much information the leader possesses that is relevant to the decision (attribute B) is reduced to a simple judgment by the leader concerning whether or not he has sufficient information to make a high quality decision.

We have found that managers can diagnose a situation quickly and accurately by answering this set of seven questions concerning it. But how can such responses generate a prescription concerning the most effective leadership style or decision process? What kind of normative model of participation in decision making can be built from this set of problem attributes?

Figure 1 shows one such model expressed in the form of a decision tree. It is the seventh version of such a model that

TABLE 2

PROBLEM ATTRIBUTES USED IN THE MODEL

	Problem Attributes	Diagnostic Questions
A.	The importance of the quality of the decision.	Is there a quality requirement such that one solution is likely to be more rational than another?
B.	The extent to which the leader possesses sufficient information/expertise to make a high-quality decision by himself.	Do I have sufficient information to make a high-quality decision?
C.	The extent to which the problem is structured.	Is the problem structured?
D.	The extent to which acceptance or commitment on the part of subordinates is critical to the effective implementation of the decision.	Is acceptance of decision by subordinates critical to effective implementation?
E.	The prior probability that the leader's autocratic decision will receive acceptance by subordinates.	If you were to make the decision by yourself, is it reasonably certain that it would be accepted by your subordinates?
F.	The extent to which subordinates are motivated to attain the organizational goals as represented in the objectives explicit in the statement of the problem.	Do subordinates share the organizational goals to be obtained in solving this problem?
G.	The extent to which subordinates are likely to be in conflict over preferred solutions.	Is conflict among subordinates likely in preferred solutions?

we have developed over the last three years. The problem attributes, expressed in question form, are arranged along the top of the figure. To use the model for a particular decision-making situation, one starts at the left-hand side and works toward the right asking oneself the question immediately above any box that is encountered. When a terminal node is reached, a number will be found designating the problem type and one of the decision-making processes appearing in Table 1. AI is prescribed for four problem types (1, 2, 4, and 5); AII is prescribed for two problem types (9 and 10); CI is prescribed for only one problem type (8); CII is prescribed for four problems types (7, 11, 13, and 14); and GII is prescribed for three problem types (3, 6, and 12). The relative frequency with which each of the five decision processes would be prescribed for any manager would, of course, depend on the distribution of problem types encountered in his decision making.

Rationale Underlying the Model. The decision processes specified for each problem type are not arbitrary. The model's behavior is governed by a set of principles intended to be consistent with existing evidence concerning the consequences of participation in decision making on organizational effectiveness.

There are two mechanisms underlying the behavior of the model. The first is a set of seven rules* that serve to protect the quality and the acceptance of the decision by eliminating alternatives that risk one or the other of these decision outcomes. Once the rules have been applied, a feasible set of decision processes is generated. The second mechanism is a principle for choosing among alternatives in the feasible set where more than one exists.

Let us examine the rules first, because they do much of the work of the model. As previously indicated, the rules are intended to protect both the quality and acceptance of the decision. In the form of the model shown, there are three

rules that protect decision quality and four that protect acceptance.

1. *The Information Rule.* If the quality of the decision is important and if the leader does not possess enough information or expertise to solve the problem by himself, AI is eliminated from the feasible set. (Its use risks a low-quality decision.)

2. *The Goal Congruence Rule.* If the quality of the decision is important and if the subordinates do not share the organizational goals to be obtained in solving the problem, GII is eliminated from the feasible set. (Alternatives that eliminate the leader's final control over the decision reached may jeopardize the quality of the decision.)

3. *The Unstructured Problem Rule.* In decisions in which the quality of the decision is important, if the leader lacks the necessary information or expertise to solve the problem by himself, and if the problem is unstructured, i.e., he does not know exactly what information is needed and where it is located, the method used must provide not only for him to collect the information but to do so in an efficient and effective manner. Methods that involve interaction among all subordinates with full knowledge of the problem are likely to be both more efficient and more likely to generate a high-quality solution to the problem. Under these conditions, AI, AII, and CI are eliminated from the feasible set. (AI does not provide for him to collect the necessary information, and AII and CI represent more cumbersome, less effective, and less efficient means of bringing the necessary information to bear on the solution of the problem than methods that do permit those with the necessary information to interact.)

4. *The Acceptance Rule.* If the acceptance of the decision by subordinates is critical to effective implementation, and if it is not certain that an autocratic decision made by the leader would receive that acceptance, AI and AII are eliminated from the feasible set. (Neither provides an opportunity for

FIGURE 1
Decision Model

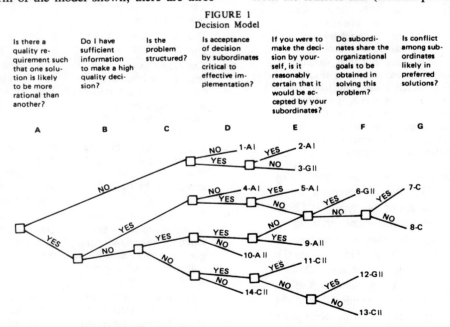

*The rules and figure 1 are reprinted from *Leadership and Decision-Making*, by Victor H. Vroom and Philip W. Yetton, by permission of the University of Pittsburgh Press. © 1973 by University of Pittsburgh Press.

subordinates to participate in the decision and both risk the necessary acceptance.)

5. *The Conflict Rule.* If the acceptance of the decision is critical, and an autocratic decision is not certain to be accepted, and subordinates are likely to be in conflict or disagreement over the appropriate solution, AI, AII, and CI are eliminated from the feasible set. (The method used in solving the problem should enable those in disagreement to resolve their differences with full knowledge of the problem. Accordingly, under these conditions, AI, AII, and CI, which involve no interaction or only "one-on-one" relationships and therefore provide no opportunity for those in conflict to resolve their differences, are eliminated from the feasible set. Their use runs the risk of leaving some of the subordinates with less than the necessary commitment to the final decision.)

6. *The Fairness Rule.* If the quality of decision is unimportant and if acceptance is critical and not certain to result from an autocratic decision, AI, AII, CI, and CII are eliminated from the feasible set. (The method used should maximize the probability of acceptance as this is the only relevant consideration in determining the effectiveness of the decision. Under these circumstances, AI, AII, CI, and CII, which create less acceptance or commitment than GII, are eliminated from the feasible set. To use them is to run the risk of getting less than the needed acceptance of the decision.)

7. *The Acceptance Priority Rule.* If acceptance is critical, not assured by an autocratic decision, and if subordinates can be trusted, AI, AII, CI, and CII are eliminated from the feasible set. (Methods that provide equal partnership in the decision-making process can provide greater acceptance without risking decision quality. Use of any method other than GII results in an unnecessary risk that the decision will not be fully accepted or receive the necessary commitment on the part of subordinates.)

Once all seven rules have been applied to a given problem, we emerge with a feasible set of decision processes. The feasible set for each of the fourteen problem types is shown in Table 3. It can be seen that there are some problem types for which only one method remains in the feasible set, others for which two methods remain feasible, and still others for which five methods remain feasible.

When more than one method remains in the feasible set, there are a number of ways in which one might choose among them. The mechanism we have selected the principle underlying the choices of the model in Figure 1 utilizes the number of man-hours used in solving the problem as the basis for choice. Given a set of methods with equal likelihood of meeting both quality and acceptance requirements for the decision, it chooses that method that requires the least investment in man-hours. On the basis of the empirical evidence summarized earlier, this is deemed to be the method furthest to the left within the feasible set. For example, since AI, AII, CI, CII, and GII are all feasible as in Problem Types 1 and 2, AI would be the method chosen.

To illustrate application of the model in actual administra-

TABLE 3

PROBLEM TYPES AND THE FEASIBLE SET OF DECISION PROCESSES

Problem Type	Acceptable Methods
1.	AI, AII, CI, CII, GII
2.	AI, AII, CI, CII, GII
3.	GII
4.	AI, AII, CI, CII, GII*
5.	AI, AII, CI, CII, GII*
6.	GII
7.	CII
8.	CI, CII
9.	AII, CI, CII, GII*
10.	AII, CI, CII, GII*
11.	CII, GII*
12.	GII
13.	CII
14.	CII, GII*

*Within the feasible set only when the answer to question F is Yes.

tive situations, we will analyze four cases with the help of the model. While we attempt to describe these cases as completely as is necessary to permit the reader to make the judgments required by the model, there may remain some room for subjectivity. The reader may wish after reading the case to analyze it himself using the model and then to compare his analysis with that of the author.

CASE I. You are a manufacturing manager in a large electronics plant. The company's management has recently installed new machines and put in a new simplified work system, but to the surprise of everyone, yourself included, the expected increase in productivity was not realized. In fact, production has begun to drop, quality has fallen off, and the number of employee separations has risen.

You do not believe that there is anything wrong with the machines. You have had reports from other companies that are using them and they confirm this opinion. You have also had representatives from the firm that built the machines go over them and they report that they are operating at peak efficiency.

You suspect that some parts of the new work system may be responsible for the change, but this view is not widely shared among your immediate subordinates who are four first-line supervisors, each in charge of a section, and your supply manager. The drop in production has been variously attributed to poor training of the operators, lack of an adequate system of financial incentives, and poor morale. Clearly, this is an issue about which there is considerable depth of feeling within individuals and potential disagreement among your subordinates.

This morning you received a phone call from your division manager. He had just received your production figures for the last six months and was calling to express his concern. He indicated that the problem was yours to solve in any way that you think best, but that he would like to know within a week what steps you plan to take.

2. PLANNING: Management Classic

You share your division manager's concern with the falling productivity and know that your men are also concerned. The problem is to decide what steps to take to rectify the situation.

Analysis
Questions—
  A (Quality?) = Yes
  B (Managers Information?) = No
  C (Structured?) = No
  D (Acceptance?) = Yes
  E (Prior Probability of Acceptance?) = No
  F (Goal Congruence?) = Yes
  G (Conflict) = Yes
Problem Type—12
Feasible Set—GII
Minimum Man-Hours Solution (from Figure 1)—GII
Rule Violations—
  AI violates rules 1, 3, 4, 5, 7
  AII violates rules 3, 4, 5, 7
  CI violates rules 3, 5, 7
  CII violates rule 7

CASE II. You are general foreman in charge of a large gang laying an oil pipeline and have to estimate your expected rate of progress in order to schedule material deliveries to the next field site.

You know the nature of the terrain you will be traveling and have the historical data needed to compute the mean and variance in the rate of speed over that type of terrain. Given these two variables, it is a simple matter to calculate the earliest and latest times at which materials and support facilities will be needed at the next site. It is important that your estimate be reasonably accurate. Underestimates result in idle foremen and workers, and an overestimate results in tying up materials for a period of time before they are to be used.

Progress has been good and your five foremen and other members of the gang stand to receive substantial bonuses if the project is completed ahead of schedule.

Analysis
Questions—
  A (Quality?) = Yes
  B (Manager's Information?) = Yes
  D (Acceptance?) = No
Problem Type—4
Feasible Set—AI, AII, CI, CII, GII
Minimum Man-Hours Solution (from Figure 1)—AI
Rule Violations—None

CASE III. You are supervising the work of 12 engineers. Their formal training and work experience are very similar, permitting you to use them interchangeably on projects. Yesterday, your manager informed you that a request had been received from an overseas affiliate for four engineers to go abroad on extended loan for a period of six to eight months. For a number of reasons, he argued and you agreed that this request should be met from your group.

All your engineers are capable of handling this assignment and, from the standpoint of present and future projects, there is no particular reason why anyone should be retained over any other. The problem is somewhat complicated by the fact that the overseas assignment is in what is generally regarded as an undesirable location.

Analysis
Questions—
  A (Quality?) = No
  D (Acceptance?) = Yes
  E (Prior Probability of Acceptance?) = No
  G (Conflict?) = Yes
Problem Type—3
Feasible Set—GII
Minimum Man-Hours Solution (from Figure 1)—GII
Rule Violations—
  AI and AII violate rules 4, 5, and 6
  CI violates rules 5 and 6
  CII violates rule 6

CASE IV. You are on the division manager's staff and work on a wide variety of problems of both an administrative and technical nature. You have been given the assignment of developing a standard method to be used in each of the five plants in the division for manually reading equipment registers, recording the readings, and transmitting the scorings to a centralized information system.

Until now there has been a high error rate in the reading and/or transmittal of the data. Some locations have considerably higher error rates than others, and the methods used to record and transmit the data vary among plants. It is probable, therefore, that part of the error variance is a function of specific local conditions rather than anything else, and this will complicate the establishment of any system common to all plants. You have the information on error rates but no information on the local practices that generate these errors or on the local conditions that necessitate the different practices.

Everyone would benefit from an improvement in the quality of the data; it is used in a number of important decisions. Your contacts with the plants are through the quality-control supervisors who are responsible for collecting the data. They are a conscientious group committed to doing their jobs well, but are highly sensitive to interference on the part of higher management in their own operations. Any solution that does not receive the active support of the various plant supervisors is unlikely to reduce the error rate significantly.

Analysis
Questions—
  A (Quality?) = Yes
  B (Manager's Information?) = No
  C (Structured?) = No
  D (Acceptance?) = Yes
  E (Prior Probability of Acceptance?) = No
  F (Goal Congruence?) = Yes
Problem Type—12
Feasible Set—GII
Minimum Man-Hours Solution (from Figure 1)—GII
Rule Violations—
  AI violates rules 1, 3, 4, and 7
  AII violates rules 3, 4, and 7
  CI violates rules 3 and 7
  CII violates rule 7

Short Versus Long-Term Models

The model described above seeks to protect the quality of the decision and to expend the least number of man-hours in the process. Because it focuses on conditions surrounding the making and implementation of a particular decision rather than any long-term considerations, we can term it a short-term model.

It seems likely, however, that the leadership methods that may be optimal for short-term results may be different from those that would be optimal over a longer period of time. Consider a leader, for example, who has been uniformly pursuing an autocratic style (AI or AII) and, perhaps as a consequence, has subordinates who might be termed "yes men" (attribute E) but who also cannot be trusted to pursue organizational goals (attribute F), largely because the leader has never bothered to explain them.

It appears likely, however, that the manager who used more participative methods would, in time, change the status of these problem attributes so as to develop ultimately a more effective problem-solving system. A promising approach to the development of a long-term model is one that places less weight on man-hours as the basis for choice of method within the feasible set. Given a long-term orientation, one would be interested in the possibility of a trade-off between man-hours in problem solving and team development, both of which increase with participation. Viewed in these terms, the time-minimizing model places maximum relative weight on man-hours and no weight on development, and hence chooses the style farthest to the left within the feasible set. A model that places less weight on manhours and more weight on development would, if these assumptions are correct, choose a style further to the right within the feasible set.

We recognize, of course, that the minimum man-hours solution suggested by the model is not always the best solution to every problem. A manager faced, for example, with the problem of handling any one of the four cases previously examined might well choose more time-consuming alternatives on the grounds that the greater time invested would be justified in developing his subordinates. Similar considerations exist in other decision-making situations. For this reason we have come to emphasize the feasible set of decision methods in our work with managers. Faced with considerations not included in the model, the manager should consider any alternative within the feasible set, and not opt automatically for the minimum man-hours solution.

As I am writing this, I have in front of me a "black box" that constitutes an electronic version of the normative model discussed on the preceding pages. (The author is indebted to Peter Fuss of Bell Telephone Laboratories for his interest in the model and his skill in developing the "black box.") The box, which is small enough to fit into the palm of one hand, has a set of seven switches, each appropriately labeled with the questions (A through G) used in Figure 1. A manager faced with a concrete problem or decision can "diagnose" that problem by setting each switch in either its "yes" or "no" position. Once the problem has been described, the manager depresses a button that illuminates at least one or as many as five lights, each of which denotes one of the decision processes (AI, AII, etc.). The lights that are illuminated constitute the feasible set of decision processes for the problem as shown in Table III. The lights not illuminated correspond to alternatives that violate one or more of the seven rules previously stated.

In this prototype version of the box, the lights are illuminated in decreasing order of brightness from left to right within the feasible set. The brightest light corresponds to the alternative shown in Figure 1. Thus, if both CII and GII were feasible alternatives, CII would be brighter than GII, since it requires fewer man-hours. However, a manager who was not under any undue time pressure and who wished to invest time in the development of his subordinates might select an alternative corresponding to one of the dimmer lights.

Toward a Descriptive Model of Leader Behavior

So far we have been concerned with the normative questions defined at the outset. But how do managers really behave? What considerations affect their decisions about how much to share their decision-making power with their subordinates? In what respects is their behavior different from or similar to that of the model? These questions are but a few of those that we attempted to answer in a large-scale research program aimed at gaining a greater understanding of the factors that influence managers in their choice of decision processes to fit the demands of the situation. This research program was financially supported by the McKinsey Foundation, General Electric Foundation, Smith Richardson Foundation, and the Office of Naval Research.

Two different research methods have been utilized in studying these factors. The first investigation utilized a method that we have come to term "recalled problems." Over 500 managers from 11 different countries representing a variety of firms were asked to provide a written description of a problem that they had recently had to solve. These varied in length from one paragraph to several pages and covered virtually every facet of managerial decision making. For each case, the manager was asked to indicate which of the decision processes shown in Table I they used to solve the problem. Finally, each manager was asked to answer the questions shown in Table II corresponding to the problem attributes used in the normative model.

The wealth of data, both qualitative and quantitative, served two purposes. Since each manager had diagnosed a situation that he had encountered in terms that are used in the normative model and had indicated the methods that he had used in dealing with it, it is possible to determine what differences, if any, there were between the model's behavior and his own behavior. Second, the written cases provided the basis for the construction of a standard set of cases used in later research to determine the factors that influence managers to share or retain their decision-making power. Each case depicted a manager faced with a problem to solve or decision to make. The cases spanned a wide range of managerial problems including production scheduling, quality control, portfolio management, personnel allocation, and research and development. In each case, a person could readily assume the role of the manager described and could indicate which of the decision processes he would use if he actually were faced with that situation.

In most of our research, a set of thirty cases has been used and the subjects have been several thousand managers who were participants in management development programs in the United States and abroad. Cases were selected systematically. We desired cases that could not only be coded unambiguously in the terms used in the normative model but that would also permit the assessment of the effects of each of the problem attributes used in the model on the person's behavior. The solution was to select cases in accordance with an experimental design so that they varied in terms of the seven attributes used in the model and variation in each attribute was independent of each other attribute. Several such standardized sets of cases have been developed, and over a thousand managers have now been studied using this approach.

To summarize everything we learned in the course of this research is well beyond the scope of this paper, but it is possible to discuss some of the highlights. Since the results obtained from the two research methods—recalled and standardized problems—are consistent, we can present the major results independent of the method used.

Perhaps the most striking finding is the weakening of the widespread view that participativeness is a general trait that individual managers exhibit in different amounts. To be sure, there were differences *among* managers in their general tendencies to utilize participative methods as opposed to autocratic ones. On the standardized problems, these differences accounted for about 10 percent of the total variance in the decision processes observed. These differences in behavior between managers, however, were small in comparison with differences *within* managers. On the standardized problems, no manager indicated that he would use the same decision process on all problems or decisions, and most used all five methods under some circumstances.

Some of this variance in behavior within managers can be attributed to widely shared tendencies to respond to some situations by sharing power and others by retaining it. It makes more sense to talk about participative and autocratic situations than it does to talk about participative and autocratic managers. In fact, on the standardized problems, the variance in behavior across problems or cases is about three times as large as the variance across managers!

What are the characteristics of an autocratic as opposed to a participative situation? An answer to this question would constitute a partial descriptive model of this aspect of the decision-making process and has been our goal in much of the research that we have conducted. From our observations of behavior on both recalled problems and on standardized problems, it is clear that the decision-making process and has been our goal in much of the research that we have conducted. From our observations of behavior on both recalled

problems and on standardized problems, it is clear that the decision-making process employed by a typical manager is influenced by a large number of factors, many of which also show up in the normative model. Following are several conclusions substantiated by the results on both recalled and standardized problems: Managers use decision processes providing less opportunity for participation (1) when the possess all the necessary information than when they lack some of the needed information, (2) when the problem that they face is well-structured rather than unstructured, (3) when their subordinates' acceptance of the decision is not critical for the effective implementation of the decision or when the prior probability of acceptance of an autocratic decision is high, and (4) when the personal goals of their subordinates are *not* congruent with the goals of the organization as manifested in the problem.

So far we have been talking about relatively common or widely shared ways of dealing with organizational problems. Our results strongly suggest that there are ways of "tailoring" one's approach to the situation that distinguish managers from one another. Theoretically, these can be thought of as differences among managers in decision rules that they employ about when to encourage participation. Statistically, they are represented as interactions between situational variables and personal characteristics.

Consider, for example, two managers who have identical distributions of the use of the five decision processes shown in Table I on a set of thirty cases. In a sense, they are equally participative (or autocratic). However, the situations in which they permit or encourage participation in decision making on the part of their subordinates may be very different. One may restrict the participation of his subordinates to decisions without a quality requirement, whereas the other may restrict their participation to problems with a quality requirement. The former would be more inclined to use participative decision processes (like GII) on such decisions as what color the walls should be painted or when the company picnic should be held. The latter would be more likely to encourage participation in decision making on decisions that have a clear and demonstrable impact on the organization's success in achieving its external goals.

Use of the standardized problem set permits the assessment of such differences in decision rules that govern choices among decision-making processes. Since the cases are selected in accordance with an experimental design, they can indicate differences in the behavior of managers attributable not only to the existence of a quality requirement in the problem but also in the effects of acceptance requirements, conflict, information requirements, and the like.

The research using both recalled and standardized problems has also enabled us to examine similarities and differences between the behavior of the normative model and the behavior of a typical manager. Such an analysis reveals, at the very least, what behavioral changes could be expected if managers began using the normative model as the basis for choosing their decision-making processes.

A typical manager says he would (or did) use exactly the

same decision process as that shown in Figure 1 in 40 percent of the situations. In two thirds of the situations, his behavior is consistent with the feasible set of methods proposed in the model. In other words, in about one third of the situations his behavior violates at least one of the seven rules underlying the model.

The four rules designed to protect the acceptance or commitment of the decision have substantially higher probabilities of being violated than do the three rules designed to protect the quality or rationality of the decision. One of the acceptance rules, the Fairness Rule (Rule 6) is violated about three quarters of the time that it could have been violated. On the other hand, one of the quality rules, the Information Rule (Rule 1), is violated in only about 3 percent of occasions in which it is applicable. If we assume for the moment that these two sets of rules have equal validity, these findings strongly suggest that the decisions made by typical managers are more likely to prove ineffective due to deficiencies of acceptance by subordinates than due to deficiencies in decision quality.

Another striking difference between the behavior of the model and of the typical manager lies in the fact that the former shows far greater variance with the situation. If a typical manager voluntarily used the model as the basis for choosing his methods of making decisions, he would become both more autocratic and more participative. He would employ autocratic methods more frequently in situations in which his subordinates were unaffected by the decision and participative methods more frequently when his subordinates' cooperation and support were critical and/or their information and expertise were required.

It should be noted that the typical manager to whom we have been referring is merely a statistical average of the several thousand who have been studied over the last three or four years. There is a great deal of variance around that average. As evidenced by their behavior on standardized problems, some managers are already behaving in a way that is highly consistent with the model, while others' behavior is clearly at variance with it.

A New Technology for Leadership Development

The investigations that have been summarized here were conducted for research purposes to shed some light on the causes and consequences of participation in decision making. In the course of the research, we came to realize, partly because of the value attached to it by the managers themselves, that the data collection procedures, with appropriate additions and modifications, might also serve as a valuable guide to leadership development. From this realization evolved an important by-product of the research activities—a new approach to leadership development based on the concepts in the normative model and the empirical methods of the descriptive research.

This approach is based on the assumption stated previously that one of the critical skills required of all leaders is the ability to adapt their behavior to the demands of the

situation and that one component of this skill involves the ability to select the appropriate decision-making process for each problem or decision he confronts.

Managers can derive value from the model by comparing their past or intended behavior in concrete decisions with that prescribed by the model and by seeing what rules, if any, they violate. Used in this way, the model can provide a mechanism for a manager to analyze both the circumstances that he faces and what decisions are feasible under these circumstances.

While use of the model without training is possible, we believe that the manager can derive the maximum value from a systematic examination of his leadership style, and its similarities to and dissimilarities from the model, as part of a formal leadership development program.

During the past two years we have developed such a program. It is not intended to "train" participants in the use of the model, but rather to encourage them to examine their own leadership style and to ask themselves whether the methods they are using are most effective for their own organization. A critical part of the program involves the use of a set of standardized cases, each depicting a leader faced with an administrative problem to solve. Each participant then specifies the decision-making process that he would use if faced with each situation. His responses are processed by computer, which generates a highly detailed analysis of his leadership style. The responses for all participants in the course are typically processed simultaneously, permitting the economical representation of differences between the person and other participants in the same program.

In its present form, a single computer printout for a person consists of three $15'' \times 11''$ pages, each filled with graphs and tables highlighting different features of his behavior. Understanding the results requires a detailed knowledge of the concepts underlying the model, something already developed in one of the previous phases of the training program. The printout is accompanied by a manual that aids in explaining results and provides suggested steps to be followed in extracting full meaning from the printout.

Following are a few of the questions that the printout answers:

1. How autocratic or participative am I in my dealings with subordinates in comparison with other participants in the program?
2. What decision processes do I use more or less frequently than the average?
3. How close does my behavior come to that of the model? How frequently does my behavior agree with the feasible set? What evidence is there that my leadership style reflects the pressure of time as opposed to a concern with the development of my subordinates? How do I compare in these respects with other participants in the class?
4. What rules do I violate most frequently and least frequently? How does this compare with other participants? On what cases did I violate these rules? Does my

leadership style reflect more concern with getting decisions that are high in quality or with getting decisions that are accepted?

5. What circumstances cause me to behave in an autocratic fashion; what circumstances cause me to behave participatively? In what respects is the way in which I attempt to vary my behavior with the demands of the situation similar to that of the model?

When a typical manager receives his printout, he immediately goes to work trying to understand what it tells him about himself. After most of the major results have been understood, he goes back to the set of cases to reread those on which he has violated rules. Typically, managers show an interest in discussing and comparing their results with others in the program. Gatherings of four to six people comparing their results and their interpretation of them, often for several hours at a stretch, were such a common feature that they have recently been institutionalized as part of the procedure.

We should emphasize that the method of providing feedback to managers on their leadership style is just one part of the total training experience, but it is an important part. The program is sufficiently new so that, to date, no long-term evaluative studies have been undertaken. The short-term results, however, appear quite promising.

Conclusion

The efforts reported in this article rest on the conviction that social scientists can be of greater value in solving problems of organizational behavior if their prescriptive statements deal with the complexities involved in the phenomena with which they study. The normative model described in this paper is one step in that direction. Some might argue that it is premature for social scientists to be prescriptive. Our knowledge is too limited and the issues too complex to warrant prescriptions for action, even those that are based on a diagnosis of situational demands. However, organizational problems persist, and managers cannot wait for the behavioral sciences to perfect their disciplines before attempting to cope with them. Is it likely that models that encourage them to deal analytically with the forces impinging upon them would produce less rational choices than those that they now make? We think the reverse is more probable—reflecting on the models will result in decisions that are more rational and more effective. The criterion for social utility is not perfection but improvement over present practice.

Why Do Employees Resist Change?

Organizations have personal compacts with their employees.
Change efforts will fail unless those compacts are revised.

Paul Strebel

Paul Strebel is a professor and director of the Change Program for international managers at IMD, the International Institute for Management Development in Lausanne, Switzerland. This article is based on part of his forthcoming book, New Personal Compacts: The Missing Link in Change Management, *to be published by the Harvard Business School Press in 1997. The material on Eisai is taken partly from a study by Liisa Välikangas, a senior business analyst with SRI Consulting in Menlo Park, California.*

Change management isn't working as it should. In a telling statistic, leading practitioners of radical corporate reengineering report that success rates in *Fortune* 1,000 companies are well below 50%; some say they are as low as 20%. The scenario is all too familiar. Company leaders talk about total quality management, downsizing, or customer value. Determined managers follow up with plans for process improvements in customer service, manufacturing, and supply chain management, and for new organizations to fit the new processes. From subordinates, management looks for enthusiasm, acceptance, and commitment. But it gets something less. Communication breaks down, implementation plans miss their mark, and results fall short. This happens often enough that we have to ask why, and how we can avoid these failures.

In the Change Program at IMD, in which executives tackle actual change problems from their own companies, I have worked with more than 200 managers from 32 countries, all of whom are struggling to respond to the shocks of rapidly evolving markets and technology. Although each company's particular circumstances account for some of the problems, the widespread difficulties have at least one common root: Managers and employees view change differently. Both groups know that vision and leadership drive successful change, but far too few leaders recognize the ways in which individuals commit to change to bring it about. Top-level managers see change as an opportunity to strengthen the business by aligning operations with strategy, to take on new professional challenges and risks, and to advance their careers. For many employees, however, including middle managers, change is neither sought after nor welcomed. It is disruptive and intrusive. It upsets the balance.

Senior managers consistently misjudge the effect of this gap on their relationships with subordinates and on the effort required to win acceptance of change. To close the gap, managers at all levels must learn to see things differently. They must put themselves in their employees' shoes to understand how change looks from that perspective and to examine the terms of the "personal compacts" between employees and the company.

What Is a Personal Compact?

Employees and organizations have reciprocal obligations and mutual commitments, both stated and implied, that define their relationship. Those agreements are what I call personal compacts, and corporate change initiatives, whether proactive or reactive, alter their terms. Unless managers define new terms and persuade employees to accept them, it is unrealistic for managers to expect employees fully to buy into changes that alter the status quo. As results all too often prove, disaffected employees will undermine their managers' credibility and well-designed plans. However, I have observed initiatives in which personal compacts were successfully revised to support major change—although the revision process was not necessarily explicit or deliberate. Moreover, I have identified three major dimensions shared by compacts in all companies.

These common dimensions are *formal, psychological*, and *social*.

The *formal* dimension of a personal compact is the most familiar aspect of the relationship between employees and their employers. For an employee, it captures the basic tasks and performance requirements for a job as defined by company documents such as job descriptions, employment contracts, and performance agreements. Business or budget plans lay out expectations of financial performance. In return for the commitment to perform, managers convey the authority and resources each individual needs to do his or her job. What isn't explicitly committed to in writing is usually agreed to orally. From an employee's point of view, personal commitment to the organization comes from understanding the answers to the following series of questions:

□ What am I supposed to do for the organization?
□ What help will I get to do the job?
□ How and when will my performance be evaluated, and what form will the feedback take?
□ What will I be paid, and how will pay relate to my performance evaluation?

Companies may differ in their approach to answering those questions, but most have policies and procedures that provide direction and guidelines to managers and employees. Nevertheless, a clear, accurate formal compact does not ensure that employees will be satisfied with their jobs or that they will make the personal commitment managers expect. Unfortunately, many managers stop here when anticipating how change will affect employees. In fact, performance along this dimension is tightly linked to the other two.

The *psychological* dimension of a personal compact addresses aspects of the employment relationship that are mainly implicit. It incorporates the elements of mutual expectation and reciprocal commitment that arise from feelings like trust and dependence between employee and employer. Though often unwritten, the psychological dimension underpins an employee's personal commitment to individual and company objectives. Managers expect employees to be loyal and willing to do whatever it takes to get the job done, and they routinely make observations and assumptions about the kind of commitment their employees display. The terms of a job description rarely capture the importance of commitment, but employees' behavior reflects their awareness of it. Employees determine their commitment to the organization along the psychological dimension of their personal compact by asking:

□ How hard will I really have to work?
□ What recognition, financial reward, or other personal satisfaction will I get for my efforts?

□ Are the rewards worth it?

Individuals formulate responses to those questions in large part by evaluating their relationship with their boss. Their loyalty and commitment is closely connected to their belief in their manager's willingness to recognize a job well done, and not just with more money. In the context of a major change program, a manager's sensitivity to this dimension of his or her relationship with subordinates is crucial to gaining commitment to new goals and performance standards.

Employees gauge an organization's culture through the *social* dimension of their personal compacts. They note what the company says about its values in its mission statement and observe the interplay between company practices and management's attitude toward them. Perceptions about the company's main goals are tested when employees

> # Employees often misunderstand or, worse, ignore the implications of change for their individual commitments to the company.

evaluate the balance between financial and non-financial objectives, and when they determine whether management practices what it preaches. They translate those perceptions about values into beliefs about how the company really works–about the unspoken rules that apply to career development, promotions, decision making, conflict resolution, resource allocation, risk sharing, and layoffs. Along the social dimension, an employee tries to answer these specific questions:

□ Are my values similar to those of others in the organization?
□ What are the real rules that determine who gets what in this company?

Alignment between a company's statements and management's behavior is the key to creating a context that evokes employee commitment along the social dimension. It is often the dimension of a personal compact that is undermined most in a change initiative when conflicts arise and communication breaks down. Moreover, it is the dimension along which management's credibility, once lost, is most difficult to recover.

Unrevised Personal Compacts Block Change

Looking through the lens of unrevised personal compacts, employees often misunderstand or, worse, ignore the implications of change for their individual commitments. At Philips Electronics, based in the Netherlands, employees' failure to understand changing circumstances drove the organization to the brink of bankruptcy.

In the early 1980s, Philips's reputation for engineering excellence and financial strength was unparalleled, and it was a prestigious company to work for. The company – which pioneered the development of the audio cassette, the video recorder, and the compact disc – recruited the best electrical engineers in the Netherlands.

Like many multidomestic European companies, Philips had a matrix structure in which strong country managers ran the international sales and marketing subsidiaries like fiefdoms. Local product divisions were organized separately, and competition for resources among the different business units was vigorous. Central control was anathema, but the size and complexity of headquarters in Eindhoven grew nevertheless.

At the same time, competition was intensifying. Despite its continued excellence in engineering innovation, Philips was having trouble getting new products to market in a timely way. Margins were squeezed as manufacturing costs slipped out of line in comparison with Sony's and Panasonic's, and market share started falling even in the company's northern European heartland, where Sony was rapidly taking over the leading position. During the 1980s, two successive CEOs, Wisse Dekkers and Cor van der Klugt, tried to redirect the company. Each, in his time, hammered home the problems that needed correcting: the pace and quality of product development, slow time to market, and high manufacturing costs. The two men communicated vigorously, reorganized, and set up task forces on change. In Philips's 1989 annual report, van der Klugt reported that he had redefined management responsibilities to give product divisions greater freedom to respond to competitive and market pressures. Yet the projected improvements in costs and market share did not materialize quickly enough. At the end of van der Klugt's tenure, Philips was facing the biggest operating loss in the company's history.

Why couldn't either of those seasoned professional managers deal with the changes in the competitive environment? They understood the problems, articulated the plans, and undertook the initiatives that we associate with change leadership. Yet each failed in his attempt to redirect the company in time because widespread employee support was missing. In fact, personal compacts in place at the time actually blocked change because there was little alignment between senior managers' statements and the practice and attitude of lower-level managers and their subordinates.

But the problem could have been predicted. During Philips's prosperous years, a tradition of lifelong employment was part of the company culture. Job security came in exchange for loyalty to the company and to individual managers. Informal rules and personal relationships dominated formal systems for performance evaluations and career advancement. Managers' job descriptions and position in the hierarchy set limits on their responsibilities, and operating outside those boundaries was discouraged. Subordinates weren't encouraged any differently. People weren't trying to meet challenges facing the company or even looking for personal growth. Position and perceived power in the company network determined who got what. And because seniority so directly affected an employee's career growth and level of compensation, workers had no incentive to work harder than people just above them or to exceed their boss's minimum expectations for performance.

Moreover, even when costs were demonstrably out of line and operating margins were declining, Philips had no effective mechanism for holding managers accountable for failing to achieve financial targets. Budget-to-actual variances were attributed to events outside the control of unit managers. And because of the limitations of financial reporting systems and a culture that encouraged loyalty over performance, no one was able to challenge this mind-set effectively.

None of that changed under Dekkers or van der Klugt. Managers and subordinates were not forced to understand how the changes essential to turning the company around would require them to take a fundamentally different view of their obligations. Neither Dekkers nor van der Klugt drove the process far enough to alter employees' perceptions and bring about revised personal compacts.

By the time Jan Timmer took over at Philips in May 1990, the company faced a crisis. Net operating income in the first quarter of 1990 was 6 million guilders compared with 223 million guilders the previous year, and the net operating loss for the year was projected by analysts at 1.2 billion guilders. Timmer was an insider from the consumer electronics division, where he had successfully stopped mounting operating losses. But the scale of Timmer's challenge to turn the company around was matched by the pressure on him to deal quickly and effectively with the potentially crippling losses.

Orchestrating the Revision of Compacts

The revision of personal compacts occurs in three phases. First, leaders draw attention to the need to change and establish the context for revising compacts. Second, they initiate a process in which employees are able to revise and buy into new compact terms. Finally, they lock in commitments with new formal and informal rules. By approaching these phases systematically and creating explicit links between employees' commitments and the company's necessary change outcomes, managers dramatically improve the probability of hitting demanding targets. To lead Philips out of its crisis, Jan Timmer had to steer the company through those phases.

Shock Treatment at Philips. Although the competitive landscape around Philips had changed, the company and its employees had not. Employees' personal compacts favored maintaining the status quo, so resistance to change was imbedded in the culture. To achieve a turnaround, Timmer was going to have to reach deep into the organization and not only lead the initiative but also closely manage it. Getting people's attention was merely the first step. Persuading them to revise the terms of their personal compacts was a much bigger challenge.

Timmer's approach was a dramatic one; in fact, it was shock treatment. Shortly after becoming CEO in mid-1990, he invited the company's top 100 managers to an off-site retreat at Philips's training center in De Ruwenberg. There he explained the company's situation in stark terms: Its survival was in jeopardy. To reinforce the message, he handed out a hypothetical press release stating that Philips was bankrupt. It was up to the group in the room to bring the company back. Everyone would have to contribute. Operation Centurion had begun and, with it, the end of life in the company as all those in the room had known it.

From the start, Timmer's terms for change were tough and unambiguous, and those who didn't like them were encouraged to leave. In Operation Centurion, Timmer captured the mind-set he wanted

and created the process he would use to focus managers' attention on the new goals. Extending the metaphor, Timmer offered his managers new personal contracts, which were like the assignments given officers by their superiors in the Roman army. In the ensuing Centurion Sessions, the terms of these new compacts would begin to take shape.

Drawing on benchmarking data on best-in-class productivity, Timmer called for an across-the-board 20% reduction in head count. He also stipulated that resources for essential new initiatives would have to come from within, despite deep cuts in expenses throughout the company. The meeting broke up to allow managers from each product division to come to grips with what they had been presented and to consider how they would respond. Before this initial session with Timmer ended, each of the division managers had orally agreed on targets for reductions in head count and operating costs. In subsequent discussions, those plans became formal budget agreements between Timmer and his Centurion managers: Each plan was signed by the presenting manager to signify his personal commitment to the terms. Performance would be measured against achievement of the targets and linked to individual bonuses and career opportunities. Personal commitments, binding agreements, and standards for performance would form the basis for the new personal compacts at Philips.

The De Ruwenberg meeting has become part of Philips's company lore. It underscored the urgency of the company's situation and set the stage for the compact-revision process that followed. In the days and weeks thereafter, Timmer maintained a high profile as he spread the message of Operation Centurion and the significance of the new personal compacts. Regular budget reviews gave him opportunities to reinforce his message about personal commitments to current goals. Ongoing meetings with Philips's top 100 managers were the forum for discussing long-term plans.

But Timmer knew that he could not accomplish his goals unless managers and subordinates throughout the company were also committed to change. Employees' concerns about this corporate initiative had to be addressed. Therefore, as the objectives for Operation Centurion came into focus at senior levels, plans to extend its reach emerged. Senior managers negotiated Centurion contracts with their business unit directors, and that group then took the initiative to the product-group and country-management teams. At workshops and training programs, employees at all levels talked about the consequences and objectives of change. Timmer reached out via company "town meetings" to answer questions and talk about the future. His approach made people feel included, and his direct

Personal commitments, binding agreements, and performance standards formed the basis for new compacts at Philips.

style encouraged them to support him. It soon became clear that employees were listening and the company was changing.

By the end of 1991, the workforce had been cut by 22%—68,000 people. Those who didn't meet the terms of their contracts were gone, including Timmer's successor in the consumer electronics division. Even at the top, the culture of patronage, social networking, and lifetime employment in exchange for loyalty became things of the past. When no one inside qualified, Timmer hired top managers from outside. As a result, by mid-1994, only 4 members of the original senior-management committee remained, and only 5 of the 14 were Dutch. A company survey in 1994 confirmed that employees had responded favorably to the changes and the new atmosphere: Morale and feelings of empowerment had soared. After fluctuating during the early nineties, Philips's financial performance recovered strongly in 1993 and 1994; operating income rose from (4.3%) of sales in 1990 to 6.2% in 1994 and the share price moved from 20.30 guilders to 51.40 guilders.

Of course, not every case is like Philips's. You do not need a crisis to revise personal compacts and get greater commitment. The contrasting example of Eisai, a Japanese health-care company, shows how far the understanding of personal compacts can take you when change is proactive.

Creating the Context for Change at Eisai. A small, family-owned company, Eisai was one of the original manufacturers of vitamin E, and it maintained a strong research commitment to natural pharmaceuticals. Over the years, it developed drugs for the treatment of cardiovascular, respiratory, and neurological diseases; by the end of the 1980s, such drugs comprised 60% of the company's sales. The company experienced steady, modest growth during that decade, and in 1989 sales reached 197 billion yen and profits approached 13 billion yen. But there were signs of potential trouble ahead. Eisai was spending a hefty 13% of sales on R & D—compared with an average of 8.5% in other companies—and between 1982 and 1991, only 12 of the company's 295 patent applications in Japan had been approved by regulatory authorities. Although it was the sixth-largest Japanese pharmaceutical company, Eisai was a relatively small player in an industry in which global competition was increasing while growth in the domestic market was slowing down.

In 1988, Haruo Naito took over as CEO and president from his father. Before that, he had chaired Eisai's five-year strategic planning committee. During that time, he had become convinced that the company's focus on the discovery and manufacture of pharmaceuticals was not sustainable for long-term growth against large, global competitors. In the absence of either a real or a perceived crisis, however, and in the face of deeply felt cultural traditions, changing direction at Eisai would require unusual leadership.

In the tradition of Japanese family companies, Eisai had few formal rules of employment. Among the 4,000 employees, lifelong employment was the norm and career advancement and authority were based on seniority. Groups made decisions because failure by an individual would mean loss of face. And employees were not encouraged to step outside established roles to take on assignments beyond the scope and structure of the existing organization. Individuals were loyal both to their managers and to group norms, so they did not seek personal recognition or accomplishment. And because other Japanese companies operated in similar ways, there was no external competitive pressure to be different. To accomplish strategic transformation, Naito would have to create a compelling context for change and an inducement for employees to try something new—without disrupting the entire organization.

> To accomplish strategic transformation, Eisai's CEO had to create a context for change.

Several years after becoming CEO, Naito formulated a radical new vision for Eisai that he called Human Health Care (HHC). It extended the company's focus from manufacturing drug treatments for specific illnesses to improving the overall quality of life, especially for elderly sick people. To accomplish that mission, Eisai would have to develop a wide array of new products and services. And that, in turn, would require broad employee involvement and commitment. Although Naito did not explicitly characterize Eisai employees' commitments as personal compacts, he clearly understood that individuals would have to accept new terms and performance standards that he could not sim-

The employees themselves would have to take the lead in designing the formal terms of their personal compacts.

ply mandate. He had to encourage entrepreneurial and innovative activity and create an environment in which such efforts would be accepted and rewarded. Indeed, for his vision of HHC to become reality, Naito knew that employees themselves would ultimately have to take the lead in designing the formal terms of their personal compacts.

In 1989, Naito announced his new strategic vision and initiated a training program for 103 "innovation managers" who were to become the agents for change in the company. The training program consisted of seminars on trends in health care and concepts of organizational change. It also gave employees a firsthand look at patient-care practices by having them spend several days in both traditional and nontraditional health-care facilities where they performed actual nursing activities. At the end of the program, Naito charged the innovation managers with turning the insights from their experiences into proposals for new products and services. Each proposal was brought before Naito and Eisai's executive management to gain high-level corporate support and, as important to Naito, to secure individual managers' public commitment to the achievement of their HHC projects' goals.

This training program and the subsequent HHC product-development efforts set the stage for the creation of a dramatically different set of personal compacts at Eisai. The innovation managers operated outside both the normal organizational structure and the company's traditional cultural boundaries. They designed new products and programs, put together multidisciplinary teams to develop their ideas, and drew new participants of their own choice into the change initiative. They reported to Naito, and he personally evaluated their performance and the contribution of individual projects to the HHC vision. As a result, junior people had a chance to break out of the seniority system and to shape the development of the company's new strategy as well as the terms of their own personal compacts. These were opportunities previously unheard of in Eisai or in other Japanese pharmaceutical companies.

The visibility and senior-management support for the first projects generated widespread enthusiasm for participating in the new movement at Eisai. The cross-functional teams established employee ownership of the HHC vision, which rapidly took on a life of its own. Soon there were proposals for 130 additional HHC projects involving 900 people, and by the end of 1993, 73 projects were under way. New services offered by the company included a 24-hour telephone line to assist people taking Eisai medications. Another brought consumers and medical professionals together at conferences to discuss health care needs. New attention to consumer preferences led to improvements in the packaging and delivery of medications.

Although personal compacts at Eisai are still dominated by traditional cultural norms, Naito's ability to lead his employees through a process in which they examined and revised the old terms enabled them to accomplish major strategic change. The effects of the new strategy are visible in Eisai's product mix. By the end of 1993, the company had moved from sixth to fifth place in the Japanese domestic pharmaceutical industry, and today Eisai's customers and competitors view the company as a leader in health care.

Culture and Personal Compacts

The extent to which personal compacts are written or oral varies with the organization's culture and, in many cases, the company's home country.

Personal compacts will need to be more explicit as companies become truly multinational.

In general, the more homogeneous the culture, the more implicit the formal dimension of personal compacts is likely to be. The same is true along psychological and social dimensions in homogeneous environments, because employers and employees share similar perspectives and expectations. For example, in Japan and continental Europe, the legal systems for settling disputes are based on a civil code documented in statutes. Those systems carry over to the underlying principles in legal contracts and to the assumptions that support employer-employee relationships. Indeed, when a compact is laid out too explicitly in Japan, it is taken as an affront and a sign that one party doesn't understand how things work.

By contrast, in countries like the United States, personal compacts tend to be supported by formal systems to ensure objectivity in the standards for performance evaluation. And more structure exists to support employee-employer relations, both in the form of company policies and procedures and in the role that human resource departments play. Similarly, as companies become more truly multinational, the importance of making the terms of personal compacts explicit increases, as does the requirement to support them formally. In my experience, this is true whether companies are implementing change to meet the needs of a culturally diverse workforce or to respond to market opportunities and threats.

Regardless of the cultural context, unless the revision of personal compacts is treated as integral to the change process, companies will not accomplish their goals. In one way or another, leaders must take charge of the process and address each dimension. Jan Timmer and Haruo Naito revised their employees' personal compacts using different approaches and for different reasons. But each drove successful corporate change by redefining his employees' commitment to new goals in terms that everyone could understand and act on. Without such leadership, employees will remain skeptical of the vision for change and distrustful of management, and management will likewise be frustrated and stymied by employees' resistance.

HAVE A BALL

Consultant Michael Gelb uses juggling to teach ways to learn, change habits of individuals and organizations, and apply more creativity in problem solving.

Tim Stevens

A BOVE THE HEADS OF SOME 200 CONVENTIONEERS, THE AIR QUIVERS WITH FIST-sized bean bags. On stage the instructor cascades three balls in a figure-eight pattern. Have we entered the International Jugglers Assn. training camp? No, it's the annual conference of the Council for Continuous Improvement in San Francisco, where keynoter and change-management consultant Michael Gelb is teaching executives how to take better advantage of their own intellectual capital. Many years ago, Gelb found that groups were more effective in applying his principles after taking a 10-minute juggling break. In fact, juggling itself serves as the perfect metaphor for his teachings in habit change, learning, and creativity.

Today Gelb consults from his company, High Performance Learning, Great Falls, Va.; has books on change and reaching full potential to his credit; and numbers among his clients such organizations as Du Pont, AT&T, Merck, Xerox, Digital Equipment, and the U.S. Army.

The essence of creativity, contends Gelb, is not to come up with something totally new, like pulling a rabbit out of a hat. "That's not how creativity works—that's a common myth," he says. "Creativity works through a new combination of things you already know, a fresh look at elements with which you are already familiar. You don't have to reinvent the wheel—you just have to give it a new spin. And the ability to shift perspective, to see the big picture without losing track of the details, is a core skill of highly creative people.

"Some people are good at seeing details, but they never see things in an unfamiliar way, so they're not very creative. Other people are very good at going off on divergent thinking and free association, and they see the big picture. But they can't pay attention to details, so they don't get anything done. The very most creative people and organizations are able to see the big picture, to be divergent and free-associative, *and* pay attention to detail and analysis. Juggling trains you to see the big picture—to

Michael Gelb (foregound) teaches businessmen to parlay juggling skills into creative decision-making.

watch the whole pattern, while paying attention to each individual ball.

"That movement back and forth between the two modes—analyzing what I'm doing that is or isn't working, and then clicking into the big picture, sensing the rhythm, the overall pattern—reinforces the tools I teach in becoming a more creative individual or organization."

One of those tools is mind-mapping, a way of generating and organizing ideas faster and more effectively. Brainstorming generates ideas, concedes Gelb, but "nothing changes after the sessions because people don't know how to link divergent, free-flowing thinking with logic and analysis. Mind-mapping is a way to wake up the brainstorming, free-flowing, unfettered process of association that leads to new insights and new combinations of what you already know."

To mind-map, first draw a colorful picture in the middle of a large sheet of paper that represents the topic you are working on. Next print key words or images, arrived at by free association, on lines radiating out from the central image. Then connect related areas or recurring themes of the map, and eliminate ideas that seem extraneous. Then put the ideas in sequence by numbering or by redrawing the map in clockwise order.

"By representing ideas in a picture, you awaken the imaginative, colorful part of the brain that is normally relegated to the realm of doodling and daydreaming," says Gelb. "To find key words, you have to use the analytical convergent part of your mind. It's an analytical-focus skill."

IN HIS BOOK *Thinking for a Change: Discovering the Power to Create, Communicate, and Lead* (Harmony Books, New York), Gelb introduces a concept called "synvergent thinking," synergistic integration of convergent and divergent thinking, with mind-mapping as the tool to accomplish it. A senior research fellow at Du Pont mind-mapped four chemical processes, saw them in a new

light, and was granted a patent based on the new conclusions. Mind-mapping has also been used at Boeing to create strategic plans, at National Public Radio to create its mission and vision, and at Amoco to draft a values statement, according to Gelb.

Key to Gelb's teachings is taking a constructive attitude toward mistakes. A person is not going to learn to juggle without dropping the balls—a lot.

"There is plenty of research to show that the most successful individuals and organizations are characterized by their resilience in the face of adversity," he says. "Many people can't learn to juggle, because they cannot deal with dropping the balls, what they perceive as repeated failure. They just give up. So I teach them to drop the balls on purpose."

That way, beginning jugglers can focus purely on the throw, and their poise, balance, and breathing. Freed from the fear of failure, they become smoother, more relaxed jugglers right from the beginning. Catching, which is instinctive, is added later in the learning process. "Quality results are a function of quality processes," says Gelb, "and I teach people how to apply quality processes in their own learning. In juggling, that means quality throws, and then the results take care of themselves."

The basic pattern of juggled balls should look like McDonald's golden arches, "but with two balls what often happens is that beginners will throw one ball up and hand the other across the bottom," says Gelb. "What's so fascinating is that you can explain to people really carefully what to do, then you can show them really carefully, then you can show them what not to do, and yet sure enough, they will hand the ball across the bottom anyway. This is perfect. This is a great learning opportunity. This is what I call 'the individual mind and body problem.' Your mind says to do one thing, and your body goes ahead and does something else. This is a fundamental problem of habit and change."

Gelb links this to a corporate situation: "Your company has all these great ideas. You have a vision, a mission. You

have the ideal of high-performance work teams and empowerment. And yet when you get out there in the real world, you notice that much of the time that stuff doesn't happen. What does happen is power politics, people looking after their own turf, rumor, gossip, disempowerment, low-performance teams, all the opposite of that idealistic jargon.

"Trying harder isn't the answer—you're just going to be doing the wrong things better," Gelb continues. "Before you can change, you have to become aware of what you are doing, usually through feedback from a partner. Being aware is the secret to changing. Then you have to interpose a delay between stimulus and response; you have to learn to pause and reflect on what you are doing. So when teaching juggling, I sometimes have people

"You don't have to reinvent the wheel—you just have to give it a new spin."

throw the first ball and then wait an exaggerated period of time—10 seconds—before making the second throw. In that period, I have them visualize where that ball should be going in space. Research shows that when you visualize, you are actually activating the neuromuscular connections that will perform the activity.

"When they are confident they can match the action with the picture that's in their mind's eye, I let them throw the second ball. That's another principle: Build confidence through creating success experiences and build success through creating confidence. Then we work on narrowing the time between throwing the first and second ball until they can do it in real time, and they have changed their habit. It's simple, but incredibly powerful, because the principle applies to changing habits in any area of life."

DILBERT'S
MANAGEMENT HANDBOOK

Scott Adams

■ *Yes, business is serious stuff, but every once in a while we need to be reminded that corporate life can get pretty ridiculous. Master satirist Scott Adams, a sort of corporate Fellini, does just that, by lampooning idiot bosses and inane management trends. His* Dilbert, *which runs in more than 1,000 newspapers, with a readership of some 60 million people, is the fastest-growing comic strip in the country. The main character is a sack-shaped, ever-threatened corporate loser named Dilbert, who, with Dogbert, his bespectacled canine companion, copes with managementspeak, teamwork, mission statements, downsizing, and all else.*

An MBA from Berkeley and a self-described cubicle-bound gearhead, Adams worked for Pacific Bell until leaving last year to pursue his cartooning full time. Most of his material comes from readers. One fan, for instance, recently E-mailed Adams about a company that purchased laptops for employees to use while traveling. Fearing they might be stolen, the management came up with a clever solution: permanently attach the laptop computers to the employee's desk. Says Adams: "No matter how absurd I try to make my comic strip, I can't stay ahead of what people are experiencing in their own workplace." Here's Dilbert on management.

Reprinted from *Fortune,* May 13, 1996, pp. 99-100, 102, 104, 108, 110. Adapted from *The Dilbert Principle* by Scott Adams.

Cubicles

Cubicles—sometimes called "workspaces" or "pods"—serve as a constant reminder of the employee's marginal value to the company. I've never seen a brochure from a cubicle manufacturer, but I think it would look something like this:

■ The Cubicle 6000™ Series

Think of The Cubicle 6000™ as a life-style, not just a big box to keep your crap in one place!!

We used nature as our guide when we designed The Cubicle 6000™. Every unit has the unmistakable motivational feel of the four most inspiring locations on earth:

► Veal-Fattening Pen

Imagine the security that those lucky young cows feel, snug in their individual living units, without a care in the world. The reaffirming message is "Live for today!"

► Cardboard Box

It's the same architecture that has transported the possessions of successful people for hundreds of years!

► Baby's Playpen

A reminder of the exuberance of youth and the thrill of being held captive by strange people who speak gibberish and punish you for reasons you don't understand!

► Prison Cell

We've "captured" the carefree feeling of a convict serving 20 to life. Experience the security that was previously available only in the penal system!

■ And look at these features!!

Open top, so you'll never miss a surrounding noise.
Small size, so you can enjoy the odors of your co-workers.
No annoying windows.
Available in battleship gray or feces brown.
Movable—discover the thrill of frequent office shuffling.
Coat hanger (only available on the Admiral Series).

Hoteling

The only drawback to the cubicle-oriented office is that some employees develop a sense of "home" in their little patch of real estate. Soon pride of ownership sets in, then self-esteem, and poof—good-bye productivity. But thanks to the new concept of "hoteling," this risk can be eliminated. Hoteling is a system by which cubicles are assigned to the employees as they show up each day. Nobody gets a permanent workspace, and therefore no unproductive homey feelings develop.

Another advantage: Hoteling eliminates all physical evidence of the employee's association with the company. This takes the fuss out of downsizing; the employee doesn't even have to clean out a desk. With hoteling, every employee has "one foot out the door" at all times. Hoteling sends an important message to the employee: "Your employment is temporary. Keep your photos of your ugly family in the trunk of your car so we don't have to look at them."

Employee Recognition Programs

Employees like to feel that their contributions are being valued. That's why managers try to avoid that sort of thing. With value comes self-esteem, and with self-esteem come unreasonable requests for money.

There are many ways to tell employees that their work is not valued. Here are some of the crueler methods, which incidentally work the best:

► Leaf through a magazine while the employee voices an opinion.

► Ask for information "urgently," and then let it sit on your desk untouched for weeks.

► Have your secretary return calls for you.

Then there are recognition programs. These send an important message to all the employees in the group, not just the "winners." Specifically, the message is this: "Here's another person who won't be downsized until after we nail you."

But that's not the only benefit. Recognition programs help identify which social caste the employees belong to.

► Employee of the Month Program—Paper Hat caste
► Certificate of Appreciation—No Overtime Pay caste
► Token Cash Award—Mushroom in the Cubicle caste
► None—Executive caste

There are no recognition programs at the highest levels of the organization. This is a motivating factor for lower-level employees. They know that if they work hard, they have a chance of reaching a level of management where recognition programs don't exist.

I once won a recognition award at Pacific Bell. As I approached the front of the room to accept my award, it became apparent that the executive running the program didn't know what I did for a living. Thinking quickly, he invented an entirely fictitious project for the benefit of the audience and thanked me for my valuable contribution to its success.

I felt "happier" after that, but my self-esteem didn't increase enough for me to think it was a good time to ask for a raise. Morale-wise, this was a home run for the company. I was so motivated that I gave serious thought to working right through my siesta that afternoon.

I'm not alone.

Here's an E-mail I received:

Re: The All-Time Most Humiliating Recognition Program Ever
From: (name withheld)
To: scottadams@aol.com
Scott,

In the wake of a recent senior staff retreat, it was announced that as a reward for outstanding work, one employee would be selected each month to receive the Fuzzy Bunny Award. Another employee, dressed in a rabbit suit (I swear I am not making this up) would visit the chosen employee's cubicle bearing balloons, a coffee mug, and a certificate of merit. This would presumably encourage us to work harder. The plan was killed (thank God) because nobody would agree to be the bunny.

Making Them Wait

One of the most effective methods of humiliation used by managers is the practice of ignoring an underling who is in or near the manager's office while the manager pursues seemingly unimportant tasks. This sends a message that the employee has no human presence. It is similar to changing clothes in front of the family pet; the animal is watching, but it couldn't possibly matter.

This tool of humiliation can be fine-tuned to any level simply by adjusting what activities are performed while the employee waits.

■ **Activity—Level of Humiliation**
► Taking phone calls—Not so bad
► Reading other things—Bad
► Flossing—Very bad
► Learning a foreign language —Very, very bad

Talk Like a Manager

If you want to advance in management you have to convince other people you're smart. This is accomplished by substituting incomprehensible jargon for common words. Example: A manager would never say, "I used my fork to eat a potato." He would say, "I utilized a multi-tined tool to process a starch resource." The two mean the same thing, but the latter is obviously from a smarter person.

Mission Statement

If your employees are producing low-quality products that no sane person would buy, you can often fix that problem by holding meetings to discuss your Mission Statement.

A Mission Statement is defined as "a long, awkward sentence that demonstrates management's inability to think clearly."

All good companies have one.

Companies without Mission Statements will often be under the mistaken impression that the objective of the company is to bicker among departments, produce low-quality products, and slowly go out of business. That misperception can be easily cured by writing one such as this:

▶ Mission: "We will produce the highest-quality products, using empowered team dynamics in a new Total Quality paradigm until we become the industry leader."

But you're not home free yet. The company Mission Statement will be meaningless until all the individual departments write their own to support the company's overall mission:

▶ Mission: "Perform world-class product development, financial analysis, and fleet services using empowered team dynamics in a Total Quality paradigm until we become the industry leader."

Individually, the Mission Statement of the company and the Mission Statement of the department might mean nothing. But taken together, you can see how they would inspire employees to greater heights.

Group Writing

Stephen King writes very scary books. Shakespeare wrote several excellent plays. Unfortunately, they worked alone. If only they had worked together there's no telling how much better the results would have been. That's the theory behind "group writing," and it's hard to find fault with the logic.

The main goal of group writing is to ensure that every sentence satisfies all the objectives of every person in the room. This can be problematic if all the participants have different objectives. You can minimize the impact of different objectives by focusing on goals all parties can agree on:

1. Don't convey any information whatsoever.
2. See No. 1.

The best of all worlds is to be asked to comment on the writing of a co-worker. You get to savor the experience of shredding another person's ego while taking no personal risk. It can be

very satisfying. For fun, suggest changes that would completely reverse the message intended by the author. This puts the author in the awkward position of having to reroute the document for further unhelpful comments or choosing to ignore your "upgrades." If your comments are ignored, you have the God-given right to ridicule the end product and claim you had no input. Your activity will look just like "work" even though it's easy. And on the off chance that the document you ridiculed becomes successful, you can claim it as part of your accomplishments.

Great Lies of Management

For your convenience, I have compiled and numbered the most popular management lies of all time. I do this as a service to the business community. Now when you're telling a story about the treachery of your managers, you can simply refer to each lie by its number, for example, "She told us No. 6 and we all went back to our cubicles and laughed." This will save you a lot of energy that can then be channeled into whining about your co-workers.

1. "Employees are our most valuable asset."
2. "I have an open-door policy."
3. "You could earn more money under the new plan."
4. "We're reorganizing to better serve our customers."
5. "The future is bright."
6. "We reward risktakers."
7. "Performance will be rewarded."
8. "We don't shoot the messenger."
9. "Training is a high priority."
10. "I haven't heard any rumors."
11. "We'll review your performance in six months."
12. "Our people are the best."
13. "Your input is important to us."

It's not always easy to tell the difference between a scurrilous management lie and ordinary

nitwitism. When confronted with an ambiguous situation, you can usually sniff out the truth by using a handy method I call the "What Is More Likely" test. Here's how it works:

State each of the plausible interpretations of reality (using humorous metaphors when possible), then ask yourself this question:

"What is more likely?"

You will discover that this technique will greatly clarify the communications of your managers. Allow me to demonstrate its usefulness on the First Great Lie of Management: "Employees are our most valuable asset." On the surface this statement seems to be at odds with the fact that companies are treating their "most valuable assets" the same way a leaf blower treats leaves. How can this apparent contradiction be explained?

An example will be useful. Let's say your boss has a broken desk chair and there's no money left in the budget to replace it. Is it more likely that your boss would

A. Sit on the floor until the next budget cycle.
B. Use a nonmanagement chair despite the lower status it confers on the sitter.
C. Postpone filling a job opening in the group, distribute the extra work to the "most valuable assets," and use the savings to buy a proper chair.

As employees we like to think we're more valuable than the office furniture. But the "What Is More Likely" test indicates that it's not the case. Realistically, we're someplace toward the lower end of the office-supply hierarchy.

Machiavellian Methods *(written by Dogbert)*

During the course of your career, many people will come to you for advice. This is your chance to steer them off the corporate speedway and—if you're skillful—help them plow into a crowd of innocent spectators.

It's not always easy to give advice. For one thing, your tail might wag uncontrollably, thus signaling your impending treachery. Moreover, your advice has to sound plausible, no matter how destructive and self-serving it really is. The best way to give bad advice that still sounds well-meaning is to "take the high road."

For example, let's say your manager has engaged in unethical conduct, and your co-worker discovers this activity and comes to you for advice. You should "take the high road." Tell your co-worker to con-

front the boss and also blow the whistle to the authorities. This will simultaneously open your boss's job for you while most likely eliminating your co-worker from competition, all in the name of what is "right."

If you're in charge of a project that's a sure loser, or if the people who work for you are losers, you must distance yourself from them as soon as possible. The direct method is to simply switch jobs or fire your bad employees. But that's settling for too little. Instead, think of your bad assets as potential viruses that can be used to infect your enemies within the corporation. All you need to do is artificially inflate their value and wait for some unsuspecting manager to take them off your hands.

Never make the mistake of giving bad performance reviews to bad

employees. That will limit their ability to switch jobs within the company and shackle them to you forever until their corrosive effect destroys you. It's better to focus on the positive aspects of every employee's performance, even if you have to assault the truth a bit. This is similar to tactics used by the Vietcong when they booby-trapped toys and waited for somebody to pick them up.

If you can't get rid of bad employees, as a last resort put the poor performers in charge of the United Way campaign and let everybody suffer with you.

Job Security

If you want to keep your job safe, take every opportunity to complain about the unreasonable demands that are being placed on you. Reinforce your message during every interaction with a co-worker or manager. Here are some time-tested phrases that you should insert into every conversation:

► "I'm up to my ass in alligators."
► "I've been putting out fires all day."
► "I had 1,500 voice mail messages today. Typical."
► "It looks like I'll be here on the weekend again."

Over time, these messages will work themselves into the subconscious of everybody around you, and they will come to think of you as a hard worker without ever seeing a scrap of physical evidence to support the theory.

Downsizing

When I entered the work force in 1979, the word "downsize" hadn't been invented yet. A new employee could burrow into the bureaucracy and make a little nest that would last for decades. I felt like a happy little termite living in a Victorian mansion that was always adding another room. I gnawed on the beams, paycheck after paycheck, and nobody ever noticed my tiny teeth marks.

I remember my first "staff" job in a big bank in San Francisco. It was 1980. My partner, Dean, and I were plucked from the management training program and put on a "special project."

The term "special project" means "All the real jobs are filled by people who, at first glance, don't appear nearly as incompetent as you." That was certainly true in my case. Dean was actually pretty good at appearing competent, but he theorized that he was being punished for something he said to somebody.

Our job was to build a computer information system for the branch banks. We were the perfect people for the job: Dean had seen a computer once, and I had heard Dean talk about it.

Our office was an unused storage room in the basement just off the parking garage, big enough to hold two beat-up desks and some squeaky chairs. It had bare, white walls, an uncarpeted floor, no windows, and an annoying echo. It was like a prison cell, but without access to a library and free weights.

Sometimes I would try to call other people in the company to get important information for our project. The response was always the same: "Who are you, and why do you want to know?"

I would try to sound important by invoking the first name of the senior vice president and describing how the fate of the free world depended on this vital transfer of information. For example, "Bill needs it … to keep our great nation independent."

But somehow they always figured out I was a 22-year-old guy with a bad haircut and a cheap suit, sitting in a storage room just off the parking garage. If I was especially charismatic that day, they would have the courtesy to swear at me before hanging up.

Eventually Dean and I degenerated into a pattern of sitting in our little bare room gossiping about co-workers, balancing our checkbooks, and fantasizing about whether the sun was out that day. When we got bored, we would hypothesize about the information we needed, talking about it for hours until we were both pretty sure we knew what it "should" be. Then we packaged it up as "user requirements" and gave it to a woman named Barbara, who programmed the system in about two weeks. The whole project took about a year, because it's not the type of thing you want to rush.

When it was done, the results of the system were notoriously inaccurate. But our manager assured us that it was okay because he only used the numbers that supported his personal opinion anyway.

It was during this year that I realized the world would run smoothly if companies employed far fewer people like me. In the years that followed, managers all over the world reached the same realization. It was the dawn of downsizing.

Global Strategic Management in a New World Order

William E. Halal

William E. Halal is a professor of management at George Washington University, Washington, D.C.

The globalization of business has become so rapid that a new field called "Global Strategic Management" has now emerged. This new field is a blend of strategic management and international business that develops worldwide strategies for global corporations. Whereas most studies in this field focus on ordinary business conditions, the revolutionary events of the past few years make it clear that the present is not ordinary. Such epoch-shattering events as the collapse of communism, the unification of Europe, the information revolution, the arrival of an environmental ethic, and other remarkable new developments signal that a new era is emerging in global affairs. This article describes a broader approach to global strategic management that encompasses these revolutionary changes.

The viewpoint presented here was developed in a project sponsored by the World Future Society called "WORLD 2000." WORLD 2000 focuses on conducting a global strategic management process among business, government, education, and other sectors of society to define the emerging global system and help institutions adapt to changes. It represents a fresh examination of the forces that are integrating the earth into a coherent global *order* as well as those that are creating the *disorder* that tends to characterize our time: the unification of markets and communications, as well as the vast differences in cultures, local problems, and values erupting around the globe. By gaining new insights into the emerging world system, social institutions may better understand how they can adapt to these changes.

This seems to be an opportune time for such an examination. The transition to a new global system is likely to be made during the next decade; the year 2000 offers a highly symbolic turning point at which the emerging global order can be shaped and molded.

Following is a global strategic plan, developed by synthesizing the literature and then reviewing the plan with groups of executives. It follows the logic of a typical strategic plan but carried to a global level. First, we summarize nine supertrends that describe a long-term trajectory toward an advanced stage of "global maturity." Second, we note five principal obstacles that must be overcome to clear the way ahead. Third, we argue that these issues can be resolved by a newly emerging perspective that recognizes the essential unity of a global community.

> *The new shape of the world requires new strategies for the management of its institutions.*

THE TRAJECTORY TO GLOBAL MATURITY

The following trends represent the principal driving forces that are now moving the world in new directions. They could be called "supertrends." Little attempt is made to offer justifications, and many other trends that capture finer details are not covered. This summarizes the major features that characterize the emerging shape of the globe as it moves along a long-term trajectory toward a new stage of global maturity.

Trend 1: A Stable Population of 10-14 Billion

The earth, which already is teeming with 5.5 billion people, is expected to double its population to reach a stable level somewhere between 10-14 billion humans by the mid-21st century. About 95 percent of this growth will occur in the less developed countries (LDCs).

From *Business Horizons*, November/December 1993, pp. 5-10. © 1993 by the Foundation for the School of Business at Indiana University. Reprinted by permission.

Trend 2: Industrial Output Will Increase by a Factor of 5-10

The aggregate level of material consumption, or industrial output, should increase by a factor of 5-10 over the next few decades as most remaining parts of the world industrialize to reach the equivalent standard of living enjoyed by Americans, Europeans, and Japanese. Industrial *throughput*, however, is likely to grow less as more efficient means are found to insure a sustainable form of development.

Trend 3: The Wiring of the Globe

Information technology (IT) is a revolutionary force that will continue to overthrow governments, restructure corporations, and unify the world. This revolution will wire the earth into a single communication network, a central nervous system for a planetary society. However, the gap between information haves and have-nots is apt to persist.

Trend 4: The High-Tech Revolution

The IT revolution is accelerating technical advances to create breakthroughs in all fields: the mapping of DNA, genetic therapy, robotics, materials research, sustainable "green technology," automated transportation, and even a "technology of consciousness."

Trend 5: Global Integration

The globe is becoming integrated into a single community connected by a common communication system, a global economy, and a shared international culture. In time, this process may unify today's growing economic blocs and political federations into a universal system of open trade, a global banking system and common currency, and some form of world governance.

Trend 6: Diversity and Complexity

It is a great paradox that global integration will be accompanied by *disintegration* into a highly diverse system. Ethnic enclaves, such as those in the former republics of the USSR, will continue to seek autonomy; various groups within nations will form pockets of self-governing subcultures; and modern societies generally will splinter into a far more complex, differentiated social order.

Trend 7: A Universal Standard of Freedom

Freedom and the recognition of human rights should continue spreading around the globe, though this movement may ebb and flow at times. A majority of nations now have political democracy and free market systems, and the number should grow to the extent that freedom becomes the accepted norm, with authoritarian systems being the exception.

Trend 8: Continued Crime, Terrorism, and War

Traumatic upheaval is likely to produce disgruntled individuals, groups, and nations resorting to a variety of crimes, terrorism, and limited wars. However, global wars and the old fear of nuclear holocaust now seem unlikely.

Trend 9: Transcendent Values

As this transformation unfolds, most people in advanced nations should strive for quality of life, community, self-fulfillment, art, spirituality, and other higher-order values that transcend material needs. Many are cynical about such claims, but as the philosopher André Malraux predicted, the twenty-first century will be the century of religion.

CRITICAL ISSUES BLOCKING THE PASSAGE AHEAD

Although this evolutionary trajectory is likely to stabilize into a mature, coherent global order in the mid-twenty-first century, business and government must resolve the following five issues, which pose barriers to this forward movement. Once again, this represents a quick survey—not a detailed summary—to highlight key issues that now present major obstacles to progress.

Issue 1: Making the Leap to a Global Order

Most of the problems the world struggles with result from the fragmented economic and political systems that continue unchanged from the industrial past. Trade barriers, fluctuating currency exchange rates, and difficulties in communicating are "old" problems that should not exist in a "new" global order managed as a coherent system; they do not exist in the United States, Germany, China, or other societies governed as coherent systems. The transition to some type of world order is monumental because it requires sophisticated global systems that integrate the world into a single whole, permitting a quantum leap to a global level of governance heretofore unknown.

Issue 2: Reconciling Economic Interests

Communism may have yielded to markets, but markets do not exist only in capitalism. The strength of Japan, for instance, hinges on a market system that is based on collaborative working relations: a "Human Enterprise System" (Ozaki 1991). In contrast, the capitalism practiced in Western nations, such as the United States, is in trouble because it exacerbates conflicts between labor and management, rich and poor, business and government, domestic and foreign trade, private and public sectors, and other basic incompatibilities. A sound global economy for the future, therefore, awaits the creation of a new economic paradigm based on some form of free enterprise that can reconcile these diverse interests into a productive and harmonious community.

Issue 3: Achieving Sustainable Development

The present conflict between economic growth and environmental protection will be resolved either rationally or through some form of decline. The anticipated five- or ten-fold increase in industrial output is incompatible with any reasonable forecast under existing conditions. Many solutions are being proposed to achieve sustainable development, but the task of implementation remains formidable. Ecological systems are suffering unsustainable stress even under today's far more modest load. Developed countries (DCs) show little inclination to alter their profligate lifestyles, and LDCs seem to be striving for Western affluence.

Issue 4: Managing Complexity

One of the most striking trends of the emerging future is the explosion of complexity that is almost impossible to contain within today's cumbersome institutions. Much of what passes for unsolvable disorder reflects an inability to respond effectively to the diversity of individual and community challenges. This problem, which toppled communism, is becoming severe in the West. Top-down corporations are struggling to diversify so they can serve myriad market niches; governments have not yet begun to grapple with the intricacies of education, poverty, crime, and other chronic social problems. Dramatically different institutions are needed to manage this complex new world, which may require an upheaval similar to the one now plaguing the former communist bloc.

Issue 5: Alleviating the North-South Gap

The enormous disparity between the wealth of LDCs in the South and the DCs of the North shows little sign of improvement, fanning an explosive antagonism between these two halves of the globe. Average income in the South is now about six percent of that in the North; little progress is being made in alleviating the misery of these people, who make up three-quarters of all humanity. Unless serious efforts are made to close this gap by bringing LDCs into the modern world, the Southern hemisphere will seethe with the same potential for violent confrontation that was released in the Los Angeles riots of 1992.

These five dilemmas are exacerbated by one of the most pervasive problems of our time: a collapse of faith in the familiar old ideology that guided humans through the past epoch with good success. It could be thought of as a "meta-issue." With the USSR now defunct and the United States in crisis, the lack of superpower leadership has left a vacuum of power, ideas, and moral guidelines at a time when the world is facing Herculean new challenges. The result is political gridlock, economic stagnation, destructive personal stress, social disorders, and many other symptoms of breakdown. From all this apparent chaos, a new paradigm, model, or belief system must somehow be formed that allows people to make sense of today's different global realities.

> "With the USSR now defunct and the United States in crisis, the lack of superpower leadership has left a vacuum of power, ideas, and moral guidelines at a time when the world is facing Herculean new challenges."

A STRATEGY BASED ON A NEW GLOBAL PERSPECTIVE

An enormous variety of policies and remedial programs are being proposed to resolve all these problems, but their sheer number and diversity scatter attention into confusing, uncoordinated, and ineffectual directions. This section synthesizes these proposals into a "master strategy" based on a different perspective now gaining increasing attention, one that recognizes the essential unity of the emerging global system.

The key to understanding the emerging world view is to see that unprecedented new imperatives have arisen—especially the revolutionary force of IT—that are unleashing powerful new forces to integrate the globe. As communication systems encircle the earth to form a central nervous system for the planet, the fragmented parts of today's failing global order are being joined together into an interconnected, coherent system. The most recent report of the Club of Rome (King and Schneider 1991) notes that current dramatic changes represent the first *global*

Table
The Transition to a New Global Perspective

	Old Perspective	New Perspective
Technological Base	Physical Technology	Information Technology
Economy	Capital-Centered	Human-Centered
Frontier of Progress	Material Growth	Sustainable Development
Institutions	Hierarchical	Decentralized
Working Relationships	Conflict	Cooperation

revolution because the entire earth is experiencing these events together at the same time. This shift to a new global perspective is summed up in the **Table**. This perspective then leads to the following elements of a master strategy required to overcome the issues defined before:

Strategy 1: Disseminate Advanced Technology to Unify the Globe

Although many people fear its effects, the relentless advance of modern technology—especially information technology—is the primary force driving the globe through its present transition. It was the ubiquitous presence of television, radio, facsimile, and video, for instance, that armed citizens of the former USSR and the Eastern Bloc with the knowledge required to overthrow their governments.

Information technologies should be diffused, therefore, by corporations selling sophisticated products abroad, governments fostering joint research and development projects, individuals sharing technical knowledge, and any other reasonable methods. There is a particular need to find ways of introducing these technologies into LDCs to advance their modernization and unite them with the world. All technology can be misused, so care is needed to ensure that it is applied appropriately. The emerging global order is being constructed on a technological foundation; the sooner that foundation is in place, the sooner this system can behave as a coherent global community.

Strategy 2: Integrate Economics and Society

The conflict between economic life and social life is being reconciled, as evidenced by breakthroughs that would have been unthinkable a few years ago. Japan has shown the world that a union of economic and social interests is *more* productive, spurring others to emulate this "human-centered" form of enterprise. Even General Motors, long regarded as the antithesis of this idea, has formed GM-Saturn as a prototype of socially responsive business, managed by a coalition of workers, customers, suppliers, distribu-

tors, and local citizens. Saturn production lines cannot keep up with demand because Saturn cars are now the best in their class, proving that social goals are compatible with economic goals.

Intense global competition should, in time, drive most economies in this direction because it is efficient. Decisions ranging from the shop floor to national macroeconomic policy may then be made collectively by all affected parties, including workers, labor, consumer advocates, governments, and citizens. If this can be done, the leaders of business and other social institutions may then act as stewards rather than managers, creating the badly needed trust, quality, mutual service, and collaborative economic relationships that can instill the essential sense of community that vitalizes society.

Strategy 3: Create a Symbiotic Society-Environment Interface

A harmonious economic-societal relationship will mean little if it is not supported by a viable ecosystem. Civilization must be carefully redesigned to form a symbiotic society-environment interface. Business firms are now competing to prove their environmental consciousness because of public pressure. Stephen Schmidheiny, Chairman of the Business Council for Sustainable Development, described the advantages (1992): "Progress toward sustainable development makes good business sense because it can create competitive advantage and new opportunities."

A wide range of difficult adjustments are under way to integrate ecological realities into economic and social life. Sustainable technologies and practices are being developed to increase economic efficiency, advance more modest but wholesome lifestyles, develop renewable energy, reforest denuded lands, convert to organic agriculture, recycle waste, and improve pollution controls. To evaluate this complex situation realistically, social indicators must be incorporated into such financial measures as GNP; social costs, such as pollution, should be internalized in the form of taxes and credits to guide balanced economic choices.

Strategy 4: Decentralize Institutions to Empower Individuals

Almost all analysts agree that social institutions need to be restructured for a knowledge-based global order, but confusion reigns over what is needed. The most useful guide can be found in a dominant imperative now sweeping through modern nations: institutions are being decentralized into networks of small, autonomous units to master complexity. This imperative is the entrepreneurial half of the new role emerging for institutions; the move toward collaborative, democratic policymaking described in Strategy 3 constitutes the other half that unifies this diversity into a harmonious whole.

For instance, large corporations are being disaggregated into small "internal enterprises" that form the equivalent of market economies *inside* organizations—"internal markets" (Halal et al. 1993). Under the pressure of limited budgets and public demands, governments are also allowing the public to choose among competing agencies. A good example is the way U.S. education is introducing market competition among schools, which are also governed democratically by teachers, parents, local citizens, and administrators.

The result of all these changes is to restructure authority relationships. Markets and democracies share the common feature of placing control in the hands of ordinary people to harness the growing diversity of thought and values into creative forces of change, with institutions providing the overarching systems that support and guide change. The decentralization of authority, then, empowers people to care for themselves more effectively, which provides a self-organizing system for managing a complex world.

Strategy 5: Foster Collaborative International Alliances

A knowledge-based society fosters pockets of collaborative problem solving in which all partners benefit, while competition drives collaborating parties together. This is why business managers and politicians are creating a flurry of strategic alliances with their competitors. Cooperation has now become the most powerful force in world affairs.

This new ethic of strategic collaboration is also being extended to forge productive alliances between business and government, economists and ecologists, and competing nations, knitting together a global community of diverse groups. Note that an ethic of cooperation implies not altruism but a reciprocity of interests that benefits all partners. It is enlightened self-interest.

The conflict between North and South, for example, could yield cooperative ventures, such as the North American Free Trade Agreement, between DCs and LDCs based on mutual advantages for both parties. LDCs gaining capital, jobs, and know-how, while DCs gain access to markets and less costly labor.

Obviously there is no assurance that the world will pursue a path of this type. And it is certainly true that difficult choices at dangerous junctures could deflect the trajectory toward maturity into other directions. However, historic breakthroughs have occurred in the past few years—the collapse of communism, a greatly reduced threat of nuclear holocaust, and worldwide concern over the environmental crisis—largely through the natural evolution of the global order. Barring unforeseen disasters, it seems reasonable to expect that the other remaining obstacles noted above could also be resolved from this same natural process, though we cannot now anticipate how or when.

This does not mean that individuals and institutions are passive observers of an immutable process of natural development: change is the sum of countless small human actions that collectively produce social transformation. A coherent new world order will emerge only if global corporations, national governments, and educational institutions are able to adopt major strategies such as those outlined above. Developing and disseminating advanced technologies, especially information technology, will be essential in forming the foundation for a mature global society. A collective model of enterprise must be defined that reconciles the interests of capital with mounting social concerns, particularly environmental sustainability. Large firms must be decentralized to empower individuals if we hope to manage a complex and diverse world. Strategic alliances must be encouraged on a global scale to avoid the conflicts that now divide the world.

Accomplishing these ambitious tasks will test us all because our individual perspectives will have to yield to a broader perspective. In our work conducting the WORLD 2000 global strategic management process for corporations, government agencies, and other management groups, we find a common theme running through all these changes: the emerging global order can be integrated into a workable whole only by accepting the legitimacy of other views, even those we feel are antithetical to our own.

The primary skill required to survive this critical transformation, therefore, is an attentive ability to reconcile the conflicting, endlessly changing, overwhelming complexity posed by today's diverse world. A crucial paradox lies at the heart of this challenge. What is involved, fundamentally, is cultivating a more transcendent mode of thought that can permit all of us to regain command over our affairs by relinquishing the illusion of self-control in favor of shared control.

References

Lester Brown et al., *Saving the Planet* (New York: W.W. Norton, 1991).

"Bruntland Report"; World Commission of Environment and Development, *Our Common Future* (New York: Oxford University Press, 1987).

Business Horizons, special issue on "Business and the Environment," March-April 1992.

Harlan Cleveland, "Birthday of a New World," address to the International Insurance Society, Tuscaloosa, Alabama, March 23, 1992.

Robert Constanza, *Ecological Economics* (New York: Columbia University Press, 1991).

Encyclopedia of World Problems and Potential (Munich, Germany: Saur Verlag, 1991).

Jay Forrester, "Counterintuitive Behavior of Social Systems," *Technology Review,* January 1971.

Ken Geiser, "The Greening of Industry," *Technology Review,* August-September 1991, pp. 64-72.

William E. Halal, "A Forecast of the Information Technology Revolution," *Technological Forecasting and Social Change* (forthcoming).

William E. Halal, "East is East, and West is West," *Business in the Contemporary World,* Fall 1992, pp. 95-113.

William E. Halal, *The New Capitalism* (New York: Wiley, 1986).

William E. Halal, "The New Management: Social Institutions for an Information Age," *Business in the Contemporary World,* Winter 1990, pp. 41-54.

William Halal et al., *Internal Markets: Bringing the Power of Free Enterprise Inside Organizations* (New York: Wiley, 1993).

Willis Harman, *Global Mind Change* (Indianapolis, IN: Knowledge Systems, 1988).

Hazel Henderson, "Beyond Economics: New Indicators for Culturally Specific Sustainable Development," *Development,* Vol. 4, No. 4 (1990): 60-68.

Samuel Huntington, *The Third Wave: Democratization in the Late Twentieth Century* (Norman, OK: University of Oklahoma Press, 1991).

Alexander King and Bertrand Schneider, *The First Global Revolution* (New York: Pantheon, 1991).

Art Kleiner, "What Does It Mean to be Green?" *Harvard Business Review,* July-August 1991, pp. 38-45.

Hans Kung, *Global Responsibility: In Search of a New World Ethic* (New York: Crossroads Publishing Co., 1991).

Donald Lesh and Diane Lowrie, *Sustainable Development* (Washington, DC: Global Tomorrow Coalition, 1990).

Jim MacNeill, Pieter Winsemius, and Taizo Yakushiji, *Beyond Interdependence: The Meshing of the World's Economy and the Earth's Ecology* (New York: Oxford University Press, 1991).

Donella H. Meadows, Dennis L. Meadows, and Jorgen Randers, *Beyond the Limits* (Mills, VT: Chelsea Green Publ., 1992).

John Naisbitt and Patricia Aburdene, *Megatrends 2000* (New York: Morrow, 1990).

Julius Nyerere, *The Challenge to the South: Report of the South Commission* (New York: Oxford University Press, 1990).

David Osborne and Ted Gaebler, *Reinventing Government* (Reading, MA: Addison-Wesley, 1992).

Robert Ozaki, *Human Capitalism* (Tokyo: Kodanshi, 1991).

Christopher Plant and Judith Plant, *Green Business: Hope or Hoax?* (Philadelphia: New Society, 1991).

Alan Rugman, ed., *Research in Global Strategic Management* (Greenwich, CT: JAI Press, 1990).

Nafis Sadik (Executive Director, UN Population Fund), "World Population Continues to Rise," *The Futurist,* March-April 1991, pp. 9-14.

Stephen Schmidheiny (Chairman of the Business Council for Sustainable Development), *Changing Course: A Global Business Perspective on Development and the Environment* (Cambridge, MA: MIT Press, 1992).

Charlene Spretnak, *States of Grace: The Recovery of Meaning in the Postmodern Age* (San Francisco: Harper, 1991).

Strategic Management Journal, special issue on global strategy, Vol. 12, Summer 1991.

Lester Thurow, *Head to Head: The Coming Economic Battle Among Japan, Europe, and America* (New York: Morrow, 1992).

Sandra Vandermerwe and Michael E. Oliff, "Corporate Challenges for an Age of Reconsumption," *Columbia Journal of World Business,* Fall 1991, pp. 6-25.

Heidi Vernon-Wortzel and Lawrence H. Wortzel, *Global Strategic Management* (New York: Wiley, 1992).

Robert Wesson, *Democracy World Survey 1987* (Boulder, CO: Lynne Rienner Publishers, 1988).

Robin Wright and Doyle McManus, *Flashpoints: Promise and Peril in a New World* (New York: Knopf, 1991).

Case II: *The Fairfax County Social Welfare Agency*

The Fairfax County Social Welfare Agency was created in 1965 to administer services under six federally funded social service grants:

- The Senior Citizens' Developmental Grant (SCD).
- The Delinquent Juvenile Act Grant (DJA).
- The Abused Children's Support Grant (ACS).
- The Job Development and Vocational Training Grant (JDVT).
- The Food Stamp Program (Food).
- The Psychological Counseling and Family Therapy Fund (Counseling).

The agency's organizational structure evolved as new grants were received and as new programs were created. Staff members—generally the individuals who had written the original grants—were assigned to coordinate the activities required to implement the programs. All program directors reported to the agency's executive director, Wendy Eckstein, and had a strong commitment to the success and growth of their respective programs. The organizational structure was relatively simple, with a comprehensive administrative department handling client records, financial records, and personnel matters. (See below.)

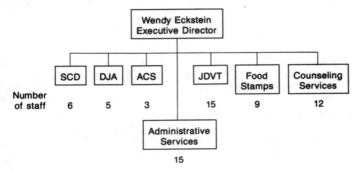

The sense of program "ownership" was intense. Program directors jealously guarded their resources and only reluctantly allowed their subordinates to assist on other projects. Consequently, there was a great deal of conflict among program directors and their subordinates.

The executive director of the agency was concerned about increasing client complaints regarding poor service and inattention. Investigating the matter, Eckstein discovered that:

1. Staff members tended to "protect" their clients and not refer them to other programs, even if another program could provide better services.
2. There was a total absence of integration and cooperation among program directors.
3. Programs exhibited a great deal of duplication and redundancy; program directors acquired administrative support for their individual programs.

Eckstein concluded that the present client or program-based structure no longer met the agency's needs. A major reorganization of this county social welfare agency is being considered.

Discussion Questions

1. What structural attributes of the agency could be causing the client complaints?
2. What actions could Eckstein take without actually changing the organization's structure?
3. Redesign the structure of the agency to improve cooperation and increase efficiency. How would you implement your newly designed structure?

Using the Case on *The Fairfax County Social Welfare Agency*

This case provides an outstanding opportunity to use Vroom's model of decision-making. Included with this discussion is some material developed by the Center for Creative Leadership, which takes Vroom's model and creates a schematic for decision purposes.

It is suggested that the instructor make a copy of the material for each of you or, perhaps, make an overhead for use in the classroom as you try to decide which decision-making approach would be best.

Questions for Discussion

1. How do you think Ms. Eckstein should proceed with making her decision?
2. What parts of the agency are going to be affected by the decision?
3. What are some of the likely outcomes from various decision-making approaches that Eckstein could use?

Exercise II: *NASA Exercise*

As you approach the moon for a rendezvous with the mother ship, the lateral dissimilar malfunctions, forcing your ship and crew to land some 17 craters, or 145 Earth miles, from the mother ship. The touchdown results in a great deal of damage to the ship but, luckily, none to the crew. Survival is dependent upon reaching the mother ship. The most critical items must be chosen for the trip.

Instructions: Below are the only 15 items left intact after the landing. Rank the items in order of importance they hold to you and your crew in reaching the rendezvous point. Place 1 by the most important item, 2 by the next most important, and so on, through all fifteen items. You should complete this section in 10 minutes.

Your Decision	Articles	Group Decisions
_____	Box of matches	_____
_____	Food concentrate	_____
_____	50 feet of nylon rope	_____
_____	Parachute silk	_____
_____	Portable heating unit	_____
_____	Two .45 caliber pistols	_____
_____	One case of dehydrated Pet milk	_____
_____	Two 100-pound tanks of oxygen	_____
_____	Stellar map of the moon's constellation	_____
_____	Self-inflating life raft	_____
_____	Magnetic compass	_____
_____	Five gallons of water	_____
_____	Signal flares	_____
_____	First-aid kit containing injection needles	_____
_____	Solar-powered FM receiver/transmitter	_____

Because you have survived as a group, the most appropriate decision-making method is group consensus. Each member of the group has to agree upon the rank order. Because the consequence of a wrong decision is so severe—death—you want to be as logical as you can and avoid arguments. In addition, you want to be sure to agree with that ranking that somewhat meets your solution. Be sure not to employ any voting, averaging, or trading techniques that might stifle and embitter one of your companions on this survival journal. (Answers may be found at the end of the Index.)

Scoring

1. Subtract the group score on each item from your individual score on each item. Write down the difference. For example, you put down an item as 3 on your list, and the group ended up ranking it 6. There is a net difference of 3.
2. Add all the net differences together to get your par score.
3. Collect all the scores in the group, add them, then divide by the number of people in the group.
   Your net difference-score _____
   Average Individual score _____
4. Now take the NASA-computed rankings and compare the group's ranking with it, computing the net difference between the group's ranking and the correct ranking.
   Net Difference Score—Group and Correct _____

What do these differences mean?

Organizing

- **Management Classic (Article 12)**
- **Elements of Organization (Article 13)**
- **Job Design (Articles 14 and 15)**
- **Designing and Changing the Organization (Articles 16 and 17)**

After the managers of an organization have planned a course of action, they must organize the firm to accomplish their goals. Many early writers in management were concerned with organization. Frederick W. Taylor was one of the first to apply scientific principles to organizing work. He was followed by Frank and Lillian Gilbreth, pioneers in the field of time and motion studies. Their work contributed to the development of the assembly line and other modern production techniques and is shown in the classic essay "Classifying the Elements of Work."

The question that constantly confronts managers today is how best to organize the firm, given the internal and external environments; how to approach the problem, not only from the company's perspective, but also from the perspective of the economy as a whole. Are large organizations better than small ones? Each has advantages and disadvantages. Which is better able to compete in the global environment against organizations from different countries with different expectations and rules? Add to this the fact that society is evolving, so that new types of organizations will be needed in the future.

There are two ways a company can grow. One is to merge with and acquire other firms. The second is to expand the current businesses internally by building on their already established business units. A recent trend in U.S. industry has been to grow via the merger and acquisition route, but growing internally can often be more rewarding and more fun, as shown in "Of Things Fundamental."

People are not machines; they are looking for fulfilling and enjoyable work. Managers, therefore, must design jobs to be interesting and rewarding. The days of assembly-line workers doing the same task over and over are numbered. Such positions are being replaced by jobs that vary in the types of tasks the worker performs each day. The content of jobs that have traditionally been low in requirements for mental ability and effort is also changing. Technology is forcing organizations to change the way they do business and the way people do their jobs, as may be seen in "The New Workplace." Another change is that quality control is now each worker's responsibility. No longer can a worker pass defects down the line for someone else to fix.

Today, firms must be designed to meet the increasingly competitive environment of a global economy. Organizations must learn to do more with fewer resources and fewer people; management overlap and deadwood can no longer be tolerated. Organizations try to be lean and mean, but is that necessarily the best way to go? This is addressed in "When Is Virtual Virtuous? Organizing for Innovation." As firms cut back, are they crippling the future of the organization by looking only at the short term? The opposite side of this coin is that the middle manager who is able to survive and prosper in this environment will be a better leader, having been tempered in a much hotter furnace than his or her predecessors.

To remain competitive in a rapidly changing environment, organizations must evolve to meet the rapidly developing global economy with which they will have to interact. These new and improved organizations will have the world as their market and as their competitor. They must be able to foresee changes in their environment and to react quickly to turn those changes to their advantage. Organizations will need strength and flexibility to meet change or they will suffer the fate of the dinosaur, which failed to adapt to a new environment.

Looking Ahead: Challenge Questions

Organizations can grow either by acquisition or internally. Which way is best for the economy? Explain your answer.

Job design is an evolving process that is leading to more interesting work. Give examples of jobs that would benefit from better and more complete job design.

Organizations are changing as they prepare to enter the future. What pressures are causing this evolution? What are the results?

Classifying the Elements of Work

Frank B. Gilbreth and Lillian M. Gilbreth

Frank Bunker Gilbreth graduated from the English high school in Boston in 1885, passed the entrance examinations at M.I.T., but decided to work for a firm of consulting engineers and to complete his technical training at night. In 1911, he established Gilbreth, Inc., an engineering consulting firm, which advanced the specialty of Motion Study. His achievements in scientific engineering were recognized by the University of Maine, which conferred on him an LL.D. degree in 1920. Gilbreth died in 1925.

Lillian Moller Gilbreth married Frank Gilbreth in 1904. Her education included a Bachelor of Letters and a Master of Letters from the University of California and a Ph.D. from Brown University (1915). She traveled widely as a lecturer on technology and human relations problems, served as president of Gilbreth, Inc., and received numerous awards and medals. Lillian Gilbreth died in 1972.

This paper presents a complete method of visualizing a classification of all the subdivisions and the true motion-study elements of The One Best Way to Do Work.

NEED FOR SUCH A CLASSIFICATION

Such a classification is vitally necessary, in order that fundamental super-standards shall be made by the scientific method of selecting and measuring the best units, for synthesis into methods of least waste.

This classification furnishes the basis of a definite mnemonic classification for filing all motion-study and time-study data for the work of the industrial engineer, the machine designer, and the behavior psychologist—that their various pieces of information, usually obtained through entirely different channels and methods of attack, may be automatically brought together, to the same filing folders, under the same filing subdivisions.

So far as we are able to learn, there are no other classifications or bases for filing that accomplish this purpose, and we have found that such a classification is absolutely necessary for our work of finding The One Best Way to Do Work, standardizing the trades, and making and enforcing standing orders for best management.

It is hoped that teachers of industrial engineering in our colleges will learn that *one* demonstration of building up The One Best Way to Do Work from the ultimate elements, in any kind of activity, will do more to teach a student the principles of motion study and most efficient methods of management than dozens of lessons dealing with generalities.

The coming generation should be taught a definite filing system for data of scientific management, laid out under a complete classification of all work; should be taught the method of selecting the right units to measure and the methods of measuring these units; and should be furnished with the devices for making the cost of measuring cheap, and with a method for synthesizing the resulting information. This would result in a general progress in world efficiency and an increase in quality of living that would mark an epoch in the history of industry and civilization.

USE OF FUNDAMENTAL ELEMENTS

The literature of scientific management abounds with examples of units of work improperly called "elements," which are in no sense elements. A classification for finding The One Best Way to Do Work must deal with *true elements*, not merely with subdivisions that are arbitrarily called "elements."

There has recently appeared a well-written biography of a great engineer[1] in which subdivisions of operations, requiring in many instances more than 30 seconds to perform, have been erroneously described as "elements." That error will again mislead many people. These so-called elements should be taken for what they really are, namely, subdivisions and not elements, and not confused with true elements, or

Originally from *Management and Administration*, Vol. 8, No. 2, August 1924, pp. 151-154 and Vol. 8, No. 3, September 1924, pp. 295-296.

fundamental units which cannot be further subdivided.

SCOPE OF THE CLASSIFICATION

This classification for finding The One Best Way to Do Work is applicable to all kinds of work. It was used by one of the authors while serving as ranking officer in the field under the training committee of the General Staff, standardizing the methods of The Best Way to Do Work for teaching the five million men and officers in the World War. It has also been used in analyzing the work of the surgeon, nurse, hospital management, large department stores, selling a great many kinds of manufacturing, accounting, office work in general, and many other kinds of work.

TRUE ELEMENTS OF WORK

The classification of all work of any and all organizations for the purpose of finding The One Best Way to Do Work may be visualized as follows:

  I. A complete organization, which consists of
 II. Processes, such as
  (a) Financing
  (b) Advertising
  (c) Marketing
  (d) Distributing
  (e) Selling
  (f) Accounting
  (g) Purchasing
  (h) Manufacturing
  (i) Planning
  (j) Teaching
  (k) Charting
  (l) Maintaining
  (m) Filing

    These processes consist of

III. Operations, which consist of
 IV. Cycles of motions, which consist of
  V. Subdivisions, or events, or therbligs[2] of a cycle of motions which consist of
  (a) Search
  (b) Find
  (c) Select
  (d) Grasp
  (e) Transport loaded
  (f) Position
  (g) Assemble
  (h) Use
  (i) Disassemble
  (j) Inspect
  (k) Pre-position for next operation
  (l) Release load
  (m) Transport empty
  (n) Rest for overcoming fatigue
  (o) Other periods of unavoidable delay
  (p) Avoidable delay
  (q) Plan

 VI. Variables of motions

  (a) Variables of the worker
   1. Anatomy
   2. Brawn
   3. Contentment
   4. Creed
   5. Earning power
   6. Experience
   7. Fatigue
   8. Habits
   9. Health
   10. Mode of living
   11. Nutrition
   12. Size
   13. Skill
   14. Temperament
   15. Training

  (b) Variables of the surroundings, equipment, and tools
   1. Appliances
   2. Clothes
   3. Colors
   4. Entertainment, music, reading, etc.
   5. Heating, cooling, ventilating
   6. Lighting
   7. Quality of material
   8. Reward and punishment
   9. Size of unit moved
   10. Special fatigue-eliminating devices
   11. Surroundings
   12. Tools
   13. Union rules
   14. Temperament

  (c) Variables of the motion
   1. Acceleration
   2. Automaticity
   3. Combination with other motions and sequences
   4. Cost
   5. Direction
   6. Effectiveness
   7. Foot-pounds of work accomplished
   8. Inertia and momentum overcome
   9. Length
   10. Necessity
   11. Path
   12. ''Play for position''
   13. Speed

Under I, a complete organization, are included all kinds of organizations, including financial, industrial, commercial, professional, educational, and social.

Under II, processes, it should be noted that processes are divided in the same way from a motion-study analyst's standpoint, regardless in which department or in which function they are found.

Under III, operations, the operations include mechanical as well as physiological, and mental as well as manual.

The reasons for these inclusions are:

1. From the motion-study standpoint there are not always clear dividing lines between the *operations of devices* and the *mental and manual operations of the human being,* for they are often mutually interchangeable, sometimes in part and sometimes as a whole.[3]

2. Records of many and probably all mental operations can now be obtained by the chronocyclegraph and micromotion photographic methods, and each year such photographic records can more and more be deciphered and used to practical advantage. Enough can already be read and used to serve our present needs. Careful examination of all our old micromotion and chronocyclegraph films taken under conditions of actual practice show that they are literally full of examples of such records of mental processes.

Under IV, cycles of motions are arbitrary subdivisions of operations. They have distinct and natural boundaries of beginning and ending. Usually and preferably there are certain sequences of therbligs that are especially suitable for standardization and transference to other kinds of work, and serve every purpose of finding The One Best Way to Do Work.

Under V, therbligs, we would emphasize that we do not place "motions" as the next subdivision under "cycle of motions" because "motions" have neither distinct and definite boundaries nor beginnings and endings. For example: It is difficult to determine correctly how many "motions" are required to take a fountain pen from the pocket and prepare to write with it. It will be found difficult to agree on just how many "motions" are made and as to where are located the boundaries of the "motions" of so simple a cycle as this, or of any other similarly common cycle of motions.

However, the 17 subdivisions, or events, or therbligs, as they are variously called, seem to be all that are necessary from which to synthesize all of the *cycles of motions* of all the *operations* of all the *processes* of all the *organizations* of every kind whatever. The science of motion study consists, therefore, of finding The One Best Sequence of therbligs for each kind of work and the science of management consists of deriving, installing, and enforcing the conditions that will permit the work to be done repeatedly the The One Best Way. It is conceivable that sometime in the future an eighteenth and possibly more therbligs will be found, and we seem near to their discovery at the present time. The discovery of additional therbligs pertaining to the phenomena of skill and automaticity seems inevitable.[4]

Under VI, variables of motions, provision is made for filing all information regarding any kind of motion made by either hand, device, or machine. It provides for all information regarding the structures in which work is performed. It provides for filing all data regarding human behavior—supernormal, normal, and subnormal. It supplies the basis of filing all data of the educator, psychologist, psychiatrist, and the expert in personnel, placement, and promotion problems.

This classification can be carried on and subdivided indefinitely. It furnishes an efficient and quickly usable plan for synthesizing the components of The One Best Way to Do Work in such shape that they can be cumulatively improved.

However, our present information regarding the 17 therbligs is sufficient to revolutionize all kinds of work, and if the industries of the various nations would eliminate the obviously unnecessary therbligs and standardize the kinds, sequences, and combinations of the remaining efficient therbligs, the resulting savings each year would be sufficient to pay the outstanding debts of most nations.

HISTORY OF THIS CLASSIFICATION

For many years we have used these therbligs as divisions for dissecting cycles of motions of a great many different kinds of work, but it was not until we began to use photography in motion study in 1892 that we made our greatest progress. It was not until 1912, when we used our first micromotion processes intensively, that we were able to make such great advances as projecting the motions of experts faster and slower, as well as at the speed of experts' demonstration. We were then also able to project and examine therbligs backwards, or in the reversed directions. This enabled us to get a new fund of information that resulted in many suggestions from seeing, measuring, and comparing the therbligs performed in the reversed sequence and opposite directions. This was used to great advantage in finding the methods of least waste and especially in the process of taking machines apart and putting them together again in front of a motion picture camera, and then running the film backwards, showing the films of assembling as dissembling and vice versa.

EXAMPLES OF PROFITABLE USE

Running films of superexperts backwards, to see what we could get for automatically suggesting inventions, or as "thought detonators" when seeing the operation done thus, presented peculiarities and combinations of therbligs never seen before. This was, of course, supplemented by examining one picture, or frame, at a time which, with motion study experts, will always be the most efficient method for getting facts from the films. Great progress was made, for example, in *pre-positioning for next operation* (therblig *k*) parts and tools so that *grasp* (therblig *d*) was performed with quite the same motions and actions and performed within a time equal to that of *release load* (therblig *l*).

As an example of the importance of recognizing the therblig as the fundamental element, the result of that particular study in 1912 was that our organization enabled a client to have his machine assemblers put together 66 machines per day with less fatigue than they had previously accumulated while assembling 18 machines per day. Because this method was synthesized from fundamentally correct units, the same methods are still in use today in this same factory.[5]

This increase in output should not be considered as an exceptional case. On the contrary, it is quite typical. In fact we have a great many illustrations that we could give where the savings were much greater. For example: One large motion-study laboratory, as a result of this method of attack, synthesized and demonstrated new methods which averaged an output of five times as much product per man. This method used in assembling carburetors enabled messenger boys to do the work in one-tenth the time required by skilled mechanics.[6] It has been used on work of assembling pumps with still greater results.[7]

THERBLIG SEQUENCES

It was early recognized that certain similar operations have similar sequences of therbligs. For example: The operations of feeding pieces into a drill press or into a punch press, time tickets into a time stamp, and paper into a printing press, have practically the same sequence of therbligs. A typical sequence of therbligs for one complete cycle of handling one piece on a drill press is *search, find, select, grasp, transport loaded, position, assemble, use, disassemble, inspect, transport loaded, pre-position for next operation, release load* and *transport empty*. This cycle of motions can and should be done with the following therbligs: *grasp, transport loaded, position, assemble, use, release load* and *transport empty,* which are half the number of therbligs of the usual method.

While the former is the usual sequence of therbligs on a drill press, it is by no means the best one. There is The One Best Sequence of therbligs on each machine and each kind of work, and it should always be found, standardized, taught, and maintained.

ANOTHER WORK CLASSIFICATION

Now let us look at another method of subdividing and classifying all work. There is another and better known type of division and classification for visualizing all activity which was early recognized. The importance of considering this simple classification can be

seen in the unfairness and trouble that have been caused by giving the same piece rate for large lots as for small. This classification divides all work, both large and small, into three parts, as follows:

1. Get ready.
2. Do it, or make it.
3. Clean up.

Now, applying this division to one piece on the drill press, we have:

1. *Get ready,* or pick up the piece and put it under the drill. This consists of all therbligs that come before *use* (therblig *h*).

2. *Drill it* (do it or make it). This consists of only one therblig, namely *use* (therblig *h*).

3. *Clean up,* or take the piece out from under the drill and inspect it and lay it down. This consists of all therbligs that come after *use* (therblig *h*).

THE IMPORTANCE OF USE

It should be recognized that the therblig *use* is the difficult one to learn in mastering a trade. It is the most productive and, therefore, the most important therblig of all.

All other therbligs of all kinds of work are desirable and necessary only so far as they facilitate, prepare for, or assist in increasing *use*. Any therbligs that do not foster *use* should be under suspicion as being unnecessary. Use is the highest paid therblig, because it usually requires the most skill. The more of the therbligs of "get ready" and "clean up" that are performed by less skilled and consequently lower priced workers the better for all workers, for they all will be employed a larger portion of the day at the highest priced work at which they are each individually capable. This is true not only in the consideration of the therbligs but also in the trades in general. For example: The bricklayer, the plumber, the steamfitter, the office executive, and many others, each have their specially assigned helpers, but they still habitually do much pay-reducing work for which in the long run they suffer a loss due to less personal activity. It will help to analyze and classify all work if it is recognized that the hod carrier bears the same relation to the bricklayer, and the secretary to the executive, as do the therbligs that compose "get ready" bear to the therblig *use;* and the laborer's work of "clean up" after the work of the bricklayer, is quite the same as the therbligs that compose "clean up" after therblig *use*.

Further investigations of a typical sequence of therbligs, such as on the drill press or other examples cited, from the standpoint of the classification of the therbligs show that *grasp* (therblig *d*) of "get ready" is used before *use* (therblig *h*) and that *release load* (therblig *l*) done after *use* may be quite the same except that it is performed in motions that are the reverse of those of *grasp*.

Table 1

PAIRED THERBLIG USUALLY PERFORMED BEFORE USE		PAIRED THERBLIG USUALLY PERFORMED AFTER USE	
d. Grasp	Use	l. Release load	
e. Transport loaded	Use	m. Transport empty	
f. Position	Use	k. Pre-position for next operation	
g. Assemble	Use	i. Disassemble	
q. Plan	Use	j. Inspect	

Table 2 Unpaired Therbligs

ORDER NO. 4		ORDER NO. 5
a. Search	Use	n. Rest for overcoming fatigue
b. Find	Use	o. Other forms of unavoidable delay
c. Select	Use	p. Avoidable delay

PAIRED THERBLIGS

There are a number of such paired therbligs which are almost always separated by the therblig *use*.

For example:

It was the absence of a therblig on the other side of *use* to pair with *inspect*, together with the fact that *plan* is actually found in the photographic records regardless of how much planning may be done prior to the beginning of an operation, that caused us to add to the list of therbligs, *plan* (therblig *q*). The therblig *plan* may occur in any place in the sequence of therbligs, but we have put it last in the list before cited because it was added last, and also to distinguish it from the "planning" that should be done before any "performing" of the operation is begun.

There are two more kinds of divisions, or orders, making a total of five orders of therbligs, namely, one consisting of *search*, *find* and *select* (therbligs *a*, *b*, and *c*) which usually come before *use*, and *rest for overcoming fatigue*, *other forms of unavoidable delay* and *avoidable delay* (therbligs *n*, *o*, and *p*) which usually come after *use*. Thus we have two orders of unpaired therbligs separated by *use*, as follows:

In analyzing an operation of any kind a simultaneous motion cycle chart is prepared. The therbligs of motion are applied to this chart in studying it for present methods and determining the altered sequence which should be adopted to establish The One Best Way to Do Work. This brought up the problem of graphic presentation of the therbligs for ready identification.

To make these 17 therbligs more real, tangible, and easier to visualize and remember, different colors are used to distinguish them on the simultaneous motion cycle chart.[8] One member of our organization, Paul M. Vanderhorst, who conceived the idea of adding *plan* to our list of therbligs, also suggested the idea of showing the 17 therbligs in the design of a wheel, and we have adopted a "Wheel of Motion" not altogether unlike the "Wheel of Life" of Hindus, for explaining therblig study to the employees of our clients. Each part of the wheel representing a therblig has its own individual color, and each of the colors has a special meaning and is also mnemonic. See Figs. 1 and 2.

It should be noted that *use* is the hub of the wheel. *Use* is the most important therblig. The more *use*, the more production.

The therbligs that have like characteristics, although they may represent reversed action, are shown as paired spokes on opposite sides of the wheel.

The rim of the wheel consists of two different kinds, or orders, of three parts each, and the cogs on the rim are shaped like the letter V, and are to remind the motion-study student that the variables affect all of the therbligs and must be all carefully considered in order to obtain The One Best Way to Do Work. There are at least a hundred variables that are important on nearly all kinds of work and our complete list contains several thousand variables. It is extremely important to recognize that information relating to the variables is applicable to all kinds of work. The application of this information is simply a matter of degree required in the particular study in hand.

The same colors are always used on the same therbligs wherever they are represented or shown. This permits instant visualization of all the therbligs of any one kind. These colors are specially important in connection with quickly visualizing, grouping, comparing, and interpreting the behavior and happenings on simultaneous motion cycle charts. The use of the standard colors enables the micromotion study engineer to acquire a proper sense of the proper time for each therblig, even before a new study is made. This is particularly important when studying an operator for his first time, as it will show whether or not he is fully cooperating.

In fact, too much stress can hardly be laid on the importance of showing each and every therblig and all possible happenings on the simultaneous motion cycle chart in finding The One Best Way to Do Work. We know of no other method in finding The One Best Way to Do Work. It answers all purposes satisfactorily.

After sufficient experience and study, preferably in a motion-study laboratory, the interrelations, peculiarities, and suitabilities of the therbligs on several simultaneous motion cycle charts of different kinds of work will be recognized by an engineer trained in motion study. When he has the proper training he is invariably able to improve and completely revolutionize any work on which the micromotion study method of attack has not already been used.

RELATION OF THERBLIG STUDY TO STOPWATCH TIME STUDY

The symbols here shown furnish a sort of shorthand which makes for greater speed in making notes regarding best sequences of therbligs and motion study in general, and for remembering the therbligs easily. The results of careful study of the peculiarities of the therbligs individually, and in combination with those that immediately precede and immediately follow, as well as those that are executed simultaneously by other anatomical members, will remove for all time any idea that scientific motion study of the behavior of the workers can be accomplished with any such obsolete device as a stopwatch, or that time study and motion study are the same thing or even similar.

The literature of scientific management is full of examples where time study and motion study are

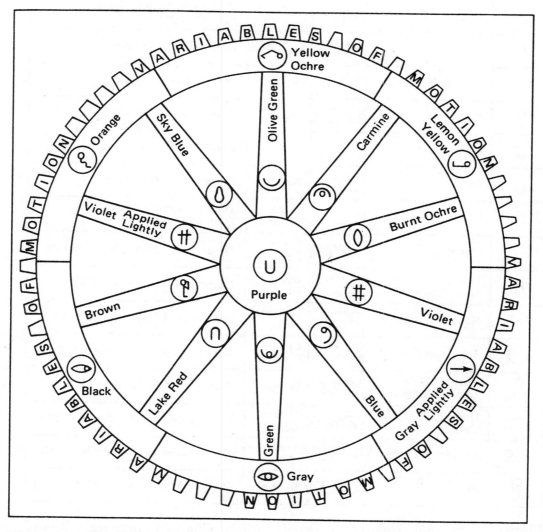

Figure 1. The Wheel of Motion

confused. This confusion abounds even in books that are considered classics. It should be recognized that "Time study is the art of finding how long it takes to do work." This was Taylor's original definition, and it is still good. Time study is the great invention of Dr. Taylor. Taylor never did any motion study[9] of any kind whatever.[10]

The definition of motion study is: "Motion study is the science of finding The One Best Way to Do Work." Of course micromotion study gives records in indispu-

table permanent form of the motions and behavior of the demonstrator of the methods and of the individual errorless times of each therblig of each cycle of motions and of the overall times of the operator.

TRANSFERABLE DATA

Intensive study of the resulting therbligs furnishes information that is interchangeable in all kinds of work for finding The One Best Way to Do Work. It is this

STANDARD SYMBOLS, COLORS AND PENCILS FOR SIMO-CHARTS
(Simultaneous Motion Cycle Charts)

Symbol	Name of Symbol	Symbol Color	Name of Color	Name and Number of Pencil or Crayon
◉	Search	▬	Black	Dixon's Best Black #331
◎	Find	▤	Gray	Dixon's Best Gray #352½
→	Select	▦	Light Gray	Dixon's Best Gray #352½ Applied Lightly
∩	Grasp	▨	Lake Red	Dixon's Best Lake Red #321½
⌣	Transport Loaded	▨	Green	Dixon's Best Green #354
᧘	Position	▨	Blue	Dixon's Best Blue #350
♯	Assemble	▨	Violet	Dixon's Best Violet #323
∪	Use	▨	Purple	Dixon's Best Purple #323½
♯	Dis-assemble	▨	Light Violet	Dixon's Best Violet #323 Applied Lightly
◊	Inspect	▨	Burnt Ochre	Dixon's Best Burnt Ochre #335½
᧙	Pre-position for Next Operation	▨	Sky Blue	Dixon's Best Sky Blue #320
⌒ᵒ	Release Load	▨	Carmine Red	Dixon's Best Carmine Red #321
∪	Transport Empty	▨	Olive Green	Dixon's Best Olive Green #325
᧚	Rest for Over-coming Fatigue	▨	Orange	Ruben's "Crayola" Orange
⌒ᵒ	Unavoidable Delay	▨	Yellow Ochre	Dixon's Best Yellow Ochre #324½
∟ᵒ	Avoidable Delay	▨	Lemon Yellow	Dixon's Best Lemon Yellow #353½
᧗	Plan	▨	Brown	Dixon's Best Brown #343

Figure 2. Symbols, Colors, and Pencils for Simo-Charts. In practice, column 3 is solid colors, not crosshatching.

feature of the great value of the interchangeability of the indisputable detailed data that makes it most desirable to select as demonstrator of a method that person only who is *the best demonstrator obtainable* of the best methods extant or the best known, and in a motion-study laboratory[11] equipped for the purpose, and under controlled conditions.

It is obvious that records of the methods of recognized champions are most desirable. It must be recognized, however, that champions are usually champions because others are so inefficient. The synthesis of the best components of the methods of two or more champions will make a method better than that of the method of the champion of champions and better than the method of *the one best demonstrator obtainable*.

Data regarding the therbligs of a champion or a superexpert in any one kind of work are usable on a great many different kinds of work, for the times and skill on each therblig are transferable. It is also desirable, but not absolutely necessary, that *the best demonstrator obtainable*, of the best method extant, shall have sufficient experience to perform the cycles of motions and the complete operation in the shortest time for that operation. However, it is often difficult to obtain anyone who can demonstrate the combination of the *best method known* and also the *best speed of performance*. Oftentimes the expert of motion study can demonstrate the sequence of therbligs which constitute The One Best Way to Do Work, yet, because of his lack of practice and speed, is not able at first to equal the times nor the relativity of simultaneity of therbligs performed by different anatomical members of those with a much poorer method, but with much greater natural dexterity, who have had so much practice that they have arrived at a state of motion automaticity.

It is here that the method of recording lateness of therbligs previously cited is of importance. Here again the detailed records of the therbligs are of great value for the correct times of individual therbligs and the proper relativity of simultaneity can be obtained even from inferior sequences where great dexterity and automaticity have been recorded under the wrong method. When the best sequence is known, the correct time for task management for performing The One Best Way to Do Work *can be prophesied before anyone can demonstrate it*. The importance of prophesying the time for accomplishing The One Best Way to Do Work before it can be demonstrated will be appreciated when it is realized that there is not a single case on record where The One Best Way to Do Work has been derived by the wasteful fumbling methods of evolution.

RELATION OF THIS CLASSIFICATION TO FATIGUE STUDY

Much has been written in generalities regarding un-

necessary fatigue. Because of the dreadful working conditions in nearly all factories, some improvements can almost always be made by anyone with good intentions and authority together with sufficient continuity of purpose. However, such improvements are only part of what could be done and often lapse after the passing of the regime of the untrained enthusiast who is merely interested in the elimination of unnecessary fatigue. The One Best Way to Do Work is that sequence of therbligs which permits the work to be done in least time, with least fatigue, and entails having the periods of *unavoidable delay* (therblig *o*) and *avoidable delay* (therblig *p*) utilized for *rest for overcoming fatigue* (therblig *n*).

The data relating to therbligs that cause or eliminate unnecessary fatigue can be filed in orderly fashion for future use under the classification shown herein.

Unnecessary fatigue should be recognized as the badge of ignorance of the therbligs and consequently of motion study. To eliminate unnecessary fatigue, there must be complete recognition that the therbligs are the fundamental elements of The One Best Way to Do Work, and are units for the application of the laws of motion study and fatigue study.

RELATION TO STANDARDIZATION

Much has been written also of standardization, and The One Best Way to make standards is to proceed from the standpoint that the best standard is the one that best complies with the laws of motion study. It is quite impossible to standardize a method for quickest achievement of the state of automaticity without recognition and standardization of the individual therbligs involved and their combinations and sequences.

Automaticity of the wrong method, so prevalent in highly repetitive vocations like those of the textile trades, is the shame and disgrace of industry today. However, it will be quite useless for executives and managers to talk standardizations of the correct sequences of the therbligs for The One Best Way to Do Work until they know from personal experience the possibilities of micromotion study, and set the example in their own duties. For this purpose the simplest device is the executive's cross-sectioned desk which serves as a permanent reminder, and if used properly will furnish a permanent proof. It permits doing all manual work with almost exactly the same motions every time. It soon becomes strikingly evident how much faster work can be accomplished when the motions are made over the same locations each and every time. The next step is the search for The One Best Way to Do Work.

Because of the rule-of-thumb methods used in the past for obtaining standards, almost anyone can make improvements in the present state of standardization encountered in all organizations. The usual standards obtained by rule-of-thumb methods will always be temporary and transitory. If standards are based upon the permanent records of indisputable knowledge of the ultimate components of the cycles obtained by the micromotion methods, they will be in shape for cumulative improvement without any additional study.

Comparatively few organizations have given proper attention to the possibilities of standardization built upon indisputable measured elements, and but few standards have been made with due regard to the extra outputs in the savings of time and fatigue that result if the standards are made to conform with the laws of automaticity, which is the greatest free asset of the working man, whatever his occupation.

RELATION TO THE LEARNING PROCESS

For greatest speed with least effort and fatigue in learning, The One Best Sequence of therbligs should be used whenever possible from the very beginning of the learning period so that automaticity may be achieved in the shortest possible learning period and with least habit interference. The study of the 17 therbligs of this classification furnishes a means to shorten the period required to learn any kind of art, trade, profession, or other activity. Hence, there will be more time available to learn more jobs and thus gain promotion, and, by reason of more knowledge of the theory combined with the practice, prolong one's earning periods by teaching others, when one is too old to do a young man's total quantity of output.

Finally, the evils of deadening monotony do not exist where there is sufficient knowledge of the therbligs and the variables affecting them. As two cycles of motions can never be made exactly alike, the quest of perfection of methods is much more interesting and absorbing than the desire to know which part of the whole structure is the piece which is being worked upon, although the latter is supposed to be the millennium by the academic enemies of standardization.

Knowledge of measuring, selecting, and studying of therbligs makes all work fascinating, for while the best method known and performed under given conditions may be called for practical purposes "The One Best Way to Do Work," a still better method with new tools and conditions is ever possible. There is no instance or example that cannot be improved with greater knowledge of the therbligs pertaining to that work. There are so many possible combinations of therbligs that the skilled worker with the knowledge of therbligs performing any work ordinarily considered monotonous has the opportunity to improve the temporary One Best Way to Do Work almost without limit.

It is not the fault of the skilled worker, if he has not been taught to visualize the therbligs, that he has not been given sufficient incentives to enlist and hold all of his zeal continuously, has not been taught the science that underlies his work, has not been induced to search for the scheme of perfection, has not been taught a filing method for his knowledge that he may have systematized improvement from his additional experience, and has not desired to teach the apprentices and other learners the best way that he knew.

The results derived under the method of attack that this classification embodies have been successful in every kind of work in which it has been used.

It is hoped that this description of this filing classification will be of service to those who are interested in efficiency, in making waste elimination attractive, and in finding and enforcing the managerial conditions which will permit The One Best Way to Do Work.

NOTES AND REFERENCES

1. See *Frederick W. Taylor* by F. B. Copley.
2. This word was coined for the purpose of having a short word which will save the motions necessary to write such long descriptions as "The 17 categories into which the motion-study elementary subdivisions of a cycle of motions fall."
3. In 1910 and the years following, we collected and specially devised in our own laboratory, many devices for supplying, mechanically, the therbligs of cycles of motions that the crippled soldiers could not perform, due to their injuries. Such collections should be made by all museums and colleges that intend to teach motion study.
4. See Society of Industrial Engineers Bulletin, November 1923, pp. 6–7. "A Fourth Dimension for Recording Skill," by Frank B. Gilbreth and L. M. Gilbreth. The lateness in starting or finishing of a therblig performed by any one anatomical member as compared with the time of beginning or finishing of a therblig performed by another anatomical member is a most important unit for measuring skill and automaticity.
5. See *Management Engineering*, February 1923, p. 87. "Ten Years of Scientific Management," by John G. Aldrich, M. E., and also his discussion of paper 1378 on page 1131, vol. 34, 1912, American Society of Mechanical Engineers Transactions.
6. See Proceedings of the Institution of Automobile Engineers (English), "The Fundamentals of Cost Reduction," by H. Kerr Thomas, Member of the Council.
7. See Society of Industrial Engineers Transactions, vol. 2, 1920, "The One Best Way to Do Work," by Frank B. Gilbreth and L. M. Gilbreth.
8. See "Applied Motion Study," by Frank B. Gilbreth and L. M. Gilbreth, p. 138.
9. See Bulletin of The Taylor Society, June 1921.
10. This can easily be proved by reading Taylor's own writings, and it is also a matter of record in our own office. This fact is entirely missed, perhaps unintentionally, by Taylor's biographer, Copley.
11. Laboratory motion study has been criticized as being done under conditions of the shop. The conditions of the shop should be changed until they duplicate the most desirable conditions of the laboratory.

OF THINGS FUNDAMENTAL

There's nothing like a crazy startup to remind you of the basics, something no gazillion-dollar firm can ever do.

Tom Peters

AS A FAVOR TO AN OLD SILICON VALLEY FRIEND, I'VE begun working with his about-to-be-born startup. It's low-tech ... and not a darling of 3000 Sand Hill Road. (Funding comes mostly from a whopping home mortgage and several shaken-down relatives.)

I don't know how it's going to work out for him (great, I hope), but I've had a helluva ride and been pointedly reminded about business basics in a way that working with a gazillion-dollar firm can never do. Here are lessons learned to date:

1 Gotta love that product. Sure it's obvious—or is it? The *Economist* recently reported on an extensive study of "product juggernauts," companies that out-innovate the competition year in and year out. They shared one thing in common: "an unnatural obsession with what they produce."

The issue is not to have just a "good product," but a product that's clearly special. Your daughter, son, spouse, aunts and uncles—and then the professional folks you talk with—have got to glow when you show them your sketches, prototypes, whatever. A *Boston Globe* columnist said of a concert by Ben Zander (conductor of the Boston Philharmonic), "It left you feeling as though you had been struck by lightning, dazzled, with all your molecules rearranged." I've adopted those words for my friend's endeavor. We're in the "dazzlement/molecule-rearrangement business"—no less a response will do. (Hey, I'm on board precisely because his idea rearranged a few of my molecules!)

2 Sales beats marketing. I believe in marketing, in knowing who your customer is and which channels you need to traverse (initially) to distribute your product. But it's become clear to my pal and me that sales comes first.

There's no bonanza for the world's greatest widget until there's a completed connection with the customer. For my friend's startup, aiming exclusively as we are for national-account business, we require a driven, proven national-account sales genius to get us going with a bang.

We began by thinking we needed an inspired marketer, with some sales background. Now we are convinced we need an inspired salesperson—with some marketing history. (And, incidentally, back to No. 1 above, the sales point

person must love our product; though the pay/incentive prospects will be good to excellent, the "job" must be a labor of passion, not a day at the office or a bullet point for the resume.)

3 Great people. "People are everything." Every business says it; only a handful live it. But in a startup, your top employees (a sales whiz and a business manager, in our case) must be "planet class." We are looking for the best people even though currently our startup is "garage class." We are in a panic. We want to hustle, hustle, hustle. There is a great temptation to: (1) hire "Joe's friend Mary, who's done this stuff before," or (2) grab the first half-intelligent warm body that walks through the door.

In this one area, we are grinding teeth, biting tongues ... and being very patient. We are leaving no stone unturned in our hyperprofessional job search and are spending gobs of time we just don't have on interviews. My friend, strategist and product designer par excellence, has tried to stiff me at the last minute on a couple of interviews. I have literally (once) dragged him in. This is the "Big Enchilada," I've insisted. (And I think I'm right.)

4 Be prototype-happy. I devoted a whole *Forbes ASAP* column to prototyping (the No. 1 "core competence" for an innovative company, I argued) last August. This is where the rubber meets the road: We're spending ourselves (himself, mostly!) half-poor on prototypes.

The best way to enthuse prospects is (surprise!) with product, not concept; moreover, give them an inkling of the breadth and depth of the eventual product line. My instinct, his instinct, and that of all our advisers tell us: prototype, prototype, prototype! We are learning, revising, impressing others ... and spurring ourselves on ... with THE REAL THING.

5 Systems aren't an afterthought. For the little (wee) firm dealing with national accounts, it's "one strike and you're out." We are already knee-deep in business systems. These include: (1) a great (not just good) accountant, and hands-on involvement in accounting; (2) a thoroughly modern inventory-management system; and (3) state-of-the-art database management systems. We simply want to know, record and be able to leverage every dollop of information we collect about every item and individual we come in contact with. We are not into gold-plating, but we are committed to systems that are solid, substantial, broad and deep.

6 **Act big from the get-go.** Yes, timing is everything. We think our timing is very right. Nonetheless, we are taking deep breaths and being somewhat too substantially patient: We're following the "think-big, act-big law of self-fulfilling prophecy strategy." That is, we are not going to expose our startup to the market (beyond numerous beta tests and a jillion conversations) until we can be a noticeable, commented-upon presence. It's said that Hewlett-Packard gave its first machine back in 1939 a high number to make it sound like the company had been around a while.

We're playing the same game—to the hilt. We're producing samples galore, generating marketing material, going big league (or at least AAA) in trade-show presence, launching a serious and classy (we think) ad campaign, and chintzing on nothing that will allow us to be perceived as "a player" from day one. (All of this is being done, of course, within the bounds of modest capitalization. It's a matter of priorities, and this is a big one.)

7 **A plan.** We have a prospectus (a little gold-plated, meant to exude some frankly unwarranted signs of gravitas), but that's not the key. Neither are the pro formas. What's turned out to be the planning essential is the humble time line. Now five single-spaced pages long, including milestones monumental and mundane, it's on everybody's computer (okay, four of ours), plastered on butcher paper on the headquarter's walls (okay, home office). It is reality. It is how we think. How we debate. It's our paramount talking document with potential partners.

8 **A philosophy.** Our product is vital and energetic. And my friend's heart and soul are in the right place. We read and reread Anita Roddick's *Body and Soul*, her account of creating Body Shop International. We really want to have a business we can be proud of in all respects (great place to work, ethical to a fault, diversity-is-our-middle-name, etc.), or we don't want to be in business at all. Again and again, call it crunch time—which happens all the time in a startup—we come within a hair's breadth of compromising on this or that; and then, so far at least, we step back. The time to do it right is from the start and all the time, not just when it becomes convenient.

At the top of the list: Work only with people you like (as well as respect). On a couple of occasions, we've met with superstars, been wowed by their command of their specialty, but not liked them for some wholly subjective reason. Our decision: not to work with them, period. Life's too short.

9 **A clear signature.** It's a variation on No. 8. In a want ad, we asked for a "wildly enthusiastic, bizarrely committed" individual. Some friends scolded us: "You can't use language like that. It's not professional!" "It's who I am," my friend said, "and what we want. Why in the hell can't businesspeople use real people's language?"

> **"Are we having fun?" We're dead tired is what we are! But alive and wired and having fun.... If anything smacks of dreary business-as-usual, we draw back in alarm.... Friends scolded us: "You can't use language like that. It's not professional!" "It's who I am," my friend protested, "and what we want. Why in the hell can't businesspeople use real people's language?"**

10 **Improv skills.** My friend knows what he is about. I agree with his rigidity about what makes his baby his baby. On the other hand, we are making fundamental decisions that take us SSE one week, NNW the next. "We run like mad and then we change direction" is the way Chairman Bert Roberts describes MCI's strategy. We, too, are trying to be masters of improv (principled improv masters, nonetheless—see No. 8).

11 **Grains of salt.** We've consulted with perhaps two dozen incredible folks—most of whom, incidentally, have been delighted to share their innermost thoughts. We have benefited enormously from their wisdom. But they all seem to be in utter disagreement (and that's only a slight exaggeration). Each has a clear theory of the market that has served him or her well. Thus we listen, learn, sift and—with fear and trepidation at eschewing such good advice—go our own sweet, determined way.

12 **Fun.** "Are we having fun?" We're dead tired is what we are! But alive and wired ... and having fun. And if anything we do smacks of dreary business-as-usual, the way "they" do it, we draw back in alarm.

That's my report from the trenches ... so far. Take it with a grain of salt. (I do, and I promise an update soon.) And, big boss reader, you might try what I've tried. It's been my best learning—relearning—experience in 10 years!

The Happiest Workers in the World

The crisis of worker confidence is as inescapable as the daily news—and we expected the first annual Inc./Gallup *survey to reflect it. Boy, were we surprised* ▪ JEFFREY L. SEGLIN

1. Fear and loathing in the new economy

Exactly when did "economic anxiety" become the emotional bumper sticker for our coast-to-coast collective unconscious?

Was it when Pat Buchanan (remember him?) won New Hampshire's first-in-the-nation presidential primary, reminding rivals in both parties that the electorate really is mad as hell? Or was it later in March, when the *New York Times* saw fit to run seven straight days of page-one stories on the downsizing of America? Or was it all the way back in 1993, when employment-for-life apostle IBM announced its first-ever five-digit layoff?

By now in any case, the supposed crisis of worker confidence is as inescapable as the daily news—and we expected the first annual *Inc.*/Gallup survey on work and the American workplace to reflect it.

In headlines that glare at us every waking moment of every working day, we are told that corporate downsizings, mergers, and other belt-tightening measures leave us hemorrhaging jobs. Politicians from both the left (Edward Kennedy) and the center (Bill Bradley) express concern as eagerly as Buchanan

did from the right. Bradley, the would-be third-party moderate, writes, "Economic anxiety eats away at people who work in America."

The statistics seem bad enough—on average, 37,000 jobs were cut every month in 1995—but perhaps the more stinging signs of unease are anecdotal and very close to home.

For instance, my own children—though successful grad school–educated teachers—wrestle with the need to work other jobs and train for other careers to feel secure. Both realize that their working lives will be a jigsaw puzzle of jobs, projects, and skills-gathering expeditions. Both, though fulfilled by their work, are exhausted and daunted by the effort of keeping the puzzle together.

Who hasn't heard similar testimony? "Everyone is a contingent worker," observes William Bridges, author of *Job-Shift: How to Prosper in a Workplace Without Jobs* (Addison-Wesley, 1994). We will come to see our times, he says, as the great dejobbing of America, leading to a day when all jobs come and go according to the changing needs of a company and its customers—a fine and flexible day indeed for those companies

and customers, but a fearful one for employees on a quest for career stability and some sense of control over the course of their lives. The unknown is a breeding ground for free-floating anxiety.

And out of that anxiety comes the brand-new conventional wisdom that the American dream—the dream that living standards will forever rise, that we'll do better than our parents, and that our children's lives will be better than ours—is ailing.

Or dead.

2. Who's to blame? Part 1

Although the news accounts of our economic unease are broad and sweeping, they are quite specific about the root of our troubles. They lay blame squarely on the shoulders of greedy, heartless, soulless business. "Is the American Worker Getting Shafted?" asks the January 22 cover headline of *U.S. News & World Report*. The implied answer is all too clear: yes. The implied culprit? Business.

The theme is pounded on repeatedly not just by journalists but by policymakers of every stripe at every level. Chief among them is Robert Reich, President Clinton's labor secretary, who passionately proclaims that the implicit social compact between employer and employee, which used to guarantee workers' job security, "has come undone" and should be put right. Legislation has been field. Theories of "new corporate citizenship" have been advanced.

It's not hard to understand why Reich's sentiments are widely shared. Given the hundreds of thousands of layoffs over the past several years, the argument goes, business must be failing us. And there is plenty of corroborating evidence that the public in fact sees our economic future as relatively bleak. The upshot? Whatever societal changes we face and whatever forces are producing them, business is simply not pulling its weight to help us through. Business—we keep being told—is harming America.

But do workers agree? They may be troubled, but do *they* think business is to blame? In the flood of coverage on economic insecurity, worker unease, and "the anxious class," we noticed an alarming absence of information about how workers see their own jobs and workplaces. Not how they see the future or the state of the economy overall—many surveys have described diminished expectations or wounded hopes—but how they assess their own situations. No one has been asking working Americans—about 118 million of us—how we are doing on the job and what we think of our employers.

AMERICANS AT WORK

Joe Kenney, 42,
police officer,
Pleasant Hills, Pa.

'I feel good about what I do, and our new police chief recognizes good work. If someone tells him, "Hey, Joe did a nice job on this," I'll get real congratulations from him.'

So we at *Inc.* did just that. In partnership with the Gallup Organization, we surveyed Americans nationwide to ask questions like these: Are you worried about losing your job? Does the stress of

work cause you to behave badly with your family? Does your management do what's necessary to make your company a great place to work?

AMERICANS AT WORK

Lori Gaunt, 28,
retail manager,
Macrina Bakery
and Café, Seattle

'I feel as if my opinions count a lot, and I've been instrumental in making changes. The owner isn't hands-off, but she loves what I do and tells me to run with it. It's neat to have that much freedom.'

The survey was conducted in November 1995. We asked randomly selected working adults throughout the United States to agree or disagree with 34 statements about their jobs, their workplaces, and their job security.

The results were nothing like what we expected.

3. What American workers really think

We expected the same answers we bet you would: hard times on the job, rough handling by employers, fears about the future. Try this test: Ask folks at your next neighborhood barbecue to predict the responses to the national survey. What percentage of Americans do they think are worried about losing their jobs? Maybe 50%? More? What percentage do they think feel fairly paid? Say, 25%? And how many people do they think would say that management does whatever's necessary to make their company a great place to work? Hmmm, 10%? On a good day.

What other kinds of answers could we expect from a citizenry that's been depicted as economically threatened?

Positive ones, it turns out.

Across the board the 34 questions prompted upbeat—sometimes even glowing—responses. Could this be the same American workforce we've been reading about? (See page 97 for a copy of

the survey questionnaire, a complete breakdown of the answers, and a description of how the poll was conducted.) A sampling of the results:

- 90% of the respondents said that they were *not* worried about losing their jobs (even though 39% said they had friends who lost jobs because of downsizing).
- 69% believed they had been compensated fairly over the past year.
- 75% said they had not had three or more days in the past month when stress caused them to behave badly with their families.
- 70% said that management did what was necessary to make their company a great place to work.
- 80% said that their company was "family friendly."
- 82% said that every day they have an opportunity to do what they do best.

Perhaps most contradictory to current popular consensus was this finding: 63% of workers felt *more* secure in their jobs than they did a year ago, compared with only 20% who felt less secure. (Seventeen percent felt about the same.) What's more, when asked to rank their level of satisfaction with their place of employment—on a scale from 1 to 5, with 5 representing "extremely satisfied"—71% rated it at 4 or 5 while only 9% rated it at 1 or 2.

Are Americans worried about the practical matter of keeping a job? No. Do they think their employers treat them fairly? Yes. And from the most personal perspective, do they feel their jobs fulfill them and enrich their lives? Yes again.

AMERICANS AT WORK

Cindy LaRue, 39,
production worker, and
Candy Smalley, 48,
production team leader,
Springfield Remanufacturing
Corp., Springfield, MO.

Smalley: 'When I first came here and the CEO not only gave us the financials but expected us to learn them, I was astounded. We felt respected. And now we use those numbers to improve.'

To better assess whether the survey results are as positive as they initially appear, we compared our findings with those of similar national surveys conducted by Gallup in 1994 in Canada, Mexico, Great Britain, Japan, and Germany. The results from the working populations of those countries were also more positive than negative, but not nearly as positive as those in the United States. And American workers are hands-down more positive about how they are treated by their employers than are workers in any other country. To the question "In the past seven days, have you received recognition or praise for good work?" 62% of U.S. workers answered yes. The next highest percentage of yes answers came from Canada, with 54%. Germany registered 36% yes answers and Japan a meager 33%. The same relative findings emerged from questions about whether someone had talked with employees about their progress at work and whether supervisors seemed to care about them as people. U.S. workers, it appears, aren't just happy. They seem to be the happiest workers in the world.

Still, interpreting survey results is sometimes a matter of how one wants to cast the light. So here's another angle: Imagine you're the manager receiving positive answers to a survey of your own workforce. (To make this proposition real, you can conduct the survey, using the questionnaire on page 97.) What would you think if you saw that 84% of those surveyed felt that their supervisors seemed to care about them as people? That a whopping 96% of them said that they knew what was expected of them at work? That 82% felt that every day they had the opportunity to do what they do best? That 87% said that the mission of their employer made them feel important? That 69% felt they were compensated fairly? That 79% were not looking for another job?

Wouldn't you be thrilled with how satisfied—even how downright happy—the vast majority of your employees appeared to be? You'd probably think you were doing a pretty good job.

4. What's wrong with this picture?

Why then do journalists, policymakers, and politicians paint such a dismal portrait of the American workplace, indicting business and business owners in the process? Are they wrong? In an environment of much-hyped public sentiment that the economy is going to hell in a handbasket, what are we to make of the positive results from the *Inc.*/Gallup survey? Does the poll give the lie to everything we've heard about economic jitters? Is *it* wrong?

The overall health of the U.S. economy is hard to read. At a time when we have the lowest unemployment rate in almost 30 years, real wages have fallen from a 1979 average of $24,000 for a high school graduate to a 1995 average of $18,000. And there is unquestionably concern among American workers about what the future holds. Still, it's difficult in the face of our survey not to conclude that there's something the gurus and opinion makers aren't getting. In his recent book, *How to Tell When You're Tired: A Brief Examination of Work* (W. W. Norton, 1995), Reg Theriault uses Karl Marx to explain the shortcomings of many economic thinkers: "Marx, it appears, lacked insight into the reality of day-to-day work, perhaps because he never really held down a job."

But amateurs appear to have trouble interpreting the work-related feelings of their compatriots, too. The regular folks we asked to read our survey results were shocked at the positive findings. Doubt and denial were the common reactions. To collect more anecdotal research and test theories about the apparent mismatch between public perception and statistical reality, we asked a number of people (staff members, relatives, passersby) to answer the questionnaire before looking at the results. Every one of them answered the majority of the questions positively—yet everyone was astounded at the overwhelmingly positive response of the nation as a whole.

It became clear that a gap has grown between how Americans feel about their daily work and how they feel about the economy as a whole. People feel good about their own jobs—but they believe that the rest of U.S. workers are about to lose *theirs*.

Why?

5. I'm okay. You're really screwed.

The simplest explanation may have to do with emphasis. Don Clifton, chairman of the Gallup Organization, reconciles the perception-reality mismatch this way: "We ought to feel good about where we are, but there's just so much opportunity to manage better. Though 75% said their work doesn't cause them to behave poorly with their families, 23% said it does. That's a lot of people."

Skeptics that we journalists are, we took a similar angle when we first got what seemed to us surprisingly positive results. Sure, only 9% of the adult work-

---

THE INC./GALLUP SURVEY

What Workers Want

Based on the survey results and an analysis by the Gallup Organization, the most critical factors bearing on employees' satisfaction and job performance seem to be the following:

- At work, employees have the opportunity every day to do what they do best.
- A supervisor or someone at work seems to care about them as people.
- At work, employees' opinions seem to count.
- Over the past year, employees had opportunities to learn and grow.
- The mission of their employer makes employees feel that their jobs are important.
- Employees have the materials and equipment to do their work right.
- Employees' companies are "family friendly."

ing population scored their work satisfaction at a level 1 or 2 on the five-point scale—but that's still somewhere between 9 million and 11 million unhappy people in our workforce on any given day. Several million unsatisfied people can make some serious noise and have a sobering effect on the public's mood about the state of the economy.

The fact remains, however, that when asked specifically about their workplaces and their own jobs, the vast majority of the working adult population in the United States is remarkably satisfied. So why do Americans appear to believe the worst about the circumstances of their neighbors, even though their own work lives are fine?

Some possible explanations:

Bad news sells. Perhaps we have a dim view of the country's prospects because, as Robert J. Samuelson observes in *The Good Life and Its Discontents: The American Dream in the Age of Entitlement, 1945–1995* (Times Books/Random House, 1995), "the nature of the modern press gives the worst side of us much more exposure and respectability than ever before."

We were reminded of just how much you can twist positive news by a front-page blurb in the "Work Week" column of the January 16 *Wall Street Journal*, soon after the publication of Samuelson's book last year. Under the boldfaced heading "Does Money Buy Happiness?" the *Journal* writes: "Samuelson . . . quotes a survey showing that 6% of people making $75,000 or more describe themselves as 'not too happy.'" It appears we're supposed to be alarmed that so many people making that kind of money are unhappy. But what about the 45% making more than $75,000 who said that they were *very* happy? Or the other 49% who said that they were *pretty* happy? Samuelson reports it all in his book. He also cites another survey in which 80% of us say that we're satisfied with our lives. Eighty percent! Ninety-four percent of those making $75,000 or more are happy! Yet the *Journal* turned the unhappy 6% into news. Funny? Yes. Unusual? No.

As recently as last fall, the Hay Group, a management-consulting firm with headquarters in Philadelphia, reported findings from its 1995–1996 employee-attitudes study suggesting that despite downsizing, workers are generally more upbeat about their employers than they were five years ago. According to the Hay report, overall job satisfaction was up

from earlier surveys, and pride in one's company was high across all job levels. The news of the Hay study seems to have fallen on deaf ears when it came to press coverage. Few media outlets picked up the findings. Good news just doesn't sell.

Bad news gets promoted even by the people making it. Consider the daily doses of news on massive corporate layoffs. While companies *are* laying off workers regularly, the job losses are more than offset by new jobs in the same industries. Why don't we hear about that? One, the media don't report it much—and when they do, they bury the good news deep in the story. Twenty-one paragraphs into a cover feature headlined "Economic Anxiety" in the March 11 *Business Week* is this information: "During the past two years, the seven regional

---

AMERICANS AT WORK

Nina Liu, 33, kindergarten/ first-grade teacher, P.S. 234, New York City

'I work in a terrific school. Collaboration is encouraged, and we're given the time to sit together and bounce ideas off one another—to be a think tank. There's a lot of debate and a sense of encouragement and support.'

---

telephone companies have slashed some 125,000 jobs, on top of the 40,000 latest cuts announced at AT&T. Nevertheless, the industry's total employment rose by 91,000 during the period, as companies beefed up employment in cellular and other fast-growing businesses."

Sometimes the new jobs are added by the same companies that announce the cuts. Last October, when AT&T announced it would eliminate 8,500 people from its personal-computer division, it also was hiring hundreds in its new consulting and systems-integration divisions. But we hear about the fires, not the hires. Corporate America has learned that a good thing happens when you broadcast a sense of prudent cost management and rigorous-if-ruthless leanness: your stock price goes up. So, got some jobs to cut? Call a press conference.

The halo effect. Isn't it curious that according to surveys, most Americans hold gloomy views about the economy at large while at the same time they've told us that as individuals they're doing just fine in their own workplaces? Curious, perhaps. But not unusual. In fact, the I'm-okay-but-nothing-else-is worldview is a predictable pattern—not just in surveys on the economy but also in surveys on religion, public schools, and almost every aspect of life that's been the subject of a poll.

For instance:

■ A recent Knight-Ridder poll of 1,200 registered voters showed that about 60% of those surveyed were pessimistic about the overall direction of the country's economy while an almost equal number were optimistic about their own personal finances, a response that was buried six paragraphs down in a *Miami Herald* report of the survey, which carried the headline "Economic anxiety now transcends class lines."

■ In its annual poll on religious trends, Gallup asks these questions: "How important would you say religion is in your own life—very important, fairly important, or not very important?" and "At the present time, do you think religion as a whole is increasing its influence on American life or losing its influence?" When asked about religion in their own lives, roughly 60% of adult Americans have responded pretty consistently in each of the past five years that religion is *very* important to them. During those same five years, almost 60% of adult Americans have also said that they believe religion is losing its influence. Trouble is, if the latter 60% had been right about religion's losing its influence year after year, the percentage of people who feel that it's very important in their own lives should have dropped. It didn't. That first 60% figure held steady.

What we're seeing is a halo effect, says Benjamin R. Barber, a political scientist at Rutgers University. "You know, people hate Congress except for their own congressperson. You read about layoffs, and you probably feel that your firm won't do that, but meanwhile you're reading stories that lead you to have a sense of foreboding not necessarily tied to anything in your own experience. That allows you to say, 'Hey, I'm exempt from all this.' Your immediate workplace doesn't give you any reason for anxiety, but the picture you're getting of the global workplace and NAFTA and downsizing makes you feel deeply anxious in some vague way."

The watercooler syndrome. You know the scenario. Four employees gather around the watercooler or coffeepot and listen to one among them gripe about how awful his job is. He's treated unfairly, never gets a competent review, and has a boss who doesn't say boo to him, let alone praise him for a job well done. You, on the other hand, are feeling pretty good about your job, your boss, your workplace—as do, unbeknownst to you, the two other listeners. But rarely, if ever, do the others look the complainer in the eye and say, "Nah, that's just you. I know your work. You stink."

Instead, the tendency is to sympathize—and worse, to join in on the complaining. The result: you leave the watercooler thinking not that one person hates his job (because he's bad at it) but that everybody but you does.

Whether it's at the watercooler, in the media, or from our politicians, we are fed a steady diet of lament about what's wrong with the institutions we depend on. Ours has become, as social critic Robert Hughes observed, "a culture of complaint." It's no wonder that the employee leaving the watercooler finds the positive results of a workplace poll running contrary to everything he's been hearing.

6. What you see isn't what you get.

Each of the hypotheses tries to explain why the *Inc.*/Gallup survey revealed such positive feelings about the economy at a time when any poll seemed destined to uncover the opposite. Yet even the pundits who find the results reasonable have a hard time accepting that the respondents are telling the whole story. "There's got to be some denial," says Professor Barber. "There's no way people can be exposed to this kind of insecurity and still feel so sound and convinced about their own relationship to their own jobs."

As we look around us—hearing what we hear, reading what we read, seeing what we see—we just can't bring ourselves to believe that workers are as positive as they appear to be about their own workplace and their role in it. How *can* they be, when we see how overworked and overwrought they are?

In his essay "Economy and Pleasure," in *What Are People For?* (North Point Press, 1990), writer and farmer Wendell

For Workers, Small Really Is Beautiful

Workers at small companies—those with 50 or fewer employees—were more positive about their jobs and their workplaces than workers at any other size companies. Here are some examples:

	PERCENTAGE RESPONDING YES	
	Small Companies	**Survey Average**
1. This past year, have you had opportunities at work to learn and grow?	89%	84%
2. Does the mission of your employer make you feel your job is important?	91%	87%
3. Do you have the materials and equipment you need to do your work right?	93%	86%
4. In terms of your potential, about what percentage of your ability do you use in your work?	81%	78%
5. Do you want to be a leader in your company someday?	51%	41%
6. Does your management do what is necessary to make your company a great place to work?	82%	70%
7. Is your company a good workplace for all of the people or for only the privileged few?	84%	74%
8. Have you ever owned your own business?	45%	28%

The positive attitudes of small-company employees toward their work environment are directly counter to the observations made by big-company pundits, such as Bennett Harrison, author of *Lean and Mean: The Changing Landscape of Corporate Power in the Age of Flexibility* (BasicBooks/HarperCollins, 1994). Harrison and others claim that the jobs created by small businesses are the scut jobs of the economy, with little security and terrible working conditions. In the early days of the Clinton administration, Robert Reich referred to those jobs as "hamburger flipper" jobs. The responses from small-company employees in the *Inc.*/Gallup survey suggest a dramatically different situation. Across the board, small-company employees share in the positive response about their jobs and workplace; in fact, they're frequently even more positive than their big-company counterparts. They may be flipping hamburgers, but they're mighty happy doing it.

Berry tells the story of a December day spent with his granddaughter, Katie: The two of them hitched a team of horses to a wagon and hauled soil to cover a barn floor. It was cold, and Berry let his granddaughter drive the team of horses for the first time:

> She did very well, and she was proud of herself. She said that her mother would be proud of her, and I said that I was proud of her.
>
> We completed our trip to the barn, unloaded our load of dirt, smoothed it over the barn floor, and wetted it down. By the time we started back up the creek road the sun had gone over the hill and the air had turned bitter. Katie sat close to me in the wagon, and we did not say anything for a long time. I did not say anything because I was afraid that Katie was not saying anything because she was cold and tired and miserable and perhaps homesick; it was impossible to hurry much, and I was unsure how I would comfort her.
>
> But then, after a while, she said, "Wendell, isn't it fun?"

Maybe, like Berry, we are too eager to project our recognition of big-picture tough circumstances onto our expectations about how people feel about their work.

7. Who's to blame? Part 2

The real lesson of the *Inc.*/Gallup survey, perhaps, is to show that people don't necessarily feel the same about their work and workplace as they do about their economic circumstances and prospects. They can feel betrayed by the country's economy and its effect on real wage levels. They can feel overwhelmed by the pace of change wrought by technological advances. But they can feel those things deeply *without* feeling unhappy with their jobs—and *without* feeling that the problems are caused by their employers. "Is the American Worker Getting Shafted?" the *U.S. News & World Report* headline asks. Not according to the people who responded to our poll.

Perhaps most Americans realize individually what collectively we as a nation too often forget: that companies aren't job banks for the lifestyle benefit of those they employ. Indeed, perhaps most workers realize that if companies were

---

AMERICANS AT WORK

Brad Braxton, 27,
pastor,
Douglas Memorial
Community Church,
Baltimore

'The black pulpit is still one of the most valued places in our culture, and those who show some competence at it are rewarded with prestige and decent pay. However, there's a high personal cost. Being a pastor is literally a 24-hour-a-day job. But there are very special rewards. The greatest one is being invited into people's lives.'

---

run that way they would fail and provide no jobs at all. Companies, workers understand, have to *compete*.

Here then is a better way to reconcile on-the-job satisfaction with overall economic angst: it's possible for individuals to like their work and feel good about their employers—to know that given the world's cutthroat competitive climate they're being cared for as well as possi-

ble—while *still* feeling that their economic circumstances fall short of what they'd expected or hoped for or simply believe they need.

Which means that even if economic anxiety is real—a consequence of structural change on a global scale—and that we as a nation, business owners included, have to address it, we should be careful when identifying its source. Although we can blame many things for the malaise about the future of the economy in the United States (and in this presidential-election year, plenty of blame will be spread around), we shouldn't lay the blame on the American workplace.

For the survey questionnaire and full results, turn to *The Inc./Gallup Survey: Americans at Work. Because rigorous surveying methodology requires anonymity of randomly selected respondents, those surveyed could not be identified to be photographed. The subjects of the pictures accompanying this article were probably not included in the national survey conducted by the Gallup Organization and Inc. They were chosen to reflect a cross section of employees at a variety of business and institutional work sites around the country. They were interviewed by Jerry Useem (jerry_useem@incmag.com), a reporter at Inc.*

Jeffrey L. Seglin (jeff_seglin@incmag.com) is an editor at large at Inc.

THE INC./GALLUP SURVEY

Are You Starting Your Own Business?

In spite of the overwhelmingly positive response to questions about their workplace, working Americans dream about starting their own business.

Thirty-two percent of the adult working population—or almost 40 million people—have never owned their own business but dream of starting one. And 19% of those dreamers—almost 9% of the adult working population, or almost 10 million people—are currently in the *process* of starting their own business.

Twenty-eight percent of those surveyed had once owned their own business, and 59% of them—representing 17% of the adult working population, or just over 20 million people—still own that business.

THE INC./GALLUP SURVEY: Americans at Work

1. On a 5-point scale, where 1 is extremely dissatisfied and 5 is extremely satisfied, how satisfied are you with your place of employment?

5	36%
4	35%
3	20%
2	5%
1	4%

2. At work, do you have the opportunity every day to do what you do best?

Yes	82%
No	18%

3. Does your supervisor or someone at work seem to care about you as a person?

Yes	84%
No	12%
No response	4%

4. Do you know what is expected of you at work?

Yes	96%
No	3%
No response	1%

5. In the past seven days, have you received recognition or praise for good work?

Yes	62%
No	36%
No response	2%

6. At work, do your opinions seem to count?

Yes	84%
No	15%
No response	1%

7. Is there someone at work who encourages your development?

Yes	72%
No	26%
No response	2%

8. In the past six months, has someone at work talked to you about your progress?

Yes	60%
No	39%
No response	1%

9. This past year, have you had opportunities at work to learn and grow?

Yes	84%
No	15%
No response	1%

10. Are your associates (fellow employees) committed to doing quality work?

Yes	87%
No	11%
No response	2%

11. Does the mission of your employer make you feel that your job is important?

Yes	87%
No	12%
No response	1%

12. Do you have the materials and equipment you need to do your work right?

Yes	86%
No	14%

13. Do you have a best friend at work?

Yes	57%
No	42%
No response	1%

14. In terms of your potential, about what percentage of your ability do you use in your work?

Average	78%

15. Do you believe you will continue with your current company until you retire?

Yes	56%
No	38%
No response	6%

16. From your most objective viewpoint, have you been compensated fairly this past year?

Yes	69%
No	30%
No response	1%

17. Are you more secure or less secure in your job than you were a year ago?

More secure	63%
Less secure	20%
About the same	17%

18. Do you want to be a leader in your company someday?

Yes	41%
No	57%
No response	2%

19. (If yes to 18) Do you think you will become a leader in your company someday?

Yes	74%
No	20%
No response	6%

20. Is your company family friendly?

Yes	80%
No	17%
No response	3%

21. Does your management do what is necessary to make your company a great place to work?

Yes	70%
No	27%
No response	3%

22. Is your company a good workplace for all of the people, or for only the privileged few?

All people	74%
Privileged few	23%
No response	3%

23. In the past month, have you had three or more days when the stress of work caused you to behave badly with your family?

Yes	23%
No	75%
No response	2%

24. Are you currently looking for a different job?

Yes	21%
No	79%

25. In the past week, have you been worried that you might lose your job?

Yes	9%
No	90%
No response	1%

26. Do members of your family worry about your losing your job in the next year?

Yes	8%
No	91%
No response	1%

27. In the past year, have any of your friends lost jobs because of downsizing?

Yes	39%
No	60%
No response	1%

28. Do you worry that your job may become obsolete because of advances in technology?

Yes	11%
No	88%
No response	1%

29. At work, has your boss ever asked you to do something unethical or dishonest?

Yes	8%
No	91%
No response	1%

30. Have you ever owned your own business?

Yes	28%
No	72%

31. (If yes to 30) Do you still own that business?

Yes	59%
No	41%

32. (If no to 30 or 31) Do you dream of starting your own business?

Yes	44%
No	55%
No response	1%

33. (If yes to 32) Are you currently in the process of starting your own business?

Yes	19%
No	80%
No response	1%

34. (If no to 33) Do you plan to start a new business in the next two years?

Yes	27%
No	69%
No response	4%

How the Inc./Gallup survey was conducted In November 1995 the Gallup Organization conducted a nationwide employee survey for *Inc.* magazine. The purpose of the study was to investigate the extent to which full-time employees agree with statements regarding their workplace experiences. All participants were required to be at least 18 years old and employed at least 30 hours a week. With the survey methods used and a sample of 803 respondents, the resulting maximum expected error range, at a 95% confidence level, is plus or minus 3.5%.

THE NEW WORKPLACE

Walls are falling as the "office of the future" finally takes shape

WITH ITS DIMPLED ALUMINUM facade and TV-screen-shaped windows, Pittsburgh's Alcoa Building once exemplified the power and pizzazz of the classic corporate skyscraper. When it went up in the 1950s, 2,000 company employees streamed into the 31-story tower every morning, each to work in a private 12-foot by 15-foot office.

But go looking for Aluminum Company of America Chief Executive Paul H. O'Neill in his office these days and you discover that he doesn't exactly have one. The executive suite has no permanent walls or doors. All of Alcoa's senior executives work in open cubicles and gather around a "communications center" with televisions, fax machines, newspapers, and tables to encourage impromptu meetings. O'Neill's own favorite hangout is the kitchen, where he and his staff nuke take-out food, huddle, and talk work. "It's like being at home in your own kitchen and sitting around the table," he says happily.

This experiment has taken place only on Alcoa's top floor. But O'Neill will soon bring kitchenettes and open offices to the whole company. Alcoa is abandoning the aluminum tower for a new three-story complex on the banks of the Allegheny. "We're going to have an opportunity to do things with the way people relate to each other. It will be freer and easier," O'Neill says. With escalators instead of elevators and plenty of meeting rooms, "there'll be a lot of places where people can gather."

Alcoa is eager to solve an increasingly urgent workplace problem: After having downsized, reengineered, customer-focused, shattered old hierarchical structures, and reorganized work around teams—all the things that were supposed to make companies more responsive and competitive—corporations such as Alcoa aren't getting the results they expected. They are, quite literally, running into walls, because the new work styles don't work in buildings designed for the old top-down corporation. "Companies feel work processes need to change, and physical environments can get in the way," says Karen Lalli, senior associate with the Hillier Group, an architectural firm based in Princeton, N.J.

Hence, the much prophesied "office of the future" is finally taking shape. From Manhattan towers to Silicon Valley tilt-ups, from behemoths, such as Mobil, IBM, and Procter & Gamble, to tiny startups, business is embracing new office designs for the 21st century. Privacy is being replaced with productivity, hierarchy with teamwork, and status with mobility.

Work anywhere, anytime is the new paradigm. Your car, your home, your office, even your client's office. Work alone, coupled, teamed. Work in real space or in cyberspace. It amounts to a massive disaggregation of work, spinning outside the walls and confines of the traditional office.

If the office of the future is a bit tardy in making its appearance, it's because technology is just catching up with economic trends. That "seamless" web of voice, fax, and phone is only now making teamwork and mobility a reality. And it took business time to grow comfortable with tools such as voice mail and E-mail, the World Wide Web and private "intranets" that link far-flung workers.

Corporations are putting their money into computer networks and other technologies that can boost efficiency and effectiveness, while cutting back on bricks and mortar. At many companies, says Lalli, technology is already surpassing facilities and real estate as the second-biggest corporate operating expense, after salaries and benefits.

Increasingly, architects, interior designers, facilities managers, and furniture companies are assuming a new role: strategic consultants familiar not only with blueprints but also with human behavior and organization. Corporations are using them to boost productivity, not stroke executive egos. "The forms of organizations that achieve competitive advantage are exploding," says Gene Rae, a principal with Studios, a Washington-based firm that has created innovative workspaces for General Electric, Silicon Graphics, and other major players.

DOING AWAY WITH OLD PERKS. Design of the office of the future is

"The freedom I've felt being here is incredible . . . I'm having weekly meetings on the stair-steppers. It's cool."

rushing simultaneously in two directions: One is reorganizing the space of employees who must still work in offices. The other is shoving everyone else out the door. For people involved in product innovation or development, for example, cutting cycle time is key. The need for speed makes it imperative for employees to team up and share information.

Consider the "cave and commons" design. The idea is to balance individual work and teamwork, privacy and community. At Minneapolis-based advertising agency Fallon-McElligott, when it's time to brainstorm, art directors, space buyers, account managers, and copywriters can now wheel special desks equipped with an employee's computer, files, and phone into what they call "virtual" or "flexible" space. The room may hold 30 employees on Monday, none Tuesday, 10 for a marathon session on Wednesday, depending on what needs to be done. Group members may all be typing silently and furiously at their stations or meeting at a center table. "It's a wonderful solution for businesses where teamwork is everything," says Rob White, director of planning.

Then there is "hoteling." As more companies rack up huge bottom-line savings (and improved customer relations to boot) by outfitting mobile workers with laptops, cell phones, and other tools, the legions who spend most of their days out of the office—telecommuters, sales personnel, consultants, and auditors—are growing. These folks still need a place to have the occasional meeting with the boss or gather for team-building. So companies are providing buildings where offices or meeting rooms can be reserved in advance. Just like a hotel.

If you haven't seen any of this at your company, you probably will

soon. According to a 1995 survey by the International Facility Management Assn., 83% of companies are embracing so-called alternative-office strategies, from cave and commons and hoteling to telecommuting and open-plan office designs.

While they may not look vastly different from conventional offices, the new workplaces repeal rules that have governed corporate office design in the past. No perk has been more sacrosanct than personal space, no status symbol more significant than big, heavy mahogany doors sweeping across deep-pile carpet and sealing executives into remote lairs with a smug ka-chunk. In many companies, when employees congregated in neutral zones such as lunchrooms, hallways, and patios, managers cast a dim eye and mentally added names to their list of slackers.

New workplace design reverses all that. Take Procter & Gamble's gleaming new $280 million, 1.3 million-square-foot building tucked into a wooded knoll 20 miles north of Cincinnati. The need to promote product development dictated the space, not trendy architectural forms or status symbols. "The facility had to become a competitive advantage," says J. P. Jones, P&G's research and development vice-president for over-the-counter health-care products. "We went about it like we were developing a new product."

CHAT-ZAPPING ELEVATORS. Project groups were the central design theme. Members of teams work in open cubicles, grouped together, and can all see each other, regardless of rank. File cases are literally on wheels, and offices are designed in "bricks" that can be reconfigured in short order if a team needs to get bigger or smaller. P&G personnel travel between floors by escalator, instead of conversation-zapping ele-

vators. So-called huddle rooms are strategically placed where teams can come together to brainstorm. P&G also equipped spaces within the building, such as lunchrooms and lounges, with electronic whiteboards that can convert scribblings to E-mail. Corridors are deliberately wide and have couches where workers can stop for a quick chat. The building opened last July, and Jones is thrilled. He's convinced it will deliver 20% to 30% productivity gains because "data sharing is immediate, and higher-quality decisions are made faster."

Linda Dudek, 33, a P&G engineer, says she was leery when she heard private offices would be verboten in the new digs. Today, she's a convert: "Things get accomplished a lot quicker because I can stand up and see everyone on my team, my manager, my manager's manager."

P&G is also among those companies using design to help dual-career families while still boosting productivity. When planning its new building, the company specifically designed in a dry cleaner, a shoe-repair shop, and a cafeteria that prepares food that employees can take home at night. It hits home for Dudek, the mother of two. "The freedom I've felt being here is incredible, and yet I'm leaving the building a lot less. I take my breaks in the fitness center. I'm having weekly meetings on the stair-steppers. It's cool."

Then there are those working either from home, a moving car, or both. These telecommuters need space and support when they tether up to home base. Hoteling gives it to them. At Ernst & Young's Washington office, when employees call, they're asked for a personal I.D. and the dates they need space. Within 30 seconds, the system confirms whether a workstation or a meeting room is available.

Like any good hotel, this one has a concierge to take care of guests. When workers arrive, their name is on a door, and any files or supplies the employees have requested will be there, too. Their phone numbers have been forwarded—even a digitized photo of their kids may be bouncing around the computer as a screen saver. "Once people get used to it, they never want to go back" because they like not wasting time traveling to and from the office, says Larry Ebert, national director of real estate for Ernst & Young. E&Y has hoteled eight offices and will soon convert seven more.

REDUCING CYCLE TIME. The longer workers "hotel," the less they seem to focus on the office and the more they focus on the customer. Deborah A. Lis, a 33-year-old, Los Angeles-based marketer from IBM, is equally comfortable in her home office, her car, or even a client's office. Since her operation shifted to hoteling two years ago, she says she has cut the time commuting on L. A. freeways in half; she spends more time with customers, and she starts work earlier, calling customers and colleagues from Tokyo to Torrance, Calif. "My customers are happy, and I'm selling," she says.

IBM now has about 20,000 sales and service professionals nationwide using shared offices—and according to a study in the *Harvard Business Review,* by shifting to hoteling, closing underutilized offices, and moving to cheaper locations, Big Blue has shaved about $1.4 billion off its real estate expenses.

Traveling salespeople, of course, have long hoteled in real hotels. And Silicon Valley pioneers such as Intel Corp. and Hewlett-Packard Co. have long favored large, open cubicle spaces to limit hierarchies and promote interaction. But the recent emphasis at the corporate level on project teams has demanded refinements in older schemes. For example, even the modest walls of conventional open-office cubicles can be too much of a barrier for some companies. That's what man-agement discovered at In Focus Systems Inc., a Wilsonville (Ore.) maker of computer-projection systems. Vice-President Allan Alley was determined to shorten product-development times but says his engineers and marketers just weren't communicating. Open cubicles were "the worst of both worlds," he found. "There were no impromptu meetings and a lot of wasted space."

The answer for Alley turned out to be perhaps the priciest and purest form of the "cave and commons" concept available today: Steelcase Inc.'s Personal Harbors. Each $7,000 Personal Harbor is like a small, cylindrical booth with a door that can be closed, and because it's curved, it actually seems to increase the interior space. There's enough room inside for a flat work surface, computer setup, phones, a file drawer, and other standard desk items. There's also a whiteboard and built-in CD player.

But the key is that the harbors are grouped around a large puzzle-like table that can be broken into several pieces. When harbor doors are open, people move in and out of the group space to talk to colleagues, participate in meetings, or just listen in. "People will never leave a [traditional] meeting room," says Alley, but with this system, they stay in a meeting just long enough to contribute and go back to work. "Personal Harbor creates an atmosphere where we can rapidly develop products," he says.

Steelcase and its rivals in the $9.5 billion office-furniture industry—Haworth, Herman Miller, and others—are scrambling to crank out the right products for the new workplaces. They're adding mobility—putting wheels on desks, tables, and file cabinets and trying to manage the spaghetti of cables that office equipment can generate. Furniture used to project an image of stability. Now lines such as Haworth's Crossings furniture, which feature large wheels, speak directly to the need for flexibility.

Designers and companies complain they still have to do a lot of custom work to get just what they want. When Fallon-McElligott wanted to create its flexible space, it couldn't find the right equipment. So interior designer Gary E. Wheeler created award-winning "free-address lockers" that resemble armoires on wheels. They hold a computer, files, phone, and a desktop, as well as a special universal plug to simplify "docking" all the electronics. Employees literally wheel them around to create a wagons-in-a-circle effect for teams scrambling to make a deadline.

Some of these new office designs don't win awards—but they do address nitty-gritty business goals quite dramatically. Inhale Therapeutic Systems, a tiny Palo Alto (Calif.) startup working on novel drug-delivery technology, is one example. In a previous job, CEO Robert B. Chess served as a White House staff member in the Bush Administration. He observed firsthand the ultimate form of "office politics." His colleagues were obsessed with their "proximity to the President," he recalls.

From the beginning, Chess decided Inhale couldn't afford such nonsense. Everyone—which includes his 65 employees and himself—sits in large cubicles that he calls "bullpens" with four other people of various ranks and functions—no walls or barriers of any kind between them. "It forces everybody to talk to each other all the time," he says. Chess says the lack of private space also limits gossip, reduces the need for memo writing, and gets top managers scattered among the troops. Every nine months or so he even stirs the pot, reshuffling everybody.

Questioning ancient assumptions has also allowed Mobil Oil Corp. to save big bucks and help employees work better. After a companywide study, Mobil realized existing office-space guidelines, which assigned space largely by company rank, were obsolete and occasionally even counterproductive. When company geologists achieved a certain rank, for example, the rules demanded they move to offices with windows—which they hated. Turns out, geologists refer constantly to big seismic charts and maps, and windowed offices give them less space to hang them.

Mobil reformulated guidelines by job function instead of rank, and the company settled on basic space sizes that were interchangeable. For example, 75 square feet is now the standard, one-person office; 150 square feet is a two-person office or a manager's office; 300 square feet is a conference room or a file-storage office. That replaces a half-dozen more staggered sizes just for personal spaces. The changes will likely cut Mobil's costs by $100 million a year.

Sometimes, a big up-front investment in redesign pays off in unexpected productivity. At West Bend Mutual Insurance Co., Senior Vice-President Ronald W. Lauret says the extremes of his local Wisconsin prairie climate make personal comfort a huge issue for his workers. Surveys show that trait is shared by 15% to 30% of office workers nationwide, who say they are uncomfortable during the day. So West Bend invested in equipment from Johnson Controls Inc. called Personal Environment Manager that lets workers adjust the temperature, fresh air, and even ambient noise in their cubicles. Researchers from Rensselaer Polytechnic Institute have studied the impact of the PEMS on West Bend's productivity. They found workers with PEMS were at least 3% more productive than other workers. Lauret thinks the gain may be more in the range of 5% to 10%. Plus, Lauret says, the novel work-stations have become an asset for recruiting and

retaining workers. He believes the fresh-air component of the systems may be keeping workers healthier, too. "To make our customers happy we have to give that level of satisfaction to our associates," Lauret says.

OVERSTIMULATED EMPLOYEES? One element of West Bend's experience that all companies would do well to heed is the value of listening to employees and trying to understand how they actually work in today's fast-changing world. At Sun Microsystems Inc., Chief Information Officer William J. Raduchel feels that American business has finally become comfortable enough with technology to make more radical office schemes possible. He and his colleagues travel constantly, often using Web pages in lieu of face-to-face meetings to keep tabs on projects. When he looks around Sun these days, he claims, "nobody's ever in their office." So why should Sun pay to provide them, heat them, and keep them clean? The company is wrestling with just those questions, Raduchel says, by providing hoteling in Europe and various team-oriented designs in new constructions.

There are still many unknowns and a few rough spots in many of these new designs. Any change, notes Ann Bamesburger, who is implementing alternative-office schemes at Sun, "can enable you and disable me." Open-plan office designs may facilitate so much interaction that some employees feel overstimulated and distracted. "Sometimes you've got to put your hand over the phone and say, 'Hey, hold it down'" admits a sales manager at Inhale.

And what makes perfect sense today could quickly be eclipsed by

changes in technology tomorrow. Bill Moggridge is a principal with industrial-design leader IDEO in Palo Alto, Calif., which is helping Steelcase integrate technology into new workplace tools. Moggridge notes that the sheer physical "volume of technology is now halving about every five years," and that will have many implications for the workspace, some unpredictable. Think about it: Roomfuls of machines once contained less computing power than a single laptop has today. Telephone switching equipment now requires only small, chip-laden panels. Elaborate videoconferencing rooms are fast giving way to desktop conferencing power. And centralized network capacities are growing much faster than the wires into homes and hotels, meaning some wired telecommuters may feel like second-class network surfers unless they're in the office.

The good news, however, is that those involved in forging the new workplace realize there is no ideal, no cookie-cutter workplace template they can plop on top of organizations. And it's a rare alternative-office space that doesn't get adapted as trial runs reveal elements that don't work or could work better. Says architect Rae: "One thing we've realized is that not only must we assess what's possible but how far and how fast it can move." That would seem to signal an end to the age of the corporate "edifice complex" and a new era of workspaces that work.

By Joan O'C. Hamilton in San Francisco, with Stephen Baker in Pittsburgh, Bill Vlasic in Detroit, and bureau reports

If You Want Your People to Buy-in to Change, You Have to Sell Them. Yes, Sell Them.

John Guaspari

JOHN GUASPARI is a senior associate at Lexington, Mass.-based management consultancy Rath & Strong Inc.

In this new, continuously improving, employee-involved, customer-focused, reengineered, empowered, bench-marked, rightsized, cross-functional world in which we live, it is no longer enough to mandate change. You must first obtain people's "buy-in."

How? If your instincts tell you that it will have something to do with "a participative process of sharing and involvement," you have been paying attention during the '90s. But, although participation and involvement may be admirable characteristics, they alone do not answer the question. Saying that you achieve buy-in through "involvement" is like saying that the way to solve national problems is "democracy." Well, democracy may be the best way to go about finding the solution, but what *is* the solution? What do you have to *do*?

Listen to What You're Saying

You say you want people to "buy-in," and you want them to "take ownership" of the change. So you have something you want people to buy and own—now what? Might not some of the techniques of selling and marketing be helpful in getting others to buy-in to and take ownership of your change efforts? Certainly, if you can get past the objections of those for whom "sales and marketing" conjure up semisavory images of fast-talking manipulation, even out-and-out deception. Let me suggest a much less loaded definition of selling and marketing: *making clear why what you are offering is better than the alternatives.*

This definition puts three significant demands on the seller/marketer:

1) It requires that you know enough about the customer to know what is, in fact, better for him or her; 2) it requires that what you are offering *be* better; and 3) it requires that you communicate that "betterness," clearly and compellingly.

Those are the criteria one must satisfy to sell products and services to customers. To the challenge of getting people to buy-in to change efforts, those requirements reduce, mutatis mutandis, to: Do you really know why the change is best for your employees? Can you deliver on those claims? Can you communicate "best," clearly, and compellingly?

Straightforward application of some sales and marketing basics can be extraordinarily helpful in answering these questions and, in so doing, help to demystify the buy-in process.

Know Your Customer

Effective marketers know that you can't be all things to all people. You must be very clear and explicit about the target market. Focus and prioritization are essential. I have had clients beg the question by saying that "we need buy-in from everyone" and conclude that such segmentation is unnecessary. But choices must be made, and they fall into two categories.

The first is demographic. Let's go back to our parallel with selling and marketing of real products. Suppose the product in question was a car, and you were given the responsibility for marketing that car in the

From *Across the Board*, May 1996, pp. 32-36. © 1996 by The Conference Board. Reprinted with permission.

Mr. Clean: McDonald's founder Ray Kroc, hosing down his first store in Des Plaines, Ill., in 1955 (*pictured below*). Kroc showed how to turn an obsession into a value proposition.

COURTESY MCDONALD'S

United States. You'd quickly bump up against the fact that no approach will work with all Americans, and you will quickly begin to develop focused marketing plans for the Northeast and Southwest, senior citizens and thirtysomethings, status seekers and penny pinchers.

Wouldn't you agree that trying to achieve buy-in—getting people's energetic support of your change effort—is at least as complicated as peddling cars? Wouldn't you need to make similar distinctions within your marketplace and take a tailored approach to each? For example, if you're trying to reach rank-and-file workers, invocations about gains in return on net equity employed will probably pack less of a wallop than they would with the executive committee. People in the R&D lab may resonate fully to "the great voyage of discovery" upon which you are about to embark, while the accounting staff might be more inclined to get behind an effort "to create some order."

And so it goes. Are you trying to reach new hires or 20-year veterans? Headquarters personnel or people in field offices? Employees from the design division or the manufacturing division? The point here is not the specific answers to such questions; rather, it's the essentialness of such questions being asked.

The second set of choices you must make is best described by a word too seldom invoked: political. It's a perfectly good word, one that doesn't have to conjure up images of scheming, conniving, and duplicity. Here the definition is a pragmatic one: what works. This is important because as much as you'd like everyone to buy-in to the change you're proposing, the fact of the matter is that not everyone will.

Given that reality, another critical set of questions suggests itself: Which people—individuals as well as groups—must you *absolutely* have buy-in from for the change to take hold? Who are the most influential constituencies in your organization who might pull others along? Which groups are closest to buy-in already and need just a slight nudge? Which groups will need a lot of time to get them there? How essential is their buy-in? Which groups aren't essential—nice-to-haves, not need-to-haves?

This may all seem rather cold-blooded, but the fact remains that you can't get buy-in from everyone—at least not to the same degree and not by the same deadlines. It helps to have a considered plan of attack as to which constituencies to go after, in what order, and with what degree of effort. Without such a plan, you may be leaving the success of your change effort dangerously exposed to chance.

Remember the Why Of the Buy

A marketing truism: Customers buy for one reason alone—to maximize value received. Here, value can be defined as what the customer "Got" weighed against what it "Cost." "Got" includes the product, plus service, plus a host of intangibles such as peace of mind, status, relaxation, etc., while "Cost" includes money, plus time, and a different host of intangibles such as aggravation, anxiety, and frustration.

Let's go back again to our car example and ask: What is of value to car buyers? It depends. A young couple trying to scrape by on a tight budget might be looking for basic transportation (a Got) at the lowest operating Cost. A late-middle-aged couple with a paid-for house and children already through college might value a luxurious ride and top-of-the-line stereo system (Gots) and be relatively unconcerned about insurance premiums and miles per gallon (Costs). How do marketers know what really makes these value differences? They expend a lot of energy employing a wide range of qualitative and quantitative research techniques in an effort to understand just what makes customers buy.

How many organizations make this kind of effort to understand just what makes its own people buy-in? I'm not talking about the occasional attitude survey or focus group in which people get a chance to vent. I'm talking about gaining an in-depth understanding of what moves people in an organization. I'm talking about a systematic way of knowing what the list of Gots (a paycheck, professional identity, colleagueship, pride of accomplishment, etc.) and Costs (time, toil, autonomy, the hassles of corporate life, etc.) are for an organization and how the value equation differs for different segments of the organization.

If people buy-in based on "value received" (and they do), how can you afford not to do a thorough employee-value analysis? If you don't do such an analysis, and buy-in is not forthcoming, why are you surprised?

Reality Intrudes

While customers would certainly love a car that got 1,000 miles to the gallon, it's unlikely anyone will be able to manufacture one, at least not until somebody gets around to repealing the second law of thermodynamics. Drawing the boundaries around what's feasible—specifying the product to be offered—is one of the main jobs of the marketer.

Similarly, just because you have a profound knowledge of what your various employee segments value, it does not necessarily follow that you can or even should provide it all for them. People might prefer a steady 9-to-5 work schedule, but if you're in a business where customers expect a 24-hour hot line, somebody must staff it. And the fact that employees would be delighted with 40 percent annual salary increases notwithstanding, the economics of your business probably won't support such generosity.

The point to be made here is this: Limits exist, and if you're not clear about the limits to what a change effort can provide employees, then you won't be clear about why what you are offering is better than the alternatives available to them. And if you're not clear about that, your chances of gaining buy-in will go down dramatically.

Have a Clear Value Proposition

When Federal Express legitimized the overnight-delivery business a couple of decades back, the service they provided was "getting your package from here to there by 10:30 tomorrow morning." Their value proposition to their customers—not the thing the supplier sells but the thing the customers buy—was a little different: "Do business with FedEx, and two things will happen: 1) Your package will be delivered by 10:30 tomorrow morning; and 2) your worries about it getting there on time tomorrow will be gone the instant you hand it over to us."

McDonald's sells burgers and fries. Its value proposition is "good food, low prices, clean facilities, and an experience that will be identical at any McDonald's you go to; there will be no surprises."

The need for a value proposition drives two useful outcomes. First, it forces you to be very clear about just what it is that you offer that distinguishes you in the eyes of your customers. Second, it provides a useful reference point to focus on in the hurly-burly of day-to-day operations. Given the company's value proposition, the stories of heroic performances by FedEx employees become far easier to understand, and McDonald's founder Ray Kroc's obsessiveness about cleanliness seems a bit less idiosyncratic.

The same logic holds with employees. If your goal is to energize them around your change effort (i.e., the product you're selling), you need to know what it is you're asking them to buy (i.e., your value proposition).

For example, here is a value proposition proffered to employees of an organization about to embark on a reengineering effort: "As a result of the new skills you'll learn in order to perform your job in the newly reengineered organization, you will have significantly increased your value internally and your marketability externally."

Here's one used by an industrial-products company that had just gone through a leveraged buyout: "The work will be backbreak-

Peace of mind: Federal Express pledged to "absolutely, positively" deliver packages by 10:30 the next morning. By keeping its promise, the company legitimized the overnight-delivery business.

COURTESY FEDERAL EXPRESS

ing. The pace will be relentless. You stand to make a ton of money."

Here's one for a company whose employee values were perfectly aligned with the market opportunity open to whoever could offer drop-dead customer service: "We are making these changes to enable us to rewrite the rules in our industry, to improve by orders of magnitude the value we can create for our customers."

The goal here is clarity and alignment, not sugarcoating. (Say what you will about the LBO example, sugarcoated it ain't.) Different organizations will have different value propositions, as will different segments of the same organization. The point is this: If they're buying into a value proposition, it is helpful if you have one to sell.

Communicate Every Minute

If there's one thing that everyone agrees on, it's that communications are an essential part of achieving buy-in. Budgets, often lavish, are created to carry out this critical task. Dedicated staffs of talented professionals are retained to ghostwrite speeches, design the brochures, and create the snappy slogans that are emblazoned on the posters, coffee mugs, oven mitts, and one-size-fits-all baseball caps.

The problem lies in bounding communications this way. By saying that the communications department is responsible for communications (a sensible position), you imply that those not in the communications department are somehow not (a dangerous one). By blocking off an hour each week to devote to communications (very enlightened), you can lull yourself into thinking that communications is not on the agenda during the other 39 hours (very naive).

The fact of the matter is this: *You're never not communicating.* What you don't say can

> Ask 100 people why communications is so essential to change, and 99 of them will say: "To get the word out." Unfortunately, the fact that this answer seems so reasonable masks the fact that it's damningly arrogant.

speak as loudly as what you do say. Where you spend your time can send out as clear a message as what you did while you were there.

We can all recite FedEx's early, memorable advertising slogan: "When it absolutely, positively has to be there overnight." But what speaks FedEx's value proposition even louder and clearer are the combined efforts of the couriers and the customer-service representatives and the mechanics and the pilots and the sorters and all the thousands of FedEx employees performing millions of individual actions, working in concert to ensure that it will, in fact, be there overnight.

McDonald's can tell you that "You deserve a break today!" until they're blue in the face. But it's only after we eat there and the food is good and there are no hassles and no surprises that the message registers.

Similarly, you can come up with the snappiest slogan going. But the fastest way to kill buy-in is to launch a communications blitz that is too slick, too glib, and too soon. By now people have been burned by enough programs-of-the-month that they will withhold their buy-in until they have proof that management has bought-in first. The only thing that four-color posters prove is that you had enough money to pay the printer. Here's a good test that some clients have used to flush out the issue of management buy-in: Establish a communications budget of precisely $0. If you can't print posters or put on a laser show at an all-hands meeting, you might have to hunker down and invest time and attention instead—a far more compelling statement of proof.

To be most effective, communication should be viewed more as validation than as exhortation: less tugging at your sleeve to pull you into the tent, more tapping you on the shoulder and reminding you about what it was like once you were inside. And time spent doing the things to ensure that being inside the tent was, in fact, a most pleasant experience is about the most effective communication of all.

Think About *Why* You're Communicating

Ask 100 people why communications is so essential to change, and 99 of them will say something like: "To get the word out." Unfortunately, the fact that this answer seems so reasonable masks the fact that it's damningly arrogant. And the purity of the motives behind this answer serves only to make the arrogance that much more dangerous.

Consider the implicit premise of this answer: "We need to get the word out. We know what is right and what is good, and if we can impart that knowledge to others, all will be well. Ultimately, our reason for communicating is 'to inform.'" From that objective, then, actions follow. Newsletters are published. Speeches are made. Videos are produced. Memos are distributed. All in an effort to set up clear, clean channels from, informationally speaking, the haves to the have-nots.

Contrast that, if you will, with the organization that sees communications not as a way to get the word out, but as a way to obtain buy-in: "We need to move people, to touch them . . . to get them to step up and grab hold of this change effort and make it theirs." Such an objective would seem to suggest a different set of actions. For one thing, instead of assuming that you have the information that they need, you will begin to find ways to gather the information from them that *you* need: What is most important to *them*? What are *their* Gots, *their* Costs? For another, you begin to gauge the success of your communications in terms not of what they know but of what they do.

And if you're still skeptical, ask yourself this question in regard to our car example. Would you be more likely to buy from a car company that went off into an ivory tower, emerged with the car that it thought you should buy, and expended its communications budget on telling you why you should buy it? Or would you be more likely to spend your hard-earned money on the car made by people who started out by getting to know you and your wants and needs, developed a car accordingly, and then communicated to make clear its understanding of how that car met your value needs? Employees will expend their buy-in in exactly the same way.

When Is Virtual Virtuous? Organizing for Innovation

Henry W. Chesbrough and David J. Teece

Henry W. Chesbrough, a former computer industry executive, is now a Ph.D. candidate at the Haas School of Business at the University of California at Berkeley. David J. Teece is the Mitsubishi Bank Professor and director of the Institute of Management, Innovation and Organization at the Haas School of Business.

Champions of virtual corporations are urging managers to subcontract anything and everything. All over the world, companies are jumping on the bandwagon, decentralizing, downsizing, and forging alliances to pursue innovation. Why is the idea of the virtual organization so tantalizing? Because we have come to believe that bureaucracy is bad and flexibility is good. And so it follows that a company that invests in as little as possible will be more responsive to a changing marketplace and more likely to attain global competitive advantage.

There is no question that many large and cumbersome organizations have been outperformed by smaller "networked" competitors. Consider the eclipse of IBM in PCs and of DEC in workstations by Packard Bell and Sun Microsystems. But while there are many successful virtual companies, there are even more failures that don't make the headlines. After many years of studying the relationship between organization and innovation, we believe that the virtues of being virtual have been oversold. The new conventional wisdom ignores the distinctive role that large integrated companies can play in the innovation process. Those rushing to form alliances instead of nurturing and guarding their own capabilities may be risking their future.

What's Special About Virtual?

What gives the virtual company its advantage? In essence, incentives and responsiveness. Virtual companies coordinate much of their business through the marketplace, where free agents come together to buy and sell one another's goods and services; thus virtual companies can harness the power of market forces to develop, manufacture, market, distribute, and support their offerings in ways that fully integrated companies can't duplicate. As William Joy, vice president of research and development at Sun Microsystems, puts it, "Not all the smart people [in the workstation industry] work for Sun." Because an outside developer of workstation software can obtain greater rewards by selling software to Sun customers than by developing the same software as a Sun employee, he or she will move faster, work harder, and take more risks. Using high-powered, market-based incentives such as stock options and attractive bonuses, a virtual company can quickly access the technical resources it needs, if those resources are available. In situations where technology is changing rapidly, large companies that attempt to do everything inside will flounder when competing against small companies with highly trained and motivated employees.

But the incentives that make a virtual company powerful also leave it vulnerable. As incentives become greater and risk taking increases, coordination among parties through the marketplace becomes more and more difficult, precisely because so much personal reward is at stake. Each party to joint development activity necessarily acts in its own self-interest. Over time, innovation can generate unforeseen surprises that work to the advantage of some parties and to the disadvantage of others. The result: Once-friendly partners may be unwilling or unable to align strategically, and coordinated development activity falters. In contrast, integrated, centralized companies do not generally reward people for taking risks, but they do have established processes for settling conflicts and coordinating all the activities necessary for innovation.

This trade-off between incentives and control lies at the heart of the decision that managers must make about how to organize for innovation. (See the graph "Finding the Right Degree of Centralization.") If virtual organizations and integrated companies are at opposite ends of the spectrum, alliances occupy a kind of organizational middle ground. An alliance can achieve some of the coordination of an integrated company, but, like players in a virtual network, the members of an alliance will be driven to enhance their own positions, and over time their interests may diverge. The challenge for managers is to choose the organizational form that best matches the type of innovation they are pursuing.

Types of Innovation

When should companies organize for innovation by using decentralized (or virtual) approaches, and

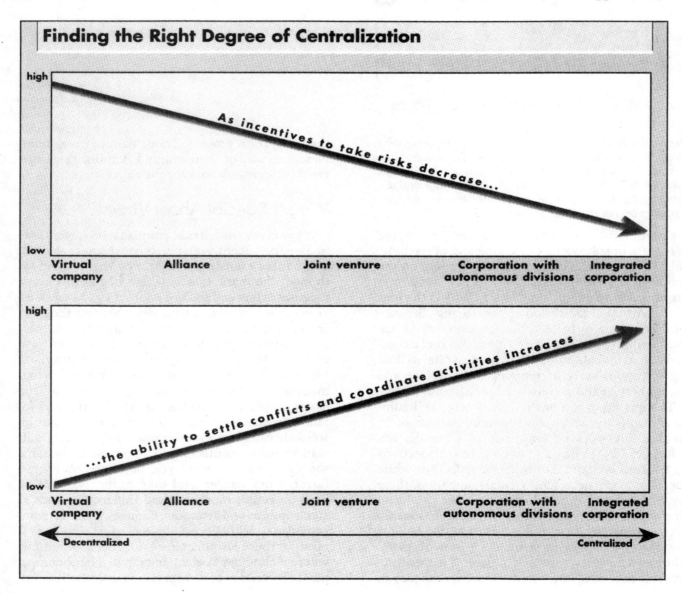

Finding the Right Degree of Centralization

As incentives to take risks decrease...

...the ability to settle conflicts and coordinate activities increases

Virtual company — Alliance — Joint venture — Corporation with autonomous divisions — Integrated corporation

Decentralized ⟷ Centralized

when should they rely on internal organization? The answer depends on the innovation in question.

Some innovations are *autonomous* – that is, they can be pursued independently from other innovations. A new turbocharger to increase horsepower in an automobile engine, for example, can be developed without a complete redesign of the engine or the rest of the car. In contrast, some innovations are fundamentally *systemic* – that is, their benefits can be realized only in conjunction with related, complementary innovations. To profit from instant photography, Polaroid needed to develop both new film technology and new camera technology. Similarly, lean manufacturing is a systemic innovation because it requires interrelated changes in product design, supplier management, information technology, and so on.

The distinction between autonomous and systemic innovation is fundamental to the choice of organizational design. When innovation is autonomous, the decentralized virtual organization can manage the development and commercialization tasks quite well. When innovation is systemic, members of a virtual organization are dependent on the other members, over whom they have no control. In either case, the wrong organizational choice can be costly.

Consider what happened to General Motors when the automobile industry shifted from drum brakes to disc brakes, an autonomous innovation. General Motors was slow to adopt disc brakes because it had integrated vertically in the production of the old technology. GM's more decentralized competitors relied instead on market relationships with their suppliers—and the high-powered incentives inherent in those relationships. As a result, they were able to beat GM to market with the new disc brakes, which car buyers wanted. When companies inappropriately use centralized approaches to manage autonomous innovations, as GM did in this case, small companies and more decentralized large companies will usually outperform them.

To understand why the two types of innovation call for different organizational strategies, consider the information flow essential to innovation. Information about new products and technologies often develops over time as managers absorb new research findings, the results of early product experiments, and initial customer feedback. To commercialize an innovation profitably, a tremendous amount of knowledge from industry players, from customers, and sometimes from scientists must be gathered and understood. This task is easier if the information is codified.

Codified information – for example, specifications that are captured in industry standards and design rules – can often be transferred almost as effectively from one company to another as it can within a single company. Because such information is easily duplicated, it has little natural protection. Sometimes bits and pieces can be protected by intellectual property rights, but those pieces, especially trade secrets and patents, are small islands in a broad ocean of knowledge.

Other information does not travel as easily between companies. Tacit knowledge is knowledge that is implicitly grasped or used but has not been fully articulated, such as the know-how of a master craftsman or the ingrained perspectives of a specific company or work unit. Because such knowledge is deeply embedded in individuals or companies, it tends to diffuse slowly and only with effort and the transfer of people. Established companies can pro-

The incentives that make a virtual company powerful also leave it vulnerable.

tect the tacit knowledge they hold, sharing only codified information. They can be quite strategic about what they disclose and when they disclose it.

The information needed to integrate an autonomous innovation with existing technologies is usually well understood and may even be codified in industry standards. Systemic innovations, on the other hand, pose a unique set of management challenges regarding information exchange. By their very nature, systemic innovations require information sharing and coordinated adjustment *throughout an entire product system*. Here is where a market-based, virtual approach to innovation poses serious strategic hazards. Unaffiliated companies linked through arm's-length contracts often cannot achieve sufficient coordination. Each company wants the other to do more, while each is also looking for ways to realize the most gain from the innovation. Information sharing can be reduced or biased, as each seeks to get the most at the other's expense. In most cases, the open exchange of information that fuels systemic innovation will be easier and safer within a company than across company boundaries. The inevitable conflicts and choices that arise as a systemic innovation develops can best be resolved by an integrated company's internal management processes.

The Case of Industry Standards

Coordinating a systemic innovation is particularly difficult when industry standards do not exist and must be pioneered. In such instances, virtual organizations are likely to run into strategic problems. Consider how technical standards emerge. Market participants weigh many competing technologies and eventually rally around one of them. There are winners and losers among the contestants, and potential losers can try to undermine the front-runner or to fragment the standard by promoting a rival. Until a clear winner emerges, customers may choose to sit on the sidelines rather than risk making the wrong choice.

By virtue of its size and scope, an integrated company may be able to advance a new standard simply by choosing to adopt a particular technology. If a large company commits itself to one of a host of competing technologies, consumers as well as companies promoting rival technologies will probably be persuaded to follow suit. Virtual companies, however, which may be struggling to resolve conflicts within their networks, won't be able to break a deadlock in a complicated standards battle. Players in a network won't be able to coordinate themselves to act like a large company.

Once a new standard has been established, virtual organizations can manage further innovation quite well. But when an industry begins to advance technology to a new level, the cycle can begin anew. Again, technically feasible choices present new strategic trade-offs. Suppliers, competitors, and customers may fail to agree on a common path. Unless a big player emerges to break the logjam among rival technologies, the existing standard will prevail long past its usefulness.

Today computer floppy disks are frozen in an old standard because no single company has been able to establish a new one. IBM pioneered the 3.5-inch hard-case diskette in 1987 when it introduced its new line of PS/2 personal computers. Within two years, the memory capacity of 3.5-inch diskettes doubled from 720 kilobytes to 1.44 megabytes, where it has remained ever since.

Why? The technical capability to expand diskette capacity is available, but no company has the reputation and strength to set a new standard. Through the 1980s, IBM was large enough to coordinate standards among the key participants in the industry: personal computer manufacturers, diskette makers, and software publishers. If IBM told the industry it would use a particular capacity on its next generation of machines, others did the same. But in the 1990s, IBM's leadership of the PC market came to an end, perhaps permanently. Today IBM is not strong enough to move the industry by itself, and it won't move ahead of the other industry players and risk being stranded if they don't follow.

A simple rule of thumb applies: When innovation depends on a series of interdependent innovations – that is, when innovation is systemic – independent companies will not usually be able to coordinate themselves to knit those innovations together. Scale, integration, and market leadership may be required to establish and then to advance standards in an industry.

The IBM PC: Virtual Success or Failure?

IBM's development of the personal computer is a fascinating example of both the advantages and disadvantages of using virtual approaches to pursue innovation. When IBM launched its first PC in 1981, the company elected to outsource all the major components from the marketplace. By tapping the capabilities of other companies, IBM was able to get its first product to market in only 15 months. The microprocessor (the 8088) was purchased from Intel, and the operating system (which became PC-DOS) was licensed from a then fledgling software company, Microsoft. In effect, the IBM PC had an "open" architecture: It was based on standards and components that were widely available. The high-powered incentives of the marketplace could coordinate the roles of component manufacturers and software vendors. IBM successfully promoted its open architecture to hundreds of third-party developers of software applications and hardware accessory products, knowing that those products would add to the appeal of the PC.

IBM also relied on the market to distribute the product. Although IBM launched its own IBM Product Centers as retail storefronts and had its own direct sales force for large corporate customers, the majority of the company's systems were distributed through independent retailers, initially Computer-Land and Sears. Eventually, there were more than 2,000 retail outlets.

By using outside parties for hardware, software, and distribution, IBM greatly reduced its investment in bringing the PC to market. More important, those relationships allowed IBM to launch an attack against Apple, which had pioneered the market and was growing quickly. The IBM PC was an early success, and it spawned what became the dominant architecture of the entire microcomputer industry. By 1984, three years after the introduction of the PC, IBM replaced Apple as the number one supplier of microcomputers, with 26% of the PC business. By 1985, IBM's shard had grown to 41%. Many observers attributed the PC's success to IBM's creative use of outside relationships. More than a few business analysts hailed the IBM PC development as a model for doing business in the future.

Indeed, IBM's approach in its PC business is exactly the kind of decentralized strategy that commentators are urging large, slow-moving compa-

More than a few analysts hailed IBM's development of the PC as a new business model.

nies to adopt. The early years of the IBM PC show many of the benefits of using markets and outside companies to coordinate innovation: fast development of technology and tremendous technological improvements from a wide variety of sources.

With the passage of time, though, the downside of IBM's decentralized approach has become apparent. IBM failed to anticipate that its virtual and open approach would prevent the company from directing the PC architecture it had created. The open architecture and the autonomy of its vendors invited design mutinies and the entry of IBM-compatible PC manufacturers. At first, competitors struggled to achieve compatibility with IBM's architecture, but after several years compatibility was widespread in the industry. And once that happened, manufacturers could purchase the same CPU from Intel and the same operating system from Microsoft, run the same application software (from Lotus, Microsoft, WordPerfect, and others), and sell through the same distribution channels (such as ComputerLand, BusinessLand, and Micro-Age). IBM had little left on which to establish a competitive advantage.

To maintain technological leadership, IBM decided to advance the PC architecture. To do that, IBM needed to coordinate the many interrelated pieces of the architecture – a systemic technology coordination task. However, the third-party hardware and software suppliers that had helped establish the original architecture did not follow IBM's lead. When IBM introduced its OS/2 operating system, the company could not stop Microsoft from introducing Windows, an application that works with the old DOS operating system, thereby greatly reducing the advantages of switching to OS/2. And third-party hardware and software companies made investments that extended the usefulness of the original PC architecture. Similarly, Intel helped Compaq steal a march on IBM in 1986, when Compaq introduced the first PC based on Intel's 80386 microprocessor, an enhancement over the earlier generations of microprocessors used in IBM and compatible machines. Even though IBM owned 12% of Intel at the time, it couldn't prevent Intel from working with Compaq to beat IBM to market. This was the beginning of the end of IBM's ability to direct the evolution of PC architecture.

By the third quarter of 1995, IBM's share of the PC market had fallen to just 7.3%, trailing Compaq's 10.5% share. Today its PC business is rumored to be modestly profitable at best. Most of the profits from the PC architecture have migrated upstream to the supplier of the microprocessor (Intel) and the operating system (Microsoft), and to outside makers of application software. The combined market value of those suppliers and third parties today greatly exceeds IBM's.

IBM's experience in the PC market illustrates the strategic importance of organization in the pursuit of innovation. Virtual approaches encounter serious problems when companies seek to exploit systemic innovation. Key development activities that depend on one another must be conducted in-house to capture the rewards from long-term R&D investments. Without directed coordination, the necessary complementary innovations required to leverage a new technology may not be forthcoming.

The Virtuous Virtuals

How have the most successful virtual companies accomplished the difficult task of coordination? The virtual companies that have demonstrated staying power are all at the center of a network that they use to leverage their own capabilities. Few virtual companies that have survived and prospered have outsourced everything. Rather, the virtuous virtuals have carefully nurtured and guarded the internal capabilities that provide the essential underpinnings of competitive advantage. And they invest considerable resources to maintain and extend their core competencies internally. Indeed, without these companies' unique competencies and capabilities, their strategic position in the network would be short-lived.

Consider the well-known battle between MIPS Technologies and Sun Microsystems for control of workstation processors. (See Benjamin Gomes-Casseres, "Group Versus Group: How Alliance Networks Compete," HBR July-August 1994.) MIPS was trying to promote its Advanced Computing Environment (ACE) against Sun's Scalable Processor Architecture (SPARC). Sun had strong internal capabilities, whereas MIPS tried to compete as a more virtual player, leveraging off of the competencies of partners such as Compaq, DEC, and Silicon Graphics. MIPS had a good technical design, but that was literally all it had, and this hollowness left the company at the mercy of its partners. As soon as DEC and Compaq reduced their commitment to the ACE initiative, the network fell apart and pulled MIPS down with it. The very reliance of virtual companies on partners, suppliers, and other outside companies exposes them to strategic hazards. Put another way, there are plenty of small, dynamic companies that have not been able to outperform larger competitors. In particular, a hollow company like MIPS is ill equipped to coordinate a network of companies. Although Sun also worked with alliance partners, it had strong internal capabilities in systems design, manufacturing, marketing, sales, service, and support. As a result, Sun can direct and advance the SPARC architecture, a dominant technology in the industry.

Many companies with superior capabilities have prospered as the dominant player in a network. Japanese keiretsu are structured that way. Consider Toyota, whose successful introduction of the lean production system – a truly systemic innovation – required tremendous coordination with its network of suppliers. Because Toyota was much larger than its suppliers, and because, until recently, it was the largest customer of virtually all of them, it could compel those suppliers to make radical changes in their business practices. In a more egalitarian network, suppliers can demand a large share of the economic benefits of innovations, using what economists call hold-up strategies. Strong central players like Toyota are rarely vulnerable to such tactics and are thus in a better position to drive and coordinate systemic innovation.

The most successful virtual companies sit at the center of networks that are far from egalitarian. Nike may rely on Asian partners for manufacturing, but its capabilities in design and marketing allow it to call all the shots. In the computer industry, Intel has effective control of the 80X86 microprocessor standard, Microsoft dominates PC operating systems, and Sun is driving the SPARC architecture. Those companies control and coordinate the advance of technologies in their areas, and in this regard they function more like integrated companies than like market-based virtuals.

Choosing the Right Organizational Design

Today few companies can afford to develop internally all the technologies that might provide an advantage in the future. In every company we studied, we found a mix of approaches: Some technologies were "purchased" from other companies; others were acquired through licenses, partnerships, and alliances; and still other critical technologies were developed internally. Getting the right balance is crucial, as IBM's disastrous experience in PCs illustrates. But what constitutes the right balance?

Consider how a successful innovator such as Motorola evaluates the trade-offs. Motorola, a leader in wireless communications technology, has declared its long-term goal to be the delivery of "untethered communication"—namely, communication anytime,

anywhere, without the need for wires, power cords, or other constraints. In order to achieve that goal, Motorola must make important decisions about where and how to advance the required technologies. Those decisions turn on a handful of questions: Is the technology systemic or likely to become systemic in the future? What capabilities exist in-house and in the current supplier base? When will needed technologies become available?

For Motorola, battery technology is critical because it determines the functionality that can be built into a handheld communications device and the length of time that the device can be used before recharging. Batteries have been a pacing technology in this area for many years.

As Motorola scans the horizon for improved battery technology, it encounters a familiar trade-off between the degree of technological advancement and the number of reliable volume suppliers. Conventional battery technologies such as nickel cadmium (Ni-Cd) have become commodities, and there are many suppliers. But few if any suppliers can offer the more advanced technologies Motorola needs. And the most exotic technologies, such as fuel cells and solid-state energy sources, are not yet commercially viable from any supplier. How should Motorola organize to obtain each of the technologies it might need? Under what circumstances should the company buy the technology from a supplier and when should it form alliances or joint ventures? When should Motorola commit to internal development of the technology? (See the matrix "Matching Organization to Innovation.")

For Ni-Cd technology, the clear choice for Motorola is to buy the technology, or to use the market to coordinate access to this technology, because Motorola can rely on competition among many qualified suppliers to deliver what it wants, when needed, for a competitive price. Motorola faces a more complex decision for fuel cells and solid-state battery technologies. Should Motorola wait until those technologies are more widely available, or should the company opt for a joint venture or internal development?

Before deciding to wait for cutting-edge battery technologies to be developed, Motorola must consider three issues. One is that Motorola could lose the ability to influence the direction of the technology; the early commercial forms may be designed for applications that do not benefit Motorola, such as electric automobiles. The second problem is that Motorola might lose the ability to pace the technology, to bring it to market at a competitively desirable time. The third issue is that if such technologies are—or become—systemic and Motorola has no control over them, the company may not be able to advance related technologies and design features to achieve its goal of untethered communication.

Those issues suggest that Motorola cannot simply wait for the technologies to be provided by the market. Rather, Motorola needs to build strong ties to suppliers with the best capabilities, thus increasing its ability to direct the path of future systemic innovation. Where Motorola itself has strong capabilities, the company should pursue the technologies on its own.

To retain its leadership over the long term, Motorola must continue to develop the critical parts of its value chain internally and acquire less critical technologies from the market or from alliances. Although networks with their high-powered incentives may be effective over the short term for an unchanging technology, they will not adapt well over the long term as technology develops and companies must depend on certain internal capabilities to keep up. The popularity of networked companies and decentralization arises, in part, from observations over a time horizon that is far too short. Remember the enthusiasm that greeted IBM's early success in PCs.

Scale and Scope

Business history presents us with a lesson of striking relevance to the organizational decisions managers face today. In the classic *Scale and Scope*, Alfred Chandler details how the modern corporation evolved in the United States, Germany, and Great Britain at the end of the nineteenth century. Managers who invested the capital to build large-scale en-

---

Ameritech's Strategy for Emerging Technologies

Ameritech, a Regional Bell Operating Company with wire and fiber assets in the Midwest, has the potential to be a major player in the development of on-demand video and interactive information services for home use. In emerging technologies such as multimedia, no one has all the information to determine what capabilities a company must develop internally or access through the market. The only certainty is that the promise of this market will depend on the co-development of many technologies, including data formats, throughput rates, wiring topologies, billing systems, and user interfaces.

Because the eventual configuration of the multimedia industry is unknown (and arguably unknowable ex ante), organizations such as Ameritech must become insiders to the discussions among a range of potential industry players. In emerging markets that are dependent on evolving technologies, considerable information sharing among a wide variety of companies will ultimately result in a road map for the industry. Virtual organizations can serve as catalysts to the development of industry directions and standards in ways that fully integrated organizations cannot.

Consider the role of alliances in Ameritech's multimedia strategy. By allying its own capabilities with those of companies with relevant and complementary skills, Ameritech can participate directly in defining and developing an architecture that will ultimately manage the emerging technologies. One such alliance is with Random House, a leading print publisher of books and magazines, with properties such as the *New Yorker*, Condé Nast, Fodor's, and Arthur Frommer Travel Guides. Random House is capable of supplying significant "content" over Ameritech's wires into the home. This alliance allows both companies to begin to explore the business and technical requirements of providing content into the home.

Ameritech and Random House have formed a joint venture to acquire a start-up virtual company called Worldview Systems, which publishes an electronic monthly current-events database of travel information about more than 170 destinations around the world. While Worldview Systems' products are now sold primarily through travel agents and an 800 telephone number, Ameritech and Random House believe that this type of product may turn out to be ideal for delivery to the home. As Thomas Touton, Ameritech Development's vice president for venture capital, notes, such exploratory investments "require support from senior management willing to move fast in investing but be patient in waiting for returns, and an investment focus that is strongly synergistic with the company's operations."

When and if the promise of the multimedia market becomes real, Ameritech will doubtless be competing against other powerful players. But Ameritech may already have an inside track in the race to deliver information and video on demand into the home. Through alliances such as the one with Random House and exploratory investments in virtual companies such as Worldview Systems, Ameritech has been able to share information and know-how with other potential industry participants and become an insider with the potential to influence the direction of this nascent industry. Until a technological direction becomes clear, companies must invest in capabilities and become active participants in the information dissemination process. Virtual organizations can be an extremely valuable tool at this early stage of market evolution.

terprises blazed the trail for the leading industries of the second industrial revolution. Markets in railroads, steel, chemicals, and petroleum were developed and shaped by major companies, not the other way around. The most successful of those companies were the first in their industries to make the massive investments in manufacturing, management, and distribution that were needed to realize the gains from innovation.

Companies that failed to make such coordinated, internal commitments during this period were soon thrust aside. The experience of British companies provides a cautionary tale for the champions of the virtual company. Many enjoyed early technological leads in their industries, but the reluctance of those family-run companies to relinquish control to outside investors prevented them from investing to build the capabilities they needed to commercialize their technologies. When German or U.S. competitors made the requisite investments, British companies lost their leadership position. In chemicals, for example, the British lead in the 1870s was completely lost by 1890. History even provided British chemical companies with a second chance when Germany's defeat in World War I temporarily cost German chemical manufacturers their plants and distribution networks. But by 1930, German chemical companies regained the lead because the British again failed to invest adequately. The lesson is that companies that develop their own capabilities can outperform those that rely too heavily on coordination through markets and alliances to build their businesses.

The leading industries of the late nineteenth and early twentieth centuries – chemicals, steel, and railroads – all experienced rapid systemic innovation. The winners were the companies that made major internal investments to shape the markets, rather than those that relied on others to lead the way. While business conditions have certainly changed, many of the principles that worked a century ago still pertain.

Matching Organization to Innovation

The capabilities you need...	Type of Innovation	
	Autonomous	Systemic
...exist outside	go virtual	ally with caution
...must be created	ally or bring in-house	bring in-house

Today leading companies like Intel and Microsoft make extensive investments to enhance their current capabilities and spur the creation of new ones. Because so many important innovations are systemic, decentralization without strategic leverage and coordination is exactly the wrong organizational strategy. In most cases, only a large company will have the scale and scope to coordinate complementary innovations. For both the chemicals industry 100 years ago and the microcomputer industry today, long-term success requires considerable and sustained internal investment within a company. The lessons of the second industrial revolution apply to the third: Adept, well-managed companies that commit the right internal resources to innovation will shape the markets and build the new industries of the twenty-first century.

Case III: *Resistance to Change*

What This Incident Is About: Employees face the threat of the unknown when consultants arrive to study their performance. The incident involves the process of successful change: gaining acceptance, coordination, use of consultants, attitudes, and morale.

As office manager of the Duncan Paper Products Corporation, Robert Hale was responsible for the work of approximately 45 employees, of whom 26 were classified as either stenographers or file clerks. Acting under instructions from the company president, he agreed to allow a team of outside consultants to enter his realm of responsibility and make time and systems-analysis studies in an effort to improve the efficiency and output of his staff.

The consultants began by studying job descriptions, making observations, and recording each detail of the work of the stenographers and file clerks. After three days, they indicated to Hale and his employees that they were prepared to begin more detailed studies, observations, and interviews on the following day.

The next morning, five employees participating in the study were absent. On the following day, 10 employees were absent. Concerned, Hale investigated the cause of the absenteeism by telephoning several absentees. Each employee related approximately the same story. Each was nervous, tense, and tired after being viewed as a "guinea pig" for several days. One stenographer told Hale that her physician had advised her to ask for a leave of absence if working conditions were not improved.

Shortly after the telephone calls, the chief of the systems-analysis team explained to Hale that, if there were as many absences on the next day, his team would have to drop the study and proceed to another department. He said that a valid analysis would be impossible to conduct with 10 employees absent. Realizing that he would be held responsible for the failure of the systems analysis, Hale began to create and evaluate alternative actions that would provide the conditions necessary for the study. He was also concerned about implementing the procedural changes that he knew would be mandated after the study was completed. Hale was astute enough to realize that policies declared and orders issued are not always followed by instant compliance, even in the military, and that this wasn't a military situation.

Using the Case on *Resistance to Change*

This case is a classic example of how people will react to situations that are imposed upon them as opposed to situations in which they themselves have been active in producing. These employees are responding in this manner because they fear for their jobs and their well-being. They have no input into the decisions leading to the study, and they are refusing to cooperate with the company by simply not showing up for work. This passive/aggressive behavior is typical in this type of situation, although mass absenteeism is a very strong form of protest, just short of mass resignation.

Questions for Discussion

1. How do you think the company could have handled the situation so as to get greater cooperation?
2. What are some of the alternatives that Robert Hale could implement to get greater cooperation from the employees?
3. What do you think Robert Hale and the company should do?

Exercise III: *Organizing*

The purpose of this exercise is to increase your awareness of the importance of structure in organization. In addition, the exercise focuses on the importance of management in organizing a venture.

The Problem

Select one of the following situations to organize. Then read the background material before answering the questions.

- The registration process at your university or college
- A new hamburger fast-food franchise
- A Jet-ski rental in an ocean resort area

Do steps 1–7, below, as homework. In preparing your answers, use your own experience or think up logical answers to the questions.

Background

Organization is a way of gaining some power against an unreliable environment. The environment provides the organization with input, which includes raw materials, human resources, and financial resources. There is a service or product to produce that involves technology. The output is to be sold to a client, a group that must be nurtured. The complexities of the environment and the technology determine the complexity of the organization.

Planning Your Organization

1. In a few sentences, write the mission or purpose of your organization.
2. From the mission statement you should be able to write down specific things that must be done in order to accomplish the mission.
3. From the list of specifics that must be accomplished, an organizational chart can be devised. Each position on the chart will perform a specific task or is responsible for a specific outcome.
4. Add duties to each job position on your organizational chart. This will form a job description.
5. How would you ensure that the people you placed in these positions work together?
6. What degree of skill and abilities is required at each position and level in order to hire the right person for each position?
7. Make a list of the decisions that would have to be made while you planned and built the organization. Make a second list of those decisions you would have to make just after your organization began operating.

In Class

1. Form into groups of up to three members that organized the same project and share your answers to the questions.
2. Come to agreement on the way to organize, utilizing everyone's responses.
3. Present your group's approach to the class.

Directing

- Management Classic (Article 18)
- Communication (Article 19)
- Leadership (Articles 20 and 21)
- Motivation (Articles 22 and 23)
- Performance (Article 24)

UNIT 4

Managers spend most of their time directing the organization. They have learned, however, that just telling people what to do is not good enough. To achieve the maximum possible results, people must first clearly understand the firm's goals, and then management must find a way to motivate them. Psychologist and educator Abraham Maslow, while not the first to recognize the importance of motivation, did categorize and define a hierarchy of needs that individuals must fulfill. Maslow's hierarchy has become the basis of a vast array of research into motivation. People who are motivated are far more likely to succeed than those who are not.

People enter business situations with a history of experiences, attitudes, and beliefs, and effectively communicating with them can be difficult. Open communication must be based upon trust. If there is fear or confusion as to where open communication leads, then communication will not be as effective as it could be. Managers must be able to communicate both in writing and orally. Effective communication involves the ability to design a letter, memo, or conversation so that both the sender and the receiver have a clear understanding of what was communicated and what is now expected of both parties. This frequently involves telling the receiver not only the message, but how the message was generated, because an employee's understanding of the reasons for an instruction can be the key to effective motivation. In today's environment, the problem is not a lack of ways to communicate, but, rather, selecting from all the information what is important and what is not, as discussed in "Overload."

Of all the various components of management, leadership is probably the most discussed, analyzed, and misunderstood. Indeed, some would argue that leadership and management are two separate and distinct activities. As revealed in "Lead, Don't Manage," leadership may be overdiscussed, but it is not well understood. Leaders come in all shapes and sizes, and two of the most successful are interviewed in the essay "Bill Gates and Paul Allen Talk." There have been good leaders and evil leaders; saints and brutes. They all share certain characteristics. One is an idea that they are able to communicate to their followers and have them accept as their own. This results in motivation of the followers. The second characteristic is genuine caring, enthusiasm, and dedication to the dream and the people involved in striving for it.

A manager who is successful in communicating with, motivating, and leading people will experience enhanced performance and productivity. The Japanese have led other nations in this area with the application of many techniques, such as quality circles. However, not all forms of worker participation have resulted in enhanced productivity, according to "The Failure of Participatory Management." American firms have also been applying new ideas in a variety of industries and settings, the topic of "Innovate or Evaporate: Seven Secrets of Innovative Corporations."

Effective managers are people who are able to successfully direct the organization. They know how to communicate, motivate, and lead, achieving enhanced productivity and performance that will accomplish the goals and mission of the organization in a fluid environment.

Looking Ahead: Challenge Questions

An effective manager must be able to communicate. How could managers communicate more effectively?

Motivating people may be the single most difficult task for a manager. In what ways could managers better motivate their employees?

Leadership may be the least understood of all the functions a manager must perform. Name at least five people who have best represented the qualities of leadership, in your opinion. What do they have in common?

The Abilene Paradox: The Management of Agreement

Jerry B. Harvey

JERRY B. HARVEY *is professor of management science at the George Washington University in Washington, D.C. He is a graduate of the University of Texas in Austin, where he earned an undergraduate degree in business administration and a Ph.D. in social psychology.*

A member of the International Consultant's Foundation, a Diplomate of the American Board of Professional Psychology, and a member of the O.D. Network, he has served as a consultant to a wide variety of industrial, governmental, religious, and voluntary organizations. He has written a number of articles in the fields of organizational behavior and education and currently is involved in the exploration of moral, ethical, and spiritual issues of work. In the pursuit of that interest, his book, The Abilene Paradox and Other Meditations on Management, *was published by Lexington Books in 1988.*

The July afternoon in Coleman, Texas (population 5,607) was particularly hot—104 degrees as measured by the Walgreen's Rexall Ex-Lax temperature gauge. In addition, the wind was blowing fine-grained West Texas topsoil through the house. But the afternoon was still tolerable—even potentially enjoyable. There was a fan going on the back porch; there was cold lemonade; and finally, there was entertainment. Dominoes. Perfect for the conditions. The game required little more physical exertion than an occasional mumbled comment. "Shuffle 'em," and an unhurried movement of the arm to place the spots in the appropriate perspective on the table. All in all, it had the makings of an agreeable Sunday afternoon in Coleman—that is, it was until my father-in-law suddenly said, "Let's get in the car and go to Abilene and have dinner at the cafeteria."

I thought, "What, go to Abilene? Fifty-three miles? In this dust storm and heat? And in an unairconditioned 1958 Buick?"

But my wife chimed in with, "Sounds like a great idea. I'd like to go. How about you, Jerry?" Since my own preferences were obviously out of step with the rest I replied, "Sounds good to me," and added, "I just hope your mother wants to go."

"Of course I want to go," said my mother-in-law. "I haven't been to Abilene in a long time."

So into the car and off to Abilene we went. My predictions were fulfilled. The heat was brutal. We were coated with a fine

From *Organizational Dynamics*, Summer 1988, pp. 17-43. © 1988 by the American Management Association, NY. All rights reserved. Reprinted by permission of the publisher.

layer of dust that was cemented with perspiration by the time we arrived. The food at the cafeteria provided first-rate testimonial material for antacid commercials.

Some four hours and 106 miles later we returned to Coleman, hot and exhausted. We sat in front of the fan for a long time in silence. Then, both to be sociable and to break the silence, I said, "It was a great trip, wasn't it?"

No one spoke. Finally my mother-in-law said, with some irritation, "Well, to tell the truth, I really didn't enjoy it much and would rather have stayed here. I just went along because the three of you were so enthusiastic about going. I wouldn't have gone if you all hadn't pressured me into it."

I couldn't believe it. "What do you mean 'you all'?" I said. "Don't put me in the 'you all' group. I was delighted to be doing what we were doing. I didn't want to go. I only went to satisfy the rest of you. You're the culprits."

My wife looked shocked. "Don't call me a culprit. You and Daddy and Mama were the ones who wanted to go. I just went along to be sociable and to keep you happy. I would have had to be crazy to want to go out in heat like that."

Her father entered the conversation abruptly. "Hell!" he said.

He proceeded to expand on what was already absolutely clear. "Listen, I never wanted to go to Abilene. I just thought you might be bored. You visit so seldom I wanted to be sure you enjoyed it. I would have preferred to play another game of dominoes and eat the leftovers in the icebox."

After the outburst of recrimination we all sat back in silence. Here we were, four reasonably sensible people who, of our own volition, had just taken a 106-mile trip across a godforsaken desert in a furnace-like temperature through a cloud-like dust storm to eat unpalatable food at a hole-in-the-wall cafeteria in Abilene, when none of us had really wanted to go. In fact, to be more accurate, we'd done just the opposite of what we wanted to do. The whole situation simply didn't make sense.

At least it didn't make sense at the time. But since that day in Coleman, I have

observed, consulted with, and been a part of more than one organization that has been caught in the same situation. As a result, they have either taken a side-trip, or, occasionally, a terminal journey to Abilene, when Dallas or Houston or Tokyo was where they really wanted to go. And for most of those organizations, the negative consequences of such trips, measured in terms of both human misery and economic loss, have been much greater than for our little Abilene group.

This article is concerned with that paradox—the Abilene Paradox. Stated simply, it is as follows: Organizations frequently take actions in contradiction to what they really want to do and therefore defeat the very purposes they are trying to achieve. It also deals with a major corollary of the paradox, which is that *the inability to manage agreement is a major source of organization dysfunction.* Last, the article is designed to help members of organizations cope more effectively with the paradox's pernicious influence.

As a means of accomplishing the above, I shall: (1) describe the symptoms exhibited by organizations caught in the paradox; (2) describe, in summarized case-study examples, how they occur in a variety of organizations; (3) discuss the underlying causal dynamics; (4) indicate some of the implications of accepting this model for describing organizational behavior; (5) make recommendations for coping with the paradox; and, in conclusion, (6) relate the paradox to a broader existential issue.

Symptoms of the Paradox

The inability to manage agreement, not the inability to manage conflict, is the essential symptom that defines organizations caught in the web of the Abilene Paradox. That inability to manage agreement effectively is expressed by six specific subsymptoms, all of which were present in our family Abilene group.

1. Organization members agree privately, as individuals, as to the nature of the situation or problem facing the organization. For example, members of the Abilene group agreed that they were enjoying themselves

sitting in front of the fan, sipping lemonade, and playing dominoes.

    2. Organization members agree privately, as individuals, as to the steps that would be required to cope with the situation or problem they face. For members of the Abilene group "more of the same" was a solution that would have adequately satisfied their individual and collective desires.

    3. Organization members fail to accurately communicate their desires and/or beliefs to one another. In fact, they do just the opposite and thereby lead one another into misperceiving the collective reality. Each member of the Abilene group, for example, communicated inaccurate data to other members of the organization. The data, in effect, said, "Yeah, it's a great idea. Let's go to Abilene," when in reality members of the organization individually and collectively preferred to stay in Coleman.

    4. With such invalid and inaccurate information, organization members make collective decisions that lead them to take actions contrary to what they want to do, and thereby arrive at results that are counterproductive to the organization's intent and purposes. Thus, the Abilene group went to Abilene when it preferred to do something else.

    5. As a result of taking actions that are counterproductive, organization members experience frustration, anger, irritation, and dissatisfaction with their organization. Consequently, they form subgroups with trusted acquaintances and blame other subgroups for the organization's dilemma. Frequently, they also blame authority figures and one another. Such phenomena were illustrated in the Abilene group by the "culprit" argument that occurred when we had returned to the comfort of the fan.

    6. Finally, if organization members do not deal with the generic issue — the inability to manage agreement — the cycle repeats itself with greater intensity. The Abilene group, for a variety of reasons, the most important of which was that it became conscious of the process, did not reach that point.

    To repeat, the Abilene Paradox reflects a failure to manage agreement. In fact, it is my contention that the inability to cope with (manage) agreement, rather than the inability to cope with (manage) conflict, is the single most pressing issue of modern organizations.

OTHER TRIPS TO ABILENE

The Abilene Paradox is no respecter of individuals, organizations, or institutions. Following are descriptions of two other trips to Abilene that illustrate both the pervasiveness of the paradox and its underlying dynamics.

Case No. 1: The Boardroom.
The Ozyx Corporation is a relatively small industrial company that has embarked on a trip to Abilene. The president of Ozyx has hired a consultant to help discover the reasons for the poor profit picture of the company in general and the low morale and productivity of the R&D division in particular. During the process of investigation, the consultant becomes interested in a research project in which the company has invested a sizable proportion of its R&D budget.

    When asked about the project by the consultant in the privacy of their offices, the president, the vice-president for research, and the research manager each describes it as an idea that looked great on paper but will ultimately fail because of the unavailability of the technology required to make it work. Each of them also acknowledges that continued support of the project will create cash flow problems that will jeopardize the very existence of the total organization.

    Furthermore, each individual indicates he has not told the others about his reservations. When asked why, the president says he can't reveal his "true" feelings because abandoning the project, which has been widely publicized, would make the company look bad in the press and, in addition, would probably cause his vice-president's ulcer to kick up or perhaps even cause him to quit, "because he has staked his professional reputation on the project's success."

    Similarly, the vice-president for research says he can't let the president or the research manager know of his reservations because the president is so committed to it that "I would probably get fired for insubordination if I questioned the project."

    Finally, the research manager says he can't let the president or vice-president know of his doubts about the project because of their extreme commitment to the project's success.

All indicate that, in meetings with one another, they try to maintain an optimistic façade so the others won't worry unduly about the project. The research director, in particular, admits to writing ambiguous progress reports so the president and the vice-president can "interpret them to suit themselves." In fact, he says he tends to slant them to the "positive" side, "given how committed the brass are."

The scent of the Abilene trail wafts from a paneled conference room where the project research budget is being considered for the following fiscal year. In the meeting itself, praises are heaped on the questionable project and a unanimous decision is made to continue it for yet another year. Symbolically, the organization has boarded a bus to Abilene.

In fact, although the real issue of agreement was confronted approximately eight months after the bus departed, it was nearly too late. The organization failed to meet a payroll and underwent a two-year period of personnel cutbacks, retrenchments, and austerity. Morale suffered, the most competent technical personnel resigned, and the organization's prestige in the industry declined.

Case No. 2: The Watergate
Apart from the grave question of who did what, Watergate presents America with the profound puzzle *of why. What is it that led such a wide assortment of men, many of them high public officials, possibly including the President himself, either to instigate or to go along with and later try to hide a pattern of behavior that by now appears not only reprehensible, but stupid? (The Washington Star and Daily News, editorial, May 27, 1973.)*

One possible answer to the editorial writer's question can be found by probing into the dynamics of the Abilene Paradox. I shall let the reader reach his own conclusions, though, on the basis of the following excerpts from testimony before the Senate investigating committee on "The Watergate Affair."

In one exchange, Senator Howard Baker asked Herbert Porter, then a member of the White House staff, why he (Porter) found himself "in charge of or deeply involved in a dirty tricks operation of the campaign." In response, Porter indicated that he had had qualms about what he was doing, but that he ". . . was not one to stand up in a meeting and say that this should be stopped. . . . I kind of drifted along."

And when asked by Baker why he had "drifted along," Porter replied, "In all honesty, because of the fear of the group pressure that would ensue, of not being a team player," and ". . . I felt a deep sense of loyalty to him [the President] or was appealed to on that basis." (*The Washington Post*, June 8, 1973, p. 20.)

Jeb Magruder gave a similar response to a question posed by committee counsel Dash. Specifically, when asked about

---

"The inability to manage agreement, not the inability to manage conflict, is the essential symptom that defines organizations caught in the web of the Abilene Paradox. That inability to manage agreement effectively is expressed by six specific subsymptoms. . . ."

his, Mr. Dean's, and Mr. Mitchell's reactions to Mr. Liddy's proposal, which included bugging the Watergate, Mr. Magruder replied, "I think all three of us were appalled. The scope and size of the project were something that at least in my mind were not envisioned. I do not think it was in Mr. Mitchell's mind or Mr. Dean's, although I can't comment on their states of mind at that time.

Mr. Mitchell, in an understated way, which was his way of dealing with difficult problems like this, indicated that this was not an "acceptable project." (*The Washington Post*, June 15, 1973, p. A14.)

Later in his testimony Mr. Magruder said, ". . . I think I can honestly say that no one was particularly overwhelmed with the project. But I think we felt that this information could be useful, and Mr. Mitchell agreed to approve the project, and I then notified the parties of Mr. Mitchell's approval." (*The Washington Post*, June 15, 1973, p. A14.)

Although I obviously was not privy to the private conversations of the principal characters, the data seem to reflect the essential elements of the Abilene Paradox. First, they indicate agreement. Evidently, Mitchell, Porter, Dean, and Magruder agreed that the plan was inappropriate. ("I think I can honestly say that no one was particularly overwhelmed with the project.") Second, the data indicate that the principal figures then proceeded to implement the plan in contradiction to their shared agreement. Third, the data surrounding the case clearly indicate that the plan multiplied the organization's problems rather than solved them. And finally, the organization broke into subgroups with the various principals, such as the President, Mitchell, Porter, Dean, and Magruder, blaming one another for the dilemma in which they found themselves, and internecine warfare ensued.

In summary, it is possible that because of the inability of White House staff members to cope with the fact that they agreed, the organization took a trip to Abilene.

ANALYZING THE PARADOX

The Abilene Paradox can be stated succinctly

as follows: Organizations frequently take actions in contradiction to the data they have for dealing with problems and, as a result, compound their problems rather than solve them. Like all paradoxes, the Abilene Paradox deals with absurdity. On the surface, it makes little sense for organizations, whether they are couples or companies, bureaucracies or governments, to take actions that are diametrically opposed to the data they possess for solving crucial organizational problems. Such actions are particularly absurd since they tend to compound the very problems they are designed to solve and thereby defeat the purposes the organization is trying to achieve. However, as Robert Rapaport and others have so cogently expressed it, paradoxes are generally paradoxes only because they are based on a logic or rationale different from what we understand or expect.

Discovering that different logic not only destroys the paradoxical quality but also offers alternative ways for coping with similar situations. Therefore, part of the dilemma facing an Abilene-bound organization may be the lack of a map—a theory or model—that provides rationality to the paradox. The purpose of the following discussion is to provide such a map.

The map will be developed by examining the underlying psychological themes of the profit-making organization and the bureaucracy and it will include the following landmarks: (1) Action Anxiety; (2) Negative Fantasies; (3) Real Risk; (4) Separation Anxiety; and (5) the Psychological Reversal of Risk and Certainty. I hope that the discussion of such landmarks will provide harried organization travelers with a new map that will assist them in arriving at where they really want to go and, in addition, will help them in assessing the risks that are an inevitable part of the journey.

ACTION ANXIETY

Action anxiety provides the first landmark for locating roadways that bypass Abilene. The concept of action anxiety says that the reasons organization members take actions in contradiction to their understanding of the organization's problems lies in the intense anxiety that is created as they think about acting in accordance with what they believe needs to be done. As a result, they opt to endure the professional and economic degradation of pursuing an unworkable research project or the consequences of participating in an illegal activity rather than act in a manner congruent with their beliefs. It is not that organization members do not know what needs to be done — they do know. For example, the various principals in the research organization cited *knew* they were working on a research project that had no real possibility of succeeding. And the central figures of the Watergate episode apparently *knew* that, for a variety of reasons, the plan to bug the Watergate did not make sense.

Such action anxiety experienced by the various protagonists may not make sense, but the dilemma is not a new one. In fact, it is very similar to the anxiety experienced by Hamlet, who expressed it most eloquently in the opening lines of his famous soliloquy:

> To be or not to be; that is the question:
> Whether 'tis nobler in the mind to suffer
> The slings and arrows of outrageous fortune
> Or to take arms against a sea of troubles
> And by opposing, end them? . . .
> (*Hamlet*, Act III, Scene II)

It is easy to translate Hamlet's anxious lament into that of the research manager of our R&D organization as he contemplates his report to the meeting of the budget committee. It might go something like this:

> To maintain my sense of integrity and self-worth or compromise it, that is the question. Whether 'tis nobler in the mind to suffer the ignominy that comes

from managing a nonsensical research project, or the fear and anxiety that come from making a report the president and V.P. may not like to hear.

So, the anguish, procrastination, and counterproductive behavior of the research manager or members of the White House staff are not much different from those of Hamlet; all might ask with equal justification Hamlet's subsequent searching question of what it is that

> makes us rather bear those ills we have than fly to others we know not of. (*Hamlet*, Act III, Scene II)

In short, like the various Abilene protagonists, we are faced with a deeper question: Why does action anxiety occur?

Negative Fantasies

Part of the answer to that question may be found in the negative fantasies organization members have about acting in congruence with what they believe should be done. Hamlet experienced such fantasies.

Specifically, Hamlet's fantasies of the alternatives to the current evils were more evils, and he didn't entertain the possibility that any action he might take could lead to an improvement in the situation. Hamlet's was not an unusual case, though. In fact, the "Hamlet syndrome" clearly occurred in both organizations previously described. All of the organization protagonists had negative fantasies about what would happen if they acted in accordance with what they believed needed to be done.

"[A]ction anxiety is supported by the negative fantasies that organization members have about what will happen as a consequence of their acting in accordance with their understanding of what is sensible."

The various managers in the R&D organization foresaw loss of face, prestige, position, and even health as the outcome of confronting the issues about which they believed, incorrectly, that they disagreed. Similarly, members of the White House staff feared being made scapegoats, branded as disloyal, or ostracized as non-team players if they acted in accordance with their understanding of reality.

To sum up, action anxiety is supported by the negative fantasies that organization members have about what will happen as a consequence of their acting in accordance with their understanding of what is sensible. The negative fantasies, in turn, serve an important function for the persons who have them. Specifically, they provide the individual with an excuse that releases him psychologically, both in his own eyes and frequently in the eyes of others, from the responsibility of having to act to solve organization problems.

It is not sufficient, though, to stop with the explanation of negative fantasies as the basis for the inability of organizations to cope with agreement. We must look deeper and ask still other questions: What is the source of the negative fantasies? Why do they occur?

Real Risk

Risk is a reality of life, a condition of existence. John Kennedy articulated it in another way when he said at a news conference, "Life is unfair." By that I believe he meant we do not know, nor can we predict or control with certainty, either the events that impinge upon us or the outcomes of actions we undertake in response to those events.

Consequently, in the business environment, the research manager might find that confronting the president and the vice-president with the fact that the project was a "turkey" might result in his being fired. And Mr. Porter's saying that an illegal plan of surveillance should not be carried out could have caused his ostracism as a non-team player. There are too many cases when confrontation of this sort has resulted in such consequences. The real question, though, is not, Are such fantasized consequences possible?

but, Are such fantasized consequences likely?

Thus real risk is an existential condition, and all action do have consequences that, to paraphrase Hamlet, may be worse than the evils of the present. As a result of their unwillingness to accept existential risk as one of life's givens, however, people may opt to take their organizations to Abilene rather than run the risk, no matter how small, of ending up somewhere worse.

Again, though, one must ask, What is the real risk that underlies the decision to opt for Abilene? What is at the core of the paradox?

Fear of Separation

One is tempted to say that the core of the paradox lies in the individual's fear of the unknown. Actually, we do not fear what is unknown, but we are afraid of things we do know about. What do we know about that frightens us into such apparently inexplicable organizational behavior?

Separation, alienation, and loneliness are things we do know about—and fear. Both research and experience indicate that ostracism is one of the most powerful punishments that can be devised. Solitary confinement does not draw its coercive strength from physical deprivation. The evidence is overwhelming that we have a fundamental need to be connected, engaged, and related and a reciprocal need not to be separated or alone. Everyone of us, though, has experienced aloneness. From the time the umbilical cord was cut, we have experienced the real anguish of separation—broken friendships, divorces, deaths, and exclusions. C. P. Snow vividly described the tragic interplay between loneliness and connection:

> Each of us is alone; sometimes we escape from our solitariness, through love and affection or perhaps creative moments, but these triumphs of life are pools of light we make for ourselves while the edge of the road is black. Each of us dies alone.

That fear of taking risks that may result in our separation from others is at the core of the paradox. It finds expression in ways of which we may be unaware, and it is ultimately the cause of the self-defeating, collective deception that leads to self-destructive decisions within organizations.

Concretely, such fear of separation leads research committees to fund projects that none of its members want and, perhaps, White House staff members to engage in illegal activities that they don't really support.

The Psychological Reversal of Risk and Certainty

One piece of the map is still missing. It relates to the peculiar reversal that occurs in our thought processes as we try to cope with the Abilene Paradox. For example, we frequently fail to take action in an organizational setting becasue we fear that the actions we take may result in our separation from others, or, in the language of Mr. Porter, we are afraid of being tabbed as "disloyal" or are afraid of being ostracized as "non-team players." But therein lies a paradox within a paradox, because our very unwillingness to take such risks virtually ensures the separation and aloneness we so fear. In effect, we reverse "real existential risk" and "fantasied risk" and by doing so transform what is a probability statement into what, for all practical purposes, becomes a certainty.

Take the R&D organization described earlier. When the project fails, some people will get fired, demoted, or sentenced to the purgatory of a make-work job in an out-of-the-way office. For those who remain, the atmosphere of blame, distrust, suspicion, and backbiting that accompanies such failure will serve only to further alienate and separate those who remain.

The Watergate situation is similar. The principals evidently feared being ostracized as disloyal non-team players. When the illegality of the act surfaced, however, it was nearly inevitable that blaming, self-protective actions, and scapegoating would result in the very emotional separation from both the President and one another that the principals feared. Thus, by reversing real and fantasied risk, they had taken effective action to ensure the outcome they least desired.

One final question remains: Why do we make this peculiar reversal? I support the general thesis of Alvin Toffler and Philip Slater, who contend that our cultural emphasis on technology, competition, individualism, temporariness, and mobility has resulted in a population that has frequently experienced the terror of loneliness and seldom the satisfaction of engagement. Consequently, though we have learned of the reality of separation, we have not had the opportunity to learn the reciprocal skills of connection, with the result that, like the ancient dinosaurs, we are breeding organizations with self-destructive decision-making proclivities.

A Possible Abilene Bypass

Existential risk is inherent in living, so it is impossible to provide a map that meets the no-risk criterion, but it may be possible to describe the route in terms that make the landmarks understandable and that will clarify the risks involved. In order to do that, however, some commonly used terms such as victim, victimizer, collusion, responsibility, conflict, conformity, courage, confrontation, reality, and knowledge have to be redefined. In addition, we need to explore the relevance of the redefined concepts for bypassing or getting out of Abilene.

• *Victim and victimizer.* Blaming and fault-finding behavior is one of the basic symptoms of organizations that have found their way to Abilene, and the target of blame generally doesn't include the one who criticizes. Stated in different terms, executives begin to assign one another to roles of victims and victimizers. Ironic as it may seem, however, this assignment of roles is both irrelevant and dysfunctional, because once a business or a government fails to manage its agreement and arrives in Abilene, all its members are victims. Thus, arguments and accusations that identify victims and victimizers at best become symptoms of the paradox, and, at worst, drain energy from the problem-solving efforts required to redirect the organization along the route it really wants to take.

• *Collusion.* A basic implication of the Abilene Paradox is that human problems of organization are reciprocal in nature. As

Robert Tannenbaum has pointed out, you can't have an autocratic boss unless subordinates are willing to collude with his autocracy, and you can't have obsequious subordinates unless the boss is willing to collude with their obsequiousness.

Thus, in plain terms, each person in a self-defeating, Abilene-bound organization *colludes* with others, including peers, superiors, and subordinates, sometimes consciously and sometimes subconsciously, to create the dilemma in which the organization finds itself. To adopt a cliche of modern organization, "It takes a real team effort to go to Abilene." In that sense each person, in his own collusive manner, shares responsibility for the trip, so searching for a locus of blame outside oneself serves no useful purpose for either the organization or the individual. It neither helps the organization handle its dilemma of unrecognized agreement nor does it provide psychological relief for the individual, because focusing on conflict when agreement is the issue is devoid of reality. In fact, it does just the opposite, for it causes the organization to focus on managing conflict when it should be focusing on managing agreement.

• *Responsibility for problem-solving action.* A second question is, Who is responsible for getting us out of this place? To that question is frequently appended a third one, generally rhetorical in nature, with "should" overtones, such as, Isn't it the boss (or the ranking government official) who is responsible for doing something about the situation?

The answer to that question is no.

The key to understanding the functionality of the no answer is the knowledge that, when the dynamics of the paradox are in operation, the authority figure—and others—are in unknowing agreement with one another concerning the organization's problems and the steps necessary to solve them. Consequently, the power to destroy the paradox's pernicious influence comes from confronting and speaking to the underlying reality of the situation, and not from one's hierarchical position within the organization. Therefore, any organization member who chooses to risk confronting that reality possesses the necessary leverage to release the organization from the paradox's grip.

In one situation, it may be a research director's saying, "I don't think this project can succeed." In another, it may be Jeb Magruder's response to this question of Senator Baker:

If you were concerned because the action was known to you to be illegal, because you thought it improper or unethical, you thought the prospects for success were very meager, and you doubted the reliability of Mr. Liddy, what on earth would it have taken to decide against the plan?

Magruder's reply was brief and to the point:

"*Conflict is a part of any organization. . . . However, analysis of the Abilene Paradox opens up the possibility of two kinds of conflict—real and phony. On the surface, they look alike. But, like headaches, they have different causes and therefore require different treatment.*"

Not very much, sir. I am sure that if I had fought vigorously against it, I think any of us could have had the plan cancelled. (*Time*, June 25, 1973, p. 12.)

• *Reality, knowledge, confrontation.* Accepting the paradox as a model describing certain kinds of organizational dilemmas also requires rethinking the nature of reality and knowledge, as they are generally described in organizations. In brief, the underlying dynamics of the paradox clearly indicate that organization members generally know more about issues confronting the organization than they don't know. The various principals attending the research budget meeting, for example, knew the research project was doomed to failure. And Jeb Magruder spoke as a true Abilener when he said, "We knew it was illegal, probably, inappropriate." (*The Washington Post*, June 15, 1973, p. A16.)

Given this concept of reality and its relationship to knowledge, confrontation becomes the process of facing issues squarely, openly, and directly in an effort to discover whether the nature of the underlying collective reality is agreement or conflict. Accepting such a definition of confrontation has an important implication for change agents interested in making organizations more effective. That is, organization change and effectiveness may be facilitated as much by confronting the organization with what it knows and agrees upon as by confronting it with what it doesn't know or disagrees about.

REAL CONFLICT AND PHONY CONFLICT

Conflict is a part of any organization. Couples, R&D divisions, and White House staffs all engage in it. However, analysis of the Abilene Paradox opens up the possibility of two kinds of conflict—real and phony. On the surface, they look alike. But, like headaches, they have different causes and therefore require different treatment.

Real conflict occurs when people have real differences. ("My reading of the research printouts says that we can make the project profitable." "I come to the opposite conclusion.") ("I suggest we 'bug' the Watergate." "I'm not in favor of it.")

Phony conflict, on the other hand, occurs when people agree on the actions they want to take, and then do the opposite. The resulting anger, frustration, and blaming behavior generally termed "conflict" are not based on real differences. Rather, they stem from the protective reactions that occur when a decision that no one believed in or was committed to in the first place goes sour. In fact, as a paradox within a paradox, such conflict is symptomatic of agreement!

GROUP TYRANNY AND CONFORMITY

Understanding the dynamics of the Abilene Paradox also requires a "reorientation" in thinking about concepts such as "group tyranny"—the loss of the individual's distinctiveness in a group, and the impact of conformity pressures on individual behavior in organizations. Group tyranny and its result, individual conformity, generally refer to the coercive effect of group pressures on individual behavior. Sometimes referred to as Groupthink, it has been damned as the cause for everything from the lack of creativity in organizations ("A camel is a horse designed by a committee") to antisocial behavior in juveniles ("My Johnny is a good boy. He was just pressured into shoplifting by the kids he runs around with").

However, analysis of the dynamics underlying the Abilene Paradox opens up the possibility that individuals frequently perceive and feel as if they are experiencing the coercive organization conformity pressures when, in actuality, they are responding to the dynamics of mismanaged agreement. Conceptualizing, experiencing, and responding to such experiences as reflecting the tyrannical pressures of a group again serves as an important psychological use for the individual: As was previously said, it releases him from the responsibility of taking action and thus becomes a defense against action. Thus, much behavior within an organization that heretofore has been conceptualized as reflecting the tyranny of conformity pressures is really an expression of collective anxiety and therefore must be reconceptualized as a defense against acting.

A well-known example of such faulty conceptualization comes to mind. It involves the heroic sheriff in the classic Western movies who stands alone in the jailhouse door and singlehandedly protects a suspected (and usually innocent) horse thief or murderer from the irrational, tyrannical forces of group behavior—that is, an armed lynch mob. Generally, as a part of the ritual, he threatens to blow off the head of anyone who takes a step toward the door. Few ever take the challenge, and the reason is not the sheriff's six-shooter. What good would one pistol be against an armed mob of several hundred people who *really* want to hang somebody? Thus, the gun in fact serves as a face-saving measure for people who don't wish to participate in a hanging anyway. ("We had to back off. The sheriff threatened to blow our heads off.")

The situation is one involving agreement management, for a careful investigator canvassing the crowd under conditions in which the anonymity of the interviewees' responses could be guaranteed would probably find: (1) that few of the individuals in the crowd really wanted to take part in the hanging; (2) that each person's participation came about because he perceived, falsely, that others wanted to do so; and (3) that each person was afraid that others in the crowd would ostracize or in some other way punish him if he did not go along.

Diagnosing the Paradox

Most individuals like quick solutions, "clean" solutions, "no risk" solutions to organization problems. Furthermore, they tend to prefer solutions based on mechanics and technology, rather than on attitudes of "being." Unfortunately, the underlying reality of the paradox makes it impossible to provide either no-risk solutions or action technologies divorced from existential attitudes and realities. I do, however, have two sets of suggestions for dealing with these situations. One set of suggestions relates to diagnosing the situation, the other to confronting it.

When faced with the possibility that the paradox is operating, one must first make a diagnosis of the situation, and the key to diagnosis is an answer to the question, Is the organization involved in a conflict-management or an agreement-management situation? As an organization member, I have found it relatively easy to make a preliminary diagnosis as to whether an organization is on the way to Abilene or is involved in legitimate, substantive conflict by responding to the Diagnostic Survey shown in the accompanying figure. If the answer to the first question is "not characteristic," the organization is probably not in Abilene or conflict. If the answer is "characteristic," the organization has a problem of either real or phony conflict, and the answers to the succeeding questions help to determine which it is.

In brief, for reasons that should be apparent from the theory discussed here, the more times "characteristic" is checked, the more likely the organization is on its way to Abilene. In practical terms, a process for managing agreement is called for. And finally, if the answer to the first question falls into the "characteristic" category and most of the other answers fall into the category "not characteristic," one may be relatively sure the organization is in a real conflict situation and some sort of conflict management intervention is in order.

Coping with the Paradox

Assuming a preliminary diagnosis leads one to believe he and/or his organization is on the way to Abilene, the individual may choose to actively confront the situation to determine directly whether the underlying reality is one of agreement or conflict. Although there are, perhaps, a number of ways to do it, I have found one way in particular to be effective—confrontation in a group setting. The basic approach involves gathering organization members who are key figures in the problem and its solution into a group setting. Working within the context of a group is important because the dynamics of the Abilene Paradox involve collusion among group members; therefore, to try to solve the dilemma by working with individuals and small subgroups would involve further collusion with

---

ORGANIZATION DIAGNOSTIC SURVEY

Instructions: For each of the following statements please indicate whether it is or is not characteristic of your organization.

---

1. There is conflict in the organization.
2. Organization members feel frustrated, impotent, and unhappy when trying to deal with it. Many are looking for ways to escape. They may avoid meetings at which the conflict is discussed, they may be looking for other jobs, or they may spend as much time away from the office as possible by taking unneeded trips or vacation or sick leave.
3. Organization members place much of the blame for the dilemma on the boss or other groups. In "back room" conversations among friends the boss is termed incompetent, ineffective, "out of touch," or a candidate for early retirement. To his face, nothing is said, or at best, only oblique references are made concerning his role in the organization's problems. If the boss isn't blamed, some other group, division, or unit is seen as the cause of the trouble: "We would do fine if it were not for the damn fools in Division X."
4. Small subgroups of trusted friends and associates meet informally over coffee, lunch, and so on to discuss organizational problems. There is a lot of agreement among the members of these subgroups as to the cause of the troubles and the solutions that would be effective in solving them. Such conversations are frequently punctuated with statements beginning with, "We should do. . . ."
5. In meetings where those same people meet with members from other subgroups to discuss the problem they "soften their positions," state them in ambiguous language, or even reverse them to suit the apparent positions taken by others.
6. After such meetings, members complain to trusted associates that they really didn't say what they wanted to say, but also provide a list of convincing reasons why the comments, suggestions, and reactions they wanted to make would have been impossible. Trusted associates commiserate and say the same was true for them.
7. Attempts to solve the problem do not seem to work. In fact, such attempts seem to add to the problem or make it worse.
8. Outside the organization individuals seem to get along better, be happier, and operate more effectively than they do within it.

---

the dynamics leading up to the paradox.

The first step in the meeting is for the individual who "calls" it (that is, the confronter) to own up to his position first and be open to the feedback he gets. The owning up process lets the others know that he is concerned lest the organization may be making a decision contrary to the desires of any of its members. A statement like this demonstrates the beginning of such an approach:

> I want to talk with you about the research project. Although I have previously said things to the contrary, I frankly don't think it will work, and I am very anxious about it. I suspect others may feel the same, but I don't know. Anyway, I am concerned that I may end up misleading you and that we may end up misleading one another, and if we aren't careful, we may continue to work on a problem that none of us wants and that might even bankrupt us. That's why I need to know where the rest of you stand. I would appreciate any of your thoughts about the project. Do you think it can succeed?

What kinds of results can one ex-

pect if he decides to undertake the process of confrontation? I have found that the results can be divided into *two* categories, at the technical level and at the level of existential experience. Of the two, I have found that for the person who undertakes to initiate the process of confrontation, the existential experience takes precedence in his ultimate evaluation of the outcome of the action he takes.

• *The technical level.* If one is correct in diagnosing the presence of the paradox, I have found the solution to the technical problem may be almost absurdly quick and simple, nearly on the order of this:

"Do you mean that you and I and the rest of us have been dragging along with a research project that none of us has thought would work? It's crazy. I can't believe we would do it, but we did. Let's figure out how we can cancel it and get to doing something productive." In fact, the simplicity and quickness of the solution frequently don't seem possible to most of us, since we have been trained to believe that the solution to conflict requires a long, arduous process of debilitating problem solving.

Also, since existential risk is always present, it is possible that one's diagnosis is incorrect, and the process of confrontation lifts to the level of public examination real, substantive conflict, which may result in heated debate about technology, personalities, and/or administrative approaches. There is evidence that such debates, properly managed, can be the basis for creativity in organizational problem solving. There is also the possibility, however, that such debates cannot be managed, and substantiating the concept of existential risk, the person who initiates the risk may get fired or ostracized. But that again leads to the necessity of evaluating the results of such confrontation at the existential level.

• *Existential results.* Evaluating the outcome of confrontation from an existential framwork is quite different from evaluating it from a set of technical criteria. How do I reach this conclusion? Simply from interviewing a variety of people who have chosen to confront the paradox and listening to their responses. In short, for them, psychological success and failure apparently are divorced from what is traditionally accepted in organizations as criteria for success and failure.

For instance, some examples of success are described when people are asked, "What happened when you confronted the issue?" They may answer this way:

> I was told we had enough boat rockers in the organization, and I got fired. It hurt at first, but in retrospect it was the greatest day of my life. I've got another job and I'm delighted. I'm a free man.

Another description of success might be this:

> I said I don't think the research project can succeed and the others looked shocked and quickly agreed. The upshot of the whole deal is that I got a promotion and am now known as a "rising star." It was the high point of my career.

Similarly, those who fail to confront the paradox describe failure in terms divorced from technical results. For example, one may report:

> I didn't say anything and we rocked along until the whole thing exploded and Joe got fired. There is still a lot of tension in the organization, and we are still in trouble, but I got a good performance review last time. I still feel lousy about the whole thing, though.

From a different viewpoint, an individual may describe his sense of failure in these words:

> I knew I should have said something and I didn't. When the project failed, I was a convenient whipping boy. I got demoted; I still have a job, but my future here is definitely limited. In a way I deserve what I got, but it doesn't make it any easier to accept because of that.

Most important, the act of confrontation apparently provides intrinsic psychological satisfaction, regardless of the technological outcomes for those who attempt it. The real meaning of that existential experience, and its relevance to a wide variety of organizations, may lie, therefore, not in the scientific analysis of decision making but in the plight of Sisyphus. That is something the reader will have to decide for himself.

THE ABILENE PARADOX AND THE MYTH OF SISYPHUS

In essence, this paper proposes that there is an underlying organizational reality that includes both agreement and disagreement, cooperation and conflict. However, the decision to confront the possibility of organization agreement is all too difficult and rare, and its opposite, the decision to accept the evils of the present, is all to common. Yet those two decisions may reflect the essence of both our human potential and our human imperfectability. Consequently, the choice to confront reality in the family, the church, the business, or the bureaucracy, though made only occasionally, may reflect those "peak experiences" that provide meaning to the valleys.

In many ways, they may reflect the experience of Sisyphus. As you may remember, Sisyphus was condemned by Pluto to a perpetuity of pushing a large stone to the top of a mountain, only to see it return to its original position when he released it. As Camus suggested in his revision of the myth, Sisyphus's task was absurd and totally devoid of meaning. For most of us, though, the lives we lead pushing papers or hubcaps are no less absurd, and in many ways we probably spend about as much time pushing rocks in our organizations as did Sisyphus.

Camus also points out, though, that on occasion as Sisyphus released his rock and watched it return to its resting place at the bottom of the hill, he was able to recognize the absurdity of his lot and, for brief periods of time, transcend it.

So it may be with confronting the

Abilene Paradox. Confronting the absurd paradox of agreement may provide, through activity, what Sisyphus gained from his passive but conscious acceptance of his fate. Thus, through the process of active confrontation with reality, we may take respite from pushing our rocks on their endless journeys and, for brief moments, experience what C. P. Snow termed "the triumphs of life we make for ourselves" within those absurdities we call organizations.

Selected Bibliography

Chris Argyris in *Intervention Theory and Method: A Behavioral Science View* (Addison-Wesley, 1970) gives an excellent description of the process of "owning up" and being "open," both of which are major skills required if one is to assist his organization in avoiding or leaving Abilene.

Albert Camus in *The Myth of Sisyphus and Other Essays* (Vintage Books, Random House, 1955) provides an existential viewpoint for coping with absurdity, of which the Abilene Paradox is a clear example.

Jerry B. Harvey and R. Albertson in "Neurotic Organizations: Symptoms, Causes and Treatment," Parts I and II, *Personnel Journal* (September and October 1971) provide a detailed example of a third-party intervention into an organization caught in a variety of agreement-management dilemmas.

Irving Janis in *Victims of Groupthink* (Houghton-Mifflin Co., 1972) offers an alternative viewpoint for understanding and dealing with many of the dilemmas described in "The Abilene Paradox." Specifically, many of the events that Janis describes as examples of conformity pressures (that is, group tyranny) I would conceptualize as mismanaged agreement.

In his *The Pursuit of Loneliness* (Beacon Press, 1970), Philip Slater contributes an in-depth description of the impact of the role of alienation, separation, and loneliness (a major contribution to the Abilene Paradox) in our culture.

Richard Walton in *Interpersonal Peacemaking: Confrontation and Third Party Consultation* (Addison-Wesley, 1969) describes a variety of approaches for dealing with conflict when it is real, rather than phony.

Abilene Revisited: An Epilogue

Jerry B. Harvey

"The Abilene Paradox" was born October 9, 1971 as part of a presentation I gave to the Organization Development (OD) Network about some variations of ideas contained in a paper Dick Albertson and I had written on neurotic organizations. I remember the date not because of the presentation, but because the Texas Longhorns suffered an ignominious 48-27 defeat at the

hands of the Oklahoma Sooners; no self-respecting Texan could forget a disappointment of that magnitude.

Two hours before the session, I was "sweating bullets" trying to think of a prototypical example of a neurotic organization, one that had done something blatantly insane. For reasons that remain incomprehensible, I suddenly thought of my family and a trip we took one hot Sunday afternoon across a godforsaken desert to eat an indigestible meal in a hole-in-the-wall cafeteria in Abilene, Texas, and . . .

The audience apparently thought the story itself was great, but they didn't seem to think too much of the remainder of the speech—primarily, I suspect, because I had only a very superficial explanation for why such craziness occurred.

Since, of course, I heard the Abilene story for the first time when I told it, I was equally puzzled about its underlying dynamics. Consequently, soon after I returned home I sequestered myself in my office and, with Dick's encouragement, a great deal of passion, and very little sleep, tried to figure it out. One week and sixty-five pages later, I thought I had.

EARLY REJECTION

Publishers didn't, however. For instance, the editor of a major monograph series in the OD field returned it to me with the comment, "The nicest thing I could say about your work is that it would make a good high school senior thesis." That hurt. Generally I'm not vindictive, but in his case I still harbor the fond hope of suckering him into a meal at the Abilene Cafeteria.

I decided to reduce the manuscript to article length. I felt as if I were applying medicinal leeches to a baby that wasn't sick. In its shrunken state, it was further rejected by a major management journal because it fit "neither the journal's editorial style nor its policy of printing material of proven value to experienced managers." Since then, representatives of the same journal have asked me to produce an article for them *exactly* like the "Abilene Paradox," but on a completely different topic. I guess they have either changed their editorial style or neglected to read Heidegger's observation that most of us human beings have to confine ourselves to developing a single thought.

Running short of courage, I nevertheless sent it to Bill Dowling, then editor of *Organizational Dynamics*, and awaited his letter of rejection. Failing to collude with my negative fantasies, he agreed instead to publish it if I would allow him to do some editorial work on it—including the removal of (1) an interview I had conducted with a group of lemmings just before they went over the cliff and (2) the word my father-in-law *really* used when commenting upon our disastrous trip to Abilene.

His argument was persuasive, and though I someday hope to remove the scar tissue from the very minor surgery he performed, I will always be in his debt. God bless Bill Dowling; I *am* in his debt. He died much too young.

THE PERIPATETIC PARADOX

Once the article was printed, it apparently "took off." In the years since it first appeared, for example, I have been inundated with cards, letters, and telephone calls from people who have described other "trips to Abilene," including couples who have gotten married when they wanted to remain single, couples who have gotten divorced when they wanted to stay married, parishioners who built church buildings none of them wanted, school systems that implemented curricula none of their stakeholders supported, and countries that went to war when their citizens wanted peace.

In a similar vein, I have frequently been thanked and occasionally castigated for facilitating marriages, divorces, promotions, demotions, good business decisions, lousy business decisions, family reconciliations, and family fights.

THE TRANSFORMING PARADOX

McGraw-Hill has seen fit to make a movie about the Paradox. Filmed in the style of *The Waltons*, with me as the narrator, the film has provided me with a number of great learning experiences, one of which occurred not long ago as I walked down the aisle of a plane bound for Dallas. As I passed a rather frumpy-appearing woman, she looked up and shouted for all to hear, "Are you the star of that movie, *The Abilene Paradox?*" Where that gorgeous femme fatale came from, I don't know, but as I modestly replied (in my suavest actor's voice), "Yes, Ma'am, I am," I thought to myself, "Robert Redford, eat your heart out."

Paradoxically, the Paradox has had its dark side, too. For example, a videotape of me (talking about the Paradox) has been reproduced and "bootlegged" literally all over the world without my permission or the permission of the organization that legitimately produced it. Consequently, every time a naïve (and sometimes not-so-naïve) person tells me, "Our organization showed the videotape of your Abilene speech at our training program and we really enjoyed it," my blood boils at the lack of ethics on the part of those who knowingly did (and do) it. I also bridle when I realize the amount of money I might have made had I known how to market it and control its distribution. Ultimately, though, I think my own sense of greed disturbs me the most because, deep down, I know I have been given a gift which is mine to share, not to hoard.

THE PARADOX AS PHANTOM

All this has occurred despite the fact that, to this day, I cannot prove scientifically that the Abilene Paradox actually occurs. For example, it is altogether possible that my in-laws really wanted to go on the original trip, but changed their stories once we arrived in Abilene and had such a lousy time. All I know for sure is that from the time the trip was first suggested I didn't want to go, and *I drove the Buick*. In that sense the problem, existentially, was mine.

So, given all that has occurred, would I change any of what I wrote? Not really. Oh, I might make a few cosmetic alterations, such as reinserting the interview with the lemmings; stressing the role which anaclitic depression plays in causing the separation anxiety central to trips to Abilene; and, exploring in greater depth the ethical, moral, and spiritual aspects of the Paradox.

Still, in Heiddeger's terms, those are extensions of the same basic idea. Whether my expression of the idea is flawed or not, I accept it for what it is—my initial effort to do the best I could with *the* thought that the Good Lord—out of confusion, compassion, appreciation, administrative errors in the Idea Assignment Division, or other reasons beyond the limits of my human comprehension—saw fit to offer me.

An Abilene Defense: Commentary One

Rosabeth Moss Kanter

Public agreement, private disagreement. "The Abilene Paradox" points out that this situation almost inevitably leads to people going along for the ride even when they know better. The result: trouble.

The Abilene Paradox has two parts. The first involves a person's inaccurate assumptions about what others think and believe. This sometimes takes the guise of what social scientists call "pluralistic ignorance"—everybody in a group holds a similar opinion but, ignorant of the opinion of others, believes himself to be the only one feeling that way. The second part of the paradox involves a person's unwillingness to speak up about what she does think and believe. It is easier, more comfortable, or safer to keep quiet and be swept along by the current. Combine pluralistic ignorance with the path of least resistance and, before you know it, you're in Abilene.

Part one, then, is a problem of data. Part two is a problem of risk. The manager's tasks are to manage communication to allow the data to surface and to manage the organizational context to enhance power and reduce risk.

MANAGE COMMUNICATION

How can communication be managed in this way? Here are some guidelines:

Establish debates. Clearly, the first task for a manager is to set communication norms—and he or she has to go first. Participative management has become a cliché, but the idea of consulting others about possible decisions and genuinely pushing to hear the negatives still makes sense. One way to encourage other people to express what they really think is to frame every issue as a debate between alternatives—a matter of pros and cons. Instead of presenting issues as matters of concurrence—"I'd like to do X, wouldn't you?"—they should be presented as matters for debate: "X has been proposed; let's examine the pros and cons." Instead of considering only one choice, always seek alternative courses of action—"What else might we be doing with that money or that time?"—and then evaluate the main choice against the alternatives. Doing this requires actively valuing the additional time that debate can take, but a "bias for action" without considering alternatives can indeed land an organization in Abilene.

Assign gadflies, devil's advocates, fact checkers, and second guessers. There are certain well-established roles whose very definition involves confrontation, contrariness, and argument. Making sure that there is always someone playing the role of questioner ("Is that conclusion accurate?") or prober ("C'mon now, you can't really believe that!") is a way to ensure that contrary opinions will begin to surface. If the role is formally assigned, some of the risk associated with speaking up is reduced, and everyone understands it's nothing personal. Making this into an assigned role also permits rotation, so that everyone gets to play devil's advocate from time to time. Gradually the questioning style will become part of the normal routine. Third parties such as consultants and facilitators often play this role. But think how effective it would be as part of the work group's own repertoire!

Encourage organizational graffiti. My colleague Barry Stein deserves credit for this idea, which he is implementing in a very large company with a tradition of bureaucracy and conformity. The problem: People were not yet ready for open communication about their concerns. What was needed was devices that would allow people to comment on their concerns regularly but anonymously. The solution was to use unattended computer terminals as a site for the corporate equivalent of "graffiti"—remarks of any kind about any issue. Although written surveys and consultant interviews often serve this function, the appeal of organizational graffiti is that it is spontaneous, ongoing, timely, free-form, open-ended, and—as people comment on each other's inputs—interactive.

MANAGE THE ORGANIZATIONAL CONTEXT

How can the organizational context be managed to enhance power and reduce risk? Here are a few ways.

Make confronters into heroes. Instead of shooting messengers, reward them. Of course, this is really hard. How many of us thank the bearers of bad news? How many whistle blowers on corporate misconduct have kept their jobs, let alone gotten tokens of appreciation? And what rewards go to people who stop the trip to Abilene—a passive result—as opposed to those who push action forward? But still, if managers learn to value the honest expression of concerns because doing so will prevent more trouble later, then there is hope. If the organization provides role models, if the prizewinners and recognition garnerers include people known for their outspokenness rather than for their conformity, then more people can be encouraged to speak up.

Develop a "culture of pride." This is one of the cornerstones of the successful, innovative companies I identified in *The Change Masters.* A culture of pride builds collective self-esteem through abundant praise and recognition. People are made visible; they are valued for their accomplishments. Standards of high performance are communicated over and over again. Thus when collective pride is high, individual self-esteem is also high. Self-identified winners feel more secure psychologically and find it easier to take risks.

Create empowering structures. If people are informed and well-connected, they can more readily exercise independent judgment and speaking up is less risky. Organizational power comes from access to information, political support, and resources; powerlessness, in contrast, means not only a lack of access to, but also a dependence on, the boss to provide everything. Some of the structures that provide power include networks of peers who provide political backing and a forum for communication; sufficient employment security so that the job is not on the line every time the person speaks up; and affiliations with more than one work unit or reporting relationships with more than one boss, so that the person always has an alternative set of ties.

CHECKPOINTS AND MILESTONES
Surfacing data and empowering people are good ways to *help* prevent starting out for Abilene, but they do not always *guarantee* that organizations won't begin some troublesome trips anyway, without full discussion of the consequences. Sometimes that's because no one really understands the consequences yet, or feelings and opinions really are not that strong. The organization can find itself partway to Abilene before anyone knows they were headed there. This situation is increasingly common as decisions become more complex.

Even harder than preventing bad decisions from being implemented is turning them around halfway to their destination. So my final thought is this: All organizational trips should include some checkpoints

to permit the travellers to pause, regroup, and consult the map one more time.

If you don't want to go to Abilene after all, it's never too late to take a road to somewhere else.

Rosabeth Moss Kanter is the Class of 1960 Professor at the Harvard Business School, which she joined in 1986 after serving on the Yale faculty for 9 years and founding Goodmeasure, Inc., the Boston-based consulting firm. Author of The Change Masters, Men and Women of the Corporation, *and 7 other books, she has most recently written the book* Creating the Future: The Massachusetts Comeback and Its Promise for America (Summit Books), *with Governor Michael S. Dukakis. She is completing a new book for Simon and Schuster tentatively titled* The Great Corporate Balancing Act: Managing the Fallout from the Entrepreneurial Explosion.

An Abilene Defense: Commentary Two

Arthur Elliott Carlisle

In educating his nephew Wormwood in the wiles of temptation, the old devil Screwtape talks of the discord that can be engendered by urging people to argue in favor of what they believe (often incorrectly) other people want to do; this in spite of their own desire to do exactly the opposite. The net result is, of course, that no one's wishes are fulfilled and attempts to develop mutually satisfying and successful joint ventures fail.

The participants become angered by their frustration and, in this particular case, a discussion on whether to have tea in the garden or in the house results in not having tea at all (C. S. Lewis, *The Screwtape Letters,* New York: The Macmillan Company, 1944, pp. 133 and 134). This oft-recurring theme provides the basis for many literary comedies of manners and, fortunately, Jerry Harvey made it operational for managers in the "Abilene Paradox."

The behaviors described by Professor Harvey are reenacted all too frequently in decision-making sessions where managers must jointly determine courses of action that are often of vital importance to their organizations. They are important symptoms—symptoms that cannot be ignored, because they demonstrate an inability to manage an organization in a truly professional manner. Indeed, they reflect deep-seated organizational problems that go far beyond questions of conflict or agreement. Effective management requires the setting of clear objectives—where possible by consensus, but occasionally by edict—after hearing *all* sides and positions.

CLIMATE OF FEAR: A FAILURE OF MANAGEMENT
A failure of management occurs when a climate exists in which organization members are unwilling to express conflicting opinions whether the boss is present or not. This reluctance results from the fear of being viewed by both peers and superiors as someone who is not a team player or as someone who does not support the boss's known pet projects. Furthermore, when

being a "yes-(wo)man" is believed to be the best route to promotion, something is profoundly wrong. This sort of behavior at best results in reduced organizational effectiveness and at worst leads to organizational decline or even dissolution.

In Western industrialized countries management has entered a new era, one in which business organizations are facing substantially increased competition—not only from abroad, but also from domestic firms seeking new markets with fundamentally different products. For example, the invasion of the electronic calculator from outside the industry caught traditional manufacturers like Marchant and Friden with a line of outmoded products. There is every reason to believe this pattern will continue. Organizational survival now requires a level of expertise beyond what has been needed in the past, and this expertise is often available only at lower organizational levels.

To an ever-increasing extent, subordinates are better-trained in analytical and technical skills than are their superiors. Both domineering and charismatic leadership have become truly dangerous as a general modus operandi. An attitude at lower levels that "(s)he may not always be right, but (s)he's always the boss" or an all-consuming desire to be viewed as a team member at whatever cost can result in the loss of contributions by truly talented personnel who could improve organizational performance.

Avoiding the Abilene Paradox requires, first, recognition of its potential as a trap—recognition at the highest organizational levels, including the members of the board of directors. (Directors are often guilty of "Abilene" behavior.) The next phase involves *both* management training *and* organization development. Managers must be reminded of their responsibility to communicate and gain commitment to the attainment of multiple objectives. Organization development is essential for maintaining a climate in which the Abilene Paradox cannot flourish, let alone survive.

THE RIGHT KIND OF CLIMATE

Managers tend to pattern their leadership styles after those of their superiors; therefore, managers at the highest levels must make it clear, by their own example, that *all* the organization's managers are responsible for creating a healthy organizational climate. This climate is one in which:

• Members are not afraid to express their opinions and, when they feel it appropriate, to challenge those of others when they have the facts.

• The "Kill the messenger who brings the bad news" syndrome is no longer part of the organizational canon.

• Dissent, if backed up with data and analysis, does not brand the dissenter as a loner, a troublemaker, or someone who is not a team player; instead, it is recognized as a *professional responsibility* and rewarded.

• Changing one's mind, particularly after new information or argument is presented, is not seen as a sign of weakness, but rather of strength and self-confidence.

• Attainment of realistic group and individual objectives, rather than pleasing the boss or being a good team member, is the basis for organizational reward and advancement.

An organization that is to avoid the destructive consequences of an Abilene Paradox requires one additional ingredient: Management training and organization development are not enough if the necessary raw materials are lacking. At managerial and technical levels, hiring and promotional practices must seek self-confident, sensitive (but *not* supersensitive), non-risk-aversive men and women, competent enough to be readily hired elsewhere. Such individuals do not play Screwtape's "Let's have tea in the garden" game.

Arthur Elliott Carlisle is professor of management at the University of Massachusetts at Amherst. He is also author of another remarkably popular Organizational Dynamics *classic: "MacGregor," which appeared in the Summer 1976 issue.*

For James Mendelsohn and his colleagues at Perdue Farms, instant and urgent communications has an almost incalculable value. The manager of marketing research and information for the Salisbury, Md.-based firm, Mendelsohn explains Perdue is a far-flung enterprise that deals in a perishable commodity. Thus, tools such as voice mail, e-mail, cellular phones, and beepers are like nerves that carry impulses, which in turn drive a timely distribution system.

This is especially important for Mendelsohn and Perdue. "As we say in our business," relates the poultry peddler, "you either sell it or smell it."

But in a lament that is increasingly common at large companies, those same tools are raising an electronic cacophony that's louder and more demanding than a henhouse at feeding hour. "When I'm faced with 50 e-mails and a couple of dozen voice mails, the chore is to sort out what's important from what's not relevant to my job," says Mendelsohn. "I find myself

delsohn, "at times, I go home realizing I haven't completed any of the tasks that I'd planned for that day."

Welcome to the world of communications overload, an environment in which a torrent of messages pelts people like a relentless Seattle rain. As the intensity of the deluge grows, we're only beginning to feel the true effects of being soaked in a surfeit of information.

A variety of services and technologies have facilitated an explosion of rapid communications, be it carried by overnight express couriers, fax machines, voice mail, the Internet, the World Wide Web, e-mail, and other systems. Changes in organizational structures have also contributed to the exchange. Self-directed teams—an evolution facilitated by easy-access e-mail—have generated a tremendous need for fast, cross-functional communications. In turn, there are fewer supervisors to filter information and serve as gatekeepers, sending out what is essential and spiking the egregiously trivial.

As a result, corporations have undergone a *sociological* change.

Call it the Great Democratization of corporate com-

> Are you and your workers really coping with the glut of e-mail, voice mail, and faxes? Here's how others deal with it.

Overload

By Jay Stuller

spending an awful lot of time these days on electronic-communications overhead."

He has also discovered that the ever-mounting backlog of requests and FYI messages is compounded by the company's electronic scheduling system, a form of "groupware." On a computer, his colleagues can see when he's available; this makes it easy for them to schedule Mendelsohn into a chock-full day of cross-functional study-team and task-force meetings. "Even though I have the right to say no," he explains, "the system is a real facilitator for bringing disparate people with complicated schedules together. So I end up going to a lot of meetings." When he's away, internal and external message senders continue to play.

"After dealing with one unexpected message or request after another," says Men-

munications. For better or worse, these systems enable thousands of employees to function as individual publishers.

For large, complex, or multinational companies, the systems are essential. But thanks to the miracle of electronic mail, a typical manager may well boot up a computer, only to find a critical report or request for information encased by 15 FYI copies from study teams, each announcing they've completed a quality process step. Whoopee. In the backlog of e-mail that's growing faster than kudzu, Sally's latest joke about Anna Nicole Smith may be considered a must-read. Among the clatter and tangle, senior management occasionally gets in a word edgewise: The CEO might make an announcement about some huge new corporate strategy.

"This is not an 'information' problem, since

From *Across the Board*, April 1996, pp. 16-22. © 1996 by The Conference Board. Reprinted with permission.

From Kazakstan With E-Love

*A*rriving at the Tengiz field for his 28-day shift after 28 days at home in the United States, Charlie Auvermann came to dread one particular task. "My computer would be stuffed with hundreds of e-mails," says the public-affairs supervisor at Tengizchevroil (TCO), a joint oil-production venture between the Republic of Kazakstan and Chevron Corp. "Important messages would be buried among reports of lost wedding rings and power shutdowns that had happened two weeks before. It seemed like I'd spend a full day on e-mail triage, sorting out the critical from the trivial."

Auvermann wasn't alone in his frustration. TCO's 1,100 e-mail users—about 30 percent of whom are expatriates working 28-day rotations—were flooding each other with missives.

"Even as the use and costs of the system increased," says Auvermann, "we started to notice that communications gaps were developing, mainly because of the information clutter."

A small quality action team was formed to tackle this rather complex technological, behavioral, and organizational issue. The team's first recommendation: Remove the "All E-Mail Users" address from the system. Whenever message-senders had the slightest doubt about the relative importance of a message, "All Users" had turned into a first and last resort, ensuring the coverage of all bases.

"Today, just about anyone who wants to reach the entire organization has to go through our Information Communications Services help desk," Auvermann explains. "The team developed guidelines for these information gatekeepers, to help them sort out the relative importance of messages. And then the team developed alternate places in which to put various announcements."

One alternate is an electronic bulletin board linked to the e-mail system. It's the place to find general TCO announcements and the latest airline and bus schedules, but, most important, the information isn't forced upon users. In addition, the bulletin board includes a monthly electronic newsletter, with material of interest of the entire employee population.

The company also put up physical bulletin boards in cafeterias and other common areas. Says Auvermann: "The old tried-and-true really works for things that are important but aren't time-sensitive or limited to one audience."

For notices of power shutdowns, lost wedding rings, and the like, TCO set up a daily "sign-on bulletin board." That is, when e-mail users sign on at the start of each day, the screen shows a list of messages, with labels ranking their urgency. A message marked with INFO, for example, may be an explanation of an operational disruption or a description of a new security procedure. A message labeled QUICK means it is more urgent—say, a notice of bad road conditions—but not of lasting interest. "This way," Auvermann says, "people can quick-scan the notices at the start of the day, use the labels for triage, and get on with the rest of their work."

Removing the "All E-Mail Users" feature from the system took away the easiest message-sending option. Yet it forced TCO's people to think in terms of narrower target audiences. "There's been a real drop in common or junk mail," Auvermann observes. "People can still locate and use what they need. The system is by no means perfect. But we may be closing some of the communications gaps that form when you get too much disorganized information."—**J.S.**

just about any piece of information is important to someone in an organization," says Dave De Long, a research fellow with Ernst & Young's Boston-based Center for Business Innovation, who interviewed subjects at nine major companies for a paper on the topic. "It's a communications concern, because of the number of channels that are available and how many people use them. The recipients of the messages are starting to feel the impact of having 8,000 chefs in the kitchen."

The upshot, adds De Long, is more than an annoyance. "This is not a case of employees whining about hard work. The complaints I've heard come from the recognition that the overload has serious implications for organizational performance." In other words, De Long maintains that the load could evolve into a true productivity crisis—if it has not already gripped American workers by their throats.

Too Much of a Good Thing

At the most senior levels of management, this threat is barely flashing on the executive radar screen. "Senior executives are among the few in corporate America who still have secretaries and assistants who help filter and manage information," notes De Long.

However, since 1987, the number of secretaries employed in the United States has declined by more than a half-million. Replaced by voice-mail systems and computers with e-mail, this has saved costs. But as a result, it's the middle managers and professionals who are forced to handle an inundation of incoming requests, FYI copies of everything imaginable, stuff from shared data bases, and all the information that pours in from trade, profession, and industry sources.

With downsizing, many professionals need these tools to do the work that once required two or more employees.

This is quite wonderful from the current business standpoint. Instant access to all the data a knowledge worker could ever want—and tight links with co-workers, vendors, and customers—is an Information Age dream come true. It's part of why during the 1990s, nonfarm U.S. productivity has increased by 2.2 percent annually, double the rate of the past couple of decades, as measured by the U.S. Bureau of Labor Statistics. In 1996, those investments in information technologies are driving per-worker output to what could be a 3.5 percent gain over 1994.

"This is what's pushing American productivity ahead of the rest of the world," says management guru Robert H. Waterman. "When I visit companies in Europe or Japan, they simply don't have the information-technology systems that are comparable." Indeed, according to the International Data Corp., America has 63 computers for every 100 workers employed, including machines at home and in schools; Japan has but 17 computers for every 100 workers. We are riding the crest of a huge wave.

"The full use of the information highway is one of the things America does right," adds Waterman. "And I've yet to see communication overload hurt productivity at any of the companies I've consulted with. On the other hand, I do worry about the human capacity to absorb such an overwhelming amount of information, especially when several channels are full and flowing at top speed."

This is also true for workers who are already stretched to the thinness of phyllo dough. And as any surfer will attest, when you fall from the crest of a big wave, it has a nasty habit of pounding you straight into the sand.

"I know people who routinely get 50 to 100 e-mails per day, and some receive as many as 500," says De Long. "If you average a minute dealing with each one, the magnitude of the volume is obvious." To avoid a larger backlog of e-mails, voice mails, and the demands for responses, a growing number of workers are now taking defensive postures, leaving their systems full. Still others simply dump the wheat along with the chaff.

"I interviewed the CFO of a large Silicon Valley company who'd just come back from a week's vacation to find 2,000 e-mails in his computer," recalled De Long. "He told me, and kind of sheepishly, that he'd erased all of them. 'If it's important,' he said, 'they'll get back to me.' A CFO can get away with this; a middle manager might end up in big trouble."

Such avoidance behavior is increasingly pervasive. Ever notice how colleagues leave voice mails at times when they know you're not around to answer calls? "It's even easier to hide behind e-mail," says Mendelsohn. "If someone doesn't want to be pulled into a dialogue, during which you might be asked to respond to even more requests, these systems provide protection. Now, I think e-mail is great for sending information to a large number of people. But I prefer the camaraderie and the give-and-take you get from personal interactions."

Superhighway Gridlock

The communications channels are embedded, systemic, and, on the whole, a great industrial plus. But if they continue to evolve without some modification in their use, says De Long, the overload creates a number of ticking organizational time bombs. "There are two broad issues," he explains. "The first is the personal impact on workers. The other is the way it influences the organization's ability to meet its goals and adapt to change."

Workers are using information technology to shift the time and place in which they deal with electronic messages. Increasingly, this is done at home, which no doubt warms the hearts of managers who need to get every second of work possible out of each employee.

Such shifting is just fine with the likes of Catherine Fanning, director of project information management for Johnson & Johnson's Pharmaceutical Research Institute in Raritan, N.J. "I'd be lost on Monday morning," Fanning explains, "if I didn't spend an hour or so on Sunday evening cleaning up my e-mail." But others are taking their responses and dedication to the extreme.

"When I give presentations on this subject," says De Long, "I ask people how many of them find themselves checking on voice mails after 10 p.m. About two-thirds of the hands go up. I worry about people who quickly shuffle young kids off to bed so they can log on to the company system. If it comes down to spending time on the Internet or with your daughter, the right choice ought to be self-evident."

Perhaps. But communications overload is starting to twist some fundamental values.

And from the coldest of business perspectives, well, tough luck, kiddies, Mom and Dad are busy. But the effects of the load also appear at the office.

De Long suggests that key value-added functions, such as sales and marketing, may fail to get a quick response from crucial but overwhelmed support functions. Strategic projects or change initiatives lose momentum or merely get lost in the clutter of communications. Because so many messages appear through so many channels, employees have a difficult time separating what is truly important from what is routine.

Longtime employees, observed De Long, are too busy to share vital knowledge with new hires about processes, customers, and the organization's history. Perhaps worst of all, senior managers who have adapted to the telecommunications environment are often distracted by an onslaught of requests, all of which appear urgent. This leaves little time to contemplate the larger issues that determine the course of their business and its future.

In fact, no one these days seems to get much time for reflection and learning. Workers have little chance to build their knowledge and skill bases—other than learning the nuts and bolts of yet another new communications system. "The tyranny of the urgent really is upon us," says Richard Hillebrecht, Apple Computer Inc.'s director, information systems & technology.

"I came in one Saturday hoping to do some planning-type work," he continues, "and ended up going 0-for-six hours doing nothing but answering leftover e-mail. During the working day, it does seem like the only 'learning time' that people now have is for instruction on yet another communications system."

Hours for deep analytical thought and reflection are indeed limited and perhaps no longer even prized. "In our culture," says Perdue's Mendelsohn, "if you're sitting in your office reading a book or paper memo, people look at you as if you're not working; the phone and computer is work. We've put a value on haste. But there are knowledge-based jobs in which what you learn from reading a book might be the most important thing you do all year."

In organizations that are operating at warp speed, that urgency makes everything, including trivial issues, seem important. While working terribly fast, employees still aren't getting as far as they can or should.

"We deliver about 1.5 million e-mails per day," says Bob Walker, Hewlett-Packard Co.'s vice president and chief information officer, "and most people in this company feel like they're getting all 1.5 million. Folks are constantly telling me, 'Bob, you've got to stop

this.' The odd thing is that we've had a classic e-mail system for 12 years; we're supposed to be sophisticated in this area. And it's not as if people are sending information maliciously. When any employee sends an e-mail to colleagues, he or she is convinced that it's important."

However, HP is not about to stanch the flow of information. "Our longstanding belief is that we empower people by telling them what we want but not how to do it," Walker continues. "With all that autonomy, we've created a whole lot of opportunities for our people to interrupt each other."

A Question of Context

This raises another productivity issue, in that different working groups assign different priorities to various channels. This makes it difficult to spread essential information to all of a company's employees.

For example, an engineering division of a company might well consider e-mail the most important form of communication. Since it's the medium that carries critical items, each member of the group knows that a missive will be checked out and receive a response. But a design group might gravitate to voice mail or printed faxes as its priority channel; with this bunch, e-mails ring no bells. Neither way is right or wrong, but assuming that another group has the same priority as yours risks miscommunication.

"A division president gave his employees a 24-hour notice about a meeting to discuss a major reorganization," relates De Long. "A lot of people didn't see the message and missed the meeting. That started a considerable swell of employee gossip about the motives behind that 'last-minute' e-mail message."

What's more, for major change initiatives and corporatewide strategies, says De Long, senior management must identify and use a channel that all employees understand is priority. "If a major issue gets squeezed into the mass of messages," he explains, "its importance and meaning will be missed."

There are also profound and often-overlooked differences between the various channels. "We simply could not operate as a worldwide enterprise without e-mail," says Johnson & Johnson's Fanning. "With all the time-zone differences, it's the only way we can get things done." And as Mendelsohn of Perdue suggests, folks have become so comfortable with electronic mail that they're using it for nearly all communications.

But the most effective form of communication—the one with the greatest power, richness and value—is direct. Aside from the thoughts expressed in a face-to-face meeting, additional nuance and meaning are conveyed

> As for the CEO, he finally took himself off the e-mail system. "The guy was getting cc'ed with every 'cover your ass' memo written."

through tone, facial expressions, and body language. What's more, the listener has a chance to respond immediately, and a consensus is reached much more quickly than with other channels.

"A phone conversation is next down the list, followed by voice mail and finally e-mails," says De Long, who cites the example of a pharmaceutical research manager who had a problem with a certain formulation. "She needed to find a consensus among the people involved and started to send out an e-mail," he recalls. "But e-mail gets awfully public, and when you don't want leaks or are dealing with a sensitive subject, an e-mail is the last channel you'd want to use."

Yet another aspect of the overload is the inappropriate use of e-mail. Electronic mailboxes have turned into "cc hell," repositories for FYIs and other data put there by individuals mainly to show their colleagues and superiors that they're producing work.

De Long has found that e-mail messages often fail to contain information that lets the recipient figure out its importance. "And senders have this habit of burying action requests deep in lengthy items," he explains. "It then takes readers longer to recognize if they have to respond right away or have some time to act upon the request." And just as constantly ringing phones can make a worker who needs reflective time downright daffy, e-mails can be equally intrusive.

But it's a fact that in some corporate cultures, the number of e-mails one receives each day is the stuff of macho braggadocio. Microsoft employees, for example, have boasted of their e-mail load for years. (Despite repeated telephone requests, Microsoft offered no company officials willing to talk with *ATB* about this.) To help people manage the information glut, the techies at Microsoft have developed an "exchange server," a filtering mechanism that collects and delivers messages from all the various channels; with preprogramming, it can sort out the stuff the recipient

thinks isn't needed. It is, of course, a technical solution to the problem.

"That's crazy, just plain nuts," says Waterman. "Why even try to develop a technological solution to what is, fundamentally, a human behavioral problem?"

Probably because the techies can't help themselves.

A Case for Quiet Time

However, some firms are trying to deal with the overload at the behavioral level, to get employees either to send fewer unnecessary or pointless e-mail memos, or free them—albeit temporarily—from the tyranny of the urgent.

One of the most notable approaches is that of Computer Associates in Icelandia, N.Y. There, chairman and CEO Charles Wang ordered the company's e-mail system to be shut down from either 10 a.m. until noon or 2 p.m. to 4 p.m. "When it first happened, it was like quitting cigarettes," says Marc Sokol, the firm's vice president of advanced technology. "We had 9,000 very edgy employees. But as we got used to it, people found that they had time to think. We now like those periods when we can concentrate on tasks at hand."

As for Wang, he finally took himself off the e-mail system. "The guy was getting cc'ed with every 'cover your ass' memo written," says Sokol. "Now, if you want to meet with the CEO, go to his office or call."

Computer Associates may well write a computer application like Microsoft's Exchange to "take out stupid e-mails," says Sokol, "even though people shouldn't be sending them in the first place."

If enforced quiet time isn't enough, a company can always use financial disincentives. At Philadelphia-based SmithKline Beecham, the pharmaceutical firm's business units are charged fees based on the number and length of the unit's e-mail message. The company's manager for electronic messaging reports that the measure has produced a "dramatic falloff in the total number of messages," especially cc's and FYIs.

Perhaps the best way to tackle this growing problem is at the small work-group or individual level. Apple's Hillebrecht generally limits himself to one hour of e-mail per day. "You've got to take a defensive stance on your working time, because if you allow all the intrusions, you'll never get that time back."

Following the model of Computer Associates, divisions and smaller groups can set aside a couple of hours a day—ignoring e-mails and phones—just to deal with their primary tasks. "In companies where people have tried this," says De Long, "I've heard the same thing over and over. That quiet time is the most productive time of the day."

Hewlett-Packard is trying to package communications better. Explains Walker: "In the past, information was just pushed at people. Now we want to put it in repositories where people know they can find it if it's needed." And in defining the most important messages from senior management, HP makes use of its professional communicators.

"We have a magazine that's published eight times a year, with articles and essays that describe trends and strategies in an analytical way," says Walker. "It's old-fashioned. But what's in the publication are messages with substance. We also have 'Newsgrams' that go out over the e-mail. These are clearly labeled as having companywide significance."

Every organization has a communications channel that carries the most powerful symbolic value. For some companies it may be a worldwide teleconference featuring the CEO; for others, it's the company magazine; for high-tech firms, it might well be e-mail. "But senior managers had better know which channel is most effective," says De Long, "and they should use it wisely."

The democratization of corporate communications is an irreversible trend. The wealth of sharing information is, on the whole, a benefit to productivity. And fresh information will keep a business from smelling like week-old chicken—just so long as workers aren't suffocated in a pile of feathers.

JAY STULLER, who lives in San Francisco, is a frequent contributor to ATB. His book How to Love a PMSing Woman: When Timing Is Everything *is published by Bridgeline.*

LEAD, DON'T MANAGE

*Peter Neff is creating value for customers by tapping into the
creativity and innovation of Rhone-Poulenc employees*

Michael A. Verespej

A MORNING WITH PETER NEFF—
even on a wintry day in New Jersey when he is fighting a cold—is
like taking a short course on what is
needed to run a 21st-century organization. Neff doesn't miss a beat as he details in rapid-fire succession what
Rhone-Poulenc Inc.—the $2.4 billion U.S.
subsidiary of France's leading chemical
and pharmaceutical manufacturer (Rhone-Poulenc S.A.)—must do to compete in an
ever-changing global world.

Understand what the customer wants.
Create a culture that fosters innovation
and creativity. Push decision-making
down closer to the customer. Break down
hierarchy and walls. Lead people; don't
manage them. Form teams. Develop values that everyone can embrace. Provide
an environment for continuous learning.

An overwhelming list? Maybe. But to
Neff, there's a common thread in each
of those approaches that makes their implementation easier. Simply put, they all
move power from top management into
the hands of Rhone-Poulenc employees.

"Our success depends on people,"
says Neff, the 57-year-old CEO of
Rhone-Poulenc who has also been its
president since 1987. "We have to focus
our people on what we are about. We
have to help our people understand that
the products we are making sustain our
business long term. We have to enable
our people to do the best they know how
to do. we have to find a way to help our
people make a contribution.

"Our success in the future will depend
on our ability to tap the collective wisdom—that is, the accumulated judgments,
perceptions, experiences, intuition, and
intelligence—of all our employees."

Yet that isn't the approach that Neff
or Rhone-Poulenc has always used. Even
though the Princeton, N.J., manufacturer
of basic chemicals and crop-protection
products had always emphasized innovation and creativity among its 7,000
employees, not much more than three
years ago it was still practicing old-fashioned top-down management.

"No single management style works
for everything," explains Neff. "Management style needs to be different for different situations." And he argues that the
now-abandoned top-down approach had
worked—and had been needed—as
Rhone-Poulenc made 18 acquisitions
between 1986 and 1990. Those deals
catapulted the company from $700 million (3% of its parent's revenues) to
more than $2 billion (15%). "We had to
integrate businesses. We had to do it
quickly. We had to convince people that
it was a good place to work, and we had
to streamline the organization."

But when that integration work was
completed and Rhone-Poulenc asked its
customers how it was doing, Neff was
dismayed to find that customers had a
far different picture of Rhone-Poulenc
"than the self-portrait we had of ourself.
Our customers said that our products
were very good, but that doing business
with us was pretty bad," says Neff.

Among the complaints: Customers
said there were "too many numbers to
call and too many people to deal with"
just to conduct routine business. But as
Neff recalls, the most disturbing comment was that Rhone-Poulenc management did not seem to "hear or respond"
to such complaints.

"That made us realize that we had to
focus on doing what is important to our
external customers—the ones who pay
the bills—not the internal customers,
who only add to costs," says Neff.

He immediately began to refocus
Rhone-Poulenc around the customer. He
split its three divisions in North America
into 19 separate enterprises—each with
its own general manager—that can focus
on "what drives value to their customers."
Each unit also surveys customers on
product quality, service quality, and invoice errors.

U NDER NEFF'S DIRECTION, RHONE-
Poulenc has also torn down walls
between functions, and put workers into teams. "You have to break down
the boundaries between different parts
of the organization. A lot of narrow silos
will kill an organization." Besides, argues
Neff, companies that can't solve problems as teams won't last very long.
Things are simply too complex to be done
by specialists. You need to have people
who know different parts of an issue get
together to solve problems as a team."

He also pushed to streamline processes and to eliminate nonessential
work. For example, he reorganized customer service so that a customer, in one
phone call, can now place a routine order in less than one minute—as opposed to four days—no matter how
many units the customer orders from.

"Our conversations with our customers convinced us that big global structures with steep hierarchies just aren't
suitable" for a rapidly changing climate,
says Neff. "The management style in a bureaucracy is its own worst enemy. It inhibits people from doing their jobs and stifles"
ideas that give customers what they want.

That's why he made the shift to 19
business units. "We realized that a lot of
our success in the future would depend
on decisions made on the spot by employees who are close to the customer.
They are the only ones who can make
the best decisions to satisfy customers.
And, to do that, they have to feel that
they are involved in the business."

The shift to a people-oriented culture
has also helped Rhone-Poulenc understand that "human creativity and innovation" aren't just the ideas that lead to
breakthrough products. Certainly, Rhone-Poulenc has had those kinds of innovations. Two recent examples: AvGard
chemical treatment for chicken that prevents salmonella bacteria from spreading to people; and its reconfiguration of
agricultural pesticides into a gel form that
can be packaged in water-soluble bags.

But the new management style helped
reinforce that "innovation and creativity are
not just confined to the research-and-development laboratories and the people in
the white coats," says Neff. "They are the
ideas, big and small,that people anywhere
in the organization have about what they
are doing and how they can do it better.

Reprinted with permission from *IW/Industry Week*, March 4, 1996, pp. 55-56, 58, 60. © 1996 by Penton Publishing, Inc.,
Cleveland.

"Innovation can mean working across corporate or geographical boundaries, having the courage to reject conventional wisdom, or simply treating people as partners rather than adversaries. Only by creating a culture that will involve and empower individuals and foster innovation will we become a better global competitor."

Shifting from a top-down approach has done more than just change the way people at Rhone-Poulenc's 56 facilities in the U.S. do their jobs. It also has changed the way Neff and the Rhone-Poulenc executive team have had to approach each other and their roles.

To force people at the top to change the nature of their relationships with each other and the workforce, Neff renamed the executive committee the leadership team and made each leadership-team member the coach or sponsor for two or three of the small business units. "We are a team of equals," says Neff. "We set our individual objectives together and guide the organization as a team, rather than through the old hierarchy of president, vice presidents, managers, and supervisors. We make team decisions."

For example, during strategic-review meetings, Neff makes sure his demeanor is that of a peer, not that of a domineering CEO. "If I see a flaw, I ask them whether they have thought of X," says Neff. "And I make sure I couch my pleasure with an good idea, so that everyone doesn't rush pell-mell to embrace it just because I am the CEO. Our meetings are open. There is not a lot of intimidation."

In addition, says Neff, he and the leadership team are now "less concerned with the day-to-day management" and more focused on "helping to create an innovative environment." Instead of making decisions, he says, "Our leadership team has become much more focused down into the organization.

"I don't look over people's shoulders anymore. Instead I scan the horizon to identify the challenges and opportunities that await us. My role now is to enable people to do the best they know how to do. I need to be an opportunity seeker, coach, facilitator, motivator, and mentor—not a problem-solver or controller. As a leader, I have to show people the consequences of staying where we are and get people to believe that I am leading them to a better place, one that will allow them to use all of their skills. It is my job to find a way for them to do that."

That's a sharp contrast to the traditional hierarchical management view that "people are naturally lazy," says Neff. "A leader has to feel that people are not lazy—that they want to make a contribution."

To underscore that need to lead rather than manage people, and to have

the people who are close to the customers make day-to-day decisions, peers and subordinates rate each leader at Rhone-Poulenc on whether he or she:

- Uses positive reinforcement.
- Asks people what questions, problems, and concerns they have and how he or she can help them.
- Asks people for input prior to decision-making.
- Provides information and feedback in a timely manner.
- Overmanages or undermanages.
- Treats people with respect.

"We need leaders—not managers—who have a vision of a better place and the ability to communicate that vision and motivate their workers to seek it," says Neff. "You cannot manage tightly or direct people into narrow areas. That stifles innovation" and discourages people from making or suggesting changes that will improve the organization or serve the customer.

H OW DOES NEFF LEAD INSTEAD OF manage? "It's a combination of things," says the Rhone-Poulenc CEO. "I have to lead by example, by working as hard as anyone else. I also have to be out with people, listening to them and understanding their problems and decisions. As a leader I have to set the expectations for the company, energize people around goals, and give the people the assurance that the company is behind them. I have to stress to them that the organization's success relies on their ideas. I have to say it, talk about it a lot, and jawbone it, if you will."

Neff—who is retiring at yearend—says a leader must reinforce that talk with action. "You have to have a lot of discussions with people so that they understand you treat them as equals." He has a column in the company newsletter, is a strong believer in face-to-face communications, and regularly visits the company's plants to meet with employees.

On plant visits he will ask employees how he can help them do their jobs. He will listen to people's concerns about job security, organizational barriers, and problems in their work area.

"The specific answers I give them are not as important as whether I am listening to them, trying to understand what troubles them, and whether I am being open to their ideas," says Neff. "People have to be able to be in the same room with the CEO and say what's on their mind and express their views without fear of retribution."

But, at the same time, cautions Neff, you can't just empower people without giving them direction. That's why he has made the five basic values at Rhone-

Poulenc—integrity, safety, innovation, partnership, and quality/customer focus—the central focal point.

"Those values are the social cement that makes change possible," says Neff. "Commitment to these values provides stability in a sea of change and gives our employees confidence that they will be treated fairly no matter what happens."

Besides, with 56 facilities, that's a far better approach than the same rules for everybody. "In a company like ours, you can't get too specific about how things will be done or have the same rules apply to everyone," says Neff. "You get buy-in and marry the different cultures through values and core objectives."

Neff is also keenly aware that ever-changing customer demands require that everyone at Rhone-Poulenc "continuously learn how to do new things" just to retain the business of its current customers. "If you're not continuously improving or continuously innovating, you can't stay competitive," says Neff. "If we stop learning, we stop growing."

That need to learn also applies to leaders, says Neff. "As leaders, we have to accept that part of our job is to lead the way in learning. We have to be open to new ideas, participate in teams, and lead teams that seek to improve the way we've done things in the past."

While the need to learn and build skills "is the responsibility of each employee," says Neff, a company must provide "appropriate training and educational programs." With that in mind he set up a resource center at corporate headquarters 15 months ago that offers training courses and helps employees assess their strengths and learn where they need to develop skills. "We evaluate the requirements of jobs, the skills people have, and the gap we need to close."

The need for continuous learning and training, says Neff, is a direct result of the need to innovate to be competitive.

"No organization can innovate without good people—people who feel challenged by change and motivated by their managers," says Neff. And, for innovation to bloom, "You need an atmosphere of openness and respect, you need to let people make mistakes, and you need to reward risk-taking." Rhone-Poulenc, for example, has a spot bonus program for employees who display creativity or innovation; creates increased organizational status for employees who are creative; and each year recognizes one or more of its employee teams for innovativeness.

"Innovation is the No. 1 priority," says Neff. "And creativity and innovation are the only lasting ways an organization can create value. We need to learn to encourage people to drive value to the customers, whether it's at the local or global level."

BILL GATES & PAUL ALLEN TALK

Check out the ultimate buddy act in business history: The multi-billionaire co-founders of Microsoft sit still for an entire afternoon to tell FORTUNE's Brent Schlender their story and speculate about the future of personal computing and telecommunications.

They're just a couple of slightly geeky middle-aged guys sitting on a patio overlooking Seattle's Lake Washington on a balmy Sunday afternoon. Jet skis and speedboats drone like cicadas as the old pals reminisce, chuckling over escapades from their adolescence. The skinny one, who at 39 is starting to look a lot like Notre Dame football coach Lou Holtz, tells what it was like to incorporate their first company while still students at a prestigious Seattle private school. The burly bearded one, who is the son of librarians and has a demeanor to match, marvels at how much pizza they ate. They may have been teenage computer prodigies, but flamboyant and rebellious they were not.

They're so nonchalant as they sip their Cokes that it's hard to believe, even though you know exactly who they are—that this pair had the will and drive to create more wealth than any business partners in the history of American capitalism, or that they are, today, the undisputed masters of the digital universe.

But then, this isn't the way Microsoft founders Bill Gates and Paul Allen usually spend their Sunday afternoons. More likely, Gates would be hunched in front of a screen, scrutinizing the latest computer code from one of Microsoft's dozens of development teams, laboring to finish another chapter of his book, The Road Ahead (1995, Viking), or making notes for a public appearance somewhere in the world to promote personal com-

puting, Windows-style. (Besides, Gates' idea of relaxation is to race his wife, fellow Microsoftie Melinda French, at identical jigsaw puzzles.)

Allen, 42, who left the hurly-burly of Microsoft in 1983 after an illness, is a little more laid back. But not much: He juggles investments in more than two dozen high-tech companies and runs a pro basketball team and four charitable foundations. If he had a couple of free hours, he might crank up his Stratocaster to jam with his rock band, The Threads, in his recording studio in downtown Seattle.

It was for a special reason that the buddy billionaires—at last count, Gates' 25% stake in Microsoft was worth $13.4 billion and Allen's 9.6% was worth $5.3 billion—invited FORTUNE to sit in on a three-hour chat. This October, Microsoft will celebrate the 20th anniversary of its founding, and the world's most notorious college dropouts wanted to mark the occasion with a wide-ranging bull session.

The meeting at Paul Allen's rambling estate was a one-of-a-kind encounter between fellows so fixated on the future that they'd really rather not look in the rear-view mirror, even for a minute. Once they got rolling, they described both the inside history of a company that has become an American entrepreneurial icon, and the symbiotic relationship of two brilliant friends with similar professional interests and dramatically different personalities, whose diverging paths are already the stuff of business legend.

GETTING TO KNOW YOU

GATES: Our friendship started after the mothers' club paid to put a computer terminal in the school in 1968. The notion was that, of course, the teachers would figure out this computer thing and then teach it to the students. But that didn't happen. It was the other way around. There was a group of students who kind of went nuts.

ALLEN: The teletype room was full of rolled-up paper-tape programs and manuals and everything else. Between classes, or whenever any of us hard-core computer types had a spare period, we would congregate there.

GATES: It was easy to spend a lot of money on computer time. One of the

REPORTER ASSOCIATE *Henry Goldblatt*

smarter teachers accidentally created an infinite loop and spent something like $60 in one shot. He was so shocked that he didn't want to go near the thing after that. We ran through the mothers' club money pretty fast.

ALLEN: When that happened, the computer service would bill the school, and then the school would charge us or our parents. It wasn't always easy to tell your parents how much you had racked up, so we paid it ourselves when we could.

GATES: At the end of the year, Paul massively overdrew his checking account. On graduation day he was with his mother, and the school officials came up and said before he could get his diploma they would have to pay $200 for all this excess computer time. One year a student's mother arranged for us to go downtown to a new, commercial computer center. We didn't have to pay for

the time as long as we could find bugs in their system and report them. They brought us in like monkeys, but it was a godsend.

ALLEN: At the end of every school day, a bunch of us would take our little leather satchel briefcases and ride the bus downtown to the computer center. Bill and I were the guys that stayed the latest, and afterward we'd go eat pizza at this hippie place across the street.

GATES: Some of the professional programmers who worked at the center hated us and would shut us out. But there were guys who actually liked us. One was this super-nice guy who would give us the manuals. Another guy was kind of quiet, but if we bugged him, he would answer questions. Paul and I always wanted to understand machine code [the fundamental level of programming on a machine]. We were confused about the difference between various operations.

ALLEN: That's because they'd parcel out the manuals and only give us one at a time. It was like a game with them. They'd give us the manual for the assembler and not the manual for the operating system or the manual for the instruction set. Then they'd wait to see how long it took us to figure out that we only had part of the picture. And then we'd come back and ask for the next manual.

GATES: Paul and I got bonded together trying to figure out that machine.

ALLEN: The computer center was having financial problems, though. It's where we first learned about bankruptcy. Bill and I were working on our programs one day when somebody came to repossess the furniture. They took the chairs out from underneath us.

GATES: Yeah, and we were still typing away, trying to save our programs on these little tapes before all the lights were turned off.

BUSINESS BASICS
. . . .

GATES: The event that started everything for us business-wise was when Paul found an article in 1971 in an electronics magazine, on page 73 or something, about Intel's 4004 chip, which was the world's first microprocessor. Paul comes up and says, "Whoa," and explains that this microprocessor thing's only going to get better and better. Sure enough, a year later Intel came out with the 8008 and it was lots better.

ALLEN: That's when it hit us how Moore's Law really worked—that each generation of microprocessor chip was basically twice as fast as the previous one and that they got cheaper too. So Bill and I went out and bought our own 8008 for 360 bucks. The chip was all wrapped up in aluminum foil, and we were almost afraid to touch it.

GATES: We thought we could use the 8008 as the heart of a special computer to do traffic-volume-count analysis. We were going to make the machines and sell them to traffic departments. So we set up our first company, which we called Traf-O-Data.

ALLEN: Even though Traf-O-Data wasn't a roaring success, it was seminal in preparing us to make Microsoft's first product a couple of years later. We taught ourselves to simulate how microprocessors work using DEC computers, so we could develop software even before our machine was built.

We were always interested in business. We'd go over to Bill's house and read FORTUNE and other business magazines his parents got. Bill would say, "Gee, what does it mean to be No. 1 in the FORTUNE 500? Can you imagine what a company that size does? What do all those statistics really mean?"

We talked about being entrepreneurs. Obviously it was on a smaller scale because we were kids. Microprocessors were instantly attractive to us because you could build something for a fraction of the cost of conventional electronics. That's essentially what we did with the Traf-O-Data computer—only it was too narrow and challenging an area to try to build a service business in.

GATES: I remember, from the very beginning, we wondered, "What would it mean for DEC once microcomputers were powerful and cheap enough? What would it mean for IBM?" To us it seemed that they were screwed. We thought maybe they'd even be screwed tomorrow. We were saying, "God, how come these guys aren't stunned? How come they're not just amazed and scared?" By the time we got to Albuquerque to start Microsoft in 1975, the notion was fairly clear to us that computers were going to be a big, big personal tool.

ALLEN: I remember having pizza at Shakey's in Vancouver, Washington, in 1973, and talking about the fact that eventually everyone is going to be online and have access to newspapers and stuff and wouldn't people be willing to pay for information on a computer terminal.

GATES: Yeah, we were also fascinated by dedicated word processors from Wang, because we believed that general-purpose machines could do that just as well. That's why, when it came time to design the keyboard for the IBM PC, we put the funny Wang character set into the machine—you know, smiley faces and boxes and triangles and stuff. We were thinking we'd like to do a clone of Wang word-processing software someday. Most personal computers back then didn't even have upper- and lower-case characters.

BOOT UP AND DROP OUT
. . . .

■ *In summer 1973 the friends landed their first real jobs, helping TRW in Vancouver, Washington, use minicomputers to manage and distribute power from hydroelectric dams. Allen, who was getting bored at Washington State University, wanted to drop everything and start a company, but Gates' parents pushed Bill, who had just graduated from high school, to enroll at Harvard.*

A year later Gates persuaded Allen to move to the Boston area to take a programming job with Honeywell. That winter Allen ran across a magazine article that would change their lives and, ultimately, just about everybody else's: a cover story in Popular Electronics *describing the MITS Altair 8800, "World's First Minicomputer Kit to Rival Commercial Models."*

Within weeks Gates and Allen convinced each other this was their big chance. The Altair was practically useless to hobbyists without an easy programming language. In designing the Traf-O-Data machine, the two had written a version of BASIC—a popular and compact language that, with a few tweaks, might work on the Altair. In weeks they cobbled together a version for the MITS machine, finishing it up on the plane, and by April had persuaded MITS to sell it. MITS offered Allen a job and provided the two with office space in its ramshackle headquarters in an Albuquerque strip mall. Soon after, Microsoft was born.

GATES: When we signed that first contract with MITS, we referred to ourselves as "Paul Allen and Bill Gates doing business as Micro-Soft." I don't remember why we spelled it with a hyphen and a capital "S." We put a credit line in the source code of our first product that said, "Micro-Soft BASIC: Bill Gates wrote a lot of stuff; Paul Allen wrote some other stuff." We never officially incorporated until 1981.

ALLEN: We had talked about a lot of different names back in Boston, and at some point I said, "Well, the totally obvious name would be Microsoft."

GATES: We also had mentioned names like Outcorporated Inc. and Unlimited Ltd., but we were, you know, joking around. We talked a lot about whether we should call it Allen & Gates, but decided that was not a good idea.

ALLEN: Yeah. Because companies like DEC and IBM weren't named after personalities, they would have a longevity and identity way beyond the founders …

GATES: … and it seemed like a law firm or like a consulting company to call it Allen & Gates. So we picked Microsoft even before we had a company to name.

ALLEN: The building where we first worked in Albuquerque was pretty low rent.

GATES: Next door was a vacuum-cleaner place, then a massage parlor. To get to our offices, you had to walk past the vacuum-cleaner guy. We stayed in this motel down the road called the Sand and Sage. We're talking real sage, not some hypothetical thing. Every morning all the cars in the parking lot had all this sagebrush and tumbleweed that blew underneath them.

ALLEN: Our management style was a little loose in the beginning. We both took part in every decision, and it's hard to remember who did what. If there was a difference between our roles, I was probably the one always pushing a little bit in terms of new tech-

> *"Life was working and maybe going to a movie and then working some more. Customers would come in, and we'd fall asleep in front of them."*

•••

nology and new products, and Bill was more interested in doing negotiations and contracts and business deals.

GATES: We learned a lot of things as we went: Okay, we have to hire people; so what do we do? Okay, we're going to rent space; how do we do that? Okay, we're going to do contracts with people now; I'd get advice from my dad [a prominent Seattle attorney].

Paul and I would talk through every decision, for six or eight hours sometimes. We didn't have many major disagreements, but there was one tiny source of tension: I would always be calling Paul in the morning to tell him it was time to come work on this stuff. He slept even later than me.

ALLEN: We used to work really late into the night. You used to sleep under your desk.

GATES: Yeah, life for us was working and maybe going to a movie and then working some more. Sometimes customers would come in, and we were so tired we'd fall asleep in front of them. Or at an internal meeting I'd lie down on the floor, because I like to do that to brainstorm. And then I'd just fall asleep.

OVERCOMMITMENTS 'R' US
•••••••••••••••••••••••••••••••••

GATES: Our basic business strategy was to charge a price so low that microcomputer makers couldn't do the software internally for that cheap. One of the bigger early contracts was Texas Instruments, where we bid $99,000 to provide programming languages for a home computer they were planning. We picked that price because we were too shy to make a bid in the six figures. Afterward we realized they would have paid a lot more, and we thought, "I guess this is what the big shots do: They bid big numbers."

ALLEN: We would almost always overestimate our competitors' ability to compete.

GATES: Or we'd assume that they were going to execute competently.

ALLEN: There were so many times when I'd find an article about a competing product and we'd get depressed for three days. Then we'd find out it wasn't as good as ours …

GATES: … or didn't even exist. We were in such a flaky business. Our biggest problem

was that we talked about so many different ideas, but we never really added up all the people we'd need. When we started selling to Japanese companies, we were so overpromised it was ridiculous. Ricoh licensed every language we had and paid us $180,000 up-front, which was incredible. And then they came back a few months later and said, "Okay, we have another budget this year, so we'd like to buy some more." Well, we'd already sold them everything we had. So we asked, "What can we develop for you?" We agreed to do our first database, a word processor, and a couple of other things. Then we had to figure out how we were going to deliver them, and had to go buy some of them from somebody else.

ALLEN: We were so late that Ricoh finally flew a guy over whose whole job was to sit in our office day and night until we delivered. He couldn't help out at all; he was just there to sit and explain to us that his career was going to be over if we didn't get this work done soon. I don't know if that was really true or not …

GATES: It could get scary. In our very first contract with MITS, we set them up to sell our BASIC to their customers, rather than us selling to computer buyers directly. We thought it was a good deal because they agreed to make "best efforts" to sell it. But later they decided not to sell to anybody at all because there were so many illegal, free copies of our BASIC floating around, so why try to charge people for it? That really made us mad because we thought it encouraged piracy. We eventually went into arbitration to determine if they were in compliance with the contract. In the meantime we were totally out of money …

ALLEN: … because MITS was withholding payments from us while the arbitration was going on.

GATES: They were trying to starve us to death. We couldn't even pay our lawyer. They tried to get us to settle, and we almost did, it

was that bad. The arbitrator took nine months to issue his damn opinion. But when it was all over, the arbitrator ripped them apart for what they had done.

ALLEN: That case really, really scared us. If we had lost, we would have had to start over. Bill would call up his dad for advice. We were on pins and needles the whole time.

GATES: But, you know, through it all, we never borrowed money. I always felt like if we had to, we could have. But we never did.

THE DEAL OF THE DECADE
•••••••••••••••••••••••••••••••••

■ *By the end of 1978, a wave of impressive personal computers, including Apple Computer's landmark Apple II, had left MITS in the dust. There was no longer any reason for Microsoft—now a dozen employees strong—to hang around Albuquerque. On January 1, 1979, Gates and Allen transplanted the business to the lush and soggy Seattle suburb of Bellevue, where it took root. Within a year the head count had swelled to more than 35 people, and Gates and Allen hired their first professional manager—Gates' old Harvard buddy, a Procter & Gamble marketing man named Steve Ballmer. (They lured Ballmer with a stake in Microsoft. He now owns 5%, worth $2.7 billion.)*

Ballmer's arrival marked a turning point. "We knew we had to systematize things," Gates recalls. "Once we had more than 30 people, it was impossible for Paul and me to review or be involved with every line of code we produced." To this day, based on that early insight, Microsoft often limits work teams to 35 people.

But 1980 will be remembered for another series of events. It was the year IBM came to call, looking for programming languages for its secret PC project; also the year Paul Allen negotiated the purchase of an obscure operating system called Q-DOS from a nearby company, Seattle Computer. In a transaction that could well be called the deal of the decade, Gates and Allen would turn around and license Q-DOS to IBM, thus opening the way for Microsoft's domination of the PC software industry.

GATES: When IBM came to us in 1980, we thought they were just talking about buying our BASIC for their new PC project. The two guys who came said, "We're just the planning guys, and most of the things we plan don't get done, so don't get too excited." But then we had this really cool discussion about where the technology was going, and

•••

> *"We were so late that Ricoh finally flew a guy over whose whole job was to sit in our office day and night until we delivered."*

> *"Paul got better, and we wanted him back more than anything. But there was just no part-time way to come back to Microsoft."*

· ·

how personal computers were about to make a great leap forward. Then they said they'd also like to buy our FORTRAN and COBOL languages, and maybe even more from us.

ALLEN: It was like they were bringing up a menu and checking off "all of the above."

GATES: So we had this meeting between Paul, Steve Ballmer, me, and Kay Nishi, our partner in Japan. It seemed just like Ricoh all over again. We had told IBM, "Okay, you can have everything we make," even though we hadn't even made it yet. This was one of those marathon meetings.

The question was: Should we also commit to doing an operating system for IBM? It was unusual because I was the one being a tiny bit conservative. Nishi was actually the one saying, "Got to do it, got to do it."

ALLEN: Nishi was egging us on because he knew I had been dealing with Seattle Computer and that I thought we could probably make their Q-DOS work for IBM.

GATES: We also knew Digital Research [maker of CP/M, the then-dominant operating system for personal computers] wasn't taking IBM seriously enough. So we decided, Why not? It got kind of tense, because there was about a 48-hour period after Ballmer and I had officially offered to license Q-DOS to IBM that we didn't really own it. Paul hadn't yet closed the deal with Seattle Computer, and I was really giving him a really hard time.

ALLEN: We were afraid they were going to find out the reason we wanted to buy it was because IBM was our primary customer. If they found that out, the price for Q-DOS would go way up. [Microsoft succeeded in buying the software for only $50,000.]

GATES: See, the contract with IBM called for us to do all this work on the design of the machine and all this software. We didn't get paid that much—the total was something like $186,000—but we knew there were going to be clones of the IBM PC. We structured that original contract to allow them. It was a key point in our negotiations.

ALLEN: We already had seen the clone phenomenon in the MITS Altair days. Other companies made machines that succeeded because they were very similar to the Altair. For us it had been easy to modify our software so it worked on those machines too.

GATES: It seemed like a really great opportunity. IBM was talking about having Sears and ComputerLand sell their machines. They'd been talking with Intel about getting a really good price on the microprocessor. IBM was so hard core about it, we knew their PC might even …

ALLEN: … leapfrog the Apple II, which was the coolest computer at the time.

GATES: We worked day and night with this IBM machine in a back room. There were a lot of ups and downs. The one tiff Paul and I had was when he wanted to go see a space shuttle launch and I didn't, because we were late. Still, these guys went to the launch and I was just …

ALLEN: It was the first one, Bill. And we flew back the same day. We weren't gone even 36 hours.

GATES: Anyway, by the end, Paul and I decided every stupid little thing about the PC: the keyboard layout, how the cassette port worked, how the sound port worked, how the graphics port worked. Between us and a few IBM engineers, we did all that stuff. We felt very intimately involved.

The weirdest thing of all, though, was when we asked to come to the big official launch of the PC in New York, IBM denied us. About four days later we got this form letter that IBM probably sent to every vendor, even the guy who had the capacitors in the machine. It said something like "Dear vendor, thank you for your help, blah, blah, blah." They eventually apologized to us for that.

ALLEN'S ORDEAL
· ·

▓ *It's hard to believe now, but the acceptance of Microsoft's DOS as the operating system for the IBM PC wasn't a foregone conclusion when the machine was introduced in 1981. IBM also offered a version of the CP/M oper-*

ating system. Produced by Digital Research of Monterey, California, CP/M had the advantage of being established on other brands of personal computer. Or was that an advantage?

Initially, since IBM was Microsoft's only operating system customer, Gates and Allen went all-out to make DOS the operating system of choice, urging other software companies to write applications for DOS first and otherwise promoting and cajoling. Within a year the battle was over, DOS ruled the U.S. market for the IBM PC, and the first of what would become a tsunami of PC clones were trickling into the marketplace.

Gates and Allen turned their attention to the nascent PC market in Europe, hoping to repeat the feat. Then the unthinkable happened.

ALLEN: We were on a trip promoting some Microsoft products in Europe in 1982, and I had this little bump on my neck. I'd had little bumps before that weren't anything. But I kept feeling stranger and stranger. Then one day in Paris, I just felt really bad and decided I had to go back to the States.

The doctor here in Seattle put me in the hospital that night. At first they told me that it looked like I had lymphoma—an often incurable cancer—and they were really glum. But after the biopsy the doctors came in smiling and said, "You've got Hodgkin's disease and you're going to be fine," which was a little hard to believe, since they also said I was going to need about 2½ months of radiation therapy.

During my treatment I tried to continue working at Microsoft. Not full-time, but I'd drop in at meetings and so forth. It was hard because cancer therapy takes a lot out of you. But it was more than that. To be 30 years old and have that kind of shock—to face your mortality—really makes you feel like you should do some of the things that you haven't done. With Hodgkin's disease or any cancer like it, there's basically a two-year window: If you can pass that period without a relapse, then it's probably not going to come back.

GATES: It was terrible when Paul got sick. Nobody talked about work or anything; it was just a matter of wondering, Was Paul going to be okay? We had always worked so closely together—I mean, you know, planned stuff together, strategized together. That's why it's always hard when people ask who did what. So it was a real change for me and a huge disappointment that Paul wasn't there. It was really sad to go by his office, because all the memos and magazines would be stacked in there.

· ·

> *"The doctors said, 'You're going to be fine,' which was a little hard to believe since they also said I'd need 2½ months of radiation therapy."*

ALLEN: I took that time to step away from Microsoft and be closer to my family, and do some traveling and other things I'd always wanted to do. After that two-year period, well, I just didn't want to go back to work. I went to Bill and said, "I want to just do something different." I know Bill wished I hadn't decided that.

GATES: It was great that Paul got better, and we wanted him back more than anything. But there was just no part-time way to come back to Microsoft. If you were going to be there, you were really going to work hard. We all knew that. It's still that way.

ALLEN: After that experience I was just in a different place.

WHAT'S NEXT?

■ "Get a life." That's the derisive expression often hurled at computer jocks and other obsessive workers. It's also a pretty good summation of what Paul Allen has tried to do since recovering from Hodgkin's disease—even as his old pal continues to eat, drink, and sleep Microsoft.

Having a $6 billion nest egg helps. Such unimaginable wealth may not buy happiness, but it has allowed Allen to amass collections of authentic Roman statuary and oil paintings by French impressionist masters; to build a massive estate on the shore of Seattle's Lake Washington complete with three houses, a full-size gym, an indoor pool and waterslide, and more garages than most people have kitchen cabinets.

He owns the NBA's Portland Trail Blazers and is building them a $262 million sports and entertainment complex called the Rose Quarter. He owns a jet, so he can take friends to a game and have them back in Seattle by bedtime.

He's a good guy too. His charities have dispensed $6 million so far this year to support libraries, hospitals, AIDS programs, prostate cancer research, and cultural programs including the Oregon Shakespeare Festival. An avid guitarist, he is the main benefactor of the Experience Music Project, a planned museum dedicated to the late Seattle rock great Jimi Hendrix and other Pacific Northwest musicians.

Then there's business. Allen was an early investor in America Online. He owns 80% of TicketMaster, the national computerized ticketing service; 6% of an animal-supply retailer called Petsmart; a piece of a children's educational-products retail chain called Zany Brainy. With Gates he has invested in Darwin Molecular, a genetics research startup.

"The Internet is exciting to me as an investor because the barrier to entry is very low. Anybody can put a product out."

"We said back then, 'Don't DEC and IBM know they're in deep trouble?' Here we are, staring at the same kind of situation."

Not surprisingly, though, the bulk of Allen's investments involve software. He has positions in nearly 20 high-tech companies engaged in multimedia CD-ROMs and software tools, satellite broadcasting, online financial and sports-data services, TV programming, wireless paging and telephony, and electronic commerce. This year he doled out $500 million for an 18% stake in Hollywood's newest studio, DreamWorks.

And, of course, Allen remains a director of Microsoft. Although he claims not to pay much attention to day-to-day affairs, you can tell his buddy Bill still listens when Allen talks about what lies over the technological horizon and the strategies behind his investments.

ALLEN: For years now, I've been interested in the information superhighway or whatever you want to call it. The approach I've chosen is to start companies or make strategic investments in companies I think are positioned to take advantage of that huge opportunity. I try to add value as an investor by building synergy between those companies.

Some have no immediate commercial potential, but others are solid businesses in conventional markets: TicketMaster is a consumer service business that sold 55 million tickets last year, and there are ways to broaden the service and deliver it on the Internet. Bill and I are investors in biotechnology too, and I have other investments for fun like Petsmart and the sports team stuff. But most of them are software related. The incredible thing about the software business is, you can create something compelling and exciting out of thin air.

GATES: Paul has gone his own way, but we still see this stuff the same way, and we debate about it and share ideas quite a bit. The thing that's totally amazing is that looking at the next 20 years, we both believe there's actually more opportunity to have a broad impact than in the past 20 years.

ALLEN: Our industry is still driven by incredible improvements in semiconductor technology that now are removing constraints on communications. You have the very real prospect of continuous high-bandwidth, two-way digital communications to people's homes and places of business coming in five years. God, what can you do with that? A lot of the constraints on our imaginations have gone away. It's like, wow, there's this fertile field; what kind of seeds am I going to plant? What are they going to grow into?

GATES: The Internet is the seed corn of a lot of things that are going to happen, and there are so many parallels to when Paul and I were involved in the beginnings of the PC. We said back then, "Don't DEC and IBM know they're in deep trouble?" Here we are, staring at the same kind of situation.

In the computer industry, there's never been a company that's led the way in two successive eras. So really, what Microsoft as a company, or Paul and I as individuals, are trying to do is to defy history and actually take our leadership from the PC era into this new communications era. The odds are against us, and that's what makes it so much fun and so challenging.

ALLEN: The Internet is exciting to me as an investor because the barrier to entry is very low. Anybody can put a product out, so success depends more than anything on the quality of the product.

GATES: For Microsoft, the Internet is an incredible new platform. Just like cheap microprocessors, cheap communications drives the demand for more great software.

How do we keep up with it all? You have to remember it's all relative—you don't really, in an absolute sense, have to keep up with all the new technologies; you just have to keep up with them better than everybody else.

Some of Paul's companies are classic startups that are getting in very early and are focused on specific content areas. Eventually you won't think of "the Internet business." You'll think of it more like news, weather, sports, but even that taxonomy isn't clear.

ALLEN: When you take sports or music and start adding video and audio to a computer database service on the Internet, and you deliver it with enough bandwidth, and make it interactive, what's the difference between that and an interactive television channel?

GATES: None.

ALLEN: All these things are being served up on the Internet and will be, in effect, a click away.

HAVE YOU EVER BEEN EXPERIENCED?
• •

■ *So much for reminiscing; so much for looking forward. What was it, after all? To what quality, trait, or circumstance do these young billionaires—already historical figures—attribute their success? Was it greed, brains, obsession, paranoia, luck? Are Gates and Allen humbled by the enormousness of their success? Do they ever pause to gloat about the revolution they helped incite?*

GATES: There's one thing I have to ask if you remember, Paul. Back in Vancouver, you once said that if you made a million dollars someday, that maybe that would be enough money for anybody. Do you remember talking about that at the apartment?

ALLEN: Sounds vaguely familiar.

GATES: Really, though, all along we were never motivated in business just because there was something we wanted to buy. Paul and I paid ourselves $36,000 a year until we incorporated, and then we took this huge boost to $60,000. It was enough because there was nothing material we really wanted.

ALLEN: That's not quite true. When I showed up in Albuquerque, I had to take an advance from MITS because I had no money to pay for a hotel room. The plane ticket took all my money. And when you got there, we used to go window shopping for fast cars.

GATES: You're right. I did buy a used Porsche 911 in Albuquerque; that was my one big desire. Paul bought a big-screen TV, which I think was a seminal event, because watching all those basketball games on it may have gotten to you …

ALLEN: We never really thought about counting our pennies in terms of "this is all the money we could squirrel away for ourselves." Success to us was just plowing it right back in and building the business more. At any time there were lots of software markets we weren't doing that well in—products like word processors and spreadsheets that we've only lately come to lead. There was always some part of the business where we felt like we were the underdog.

GATES: The outside perception and inside perception of Microsoft are so different. The view of Microsoft inside Microsoft is always kind of an underdog thing. Today the worry would be: Oh, God, what can we do in the world of the Internet?

In the early years that underdog, almost paranoid attitude was a matter of survival.

ALLEN: Yeah. We were always worried that IBM would put a thousand guys on word processors or spreadsheets or BASIC or something like that.

GATES: Even though if you look back and see that our sales and profits grew by basically 50% a year for all these years, what I really remember is worrying all the time. If you ask about a specific year, I'd tell you, oh, that was the awful year we had to get Multiplan [a financial spreadsheet] out and establish it, or that was the terrible year we brought out the Microsoft mouse and it didn't sell so we had a warehouse full of them, or it was the miserable year we hired a guy to be president who didn't work out.

ALLEN: We were always worried. Sure, we could see the upside, but we could always see the downside. We're both pretty good at being devil's advocates. If Bill would start getting too optimistic, I would say, "Well, wait a moment, aren't you worried about A, B, and C?" I kind of wonder if that doesn't go back to our experiences at that computer center in Seattle where we had the chairs repossessed from under us. Or because Traf-O-Data never succeeded like we thought it would.

GATES: We've seen so many failures. This is an industry scattered with failure. But despite that, I still believe in our vision—a computer on every desk and in every home, all running Microsoft software.

And I still believe in the importance of software. We said 20 years ago that eventually people will pay more for their software than they do for their hardware. That isn't yet true.

ALLEN: It will be true, though.

GATES: I promise it will. We just have to raise our prices … No, I'm just kidding.

But if you had asked me at any point how big Microsoft could be, Paul and I once thought we could write all the software in the world with 100 people. If you had told us that someday we would have more than 5,000 people writing software, we would have just shaken our heads.

I remember coming to work in the morning when our sales were $20 million, and I'd tell myself: "This means we have to sell $100,000 of software before I go home." And I'd think: "How can I

possibly do that?" So if in the morning I closed a big deal, I'd think, "Wow, today I did it."

I don't do that so much now because Microsoft is more of an institution. The numbers are so big now, it's crazy. Just to keep the thing running at breakeven we have to sell $15 million a day.

ALLEN: Remember that day back in 1980 or so, when we figured we'd shipped a million copies of BASIC? We really felt a sense of accomplishment. And we were marveling that, wow, a million people are using our code to do God-knows-what-number of interesting things. That was such a gratifying thing to realize, that you have been able to affect other people's lives in a positive way.

GATES: Then we did something kind of funny. Paul and I were in such a different world that we had always stayed away from the normal mainframe software industry. They had a big trade organization—it doesn't exist anymore—and an annual trade show where they gave out a special award if you sold 10,000 copies of a program. Just for the heck of it, we filled out one of these forms and said we shipped a million copies. They didn't even have a category for selling that many. But they sent us this fancy plaque anyway, saying yes, indeed, Microsoft had shipped 10,000 copies of BASIC. It was our first big award.

ALLEN: Generally, we don't look in the rear-view mirror much.

GATES: Right. Because it's a waste of time, basically.

The irony of sitting down like this on our 20th anniversary is that we hardly ever do this. On those rare moments when we do look back, we kind of go, "Whoa." We've been climbing a steep mountain here, and you know, there's still lots there ahead of us. It really is pretty amazing.

ALLEN: Geez, it was only 20 years ago that we were sitting there, eating pizza, talking about what we thought a PC would be like, and what we could do.

GATES: Still, we're only about halfway to achieving our original dream of a computer in every home and on every desk. I believe that 20 years from now, before we're too old, the industry will have fulfilled that promise.

ALLEN: I would hope so before then.

GATES: Yeah, but who knows whether we'll be able to maintain our leadership role in it until then.

Opening Up Books to Employees Boosts Profits

Laurel Shaper Walters

Staff writer of The Christian Science Monitor

SPRINGFIELD, MO.

IN the gritty plants of Springfield Remanufacturing Corp., janitors pick up stray screws from trash heaps and factory workers know the cost of every part they touch.

Employees here have an eye on the bottom line. "Everybody's bonus is on the line if parts don't move," says Rick Biggs, who assembles rebuilt truck engines in one of the company's divisions.

Springfield Remanufacturing (SRC) pioneered the concept of "open-book management" in the early 1980s. Now, executives of large and small companies around the world are flocking to Springfield, Mo., to learn how SRC transformed itself from a struggling $19 million division of International Harvester with 170 employees to a thriving $100 million company employing more than 800 people. For the past 14 years since it's been independent, SRC has seen increasing profits and at least 15 percent growth.

"There's nothing magical about this," says chief executive officer Jack Stack, an energetic proponent of turning employees into partners. "What we've got to do is teach people how they are evaluated. The tea leaves of business are the financials."

Under the theory of open-book management, Mr. Stack provides every employee with a copy of the company's financial balance sheet. He also expects them to help improve those numbers. In return, quarterly bonuses and an employee stock-ownership plan allow employees to share in whatever wealth they help create.

Open-book management is more than the latest fad in business management,

(JOHN S. STEWART/AP)

KEEPING TABS: *Candy Smalley rebuilds fuel injectors at Springfield Remanufacturing Corp., a company with open-book management. She says she can make a difference for the firm's bottom line by improving material usage.*

says Corey Rosen, executive director of the National Center for Employee Ownership in Oakland, Calif.

"Usually big trends have their roots in management consulting or universities and are sold to companies," Mr. Rosen says. "Open-book management developed more from the ground up."

"I've seen a lot of management ideas come and go," he says. "But . . . this is going to become, if not the norm, at least very common in business in the next decade."

Such a change requires turning the traditional corporate hierarchy on its head. "Most business plans are put together by two people—the CEO and CFO [chief financial officer]," says Denise Bredfeldt, an SRC employee who once rebuilt engines on the factory floor and is now a top manager.

Everyone gets involved

Under open-book management, everyone from janitors and receptionists to line workers and executives gets involved in producing the annual business plan and tracking the numbers.

At SRC, each division meets weekly to compile financial statistics. Every other week, representatives from all 22 divisions gather at the corporate headquarters to share their numbers.

But no matter what, everyone in the company knows how things look and what the prime areas of focus should be.

"I'm trying to get management to get out of the way," says CEO Stack. "Most people that are hired are given a safety program. They are shown the mechanics of the job." But no one ever explains how the business makes money, he says, and that its financial health affects workers' job security.

Getting everyone in a company to understand even the basics of business takes some education, however. "Understanding financial concepts is not a simple matter; it's much more than just looking at a simple balance sheet," says management expert Arthur Pell. In fact, SRC spends more each year training employees about business than providing job-skills training.

"It was all Greek to me in the beginning," says Mr. Biggs, who has worked for the company nearly 11 years. "It takes a while to understand it all." Now,

when Biggs sees the company financial statements, he zeros in on the cash-flow situation. "That tells you a lot about the health of the company," he says.

Candy Smalley, who works in the same factory, focuses on material usage and production volume. "We know how many parts we need to move per day," she says. "I can't go and make more sales since I'm on the floor. But I understand where I can make a difference."

Biggs is convinced that "knowing what's going on makes a person a better employee." Peer pressure plays an important role as well, he says. "If I can't get the parts I need, I'm going to come over here and say something."

Biggs says he will take an engine apart himself to get the part he needs. "It's best to get it out and turn it into cash rather than having it sit in the shop," he says.

Despite the general enthusiasm on the factory floor, some workers are not convinced SRC's executives are putting everything on the table. "Some of us still think there's a separate set of books somewhere that we don't see," says one assembly worker.

Stack insists that his only goal is to be as honest as possible and enlist the help of all his employees. Yet he is well aware that most company owners and top managers have little interest in revealing their numbers. "It's a cultural thing," he says.

"Business people get overly concerned that their numbers are going to be used against them," adds CFO Don Ross. But Stack says that has never happened to SRC.

Still, "many companies are reluctant to open books to anybody, particularly employees," management expert Mr. Pell

says. "Often it's because managers are making more money and owners are taking more out of the business than they like employees to know."

Living in a glass house

Opening the books does raise employees' expectations, Bredfeldt says. "When you open the books, you begin living in a glass house," she says. "You get a lot of questions." Company owners and managers have to be prepared for that, she advises.

The many firms that have come to SRC to learn about open-book management and to implement it themselves are finding that the payoffs require patience and persistence.

At Mid-States Technical Staffing Services in Davenport, Iowa, the boss began opening the books to everyone three years ago.

Brenda Wiese, the company's bookkeeper, says the new approach makes her job easier. "People know what I'm talking about now," she says.

Under the old system, only Ms. Wiese and the company owner knew the company's financials. Now everyone does.

"It definitely takes extra time" to hold meetings and share information, says Mid-States employee Don Miehe. "But then people know how to react to changes." For Mr. Miehe, it's made a significant difference in his personal life as well.

"Knowing that the company is doing well has given me the confidence to buy a house," he says. "We're closing in about two weeks."

The Failure Of Participatory Management

What was supposed to reduce bureaucracy and organizational politics has had the opposite effect.

Charles Heckscher

CHARLES HECKSCHER chairs the Labor Studies and Employment Relations Department at Rutgers University. He is author of White-Collar Blues: Management Loyalties in an Age of Corporate Restructuring *(Basic).*

Participatory management has been one of the longest-running management trends of the post-'50s era. While fads have come and mostly gone—job enrichment, quality of work life, quality circles, autonomous teams, and more recently TQM and reengineering—one underlying theme has steadily picked up momentum: increasing the involvement of lower levels in decision making.

The reason is clear: Bureaucracy has reached its limits. The simplicity and power of top-down, rule-based administration created competitive advantage in the past, but it blocks the responsiveness and continuous innovation that are keys today. That is why "teamwork" and "empowerment" are seen almost everywhere as the road to success.

But does that road really lead to success? For five years I have interviewed middle managers in companies that are downsizing and restructuring; I've talked to more than 250 managers in 14 large organizations, including divisions of General Motors Corp., AT&T Co., Pitney Bowes Inc., Honeywell Inc., and DuPont. One thing I can say is that from their viewpoint participatory management has generally *not* accomplished much. It is rarely successful in breaking the walls of bureaucracy.

In fact, downsizing and restructuring as they are normally practiced have the opposite effect: As middle managers have consistently told me, these changes *increase bureaucracy and increase organizational politics.* Their experience is that the organizations they work in have become more rule-bound and narrowly focused rather than less, and less entrepreneurial rather than more.

There is a huge gap between the views of the middle and the top. Top managers consistently believe they are breaking down old cultures and creating a new environment of collaboration and innovation. They talk of education, increased information-sharing, systems of teamwork, and communication. In most cases little of this has actually penetrated to the middle layers. The rhetoric and the programs talk of one thing, but the reality in the heart of the organization is another.

Hence, as a growing series of studies has found, the enormous efforts at restructuring are yielding mostly disappointing results. While they usually produce some short-term cost reductions, executives looking for fundamental increases in organizational effectiveness aren't finding them.

Restructuring has great potential, but many current approaches only undermine the long-term strength of organizations. Instead of transforming bureaucracy, they unwittingly reinforce it. I have seen just a few cases that avoid the bureaucracy trap.

The Empowerment Double Play

Part of the problem is that there are two sharply different meanings of "teamwork" or "empower-

From *Across the Board*, November/December 1995, pp. 16-21. © 1995 by The Conference Board. Reprinted with permission.

ment": One of them creates something new, but the other just reinforces bureaucracy. By confusing the two, many organizations set themselves on the wrong path.

The basic problem with bureaucracy is that it operates by dividing work up into small pieces and building walls between the pieces. That is the foundation for the control system: Each person is supposed to focus on a particular set of programs, skills, and objectives. When an individual completes his piece, he throws it "over the wall" to the next step in the process.

Instead of tackling this problem, the most popular version of "empowerment" simply gives individuals bigger pieces: It gets rid of micromanaging superiors and unnecessary rules, and it allows people to do the job they are assigned without interference. "Delayering" is often seen as a way to get rid of micromanagement and restore some real power to the front lines.

That sounds good, but it's not new: Alfred Sloan recommended that back in the 1920s when he was creating the classic bureaucratic structure of General Motors. Letting people do their jobs is nothing more than a principle of good bureaucratic management. Sure, organizations tend to build up unnecessary layers and rules, and it is wise to prune them periodically. But this approach increases the autonomy of different parts of the organization rather than helping them to work together. It therefore *strengthens* the walls that block systemic innovation and responsiveness.

Another version goes a step further, but only a step. I am referring to "autonomous team" systems that get rid of an immediate supervisory level and create a team from those who would normally be a bunch of subordinates. This has the advantage of reducing layers and, to some extent, increasing flexibility within the group—people can cover for each other and share information more directly. But this kind of team, being permanent, quickly builds its *own* walls around itself. The members begin to share an identity that leads them to resist breaking up and recombining, and they don't generally deal well with "outsiders." I have come across many cases of autonomous teams fighting to protect their turf and unity against change efforts. While this kind of teamwork increases immediate flexibility, it again raises the barriers to larger-scale responsiveness.

The kind of empowerment that really breaks the bureaucratic mold is something different: Instead of increasing autonomy, it increases the ability to *work together effectively across walls*. These walls exist between levels, blocking open communication, and they exist between functions, blocking effective cooperation on complex problems. The organizations that are starting to leap beyond bureaucracy are the ones who have built a capacity to pull people together quickly, from different parts of the system, with different skills and knowledge, into effective *temporary* teams working on a task. This capacity to quickly bring together diverse expertise into an effective unit is *the* characteristic that marks a quantum leap beyond bureaucracy and that will create competitive advantage for the next economic phase.

Very few companies in my experience can do this well. Though many have been trying cross-functional, task-focused teams, the middle managers I have spoken to widely regard them as ineffective and distracting. Empowerment programs that expand *autonomy* make the situation worse, not better.

Restructuring Pitfalls

Restructuring not only fails to create the new kind of participation just described; it has also undermined the *old* forms of participation that kept good bureaucracies working reasonably effectively in the past.

In traditionally effective organizations, a key form of participation was through the direct supervisor. That was the position responsible for listening, for supporting, and for representing people to the organization. Studies have always shown that most people are pleased with their supervisors, and that this is their most important relationship in the corporation. Again, new programs to create "participatory" relations between managers and their subordinates may be helpful in systematizing past practice, but they do not bring anything fundamentally new.

But at the same time that these programs try to build those "coaching" relations, the larger restructuring process undermines them. Delayering widely increases the span of control and reduces direct supervision. That may mean that people control their own jobs more but are *less* able to bring up concerns and issues to someone they trust. Focus groups and skip-level meetings do not substitute for the personal relations that used to give people a sense that they had someone to go to in a pinch.

The old organization also had another crucial form of "teamwork." Middle managers were never the narrowly job-focused, rule-following automatons they were made out to be. Fortunately for the companies they worked for, they have always stretched their job limits by building communication *networks* throughout the system, cutting across official lines.

These management networks were informal, based on personal trust and hit-or-miss contacts. You might go through your first orientation session with Joe from engineering. A few years later, when you're handed a project that needs more engineering talent than you can muster from your own people, you call Joe up and ask for help. He might give you some tips; he might even lend you one of his people for a few weeks. And, of course, you'd do the same for him.

Now, any bureaucratic organization that didn't have these informal networks was doomed to fail. If middle managers really had to go through every channel and follow every rule to get what they needed, the whole system would quickly come to a grinding halt. It was because people *found ways to cross the walls* that bureaucracies functioned at all.

What happens in a downsizing or restructuring? One manager summed it up nicely: "The changes did two things: They destroyed networks, and they destroyed career paths. Now, more and more, people don't trust each other."

The first thing is that the networks are disrupted: Joe is gone. The second thing is that the wider basis for trust is destroyed. The main reason Joe was willing to help you was that he knew you were both in this for the long haul, and that when he came back to you for a favor you'd still be around. If he was lucky, you might even have gotten promoted and be

> In the absence of trust,
> people feel more
> isolated, more lonely,
> more vulnerable; they
> rely more on formal
> rules than before, and
> they are quicker to
> protect their turf.

able to help him more extensively. Now his replacement, if there is one, doesn't know any of that. He's got enough problems of his own; he can't spare time or people. Why should he help you out?

Things are even worse if, as in many companies, there is increasing short-term pressure to meet objectives. What that means is that the *formal* requirements of the organization are being rewarded more than ever, but the *informal* teamwork that gave it life is pushed further under the surface. It becomes still harder to go out of your way to help someone in the expectation that it will all work out for the best in the end.

In the absence of trust, people feel more isolated, more lonely, more vulnerable; they rely more on formal rules than before, and they are quicker to protect their turf. All of that is the opposite of what is intended, of course. But in the absence of trust, no amount of training, of participatory programs, or of communication makes much of a difference.

The Loyalty Trap

There is more: Restructuring not only disrupts middle managers' traditional forms of involvement and collaboration; it pushes them into a defensive mentality that blocks new forms.

Nearly every company I have been involved with has been trying to get managers more involved in the business. They have elaborate programs to distribute strategic information on a far wider scale

than ever before, and they have set up all kinds of systems to encourage critical feedback and discussion. The logic is that it is not enough anymore for people to work together on particular tasks: They need to feel an ownership in the whole and to understand its relevance to their work. It is a noble objective that is seldom realized—because managers *flee* from this level of participation.

Despite all the programs, two widespread problems appear. First, middle managers do not understand the business; they have little or no conception of the competitive environment and the strategic positioning of the firm. They understand their own piece extremely well, but not more. The whole set of changes threatening them makes very little sense.

Most of the top-level managers to whom I report this find this hard to believe. "We tell them all the time; we tell them everything," they say—and they're largely right. The problem is not usually that middle managers haven't *been told* about the business; it's just that they haven't *heard* it.

Second, though they have deep private doubts about their leaders' competence, they refuse to express these doubts in public. They almost refuse to admit them to themselves: The same person will commonly in one breath criticize top management and in the next say that he has complete faith in them. Though many companies are going all out to provide opportunities for dialogue, middle managers are reluctant to use them fully.

This is an irrational pattern but a typical one. It's partly due to fear of retaliation—but only partly. A more basic source is, surprisingly, the loyalty that managers continue to feel towards their companies. Despite the downsizings, despite the violations of long-term expectations, most of the people I have talked to care deeply about their organizations and want to hold on. But they are *trapped* by their own loyalty.

Let me try to interpret what they are feeling. The deal in loyalty is that if you do your job well the organization will take care of you—you do your part and the higher-ups will do theirs. Now a bunch of your superiors are coming down and saying to you, "We want you to know what's happening. We want you to know the information we have. We want you to know how difficult and confusing the environment is. And we want you to tell us honestly what we're doing wrong and what we can do better." What middle managers hear is: *They don't know what they're doing.*

That's not a message the middle managers want to hear; they actively resist hearing it. When their superiors come out with another batch of business information, it basically means that more layoffs and disruptions are on the way. They can't do anything with the knowledge, and it just makes them anxious. "I think what we all struggle with," one manager said, "is how much we can influence the business—because we know the business can influence *us*."

So most don't want to hear too much or criticize too

much; they don't want to come face to face with the fact that the situation is no longer in control and no one quite knows what is going on. Even the private water-cooler conversations are contradictory: On the one hand they say the top is making all sorts of stupid decisions that don't make any sense; on the other they say (or hope) that the top probably does know what it's doing.

> # The situation is one of loyalty without trust. People hang onto their attachment to the company as a kind of security blanket in a world gone mad.

The situation is, in short, one of *loyalty without trust*. People hang onto their attachment to the company as a kind of security blanket in a world gone mad, but they no longer have the network of trusting relationships so crucial in the past. They cope by withdrawing into a narrow world, putting their heads down, getting by, waiting it out:

"I have no doubt that it's going to get worse, but I have no doubt that we will recognize it and turn it around," a manager told me. "The only thing we can do is just wait. We have a good organization here, when we get directed to do it, we do it. I can't help but think that the pendulum will swing back. We will just have to wait it out, because there is really nobody to talk to."

Overcoming the Barriers

All of this adds up to a pattern in which no matter how hard you try, you stay stuck within bureaucracy. Downsizing and restructuring produce quick benefits because they cut costs and temporarily improve the alignment between structure and strategy. But they don't increase the basic flexibility of the system; in fact, they reduce it by *increasing* the barriers between people. So most organizations end up putting people back on (though they may hide it by changing the categories) or restructuring over and over to try to keep up with change.

As I've said, few in my study have escaped the trap. The ones that have are the ones that have changed the *most*. They have created a kind of teamwork that is not just a modification of bureaucracy, but that truly has brought down the walls. Most managers have served on multiple teams—some lasting for a few hours, some for a few years, many of them spontaneously created from the middle, all focused on solving problems.

I have never found this kind of management through an entire corporation: It has appeared so far only at the level of plants and divisions. In my own study one of the successes is a General Motors plant, another a Honeywell division; and recently I have been impressed by AT&T's Network Services Division. I have also heard convincing case studies of similar units at General Electric Co., IBM Corp., and a few others. But it clearly remains rare.

In these organizations the managers I have interviewed are not putting their heads down and avoiding reality; they are working together to master it. They are not looking for more *autonomy* but are enjoying a sense of *interactivity*.

"The middle managers really make this place run," one manager said. "There's a strong desire among all of us to work the problem. We work together, we're friends, we have a lot of kinship in getting a job done."

How have they done it? One element is simply to be clear about what you're doing—about the difference between "empowerment" *within* bureaucracy and breaking bureaucracy. Increasing autonomy—leaving people alone—leads the *wrong* way; increasing interdependence and interaction across walls leads the right way.

At least two other things seem crucial:

A focus on purpose. The new environment does increase the mobility and independence of managers. They can no longer rely on personal contacts and informal networks as a basis for trust, and they need to pay attention to their own needs rather than counting on the company to take care of them. The problem is how to get these more individualistic employees to work together. A major answer seems to be to a focus on the organization's *purpose*. The most successful organizations in my sample have created a rich and thoroughly shared picture of what they are trying to accomplish together in the next few years.

The purpose, in this sense, is different from most definitions of "vision," "goals," or "mission."

- On one side, "visions" tend to be simple, eternal statements of the organization's identity that can be put on a wall: Mazda Inc.'s, to take one classic example, is "Everlasting effort for everlasting cooperation." That supports traditional loyalty, but it doesn't create a sense of working on a *problem* together.
- On the other side, many organizations heavily emphasize this year's goals or numbers. That gives a visible target but is too short-term to sustain a sense of shared commitment and enthusiasm; it quickly degenerates into "just hitting the numbers."

A purpose is something in the middle: a complex statement of the organization's challenges and objectives *over a three-to-five-year time frame*. It usually can't hang on a wall, because it is far too complicated. The limited time frame keeps the purpose concrete, away from airy abstractions, but it's long enough to provide a challenge worth *caring* about.

People who understand the purpose can talk knowledgeably about competitive positioning, comparative advantages, and strategic objectives. This has been the clearest difference in my sample: In the troubled companies middle managers cannot talk about those issues; in the dynamic ones they can, and that sense of purpose pulls them together.

Telling the truth. All corporate leaders say they want to communicate the reality of change, but most are held back by their end of the loyalty bargain. They are supposed to protect "their people"; they are almost unconsciously reluctant to admit that they can't do that, and they worry that their people won't be able to deal with the full reality of what's happening. So they pull their punches. They try to reassure people: "We may not be able to guarantee you a job, but we'll do everything we can to take care of you." They also tend to hold back the full picture, doling out reality a bit at a time, allowing people to believe that things may return to "normal."

The dynamic companies don't do that. They tell the full picture of competitive problems, and they make clear that promises of security are no longer possible. For most managers, including lifelong loyalists, this has the effect of a bracing dose of

Layoffs and downsizings do not shatter the contract of loyalty. Managers are able to rationalize these for a long time as responses to crisis, and to settle into a waiting posture.

truth: The world *makes sense*, even if it isn't entirely pleasant.

I don't mean that the solution is to be cruel: Hauling people out of buildings under armed guard, or refusing to do anything to help those laid off, may be ways of getting the truth across, but they don't contribute a sense of shared purpose. The problem is to replace the paternalistic ethic of *caring for* people with a professional ethic of *mutual commitment.*

Companies with a sense of honesty and purpose have high levels of participation. They don't do it with participative programs, but they create an environment in which understanding and criticizing the business direction are important to people's daily jobs. In that situation people work together rather than fragmenting into isolated pieces.

Establishing New Relationships

"Participation" is one of those words that can mean almost anything. In this case it can mean at least two opposite things: reinforcing bureaucracy or overcoming it. Managers and others have no difficulty in "participating" within the traditional framework: That is, they want to be left alone to do their jobs, to get out from under unnecessary rules; and they are delighted to discuss with superiors how their jobs can be done better. These kinds of "participation" date back at least to the 1920s.

Flexible organizations, however, require that people participate beyond their jobs: Everyone needs to understand and contribute creatively to the overall purpose of the organization. That kind of participation profoundly threatens traditional relationships.

Surprisingly, this is the crux of the change in expectations. Layoffs and downsizings do not shatter the contract of loyalty. Managers are able to rationalize these for a long time as responses to crisis, and to settle into a waiting posture. They don't fundamentally give up the expectation that, if they can just get through this period, things will return to normal.

Being asked to get involved in strategic purpose is a far more serious threat, because it establishes new relationships. If middle managers (and others) have real involvement in issues beyond their jobs, it means that the whole system of bureaucratic coordination needs to be reconstructed. It means that middle managers have to be treated far more as independent agents than before.

It means that the uncertainty and threats of the "outside" world have to become a daily reality for everyone, not just the top.

INNOVATE *or* EVAPORATE

Seven Secrets of Innovative Corporations

Some organizations constantly create new and better products and services, delighting their customers and jolting their competitors. Here are some of the ways that successful businesses have profited from their innovative culture.

James M. Higgins

Rubbermaid is a veritable juggernaut when it comes to putting out new products: 365 a year, or almost two new products every workday. Each year it improves over 5,000 existing products. Wolfgang Schmitt, Rubbermaid's CEO, has established lofty objectives for the firm: He wants Rubbermaid to enter a new-product category every 12 to 18 months (recently it has introduced hardware cabinets and garden sheds); to obtain a third of its sales from products introduced within the past five years; and to obtain 25% of its revenues from markets outside the United States by the year 2000, up from the current 18%. To achieve these objectives, Schmitt will continue to pursue Rubbermaid's long-established strategy of innovation.

Rubbermaid excels in making mundane items seem interesting and functional, and it also makes them profitable. It produces mailboxes, window boxes, storage boxes, toys, mops, dust mitts, snap-together furniture, ice-cube trays, stadium seats, spatulas, step stools, wall coverings, sporting goods, dinnerware, dish drainers, laundry hampers, and many other useful products. However mundane those items may seem, Rubbermaid's engineers hover over their products as intently as would General Dynamics' engineers over an F-111 fighter. It is this serious approach to what others dismiss as trivial that has helped make the firm so successful.

Most of Rubbermaid's new products come from 20 cross-functional teams, each with five to seven members (one each from marketing, manufacturing, R&D, finance, and other departments, as needed). Each team focuses on a specific product line so that someone is always thinking about key product segments. But innovation doesn't stop with the teams. Individual employees are geared toward creating new products as well.

Rubbermaid has taught its employees to think in terms of letting new products flow from the firm's core competencies—the things it does well. It encourages its managers to find out what's happening in the rest of the company, continually looking at processes and technologies. For example, while running a different Rubbermaid subsidiary, Bud Hellman toured a Rubbermaid plant that made picnic coolers. As he watched the plastic blow-molding equipment, he realized that he could use that process to make a line of durable, lightweight, inexpensive office furniture. Within a couple of years that line accounted for 60% of the furniture division's sales.

Top management often contributes ideas as well. When CEO Schmitt and Richard Gates, head of product development, toured the British Museum in London in 1993, they became extremely interested in an exhibit of Egyptian antiquities. They came away with 11 specific product ideas. Gates says admiringly of the Egyptians, "They used a lot of kitchen utensils, some of which were very nice. Nice designs."

Innovation and Competitiveness

Innovation gives Rubbermaid a competitive advantage. Now and in the future, more than at any time in history, the secret to competitive advantage is innovation. Businesses face many strategic challenges as they approach the twenty-first century, such as accelerating rates of change, increasing competition (especially global competition), rapidly advancing technology, a more diverse work force, and a change from an industrial to a knowledge-based economy.

Creativity is necessary to produce innovation, but the organization's culture must also foster creativity and then turn it into the innovation that leads to competitive success. Rubbermaid has understood this principle for many years and has built an organizational culture that fosters innovation. Your organization should, too, if it expects to survive into the twenty-first century.

Let's think about some of the more innovative firms.

• The 3M Company is famous for its never-ending series of new products, which have included Scotch

---

Waiter, There's a Fork in My Soup!

In free association—one of many techniques used to generate useful new ideas—you say whatever comes into your mind relative to a word you just wrote or relative to a one- or two-word definition of a problem. It's a good group exercise as well as an individual one.

The purpose is simply to get thoughts down on paper that will trigger new thoughts about the problem. You don't expect to find solutions per se; rather, you are looking for thoughts that might lead to solutions.

At Campbell Soup Company, product developers began by randomly selecting the word *handle* from a dictionary. Through free association, the word *utensil* was suggested. This led to *fork*. One participant joked about a soup that could be eaten with a fork. The group reasoned that you couldn't eat soup with a fork unless it was thick with vegetables and meat . . . and Campbell's Chunky Soups, an extremely successful product line, was born.

Source: *101 Creative Problem Solving Techniques* by James M. Higgins.

---

brand cellophane tape and the ubiquitous Post-It Notes.

• General Electric files more U.S. patents than almost any other U.S. firm year after year.

• Bell Laboratories has consistently produced a large number of successful new products, among them the transistor and fiber optics. The company is currently developing an "optical computer" that would revolutionize the computer industry.

• Apple Computer gave us the Apple II, followed by the Apple Macintosh. Now the company is pursuing a visionary personal computer that will incorporate voice command, permit remote database searches, and include a video telephone. All of these functions will fit in a unit the size of a notebook. The Power Macintosh and the Newton are first steps toward fulfilling that vision.

• Sony is the recognized world leader in consumer electronics, introducing some 1,000 products each year; 800 of those products are new versions of old products, but 200 are totally new.

• Hewlett-Packard continues to dazzle the industrial world because, despite its size ($24 billion in sales and 96,000 employees), it continues to grow at a staggering pace, launching successful new products at a rate few competitors can match.

These firms have all shown a remarkable proclivity for innovation. By contrast, many firms fail to produce much that's new or to improve the processes by which they provide their products or services. Is there something different about organizations that are consistently innovative? Absolutely! Studies have revealed a set of characteristics that are shared by innovative firms, despite differences in their organizational cultures. These characteristics will enable a firm to survive and prosper in the future, and they constitute the profile of the innovative organization.

Organizations may assess their innovativeness through the Innovation Quotient Inventory, which includes 49 characteristics of innovative companies. (See my book *Innovate or Evaporate.*) Here I will discuss seven of these characteristics and show how they are exemplified by specific corporations.

Seven Characteristics of Innovative Organizations

1. A Stated and Working Strategy Of Innovation

It's not necessary to be a big corporation in order to have a stated and working strategy of innovation.

Take the case of Super Bakery, Inc., which has sales of $6 million a year and whose majority owner is former Pittsburgh Steelers legend Franco Harris. Formed in Pittsburgh in 1983, the company manufactures doughnuts and baked goods for institutions, mainly schools.

In the early 1980s, Super Bakery followed the conservative strategy typical of its industry. With sales and profits going nowhere, the firm decided in 1987 to use a new strategy emphasizing innovation in both its products and its services. For instance, it began stressing relationship marketing with food distributors, looking for ways to make their jobs easier. Super Bakery went into partnership with noncompeting suppliers and got its doughnuts put into a prepackaged meal. The company also educated school systems on ways of receiving government funding that they had not thought of before. Finally, Super Bakery looked to its customers' customers and tried to provide a product that they would demand, thereby pulling Super Bakery's products through the supply chain. All of these actions, and others, which are standard fare for many firms, were innovative activities for this industry.

The firm now has its own R&D facility, which created the "Super Donut," a reduced-fat, reduced-sugar, protein-enriched, and vitamin-fortified product that was a major success from the start. This and a slightly lower-fat doughnut, the "Ultra Donut," were the first such foods to be approved by the U.S. Department of Agriculture for school breakfasts.

The results of all of this innovation have been nothing short of spectacular. Super Bakery's 1993 sales totaled about $6 million, representing 4 million doughnuts a month. From 1983 to 1992, the firm cut its costs by an average of 2% per year, despite inflation. Most of the savings came through increased productivity. Customer service measures, such as accuracy of sales orders, meeting product quality standards, on-time delivery, total order-processing time, and accurate shipments, have also improved.

2. Forming Teams

A customer of the Honeywell Corporation threatened to take his business elsewhere if the firm could not produce a new climate-control device quickly. Honeywell responded by forming a "tiger team" consisting of people from the marketing, design, and engineering departments. The company allowed the tiger team to break the usual rules in order to reduce product-development time from four years to one. As a result, the company kept the customer.

Managers at Milliken & Company, a cloth manufacturer, team with customers to develop new products and services. This very successful strategy has proven especially effective in making the firm more competitive with non-U.S. firms, which almost always have an advantage in the form of lower labor costs. One result: Milliken now loads its cloth products onto trucks so that when they arrive at Levi Strauss's clothing plants the goods can be unloaded in the order in which they are needed. The trucks thus become mini-warehouses for Strauss, which does not have to establish its own inventory of raw materials.

3. Rewarding Creativity And Innovation

Until recently, many experts believed that researchers, scientists, engineers, and other professional inno-

---

Promoting Innovation at General Electric

General Electric is already the company of tomorrow. In a bold set of management actions aimed at improving productivity (and hence competitiveness), GE has set the trends for increasing innovation that others will follow into the twenty-first century.

Three tools form the core of this management revolution: the Workout, Best Practices, and Process Mapping.

• **The Workout:** Manager and subordinates gather for a three-day retreat. The subordinates work on problems with the help of an outside facilitator; the manager does not participate in these sessions. On the third day, the manager is asked to respond to solutions proposed by subordinates with a yes, no, or a deferral for further study. (Managers are encouraged to limit the number of deferrals.)

• **Best Practices:** In this technique, GE compares itself with the firms that are best at performing a particular function. Then GE attempts to improve its performance levels by emulating the best practices in other firms. Significant improvements have been reported throughout GE's many businesses as a result of best-practices analyses.

• **Process Mapping:** Employees create a flowchart of a process such as making a jet engine. The flowchart shows how all the component tasks are interrelated. Then the employees try to see how much time they can cut from the process. In the case of jet engines, which GE has been making for years, the firm was able to cut the manufacturing time in half through process mapping.

Other GE techniques:

• Friday evening beer-and-pretzel parties to increase cross-functional exchange of ideas.

• Allowing researchers who come to a dead end in one department to move to another to develop their ideas.

• Having teams from successful units tour other GE companies, providing seminars on how they achieved their success.

—*James M. Higgins*

vators were best motivated by the work itself—by the technical challenge, the opportunity to create, and autonomy. In most instances this may still be true. But corporations have discovered that their professional innovators are also very receptive to financial and other nonintrinsic rewards.

"IBM has a program called the IBM Fellows," says George S. Howie, former director of IBM's technical personnel programs. "The fellows are typically engineers who have worked for the company 15–20 years and who have been extremely creative and productive. They are given executive salaries and five years to work on what they want to with the resources needed to support that research."

The 3M Corporation has its version of a Nobel Prize for innovative employees. The prize is the Golden Step award, whose trophy is a winged foot. Several Golden Steps are given out each year to employees whose new products have reached significant revenue and profit levels.

In addition, 3M has a dual-ladder promotion program: One ladder is for management while the other honors professional success. "Some innovative people would rather face mustard gas than budget forecasts," former CEO Allen Jacobson once said. "What these people need is a system that rewards them for their innovative abilities without forcing them into a manager's desk where they'll be miserable." Art Fry, inventor of the famous Post-It Notes, was promoted through the dual ladder, eventually attaining the position of corporate scientist, the highest rung on the technical side of the company.

4. Allowing Mistakes

At Johnson & Johnson, a mistake can be a badge of honor for an innovator. Back in the 1960s, CEO Jim Burke failed with the first major product he tried to launch for the company, but he received congratulations from the company chairman, Gen. Robert Wood Johnson, for taking a risk. Burke never forgot that

The Post-It Notes Story

Post-It Notes™ can be found in almost any office in the United States today, and they are a $200-million-a-year success for the 3M Corporation. But it did not come easy.

The idea originated with Art Fry, a 3M employee who used bits of paper to mark hymns when he sat in his church choir. These markers kept falling out of the hymn books. He decided that he needed an adhesive-backed paper that would stick as long as necessary but could be removed easily. He soon found what he wanted in the 3M laboratory, and the Post-It Note was born.

Fry saw the market potential of his invention, but others did not. Market-survey results were negative; major office-supply distributors were skeptical. So he began giving samples to 3M executives and their secretaries. Once they actually used the little pieces of adhesive paper, they were hooked. Having sold 3M on the project, Fry used the same approach with other executives throughout the United States. He mailed samples to the secretaries and CEOs of Fortune 500 firms. They soon became hooked, too. As demand grew, Post-It Notes became a huge financial success.

—James M. Higgins

Mind Mapping: Brainstorming by Oneself

Mind mapping is an individual brainstorming process. Just write or otherwise record whatever comes into your head as it occurs. Quantity, not quality, is what you are after. No criticism is allowed during the brainstorming itself. Later you can go back and critique your inputs (or those of others in a group situation). You can also generate new ideas by looking at what you have already written.

To begin a mind-mapping session, write the name or description of the object or problem in the center of a piece of paper and draw a circle around it. Then brainstorm each major facet of that object or problem, drawing lines outward from the circle like roads leaving a city.

You can draw branches from those "roads" as you brainstorm them in more detail. You can brainstorm all the main lines at once and then the branches for each, or brainstorm a line and its branches, or jump from place to place as thoughts occur.

Mind mapping is an excellent technique not only for generating new ideas but also for developing one's intuitive capacity. It is especially useful for identifying all the issues and subissues related to a problem, as well as the solutions to a problem and their pros and cons. Mind mapping also works well for outlining presentations, papers, and book chapters.

About half of the people who learn mind mapping find it extremely useful; the other half find it uncomfortable to use. The latter seem to object to the lack of structure and find it difficult to be as spontaneous as the process requires. But for those who are comfortable with it, it can be a very useful and versatile tool, applicable not only to business problems, such as when to terminate an employee, but even to one's personal relationships and future plans.

Source: *101 Creative Problem Solving Techniques* by James M. Higgins.

lesson and went on to achieve many successes later.

5. Training in Creativity

Corning and Exxon are among the increasing number of firms that have trained their employees in creative processes and encouraged their use. Corning has trained 26,000 employees in these techniques, and Exxon, 7,000.

DuPont trains all its employees in the use of five techniques: lateral thinking, metaphoric thinking, positive thinking, association trigger, and capturing and interpreting dreams. Use of these techniques has been very profitable. For example, DuPont researchers were trying to figure out a way to dye Nomex fibers, which had proved to be impervious to dyes. Using the metaphor of a mine shaft, one researcher realized that timbers (metaphorically speaking) were needed to hold the fibers apart so that the dye could take effect. He then found a chemical agent that acted much like a timber in a mine shaft—holding the hole open until dyes could take effect.

Sometimes various groups of employees respond to certain processes better than others. For example, Amoco Chemical has found that its researchers prefer brainwriting (writing ideas on slips of paper for modification by others) over brainstorming because it helps cut down on self-censorship. General Motors has an automated brainwriting facility that uses networked PCs.

6. Managing the Organizational Culture

Microsoft became the world's leading software producer through a lot of hard work, astute technological and business acumen, and careful management of its organizational culture. Microsoft's founder and CEO, Bill Gates, based the firm's culture on the principle of empowerment. Managers delegate power to the developers, who write and design software. The firm is managed in such a way that managers interact as little as possible with the developers, although the managers do provide mentors to help newly recruited developers to understand the firm's culture.

Microsoft's physical layout facilitates creativity and innovation. Corporate headquarters resembles a college campus, with playing fields, an outdoor eating area, and a basketball court. Almost every office has a window, and almost every door is open. Employees work hard (80-hour weeks) and play hard (parties, pranks, picnics, sports, and good-natured fun).

7. Creating New Opportunities Proactively

Silicon Graphics, the California-based computer graphics firm, shook up the entire computer industry with its 3-D graphics. Its alliances with Nintendo, Time Warner, and Kodak are helping revolutionize the computer game, home video, and film industries respectively.

Nucor Steel first made the mini-mill successful, forever changing the U.S. steel industry by making U.S. steel cost-competitive on a global basis. Then it developed a flat-rolled steel process that is revolutionizing the steel industry for a second time.

American Airlines set the industry standard for reservation systems with its Sabre system, changing the way the industry booked seats and giving the company a tremendous strategic advantage. American Airlines also created the "frequent flyer" program, another first in the industry.

Chrysler reintroduced the convertible to the American consumer; it created the mini-van; and most recently, it developed the "cab forward" design. All of these wreaked havoc on competitors.

What all of these innovative companies know is that they can either move ahead, or decline. Understanding the future is important, but creating the future is even more important. If firms are to survive and prosper in the twenty-first century, they must assess their innovation capabilities, and then take strategic action to improve their innovation skills.

About the Author

James M. Higgins is professor of management at the Roy E. Crummer Graduate School of Business at Rollins College in Winter Park, Florida. He is the author of six college texts on strategy, management, and human relations. His address is The New Management Publishing Company, 400 North New York Avenue, Suite 215, Winter Park, Florida 32789. Telephone 407/647-5344; fax 407/647-5575.

Books by the Author

Portions of this article are excerpted from two of author James Higgins's recent books:
• *101 Creative Problem Solving Techniques: The Handbook of New Ideas for Business* (1994. 223 pages. Paperback. $17.95).
• *Innovate or Evaporate: Test & Improve Your Organization's IQ—Its Innovation Quotient* (1995. 388 pages. Paperback. $19.95).
Both books are published by The New Management Publishing Company and are available through the World Future Society's book service.

The first book was described in THE FUTURIST's November-December 1994 issue as "probably the best currently available introduction to creativity methods."

The second volume focuses on what major corporations are actually doing to innovate. The book lists the 49 characteristics of innovative organizations and provides a test so readers can assess their own organization's innovation quotient. The book is packed with fascinating case histories of innovative organizations.

Case IV: *Cub Scout Pack 81*

Things certainly have changed over the past six years for Cub Scout Pack 81. Six years ago, the pack was on the verge of disbanding. There were barely enough boys for an effective den, and they had been losing membership for as long as anyone could remember. The cub master was trying to pass his job on to any parent foolish enough to take the helm of a sinking ship, and the volunteer fire department that sponsored the pack was openly considering dropping it.

But that was six years ago. Today the pack has one of the largest memberships of any in the Lancaster/Lebanon Council. It has started its own Boy Scout troop, into which the Webelos can graduate, and it has received a presidential citation for its antidrug program. The pack consistently wins competitions with other packs in the Council, and the fire department is very happy about its sponsorship. Membership in the pack is now around 60 cubs at all levels, and they have a new cub master.

"Parents want their boys to be in a successful program," says Cub Master Mike Murphy. "Look, I can't do everything. We depend on the parents and the boys to get things done. Everybody understands that we want to have a successful program, and that means that we all have to participate to achieve that success. I can't do it all, but if we can unleash the energy these boys have, there isn't anything in the Cub Scout Program we can't do!"

It was not always like that. "About five years ago we placed fourth for our booth in the Scout Expo at the mall," says Mike. "Everybody was surprised! Who was Pack 81? We were all elated! It was one of the best things to happen to this pack in years. Now, if we don't win at least something, we're disappointed. Our kids expect to win, and so do their parents."

Fourth place at the Scout Expo eventually led to several first places. Success leads to success, and the community around pack 81 knows it.

"Last year, we made our annual presentation to the boys and their parents at the elementary school. We were with several other packs, each one trying to drum up interest in their program. When everyone was finished, the boys and their parents went over to the table of the pack that most interested them. We must have had well over half of the people at our table. I was embarrassed! They were standing six or seven deep in front of our table, and there was virtually nobody in front of the others."

Using the Case on *Cub Scout Pack 81*

This case shows what can happen to any organization when the people in the organization are motivated and have goals. Success builds upon success, and pack 81 is now successful. The role of the leader is to ensure the success of the organization by creating an environment in which the participants (the Cubs and their families) can continue to be winners.

Questions for Discussion

1. What do you think was the major change in pack 81's situation?
2. How does the cub master "spread the wealth"? That is, the credit and the work associated with operating the pack?
3. How do you think the success of pack 81 has affected the other Cub Scout packs in the area? Why?
4. If you were a potential Cub Scout, or a parent of a potential Cub Scout, why would you be interested in pack 81?
5. Part of leadership has been defined as getting others to accept your goals as their own. Do you think that Cub Master Mike Murphy has been successful in doing that? Why or why not?

Exercise IV: *Listening*

Procedure

The instructor should:

1. Instruct the students to write down the numbers 1 through 10 on a sheet of paper.
2. Advise the student that the questions will be read to them twice, and their task is to record an answer to each question on the sheet of paper.
3. Emphasize to the students that they will *not* be allowed to ask for any clarification. Likewise, they may *not* discuss the question or answer with any other student.
4. Read each of the following questions (twice) aloud to the class.

Questions

1. Does England have a fourth of July?
2. Why can't a man living in Winston-Salem, North Carolina, be buried west of the Mississippi River?
3. If you had only one match and entered a room in which there was a kerosene lamp, an oil burner, and a woodburning stove, which would you light first?
4. Some months have 30 days, some have 31; how many have 28?
5. If a doctor gave you three pills and told you to take one every half hour, how long would they last?
6. I have in my hand three U.S. coins totalling 55 cents in value. One is not a nickel. What are the coins?
7. Is it legal in Louisiana for a man to marry his widow's sister?
8. How many two-cent stamps are there in a dozen?
9. How many animals of each species did Moses take aboard the Ark with him?
10. An archaeologist claimed to have discovered some gold coins dated 46 B.C. Do you believe that she did? Why, or why not?

Alternate Question A: An aircraft flying south crashes so that the wreckage is half in the United States and half in Mexico. In which country would you bury the survivors?

Alternate Question B: How many birthdates does the average woman have?

Alternate Question C: A farmer had seventeen sheep. All but nine died. How many did he have left?

Alternate Question D: How far can a dog run into the woods?

When all the questions have been answered, provide the students with the correct answers (found at the end of the Index).

Questions for Discussion

1. Think about the barriers to effective communication. Which, if any, of these barriers affected the communication process in this exercise (perceptual differences, language and meaning, noise, etc.)?
2. How did the medium of communication affect the communication process? Do you think you could have done better if the questions had been presented in written form rather than vocal form?
3. What effect did the time constraint have on your interpretation of the message?

Controlling

Managers must plan, organize, and direct the organization, but how do they know if they are doing a good job? Controlling is the function of management that evaluates their efforts. Is the plan a good one? Is the firm adequately organized to effectively implement the plan? Is the plan being implemented so as to maximize the desired results? What changes need to be made in the plan, or the organization, or the implementation, or any combination thereof, to help the firm better achieve its goals?

It is necessary to evaluate the results the firm is getting against some sort of criteria. For most firms, those criteria are often financial, defined in terms of profits. However, it is necessary to define and truly understand control, as

Douglas Sherwin discusses in his classic article, "The Meaning of Control."

Profitability is not the only measure of effectiveness. In fact, the entire not-for-profit sector of the economy refuses to use profitability as a measure of success. Its measures come in other ways, as exemplified by the unqualified success of the March of Dimes in winning the battle against the deadly, crippling disease of polio. The March of Dimes was a success by any standard, but profitability would not be an appropriate criterion for it or other similar ventures. The key is whether or not the organization has achieved its goals, which may or may not include profitability.

When managers talk about control in the modern corporate sense, they really are talking about two different levels of control. The first is the traditional approach to controlling the firm's operation. This control is centered around the flow of information to determine what is going on in the organization, and often that information is generated on the shop floor. The second form of control deals with the organization as a whole. In this era of hostile takeovers, mergers, and acquisitions, managers are seeking to maintain control of their firms and not lose it to someone else in some new financial arrangement. Shareholders are also awakening to this realization in terms of profitability and other issues with which management has to deal. Management is discovering that decisions concerning the firm can no longer be made solely on the basis of a good financial return. Decision makers must consider what is socially and politically acceptable to the stockholders. The decision of many firms to leave South Africa to protest apartheid was just one manifestation of the new awareness of nonfinancial goals and objectives. With the new government in South Africa, several firms have decided to return to South Africa.

But financial control is important. It is obviously a chief concern of many firms, especially small ones, because it is usually the area where they run into trouble. Financial control is the basis of all the other types of control in the organization, since the people who own it have the final say in what the firm does. Such control makes it possible for management to protect itself from corporate raiders.

Security has also taken on new importance. With the advent of the computer and the World Wide Web, much information that was once the sole possession of the organization may now become public knowledge. This issue is addressed by Jeffrey Young in "Spies Like Us."

Production control is probably the area where the Japanese have made the most strides in recent years. U.S. and European firms have imported many of the ideas and techniques used in Japan over the past 20 years, and the Japanese themselves have set up their own plants in the United States, demonstrating that their techniques are transferable. Many changes have taken place in the area of production, including the introduction of computers and robots. Developments do not just involve machines; they include standards, policies, and, most especially, people. But not all manufacturers have adopted these techniques. Indeed, some of them have become even more retrograde than in the past, with very serious consequences. This is explained in "Why Markets Tolerate Mediocre Manufacturing."

Total Quality Management (TQM) is now one of the hottest topics in management. Its basic idea is that everyone is responsible for quality, but most especially senior management. The key to TQM is expressed in the title of one reading, "The Business of People Is People."

Looking Ahead: Challenge Questions

Managers are constantly evaluating how the organization is doing. What are some ways to evaluate an organization's performance besides profits?

Industry is concerned with being more efficient and productive. How can this be accomplished?

The Meaning of Control

Douglas S. Sherwin

"What exactly do you mean by management control?" When this question was asked of a number of managers, in both government and industry, the answers showed a surprising lack of agreement—surprising, since in a field for which theory has been developed to the extent it has in business management, terms should be precise, specific, and unambiguous. The literature, as one might expect, reflects about the same variety of views as entertained by management men themselves, and so does little to clarify the situation.

Is it important that managers have a clear understanding of this concept? The question almost answers itself. A manager who does not understand management control cannot be expected to exercise it in the most efficient and effective manner. Nor can staff men whose duty it is to design systems and procedures for their organizations design efficient systems unless they possess a clear understanding of management control. And certainly (though the truth of this is seldom sufficiently appreciated) anyone who is subject to control by others has to understand clearly what that means if he is to be contented in that relationship.

Indeed, when management control is *not* understood, good management is a very improbable result. This is especially true when—as frequently it is—control is identified with management, or is confused with certain devices of management, such as objectives, plans, organization charts, policy statements, delegations of authority, procedures, and the like. The manager who believes managing and controlling are the same thing has wasted one word and needs a second to be invented. And one who believes he has provided for control when he has established objectives, plans, policies, organization charts, and so forth, has made himself vulnerable to really serious consequences. A clear understanding of control is therefore indispensable in an effective manager.

Understanding control really means understanding three principal things about it: What is control? What is controlled? And who controls? By proposing answers to these questions, I will try to frame a concept of control that will be useful to practitioners of the managerial art.

The conception of control which I advocate can be simply and briefly stated as follows:

The essence of control is action which adjusts operations to predetermined standards, and its basis is information in the hands of managers.

We have a ready-made model for this concept of control in the automatic systems which are widely used for process control in the chemical and petroleum industries. A process control system works this way. Suppose, for example, it is desired to maintain a constant rate of flow of oil through a pipe at a predetermined, or set-point value. A signal, whose strength represents the rate of flow, can be produced in a measuring device and transmitted to a control mechanism. The control mechanism, when it detects any deviation of the actual from the set-point signal, will reposition the valve regulating flow rate.

BASIS FOR CONTROL

A process control mechanism thus acts to adjust operations to predetermined standards and does so on the basis of information it receives. In a parallel way, information reaching a manager gives him the opportunity for corrective action and is his basis for control. He cannot exercise control without such information. And he cannot do a complete job of managing without controlling.

As mentioned earlier, some students of management have defined control as what results from having objectives, plans, policies, organization charts, procedures, and so forth; and they refer to these elements of the management system, consequently, as controls or means of control. It is not difficult to understand why these devices of managing are so described by proponents of this point of view. Without objectives, for example, we all know results are likely to be other than desired, so it is assumed they function to control the results. And so it is with the other elements of the system.

Nevertheless, these elements are neither controls nor means of control. They do have, however, as we shall see later, an important role to play in a control *system,* and we can therefore examine them now in a little detail.

Certainly, to accomplish a task except through accident, people must know what they are trying to do. Objectives fulfill this need. Without them, people may work quite industriously yet, working aimlessly, accomplish little. Plans and programs complement objectives, since they propose how and according to what time schedule, the objectives are to be reached.

But though objectives, and plans and programs are indispensable to the efficient management of a business (or, for that matter, to the management of almost any human endeavor) they are not means of control. Control is checking to determine whether plans are being observed and suitable progress toward the objectives is being made, and acting, if necessary, to correct any deviations.

Policy is simply a statement of an organization's intention to act in certain ways when specified types of circumstances arise. It represents a general decision, predetermined and expressed as a principle or rule, establishing a normal pattern of conduct for dealing with given types of business events usually recurrent. A statement of policy is therefore useful in economizing the time of managers and in assisting them to discharge their responsibilities equitably and consistently.

POLICY VERIFICATION

Nothing in these advantages, however, makes policy a means of control. Indeed, by their very nature, policies generate the need for control; they do not fulfill that need. Adherence to policies is not guaranteed, nor can it be taken on faith. It has to be verified. Without verification, there is no basis for control, no control, and incomplete managing.

Organization is often cited as a means of control. This detracts both from its own significance and from the concept of control.

Organization is part of the giving of an assignment. The organization chart, for example, is a first crude step in the defining of assignments. It gives to each individual, in his title, a first approximation to the nature of his assignment, and it orients him as accountable to a certain individual. But it is not in a fruitful sense a means of control. Control is checking to ascertain whether the assignment is being executed as intended—and acting on the basis of that information.

The relation between 'internal check' and 'internal control' is likewise not well understood. The two terms refer to quite different aspects of the managerial system. 'Internal check' provides in practice for the principle that the same person should not have responsibility for all phases of a transaction. This makes it clearly an aspect of organization, rather than of control. For how do we provide for internal check? We provide for it through segregating the duties of recording and those of custodianship and assigning them to different employees or groups of employees.

Assigning duties is, of course, the very essence of organizing, and thus internal check is simply organizing in a special way in order to realize special objectives. Internal control, on the other hand, observes the actual performance of duties as against the assigned duties and acts, where necessary, to correct deviations of the actual from the assigned.

Internal check and internal control are obviously both very necessary in an enterprise. But they operate differently. The objective of internal check is to reduce the opportunity for fraud or error to occur. The objective of internal control is to restore operations to predetermined standards. Internal check is thus static or built-in; it is provided before the fact; and its operation is preventive in its effect. Internal control, in contrast, is active and continual; it is exercised after the fact; and its operation is corrective in its effect.

Assignments are far from defined, however, by the preparation of an organization chart. Among the ways we have for supplementing the titles and lines of authority of an organization chart are delegations of authority. Delegations of authority clarify the extent of authority of individuals and in that way serve to define assignments. That they are not means of control

is apparent from the very fact that wherever there has been a delegation of authority the need for control increases, and this could hardly be expected to happen if delegations of authority were themselves means of control.

MANAGER'S RESPONSIBILITY

Control becomes necessary whenever a manager delegates authority to a subordinate, because he cannot delegate, then simply sit back and forget all about it. A manager's accountability to his own superior has not diminished one whit as a result of delegating part of his authority to a subordinate. It is therefore incumbent upon managers who delegate authority to exercise control over actions taken under the authority so delegated. That means checking results as a basis for possible corrective action.

The question whether budgets are a means of control does not yield a straightforward answer because budgets perform more than one function. They perform three: they present the objectives, plans, and programs of the organization and express them in financial terms; they report the progress of actual performance against these predetermined objectives, plans, and programs; and, like organization charts, delegations of authority, procedures, and job descriptions, they define the assignments which have flowed down from the chief executive.

In expressing the objectives and plans of the organization, budgets are of course not means of control, for reasons examined earlier when objectives and plans were considered. Nor do budgets qualify as means of control in their function of defining assignments. Though this service of budgets is frequently overlooked, defining an assignment, as I have suggested previously, is neither a means of control nor the exercise of control.

Budgets are a means of control only in the respect that they report progress of actual performance against the program—information which enables managers to take action directed toward bringing actual results into conformity with the program.

In the previous paragraphs I have tried to show that objectives, plans and programs, organization charts, and other elements of the managerial system are not fruitfully regarded as either 'controls' or 'means of control.' They nevertheless do bear a very important relationship to the control function. They are the preestablished standards to which operations are adjusted by the exercise of management control.

It may seem unfamiliar to some to view these devices of management in that light. Perhaps 'standards' is not the very best word. Yet these elements of the system are standards in a very real sense, for they have been laid down by competent authority as models or standards of desired performance.

These standards are, of course, dynamic in character, for they are constantly altered, modified, or revised. But for a moment let us give our attention to their static quality.

An objective is static until revised; a plan or program is static until it is abandoned. They possess a kind of temporary durability or limited permanence. They are in force until superseded. This same static quality inheres also in the other elements of the managerial system we spoke of. Policies, organizational setup, procedures, delegations, job descriptions, and so forth, are, of course, constantly altered and added to. But, like objectives and plans, they retain their force until they are either abandoned or revised.

Suppose, for convenience, we use the phrase 'framework of management' to mean all the elements of the managerial system taken together—objective, plans and programs, policies, organization, and the like. Doubtless, a more descriptive phrase could be invented, but this one at least suggests the notion that there is something of a semipermanent nature in the managerial system. Now we can in a new way identify what is controlled. Managers control adherence to the objectives, plans, policies, organizational structure, procedures, and so forth, which have been laid down. In brief, managers control adherence to a predetermined 'framework of management.'

Now we can turn to the very important question that must be answered: "Who should act?"

It has become almost axiomatic as a management principle (which is unfortunately not always given effect in practice) that that person should act who is responsible for the results. 'Results' has to be interpreted here in a broad sense. For results include not only profits and costs—obvious items—but the conformity of all operations with all standards. Hence, whoever had responsibility for specifying and establishing a particular standard has to be ultimately responsible for controlling adherence to it and responsible, therefore, for such corrective action as is necessary. Of course, those below him in the chain of command may help him, but they cannot relieve him of final responsibility for control. Therefore, authority for managers to establish standards should be delegated as far down in the organization as practical wisdom permits. It then becomes their responsibility to control adherence of operations to the system they establish.

It is not only a responsibility, but a right; and it is asking for trouble to place in anyone else's hands the responsibility for controlling results in the operating manager's sphere of responsibility.

If the basis of control is information in the hands of managers, 'reporting' is elevated to a level of very considerable importance. Used here in a broad sense, 'reporting' includes special reports and routine reports; written, oral, and graphic reports; staff meetings, conferences, television screens, and any other means whereby information is transmitted to a manager as a basis for control action. Even the nonreceipt of information, as where management is by exception can be informational and imply the existence of control.

We are often told that reports should be timely and designed to meet the needs of managers. We are in a better position to appreciate this when we realize the important role that reporting plays in the control function. Certainly if it is to be the basis for control, information should be assembled with that objective in view. It should exclude material extraneous to the problem of control and must be placed at the disposal of managers quickly so that operations do not deviate any further from the desired norm—or for a longer period—than can be avoided.

That control occurs after the fact is a point that sometimes troubles managers. It should not—since this is simply part of the nature of the concept. The situation is entirely comparable in the process control system described earlier. In that system the detecting device continuously evaluates results and transmits them back to the control mechanism, which, sensing the difference between the actual and the desired results, acts to restore results to the desired value. The results, just as in management control, precede the exercise of control. Control systems, human or mechanical, deal with transfers of energy and a transfer of energy takes time. We learn from this—and it underscores the importance of speed in reporting—that all we can do for the management problem is to minimize the time lag between results and action.

CONTROL SPECTRUM

There is another sometimes troublesome aspect of control, namely, that control over some things must be relinquished as successively higher echelons of management are reached. This again we must simply face. Managers in the first echelon require certain information as their basis for controlling. But in the next higher echelon, the character of required information changes; some information is dropped, some is added. There is thus a kind of 'control spectrum.' For the process of fading out and shading in of information as you move up the pyramid until, just as in the visible spectrum the colors at one end are wholly unlike those at the other, the information reported to the top is wholly different from the information reported to first line managers.

This would hardly be worth pointing out except that some managers are burdened with a persistent sense of insecurity which undermines their self-confidence and ability to do the job, because they are unable to keep track of all the details under their management. Of course, they should not be able to keep track of all the results, or more accurately, should not allow themselves to do so. Relinquishing control over some operations is a calculated risk, taken so that managers can assume more important tasks.

It will bear mentioning that information serves other purposes than as the basis for control. The notion of a 'framework of management,' which we suggested earlier, is helpful in describing one of these purposes. This 'framework,' we said, is constantly undergoing change in one or another of its aspects. Such change takes place, not accidentally, but following conscious decisions for change by those responsible for such decisions. And decisions for changes in the framework are based on information that is conceptually different from information used for controlling adherence to the framework.

WHERE FORECASTS FIT

Forecasts and projections, for example, have no place in the problem of control (since control is after the fact while forecasts are before) but they are very important for setting objectives and formulating plans. Of course, information for aiming and for planning does not have to be before the fact. It may be an after-the-fact analysis proving that a certain policy has been impolitic in its effect on the relations of the company with customer, employee, or stockholder; or that a certain plan is no longer practical; or that a certain procedure is unworkable. The prescription here certainly would not be 'control' (since in these cases control would simply bring operations into conformity with obsolete standards), but the establishment of new standards—a new policy, a new plan, and a new procedure—to be controlled to.

Besides furnishing evidence of a need for reconstructing the managerial framework, information is, of course, the basis of all communication. But since that subject is one of the most discussed in the management field today, there is no need to discuss it further here.

Control, we have seen, means something quite specific in the managerial art. This is certainly as it should be in an area of thought as well developed as business management. For in any field for which theory has been developed to an appreciable extent, terms should be precise and unambiguous. Control, when used in a management context, should mean one thing and one thing only. I have suggested that it means action directed toward bringing operations into conformity with predetermined standards and goals; that it is exercised by managers; and that its basis is information in their hands after the fact.

In addition to being a specific part of managing, control is also, quite evidently, an extremely important part of managing. In organizations, therefore, where the responsibility for control is not placed in the hands of managers, or not accepted by them, difficulties are certain to arise. Managers must control. Staff members of the organization may, by furnishing information, help a manager discharge this responsibility, but may not share in it. Where this philosophy is adopted by top management as the policy of the organization, the probability is enhanced that the energies of the organization will be channeled in fruitful directions.

TERMINOLOGY

Control is admittedly a term with emotional connotations. The denotation of the term, however, suffers from no such objection. Control is not supervision. Experienced managers perceive that as their authority is broadened, their superiors must place increased reliance on control as a means of safeguarding their own accountability. But at the same time, supervision of their activities by superiors become[s] less close. There seems every reason to believe, therefore, that as the real nature of control becomes better understood, managers will come to recognize that their being subject to it in increasing measure is as sure a sign as any of their progress in the organization and in the fulfillment of their position.

The Power of Voice and Touch

Disparity between a company's voice and its touch is a silent slayer of organizational renaissance.

C. JAMES NOVAK

C. James Novak is human resource manager for Syracuse China Company, a manufacturer of commercial chinaware in Syracuse, New York.

"She has to be able to connect your voice to your touch," leadership maverick and author Max De Pree is counseled in the prologue of his book, *Leadership Jazz.* Responding to the nurse's advice, he gently massages a fragile 23 ounces of premature life named Zoe, repeatedly telling his new granddaughter how much he loves her. The child survives those perilous first days and grows up healthy and energetic.

For De Pree, the experience illustrates the power of matching actions with words and tone. It is a power he readily applies to leadership, "At the core of becoming a leader is the need always to connect one's voice and one's touch," he writes. The same realization can help HR professionals in their stewardship of dynamic, team-based change initiatives.

Disparity between a company's voice and its touch is a silent slayer of organizational renaissance more lethal than any of the traditional team-building poisons. The impact of a leadership that speaks with one tone and acts with another is devastating to empowerment efforts. Companies serious about pushing down decision making, opening new channels of communication, and sparking creativity must be able to recognize and react to the inevitable inconsistencies in corporate voice and touch that accompany every transition to a team-based culture.

BARRIERS TO CONSISTENCY

Corporate voice and touch drift apart for a number of reasons. One critical area is communications. "Team building starts with a clear vision, a sense of mission and a credible long-term commitment," observes Anthony Sgarlatta, human resource manager at New Venture Gear (NVG), an auto component manufacturer employing more than 3,100 people in Syracuse, New York. NVG is jointly owned by Chrysler Corporation and General Motors.

New Venture Gear has been a model of union-management team-building expertise for more than 15 years. "For employees to act on a message they have to understand the talk," Sgarlatta notes. "What are the expectations and boundaries for this change process and have they been clearly communicated? Often, it is not that the voice is inconsistent, but rather that it's misunderstood." NVG communicates its vision through plant meetings, area manager meetings, skip-level meetings, newsletters and a sincere open-door policy.

IF THE MESSAGE IS TEAMS BUT THE STRUCTURE IS TOP-DOWN, EMPLOYEES PERCEIVE A LACK OF TRUST IN THEIR ABILITIES.

Union and plant leaders are highly visible.

Employees unable or unwilling to make a sustained change in style present a serious roadblock to team-building initiatives. They embody the perceived disparity in voice and touch and create a frustrating clash of corporate vision and day-to-day reality that erodes confidence in management's commitment to change. "Managers whose style of supervision is not compatible with teams also make it easy for a company's voice and touch to appear out of sync," Sgarlatta continues. "These individuals receive training on working inside a team paradigm, but in a crisis they revert back to their old dictatorial style."

Barry Roach, Ph.D., human resource development manager at Welch Allyn, knows that failing to train employees in team skills is another reason corporate voice and touch become inconsistent. Welch Allyn is an ISO 9001-certified manufacturer of precision medical equipment and a recognized leader in team-based, total quality initiatives. This global company employs about 1,300 people at its headquarters in Skaneateles, New York.

"Team building is an organic process that starts small and grows," observes Roach. "It's an oxymoron, then, to declare, 'Thou shalt be a team' since teams are a way to empower people. By definition, it's a participative rather than dictatorial process." Roach notes that supporting teams at Welch Allyn is synonymous with quality training, performance orientation and clear vision. Training is an essential part of providing employees with the tools to understand and contribute to Welch Allyn's team environment.

Companies that implement a team environment within the confines of a hierarchical structure create another disconnect in voice and touch. If the message is teams but the structure is top-down, employees perceive a lack of trust in their abilities. "When teams are introduced in combination with other organizational changes, they work," according to Paul Osterman, a professor

---

Managers whose style of supervision is not compatible with teams make it easy for a company's voice and touch to appear out of sync.

Anthony Sgarlatta,
New Venture Gear

---

of management at MIT's Sloan School, "when they're introduced as an isolated practice, they fail."[1]

Seattle-based aerospace giant Boeing addressed the organizational structure problem when it created teams to coordinate 10,000 employees and 500 suppliers working to design the new 777 jetliner. Five or six senior managers from each major discipline oversee a group of about 50 leaders drawn from engineering and operations who in turn guide the 200-plus individual component design teams. Aircraft integration teams facilitate horizontal communications among all participants. It is a structure that encourages employees to seize initiative.

"We have the no-messenger rule," says Henry Shomber, a Boeing chief engineer, "team members must make decisions on the spot. They can't run back to their functions for permission."[2] The new structure helped ensure that the 777 completed its first test flight in the summer of 1994 with fewer than half the number of design problems experienced by earlier programs.

GETTING BACK ON TRACK

At the heart of correcting a disparity in voice and touch is understanding that team building is a continuing confirmation of trust. "The whole thing operates on trust," NVG's Sgarlatta notes, "and trust is something that takes a long time to build." When senior management extends to workers the privilege to make mistakes as they pursue well-inten-tioned efforts, employees see decision making as a valued opportunity to contribute, rather than a career-limiting risk. Trust from the top means confidence in the talent, training and motivation of team members. It also means recognizing that both success and failure are part of the dynamics of moving together toward challenging goals. Trust is the most accurate bellwether of a consistent voice and touch.

Company leaders who "walk the talk" send a powerful message that the emphasis on team building is not a passing fad. The authors of a *Harvard Business Review* article, "Why Change Programs Don't Produce Change," observe that "Senior managers must make an effort to adopt the team behavior, attitudes and skills that they have demanded of others in earlier phases of change. Their struggle with behavior change will help sustain corporate renewal . . . (and) lend credibility to top management's continued espousal of change."[3]

The presence and accessibility of senior managers also reassures team members that setbacks are part of the process. "It's two steps forward and one step back," says Welch Allyn's Roach. "You move from A to Z not in one step, but one step at a time."

The performance review process is another useful tool in underscoring a team-based environment and reinforcing a consistent voice and touch. At New Venture Gear, Sgarlatta notes that "salaried evaluations emphasize team support, linking ratings to team participation and performance." This process, he says, "promotes a system where rewards are tangibly linked with results." Likewise, individuals who are not supporting the team-based culture place their job in jeopardy. "It is important to remove people who are barriers to the team process," Sgarlatta adds.

Similar accountability is evident at Welch Allyn. "When things go wrong, some people say, 'Take the individuals back and retrain them,'" says Roach, "but that is not the

AT THE HEART OF CORRECTING A DISPARITY IN VOICE AND TOUCH IS UNDERSTANDING THAT TEAM BUILDING IS A CONTINUING CONFIRMATION OF TRUST.

answer. They've already been trained and trained well—the answer is to just do it." Roach points out that an overwhelming number of people are successful at aligning their behavior with the Welch Allyn culture. Those that struggle usually leave of their own accord. A few are removed.

Finally, standing firm on the common ground that initially launched an organization's commitment to teamwork can help a company overcome credibility tremors. For both New Venture Gear and Welch Allyn, quality was the team-building spark. "We started on the quality theme around 1980," Sgarlatta remembers, "because it was the one area all of us could agree on immediately. Who was going to argue against quality?"

Roach agrees. "Quality was our overarching goal," he says. "We went away from inspection points and made people responsible for their own quality." As a result, he says, resources and communications are focused on a common goal whose message is clearly understood by all employees.

Human resource professionals must have not only the ability to recognize a disparity in corporate voice and touch, but also the leadership skills to intervene and restore faith in the team process. Max De Pree believes Zoe found strength in connecting the tone of his voice with the reassuring touch of his hand. The same connection has the power to revitalize an organization's collective commitment to continuous improvement.

Signs of Disparity in Corporate Voice and Touch

As active corporate-change agents, human resource professionals are in an ideal position to recognize warning signs that employees perceive an organization's voice and touch as being out of sync. Recognizing this perceived disparity permits early intervention and can be crucial in restoring credibility to a team-building process. Some warning signs that corporate voice and touch may be inconsistent include the following:

• Communication flows from the top down only.

• Training is not made a visible priority.

• Mistakes are criticized unduly.

• Teams are not given the time, tools or training to be effective.

• Nearly all significant decisions require top-level approval.

• Exit interviews question the company's commitment to teams.

• Teams are implemented without any accompanying alterations in structure that are needed to support them.

• Performance appraisals do not attempt to link team participation and performance to promotions and raises.

Notes

1. Brian Dumaine, "The Trouble With Teams," *Fortune Magazine* (Sept. 5, 1994): 86.

2. Brian Dumaine, "The Trouble With Teams," *Fortune Magazine* (Sept. 5, 1994): 88-90.

3. Michael Beer, Russell A. Eisenstat, and Bert Spector, "Why Change Programs Don't Produce Change." *Harvard Business Review* (November-December 1990): 166.

Financial Reporting on the World Wide Web

SIMON PETRAVICK, CPA, AND JOHN GILLETT, CPA

Publishing on the Internet offers an inexpensive, timely platform that wraps around the world.

As of May 1996, 103 (or 69%) of the Fortune 150 have World Wide Web sites on the Internet. Of these 103, 83 (or 81%) make financial information available on the sites.

Until recently, this information was distributed primarily through printed media such as quarterly and annual reports. Current technological developments, particularly those related to the Internet and World Wide Web (Web), are providing new platforms for distributing financial information. Because management accountants are responsible for the preparation and distribution of financial information to creditors, shareholders, potential investors, and other external parties they should be particularly interested in this shift.

WHAT ARE THE INTERNET AND WORLD WIDE WEB?

The Internet is an international collection of more than 50,000 independent communication networks that are owned by a variety of public, educational, and governmental entities. These networks are linked to each other, creating a global weblike communications system. Information passes easily among them because all connected networks use a common communications protocol. This process works so well that the Internet functions as though it were one large computer.

The Web is one method for accessing information on the Internet. Web users employ software called Web browsers to connect and communicate with other Internet sites. Because the Web supports multimedia, information can be transmitted as text, graphics, audio, or animation in an efficient and user-friendly way.

Rather than rely on communications via printed media, which can become outdated quickly, many organizations are building sophisticated Web sites. These sites hold a great deal of information, which can be updated as needed. Individuals with Web access can obtain this information from those organizations that provide addresses for their sites. The development of high-capacity telecommunications networks, low-cost computer hardware, user-friendly software, and a computer savvy generation have made the Internet an effective option for distributing information. For additional information, see "Connecting Your Company to the Internet" in the September 1995 issue of MANAGEMENT ACCOUNTING®.

CURRENT STATE OF FINANCIAL REPORTING

Information disseminated by the 83 Fortune 150 companies falls within the following categories: advertisement, limited information, and comprehensive information. Table 1 shows examples of each category and the

Table 1. OVERVIEW OF FINANCIAL REPORTING ON THE WEB

Advertisement	Limited	Comprehensive
Example: No information available directly from the Web. Users can send e-mail to order information. Users are given a phone number to call to order information.	**Example:** Only certain items are reported, e.g., total revenues, net income, or earnings per share. Reports are limited to a narrow time period, such as the current quarter.	**Example:** Users can obtain: Full annual reports and 10-K. Quarterly reports and 10-Q. Current stock price. History of stock price. Audio and animated messages.
Number of companies using this option: 3	**Number of companies using this option:** 34 In eight cases, the limited information was supplemented by an advertisement that allowed users to order comprehensive information.	**Number of companies using this option:** 46 In nine cases, comprehensive information was available in formats such as WordPerfect or Microsoft Word that could not be viewed by a Web browser.

number of companies using each option.

Three organizations provide no information over the Web. Rather, they use it to advertise the existence of financial reporting information. Interested parties can e-mail requests for the information and have it delivered by regular mail. Another option instructs the users to phone in requests for the information.

Within the next category are 34 organizations that provide information that is limited in one of two ways. The first limitation concerns the time period covered by the reports. For example, through the Web, users may find information about the previous quarter only. Information about other quarters or annual periods are not available. The second limitation relates to the amount of information provided. Here, only certain elements of financial reports are available, such as total revenues or net income. Complete statements of operations or financial position are not shown. In eight of these 34 cases, the limited information was supplemented by an ad that gave users the option to order comprehensive information.

Finally, 46 organizations make comprehensive financial reports available on the Web. The typical presentation we saw included the most recent annual report prepared in accordance with generally accepted accounting principles, the corresponding independent auditor's report, and management discussion and analysis. A few organizations presented their annual reports for two to four years. In some cases, the 10-K also was available. Eight of the 46 organizations provided comprehensive information, but in a format that could not be viewed by a Web browser. This information had to be downloaded and imported into another application such as WordPerfect or Excel.

Many comprehensive presentations also provide reports for each quarter following the last annual report. Typically, they include quarter-to-date and year-to-date comparative information supplemented by footnotes. It also is common to find copies of the 10-Qs.

HOW FINANCIAL INFORMATION IS PRESENTED

The ideal presentation begins by offering links to the financial reports from the home page. (The home page is the first screen that is seen by anyone visiting a Web site.) These links are important because the construction of quality financial reports is for naught if individuals looking for them cannot find them easily.

Figure 1 shows Digital Equipment Corporation's home page. Digital leaves no doubt about the availability of financial information. Anyone interested in reaching this information only needs to point and click his or her mouse on the words *Company Financials & Contacts*. This procedure is possible because programmers who create Web pages can link a graphic or text to additional information about that subject. The linked references are called hypertext. They appear on the screen in a different color from the regular text. For example, regular text will use black letters while hypertext uses blue underlined letters. The referenced information might be located on the

Figure 1

same computer system or anywhere on the Internet. By clicking on the graphic or hypertext, users leave the current screen and open the additional information screens. Then they can follow additional links out and away, or they can backtrack one step (screen) at a time to the information they were viewing previously.

Another common method for referencing financial reports is to have a "Corporate Information" category listed on the home page. A click of the mouse on this category usually leads to another menu containing a "Financial Reporting" category. It is a mistake for a designer to use nonintuitive labels or confusing paths to financial reporting because visitors to the site will become frustrated. For example, financial reports should not be listed under categories such as "Products & Services" or "Service, Training, & Support."

In the actual financial reporting section, it is useful to have a summary of the information available there. Figure 2 shows how Digital describes its information. As with the home page, each graphic leads the user to additional information about that subject. For example, after clicking on *Annual Report Online*, users can read either the 1995 or 1994 annual report.

Figure 2

Figure 3 shows how Digital uses hypertext rather than graphics to create a table of contents for an annual report. Each blue underlined phrase is a hypertext link. To get to the statement of interest, users click the mouse on the statement of their choice. While viewing Figure 3, users can scroll down and see other hypertext links to the notes for the consolidated financial statements and several types of supplementary information: quarterly financial data, officers and management, directors, committees of the board, corporate consulting engineers, and investor information.

Figure 3

Hypertext also can be used to make the reading of financial reports easier. For example, the footnote references found in the line item descriptions of financial statements or auditor's report can be linked to the corresponding note. This feature indicates the existence of important additional information and allows the readers to access it immediately. Another possibility is to link the name of the auditor's group or firm with the auditor's home page, providing unsophisticated users with supplementary information about the assurer of the statements.

MORE THAN REPORTS

Many organizations use the Web to provide more than just annual and quarterly reports. The Web can deliver real-time information, audio and animated messages, and information in formats other than the hypertext that is viewed through the Web browser.

Because the Web is an electronic medium, it can be updated at any time, thereby providing information in real time. We found that the most common type of information presented in real time is the current stock price. For example, users can click on the *Stock Price* graphic (Figure 2—Digital Financial News & Investor Information) and receive the information shown in Figure 4. This real-time information complements the historical financial statement reports, and it provides the users with an up-to-date picture of operations. It also is more efficient because it eliminates the need for the user to go elsewhere for the information.

Digital provides this service by linking Figure 2's Stock Price graphic to another site on the Internet that tracks this information. Remember, graphics and hypertext can be linked to any site on the Internet. Figure 2 also shows another illustration of this linking. After clicking on the graphic *Stock Performance Chart*, users can view charts that show the price and volume of Digital's stock over the past 12 months. The charts are obtained through a link to another Internet site that tracks that information.

Clearly, linking is a powerful tool, but this dependency on another Internet site is not without the potential for trouble. If the remote Internet site is busy or not available, then the information is not available either. Therefore, the performance of all third-party links should be monitored and tested periodically. If responses are not received in a satisfactory manner, it may be necessary to obtain the information from another source.

Here's an example of poor monitoring of third-party links. Some organizations used this feature to provide copies of 10-Ks and 10-Qs from the Securities & Exchange Commission's (SEC) Internet site. The address of this site changed recently

tor 2.0 is available free on the Internet (http://home. netscape. com), the program does so much that it makes sense to have the best manual you can get for it, and that would be Ventana Press's *Official Netscape Navigator 2.0 Book.* Bundled with the manual is the latest version of the Navigator software.

Navigator 2.0 will handle most situations, but not all. The second solution covers the rest of the field. There are free programs on the Internet that allow you to watch, hear, download, zip/unzip, encode/decode, and check any file for viruses. Two popular sites for the programs are http://www.jumbo.com (49,446 titles free to all), and http://www.shareware.com/. The catch is that these programs make handling files on the Internet easy, but to get them you have to download them from the Internet, and many are compressed (zip files) and probably should

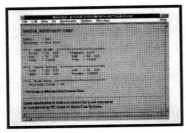

be virus checked, and so on. Luckily, Prentice Hall PTR has published *The Downloader's Companion.* Six of the most useful downloading and file managing/ viewing programs are included on disks, and with the text you get something you don't get from the Internet—a manual that includes step-by-step instructions for everything from loading the programs on your machine to using each of the utilities. The manual is the key, and it is well written.

If your screen often locks up on the highlighted request, or charts appear as kaleidoscopes of code on your screen, consider one of these solutions. Like so many other things on the Internet, the cost is ridiculously low for what these programs provide.

to http://www.sec.gov. Unfortunately, during our research we found that several organizations were still using the old address, and users were not redirected to the new site.

In addition to providing real-time capabilities, the Web supports multimedia presentations. Visitors to the Ameritech site who have a sound card and Real Audio 2.0 plug-in (see sidebar) can hear a guided audio tour with the 1995 annual report (http://www.ameritech.com/news/annuals/ annual_95/). Further, the narrative descriptions of an entity's operations can be replaced with animation and video, providing possibly an even richer explanation of activities.

Finally, the Web supports the distribution of information in other formats besides hypertext markup language (HTML), the language used to create most Web documents. At IBM (http://www.ibm.com/ibm/ar95/AR-static/ Financials/review.html), users can obtain the financial statements in either a spreadsheet (Excel or Lotus 1-2-3) or Adobe Acrobat format. Acrobat is software that can display documents in their original format. Thus, through the In-

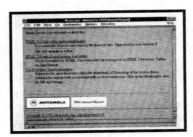

Figure 4

ternet, an interested party can obtain an annual report in the form in which it was printed originally. The user simply downloads the file from the Internet and, with Acrobat, or a similar program, opens the file in its native application (into his or her copy of Lotus 1-2-3, or Microsoft Word, for instance). CSX Corporation provides users with financial statements in Rich Text, Word, or WordPerfect formats (http://www.csx.com/docs/csx95ann.html). Because HTML documents are saturated with proprietary formatting codes they are not directly transferable to most personal and business computer applications. The ability to download the equivalent word processing and spreadsheet documents invests the information with portability. The downloaded file can be carried to, read by, or printed from any computer that is loaded with the appropriate program.

SIX SUGGESTIONS FOR SUCCESSFUL FINANCIAL REPORTING

One: Avoid software incompatibility. Without question, the software used to create and distribute information on the Internet will continue to

evolve. It is possible, however, that the software used to create financial reports will not be compatible with the viewer's software. We found that certain tables turned to garbage on the screen when viewed with older versions of Netscape Navigator or the America Online browser. This incompatibility prevents access to the information and defeats the original purpose of providing access over the Internet.

Incompatibility can be avoided by giving users a description of the software they need to view the reports. Individuals without much computer experience, however, may not understand the differences among various versions of software. A more desirable alternative is to build in guides that direct users to a presentation their systems can handle. Figure 5 shows how Motorola addressed this issue.

Figure 5

In either case, when systems conflict it is good to point users to sites that allow them to obtain the software they need to view or hear a company's information. Links can be created from home pages to Internet sites that offer the software free. For example, Chrysler Corporation provides a software library at http://www. chryslercorp.com/help/help.html. (For additional help with downloading files and Web sites for software, see "It Won't Play the Movie, and I Can't Hear the Sound.")

Two: Financial statements should be designed for on-screen viewing. A very wide display will force users to scroll to the right, moving the left-hand information off the screen. Because the left side usually has descriptions of the line items, once they are moved off the screen it is no longer possible to know what is being viewed. We found this problem was most common when viewing income statements that presented three years of operations.

Three: Financial information should be displayed against a neutral background that facilitates reading. Black letters set on a light gray or white background work well. Elaborate graphics should be avoided. For example, at one site, we struggled to read financial statements printed in black letters set on a yellow and black herringbone background. This choice of graphics made it nearly impossible to view the information.

Four: Users should be able to use e-mail to request information they cannot find. This service is useful for the viewer, and analysis of these requests allows the company to identify any omissions from information it is providing. These requests also may suggest enhancements for the current presentation.

Five: It is important for companies to advertise the existence of their site because the information is of no value unless users know it is there. Sites can be advertised in two ways. The first is to list the company in the major Internet directories such as Yahoo (http://www.yahoo.com) or Lycos (http://www.lycos.com). These directories serve as online catalogs of information/services that can be found on the Internet and are a common starting point of many Internet searches. Also, users can be made aware of the fact that information is available on the Internet by including the address of the company's home page in communications such as advertisements, letters to shareholders, or press releases.

Six: A Web site should count the number of times it answers requests for the various types of financial information it provides. This tracking ability tells a company what Internet users are interested in and, just as important, what is not being viewed. These numbers may indicate a need for corrective action if information that is expected to be popular is underutilized.

THE FUTURE

Every indication we've seen is that the phenomenal growth of the Internet will continue. Across the entire Web, there are more than 100,000 sites with hundreds being added each week. In fact, From October 1995 to May 1996, 37 Fortune 150 companies added home pages. Decision makers increasingly are using the Internet as a new source of obtaining traditional information. To meet the needs of a computer sophisticated generation and to provide easy, real-time access to information, high-quality financial reports will have to be an integral part of every organization's Internet presence.

Simon Petravick, Ph.D., CPA, is an assistant professor of accounting at Bradley University, Peoria, Ill. He can be reached at (309) 677-2286 or simonp@bradley.edu.

John Gillett, Ph.D., CPA, is an associate professor of accounting at Bradley University, Peoria, Ill. He can be reached at (309) 677-2290 or jwg@bradley.edu.

SPIES
Like Us

The wired worlds of the Internet and the World Wide Web provide a new back door for competitors to plunge into your computer network and electronically snoop around your data. You may even be tempted to return the favor.

Jeffrey Young

FORGET EVERYTHING YOU THINK you know about high-tech crime: teenage hackers, foreign spies, gangs hijacking components, forgers making phony $100 bills on the copy machine. The biggest danger to any company's intellectual crown jewels—trade secrets, R&D plans, pricing lists, customer info—comes from other U.S. companies.

"Competitors are the single greatest threat in computer crime," says Richard Power of the Computer Security Institute (CSI) in San Francisco. In a recent computer-crime survey conducted by CSI and the FBI, more than 50% of the 453 respon-dents identified electronic snooping by competitors as a major concern. Thirty-six percent had experienced an electronic break-in during the past year.

The situation is expected to get much worse. In 1990, less than 15% of personal computers were networked, according to International Data Corp. Today, more than 50% are. Meanwhile, the number of PCs soared from 10 million to more than 100 million. As companies rush to establish a World Wide Web site, they put untrained and unsophis-ticated computer users in charge of Web servers and system administration. They also inadvertently

CRIMINAL PROBE, CIVIL SUIT HIT HIGH-FLYING IC-CAD VENDOR

Police raid stuns Avant!

BY RICHARD GOERING

Sunnyvale, Calif. — In a legal double-whammy, Avant! Corp.—the recent merger of ArcSys and Integrated Silicon Systems (ISS)—was hit last week with a criminal investigation by Santa Clara County and a civil suit by Cadence Design Systems (San Jose, Calif.) over alleged theft of source code. The dramatic devel-opments could pose a for-midable challenge to the high-profile IC-CAD ven-dor, which has been erod-ing Cadence's market lead.

Avant! headquarters was raided Tuesday by the Santa Clara County Dis-trict Attorney's high-tech crime unit. Twenty-five officers from the FBI and local police agencies seized unspecified evi-dence for a continuing criminal investigation. But no charges were filed, and little public infor-mation was released.

The following day, Cadence issued a civil suit against Avant! and four individuals, including

vertising. A restraining order was issued later the same day to prevent tampering of evidence.

"We believe we have incon-trovertible evidence that Avant! is a company built and sustained with intellectual property stolen from Cadence," declared Joe

Cadence's Costello (left) claims Hsu's (right) firm stole intellectual property.

Costello, Cadence president and CEO. Costello claimed that Avant! has engaged in a "con-certed campaign" to induce Ca-dence employees to leave the company and steal key place-ment-and-routing routines.

Avant! vigorously denied all charges. "Through this civ-il lawsuit, Cadence has ad-mitted that it can't compete in the marketplace," said Gerald Hsu, Avant! presi-dent and CEO, in a pre-pared statement. "The law-suit is without merit. Allegations that Avant! is built on Cadence technolo-gy are laughable. No one wants Cadence technology."

Continued on page 8

Intel Engineer Admits To Stealing Chip Designs

By David Einstein
Chronicle Staff Writer

Leland Altschuler, chief of the U.S. Attorney's office in San Jose. "The consequences of this crimi-

...

Man Charged With Entering Computer Files

U.S. Uses On-Line Wiretap Of Harvard's System To Monitor Argentine

By ROSS KERBER

Staff Reporter of THE WALL STREET JOURNAL
Federal authorities filed fraud charges against a 22-year-old Argentine university student who allegedly broke into secret

Cadence Design Accuses A Rival of Stealing Secrets

Avanti Calls Suit Baseless, but Stock Falls

E M. FISHER

O, Dec. 8 — Ca-ms Inc. said to-1 the Avant! Cor-it of the theft of yright infringe-ncy. The compa-e market for the ign software nputer chips. dropped by $5.75,

Cadence's suit seeks unspecified damages and a court order blocking the sale of Avant!'s programs.

Late yesterday, the court issued a restraining order blocking Avant! from modifying or destroying any software code related to the case.

Joseph B. Costello, the president and chief executive of Cadence, said the company had become suspicious that code was stolen when an engi-neer reported having seen one of Avant!'s products operating at a cus-

As part of its fil District Court in Sar included an affidavit tor of computer-aide Cypress Semicondu tion, who in evalu from Cadence and had found thousands gryprints" indicatin had taken place. "In results of this come that portions of the have originated fro

Cadence Goes for the Jugular in Theft Suit Against Avant!

Also, annual reports and another update on the stock contest

Don't let Avant! slip off your radar screen.

Last December its Sunnyvale head-quarters were raided by the FBI, the San-ta Clara County District Attorney's office and local police. They were looking for evidence connected to charges that

Chairman, CEO and founder Gerald Hsu.

The raid caused Avant!'s stock to fall from around 45 to 14 in a matter of days. The company has subsequently tried to put a positive spin on the situation, and at one point said it had received $1 million in new orders. And its stock now trades at 22¾.

But all is not calm on the Avant! front. On April 19 Cadence will file a motion to seek a permanent injunction against Avant! Unless there are delays, a hearing

HERB GREENBERG
Business Insider

And this tidbit, from the conveniently overlooked department: When Avant! went public, the only employment back-ground given in the prospectus for Hsu started in 1988 when he went to work for

Telecommandos *The rush to get wired has provided scores of fresh opportunities for competitive snooping. Numerous computer break-ins are reported every week. And what you read in the papers may be only the tip of a rapidly growing menace.*

provide a handy electronic back door through which competitors can peek at a company's most intimate secrets. Result: The American Society for Industrial Security reports that electronic security breaches rose from fewer than 1 every three months before 1980 to more than 30 per month in 1995.

The problem, say security experts, is that the effervescent nature of electronic data may soften, or even erase, guilty feelings. "People do things in the computer environment that they would never do outside," says John Williams, a criminal attorney in San Jose, Calif. "An attorney in a courtroom would never look in the briefcase of another who stepped out of the room. And yet I have a case in which one attorney looked at the computer files of another. There is something [alluring] about the anonymity."

Most people wouldn't dream of breaking into an office in the dead of night and rummaging through a file cabinet. But what about shuffling through another person's e-mail from the cozy warmth of your home office? Most people wouldn't steal a car, whether locked or not. But what about copying a customer database file or the internal pricing spreadsheet of a competitor? Nothing tangible has really been taken, has it?

It sure has. Computer crime accounts for estimated losses of more than $10 billion per year, according to Management Analytics, a Hudson, Ohio, consulting company that specializes in information assurance and security.

Vital corporate data is stored on servers with wildly varying degrees of security, and employees frequently discuss confidential projects on companywide e-mail systems, say officials at the Computer Emergency Response Team at the Software Engineering Institute in Pittsburgh. Meanwhile, competitors as well as disgruntled workers troll through this data, using sophisticated search engines and powerful tools to gather everything they can get their hands on.

Computer break-ins have increased 323% since 1992. Nearly 700 attacks have been reported.

Experienced law enforcement officers say technopiracy is almost undetectable and anyone can easily get the necessary tools from electronic bulletin boards. Even if you aren't quite ready yet to edge over the line, how can you stop a competitor who doesn't have the same sense of morality?

CIRCUIT BREAKERS

CADENCE DESIGN SYSTEMS, a $500 million San Jose-based company, competes in the cutthroat business of electronic design automation. This is the world of integrated circuit design, where software tools help engineers create, craft and debug mindachingly complex blueprints for electronic devices that take years to perfect.

TESTED RECIPE FOR DISASTER

Put an insecure system into a hostile environment. Staff it with people who don't understand security.

Distributed untrusted computation. Arbitrary servers at unknown locations operated by unknown organizations provide information to an array of browsers at unknown locations operated by unknown organizations.

Remote execution of untrusted software. Web extensions such as Adobe PostScript, Java and MIME allow internal access and manipulation of data from outside the company.

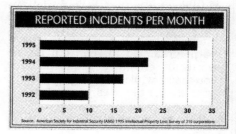

REPORTED INCIDENTS PER MONTH

Source: American Society for Industrial Security (ASIS) 1995 Intellectual Property Loss Survey of 319 corporations

Remote interpretation of unstructured and unverified content. Most browsers and servers assume that incoming information follows the HTTP protocol. If incoming information does not conform, however, it can cause incorrectly routed requests or facilitate system attacks.

5. CONTROLLING: Security

In September 1994, Cadence grew suspicious of engineer Mitsuru "Mitch" Igusa when he left the company and refused to sign a confidentiality agreement. Checking computer logs, the company's internal networking staff discovered several very large computer file transfers to Igusa's home machine, recorded days before his departure. Believing they were e-mail messages with file attachments,

the company contacted the Santa Clara County district attorney.

Three months later, the police raided Igusa's home in San Jose. They allegedly found Cadence source code running in his Unix workstation. Some of its copyrights, logos and identifying information were removed. In August 1995, the Santa Clara County District Attorney's Office charged Igusa

---

POROUS AS SWISS CHEESE

Think your Web server is safe? Your browser? Don't kid yourself.

THE ASTONISHING GROWTH of the World Wide Web has introduced security challenges that regularly defeat even the best corporate defenses. These attacks target three main areas: the servers that provide requested information; the browsers that retrieve and view information; and the network infrastructure linking the two.

BROWSER ATTACKS

■ Browsers are used to forge e-mail. An attacker can easily send false or incriminating electronic mail and make it seem like it's coming from you.

■ Many browsers automatically process and present documents, pictures, sound files and Word documents using "helper" applications like Microsoft Word and Ghostscript. But watch out if your document has a virus, or if the PostScript file includes hidden commands. Viewing these images can cause your computer to overwrite configuration files, delete critical information or even transmit company secrets.

■ Applets are Java programs that you can automatically load onto your computer and run at the push of a button. But they can also be programmed to send out passwords or credit card information you used while cruising the Web, or to list all the sites you visited.

SERVER ATTACKS

■ One favorite technique attackers use is to break into a Web server and change the information on a Web page. For example, they type in misspellings, steal and alter

credit card information, redirect shipments, change delivery addresses, add new orders, alter online catalogs and secure internal price lists.

■ Most Web servers are fairly easy to crash. For example, an attacker can cause a Web server to deny services by sending a very big Universal Resource Locator in a user request. Suddenly, the fancy Web page you spent hundreds of thousands of dollars creating is gone and your main source of electronic commerce dries up.

■ Attackers can send thousands of erroneous requests and overrun the disk area that's available on a Web server for logging activities. Most servers keep error logs in disk areas that are critical to system operation. By sending error requests, attackers can exceed the available space, causing server crashes.

■ Many Web servers provide search engines to let visitors find what they are looking for quickly, but in many cases, attackers searching for strings like "root:" end up getting copies of entries from the server's password file. The attacker then runs a password-guessing tool, such as Crack,

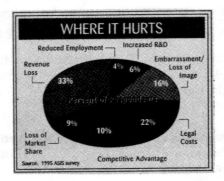

WHERE IT HURTS

Reduced Employment — Increased R&D

Revenue Loss

4% 6%

Embarrassment/ Loss of Image

33%

16%

Percent of Respondents

9% 10% 22%

Loss of Market Share

Legal Costs

Competitive Advantage

Source: 1995 ASIS survey

and gains unlimited access to the server and its data.

NETWORK ATTACKS

■ The Web uses the Transmission Control Protocol (TCP) to transport information, but the TCP design has a flaw. When a session starts, an attacker can send a request and ignore the server's response. Result: The server waits indefinitely for the protocol to finish. Servers have limits on the number of processes that can be in this state at any given time. If an attacker repeats this process many times, all further TCP ports open to Web services will fail. In some systems, this failure will last until you reboot.

■ A network attacker who gets into your system's infrastructure can record all of your Web transactions. For example, when your marketing department starts researching the competition to prepare for a new product launch, a snooper can discover your intentions.

■ Remote site (Internet Protocol) addresses are just numbers sent over the Internet. Many people are able to forge IP addresses to make it appear as if they are coming from a friendly site. This may allow access to critical files, such as R&D plans and financial records.

—*Fred Cohen*

Fred Cohen is an information security consultant and author of Protection and Security on the Information Superhighway *(John Wiley & Sons). Visit his Web site (http://all.net/) for data-protection tips.*

GLOSSARY

Audit Trail: Chronological record of system activities that allows activities to be reconstructed.

Authentication: Determining the identity of a communicating party.

Biometric Device: Authenticates a user by measuring some hard-to-forge physical characteristic, such as a fingerprint or retinal scan.

Blue Box: A device that breaks into a telephone system to make calls that bypass billing procedures.

Brute Force Attack: Hurling passwords at a system until it cracks.

Challenge-Response: A type of authentication in which a user must respond correctly to a challenge, usually a secret key code, to gain access.

Computer Fraud: Deliberate misrepresentation, alteration or disclosure of computer-based data to obtain something of value.

Controlled Access: When access to a system is limited to authorized programs, processes or other systems (in a network).

Cracker: A person who engages in computer and telecommunications intrusion.

Data Diddling: Unauthorized altering of data before, during or after it is input into a computer system.

Denial of Service: Any action or series of actions that prevents any part of a system from functioning in accordance with its intended purpose. Includes any action that causes unauthorized destruction, modification or delay of service.

Dumpster Diving: Searching for access codes or other sensitive information in the trash. Crackers may also recover erased data from tapes or disks.

Encryption: A mathematical manipulation of data that transforms original text (called plaintext) into unintelligible text (called ciphertext).

Entrapment: The deliberate planting of apparent flaws in a system for the purpose of detecting attempted penetrations.

Firewall: A hardware and/or software system that protects an internal network from the outside world or protects one part of a network from another.

Hacker: Someone who plays with computers for the pure intellectual challenge (as distinguished from a cracker).

High-Energy Radio Frequency (HERF) Gun: Shoots a highpowered radio signal at an electronic target (such as a computer) and puts it out of commission.

Logic Bomb: A resident computer program that lies dormant for a period, and then triggers an unauthorized act when a certain event, such as a date, occurs.

Penetration: Bypassing the security mechanisms of a system.

Penetration Testing: Attempting to circumvent a system's security features to identify weaknesses.

Phreaking: Employing technology to attack the public telephone system.

Pseudo-Flaw: A loophole planted in an operating system as a trap for intruders.

Risk Management: The process of identifying, controlling, and eliminating or minimizing uncertain events that may affect system resources.

Sniffer: A program that monitors all traffic on a network. Sniffers typically collect a certain number of bytes from the beginning of each session, usually where the password is typed unencrypted.

Social Engineering: Gaining privileged information about a computer system (such as a password) by skillful lying—usually over a telephone. Often done by impersonating an authorized user.

Spoofing: Sending electronic mail so that it looks like someone else sent it. Can be used to send false or damaging messages.

Stair Stepping: Using a low-level account to gain ever-higher levels of access.

Threat Analysis: Examination of all actions and events that might adversely affect a system or operation.

Tiger Team: A group hired by an organization to defeat its own security system to learn its weaknesses.

Trap Door: Hidden software or hardware mechanism that, when triggered, allows system-protection mechanisms to be circumvented.

Trojan Horse: Hidden function in a computer program that surreptitiously exploits security or integrity.

Van Eck Detection Kit: A receiver that monitors the electromagnetic radiation given off by a computer screen, allowing an eavesdropper to monitor the contents of a victim's screen from a distance (say, in the bushes outside a company).

War Dialer: A program that tries a set of sequentially changing numbers (i.e., telephone numbers or passwords) to determine which ones respond positively.

MOST WANTED

Ninety-one percent of all thefts target proprietary information.

1. **R&D data**
2. **Customer lists**
3. **Pricing schedules**
4. **Sales info**
5. **Manufacturing processes**

Losses (1995): more than $3 billion

with six felony counts for the misappropriation of trade secrets and related crimes.

A month before his arrest, Igusa set up a consulting company—K2 Design Services—across the street from Sunnyvale, Calif.-based Avant!, Cadence's $38 million archrival. Shortly thereafter, a Cadence engineer went to a customer site to resolve software discrepancies between a Cadence product and a competing application from Avant!. He noticed a bug in Avant!'s software—a bug he had originally created in the Cadence program.

PAY TO HACK YOUR OWN SYSTEM?

Why smart companies are hiring "tiger teams" to infiltrate their own security walls.

IRA WINKLER CALLS himself "a very good bullshitter." Winkler is director of technology at National Computer Security Associates in Carlisle, Penn. He specializes in social engineering, the art of talking employees out of passwords and information. Major corporations hire him to attack their computer security infrastructure. With the information gleaned from such "tiger teams," the companies hope to patch holes in their systems so the real bad guys never get in.

Last December, Winkler was hired by a multibillion-dollar company. His only cover (provided by the corporation's security manager) was as a "temp." He had no additional special access or privileges. By the end of his first day, he had acquired all the files necessary to compromise the company's most secret and valuable research project—"One billion dollars' worth of information," he claims.

Before He Arrives Using the company's annual report and company phone directory—both sent to him by the company upon request—Winkler makes a list of key personnel and areas of interest. He also creates business cards at a local print shop, indicating that he is "Supervisor for Information Security."

VALUE OF LOST INFORMATION

Strategic Plans
R&D
Manufacturing Process
Marketing Plans
Intellectual Property
Financial Data
Merger/Acquisition
Other   Total: $5.1 billion
Customer Lists
Personnel Plans

Source: 1995 ASIS survey   0 $500,000 $1M $1.5M

Social Engineering—Day One Upon arriving, he applies for an access badge. He enters fictitious data. It goes unchecked. He receives an office with a PC and an e-mail account. He gets access to the network and begins to work. Because there is an internal caller ID system, people know he is phoning from inside the company, but there is nothing to indicate his temporary status. He calls the researcher in charge of the company's most sensitive development project, telling her he's been hired to head security operations. He refers to a recent series of security breaches—all gleaned from newspaper reports. When he asks for suggestions on improving security, she recommends that he talk with the team leader.

Using the woman's name as a reference, he wangles a meeting with the team leader, then asks which information is most sensitive and where it is stored. Before leaving, he receives minutes of meetings detailing the project. Only hours into his assignment, he knows the location of the most sensitive files on the network.

The minutes include the password and log-on ID for a master document required by a government agency. The document includes detailed manufacturing instructions and "problem report" data. Winkler immediately copies the file to his machine.

Electronic Theft—Night One After dinner, Winkler returns to the office. He looks for unlocked offices, concentrating on the licensing, legal and R&D departments. A janitor ignores him. He finds patent applications and legal papers outlining strategies for lawsuits; all the paperwork is either lying in the open on unsecured desks or in unlocked offices. Using computers that were left on, he rifles through e-mail and file directories, copying anything that looks promising.

Day Two He returns to his office and hooks up a portable Unix workstation to the network. The portable is loaded with programs, including one that identifies accounts with easily guessed passwords. Using one of these accounts, Winkler logs onto a server, and with another hacker tool attains superuser status, giving him complete control of the server. He copies classified documents and leaves an electronic "back door" so he can return. Winkler also pulls a ruse with another key manager working on a different project. After persuading her to log off her computer and then log on again, he is able to guess her password. Back in his office, he logs on using her ID and accesses central files detailing manufacturing, development, problems and budgets for 95% of the company's projects.

As yet, no one has verified his identity. But he's taking no chances. Earlier, he scanned the company president's signature from the annual report and is prepared to forge a letter on company letterhead authorizing "complete access to the company and personnel at my direction."

By now, Winkler has detailed information on top-secret projects, as well as legal and licensing data. He has compromised the entire computing system from within, and left himself trapdoors and connections for future penetration. He has been at the company less than two days.

—Jeffrey Young

Cadence accused Avant! of stealing source code for its "place and route" software. The software helps design engineers lay out the electrical connections inside an integrated chip. Cadence licenses the software for between $50,000 and $200,000, depending on the configuration. "They copied our code down to the grammatical errors in the documentation," charges Cadence's CEO and president, Joseph B. Costello. "Their business was built on intellectual property stolen from us. Someone

CYBERDICKS AND VIRTUAL GUMSHOES

She had a kiss like a left hook. And a pearl-handled HERF gun in her garter.

JOHN JESSSEN is a Philip Marlowe for the '90s. But instead of a snub-nosed revolver and a trench coat, the tools of his trade are hard drives, back-up tapes and network log files.

For the past eight years, Jessen's firm, Electronic Evidence Discovery, headquartered in Seattle, has gathered electronic evidence for attorneys across the country, amassing more than 400,000 software programs and several hundred computer systems. His forte is discovering where the digital bodies are buried. "Electronic data isn't like paper," he says. "A shredded document no longer exists physically. Computers, however, keep trace of data with extremely precise audit trails. Somewhere there is an electronic record. We've learned how to find and unravel it."

Here are a few of Jessen's tricks:

Erased Files Erasing a file can take place on many levels. Simply deleting it only changes the name in the File Allocation Table (FAT) by replacing the first character of the file name with a character that cannot be replicated. The computer is instructed not to show on the screen any file starting with that character. Consequently, the deleted file only appears erased. The program knows it can write over the deleted file if it needs storage space, but sometimes it won't. Through a careful analysis of the data on a hard drive, the FAT can let some or all of a deleted file be resurrected.

Every read-write head also has its own "electromagnetic fingerprint." Different floppies have different patterns that can be revealed under an electron microscope.

The physical layout of data written on a hard disk also tells a lot. Early versions of DOS used an odd method of file storage. When looking for a place to save a new file, the operating system ran down a list on the hard drive until it found a location that was blank. That created mixed-up file tables. More recent versions start from where the last file was saved, producing more structured file collections.

"If someone claims a file was created five years ago," Jessen says, "but it is saved in the midst of documents from this year, I can be pretty certain that they're lying."

File Headers In some software applications, when a document is altered, the program updates the file with the last date and time it was altered. Even if a document is saved with the same name, a new version number is created. All of this is coded in the header of the file, which is not normally interpretable for the user. In one criminal case, for example, a man accused of rape provided a document to establish an alibi. That document showed the exact date and time of the rape. But Jessen found a deleted copy of the same document with an earlier version number and a later date and time stamp than the "ailbi document." The display in the two documents was proof positive that the suspect had fabricated his story.

Bug fixes often provide another important clue. "Finding a particular bug that was later fixed can give us precise data on when something was created," Jessen says.

E-mail Most e-mail systems store messages in a specific format in a single large file. Usually all messages remain on back-up tapes. Deleting a message doesn't necessarily erase it. The text remains in the large file.

"To actually remove [an e-mail] message requires a 'pack and compression' routine," he says. "The system administrator can do this, but it typically takes between one and three hours per user, and during that time no one can use their computers." This routine is rarely run, so previously erased messages are present on most back-up tapes.

—*Jeffrey Young*

READ ALL ABOUT IT

Security and Privacy Publications

Computer Law Observer: 800–963–5297
Computers and Security: 011–441–865–843654
Computer Security Digest: 313–459–8787
Infosecurity News: 508–879–9792
International Journal of Intelligence and Counterintelligence: 212–737–7923
International Privacy Bulletin: 202–544–9240
Monitoring Times: 704–837–9200

Privacy Journal: 401–274–7861
Privacy Times: 202–829–3660
Security Industry Buyers Guide: 800–777–5006
Security Magazine: 847–635–8800
Security Management: 703–522–5800
2600 Magazine, The Hacker Quarterly: 516–751–2600
Virus Bulletin: 011–441–235–555139

YOUR FIREWALL WON'T SAVE YOU

A NETWORK FIREWALL is a set of information systems that protects internal systems and networks from outside intrusions. Don't trust it. Here's why:

1 According to a survey by the American Society for Industrial Security, the majority of attacks on Web servers come from company insiders. Since most firewalls only protect against outsiders, even a perfect firewall is effective only part of the time.

2 Firewalls rarely prevent denial-of-service attacks or assure integrity. Even if outsiders can't get inside your system, they can often make your site inaccessible.

3 Most Web attacks are based on the content of messages, not their form. Since content is governed by the application program, no firewall adequately protects against all content-based threats (and probably none every will).

4 Many Web servers and browsers are already within firewalls and thus can act as springboards for other malicious attacks on internal systems.

—*Fred Cohen*

Fred Cohen is an information security consultant in Hudson, Ohio, and author of Protection and Security on the Information Superhighway *(John Wiley & Sons). You can visit his Web site at http://all.net/.*

---

has to be responsible for the behavior of a rogue company."

On December 5, 1995, the Santa Clara County District Attorney's Office, with the assistance of law enforcement officers, served a search warrant on Avant!, walking off with numerous tapes and hundreds of computer files. A day later, Cadence sued Avant! in federal court, charging copyright infringement, unfair competition, misappropriation of trade secrets, conspiracy and more. Avant!'s stock, which had its initial public offering less than a year earlier, dropped from 50 to 12.

Avant! shot back a lawsuit of its own, charging Cadence had destroyed its business and reputation. "We were beating them in the marketplace with a better product, and this was the only way

they could compete," says Gerald C. Hsu, Avant!'s president.

Hsu says similarities are inevitable in esoteric software programs. Both applications, in fact, depend on the same underlying published algorithms. Even dissimilar programs can have bits of code—strings—in common. "Can I absolutely tell you that none of our 115 R&D engineers did this?" Hsu asks. "No. But this isn't a case about industrial espionage; it's about marketplace competition."

Another case pitted two well-known multinationals against each other. The smaller, $5 billion corporation thought it was years ahead on a particular product line—until its larger, $25 billion competitor suddenly introduced a similar device. Suspecting dirty tricks, the company convinced a judge to

---

SO PROTECT YOURSELF

Be extremely wary of Intranets. Companies put up Intranet home pages and employees think that everything from the internal network can be posted there. Anyone who has access to your system can get to everything.

Be cautious of remote access. Many employees work from home. If they have widespread access to corporate data and they use automated log-on procedures, everything can be compromised by a simple burglary.

Have someone monitor references to your company on the Web. Also keep an eye on Usenet newsgroups for slander, libel and unwitting disclosure of proprietary information by employees.

Agree on a single companywide encryption product. Use a product that provides for a central "key" repository. If employees leave, their work product can be impossible to resurrect.

Institute a general e-mail policy. Several states won't allow you to le-

gally read e-mail unless both parties agree. This can be a big problem in the case of a dispute.

Get rid of old e-mail. In a lawsuit, the plaintiff may have the right to search through all e-mail. If you have vaults filled with back-up tapes of e-mail, who knows what they'll find.

—*Kenneth Shear*

Kenneth Shear is general counsel for Electronic Evidence Discovery in Seattle.

INSIDER TRADING

WANT THE DIRT on computer security? Subscribe to any of these Usenet newsgroups and listen up.

alt.cellular
alt.cyberpunk
alt.dcom.telecom
alt.hackers
alt.hackers.malicious
alt.os.multics
alt.privacy
alt.privacy.anon-server
alt.privacy.clipper
alt.security
alt.security.index
alt.security.keydist
alt.security.pgp
alt.security.ripem
alt.society.cu-digest
alt.2600
bit.listserv.security
comp.dcom.telecom
comp.privacy
comp.security.announce
comp.security.misc
comp.security.unix
comp.virus
de.comp.security
sb.security
sura.security
uwo.comp.security

grant an ex parte order. Such orders—which are granted without the other party's knowledge—are helpful in litigation involving electronic evidence. It allows the computer system to be reviewed before anyone can tamper with the data. Investigators can show up at the party's door unannounced, with order in hand, and access their system as well as all backup information.

During the raid, investigators discovered more than 15,000 electronic files filched from the smaller company, including marketing plans and R&D documents. They even found e-mail and a purchase order for the CD-ROM bought for the inside man who had copied the files. Within days of the execution of the order, the CEO of the larger company settled the case, which included millions of dollars in damages and a royalty on every sale.

Crime knows few limits when greed is at stake, and technology is a weapon. An Intel employee, William Gaede, wanted to steal blueprints for the Pentium. But Intel's internal computer system in Santa Clara, Calif., wouldn't allow critical files to be downloaded to remote sites—they can be viewed remotely by authorized people, but they cannot be

moved. That didn't stop Gaede. He brought the files up on his home computer and videotaped each screen. He then left the country with the tapes and was arrested. He recently pleaded guilty to transportation of stolen property and mail fraud.

INSIDE JOB

THE GAEDE CASE highlights an alarming trend: Competitors may be your greatest threat, but the dirty work is often done by insiders. According to the CSI/FBI survey, insiders were involved in 46% of electronic espionage cases.

Insiders are involved in 46% of electronic espionage cases.

If an employee already has access to a company's network, even if it's only a small corner, peeking at proprietary information can be awfully tempting. Randal Schwartz, a contractor, was caught cracking passwords on a system he wasn't authorized to access. Intel discovered this activity and reported it to local authorities, who prosecuted him under the Oregon Computer Crime Statute. On July 25, 1995, a jury found Schwartz guilty on three felony counts: one of knowingly and without authorization altering Intel's computer system and two of knowingly using a computer system to steal passwords. On September 11, 1995, Schwartz was sentenced to five years' probation with special conditions. Among other conditions, he has to inform future employers of these convictions if he accepts a job in high-tech.

How can you spot a potential electronic turncoat? "Don't go searching for the janitor as the inside man," says Ray Jarvis, who runs Jarvis International Intelligence, a training academy and security consulting operation in Tulsa, Okla. "It is much more likely to be a disgruntled manager looking ahead to his next job."

Such was the case more than three years ago when Borland International employee Eugene Wang allegedly supplied Symantec, a competitor, with electronic records of Borland International's new product marketing plans. Then Wang was offered a job at Symantec, and in 1992, Borland sued Wang and Symantec.

The case is still in litigation, no one has been tried, and the once-critical competitive issues are now moot. Wang's lawyer, James Pooley, admits

SEARCH AND EMPLOY

There's plenty of info on the Web about competitors. You just have to know where to look.

Alta Vista
http://www.altavista.digital.com
Powerful index tool used to locate information about products and companies. Includes full-text index of Usenet news-group archives. Offered by Digital Equipment.

Babson College Business Resources
gopher://info.babson.edu:70/11/.bus
Sources and sites for information about business, resources, entrepreneurship, market reports and government.

CareerPath.com
http://www.careerpath.com
Newspaper employment ads from major U.S. cities. A good place to find out how the competition plans to expand. A free service but it requires registration.

Deja News
http://www.dejanews.com
Search for discussion groups by keyword, personal name or discussion group name.

The Federal Web Locator
http://www.law.vill.edu/Fed-Agency/
Government information compiled by the Villanova Center for Information Law and Policy. Extensive listings categorized by government branch.

Competitive Intelligence Guide
http://www.fuld.com/
Fuld & Co.'s competitive intelligence site. Offers analytical tools, links to other intelligence sites.

Hoover's Online
http://www.hoovers.com
Company directory listings searchable by company name, location, industry and sales figures. Includes links to Web sites, if available.

Infoseek
http://www.infoseek.com
Includes Usenet newsgroups and non-Internet databases. Offers additional databases, including wire services, for a fee.

Library of Congress Catalog
http://www.loc.gov
The ultimate library catalog. Can help locate obscure books.

Lycos
http://www.lycos.com
One of the top search tools. Includes summaries of pages.

The NETworth Equities Center
http://networth.galt.com/www/home/equity/irr/

Its Investor Relations Resource is a searchable index of Web pages published by public companies.

NewsLink
http://www.newslink.org
More than 3,000 links to news-oriented sites.

Patent Portal
http://www.law.vill.edu/-rgruner/patport.htm
Site for patents and patent law.

Society of Competitive Intelligence Professionals
http://www.scip.org
Home page features publications, electronic discussion groups, expert/speaker database and events calendar.

Starting Point
http://www.stpt.com
Home page links to major companies in the U.S.

U.S. Securities and Exchange Commission
http://www.sec.gov
Offers 10-K and reports filed by public companies.

Compiled by Fuld & Co., a Cambridge, Mass., firm offering competitive monitoring services and seminars.

---

his client "may have done something stupid but not criminal."

"YOU THINK YOU'RE PRETTY SAFE?"

IF YOU'RE INTERESTED in electronic snooping, the means aren't hard to come by. Hacker bulletin boards offer a variety of free electronic tools. Want to get into your obnoxious boss's computer after he or she leaves work? Install Peeptom, which records keystrokes so you can go back and see everything your boss did to gain access to restricted files. An application called Cloakshare, for instance, hides your presence on an Apple network. CBI-Hack, CBILogin and CBIMan offer step-by-step instructions on how to locate terminal dialup locations and break in to one of the nation's largest credit data repositories, CBI.

BEGINNER'S GUIDE TO WORLD-CLASS SNOOPING

1 Know your questions. Focus, focus, focus. The Net won't help you narrow your options. Rather it can represent information overload.

2 Understand the chaos. Although the Net offers a free information flow, it also carries a lot of nonsense and informational static.

3 Swing like Tarzan. Hyperlinks can lead you to unexpected information pools. Use them.

4 Expect bad data. Inaccurate data are plentiful on the Net, particularly in the Usenet discussion groups. Verify rumors and double-check the so-called facts.

5 Don't expect analysis. You'll have to interpret the information you find.

6 Appreciate the power of electronic chitchat. Freewheeling Usenet discussion allows you to catch sight of industry trends or technology developments far ahead of official government filings or traditional news reports.

7 Let your fingers do the walking. Indexes such as Lycos, Yahoo! and Deja News can be powerful time-saving information-gathering tools.

8 Appreciate Web self-promotion. Corporate home pages are usually self-aggrandizing and filled with the kind of detailed information that the official media dismiss as not newsworthy and that they don't bother to report. But you can often glean enlightening tidbits about the company and the market it serves.

9 Recognize patterns. Conduct word searches on downloaded documents. Look for patterns. How many times does a particular word of phrase appear? Words such as agreement or alliance reveal strategies a company may not explicitly state but implicitly describes.

10 Instant information does not mean current information. Just because the information instantly pops up on the screen doesn't mean it's timely. Note the dates on the files you download.

—Leonard Fuld

Leonard Fuld is founder of Fuld & Co., a corporate research and analysis firm in Cambridge, Mass. His books include The New Competitor Intelligence *(John Wiley & Sons, 1995).*

With so many ways to probe, it doesn't take much sophistication to dig into someone else's files. Just a willingness to bend the rules.

Security experts warn against putting too much trust in supposedly impenetrable security systems. Within the past year, severe security flaws have been unearthed in the way public and private key encryption schemes were installed on Netscape Communications' Navigator. Admittedly, it takes a mathematician's mind and endless time to crack many of these security systems. But an entire generation of twentysomethings has grown up surrounded by digital gear and has no fear of it whatsoever.

"You think you're pretty safe because it would take hundreds of computer years' worth of hacking to breach your system?" snorts Allan Schiffman, chief technical officer at Terisa Systems, which produces communications Security software for the Internet and is owned by several companies, including RSA Data Security. "Imagine the college sophomore whose job is to run maintenance on a big technology company's internal network at night. All those high-powered engineering workstations idle but chained together. It won't take him long to crack your system."

Last summer, a French student did just that. Linking 120 computers into a network—including two super-computers—the student at the National Institute for Research in Computer Science and Control in France cracked an encrypted message from Netscape Navigator's exportable Version. It took eight days.

Electronic data pilfering often occurs in unlikely places. Q Studios is a classic garage startup in Redmond, Wash.: Two computer game designers, with a new game called Blood, worked feverishly at night after coming home from their regular jobs. They bought a new Pentium PC to use in coding the game. The hard drive crashed. So they took it back to the shop where they had bought it: Hard Drives Northwest.

INDUSTRIES MOST OFTEN HIT
- **Industrial/Manufacturing**
- **Software**
- **Pharmaceutical**

"We couldn't boot it up to even erase our source code," says the studio's president, Nicholas Newhard. The day after they got their repaired machine back, their publisher, Apogee Software Limited, called to say that the entire game—all the artwork, sounds, source code, tools and three-dimensional audio system they had hoped to license to other game developers—was available for free on the Internet.

Newhard and cofounder Peter Freese sued Hard Drives Northwest, the employee they believed was responsible for the leak and the "software pirate" who they thought released it to the Internet. But years of hard work are down the tubes. (Hard Drives Northwest has since fired the employee. The civil case is pending.)

These cases are not unusual, but "prosecuting them is nearly impossible," says William Galkin, a Baltimore attorney who publishes the *Computer Law Observer*. Although computer crime laws are clear and well defined, catching the culprits is tricky. Santa Clara County District Attorney's High-Tech/Computer Crime Unit, for instance, took months to gather enough evidence to raid Avant!.

John Jessen is founder of Electronic Evidence Discovery, a company headquartered in Seattle that specializes in "computer forensics," or the art of piecing together the electronic provenance of documents, resurrecting their electronic trails by analyzing encrypted minutiae. "We've seen our business explode in the past few years," he says. "We worked on about 300 cases last year Alone."

LIES, DAMN LIES

ONE FAVORITE TRICK: posting misleading messages on electronic bulletin boards. A notorious case involved an investment banking house. An anonymous user on Prodigy's Money Talk bulletin board accused a company called Stratton Oakmont of criminally fraudulent conduct in connection with a public stock offering. The message read:

"The end of Stratton Oakmont will finally come this week. This brokerage firm headed by president and soon to be proven criminal—Daniel Porrush [sic: actually spelled Porush]—will close this week. . . . This is fraud, fraud, fraud and criminal!!!!!!!"

Stratton Oakmont sued Prodigy for $200 million, claiming libel and gross negligence on the part of the on-line operator. Soon after, the stock price of the IPO dropped from $7 a share to $3. "In a libel case no amount of money can restore your reputation," says Jacob H. Zamansky of Singer, Bienenstock, Zamansky, Ogele & Selengut, a Wall Street firm. "We wanted to send a message to the on-line industry about the serious consequences of defamation on line. They are responsible for the mes-

sages that are posted and must screen or remove libelous messages from the board."

The suit claimed the on-line service provider was more like a publisher (with a responsibility to verify the accuracy of what is presented before publication) than a distributor (whose liability begins only after being notified that material is libelous or defamatory). In a landmark ruling, the judge held that Stratton was right. Eventually Stratton Oakmont settled for an apology from Prodigy.

Only 40% of companies properly dispose of proprietary material.

Tracking people on the Internet is nearly impossible if they try to conceal their identity. Each time a user logs on, he or she gets a unique IP, or Internet Protocol, address. Sophisticated hackers log on and then change their account's IP address. This technique, called IP spoofing, fools a target computer into believing a hacker's messages and commands are from an authorized user. Tracking is almost impossible.

The conclusion: Anyone can say whatever he or she wants about you on line, and there's little you can do about it. The possibilities for competitive mischief are enormous.

VAPOROUS BORDERS

CATCHING ELECTRONIC SNOOPERS is only half the battle. Once snagged, it is difficult to punish an electronic trespasser. The trickiest part concerns jurisdiction. "Where does the cybercrime take place?" asks Robert Morgester, deputy district attorney for Sacramento County, Calif., who prosecutes high-tech crimes. "Is it in the user's computer? Or where the computer that is breached is located? This is a nightmare of competing law-enforcement fiefdoms and investigators who are months, if not years, behind the sophisticated users they're chasing."

Attorneys who prosecute digital theft frequently use statutes that cover interstate transportation of stolen property. For instance, if you rifle another company's database and later move the information across state lines, prosecutors could indict you on federal charges. But the 10th U.S. Circuit Court of Appeals in Denver, which handles appellate cases

KILL OR BE KILLED

Think you're a character in a Tom Clancy novel? You are! And there's just about nothing—nothing!—you can do about it. Welcome to Corporate Spying circa 1996.

MY GOODNESS, CORPORATE spying is romantic! "We're living in Tom Clancyland," one executive told me. It sounds a little befuddling . . . and scary: What does one do in Tom Clancyland? What's the food like? Does everyone have a paunch and wear aviator sunglasses? The executive went into a spiel about how former CIA, Stasi and KGB agents were hiding behind every potted plant in corporate America. The White House Office of Science and Technology backs him up. According to the agency, business espionage costs U.S. companies $100 billion a year in lost sales, but here's the fillip: Most of the espionage is done by U.S. companies. We no longer spy on countries behind the Iron Curtain but we spy on each other. The Cold War has been inverted.

Conventional spying wisdom dictates that your competitors will stage late-night raids and use wily agents to ply your secretary with flowers in order to give out phone numbers from your card file. But we're entering a new age of spying. Corporate espionage has taken a different tack because of computer networks. Hack into a system and you can find out a company's secrets—click!—just like that.

Here's the kicker: Although the proliferation of computer networks makes companies more susceptible to break-ins, much of the snooping, stealing and (info) selling come from within.

Consider this: When Bernard Mayles left jobs with Merck & Co. and Schering-Plough, he took their drug manufacturing secrets with him. In 1991, Mayles was convicted of trying to sell those secrets for $1.5 million.

Or this: General Motors filed a civil lawsuit against nine ex-employees, claiming they took confidential reports on future car development plans with them when they joined Volkswagen. One of those accused, now VW's chief of worldwide manufacturing, denies the charge.

Just listen to what David Remnitz, 30, the chief executive officer of Interactive Futures, a respected security company says: "You can't trust your own people." That's a fact that keeps $1 million pouring into his company's coffers every year.

Most security experts estimate that 50% to 80% of the information that's stolen comes from insiders. Maybe the thief is a disgruntled employee or a backstabbing profiteer. Workers have some justification for being turncoats: Large companies have shown a lack of loyalty to their employees by downsizing zillions of workers. The result? Kill or be killed.

Usually, however, the moral circumstances are much more ambiguous. Maybe it's the guy who wants to evaluate his own evaluation, then gets steamed by his low marks ("I did not 'screw up' that project!") and changes the comments because he worries he won't get promoted. Some companies put two teams on the same project, pitting them against each other. The rivals—fellow workers really—hack into the other team's plans and mess with them. (That actually happened at a database company.) Or how about the guy who keeps getting the evil eye from clients whenever he shows up for appointments? One day he notices that changes have been made to his schedule. A menacing hacker? Nope. He strongly believes "Albert"—the sales guy down the hall who wants his job—did the dirty work.

Many executives just sniff at the idea that espionage is even going on. These Naive Waifs don't take security precautions and would never spy on a competitor. (Yo! Naive Waifs: Start getting your resumes together.) Then there are the Blind Isolationists: Companies that fortify so much that they become paranoid. Finally, we have the Spy Catchers: companies that actively spy on other companies.

Naive Waifs bring morality to the spying game; Blind Isolationists know how to protect themselves; and the Spy Catchers are aware of their competitors' moves.

Use a combination of these approaches. Put together a security committee to address risks. Hire an outside computer security company that can pinpoint your weaknesses. Plan countermeasures. If a competitor starts stealing information, then you can have something up your sleeve to try to stop the leaks. Yes, I'm advocating blackmail: Have "something" on everyone. If could be your competitor's extramarital affair, love of LSD or association with Pat Buchanan.

Don't kid yourself. People will try to break into your system. Don't sit in your corner office believing in the goodness of humanity. That's idiotic—you're in Tom Clancyland.

—Gary Andrew Poole

for Colorado, Kansas, New Mexico, Oklahoma, Utah and Wyoming, ruled that the mere copying of data and taking it across state lines did not constitute theft. In its decision, the court defined a personal computer as a tangible item, but not data, whether on a floppy disk or sent over a wire. The Department of Justice is trying to amend the law, which has left a new kind of computer confusion.

"If you steal data and then post it anonymously on a bulletin board, how can I prove that it is still a trade secret?" asks Kenneth Rosenblatt, deputy district attorney in Santa Clara County and the author of *High-Technology Crime: Investigating Cases Involving Computers*. "If you happen upon [data], what is to stop you from making use of it?"

Says Leland Altschuler, chief attorney in the San Jose office of the U.S. Attorney for the Northern District of California, "Unless national security is involved, we generally need to see substantial damages before we'll take on a case."

Jim McMahon, founder of the San Jose Police Department's High-Tech Crime-Squad and now a private security consultant in Santa Clara, Calif., is more direct: "One, hundred fifty thousand dollars is the minimum before the Feds will notice."

What about a small-time, white-collar snooper who roots around a competitor's database looking for useful information?

"We'll take a hard look at any case that comes to our attention," Altschuler answers quickly, then pauses. "But a lot of companies have no interest in pursuing the cases. Publicity about security flaws and breaches is almost certain to bring about unwelcome repercussions either on Wall Street or in shareholder litigation."

Tracking electronic perpetrators requires persistence as well as technical flair. If the tracking is not going to be introduced as evidence in court, an Internet service provider (ISP) can link an account to a particular session's IP address so any further espionage can be traced back to that address.

But it's a complicated process that requires tapping the outgoing line (called attaching a "pen register" in the trade) while simultaneously logging the account through a maze of POPs (points of presence) and ISPs.

That doesn't mean the police aren't trying to apply wiretap laws to the Internet. Late in 1995, the district attorney's office filed the first case that involved a wiretap on an e-mail account. The indictment followed a seven-month surveillance of a CompuServe account.

Nevertheless, the advantage still lies with the snooper. "I'm very pro-law enforcement," explains security consultant Ray Jarvis, "but it is very difficult to get the cops to take on any high-tech cases. The good guys just don't have the tools and the sophistication to tackle computer frauds."

The bottom line? Few intellectual crime cases get filed.

A GREAT PLACE TO BE A CRIMINAL

AFTER A NIGHT OF TROLLING through the Internet, logging on to hacker bulletin boards and joining several Internet relay chats about "warez" (tools for snooping), Detective Michael Menz of the Sacramento Valley High-Tech Crime Task Force is tired. He has talked one hacker into giving him his e-mail address by pretending to have software to trade, after watching thousands of illicit conversations scroll along his screen.

But realistically, would this cybercop ever catch a crook like this? Menz winces. "You must be crazy. There are millions of otherwise responsible citizens dabbling in this kind of thing. There are probably less than 100 trained investigators monitoring the Net with any regularity.

"If you want to get away with a crime today, do it using a computer."

Why Markets Tolerate Mediocre Manufacturing

Daniel Luria

This management consultant traces the pressures on smaller manufacturers that have led to their hesitation to invest, upgrade their work force, and adopt the best technologies. There is indeed a low road, he writes, and most manufacturing shops are on it.

DANIEL LURIA is Director of the Performance Benchmarking Service, a unit of the Industrial Technology Institute, a not-for-profit think-tank in Ann Arbor, MI.

Government statistics trumpet the comeback of U.S. manufacturing. Bolstered by foreign direct investment, the current recovery was, until late 1995, the most investment-led in decades. Even when you include data revisions illustrating that manufacturing output bounced back less well in the 1990s than was previously believed, the rate of productivity advance in manufacturing *has* rebounded.[1] But the sector's output has not grown enough to stem the continued erosion in its share of the economy. With rapid productivity growth and only modest output growth, it is not surprising that there are today nearly three million fewer manufacturing jobs in the United States than in 1979. What is surprising, however, is that rapid productivity growth has not led to any significant increase in real manufacturing wages.

Or is it surprising? When the data are examined by size of plant, it becomes clear that there have been large increases in productivity in plants with 500 or more employees. In these larger plants, productivity growth, which slowed from a 4.1 percent annual pace in the 1947–67 period to a still-respectable three percent rate in 1967–87, has since then been growing at well over four percent a year. But such plants constitute fewer than 1.4 percent of the total, and account for only 45 percent of manufacturing value added.[2] The other 98.6 percent of shops, invisible though they remain to most business observers and nearly all economists, must be performing on average much less well if one is to make sense of the aggregate manufacturing performance numbers.

WHAT DO REAL DATA TELL US?

This article reports on analyses of proprietary data for the manufacturing plants of 3,000 firms with fewer than 500 employees. The data are maintained by the Performance Benchmarking Service, a unit of Industrial Technology Institute, an Ann Arbor consulting firm. Although in a statistical sense they are not a true random sample of all such firms, these data are the nation's

From *Challenge*, July/August 1996, pp. 11-16. © 1996 by M. E. Sharpe, Inc., Armonk, NY, 10504. Reprinted by permission.

only window on the performance of smaller manufacturing shops. The Performance Benchmarking data are compiled through annual surveys sent each year since 1992 to 1,000 smaller establishments, each of which receives in return for its effort a confidential, customized "benchmarking" report that tells it where, according to more than 100 measures, it stands compared to other small shops with similar production processes, piece prices, order volumes, and customer types. Analysis of the 3,000 records in hand as of April 1996

Many large U.S. manufacturers contract out a large proportion of their orders to small-firm suppliers. Not only do large firms put intense pressure on their smaller, weaker suppliers to reduce prices, but they ask their smaller suppliers to bear much of the brunt of upturns and downturns in demand for their products.

---

suggests a consistent, and troubling, story about the hidden underbelly of American manufacturing.

Especially since the late 1970s, many large U.S. manufacturers have contracted out a large proportion of their orders to small-firm suppliers. Not only do large firms put intense pressure on their smaller, weaker suppliers to reduce prices, but they ask their smaller suppliers to bear much of the brunt of upturns and downturns in demand for their products. The instability of small shops' production schedules has therefore increased dramatically in recent years. They must provide the buffer inventories that enable large firms to keep their inventories lean. Big companies demand that the small suppliers meet their needs quickly, if not immediately, enabling them to practice enviable "just-in-time" methods. Thus, while large firms' sales typically rise or fall by 15 to 25 percent from peak to trough, many smaller shops' sales gyrate dramatically. Fully one in four small shops saw its sales rise more than 50 percent between 1992 and 1994, and only half had sales changes, up or down, of less than 25 percent. As a result, small firms' capacity utilization also rises and falls dramatically.

These huge swings in capacity utilization make it imperative that small shops keep as much as possible of their cost structure "variable" (i.e., composed of unskilled labor and materials and other factors of production that can be added or shed as needed rather than becoming permanent features of the business). That means minimizing capital investment; otherwise, expensive machinery would sit idle whenever orders fell, driving costs per unit through the roof. It is no surprise, then, that most small shops are much less capital-intensive than their large-plant counterparts. In 1995, the typical small shop reported a replacement value on its equipment stock that averaged just $24,300 per employee, compared to $77,300 per employee in manufacturing overall and $175,000 in plants with 500 or more employees.

For the same reason, where the typical large company spends about 2 percent of payroll on training shop workers in its large plants, the training investment in a typical small-plant employee is less than 0.5 percent of payroll.

It is thus not surprising that the productivity gap between small and large shops has been widening. According to our data, in 1967, plants with fewer than 500 employees averaged 80 percent of the productivity of plants with 500 or more; in 1992, the figure was down to 66 percent. As expected, most of the widening gap can be explained by diverging trend rates of unit growth per labor hour. But some also comes from the fact that the value added for small shops, which is the numerator of the productivity measure "value added per employee-hour," is constantly being squeezed by their big customers' demands for regular price reductions.

Many suppliers have reacted, and are continuing to react, to these capacity management and pricing pressures as one would expect. They try to minimize variable costs as well as fixed investment. The methods are well-known: union-busting, shutting down mature metropolitan plants in favor of exurban ones, freezing or cutting wages, and in general employing what is sometimes called a "low-road" strategy. In a clear sign of this, 25 percent of small shops had lower value added per full-time-equivalent employee in boom year 1994 than in still-recessionary 1992; 29 percent had lower nominal payroll per full-time employee.

As more smaller shops forgo the capital investments needed to remain modern and, more generally, opt to travel the low road of unskilled labor and skimpy capital investment, they do not differentiate or improve the quality of their products, and the relationship between large and small firms changes. The latter come to be seen as an undifferentiated set of low-cost sources of commodity inputs. Despite all the talk of "partnership" among customers and suppliers, two-thirds of the small shops in our database report that in 1995 they were quoting each job against five or more competitors, whereas in 1991 and 1992 fewer than half reported that many competitors. Far from partnering in order to raise the quality of supplies and parts, small suppliers are too often reduced to competing merely in terms of price.

ARE PRODUCTIVITY AND WAGES DIVERGING?

This analysis is superficially consistent with today's academic and policy consensus. The economy's increasing openness to international trade has put less-educated and less-skilled American workers into a global scramble for "routine" jobs, with only an educated elite of doctors, lawyers, and other "symbolic analysts" able to hold their own.

But the consensus view also implies falling wages for less-skilled workers and a rending of the tie between productivity and wage growth in all sizes of plants and firms. At a disaggregated level, the data do not support this. Our data on large manufacturing plants suggest, instead, that:

- There has been virtually no growth in the pay disparity between low- and high-skilled workers;
- Productivity and wages nearly always move together; and
- Both are rising—productivity at about 3 percent per year and real wages at about 1 percent per year.

The conclusions we can draw about smaller plants are perhaps even more interesting. In the smaller shops, productivity and wages also remained substantially linked, though somewhat less so than in large plants. The difference is that productivity and wages are flat or falling in roughly half the small shops on which we have data, and in about one-third of these they are falling far and fast. Our data on 116 small metal-forming shops, for example, show that mean productivity was unchanged between 1992 and 1994. The median (the productivity of the plant at the fiftieth percentile), however, was 6 percent lower in 1994, showing that there was a higher proportion of lower-productivity shops in the sample. A shop that was in the seventy-fifth percentile in 1992 could have maintained its position even with a 7-percentage-point drop in its value added per full-time employee.

Table 1 Value Added Per Employee Metal-Formers

| | Lowest Value In | | | |
	Top 10%	Top Qtr	Top Half	Mean
1992	$105,844	$84,177	$66,666	$69,473
1994	127,406	78,670	62,462	69,119
Difference	+20%	−7%	−6%	−1%

However—and here is the good news—to stay in the top 10 percent of the industry from 1992 to 1994, a metal-former would have had to increase value added per full-time employee by a whopping 20 percent. In other words, some 15 to 20 percent of smaller shops are becoming more productive and are doing so at a rate of nearly 10 percent per year. In those shops, wages are also rising, although at about half that rate. Analysis of these high- and growing-productivity firms also reveals them to have uniformly high capital per worker, to pay high wages across their work force, to use more advanced technology, and to spend much more per worker on technical training. In short, while many, if not most, smaller shops have opted for a low-road recipe of sweated labor and meager investment, some have not. By legacy or choice, they are investing in their workers and their facilities.

Lest one be tempted to believe that there is one, best way to make a proverbial widget, consider the sheer range of performance within smaller shops and within industries. Metal-formers making the same products for the same customers have value added per employee anywhere between $40,000 and $140,000. Indeed, in every industry the productivity level achieved by the most productive 10 percent of shops is at least 160 percent of the industry median. The seventy-fifth percentile is invariably twice the twenty-fifth percentile value. While less pronounced than for value added per employee, the huge dispersion in performance applies to nearly every metric the database supports, from on-time delivery to scrap rate to inventory turnover.

Moreover, there is no obvious consistency within firms. Companies that score in the top quartile on one metric, such as the sales–inventory ratio, are no more likely than other firms to score well on any other given measure. Few shops are either all good or all bad. Moreover, low-productivity firms often grow as fast as high-productivity firms. So, what are we to make of the small-firm economy?

TOWARD A THEORY OF SMALL-MANUFACTURER PERFORMANCE

It turns out that there *are* patterns in the data, even though they are far from obvious. Our analysis of the ways in which performance varies across shops suggests that they may be ranked usefully on three scales. The first, which we call "systematic," gives companies points for tracking, among other things, how often parts are faulty, how long it takes to set up machines for a new job, and how quickly action is taken in response to equipment breakdowns. Companies can score additional points in this systematic category if they regularly undertake new programs involving work teams, statistical quality measures, just-in-time delivery, and preventive maintenance.

We call the second scale "modern." High scores require firms to invest in the hardware and software that automate the many parts of the business, including scheduling, manufacturing, and quality assurance.

The third and last scale we call "distinctive." Points on it are earned for those who have new, proprietary, or design-intensive products, or who are able to perform sophisticated processing procedures that most shops cannot. An example is ultra-tight-tolerance machining.

Shops' scores on the three scales are modestly correlated, but mostly at the bottom end. That is, about half of smaller shops have low scores on all three of the scales. Clearly, these are the low-roaders. They are unsystematic, unmodern, and undistinctive. Only about one shop in five scores high on both the modern and distinctive scales, but they may be all over the lot on the systematic scale. These are the high-roaders.

Finally, about one-third of smaller shops look like the mirror image of the high-roaders—they score high on the systematic scale, but nearly as low on the modern and distinctive scales as the consistent low-roaders. We dub this last group "lean commodity": these are shops that are actively taking steps to improve—i.e., to get "lean,"—but not to adopt new advanced procedures or to introduce new or better-designed products. Shops in the latter group focus on rooting out waste as a way to minimize variable costs: such shops require less material (because they scrap fewer parts), less indirect labor (operators do their own machine setups), and less machinery (preventive maintenance and faster setups mean each machine runs more hours) than typical low-roaders.

Table 2   Selected Data Elements Used in Calculation of Performance Scales

Systematic	Modern	Distinctive
Formal tracking and routine reports on:	Percentage of machines with computer controls	Percent of sales from:
• Scrap rate by machine		• New products
• Percent of jobs bumped from schedule (−)	Keyboarded devices per employee	• Self-designed products • Assemblies (vs parts)
• Percent of preventive maintenance performed on schedule	Percentage of employees using computers or programmable machine controllers	Ratio of tightest tolerance to industry median (−)
Formal program in:	Technical training expenditures per shop employee	Number of shops quoting against (−)
• Statistical quality assurance • Job scheduling • Machine break-down prediction	Percent of jobs with machine instructions driven by product data (CAD) files	Ratio of skilled to unskilled shop labor

These lean commodity shops do many of the things that professional advocates of "high-performance work organization" admire, but they do them *not* to become more modern or distinctive. Indeed, they become lean precisely as an alternative to undertaking the investment required to become more capital intensive and capable. The consequences are in the numbers. The firms are not distinctive. Rather, they are the best-run firms among the huge set of pedestrian shops that bid for relatively easy-to-make "commodity" jobs. By being systematic, they lower their costs and win orders based on price alone. But they cannot improve either wages or productivity in the process. The proof lies in the value added per worker measure. Lean commodity shops do not attempt to raise value added per worker except by lowering the demoninator of the equation—the number of hours worked. Thus, these shops should not be thought of as an acceptable hybrid simply because they are systematic. They are simply the best managed of a pedestrian group—the low-road players.

The proportion of low-road, high-road, and lean commodity shops varies, of course, by sector. The 70 percent of smaller shops that function mainly as suppliers to larger manufacturers (i.e., those that make so-called intermediate goods) are most likely to be low-road. The 15 percent that make so-called capital goods (machines, tooling, etc.) for other manufactur-

Table 3

Table 3   Approximate Distribution of Shops, 1994

	Intermediate Goods	End-Use Products	Capital Goods
Low Road	55%	50%	10%
Lean Commodity	33%	25%	30%
High Road	12%	25%	60%

ers are much more likely to be high-road. Lean commodity shops make up roughly a third of both the intermediate and capital goods populations and of the 15 percent that make end-use products (suitcases, brooms, and the like).

WINNING UGLY

Falling average real wages in the shops that provide us with data make clear that the high-roaders are a declining proportion of the small-manufacturer population. Our data suggest that, as measured by value added per employee, both the low- and high-roaders are gradually ceding market share to the lean commodity shops. With low-road shops quoting low-ball prices to win jobs, managers of better-run, smaller manufacturing companies face the huge strategic decision of whether to join them or fight them. An increasing number opt to join. As depicted by the numbers, the impact is clearly negative for wages and only slightly less so for productivity. Moreover, these trends are self-reinforcing and are likely to worsen. As they lose business to low-ballers and therefore operate at lower levels of capacity utilization, the high-roaders with high capital investment rates and highly paid workers become less competitive vis-à-vis the lean commodity shops.

With a dwindling base of modern, distinctive suppliers, more large manufacturers are encouraged to treat all purchased inputs as commodities. They are therefore even further encouraged to seek six, eight, or even ten quotes for each job they subcontract, intensifying price competition. The likely winners are the worst of the low-road shops (the efflorescence of sweatshop apparel districts in many cities) and the best of the lean commodity companies. The clear losers? The shops that do precisely what common sense says they should do: invest, train, and innovate.

Clearly, in most industries, firms can now adopt recipes with very different mixes of wages, skill, technology, training, and basic management discipline. They incur no penalty in lost profits or slower growth

if they choose the low-road or the lean commodity route. Therefore, the markets are not offering meaningful incentives for "good" manufacturing behavior. Yet the low frequency of such behavior in the small-shop economy is costly, resulting in lower wages, lower productivity, less technical change, and a composition of output that has too few products that command price premiums in global trade.

ELEMENTS OF A PERFORMANCE POLICY

This contradiction raises the possibility that improved small-manufacturer performance may be a classic public good, and hence something that only government policy can or would address. The goal of such policy should be to change the mix from low-road and lean shops to high-road shops. Specifically, high-road shops need to be helped to get costs down while still retaining a high rate of capital investment. A government policy to encourage this change in mix would forestall low-road shops from winning orders on the strength of low wages and low capital investment. And lean commodity shops should be encouraged to take the risks associated with moving beyond producing commodity products by investing more in equipment, technology, and product development. It would be easy to present a laundry list of zero-probability prescriptions for government, but that is like suggesting that the Federal Reserve drop the discount rate by four points. In this case, however, four modest proposals could make a good start and are worth at least putting on the table.

- To give an advantage to mature, capital-intensive shops vis-à-vis other small shops, there should be an investment tax credit that applies only to machinery placed in plants of fewer than 500 workers that have been in operation since at least 1980. (Many large firms might back this "small business" program, since nearly 50,000 small plants are units of companies with more than 500 employees.) This would discourage shutting down older (often metropolitan) plants in favor of rural ones. Note that it would also reduce the risks for a lean commodity shop to take the leap into greater capital intensity—so long as it keeps the jobs where they are.
- That risk could be reduced further by changing the focus of public programs that assist smaller manufacturers from general business "competi-

tiveness" to modernization and distinctiveness. These so-called "manufacturing extension centers" (more than sixty of them are now coordinated by the National Institute for Standards and Technology), work with close to 20,000 small shops each year. But their activity mix is tilted heavily toward the demands of small shops, which usually means satisfying demands of their big customers. An example is complying with the international quality documentation standards. Focusing the work of these centers instead on helping high-road shops become more systematic, and lean commodity shops to get more modern and distinctive, could yield big payoffs.

- To block the worst low-road behavior, there should be a higher minimum wage. Any increase will help, and in my view the bigger the better. While manufacturing wages still average 110 percent of the private-economy average, the sector still hosts more than 2.5 million slots that pay $6 an hour or less. Along the same lines, requiring shops to provide health insurance to all employees would, by itself, shake out thousands of sweatshops whose continued viability today limits the growth prospects of many good firms. Properly pitched, such a requirement might well make its way into today's modest proposals to make existing coverage more portable.

- Reward and responsibility should be linked in the workplace. To this end, a modest deal should also be cut between capital and labor. Today, business owners have a rational fear that if their plants are unionized, labor costs will rise more than productivity. The ideal deal would make it easier for unions to organize and achieve first contracts, but would tie future wage increases to productivity growth. One effect of this would be to make more unions do what many European but few American unions have: develop and provide expertise to the shops whose workers pay them dues in

order to help raise productivity. Closer links between unions taking on that mission and a reoriented manufacturing extension community could aid in this process.

Modest though they seem, these proposals would face a tough legislative fight. Manufacturers, like other businesses, lobby with one voice, so their positions are often least-common-denominator endorsements of anything that will keep labor costs down. But this lobbying approach results in an implicit subsidy to low-road firms and hence a relative burden on those who want to follow the high road. A policy that combines support for smaller shops with initiatives that provide extra incentives to those resisting the low-road temptation might just help split a self-interested fraction of CEOs away from the current lobbying consensus. It is the absence of such a self-conscious fraction of employers that today makes the pursuit of high-wage economic growth appear a parochial trade union demand, rather than the general interest it once was and could be again. That alone makes it worth the effort to try.

NOTES

1. To some extent, solid productivity growth has become a tautology for U.S. manufacturing. Since the 1970s, a sharply higher share of manufacturing output has become subject to international competition. In response, capital has become more footloose, exiting businesses that do not produce acceptable returns. It is not surprising that a disproportionate share of the manufacturing activities exited (e.g., apparel, boots and shoes, wire harnesses) are at the low end of the sector's productivity distribution.

2. This paper presents data on plants rather than firms. Our data, as well as a comparison of the establishment (plant) and enterprise (firm) series of the Census Bureau, suggest that large firms' smaller plants exhibit the same productivity and wage distributions as the smaller plants of small firms.

The Business Of Business Is People

TOTAL QUALITY MANAGEMENT

Address by LAURIE A. BROEDLING, *Senior Vice President, Human Resources and Quality,*
McDonnell Douglas Corporation

Delivered to the Quality Conference, Washington Deming Study Group, George Washington University, Washington, D.C.,
April 8, 1996

Today I want to talk to you about reaffirming quality. By that I mean breathing new fire and spirit into the quality movement.

According to an old Chinese proverb, whom the gods would destroy, they first condemn to 30 years of success.

As part of the quality movement inspired by W. Edwards Deming, we have been "condemned" to 30 years of success.

Over the past several decades — and in the last decade, most particularly — some of the ideas that are central to our movement have gained widespread acceptance throughout the corporate world. In the process, they have gone from being revolutionary in their content to being perceived as part of the conventional wisdom.

As you all know, one of Deming's 14 points is to eliminate "slogans." Nonetheless, it is a sad fact that many of us in the quality movement have been guilty of sloganeering.

But if we have sometimes been guilty of sloganeering, we have other problems as well in trying to communicate an effective quality message.

The biggest of those problems — to my way of thinking — is that some people in the business consulting field have drawn some ideas and concepts from Deming, while discarding others. The total effect of this has been to distort ... to dehumanize ... and, I fear, to detract from the quality movement.

I am thinking, in particular, of the re-engineering movement — or at least of some expressions of it.

Re-engineering is sometimes presented as a kind of turbo-charged version of Deming — promising fast and dramatic results. In fact, exponents of re-engineering are sometimes critical of Deming and TQM as offering too much of a gradualist approach to change and improvement.

Re-engineering — often done with the help of outside consultants — is very much of a top-down phenomenon. Re-engineering seeks breakthroughs, not by enhancing existing processes, but by creating new and wholly different processes. Because it has often been associated with radical downsizing,

re-engineering has become almost a code word for pushing up profits by pushing people off the payroll and out the door.

In all of this, there is much that is contrary to the thinking of Deming — and, indeed, to the whole concept of quality, as I see it.

Dr. Deming took a holistic approach to quality ... and a holistic approach to management. As he saw it, improvements in quality led to improvements in productivity, which in turn led to lower prices, greater market share, and future growth.

In his view of the world, the interests of the employees and the shareholders were complementary, rather than antithethical.

Deming was highly explicit on this point. In "Out of the Crisis," he stated, and I quote, "The job of management is inseparable from the welfare of the company.

Management must declare a policy for the future, to stay in business and to provide jobs for their people, and more jobs."

According to Deming, loss of market, and resulting unemployment, were seldom, if ever, foreordained or inevitable. They were management made.

In Deming's view, the problem was never people — in the sense of the multitude of people working for an organization. It was always management.

Re-engineering turns that view of the world upsidedown and inside-out. When a company is "re-engineered," it seems that it is the people who are to blame for bad performance, while management is presumed to have all the answers.

This reminds me of a line in a Bertolt Brecht play, where one of the characters says, "The people have lost the confidence of their leaders. They must be punished."

Ladies and gentlemen, quality is not something that comes about as a result of all-powerful leaders punishing their people for failing to follow.

Quality presupposes integrity — integrity that is present at all levels in an organization.

There is no better or fuller description of the meaning of quality than that offered by Max DePree, the chief executive of

Herman Miller, Inc., which is perennially ranked at the top of the list of the most admired companies in its category in the annual Fortune magazine survey. In his book, "Leadership Is An Art," Depree wrote:

"When we talk about quality, we are talking about the quality of product and service. But we are also talking about the quality of our relationships and the quality of our communications and the quality of our promises to each other. And so, it is reasonable to think about quality in terms of truth and integrity."

Looked at in those terms, quality is a good thing, in and of itself. In addition — as Deming pointed out quality is efficient — in a way that mere power can never be.

Consider a story that is told of Jose[f] Stalin. At the height of the terror in Russia, Lenin's widow — a revered figure in the Communist Party — attempted to criticize some of Stalin's actions. Stalin brought her to heel with the magnificent threat — "If you don't shut up, we'll make somebody else Lenin's widow."

The point here is that any system built on coercion and control, such as Stalinist Russia, impedes the flow of critical information (in both senses of the word 'critical'). And that is not the only disadvantage of coercive versus cooperative systems.

Sydney Pollack, the Academy-award winning film director, was eloquent in expressing some of the limitations of authority in speaking to management guru Warren Bennis. Pollack noted:

"Up to a point, I think you can lead out of fear, intimidation, as awful as that sounds. There is a lot of leadership that comes out of fear, dependence, and guilt. But the problem is that you're creating obedience with a residue of resentment. If you want to make a physics analogy, you're moving through the medium, but you're creating a lot of drag, a lot of backwash."

If I were living in a monastery in Tibet, in charge of the monastery's TQM program, I might consider advocating quality solely on the basis of it being a good thing. However, since I work for a large corporation that is very much in the business of making money, I advocate quality programs and people-centered policies on the basis that they contribute not just to attitudes and morale but also very importantly — to improving the bottom line and winning new business.

Unlike re-engineering, which begins by discarding existing processes, Total Quality Management follows a path of engaging people at all levels in continually enhancing the processes that determine the flow of work. That will succeed if, and only if, people buy into the need for improvement . . . and the opportunity to make it.

In recent years, the idea of Kaizen, striving for a large number of incremental improvements, has taken something of a back seat to the idea of making big one-time breakthroughs through superior innovation and creativity.

Deming believed that both Kaizen and breakthroughs (big one-time improvements in products and processes) are very important.

The trick, then, is not choosing between the one or the other, but learning how to pursue both at once. A good place to begin is in recognizing that creativity exists in all people ... in all levels of an organization.

Here is another area where I believe that re-engineering tends to be both de-humanizing and destructive in its thinking. It has embraced the idea of a few Nietzchian supermen who determine all real change and progress.

But innovative or creative thinking is something that goes on all the time in a dynamic organization. It is a terrible (though common) mistake to think of creativity and imagination as the exclusive province of the gifted few.

There is a growing body of research showing that creativity is almost universally present in people — at least in childhood. The pre-school years have been described as a kind of golden age of creativity, when every child sparkles with artistry and innovative problem-solving skills. Young children paint in bold and daring strokes. They are able to master two or more languages with little difficulty.

After that, however, with exposure to more structure and discipline, and with more peer group pressure, a kind of rot sets in, and most of us grow into artistically stunted adults. It starts with school and it gets a whole lot worse as one enters corporate life. As part of the maturation process, as we advance in our analytic skills — or what is sometimes called linear thinking — all but a few of us become markedly weaker on the artistic or creative side — in so called non-linear thinking.

No less a genius than Pablo Picasso paid homage to the creativity that we all begin with. At an exhibition of children's work, he observed: "When I was their age, I could draw like Raphael, but it has taken me a whole lifetime to learn to draw like them."

In a similar vein, Albert Einstein was acutely aware of parallels between his thought patterns and those of children. He told one interviewer:

"How did it come to pass that I was the one to develop the theory of relativity? The reason, I think, is that a normal adult never stops to think about problems of space and time. These are things which he has thought of as a child. But my intellectual development was retarded, as a result of which I began to wonder about space and time only when I had already grown up. Naturally I could go deeper into the problem than a child with normal abilities."

If creativity is something that can be unlearned, it is also something that can be re-learned. It can be exhumed — from the slag heap of institutional thinking — and brought back to life, with careful nurturing.

That is something we have tried ... and are trying to do ... at McDonnell Douglas. Through integrated product teams — spanning various disciplines and disregarding hierarchical rank — we are endeavoring to capture more of the creativity, imagination, and motivation of all of our people.

I could cite a number of examples where we have achieved extraordinary progress through the work of ordinary people released from the constraint of ordinary expectations.

To cite just one example: Thanks to the work of integrated product teams, the new E/F Super Hornet version of our F/A-18 — due to enter service with the Navy before the turn of the century — is able to provide 40% more range, greater versatility, and more firepower than earlier versions of the Hornet at a fraction of the cost of a new program.

Having said this, let me go a step beyond and address the need for creativity of the highest order — meaning the kind of creativity that resulted in the discovery of penicillin, the polio vaccine, or the computer chip.

Clearly, there is more than one kind of innovation. There is the kind we have already discussed that expands the envelope of an existing product or an existing concept.

But there is another kind of innovation — which not only builds upon previous innovations, but also, in some important way, departs from them.

Breakthrough thinking of this kind often depends more on individual output than on group or team work. After all, a brain is a unitary thing. Sometimes it does its best work in an informal environment where there are no committees or task forces ... where people, working on their own, are free to experiment and to think the unthinkable. Dr. Deming often referred to Bell Labs as such a place.

At McDonnell Douglas, we have encouraged that kind of thinking at our Phantom Works advanced R & D facility in St. Louis.

Just a few weeks ago, some of the top officials in NASA were in St. Louis for the roll-out of an experimental aircraft, called the X-36, which was designed and developed at the Phantom Works. This aircraft — which has no horizontal or vertical tail and a severely shortened wing structure — may truly change the shape of things to come in fighter aircraft. It is extraordinarily light and agile. Its design represents the kind of radical simplicity which is characteristic of breakthrough thinking.

There is no single answer to the question of how to encourage breakthrough thinking in the midst of large and all-too-often cumbersome organizations.

Clearly, there are some areas where empowerment is appropriate and others where it is not. For instance, you would not want to rely on empowered teams — given the freedom to ignore established procedures and processes to install nuclear devices on a submarine.

Management must use common sense and good judgment in striking a balance between the need to let go in some areas and the need to exercise oversight in others.

On the topic of striking a balance between the one and the other, I read an interesting article entitled "TQM, Re-engineering, and the Edge of Chaos," in a recent issue of *Quality Progress* magazine. I would urge all of you to read it.

As defined by the author — Lawrence Leach, the head of a consulting firm in Idaho Falls — "the edge of chaos" is a constantly shifting battle zone between stagnation and anarchy." For most purposes, this is where you want your organization to be ... because systems that are too stable will die as the environment evolves, while systems that are too chaotic will tend to self-destruct.

One set of forces (the need for order and control) pulls every business toward stagnation, while another set of forces (the need for growth and creativity) drives it toward disintegration.

Deming's philosophy allows organizations to alter their control systems to avoid attraction either to disintegration or ossification.

"TQM provides both sets of forces needed to keep a company together," he writes. "Continual improvement provides the force to drive the system toward disequilibrium, while other aspects of TQM — such as constancy of purpose, managing the business as a system, and joy in work — provide the restraining forces to keep the organization together."

By building in a process of continual improvement, Dr. Deming's philosophy makes change the norm within an organization. People who learn how to change their organization in small steps gain the confidence and skill to succeed at larger changes.

At the outset of this talk, I noted that many of us in the quality movement have been guilty of resorting to slogans. Without a doubt, one of the reasons Deming bothered to include the elimination of slogans in his 14 points is the fact that he was espousing a profoundly humanistic approach to achieving improvement and creativity in the workplace. He did not want people to become the slaves of any theory — his own included.

Deming concluded every seminar with the same five words, saying, "I have done my best."

It is up to each of us to do our best in reaffirming quality within our own organizations.

To do that, there are three things that we must do very well.

First, we have to promote the understanding that quality makes good sense from a business perspective. To be understood ... and to be persuasive ... we must speak in the language of business, plainly and clearly.

Second, we must continue to emphasize the need for incremental improvements as well as breakthrough achievements. Total Quality is a journey, not a destination. Like many journeys, it is a journey that carries the hope of self-renewal without self-destruction.

And last, we must never forget that the real bottom line is people. At the end of the day, the success or failure of a business depends on management's ability to harness the willing participation and creativity of people.

Now perhaps more than ever the business of business is people. That is an awesome responsibility and for all of us in this room an inspiring challenge.

Case V: *Evaluation of Organizational Effectiveness*

The American Corporation, a $2.4 billion diversified conglomerate, acquired the $130 million Cordle Manufacturing Company. At a private luncheon with Sam Priest, American's chief executive officer, Carla Judson, a strategic planner with American's Division of Strategic Planning, learned that she was one of several persons being considered to replace, on an acting basis, Cordle Manufacturing Company's president, whose resignation was part of the acquisition agreement. Priest informed Judson that if the acting president could function effectively, the position would be permanent. He indicated, however, that one troublesome problem would have to be eliminated within six months. The problem had been revealed through a confidential survey conducted among 25 members of Cordle's middle management group. Judson was told that the survey results would be available to her and that a meeting of all officers would be held in two weeks to select the acting president. At that time, all candidates would be required to make a presentation outlining how problems revealed by the survey could best be handled.

In studying the survey results, Judson learned that each of the middle managers had been asked to evaluate other departments. The survey was designed to determine, if possible, the respect, cooperation, and goodwill generated between departments. Of the departments evaluated, all were rated satisfactory in efficiency, organization, work relationships, and cooperativeness, except for the sales department. From the 25 questionnaires returned, 18 participants said the sales department needed reorganizing. They said department members were difficult to work with and rarely cooperated with other departments.

As a strategic planner, Judson knew there were a number of feasible strategies she could present to American's officers. She knew that the survey results might be challenged as unreliable and invalid. On the other hand, she was aware that the distinct nature of the objectives, activities, and responsibilities associated with various departments often led to conflict between individuals in various areas. If she acknowledged the survey's validity, she would have to outline a plan for achieving efficient integration and coordination among departments and functional areas. Judson realized her future at American would be decided in the next few days by how her strategies would be perceived by American's officers and then by how effectively she could implement her strategies. What to decide on was her major task.

Using the Case on *Evaluation of Organizational Effectiveness*

Carl Judson is faced with the problem of trying to propose an organization for the new Cordle Manufacturing division of the American Corporation based upon the results of a study that was recently completed at the newly acquired business. The study indicates that most of the departments work well together with one major exception—sales. Ms. Judson's task is to develop a strategy to address and rectify this condition.

Discussion Questions

1. Should Ms. Judson challenge the validity and reliability of the study?
2. If Ms. Judson accepts the study, what are some of the possible strategies she could use to address this situation?

Exercise V: Win As Much As You Can!

1. Divide the group into groups of eight and have each group (cluster) divide into teams of two (dyads).
2. The goal of this exercise is to win as much money as you can.
3. Using the chart at the top of the tally sheet, each dyad is to decide whether it will choose an "X" or a "Y" (with the hope of winning money). The dyads then write their choices on their tally sheets for round 1 while not letting any other dyads see their choices. No conversation among dyads should occur, except when provided for in rounds 5, 8, and 10.
4. After the allotted time for round 1 (2 minutes) has passed, each dyad will show its choice to the other dyads in the cluster. Using the chart on the tally sheet, each dyad should determine how much money it won or lost in round 1, and record this amount on the tally sheet. No comments among dyads are allowed. Proceed immediately to round 2, then 3, and so forth, as outlined on the tally sheet. Note that in rounds 5, 8, and 10, dyads can confer with each other at the beginning of the round. Note also that the amounts won or lost in these rounds are multiplied by three, five, and ten.
5. At the end of the exercise, determine which dyad won the most and which ended up furthest behind. Then compare clusters.

4 X's:	Lose $1.00 each
3 X's: 1 Y:	Win $1.00 each Lose $3.00
2 X's: 2 Y's:	Win $2.00 each Lose $2.00 each
1 X: 3 Y's:	Win $3.00 Lose $1.00 each
4 Y's:	Win $1.00 each

Strategy: You are to confer with your partner(s) on each round and make a joint decision. Before rounds 5, 8, and 10, you confer with the others in your cluster.

Questions for Discussion

1. How was the goal defined? What conflict did it create? (Do I win for my dyad or my cluster?)
2. Do people react differently in games than they do in real life? Do goals in life create conflict?
3. How does trust relate to influence? How many times can one person betray another and still retain his/her confidence? Did anyone stick to her/his word throughout?
4. What effect did communication have on the influence process?
5. What strategies were used to win? What conflict did these strategies create? What strategies were used to manage the conflict?
   - The win/lose approach = self-oriented. (I win at your expense.)
   - The lose/win approach = martyrdom. (You win at my expense.)
   - The lose/lose approach = pride and revenge. (I may lose, but you do, too.)
   - The win/win approach = trust. (We both win.)
6. Why is the win/win approach the most effective strategy in life?

Round	Time Allowed	Confer With	Your Choice Circle	Clusters Patterns of Choices	Payoff	Balance	
1	2 mins.	partner					
2	1 min.	partner					
3	1 min.	partner					
4	1 min.	partner					
5	3 mins. 1 min.	cluster partner					Bonus round payoff × 3
6	1 min.	partner					
7	1 min.	partner					
8	3 mins. 1 min.	cluster partner					Bonus round payoff × 5
9	1 min.	partner					
10	3 mins. 1 min.	cluster partner					Bonus round payoff × 10

Staffing and Human Resources

- Management Classic (Article 31)
- Developing Human Resources (Articles 32 and 33)
- Organized Labor (Articles 34 and 35)
- Maintaining an Effective Workforce (Article 36)

Managers of organizations get things done through people. Managers can plan, organize, direct, and control, but the central focus of all their efforts is people. People determine whether or not an organization is going to succeed, and the way people perceive their treatment by management is often the key to that success. Douglas McGregor demonstrated this principle in "The Human Side of Enterprise," with his Theory X and Theory Y. These two approaches represent opposite ends of the same continuum. Theory X states that people have to be watched, that they cannot be trusted, and that management needs to be supervising them constantly. Theory Y, on the other hand, states that people need to enjoy their work, that they want to do a good job, and that they can be trusted to perform. Most people tend to be in between these two extremes. Situations vary, and the managerial approach that favors Theory Y may or may not be appropriate. The same can be said for Theory X. Neither approach is good or bad; it is a question of appropriateness to the situation.

Since human resources are a key to the success of any organization, firms need to hire the very best people they can find, because it is human beings who make the plans, organize the operation, direct the processes to accomplish the organizational goals, and evaluate the results. But while people contribute directly to a firm's success, they also represent a significant cost to the organization. Not only salaries, but also the cost of benefits are rising at an alarming rate. Benefits cost more today than just a few years ago, and workers not only want to keep the benefits they have, but seek to add others. Some of their demands include dental plans, eye care plans, child care, and senior care for their relatives. Organizations such as Gannett have had to address these issues, as explained in "Gannett's Views on Managing Employees as Individuals."

The workforce is changing. There are more minorities, women, and other groups with different needs, and if a corporation wants to hire these people, many of whom are outstanding, then they are going to have to meet their needs. Otherwise, these potential employees will go elsewhere, frequently to the competition, and put their skills, expertise, and ambition into driving the recalcitrant firm out of business. "Building a Global Workforce Starts with Recruitment" demonstrates that no organization can afford to turn its back on such a large pool of potential talent.

Human resources often involve labor unions. While unions in North America have suffered in recent years with declining membership and plant closings, they have nevertheless served an important historical role as well as providing a balance for the potential excesses of management. Today, as explained in "Labor Adversaries Bury the Hatchet," American labor unions need to define their roles in industry, and their leaders must implement these changes. Unions will have to change the way they conduct business if they plan to survive in the future.

Because of the increasing demand for qualified employees, organizations will have do everything possible to retain good workers. Firms are responding to changes in the workforce in a variety of ways. To meet the needs of the future, management must recognize that people, organizations, and the environment will continue to evolve.

Looking Ahead: Challenge Questions

People are the keys to the success of any organization. What approaches can managers use to direct individuals?

Labor unions are in transition. How do unions need to change to meet the changes in the environment?

The workforce is changing. What do managers of firms need to do to meet the changes?

UNIT 6

The Human Side of Enterprise

Douglas M. McGregor

Douglas M. McGregor was born in 1906. He was graduated A.B. from City College of Detroit (later Wayne University) in 1932 and was graduated A.M. from Oberlin College in 1933. He earned a Ph.D. from Harvard University in 1935. He is best known for his book, The Human Side of Enterprise, *published in 1960. McGregor died in 1964.*

It has become trite to say that industry has the fundamental know-how to utilize physical science and technology for the material benefit of mankind, and that we must now learn how to utilize the social sciences to make our human organizations truly effective.

To a degree, the social sciences today are in a position like that of the physical sciences with respect to atomic energy in the thirties. We know that past conceptions of the nature of man are inadequate and, in many ways, incorrect. We are becoming quite certain that, under proper conditions, unimagined resources of creative human energy could become available within the organizational setting.

We cannot tell industrial management how to apply this new knowledge in simple, economic ways. We know it will require years of exploration, much costly development research, and a substantial amount of creative imagination on the part of management to discover how to apply this growing knowledge to the organization of human effort in industry.

MANAGEMENT'S TASK: THE CONVENTIONAL VIEW

The conventional conception of management's task in harnessing human energy to organizational requirements can be stated broadly in terms of three propositions. In order to avoid the complications introduced by a label, let us call this set of propositions "Theory X":

1. Management is responsible for organizing the elements of productive enterprise—money, materials, equipment, people—in the interest of economic ends.

2. With respect to people, this is a process of directing their efforts, motivating them, controlling their actions, modifying their behavior to fit the needs of the organization.

3. Without this active intervention by management, people would be passive—even resistant—to organizational needs. They must therefore be persuaded, rewarded, punished, controlled—their activities must be directed. This is management's task. We often sum it up by saying that management consists of getting things done through other people.

Behind this conventional theory there are several additional beliefs—less explicit, but widespread:

4. The average man is by nature indolent—he works as little as possible.

5. He lacks ambition, dislikes responsibility, prefers to be led.

6. He is inherently self-centered, indifferent to organizational needs.

7. He is by nature resistant to change.

8. He is gullible, not very bright, the ready dupe of the charlatan and the demagogue.

The human side of economic enterprise today is fashioned from propositions and beliefs such as these. Conventional organization structures and managerial policies, practices, and programs reflect these assumptions.

In accomplishing its task—with these assumptions as guides—management has conceived of a range of possibilities.

At one extreme, management can be "hard" or "strong." The methods for directing behavior involve coercion and threat (usually disguised), close supervision, tight controls over behavior. At the other extreme, management can be "soft" or "weak." The methods for directing behavior involve being permissive, satisfying people's demands, achieving harmony. Then they will be tractable, accept direction.

This range has been fairly completely explored during the past half century, and management has learned some things from the exploration. There are difficulties in the "hard" approach. Force breeds counterforces: restriction of output, antagonism, militant unionism, subtle but effective sabotage of management objectives. This "hard" approach is especially difficult during times of full employment.

There are also difficulties in the "soft" approach. It leads frequently to the abdication of management—to harmony, perhaps, but to indifferent performance. People take advantage of the soft approach. They continually expect more, but they give less and less.

Currently, the popular theme is "firm but fair." This is an attempt to gain the advantages of both the hard and the soft approaches. It is reminiscent of Teddy Roosevelt's "speak softly and carry a big stick."

IS THE CONVENTIONAL VIEW CORRECT?

The findings which are beginning to emerge from the social sciences challenge this whole set of beliefs about man and human nature and about the task of management. The evidence is far from conclusive, certainly, but it is suggestive. It comes from the laboratory, the clinic, the schoolroom, the home, and even to a limited extent from industry itself.

The social scientist does not deny that human behavior in industrial organization today is approximately what management perceives it to be. He has, in fact, observed it and studied it fairly extensively. But he is pretty sure that this behavior is *not* a consequence of man's inherent nature. It is a consequence rather of the nature of industrial organizations, of management philosophy, policy, and practice. The conventional approach of Theory X is based on mistaken notions of what is cause and what is effect.

Perhaps the best way to indicate why the conventional approach of management is inadequate is to consider the subject of motivation.

PHYSIOLOGICAL NEEDS

Man is a wanting animal—as soon as one of his needs is satisfied, another appears in its place. This process is unending. It continues from birth to death.

Man's needs are organized in a series of levels—a hierarchy of importance. At the lowest level, but preeminent in importance when they are thwarted, are his *physiological needs*. Man lives for bread alone, when there is no bread. Unless the circumstances are unusual, his needs for love, for status, for recognition are inoperative when his stomach has been empty for a while. But when he eats regularly and adequately, hunger ceases to be an important motivation. The same is true of the other physiological needs of man— for rest, exercise, shelter, protection from the elements.

A satisfied need is not a motivator of behavior! This is a fact of profound significance that is regularly ignored in the conventional approach to the management of people. Consider your own need for air: Except as you are deprived of it, it has no appreciable motivating effect upon your behavior.

SAFETY NEEDS

When the physiological needs are reasonably satisfied, needs at the next higher level begin to dominate man's behavior—to motivate him. These are called *safety needs*. They are needs for protection against danger, threat, deprivation. Some people mistakenly refer to these as needs for security. However, unless man is in a dependent relationship where he fears arbitrary deprivation, he does not demand security. The need is for the "fairest possible break." When he is confident of this, he is more than willing to take risks. But when he feels threatened or dependent, his greatest need is for guarantees, for protection, for security.

The fact needs little emphasis that, since every industrial employee is in a dependent relationship, safety needs may assume considerable importance. Arbitrary management actions, behavior which arouses uncertainty with respect to continued employment or which reflects favoritism or discrimination, unpredictable administration of policy—these can be powerful motivators of the safety needs in the employment relationship *at every level,* from worker to vice-president.

SOCIAL NEEDS

When man's physiological needs are satisfied and he is no longer fearful about his physical welfare, his *social needs* become important motivators of his behavior—needs for belonging, for association, for acceptance by his fellows, for giving and receiving friendship and love.

Management knows today of the existence of these needs, but it often assumes quite wrongly that they represent a threat to the organization. Many studies have demonstrated that the tightly knit, cohesive work group may, under proper conditions, be far more effective than an equal number of separate individuals in achieving organizational goals.

Yet management, fearing group hostility to its own objectives, often goes to considerable lengths to control and direct human efforts in ways that are inimical to the natural "groupiness" of human beings. When man's social needs— and perhaps his safety needs, too—are thus thwarted, he behaves in ways which tend to defeat organizational objectives. He becomes resistant, antagonistic, uncooperative. But this behavior is a consequence, not a cause.

EGO NEEDS

Above the social needs—in the sense that they do not become motivators until lower needs are reasonably satisfied—are the needs of greatest significance to management and to man himself. They are the *egoistic needs,* and they are of two kinds:

1. Those needs that relate to one's self-esteem—needs for self-confidence, for independence, for achievement, for competence, for knowledge.

2. Those needs that relate to one's reputation—needs for status, for recognition, for appreciation, for the deserved respect of one's fellows.

Unlike the lower needs, these are rarely satisfied; man seeks indefinitely for more satisfaction of these needs once they have become important to him. But they do not appear in any significant way until physiological, safety, and social needs are all reasonably satisfied.

The typical industrial organization offers few opportunities for the satisfaction of these egoistic needs to people at lower levels in the hierarchy. The conventional methods of organizing work, particularly in mass production industries, give little heed to these aspects of human motivation. If the practices of scientific management were deliberately calculated to thwart these needs, they could hardly accomplish this purpose better than they do.

SELF-FULLFILLMENT NEEDS

Finally—a capstone, as it were, on the hierarchy of man's needs—there are what we may call the *needs for self-fulfillment*. These are the needs for realizing one's own potentialities, for continued self-development, for being creative in the broadest sense of that term.

It is clear that the conditions of modern life give only limited opportunity for these relatively weak needs to obtain expression. The deprivation most people experience with respect to other lower level needs diverts their energies into the struggle to satisfy *those* needs, and the needs for self-fulfillment remain dormant.

MANAGEMENT AND MOTIVATION

We recognize readily enough that a man suffering from a severe dietary deficiency is sick. The deprivation of physiological needs has behavioral consequences. The same is true—although less well recognized—of deprivation of higher level needs. The man whose needs for safety, association, independence, or status are thwarted is sick just as surely as the man who has rickets. And his sickness will have behavioral consequences. We will be mistaken if we attribute his resultant passivity, his hostility, his refusal to accept responsibility to his inherent "human nature." These forms of behavior are *symptoms* of illness—of deprivation of his social and egoistic needs.

The man whose lower level needs are satisfied is not motivated to satisfy those needs any longer. For practical purposes they exist no longer. Management often asks, "Why aren't people more productive? We pay good wages, provide good working conditions, have excellent fringe benefits and steady employment. Yet people do not seem to be willing to put forth more than minimum effort."

The fact that management has provided for these physiological and safety needs has shifted the motivational emphasis to the social and perhaps to the egoistic needs. Unless there are opportunities *at work* to satisfy these higher level needs, people will be deprived; and their behavior will reflect this deprivation. Under such conditions, if management continues to focus its attention on physiological needs, its efforts are bound to be ineffective.

People *will* make insistent demands for more money under these conditions. It becomes more important than ever to buy the material goods and services which can provide limited satisfaction of the thwarted needs. Although money has only limited value in satisfying many higher level needs, it can become the focus of interest if it is the *only* means available.

THE CARROT-AND-STICK APPROACH

The carrot-and-stick theory of motivation (like Newtonian physical theory) works reasonably well under certain circumstances. The *means* for satisfying man's physiological and (within limits) his safety needs can be provided or withheld by management. Employment itself is such a means, and so are wages, working conditions, and benefits. By these means the individual can be controlled so long as he is struggling for subsistence.

But the carrot-and-stick theory does not work at all once man has reached an adequate subsistence level and is motivated primarily by higher needs. Management cannot provide a man with self-respect, or with the respect of his fellows, or with the satisfaction of needs for self-fulfillment. It can create such conditions that he is encouraged and enabled to seek such satisfactions for *himself,* or it can thwart him by failing to create those conditions.

But this creation of conditions is not "control." It is not a good device for directing behavior. And so management finds itself in an odd position. The high standard of living created by our modern technological know-how provides quite adequately for the satisfaction of physiological and safety needs. The only significant exception is where management practices have not created confidence in a "fair break"—and thus where safety needs are thwarted. But by making possible the satisfaction of low level needs, management has deprived itself of the ability to use as motivators the devices on which conventional theory has taught it to rely—rewards, promises, incentives, or threats and other coercive devices.

The philosophy of management by direction and control—*regardless of whether it is hard or soft*—is inadequate to motivate because the human needs on which this approach relies are today unimportant motivators of behavior. Direction and control are essentially useless in motivating people whose important needs are social and egoistic. Both the hard and the soft approach fail today because they are simply irrelevant to the situation.

People, deprived of opportunities to satisfy at work the needs which are now important to them, behave exactly as we might predict—with indolence, passivity, resistance to change, lack of responsibility, willingness to follow the demagogue, unreasonable demands for economic benefits. It would seem that we are caught in a web of our own weaving.

A NEW THEORY OF MANAGEMENT

For these and many other reasons, we require a different theory of the task of managing people based on more adequate assumptions about human nature and human motivation. I am going to be so bold as to suggest the broad dimensions of such a theory. Call it "Theory Y," if you will.

1. Management is responsible for organizing the elements of productive enterprise—money, materials, equipment, people—in the interest of economic ends.
2. People are *not* by nature passive or resistant to organizational needs. They have become so as a result of experience in organizations.
3. The motivation, the potential for development, the capacity for assuming responsibility, the readiness to direct behavior toward organizational goals are all present in people. Management does not put them there. It is a responsibility of management to make it possible for people to recognize and develop these human characteristics for themselves.
4. The essential task of management is to arrange organizational conditions and methods of operation so that people can achieve their own goals *best* by directing *their own* efforts toward organizational objectives.

This is a process primarily of creating opportunities, releasing potential, removing obstacles, encouraging growth, providing guidance. It is what Peter Drucker has called "management by objectives" in contrast to "management by control." It does *not* involve the abdication of management, the absence of leadership, the lowering of standards, or the other characteristics usually associated with the "soft" approach under Theory X.

SOME DIFFICULTIES

It is no more possible to create an organization today which will be a full, effective application of this theory than it was to build an atomic power plant in 1945. There are many formidable obstacles to overcome.

The conditions imposed by conventional organization theory and by the approach of scientific management for the past half century have tied men to limited jobs which do not utilize their capabilities, have discouraged the acceptance of responsibility, have encouraged passivity, have eliminated meaning from work. Man's habits, attitudes, expectations—his whole conception of membership in an industrial organization—have been conditioned by his experience under these circumstances.

People today are accustomed to being directed, manipulated, controlled in industrial organizations and to finding satisfaction for their social, egoistic, and self-fulfillment needs away from the job. This is true of much of management as well as of workers. Genuine "industrial citizenship"—to borrow again a term from Drucker—is a remote and unrealistic idea, the meaning of which has not even been considered by most members of industrial organizations.

Another way of saying this is that Theory X places exclusive reliance upon external control of human behavior, while Theory Y relies heavily on self-control and self-direction. It is worth noting that this difference is the difference between treating people as children and treating them as mature adults. After generations of the former, we cannot expect to shift to the latter overnight.

STEPS IN THE RIGHT DIRECTION

Before we are overwhelmed by the obstacles, let us remember that the application of theory is always slow. Progress is usually achieved in small steps. Some innovative ideas which are entirely consistent with Theory Y are today being applied with some success.

Decentralization and Delegation

These are ways of freeing people from the too-close control of conventional organization, giving them a degree of freedom to direct their own activities, to assume responsibility, and, importantly, to satisfy their egoistic needs. In this connection, the flat organization of Sears, Roebuck and Company provides an interesting example. It forces "management by objectives," since it enlarges the number of people reporting to a manager until he cannot direct and control them in the conventional manner.

Job Enlargement

This concept, pioneered by IBM and Detroit Edison, is quite consistent with Theory Y. It encourages the acceptance of responsibility at the bottom of the organization; it provides opportunities for satisfying social and egoistic needs. In fact, the reorganization of work at the factory level offers one of the more challenging opportunities for innovation consistent with Theory Y.

Participation and Consultative Management

Under proper conditions, participation and consultative management provide encouragement to people to direct their creative energies toward organizational objectives, give them some voice in decisions that affect them, provide significant opportunities for the satisfaction of social and egoistic needs. The Scanlon Plan is the outstanding embodiment of these ideas in practice.

Performance Appraisal

Even a cursory examination of conventional programs of performance appraisal within the ranks of management will reveal how completely consistent they are with Theory X. In fact, most such programs tend to treat the individual as though he were a product under inspection on the assembly line.

A few companies—among them General Mills, Ansul Chemical, and General Electric—have been experimenting with approaches which involve the individual in setting "targets" or objectives *for himself* and in a *self*-evaluation of performance semiannually or annually. Of course, the superior plays an important leadership role in this process—one, in fact, which demands substantially more competence than the conventional approach. The role is, however, considerably more congenial to many managers than the role of "judge" or "inspector" which is usually forced upon them. Above all, the individual is encouraged to take a greater responsibility for planning and appraising his own contribution to organizational objectives; and the accompanying effects on egoistic and self-fulfillment needs are substantial.

APPLYING THE IDEAS

The not infrequent failure of such ideas as these to work as well as expected is often attributable to the fact that a management has "bought the idea" but applied it within the framework of Theory X and its assumptions.

Delegation is not an effective way of exercising management by control. Participation becomes a farce when it is applied as a sales gimmick or a device for kidding people into thinking they are important. Only the management that has confidence in human capacities and is itself directed toward organizational objectives rather than toward the preservation of personal power can grasp the implications of this emerging theory. Such management will find and apply successfully other innovative ideas as we move slowly toward the full implementation of a theory like Y.

THE HUMAN SIDE OF ENTERPRISE

It is quite possible for us to realize substantial improvements in the effectiveness of industrial organizations during the next decade or two. The social sciences can contribute much to such developments; we are only beginning to grasp the implications of the growing body of knowledge in these fields. But if this conviction is to become a reality instead of a pious hope, we will need to view the process much as we view the process of releasing the energy of the atom for constructive human ends—as a slow, costly, sometimes discouraging approach toward a goal which would seem to many to be quite unrealistic.

The ingenuity and the perseverance of industrial management in the pursuit of economic ends have changed many scientific and technological dreams into commonplace realities. It is now becoming clear that the application of these same talents to the human side of enterprise will not only enhance substantially these materialistic achievements, but will bring us one step closer to "the good society."

Gannett's Views on Managing Employees as Individuals

The media giant has become a role model for its commitment to diversity. Here, the vice president of personnel outlines some points to ponder when assessing an organization's own commitment.

Madelyn Jennings

Madelyn Jennings is senior vice president of personnel for Gannett Co. Inc., a news and information company based in Arlington, Va., that publishes 83 newspapers. Jennings previously held executive positions at Standard Brands and General Electric. She also serves on numerous committees, including the Business Roundtable's Employee Relations Executive Committee. She has a bachelor's degree from Texas Woman's University.

Diversity is a hot topic today and for good reason. You've all read about the demographic trends in our country. Some are referring to the work force of the 90s as one mainly composed of minorities: black, white, Hispanic, Asian, Native American.

But it's also a time of divisiveness.

A recent survey showed older and younger white Americans are more extreme in their biases than people aged 30 to 50, probably because the older are less educated and the younger people feel a need for belonging to a group, giving them a chance for respect, approval, affiliation. That means the number of Klu Klux Klanners and Skinheads is growing because of the number of *young* people joining up.

In the newspaper business, almost two out of three black journalists in a survey said promotion standards are higher for them. Three out of four said black employees are less likely to be considered for career opportunities.

They said minorities are "shown the stairs" and white men are "shown the elevator." Black journalists said the "one best power model" is limited to the white male standard. Anything different is defined as dysfunctional and uncomfortable.

Diversity Defined

Let's examine three key terms, EEO, affirmative action and diversity as defined today.

• Equal employment opportunity is the law and it's a neutral term. The emphasis is on everyone being treated the same. When they are not, complaints follow. Even if a discrimination complaint is found to be frivolous, it is always expensive. Ask any operating unit head about the time and dollars involved and the scrutiny of lawyers into your activities when you undergo a discrimination investigation.

• Affirmative action, according to some, is about giving protected groups the opportunity to be treated the same insofar as what is expected. Others contend that affirmative action is really about giving protected groups preference when all else is more or less equal.

Affirmative action was first used in a 1961 Executive Order. It was targeted at forcing government contractors to have plans in place and aggressive positive programs laid to equalize job opportunity and fix any disparate situations. In 1962, President Kennedy invited the business community to get involved, to give minorities what was called "access."

At the time, some of the biggest companies joined forces in a program called "Plans for Progress." One of the Plans for Progress companies was General Electric, where I worked at the time and was involved in a program we called PIMEG, a Program to Increase Minority Engineering Graduates. This was more than 30 years ago.

At Gannett Co. today, our numbers, from an affirmative action standpoint on the broad basis of our top four job categories, look pretty good. Our main focus is minorities and females ready to move up, and the number of minorities and females at the department head and general management levels. That's the challenge, to shatter the so-called "Glass Ceiling."

• Our often-stated corporate goal is a work force that reflects the communities where we do business. As President Clinton put it, a work force that looks like America. Only if you view each opening as an opportunity for progress will progress happen.

Diversity today. Diversity is qualitative — it's more than equal employment opportunity or affirmative action. It's recognition of all the differences among workers and the variety of perspectives and values that are part of the package.

Managing diversity involves recognizing and respecting those differences and making them a powerful resource to achieve business goals. It's not a soft-headed, knee-jerk, liberal idea. It has to do with getting the most out of our talent for the good of the shareholders.

Managing diversity well means you actually review all your practices, such as recruitment, promotion and employee development and take action to make sure those practices don't hinder and, in fact, support a diverse workplace.

Diversity initiatives should not create or underscore group stereotypes. Group stereotypes promote sensitivity to each possible slight and an ability to see malignant discrimination as the reason for everything that happens to one.

Diversity has to do with respecting individual differences not group stereotypes. When we make value judgments, they should be about the person. They should not be based on value judgments you've already made about a group the person may represent.

What Are Your Beliefs?

Do you assume:

• That if your college freshman son brings home a date for the holidays, that person will be a woman?

• That younger workers have more energy than older ones?

• That your new employee will have food or transportation money before his or her first paycheck?

• That no one you work with has ever been physically or sexually abused?

• That the older man who asks you about the safety rules does so because he's just friendly and not because he can't read?

• That secretary jobs are women's jobs?

Diversity has to do with lots of differences, including: age and generation, race, ethnicity, gender, physical ability/disability, sexual orientation, work background/profession, income, marital status, military experience, religion, geographic background, parental status, family background, education, conformity vs. nonconformity, personality, political party, language group/background, and social class.

Think about two of the differences on the list you think about the most; the least; as assets at your company; as assets in your career; as barriers at your company; as barriers in your career.

Gannett's Approach

Across the United States consultants are making a fortune on diversity training. For me, some of it smacks of the "I'm okay, you're okay" sensitivity training of the 1960s. It felt great at the time but had a half-life of about two weeks.

Managing diversity involves recognizing and respecting differencees and making them a powerful resource.

At Gannett, we see diversity as a part of everything we do, from our recruiting ads to our interview process to who gets promoted and who gets dismissed to the success we have working together in groups.

We start at the top where one-third of our board of directors is female and one-third are minorities. About one-third of our general managers are female and about 10 percent are minorities. That's part of our corporate culture.

We understand that there's a democratic distribution of smart and dumb and we believe that the broader our search for star talent the better a chance there is to have star talent.

We celebrate our diversity in all our corporate publications and communications, at board meetings, at shareholder meetings.

People hear how we are doing and who our talent is — and they are diverse and great role models for junior players.

Our development programs provide broadened exposure and we make sure there is diversity in those programs. And we target for improvement the weak parts of our people pipeline, those areas where we lack diversity. We expect diversity in our candidate slates. We track professional openings each year to make sure people hired and promoted reflect the make-up of our communities.

We have an open door policy for complaints and we expect managers to protect its integrity by preventing recrimination against people who use it to voice their concerns.

We have diversity committees across the company at each location and they are helping us create a more hospitable environment for all kinds of people.

I like the mission of our Battle Creek, Mich., newspaper committee. It says, "We are committed to shattering barriers — cultural, racial, gender and departmental — freeing us to learn, teach and interact — to expand our individual and collective goals and produce the highest caliber newspaper possible."

And, of course, executive bonuses are based, in part, on their progress in the area of diversity.

What's most important to success in diversity and, indeed, to overall business success, is the skill of our managers and supervisors. To get to be a department head takes supervisory experience, so the people in supervisor jobs need attention through coaching, career counseling, special project experience, and exposure to the core management training programs. Human resources should make sure that happens.

More Than a Number

Attitude surveys, exit interviews and business articles across the country point to some workplace conflicts and tensions that suggest we *must* develop better bosses. Think about this: If our employees don't feel good about themselves and coming to work in the morning, how can we be excellent?

Complaints of reverse discrimination suggest a lack of understanding of the *why* of our commitment to diversity.

There are perceptions in some places that white males are the only group not getting favoritism and promotions. Some managers don't listen or understand the need for some flexibility in scheduling, such as compressed work weeks, job sharing, telecommuting and flex time, when business needs permit. Disabled employees are, on the one hand, highly visible; and on the other hand, invisible.

Whom do you include in your group activities, from brainstorming to athletic outings to

---

Diversity Stats

Do you know the answers to these questions?

■ What percent of the U.S. work force is female? (47 percent)

■ How much on average does a woman make for each dollar a man makes? (71 cents — one cent less than in 1990)

■ What percentage of American households have a working father and a mother at home caring for the children? (9.3 percent)

■ What are the most common three ancestries reported in the 1990 census? (German, 23.3 percent; Irish, 13.6 percent; and English 13.1 percent)

■ What will be the percentage of Hispanics in the work force in the year 2000? (11.1 percent)

■ How many people in the U.S. are considered disabled? (43 million)

---

task forces?

Too often, there is splintering into special interest groups with each agenda fighting for consideration and resources. And, some minorities complain that they're only a number, suggesting the need for understanding that we value diversity for the *variety of ideas* it brings rather than only the numbers it brings.

I once saw an anonymous letter alleging, "Diverse people are promoted over their heads, generally aren't seeking help and neither is the company offering any. They don't act with notes or written materials because their communications skills are so bad. Yet they are tossed into the water with no swimming lessons."

Then the white guys turn around and walk away from the water with everyone patting each other on the back for being such forward-looking and generous and kind people."

In today's "politically correct" era, while the goal may be to eliminate prejudice, censorship has too often become the strategy. Censors think they represent the common good. But censors cause fear of speaking up and growing restraint on free speech.

Freedom comes not from squelching dissent but from tolerating it. From being prepared to stand up for those whose very existence you may find intolerable instead of all being afraid to speak up honestly and learn together.

Max Du Pree's metaphor for today's outstanding business organizations is the jazz band, where each member has a specific contribution to make, but each is dependent in its moment of performance on the other members and innovation is the rule.

Consider these questions and apply them to your own organization:

• Is yours an environment where people feel free to speak up and take risks? How do your managers react to staffer mistakes or what may seem like dumb ideas?

• Is your diversity committee being utilized to the fullest extent? Many committees are doing some fine work, including crossing over into areas related to customer service, quality initiatives, improved communications and community outreach. Are you taking advantage of your diversity committee's ideas?

• Do you have a local management development program? They are not costly and we should have more of them.

• Are your supervisors well trained in the basic training programs? In fact, *pre*-supervisory training programs are also needed and a great way to spot future leaders.

Fostering Ideas

Diversity today is many faces... older, younger, disabled, minority, female, fifty-year-old white males. Cookie-cutter approaches are out. Handling individuals as individuals is in. Fairness rather than favoritism is critical.

Developing skilled, agile, trained supervisors and managers who understand diversity is in our best interest can be our best answer to staying a leader in diversity and in our overall results.

Something to remember is that not everyone wants to be like you. The goal should be to allow for and value differences instead of lumping employees in groups. Our chairman told a group of new employees recently that the first characteristic that came to his mind to describe our managers' style is individuality. That's worth celebrating.

But, we must be careful. If we end up overemphasizing our diversity and under-emphasizing our inescapable mutuality, we miss the point.

Instead we should think hard about recent research which shows homogeneous groups get to answers quicker, but diverse groups, though they may take more time, are more creative in their solutions.

Diverse groups are more creative in their solutions. We are all in the business of ideas — what better reason for diversity? It could be the strongest strategy a company has to compete against other firms.

I would like to toss the word diversity out the window and replace it with the word community. What built this great country was community — the willingness of people to build together, to link together.

You can make your community even more successful than it is today if you remember the answer to Kermit the Frog's question: "What if we all lived in the same house?" The answer is, "We do."

This article was excerpted from a speech by Madelyn Jennings to upper-level managers at Gannett Co. Inc.

Building a Global Workforce Starts With Recruitment

Your company will never be truly global until every employee has a global mindset. If you recruit with this in mind, you'll have global-thinkers—and doers—worldwide.

If you're an HR professional in an international corporation, which members of your workforce are global employees? U.S. citizens living abroad? Japanese employees working in the United States? Swedish managers who are helping to set up operations in Portugal? Or every single member of your workforce?

Without hesitation, most HR professionals would include the first three categories of employees in their answer. Expatriates, usually defined as those living and working outside their home countries, are obviously global: They're key to the success or failure of international business, whether they remain abroad long term or work short stints while operations are being established. Selecting the right people for these assignments is a matter of great concern, as early return or failure is costly and can be damaging to business relations with international partners or customers.

But, where do you find these expats? Do you go out and hire them for the job, or do you select them from among your workforce? Most often, expatriates are selected from within the corporation. Why? Current employees usually are more in sync with a company's organizational culture, and they also have the skills necessary to do the job.

As many HR professionals are learning, however, employees need more than technical expertise to succeed. And, unless every member of an organization is looked upon as a global employee, it may be difficult to find people who have the skills necessary to perform well in the international environment. By keeping long-term goals in sight during recruitment efforts, multinational firms can build a globally aware workforce—one composed of talented members who support the company's global philosophy, have expat potential and can propel the business into the 21st century.

Make every hire a global effort.
Every year, hundreds of companies expand their operations into the global marketplace. At the same time, corporations that are established in the international sphere redefine their business to maintain a competitive edge. For organizations in both categories, recruitment and international assignment are key determinants of long-term success.

For many corporations, international recruitment is synonymous with expatriate selection. Within this area, significant progress has been made to ensure candidates are screened for global competency, which—according to most experts—includes such qualities as flexibility, open-mindedness, technical expertise, multiple language proficiency and the willingness to take risks. Says Shirley Gaufin, vice president of HR for Bechtel Group Inc. in San Francisco: "Global awareness is a subtle characteristic, but it's absolutely essential for expatriate success. It's part of someone being a good leader, part of someone being flexible and adaptable."

Today, HR professionals in progressive global companies are discovering that it isn't enough just to look for these skills among members of the expatriate community. Rather, every employee needs to have a certain level of global awareness, and many companies are finding that screening must begin at recruitment. Take, for example, Tetra Pak Inc., a multinational corporation based in Lund, Sweden. At the company's U.S. headquarters in Chicago, personnel manager Barbara Shimkus looks for expat potential every time she makes a hire. "We don't often go out and search for someone to go abroad next year. Expatriates are selected from within the company," Shimkus says. "But when we recruit, we always look for candidates who have global potential. We're interested in people who eventually could relocate internationally and handle that adjustment well."

Overall, Shimkus says candidates with international backgrounds are best suited for careers with the company. She says: "Business is changing, and companies can no longer seek out employees who have limited themselves to a domestic view of the world. Employees who will lead us into the future are those who understand business in the international arena."

Gaufin agrees. At Bechtel, she works with approximately 25,000 people who are handling diverse projects in more than 70 countries worldwide. Recently, Bechtel went through a major restructuring, giving its international regions more autonomy. Instead of ruling from above, the company is focusing on multinational awareness and cultivation of its global talent. Gaufin explains: "In the past, we were more of a U.S. firm doing business internationally. We are now becoming more 'global.' As part of that, we're working to develop a stronger global workforce." What does this mean for recruitment? Bechtel is placing more emphasis than ever before on global competencies, assuring that every member can contribute to future multinational growth.

As Gaufin and Shimkus note, it's to every company's best advantage to consider the future and hire those who can support upcoming needs. But in addition to recruiting for expatriate potential, HR professionals are finding that employees who have international experience and language proficiency help the company function on a day-to-day basis. To see why this is true, just look at the operations of an average global company. Managers must understand differing cultural norms to perform well on business trips and short-term assignments in other parts of the world. HR professionals need to be aware of legal differences surrounding benefits and compensation, as well as local norms regarding vacation and child care. Receptionists and other staff members must answer daily phone calls and correspondence from overseas.

At Tetra Pak, global interaction is common, and employees with multiple-language skills are in high demand. "It seems like every day we're searching the office for someone who speaks Swedish or German or Spanish to translate a fax or interpret a phone call," says Shimkus. Bechtel's internal communications staff are regularly reminded that their employee newsletter reaches an international audience: "We're very careful to avoid mention of the seasons, for example, because they differ with the hemispheres," Gaufin says. This type of awareness is needed by every employee. "Every day, our employees have to consider the fact that they're working within a global framework. There are time changes, cultural variations—small differences that matter."

Gaufin says the more capable employees are at understanding these everyday differences, the more successful the business will be on a global level. "Every employee needs to have a global state of mind, whether it's someone who works overseas or in the United States," Gaufin says. "Employees have to be able to look at the company—and our business—in a global way."

Realign your recruitment strategies. Identifying the need for these employees is just one-half of the battle: Finding them is the other. Not all applicants have the flexible personalities needed to perform well in a global environment—and even fewer have any sort of international training. In fact, according to the American Institute for Foreign Study, just 5% of college graduates are proficient in a foreign language, and less than half of all students studying business take a course that's internationally focused. Without a recruitment effort that's designed to attract those with global competencies, HR professionals are unlikely to find top talent.

John Amato, former manager of global assignments for St. Louis-based Monsanto Corporation, says that small changes to recruitment advertising can help companies identify global potential. "In writing job descriptions, get away from focusing only on the job's technical skills," Amato says. "Of course, technical expertise is important. But recruitment advertising can tell the applicants a lot more about future potential of the position when you describe behavioral traits needed for the job."

Changes of this type can help companies get a more globally qualified pool of applicants for every hire. This is especially true when recruiters combine the new job criteria with expanded international networking efforts and targeted recruitment campaigns. As Amato recommends: "Network among the global community. Attend conferences where you can meet other specialists. This can help you expand your global applicant pool." Amato also says to look among the college ranks, especially at schools that specialize in international education. Shimkus agrees. "When we recruit from these colleges, it gives us confidence we're identifying people who have a global foundation and a wider understanding of the world," she says.

Identification of global talent is essential to Mary Scelba's recruitment efforts. As assistant vice president of strategic staffing and planning for Warren, New Jersey-based Chubb & Son Inc., she looks for international competency during every recruitment effort. With more than 15% of the company's employees outside of the United States—and rapid overseas growth—Chubb & Son considers global awareness a must-have criterion for every new hire. "An ideal employee is one who is open to other cultures, someone who has multiple-language skills, someone who's flexible and adaptable to meet our changing business needs," Scelba explains.

No positions are less vital to Chubb's global development than the company's international branch managers. To be assured of the highest quality employees in these positions, Chubb recruits globally minded people to participate in the company's international trainee program. After an extensive training in Chubb's practices and standards, these employees move into management slots.

Recruitment efforts for trainees are initially conducted locally, using traditional methods—local campus recruiting, newspaper advertisements and employee referrals. However, Scelba frequently supplements the branches' efforts by identifying potential within the United States. She says that universities offer a concentration of qualified applicants: "We attend international career consortiums that are held specifically for international students. The attendees are ideal applicants." Why? Chubb is looking for people who have just completed master's degrees and who also have three to five years experience working in their home countries. Because the attendees have studied in the United States, they offer additional benefits to the U.S.-based company:

"Most are fluent in English and understand U.S. culture. They're bilingual, globally minded and already have international experience to build upon," Scelba says. "But many of them are planning to return to their home countries to work. We source them here, interview them, then refer them to our overseas branches for potential hire."

Make recruitment a first step.
Whatever your methods for identifying talent, efforts to build your company's international potential must continue long term. Recruitment is just a first step in developing a global workforce, a first stage in cultivating global leadership and supporting your international business. For employees who are already on board, multicultural training and international

exposure can strengthen global competencies that already exist. Career planning and internal networking can help top-potential employees excel. And, when overseas assignments are necessary, expats can perform most successfully with a comprehensive expatriation and repatriation program. But, the whole process begins with early identification of potential. "Employees who have strong global skills are a requirement—not only for expatriate positions, but to support immediate needs," says Amato. "Selection of the right people is crucial to the success of international business."

The global business environment is growing so rapidly, you can't afford not to recruit people with global mindsets. If it isn't crucial to your company today —it probably will be tomorrow.

New Bargaining Process Eases Headaches

Labor Adversaries Bury the Hatchet

A new contract negotiation process, called *target-specific bargaining*,
is helping organizations make contract talks easier—with fewer headaches.
Learn how this team-based, interactive process helped one organization and its
bargaining units bury old tensions and sign longer-term agreements.

**Donald D. Tippett
and Joseph Costa**

Donald D. Tippett, Ph.D. is an associate professor at The University of Alabama in Huntsville.

Joseph Costa, formerly the division manager for machine and fabrication services at Arnold Engineering Development Center with SSI Services, Inc., is the manager of quality assurance & safety for ACS, which took control of the mission support contract in 1995.

The end of a strike doesn't always mean the end of problems. Often, the end of a strike is just the beginning of workplace tension. For SSI Services Inc., the end of a nasty strike in 1990 was just the beginning of difficulties between the bargaining units and management.

By 1992, relations had eroded to the point at which workers didn't trust management—and management was suspect of workers' motives. Bitterness, anger, frustration and fear were commonplace. No matter what issue landed on the bargaining table, people couldn't look at it objectively without the veil of resentment clouding their thoughts.

At best, it was a difficult situation. At worst, it was another strike waiting to happen. If worker-management relations—including the bargaining process—didn't improve, both sides were headed for disaster. SSI needed a fresh approach to union relations—and fast.

A divisive strike leaves the workforce tense and bitter. Winning the contract from PanAm World Services in 1985, SSI, based in Bridgeville, Pennsylvania, became the mission support contractor for the U.S. Air Force Materiel Command's Arnold Engineering Development Center (AEDC) located at Arnold Air Force Base near Tullahoma, Tennessee. The AEDC is responsible for developing, certifying and testing of aircraft, missile and space systems for the Air Force. After signing on as one of three government contractors supporting the base, SSI took over many responsibilities on the base, such as facilities maintenance, fire protection, security, logistics and running both a precision machine shop and a fabrication shop.

To complete all these responsibilities, SSI hired 1,350 workers who were represented by 13 different unions—headed by the Air Engineering Metal Trades Council (AEMTC). Most of the workers had been employed formerly by PanAm, and were hired by SSI when it took over the contract. The workers' had a strong allegiance to the base itself, rather than to the employer of the moment (SSI)—because contractors come and go, but the base remains their "home." In addition, management operated within a very bureaucratic organization which placed laborers at the bottom of the pyramid.

During labor negotiations in 1990, SSI sought to improve its work rules to boost productivity and cut costs. The AEMTC, however, wanted to ensure job security, increase benefits and improve the overall quality of life for its members. Negotiations ended in a disruptive 57-day strike right before the year-end holiday season.

Concessions by both parties eventually ended the strike. However, the fallout of mistrust and animosity lasted several years. By 1993, SSI and the AEMTC decided that enough was enough. It was time to radically change the way they dealt with each other.

They realized they had a problem they couldn't ignore and set out to fix it. Both sides (SSI and the AEMTC) realized there were extremely bad feelings throughout the workforce. They needed to improve relations and prevent future walkouts.

So, SSI's general manager, John Stubbs, and six union leaders got together to talk about the 1990 strike and its long-term effects on morale, trust and teamwork. Key to the discussions was Anthony J. Taylor, SSI's human resources manager and labor relations manager at the time. He's now the HR management specialist for Tullahoma, Tennessee-based ACS, which took over the support contract in 1995. During the very first session, called the "Workforce Effectiveness Workshop," work issues were discussed openly and honestly, without regard to individuals' status or position.

These individuals, and others—including union representatives, managers and HR staff—continued to meet monthly, and sometimes even weekly, for approximately one year. In these subsequent meetings or workshops run by their consultant, Matt Taylor Associates, approximately 40 to 75 people would separate into "breakout teams" of approximately 10 people each to talk about specific options for solving work problems. They tackled problems identified in the sessions by exploring the facts, focusing on the causes and then providing recommendations.

These workshops, which Matt Taylor Associates calls DesignShops™, were assisted by their team of facilitators who were specialists in organizational culture transformation. The facilitators kept the interaction moving, focused and pleasant. Each session lasted 16 to 32 hours, spanning two to three days. Clear agendas were established and followed with separate modules that included team-building and problem-solving exercises.

Whenever a team needed more data, it would turn into a "problem-solving team" and went out to collect more information about the specific issue. Problem-solving teams worked on many issues such as identifying options to reduce health-insurance costs and figuring out possible ways to implement a four-day workweek. This all happened before the actual bargaining talks began so as to identify the issues and to come up with options to discuss during negotiations.

For example, one of the issues a breakout team handled was sick leave. "Many workers felt they were being treated like stepchildren and that management didn't really trust them," says SSI's Taylor, who served on several of the breakout teams, along with various union representatives, company managers and HR staffers.

---

5 Recommendations For Better Labor-management Negotiations

New methods to enhance workplace productivity must be sought out and tailored to an individual organization. Through joint labor and management teams, cooperation and employee participation can be achieved and successfully used to address and to solve issues that were previously major obstacles—such as wages, benefits and job security—for true win-win results. The following recommendations will facilitate the process:

1. Involve the HR organization from the beginning.
2. Evaluate the organization's history and culture to better understand the people and the obstacles it will have to overcome. Is the culture co-operative or adversarial in nature? Cultural audits are now common and provide this type of information.
3. Look at the organization's structure. Does it allow clear and open communication lines between upper management and the front-line workers? If not, those lines must be established through a flatter structure and joint problem-solving teams.
4. Create a labor-management relations committee (LMRC) to oversee these efforts. This LMRC should establish a clear vision, goals and objectives—a partnering agreement if you will—that can serve as the committee's guide.
5. Finally, adopt a systematic approach to negotiations, and then follow it for optimum results.

—DT, JC

"They felt that because they couldn't take sick leave the very first day [they were sick], they were being treated differently [from nonrepresented employees]." The old policy stated that employees couldn't begin using sick leave until two days after they became ill. The team came up with the idea to give employees a pool of 48 hours to use toward their first two days off (charged against their sick leave). The idea was later embraced by both sides as part of an agreement to keep sick leave usage down and to provide a similar benefit as the nonrepresented personnel.

Communication between labor and management during these sessions enabled each side to see the world from the other's perspective. During one of the sessions, team members decided to go ahead and "bury the hatchet" (literally). A procession of several managers, union representatives and HR staff marched out to a grassy area on the base grounds to the tune of a funeral march. They buried a tiny coffin bearing an actual hatchet.

"It was very poetic," says SSI's Taylor. "We all agreed that we would never, ever again allow the relationship [between labor and management] to deteriorate to the point that we would have another strike." He adds: "That was the first step in opening lines of communication and developing trust." The symbolic gesture of performing a mock funeral and burying the past helped everyone focus on the tasks at hand.

Implementing a new collective-bargaining process for a new era. After burying the hatchet, the HR manager and general manager traveled to Washington, D.C. to the National Labor Management Conference to seek out better ways of collective bargaining. There, they heard about a new team-based bargaining process that was helping organizations improve labor-management relations and negotiations. *Target-specific bargaining*, developed by Don Powers of the Federal Mediation and Conciliation Service based in Washington, D.C., seemed to be just what SSI and the AEMTC were looking for. Target-specific bargaining principles dictate that the negotiating parties focus on narrowing down work problems to only a few key issues, and work for their resolution by using joint data-gathering and problem-solving teams that bring recommendations back to the main negotiating committee—something SSI and the AEMTC had already been experimenting with. They were on the right track, but learned new techniques to help them on their way.

Under Powers' model, work issues are identified *before* the actual contract talks begin. In this way, similar topics are merged together and options are identified long before negotiations start. The basic open and honest communications learned during SSI and the AEMTC's DesignShops, became the basis for a unique and successful new approach to bargaining. So, when SSI and the AEMTC sat down for contract talks with this new process in 1993, they had only 13 issues to tackle—the bargaining unit had eight issues and SSI management had five. "That's really different from the 40 to 50 that people usually have," says Taylor.

"In this particular model, everybody's empowered to talk and voice their opinion," he adds. "And if there was an issue we couldn't agree on, we'd assign a team to work on it."

The negotiating committee consisted of top-level managers from SSI, led by Taylor and the chief stewards from the AEMTC. Facilitation was provided by an SSI manager who was selected by consensus of both sides for his objective nature and valuable experience in dealing with people—both labor and management, throughout his career in the military and in business. Information and training was provided to the committee from various sources—including in-house HR personnel—on benefits, target-specific bargaining, group problem solving and data gathering.

Going into negotiations, the joint data-gathering and problem-resolution teams were met with skepticism by both sides. However, things improved as several separate breakout teams formed to gather data and provide recommendations on such issues as sick-leave benefits, workers'-compensation allowances, and temporary promotions.

Communication between, and among, negotiating committee members was emphasized by the facilitator. The com-

mittee met during normal working hours two to three times each week. Meetings usually were conducted for a maximum of four hours to minimize fatigue, unlike former negotiating sessions that dragged on into the wee hours of the morning resulting in agreements rooted in desperation. The facilitator was invaluable in keeping meetings on track and objective.

Other than breakout teams specifically commissioned by the negotiating committee, small sidebar meetings of labor and management personnel were prohibited. Separate labor or management meetings were kept to a minimum to ensure maximum communication during joint negotiating sessions rather than outside of them.

Moving toward a team-based organization.
One of the issues identified during the new open communication process was that there wasn't enough voice from labor about what was going on within the organization. Workers didn't have enough say in things like project execution, the way the business was run and choice of tools to get their jobs done right. So, as part of the new worker-involvement philosophy, SSI initiated teams.

Approximately 20 employee-involvement teams formed with the support of the HR and Quality departments, bringing expertise and experience from labor and management together to accomplish common objectives. Several total quality (TQ) teams were initiated and followed established problem-solving processes such as those described in books like Joseph M. Juran's "Roadmap to Quality Improvement" and Phillip Crosby's "Natural Work Teams." Some of the team's goals were to cut down cycle time and save costs. Everybody (both labor and management) looked at the processes they were involved in and made changes for improved performance and greater customer satisfaction. Overall, this enabled day-to-day operations to be conducted without direct supervision in the printing plant, a small machine shop, an instrument lab and a graphics group.

For the first time, craft employees recommended solutions to technical problems, and helped in long-range planning, both implemented through various cross-functional teams. In effect, the entire internal environment of the organization evolved from adversarial to cooperative.

Implementing a skills update.
One of the concerns raised by the bargaining unit was that its members weren't given the opportunity to improve their skills. The assumption was that craft personnel had received all the training they needed when they originally trained for their professions. "With the technological environment that we're in today, [craft personnel] felt they should know some of the basics associated with personal computers, for example," says Taylor. "So we set out to make sure that not only our non-represented employees received that type of basic training, but that our represented employees had that training as well."

The HR training coordinator assessed training requirements for craft personnel, addressing those needs equally for management and technical professionals. Basic computer courses were developed for those with minimal PC backgrounds. Adds Taylor: "We trained 100% of all bargaining employees in computer skills." Also added were courses in technical drawing interpretation, welding inspection, and major equipment operation and repair. The company also introduced advanced training requirements for craftspeople and organized classes for achieving those skills.

Any other training workers received would be job-based, because, as Taylor says: "The organization doesn't have the resources to make it perpetual training—there has to be a need. Those who have to use computers in their jobs will continue to receive training to [maintain productivity] in their particular work environment."

Eureka! They've got a contract.
With all this cooperation, negotiations with the AEMTC were completed in record time—three months prior to contract expiration with a five-year agreement (the longest in AEDC history) and an attitude that the best was yet to come. In one-third of the time of previous talks, the negotiating team agreed on topics such as overtime administration, temporary employment guidelines, job-posting procedures, implementation of a four-day workweek, sick leave, workers' compensation and wages.

Influenced by this success, subsequent negotiations between SSI and the International Guards Union of America followed a similar methodology. At the time, there were 50 workers in the union. This time a member of the AEMTC was chosen as the facilitator. Negotiations concluded with a historic 10-year agreement, also months ahead of contract expiration.

An ongoing process of communication, training and joint problem resolution goes on today. A Labor and Management Relations Committee (LMRC) evolved from the 1993 negotiating committee. It's co-chaired by the HR manager and a chief union steward. The LMRC meets monthly to address the most pertinent concerns of its members. In addition to their training in target-specific bargaining, teamwork and TQ basics, LMRC members have also traveled to labor-management conferences on the local, state and national levels. In-house seminars have been expanded to include alternate dispute resolution methods and procedures from Stephen R. Covey's "The Seven Habits of Highly Effective People." Both have been facilitated by HR staff.

The LMRC is kept separate from formal administrative processes established by the contract, and therefore doesn't infringe on matters defined within the contract. Instead, the LMRC heads off problems before they develop into violations.

The atmosphere of mistrust that existed after the strike of 1990 has disappeared.

VITALS

ORGANIZATION
SSI Services Inc.

TYPE OF BUSINESS
Government support contractor

HEADQUARTERS
Bridgeville, Pennsylvania

EMPLOYEES
2,000

PRESIDENT
Matt Schneider

VICE PRESIDENT OPERATIONS
Cass Schichtle

VICE PRESIDENT HR
Andra Tokarsky

YOU SHOULD KNOW
SSI formed an alliance with the Federal Mediation and Conciliation Service, who recognized SSI's approach to target-specific bargaining as a benchmark for international and U.S. companies. SSI has presented its model to many businesses worldwide including some in South Africa.

The culture has turned into one focused on continuous improvement—even as resources shrink. Problem-solving teams composed of labor and management are now the norm, whereas they were nonexistent before 1990. By working together, the mission support contract expected to yield approximately $5 million in cost savings and efficiencies for fiscal 1995.

The biggest key to success was achieving an atmosphere of trust and open communication prior to the negotiating process. If labor and management aren't working together before negotiations, they certainly aren't going to work well during the process. Also, bringing a minimum number of issues to the table did a great deal to enable the committee to focus, solve each problem and move on. Using joint data-gathering teams to collect facts and bring well thought-out recommendations to the bargaining table shortened negotiating time and ensured consensus.

Issues were solved on the basis of facts vs. feelings. Without the support of HR personnel bringing all the facts, training, and leadership for change to the table, the success realized would never have been achieved.

Comparing Traditional and Target-specific Bargaining

TRADITIONAL	TARGET-SPECIFIC BARGAINING
• Adversarial	• Nonadversarial
• Individual	• Group generates a list of meaningful issues using the brainstorming process
• Individual sent out to solve problem	• Data is gathered to validate or invalidate the above issue by a group of labor-management representatives
• High failure rate with unresolved issues	• High success rate because the group solves problems together and no issue is left unresolved
• Chief spokesperson on both sides does all the talking	• Recognizes a chief spokesperson but all members are empowered to discuss issues
• No neutral facilitator	• Uses a facilitator
	• Total disclosure of information—no witch hunts.
• Bargaining members are seen but not heard	• Total participation of all bargaining team members is required
• Secret side-agreements between parties	• No sidebars are permitted based on the premise that what can't be said across the table isn't worth discussing
• Bargaining members sit opposite each other at the table	• Bargaining seating arrangement alternates labor and management representatives
• Limited bargaining rights	• Expanded bargaining rights

Source: Anthony J. Taylor

Labor's Last Stand

In the face of unrelenting attacks on the federal government, labor leader John Sturdivant wants to create a "fighting union" to defend its workers.

Lucius Outlaw

"**A** funny thing happened on the way to reinvention," says John Sturdivant, president of the American Federation of Government Employees. "The Republicans took control of Congress."

Federal employees now find themselves between the rock of the Clinton Administration's crusade to reinvent government and the hard place of a budget-cutting Congress. With reductions-in-force, benefit cuts and agency closings looming, the future for the average civil servant seems bleak. But the employees are not going without a fight.

Much of the ammunition for that fight comes from the federal employees union, and Sturdivant's AFGE is the biggest of them all, representing more than 700,000 federal employees across the nation.

Sturdivant is used to being the voice of opposition to what he perceives as assaults on federal employees, having served in top leadership positions at AFGE during both the Reagan and Bush Administrations. This fall, as yet another arduous budget battle played out in the White House and on Capitol Hill, Sturdivant insisted that federal employees be recognized not as bargaining chips in the budget battle between Congress and the President, but as people who provide valuable services and keep the government running.

Still, this isn't what Sturdivant imagined life would be like under the first Democratic presidential administration in 12 years. Indeed, when President Clinton moved into the Oval Office in 1993, it looked like organized labor's day had finally arrived in the federal government. Putting aside a bitter rivalry, AFGE and the second-largest federal union, the National Treasury Employees Union, teamed up and demanded a voice in Vice President Gore's National Performance Review.

Working together, the unions convinced the Administration to create the National Partnership Council (NPC), a panel of high-level Administration officials and union representatives. The council developed policy for revamping the federal civil service system and facilitated the adoption of labor-management agreements in agencies around the government. As a result, the first phase of the Administration-ordered downsizing of government was an employee-friendly process, in which buyouts, attrition and early retirements were the main tools by which 160,000 jobs were eliminated.

But everything changed when the Republicans took over Congress. In contrast to the Administration's downsizing initiatives, Republicans in Congress pushed for large-scale job cuts and the elimination of entire departments and agencies. Arguing that the Administration's reductions are too heavily concentrated in the Defense Department (DoD accounts for 75 percent of the Administration's cuts so far), congressional leaders have insisted on steep cuts at domestic agencies, too.

Sturdivant says the new party alignment requires a "more proactive political strategy." Sometimes that means outright confrontation. Last September, for example, as federal employees faced the possibility of reductions-in-force, furloughs and a government shutdown, more than 30 AFGE locals across the country held protest rallies, and the union's headquarters office in Washington launched a media and public relations blitz against the Republicans' proposed budget cuts. Sturdivant himself accused Members of Congress of playing "chicken" with the budget and holding federal employees hostage.

Sturdivant and other union leaders say that Republicans are taking a "slash and burn" approach and setting downsizing goals that can't be achieved without seriously damaging the quality of federal services. "Poppycock," answers George Nesterczuk, staff director of the House Government Reform and Oversight Subcommittee on the Civil Service. The cuts Republicans envision, he argues, are "eminently achievable. The unions' agenda is to have government grow to create more jobs so they can attract more members. Unions have a hard time accepting RIFs because they live off the workforce. They need to be realistic."

Faced with such stiff and blunt opposition, Sturdivant has chosen to make what may well be the federal labor movement's last stand. "We are in the process," he said in a recent interview, "of building a fighting union. Not a whining union, not a complaining union, not a bitching union, but a fighting union."

Following is an edited transcript of the interview.

Q *What does reinventing government mean to the people you represent?*

A Many of us who have worked or are working for the federal government have seen the arcane rules, procedures, the crazy processes that keep us from doing the best possible job for the taxpayers that we really want to do. What reinventing government means for the unions is they've tried everything else. They've tried making it easier to fire government employees. They've tried a performance appraisal system that is for the most part a legalized buddy system. They've tried pay for performance, then they didn't fund it. So why not

try something innovative, why not try listening to the workers through their unions and putting a lot of those ideas into place, and seeing whether it works? We are all taxpayers, so we all see the waste. We all should want to do a better job, and reinventing government and the partnership process in labor-management relations gives us a non-adversarial, productive way to bring those ideas to the table.

Q *With the creation of the National Partnership Council the unions played a significant role in influencing Administration policy-making . . .*

A I wish I had as much power as you all keep telling me I've got. I've got Members of Congress who say that the Administration has caved in to the unions. I wish I had half the power that you all say I've got.

Q *How would you characterize your relationship with the Administration?*

A We are supportive of the Administration, most of the time. We have a unique situation in that we are able to help elect our boss. We played a significant role in that effort in 1992, and as a result, when the transition started, we were able to put people on the transition team, because we know how the government works. When they started talking about reinventing government, we said, "Wait a minute. Who knows how better the government works, or doesn't work, than government employees?" So we were able to tell the Vice President to make the connection with the private sector. And all of those corporate executives from Xerox, Harley Davidson, Cadillac, Saturn—when they shared their ideas with the Vice President, they told him up front that you've got to have a partnership with the unions to make this work. We were able to make the connection with him that that's what we want to do in the federal sector.

Q *The Administration has used buyouts, attrition and early retirements to reduce the federal work force by 160,000 positions. How do you think the downsizing strategy will change now that Members of Congress are proposing deeper cuts?*

A Early on, we tried to work through a non-adversarial partnership process, where basically we made a policy decision that we were going to have a smaller government. And I have told my members— and I took a lot of heat on this—I said, "don't ask me to go out and try to make the case to the American people, after they've looked at

IBM, after they've looked at the auto industry, after they've looked at the steel industry, after they've looked at just about every other industry in this country and seen the downsizing, the rightsizing, the jobs disappearing, don't ask me to try to make the case that government can't slim down." It can slim down. The question is "how do we do it?" How do we do it in some kind of a rational, reasonable manner, where we take a look at our programs and we shrink them, some of them we eliminate, but not just slash and burn.

Q *AFGE, NTEU and the other unions put aside their rivalry to work together on the National Partnership Council. Are the unions still working together?*

A Definitely.

Q *Has the relationship changed since the Republicans took control of Congress?*

A Yes. We have come closer together. [NTEU President] Bob Tobias and I, you know we had the whole situation with NTEU trying to take that Social Security unit away from us. Of course, that collapsed, and they spent a lot of money on it. But early on Bob Tobias and I recognized that with the Administration moving on reinvention and a lot of other new initiatives, we needed to focus our resources on working together for the benefit of the federal employees we represent, rather than fighting each other.

I would say it has been a good partnership. One of the things you do in a partnership is you ask people to change their behavior, and make a culture change. Well, the unions recognized early on that if we were going to be able to deal with large challenges and the things that were coming down the pike, we needed to change our own behavior, and we did. It took awhile for the staff to get up to speed, and there is still some roughness among the rank and file, but I would say that Bob Tobias and I have a good working relationship. In fact, I will not go to a top-level meeting with the Administration without him.

Q *Some say that it appears that AFGE has adopted a more traditional union strategy of protest and direct confrontation in dealing with Congress. Is that accurate?*

A I don't know that we are in a confrontational role with them. We philosophically disagree with a lot of the things this new Congress is doing, but we try to work with them. We try to be bipartisan, but it's just that there are more Democrats that support our views and goals than Republicans. But we are constantly working to try to find Republican supporters. As the saying goes: "No permanent friends, no permanent enemies, just permanent interests."

I would say that we have adopted a more proactive political strategy for dealing with this Congress. This Congress has been helpful in enabling us to focus on our goals, helpful for enabling us to do strategic planning. It's been useful, with the things they have been proposing, in organizing. If I didn't have this Congress, I would probably have to invent it to get people's attention.

I would say that we use different tactics. The rallies came out of our task force to get people to begin doing some things around this effort. What we don't want our people to do is to feel like victims. I haven't thought about it as traditional union tactics, because I'm a guy who likes to cut a deal and reach consensus. But on the other hand we are building a fighting union. And that means getting folks to understand that they have a role to play, that they can do some things for themselves to fight for their pay, to fight for their jobs.

Q *The number of dues-paying federal union members has been falling in recent years. Is the Republican takeover over of Congress making it easier to attract new members?*

A Our membership is up. Of course our membership is up, because we spend a lot of time organizing. You have to go out, you have to look people in the eye, you have to tell them about your union. Remember, we are carrying close to half a million people in our existing units that are not paying dues, so even when they finish all the down-sizing, I'll still have plenty of growth opportunities. We have a strategy of getting out into the workplace. I spend about fifty percent of my time out with the rank and file. You can't run this union sitting in this office.

Q *If you could convince the Administration, Congress, and the American public of one thing about federal employees, what would it be?*

A That federal employees are good citizens. If anything positive can come out of the despicable act in Oklahoma, it is that we are not bureaucrats. We are mothers and fathers, we have kids, we work hard for our money, we are dedicated to doing our jobs for the American people, and we should not be bashed, and we should not be attacked. And if you do, if you are a politician, we are going to see you at the ballot box.

"How Accommodating Do You Have to Be?"

You might find yourself
asking that question as you try to align
good management practices with the
Americans with Disabilities Act.

John R. Allison

JOHN R. ALLISON is Mary John & Ralph Spence Centennial Professor of Business Administration and Professor of the Legal Environment of Business at the Graduate School of Business at the University of Texas at Austin.

Amanda, regional vice president for sales at a well-known U.S. food-processing company, is in a bind. George, one of her district sales managers, has been very effective during his four years in the position. He has always been overweight, but it never interfered with his performance. In the past 10 to 12 months, however, his weight has ballooned. After her latest visit to the field, Amanda spoke confidentially with several trusted senior salespeople under George who have always had good professional and personal relationships with him. They confided to Amanda their concern for George's alarming weight gain in the past year; they worried both about his health and about his job performance. He used to be constantly energized despite his weight. Now, they said, George fatigued much more easily and frequently. Moreover, although sales in his district had not slipped recently, they worried that his condition might have an adverse effect on business. In recent months, buyers for several large customers and potential customers had seemed somewhat "put off" by George's appearance and increasingly apparent lack of energetic enthusiasm.

> Even if disabled, an employee must be able to perform the essential functions of the job and can be held to the same standards as other employees.

The Americans with Disabilities Act of 1990, as interpreted by court decisions and the guidelines of the Equal Employment

Opportunity Commission, was passed by Congress to bring an estimated 43 million Americans with some type of disability into the nation's economic mainstream by removing physical barriers, diminishing the effect of stereotypes, and prohibiting job discrimination. A common initial response to this is, "Well, sure, it's a good idea. If someone in a wheelchair can do the job, I'm all for it. But 43 million? That's almost a sixth of the population. There just aren't that many people in wheelchairs!" Quite right. The response highlights some common misconceptions held by even the intelligent, informed, and progressive about what constitutes a disability in fact, and about what the ADA treats as a disability. And the ADA, supplemented by the EEOC's guidelines that seek to shed light on fuzzy areas, still leaves plenty of room for confusion and second-guessing.

What Is a Disability?

The ADA's definition intends to reach all forms of discrimination, whether flagrantly intentional, purely innocent, or unintentionally based on erroneous stereotypes about people's capabilities. If you think this is a tall order, you are not alone. In seeking to achieve such a broad societal objective, the ADA has defined a person with a disability as one who either has a "physical or mental impairment that substantially affects one or more of life's major activities," has a "record of such impairment," or is "regarded as having such an impairment." Even if you believe that the first and obviously main portion of the definition is unrealistically broad and includes vague terms that invite uncertainty and probably litigation, you can at least see what Congress was trying to do.

Discerning what Congress was getting at in the second and third parts of the definition may require some more thought. Why put people who may have no physical or mental impairment at all in a legally protected class? In referring to someone who has a "record of such an impairment," legislators were aiming at two problems. First, medical records can be mistaken, and once a medical record finds its way into the system, correcting it in all the places where it is likely to end up can be a nightmare for the person affected. Second, in the process leading up to the formulation of this part of the definition, there was much evidence that people who once had disabling conditions but no longer have them can encounter many problems in overcoming the presumption that they are still afflicted. Just ask people who have been cured of cancer.

The last part of the ADA's definition of disability, encompassing those "regarded as having such an impairment," is targeted at stereotypically based decisions. A person may be protected by the ADA because he is "regarded" as having a disability because of a mistaken record or a now-cured disability. Obviously there is some overlap between "having a record of" and "being regarded as having." The main point of the last part of

What Can You Ask When You're Hiring?

Once upon a time, if a job applicant was sitting on the other side of your desk, you couldn't ask her about her disabilities and what it might take to accommodate her in your company. This was true even if the applicant's disability was obvious because she was in a wheelchair or using a seeing-eye dog. Even if the applicant herself made reference to her disability, the employer was limited in what he could ask.

But things changed in October 1995. The Equal Employment Opportunit[y] Commission revised its guidelines for the Americans with Disabilities Act (ADA). With the new guidelines in place, it is possible for employers to make inquiries about obvious disabilities or ask questions if the applicant discloses she is disabled or will require reasonable accommodation.

The idea behind the new guidelines, called "ADA Enforcement Guidance: Pre-employment Disability-Related Questions and Medical Examinations," is to allow employers to address the accommodation issue at the initial interview stage. However, the guidelines do not allow an employer to go on archeological digs through their applicants' pasts. For example, an applicant's workers-compensation history can be tricky territory. And some questions about drug and alcohol use are off-limits, while others are not. An employer *may* ask about current illegal use of drugs ("Do you snort cocaine on a daily basis?"), because it's not protected under the ADA. On the other hand, the employer needs to be very careful asking about drinking habits—information on *how much* the applicant drinks ("Well, I usually have a bottle of burgundy every evening, just to unwind") could indicate alcoholism, and that *is* protected.

The guidelines are available in a question-and-answer format from the EEOC. Asking the right questions at an early stage of the job-application process could save you, and your applicant, a lot of bother later on.

—GEOFFREY LOFTUS

ADA's definition, however, is to protect people from adverse employment actions because of some trait or condition that is not an impairment but leads a manager to treat them as disabled. An example might be a mild but noticeable case of strabismus (crossed eyes).

How Bosses Get Involved. Isn't disability a matter for HR departments? Yes and no. Certainly most HR departments know and basically understand the various concepts of disability under the ADA. Likewise, they know that job applicants and employees cannot be discriminated against because of a disability, as long as the person can perform "the essential functions of the job," either without any accommodation at all or with some reasonable accommodation for the person's disability. An accommodation for a person's disability is unreasonable if it would cause undue hardship for the employer. However, there are enough murky situations that this part of the ADA by itself eats up more than its fair share of HR's time and budget at many companies.

Despite the good job HR people are doing, senior executives cannot seem to avoid ADA issues. While HR takes care of almost everything ADA-related at the hiring stage, some of the tougher problems involve current employees, and some of the toughest of all have to do with proven managers whose skill and judgment senior executives themselves must continually rely upon. They cannot just ship the problems over to HR without paying significant personal attention to them.

How Fat Is Too Fat?

Amanda must take the ADA into account because obesity recently has been characterized by the EEOC as a disability if it is sufficiently severe. The EEOC attempted to make the abstract statutory definitions of the ADA more concrete. In these guidelines, the agency stated that an extremely overweight person has a disability for ADA purposes if he or she is "severely" obese, that is, weighs at least 100 percent over that in the standard height-weight tables, regardless of whether it is caused by an underlying physiological (i.e., glandular) disorder. Although courts are not bound by EEOC guidelines as they are by typical federal agency regulations, the guidelines are followed more often than not—a company ignores them at its peril.

Treating obesity as a disability and defining it by *how much* a person weighs can create some rather strange situations. For example, an overweight employee sometimes might be disabled under the ADA and sometimes not, depending on weight fluctuations. Moreover, the EEOC may have even created perverse

incentives for some employees, especially those who constantly lose the diet battle. If George is continually close to the critical point and knows about the definition, he might fall back into the "comfort" of ADA protection.

Regardless whether the EEOC may have made a highly questionable public policy call, the question still remains: Can Amanda talk frankly with George about the problem? Yes, she can, and she should. Nothing in the law or the guidelines restrains her from talking to an employee about a condition that apparently is affecting the employee's performance, let alone his health. Even if disabled, an employee must be able to perform the essential functions of the job, and can be held to the same standards of performance and conduct as other employees. Amanda might be on shaky ground were she immediately to make a decision that negatively affected George's employment status, but a good manager would not do so in this case anyway. Her discussion with George should include sensitive inquiries about why he thinks his weight problem has accelerated so much recently and whether he has been to the doctor. She should not shy away from pointing out in a clear yet gentle way that there is concern about both his health and his job performance. If the company has an employee assistance program, Amanda probably should emphasize that he use the resource. If George cooperates, the EAP would place him under a doctor's care and might even propose some time off to deal with his problem and possible underlying causes. If he denies that there's a problem, or otherwise refuses to cooperate, Amanda should take careful steps. By requiring him to see a physician, Amanda would be able to find out whether George is protected by the ADA, and hopefully George's visit to the doctor might provide the wake-up call that he has not yet gotten, both about his health and about his job. If George refuses to see a doctor under these circumstances, he is guilty of insubordination and Amanda can demote, fire, or otherwise discipline him because of his *conduct*, not because of his obesity (even if his obesity constitutes a disability). What if George does cooperate and Amanda finds out that his obesity is in fact severe enough to constitute a disability, but he is unsuccessful in trying to bring his weight down? Here, the issues become more complex.

Is George's condition truly affecting his job performance? The fact that some clients are apparently "turned off" by his obesity is probably not enough to demonstrate that he is unable to perform the essential functions of his job. If there is evidence, however, that his decreased energy level or some other by-product of his obesity actually cost the company an account, or if overall sales in George's district slip significantly, Amanda probably will be acting lawfully in either demoting or firing George. In the case of a significant sales drop, Amanda's actions legally could be based on his failure to perform rather than his condition. An employer's obligations under the ADA include a "reasonable accommodation" for the employee's disability if such accommodation would enable the employee to perform the essential functions of the job. Here, Amanda has done everything for George that she can do, and it is difficult to envision any other accommodation that would bring George's performance back up and that would not cause an undue hardship to the company.

In most situations like this, the problem would be resolved before it actually resulted in lost sales, but carrying the scenario to an unhappy yet quite plausible ending proves that ADA compliance can be complex and confusing.

A Difficult Choice

Jim is director of product development at a company whose primary business is the design and manufacture of power tools, lawn and garden equipment, small appliances, and other products for consumer use. Answering directly to him are five assistant directors who supervise teams of designers, engineers, and various support staff. Mike, one of Jim's five assistant directors, has a double degree in mechanical and electrical engineering, and has worked for the company in several capacities for almost 10 years. He has performed superbly in every job, receiving several promotions before becoming an assistant director four years ago. He is probably the best assistant director in Jim's group. However, about five years ago, while working as chief engineer on product-development teams, Mike cultivated a taste for cocaine. After becoming aware that his casual use had become an addiction, Mike took all of his accrued vacation and sick leave and checked himself into an in-patient rehabilitation program. He told his supervisor what he was doing and requested and received the opportunity to go through rehab and return to his job. He was able to complete the program without having to ask for time off beyond his accrued vacation and sick leave because he had used almost none of either for several years.

After returning to his job as chief engineer, he continued to perform at an outstanding level and was promoted to assistant director one year after he had completed his rehab.

That was four years ago, and Mike has apparently been drug-free ever since. Recently, however, Jim has become concerned about Mike. Based on his own observation, as well as conversations he's had with several highly reliable people working with Mike, Jim is starting to wonder whether the drug problem has resurfaced. About a year ago, Mike's dad died after a tough bout with cancer. Within two or three months after his dad's death, Mike and his wife began having some marital difficulties. During these times, Mike did show some expectable signs of stress, but his work performance never slipped. He did take a day off on several occasions to deal with his personal situations, but the job always got done. According to several people close to Mike, he and his wife worked out their problems, and their marriage has been going smoothly for at least six months.

Until recently, Mike has appeared to be fine, and his work has been as good as ever. In the past three to four weeks, however, his behavior has changed abruptly. He doesn't have the drawn or strained look of a person under great stress; instead, on a number of occasions, Mike has appeared rather glassy-eyed and distant. Other times he has seemed almost hyperactive, showing a "fast-forward" type of behavior beyond even his usual high-energy level. Moreover, he has been uncharacteristically late for several important meetings.

Perhaps surprising to many people, there are ADA issues involved. Drug addiction, as well as clinically diagnosed alcoholism, is considered a disability by the ADA. Other provisions of the act, however, provide employers with some latitude. For example, casual use of controlled substances short of addiction is not a disability. Likewise, drinking too much is not a disability if the employee is not diagnosed as being an alcoholic. An addict or alcoholic enjoys no ADA protection from an adverse employment decision if the employee is a "current user" of illegal drugs or alcohol.

Just because the ADA gives employers significant latitude in dealing with drug use does not mean that individual decisions are easily made. Sure, HR can drug-test all applicants—a drug test is not treated as a prohibited preoffer medical exam by ADA—and reject anyone who isn't clean. But Mike has been a top performer in every job he's had at the company for years, and after getting clean has been the best of five assistant directors. *Can* Jim give Mike an unannounced drug test? Yes. *Should he?* Yes—for everyone's sake—a potential drug problem can't be ignored or soft-pedaled. Mike should be confronted about the behavioral changes his co-workers have noticed. He might have a plausible explanation. He may admit that drugs have got him again. Whether he admits it or not, Jim should have a technician who works with the company's regular drug-testing program administer a test to Mike immediately. It's legal to test him under the ADA, and in those few states that regulate work-place drug testing, there's enough evidence to create an individualized suspicion of drug use. If Mike tests positive, a second confirming test should be done immediately—the tests are not 100 percent accurate.

> According to the ADA, having the blues is not a disability. Medically diagnosed chronic depression is, however, considered a disability.

If Mike tests positive, then Jim faces a tough "can-should" decision. Mike can be fired immediately; he is a "current user" and therefore not protected by the ADA. Also, while substance abuse is treated as a serious illness under the 1993 Family and Medical Leave Act, for which an employee can get 12 weeks unpaid leave, current users of controlled substances or alcohol are excluded by the act. Jim's decision is thus reduced to one of life's most difficult denominators: Is Mike as an employee and a human being worth a legal risk?

Jim is probably on safe legal ground if he fires Mike, and probably will receive the support and maybe even the accolades of superiors. If Jim gives him another shot by allowing him leave to enter a rehab program, the legal options are more difficult. Once he has checked into rehab, either on his own or at Jim's urging, and has become clean for some period of time that the law has not seen fit to define, he is no longer a current user. Now he has a record of a disability, as well as perhaps being "regarded" as having a disability, and is now protected by the ADA from adverse employment action based on his impairment, record of impairment, or being regarded as having an impairment. This protection is, of course, dependent on Mike's successful completion of rehab and demonstration of the ability to perform the essential functions of his job, either without any accommodation or with a reasonable accommodation. In this case, the company's legal obligation of providing a reasonable accommodation is probably limited to giving Mike the opportunity to complete his re-

hab program and determining whether it is successful.

But the gut-level decisions are more fundamental. What is Mike worth as an employee and a human being? Other managers and professionals can and should be consulted before reaching a decision. Any information related to Mike's problem is privileged as long as Jim only talks to those who have a legitimate interest in the information. Exchanges of information of this type are subject to some pretty good legal protection against an invasion of privacy claim or, if something false and defamatory is said, against a defamation claim. The problems in this scenario are not primarily legal. After careful review of Mike's history, an extremely tough judgment call is at hand.

Shades of Blue

Reynaldo is the clean-room quality director for a major semiconductor-chip manufacturer. His job entails managing the operations of several "clean rooms" where chips are made in a highly sanitized environment. Working directly under him is a supervisor of each clean room, whose responsibility is partly to oversee production but primarily to ensure that each employee adheres assiduously to clean-room protocol. If clean-room procedures are not observed with the utmost rigor, critical flaws may occur in microprocessors and other chips that serve as the mainstay of the company's product lines.

One of Reynaldo's four clean-room supervisors, Joyce, has a superior educational background and an exemplary record. However, in the past three months or so, Joyce has begun to show distinctive signs of stress and perhaps depression, although Reynaldo knows he is not qualified to diagnose mental illness. At least two or three times a week during this period, Joyce has shown a haggard, wan look and has not exhibited her normal enthusiasm. She looks like she hasn't been sleeping very much, although Reynaldo knows Joyce is very serious and conscientious and not the partying type. The most ominous sign, however, is her apparent lack of interest in her job, the company's performance, and the lunches she used to enjoy so much with her co-workers. Now she usually does not eat lunch at all, or gets something from the vending machine and eats alone. Unlike as in the past, she now seems to talk only when it is necessary to do her job. There have not yet been any problems in Joyce's clean room, but Reynaldo senses impending disaster: She seems just to be going through the motions. A clean room has to be run with almost paramilitary discipline and efficiency; both the competence and the *attitude* of the leadership is absolutely crucial.

According to the ADA, having the blues is not a disability. Being depressed also is not a disability if it's the common type that is brought on by some traumatic event or disappointment and will run its course in a few weeks or months. Medically diagnosed chronic depression is, however, considered a disability.

The nature of Joyce's job dictates that Reynaldo must act, and soon. He has to talk to her. Whether she will open up to him depends on their relationship, her personality type, and the nature of any underlying cause if there is one that can be pinpointed. Even if Reynaldo finds out enough to form an opinion about her condition, he should not try to diagnose it or suggest a remedy. He

> A good manager
>
> appreciates valuable
>
> employees and recognizes
>
> that it is not easy or
>
> cheap to acquire, train,
>
> and keep them.

must insist, sensitively but firmly, that she see a doctor, preferably by route of an EAP. Not only is temporary depression treatable, but today most chronic depression can be treated with medications that should not affect Joyce's ability to perform even a highly sensitive job like hers.

Whether Joyce needs time off is a call the doctor, not Reynaldo, should make. If the doctor prescribes time off, does the company have to grant it? If the diagnosis characterizes Joyce's depression in a way that constitutes a disability under the ADA, time off for a reasonable period would probably be required as the company's reasonable-accommodation obligation. How long is a reasonable time? If Joyce feels ready to come back to work relatively soon, and her doctor agrees, this question may answer itself. Reynaldo just needs to watch her at work in the same way he watches all of those under his supervision; that is, being observant without acting like he's on a stakeout.

The real difficulty arises when Joyce's absence begins hurting the company. An accommodation for an employee's disability ceases to be reasonable when it causes an undue hardship to the employer. The more responsibility the job entails, and the more difficult it is to cover for the employee, the more quickly the time off will cease to be reasonable. Keep in mind that chronic depression will be treated as a serious illness under the FMLA. The FMLA requires an employer with 50 or more employees to grant up to 12 weeks unpaid leave for several reasons, including serious illness. Either at the employee's request or at the company's insistence, the employee can be required to use up any accrued sick leave and vacation time as part of the 12 weeks. If Joyce is diagnosed with only temporary, trauma-induced depression, there is probably not an ADA disability, and any possible FMLA coverage would probably require only a few days off to adjust to the medication, so decisions are almost purely managerial.

A good manager appreciates valuable employees like George, Mike, and Joyce and recognizes that it is not easy or cheap to acquire, train, and keep employees like them. Had any been poor or even average employees, the decisions might have been different. In all of these cases, however, human and even economic aspects may overshadow the legal implications.

Case VI: *The "Homes" Is Where the Union Is*

Recently 700 employees of a city nursing home and the city home for the aged (two facilities located on the same plot of land) voted overwhelmingly to be represented by a union. The bargaining unit includes a great variety of employees, from custodial and maintenance to social workers and professional nurses. When interviewed after the union had won bargaining rights, the employees claimed that arbitrary and inconsistent treatment by management, and the supervisors in particular, comprised the main reasons for their voting for the union. They charged discriminatory treatment and flagrant favoritism. They also charged that the supervisors made it a practice to discharge employees for trivial reasons or without adequate prior warnings. Employees were subjected to frequent criticism by their supervisors with regard to their job performance. Although many of the supervisors had been promoted from the "ranks," many of them seemed to abuse their authority in dealing with their subordinates.

Top managers in both locations were genuinely surprised when they first learned during negotiations about this serious and widespread employee discontent.

Using the Case on *The "Homes" Is Where The Union Is*

For this case you should consider yourself an arbitrator who has been presented with this case. After reading the case, what decision would you give, knowing that other people had had time off and that memos were only requested at varying intervals?

Go over the review questions at the end. How does the class feel about this as a group? Why?

Exercise VI: *Assumptions About People at Work*

Instructions

The purpose of this exercise is to help you better understand the assumptions you make about people and their work behaviors. On the following questionnaire, you will find 10 sets of questions. Assign a rank from 0 to 10 to each item in each pair. (0 indicates that you completely disagree with the statement, and 10 means that you completely agree with the statement.) Answer each question as honestly as you can. There are *no correct answers,* so don't give a response to a question that will sound good to others or that you think is the way you are supposed to answer.

Questions

1. It's only human nature for people to do as little work as they can get away with. _____ (a)
   When people avoid work, it's usually because their work has been deprived of its meaning. _____ (b)
2. If employees have access to any information they want, they tend to have better attitudes and behave more responsibly. _____ (c)
   If employees have access to more information than they need to do their immediate tasks, they will usually misuse it. _____ (d)

3. One problem in asking for the ideas of employees is that their perspective is too limited for their suggestions to be of much practical value. _____ (e)
   Asking employees for their ideas broadens their perspective and results in the development of useful suggestions. _____ (f)
4. If people don't use much imagination and ingenuity on the job, it's probably because relatively few people have much of either. _____ (g)
   Most people are imaginative and creative but may not show it because of limitations imposed by supervision and the job. _____ (h)
5. People tend to raise their standards if they are accountable for their own behavior and for correcting their own mistakes. _____ (i)
   People tend to lower their standards if they are not punished for their misbehavior and mistakes. _____ (j)
6. It's better to give people both good and bad news because most employees want the whole story, no matter how painful. _____ (k)
   It's better to withhold unfavorable news about business because most employees really want to hear only the good news. _____ (l)
7. Because supervisors are entitled to more respect than those below them in the organization, it weakens their prestige to admit that a subordinate was right and they were wrong. _____ (m)
   Because people at all levels are entitled to equal respect, a supervisor's prestige is increased when s/he supports this principle by admitting that a subordinate was right and s/he was wrong. _____ (n)
8. If you give people enough money, they are less likely to be concerned with such intangibles as responsibility and recognition. _____ (o)
   If you give people interesting and challenging work, they are less likely to complain about such things as pay and supplemental benefits. _____ (p)
9. If people are allowed to set their own goals and standards of performance, they tend to set them higher than the boss would. _____ (q)
   If people are allowed to set their own goals and standards of performance, they tend to set them lower than the boss would. _____ (r)
10. The more knowledge and freedom a person has regarding his job, the more controls are needed to keep him/her in line. _____ (s)
    The more knowledge and freedom a person has regarding his/her job, the fewer controls are needed to ensure satisfactory job performance. _____ (t)

After Completing the Questionnaire

When you have completed all of the questions, you may score the questionnaire in the following manner. Add together the scores of items: (a), (d), (e), (g), (j), (l), (m), (o), (r), and (s). The sum of these scores will provide you with your "Theory X" score. Then add together the remaining scores: (b), (c), (f), (h), (i), (k), (n), (p), (q), and (t). The sum of these scores will give you your "Theory Y" score.

In a group, discuss the relative strength of each of your scores. Is there a significant difference in the two scores? What might this mean? How do you believe your assumptions might affect your actions as a manager? Do your past experiences support the self-profile that has emerged from your discussion? Discuss with other members of your group how your scores may be related to the concepts of "espoused theory" and "theory-in-use."

Perspectives and Trends

Managers are facing new challenges. While it is never possible to determine exactly what the future will hold, there are certain trends and movements that can be perceived by an aware and thoughtful manager. Derek Bok, former president of Harvard University, offered some interesting insights into possible future trends for prospective managers in his June 1982 baccalaureate address, which has been adapted in the reading "Social Respon-sibility in Future Worlds." Bok speaks from two perspectives here, for not only was he an academic trying to look into the future, but he was also the manager of a very old and reasonably large and diverse organization, Harvard University.

Most people recognize the movement toward the internationalization of the economy. The North American continent no longer stands alone, as it did at the end of

World War II, as the main source of manufactured goods. As the world enters a new millennium, Japan and Europe are making their economic muscle felt. Japan is not alone in the Far East in the manufacture of goods. Taiwan, Korea, and Singapore, not to mention the awesome potential of China, are also factors. This is not, however, a huge monolithic bloc. It is a collection of similar countries and societies, roughly comparable to Great Britain, France, and Germany. Each establishes and maintains business relationships in it own individual way.

While most of the world was focusing on the occurrences in Eastern Europe and the former republics of the Soviet Union, important events were already in progress in Western Europe prior to the 1989 opening of the Berlin Wall. In 1992, the European Economic Community became, for the first time since the days of the Roman Empire, a truly integrated economy. This, of course, represents a significant change and presents American firms with more ways to do business than even a planner of the Common Market could foresee.

Another development in American society has been the rise of the small businessperson. Over the past decade, the number of people employed by Fortune 500 industrial companies has declined, while the size of the workforce has increased. Many of these new workers entered small firms. Small businesses tend to be family businesses, and it is often difficult to determine where the business ends and the family begins. In addition, these businesses are entrepreneurial in nature. Entrepreneurs serve the highly creative function of creating new jobs and new businesses. They develop and market new products and services and are often on the cutting edge of the new technology of tomorrow, both technical and managerial.

Managers and their organizations have been criticized in the past several years for a lack of ethics and morality. A small, and, when they are caught, highly publicized minority have indeed played fast and loose with the law and ethics. This has caused all managers to look more closely at their behavior, and the courts are starting to take a dimmer view of white-collar crime, to the point of sending some executives, such as Charles Keating and Michael Milkin, to prison.

While the study of management tends to focus on profit-making organizations, not-for-profit organizations also need to be managed effectively. This sector of the economy is very large and includes all levels and functions of government, churches, associations, schools, charities, and many health care facilities. It is a very large piece of American industry.

Information technology and data processing have also played an important role in the recent developments in management. Managers now get information more often and more quickly than they did in the recent past. According to the essay "Tapping Your Hidden Assets," there is a great deal of potential information inside the organization that managers could use but are not now using.

Finally, managers are starting to examine their careers in light of the new developments in the marketplace. In earlier generations, managers would work for the same firm for their entire working lives. That is no longer the case. Managers in today's environment must be flexible. They have to be responsible for their own careers, because the firms they join could go out of business or be purchased, and they could be left without a job. Managers must look after themselves and make career moves independently, if they hope to succeed. This is addressed in "How Job Seekers Should Approach the New Job Market."

Looking Ahead: Challenge Questions

Many new developments are facing managers in the near future. What areas of controversy do you expect to see soon?

As a prospective manager, what do you expect to be doing in the next five years? Ten years?

Social Responsibility in Future Worlds

Derek C. Bok

Derek C. Bok, President, Harvard University, Cambridge, Mass.

PROFESSIONAL STUDY

If the past is any guide, more than 90 percent of you will eventually find yourselves studying law, business, or medicine or enrolling in some other kind of graduate or professional school. The training you receive will open the door to a vocation of your choice. But what sort of experience will you find there? What will it do for you? And what kinds of dangers should you be on guard to avoid?

Many people have a slightly distorted view of what a good professional training can achieve. Some feel that it stocks the mind with a vast supply of specialized knowledge—about legal rules and procedures, about corporate organization and behavior, or about the human body and how it functions. Others think that professional training gives students a set of special tools and advanced techniques with which to pry open problems impervious to the lay mind. Both these notions are partly true, but both are incomplete. A good professional education does convey a lot of special knowledge and a grasp of sophisticated technique but it incorporates them into something greater and more important—an instinctive ability to recognize the characteristic problems of the profession and to break them down into manageable parts that can be thought through systematically. The normal way to develop this ability is to subject students to a period of total immersion in which almost all their time is spent

Based on the Baccalaureate Speech by [then-] President Derek C. Bok at the Commencement Ceremony of Harvard University, Cambridge, Mass., June 1982.

in studying, going to class and living and talking and arguing about the problems of the profession with other students like themselves.

Such training brings great benefits to those who pursue it diligently. Not only can you receive the proper credentials of your calling; you gain a power of analysis not available to people outside your profession. That power in turn opens up opportunities to render great service to others, to achieve the satisfactions of good craftsmanship, to find an identity to define your role in life, not to mention gaining your economic security and material rewards.

Along with all these benefits, however, come certain dangers. As Richard Wilbur once remarked, the genie is powerful because we have pressed him into a bottle. The pressures imposed by a good professional education can be a transforming experience. But few transformations occur without the risk of losing something of value along the way. In graduate education, the risk you run is of acquiring a somewhat distorted perspective, a set of values that seem slightly askew, a cast of mind that evidences what the French describe as "deformation professionelle."

THE DEFORMATION OF PROFESSIONALISM

And what, precisely, are these deformations? One of them surely is a tendency to grow less concerned about society's problems and more preoccupied with the special predicament of your client. It is the client, after all, to whom you will owe your loyalty and it is the client who pays the fee. Most of all, it is the client's problem that has

immediacy and concreteness. What are the distant issues of national health insurance or neighborhood clinics compared with the urgent details of a swelling tumor, a baby's cleft palate, or a damaged heart? How long can you be distracted by the injustices of our penal system or the wasteful delays of our trial courts in the presence of a corporate client facing a union election, a company take-over, or an antitrust decree?

TENDENCY TO WITHDRAW FROM SUFFERING

As you address the problems of your clients, it is also tempting to conceive of their predicament in terms that are more and more intellectual and less and less human. All professional schools tend to turn human situations into problems that can be picked apart and analyzed rationally. Professional life often supports this view of the world. Most of you who enter law or business will offer your services to banks, manufacturing companies, or retail stores—and it is easy to perceive these organizations as hollow abstractions rather than communities of living people. In medicine, the process of abstraction is even more understandable and compelling. As every study of medical education reveals, few students have feelings tough enough to cope with the terrifying immediacy of death and disease. Many tend to withdraw from the suffering and abnormalities of their patients and begin to conceive of them less as frightened, vulnerable human beings and more as a puzzling deficiency in red blood cells, an unusual kidney malfunction, an odd lesion in the lower intestine. Reinforcing these pressures is the image of success that society has imposed on all of our professions, the image of the emotionless practitioner—cool, detached, objective, and totally in control.

Still another tendency in graduate or professional school is to become so steeped in its special methods of analysis that one ignores other ways of apprehending human experience. Each of these schools arouses an immediate insecurity in its students and a corresponding desire to prove themselves by mastering the technical apparatus of the profession. As you grow more and more adept in these techniques, it is only natural that you be tempted to press these methods on problems where they do not fit. Business school students may cease to wonder about how to work with other human beings and begin to think about the efficient management of human resources. Law students may seize their yellow pads and jot down all the arguments for and against marrying their high school sweethearts. Psychiatrists often see every conceivable human situation as a product of repressed sexual desires.

The quirks I have described may strike you as quaint, but they can have serious effects, not only on your personal and family life, but on your careers as well.

HUMAN DIMENSIONS

I mentioned that most professional schools tend to emphasize the intellectual aspects of practice and to set aside the personal, the emotional, the deeply human dimensions of their calling. The bias is understandable, since formal learning is much more suited to dealing with intellectual and analytic problems than with the more intuitive and psychological aspects of experience. And yet, if you begin to accept this view of the world, you may lose many of the greatest rewards of professional life by failing to perceive much of the human interest and drama that arise in every professional practice. Not only can your work grow colorless and dull; you may accomplish less as well. After all, solutions to most legal disputes and most corporate problems cannot be found through analysis alone but depend on being aware of the feelings, the motives, the needs and aspirations of all the human beings involved. The same is even true in more

technical fields such as medicine. How can anyone expect to cope effectively with human health by scientific methods alone when one-third of all patients fail to take the drugs their doctors have prescribed, when half of all illness results from drinking, smoking, and other personal habits; when one-third to a half of all cases in general medicine practice have a strong psychosomatic base.

GREAT SOCIAL CONTRIBUTIONS

Apart from the effects on your careers, the deformations I have described can also have consequences for the professions themselves. For example, if you come to regard the problems of your clients as an intellectual challenge and not as an intensely human predicament, you are likely to move toward certain kinds of careers where the intellectual demands seem greatest—toward the sophisticated specialties in medicine; toward corporate legal practice; toward finance, planning, or consulting in business. While there is nothing inherently wrong with these lines of work, they are not necessarily the fields in which the greatest social contributions lie. For the next generation at least, our health care system will probably need able practitioners in primary care and family medicine more than specialists in cardiology or neurosurgery. As attorneys, you may serve society better as public interest lawyers and neighborhood practitioners, or dare I say it—by not becoming lawyers at all, than you will by being fresh recruits for corporate tax, securities regulation, and antitrust litigation. The economy, with its lagging productivity, may benefit more from production managers than from investment analysts, corporate planners, or roving consultants.

ETHICAL DILEMMAS

Another byproduct of professional training is that the constant emphasis on solving problems through conventional modes of analysis may cause young professionals to ignore the ethical dilemmas of their practice. Alas, you are not likely to detect much serious attention to ethics in the professional school you enter. And that is a serious deficiency at a time when every profession bristles with moral di-

lemmas and the public trust in professionals has everywhere declined. As a "New York Times" article recently concluded: "If medical education does not come to grips with the ethical as well as the technical problems of the field, society may soon discover that modern medicine has given a relatively small number of men and women enormous power—which they have not been adequately trained to wield." Exactly the same could be said of all the other major professions as well.

There is a final danger to consider that may be even more important. I have already observed that students in professional schools grow more and more preoccupied with the needs and problems of the clients they serve and less and less concerned with the impact of their profession on the larger society. That would be a problem in any era. It is a particularly serious problem today.

SOCIETY'S CONCERNS

I cannot remember a time when society's concerns about the professions have seemed more distant from the daily preoccupations of our professional schools and the body of practitioners they serve. In medicine, for example, the public is not greatly troubled by the technical quality of service that doctors offer their patients. What does concern the public is how medical services can be organized to extend adequate care to all segments of society; how to contain medical costs so that they cease to rise at much faster rates than those of other goods and services; and how to address the great moral dilemmas of euthanasia, abortion, and artificial insemination. What troubles thinking people most about our legal system is not that lawyers are poorly trained but that we rely too much on law and litigation in most of our institutions while failing to insure that poor people have proper access to basic legal services at prices they can afford. In business, our principal concern is how our corporations can work more effectively with government to increase productivity and address social problems and how business can be kept accountable to the public interest in an age when markets do not provide a perfect discipline and government regulation is often inefficient and ineffective.

FAILURE OF GOVERNMENT REGULATION

These are not problems that receive much attention in our professional schools today despite their high priority in the public mind. And that is a serious matter, for there is one thing that we have surely learned from the failures of government regulation over the years. If we wish our professions to serve the public better, we must enlist the active cooperation of professionals themselves. Without their help, little of lasting value can occur.

The problems I have described are not your problems now, but they will be your problems very soon. I hope that you will address them boldly and never regard yourselves as human clay to be molded and shaped by your professional school experience. There was a time when I could not have brought myself to utter this last remark: it would have seemed too obvious and banal. But I was startled to find in my last years as a faculty member that many students had managed to persuade themselves that the Law School was "programming them" for lucrative corporate practice and co-opting them from careers fighting for noble causes or serving the needy. Such attitudes are not merely far-fetched; they are extremely dangerous, for they offer easy rationalizations to avoid responsibility for what you make of your lives. Pro-

fessional schools graduate every kind of practitioner serving every conceivable segment of society. They give you tools with which to work. But the ends and values to which you direct your talents are yours and yours alone to decide, and professional maturity begins with that realization.

FRESH FIELDS AND PASTURES NEW

In making these decisions, you begin with a strong defense against narrowing tendencies of professional training, for you would not have been admitted to Harvard College had you not been interested in a broad range of human and social questions, and four years here should have helped to cement that foundation. In one respect, however, I fear that your Harvard experience may not have served you well. By gaining admission here you prevailed in a remarkably stiff competition. By working hard to win acceptance by a professional school, you have continued to run in a demanding race. Fresh opportunities lie before you to compete for the best residencies, the best law firms, the best positions in the best corporations. These competitions are excellent motivation devices that call on powerful human instincts.

A LIFE THAT ENGAGES ALL OF YOUR INTERESTS

But it is a characteristic that one must

play by other people's rules and compete for prizes that other people have chosen. And that is a poor preparation for life, especially if you mean to live an independent existence and resist the deformations I have tried to describe.

To guard against these dangers, I hope that you will pause now and then to free your minds from your immediate problems and ambitions and imagine how your lives will seem to you at the end of your careers. If you can somehow manage the feat of looking back upon your future lives, I suspect that you will begin to feel less concerned with whether you succeed by narrow professional standards. Instead, I suspect that you will hope more and more for a life that continuously engages all of your interests and absorbs all of your energies. And as you think further, I suspect you will come to realize that no life can engage you fully unless it is open to the feelings of everyone around you and that no career can absorb your energies for very long unless it allows you to contribute generously to the welfare of others. If these be your sentiments, I hope that you will guard them well so that you can make a life that is worthy of your talents and equal to this brave beginning. Congratulations to you all. You deserve the very best. I feel sure that you will find it.

PANGS OF CONSCIENCE

Sweatshops haunt U.S. consumers

Overnight, it seems, the use of cheap-labor factories in developing nations has sparked a First World debate. In the U.S., the issue is being politicized and Hollywood-ized in a distinctly American way. On July 16, talk-show host Kathie Lee Gifford—whose clothing line touched off the latest furor—shared top billing with Labor Secretary Robert B. Reich at a confab in Arlington, Va., where Wal-Mart Stores Inc. and Kmart Corp. announced new codes for overseas contract labor.

Why the outcry now? Credit the rapid globalization linking manufacturers, investors, and consumers everywhere. Increasingly, consumers can see how their shirts and sneakers actually are made, peering into the Indonesian factories where Nike will produce 70 million pairs of shoes this year and the Honduran maquiladoras that spawned Kathie Lee's dustup. BUSINESS WEEK correspondents visited these two countries to assess conditions.

INDONESIA
'ON THE INSIDE, IT'S HELL'
Despite improvements, Nike workers face tough conditions

The Nikomas Gemilang factory in Serang, 50 miles west of Jakarta, isn't owned by Nike itself, but it produces 1.2 million pairs of Nike sneakers every month. Like footwear factories everywhere in Asia, conditions are tough. Overtime is mandatory. Workers say exhausted colleagues regularly faint from overwork. Punishment for misdeeds consists of petty humiliation. A supervisor who skipped work one Sunday to care for his sick wife and child was forced to clean toilets and then was demoted. Another worker had to run laps around the factory because shoes she assembled had defects. "From the outside, Nikomas looks like heaven, but for workers on the inside, it's hell," says Sumantri, a 25-year-old activist who like many Indonesians uses one name.

The marketing pizzazz of Nike Inc.'s "Just Do It" U.S. campaign is nowhere evident in the 12 Indonesian factories run by the company's Taiwanese, South Korean, and Indonesian subcontractors. Although these are some of the most modern factories in the industry, they are drab and utilitarian. Vast sheds house row upon row of mostly young women, who will glue, stitch, press, and box 70 million pairs of Nikes this year. Here, a pair of Pegasus running shoes, which retails for $75, costs just $18.25 to put together and ship to the U.S. Indonesia's military police deal harshly with those who rebel, and independent unions are outlawed.

LIGHTNING ROD. The stark contrast between the tens of millions of dollars that Nike icon Michael Jordan earns and the $2.23 basic daily wage in Indonesia paid by the company's subcontractors has helped make Nike a lightning rod for concern about overseas manufacturing standards. Although Nike claims it's a leader in improving conditions, its Indonesian subcontractors secured an exemption from a minimum-wage increase that would have forced them to pay $8.91 a month extra to each worker at a time when Nike has reported record profits.

More damning, says critics, is Nike's refusal to allow independent monitoring of its factories. Nike Chief Executive Philip H. Knight defends the Indonesian operations, saying that sneaker assemblers in Indonesia earn an average of double the minimum wage. But that's because they have no choice but to do overtime. As for how subcontractors treat the workers, Knight says, "There's some things we can control and some things we can't control."

To its credit, the Beaverton (Ore.) sneaker giant, under intensifying scrutiny from U.S. labor groups, has done much to clean up more egregious violations, such as underpayment of wages that prompted workers at one factory to strike in 1994. No more do Taiwanese or Korean managers hit or verbally abuse local workers. "It's a different ball game today," says Tony Nava, a 16-year Nike veteran. Indeed, union activists at Nikomas say that a security guard who hit a worker in May was quickly fired.

Nike says it's setting high standards for others to follow in Asia, and cites as evidence the low turnover of workers at places like Feng Tay Indonesia Enterprises, a quiet, well-ventilated, $45 million factory near the central Java city of Bandung, where a Taiwanese subcontractor manufactures Nikes. At Feng Tay, every building displays a speech in English, Chi-

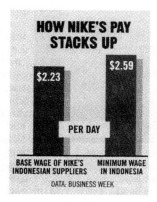

HOW NIKE'S PAY STACKS UP

$2.23 — BASE WAGE OF NIKE'S INDONESIAN SUPPLIERS

$2.59 — MINIMUM WAGE IN INDONESIA

PER DAY

DATA: BUSINESS WEEK

CHART BY ERIC HOFFMAN/BW

nese, and Bahasa Indonesia promising that workers won't have to pay anyone to get a job at the factory and forbidding managers from withholding pay.

Even some critics give Nike credit. Muchtar Pakpahan, Indonesia's most prominent labor activist whose outlawed Indonesian Prosperity Trade Union is trying to organize several Nike factories, says that the company's Nasa facility is "the best factory that I've ever visited." After an audit by Ernst & Young, ordered by Nike last year, subcontractors now are keener about ensuring that workers wear protective gloves and masks and that fire extinguishers are properly maintained.

Still, Nike has a long way to go before it lives up to its stated goal of providing a fair environment for all. Nike says it warns workers before they are hired that overtime is compulsory. But Fitri, a 19-year-old junior high school graduate from Sumatra who paid a job broker nearly a month's basic wages to get her job at Nikomas, says she was told work finished at 3 p.m. when she applied. Instead, she regularly must stay until 9 p.m. or later. Only one worker out of more than a dozen interviewed at Nikomas had ever heard of Nike's code of conduct.

There is also a not-so-subtle relationship between the managers of the factories and police, who help keep workers under control. This reporter got a taste of that power, and of the government's nervousness about the country's burgeoning labor movement, after a series of interviews set up by Pakpahan's union in Serang. Eigh-

teen plainclothes police detained me, along with three union members and an interpreter, for almost four hours, demanding an explanation of what I was doing. Two questions during my interrogation betrayed the regime's anxiety: What did the workers say about their conditions? Did I think the minimum wage was high enough? Union activists say it's typical of the chronic harassment they endure.

Nike says it does what it can to keep police, a branch of the armed forces, out of its factories. But that's virtually impossible in Indonesia. After Muchtar Pakpahan visited the sprawling Nasa factory, at the invitation of management, he says the authorities forced the factory to fire three of his union's members and banned further contact with his group. "Employers

cannot avoid a relation with the military, because it is the real power here," says human rights lawyer Teten Masduki, an attorney at the Indonesian Legal Aid Foundation.

Nike concedes its shortcomings in this arena. "We're dealing with governments that are less than ideal," Knight says. Although Nike's image is that of an on-the-edge rebel that likes to tweak authority, it has not challenged the Indonesian government's control over labor. As rumblings from workers grow louder, Nike would do well to be as much of a trendsetter in labor as it is in footwear fashion.

Mark L. Clifford in Serang, with Michael Shari in Jakarta and Linda Himelstein in San Francisco

HONDURAS
CLEANUP AT THE *MAQUILADORA*
When U.S. clients complain, sweatshops make changes

ShinWon Honduras is cleaning up its washrooms. The South Korean clothing subcontractor in San Pedro Sula is buying fire extinguishers, installing emergency exits, and checking the ventilation—all in hopes of winning business from J. C. Penney Co. "Penney wants so many things," says manager Heung-Tae Kim. Meanwhile, other customers, among them Reebok International and Sears Roebuck, have laid down the law: No underage workers. So ShinWon has laid off 50 teenage girls.

Such is the fallout from TV personality Kathie Lee Gifford's tearful admission that clothes bearing her label were made under sweatshop conditions in Honduras. Most Hondurans have no idea who Gifford is, but some 74,000 people work in 200 *maquiladoras* clustered around San Pedro Sula, and many depend on U.S. apparel contracts. Since revelations of labor abuses surfaced in May, the Americans have tightened codes of conduct and stepped up the factory inspections. A Honduran government commission, U.S. human rights groups, and unions now sweep weekly through the city.
UNIONS BARRED. The attention showered on Honduras may well be improving the lot of its people. "Things have gotten better over the past couple of years," says Israel Salinas, president of the Independent Federation of Honduran Workers. The government, for one, appears more likely to recognize local organizing efforts. And local contractors are scrambling

to deliver on demands from their U.S. customers for improvements.

The question in Honduras is whether the pressure will stay strong—and how much improvement the workers will actually see. María Herrera sews 1,500 cuffs a day on cotton knit shirts, typically earning about $20 a week to support her six children. Even the most militant unions can't force her wages up much in a country where the official unemployment is 35% and where most workers boast no more than a sixth-grade education. Government inspectors are slow to respond to allegations of forced overtime and unjustified suspensions, and Labor Minister Cecilio Zavala suspects that many of the plants are still preventing workers from organizing.

Nor does the economic pressure from abroad guarantee higher wages. J. C. Penney, for instance, now pays $5 for the same two-piece toddler's outfit it bought at $5.75 four years ago (retail price: two for $16, on sale), forcing its U.S. manufacturer to find subcontractors in Central America. The labor component of such clothing might amount to just 70¢ or less; the rest is a function of materials, shipping, and overhead.

Most Honduran *maquiladoras* are vast concrete-block sheds, with only fans to combat the heat that settles over the coastal plain by 8 a.m. Salsa and *ranchero* music blares all day, while hundreds of workers cut, stitch, and press apparel. Most are young women, often single mothers, usually migrants from Honduras' impoverished coffee-growing areas. Most, too, have little education and aren't encouraged to acquire any: When Oneyda Judith Rivera Flores, 20, asked her supervisor at Galaxy Park for time off to attend night classes, she was asked why she would want to study and was told she was needed for overtime.

ABOVEBOARD? The buzz at San Pedro Sula is that *maquiladoras* in the well-groomed industrial parks developed by Juan M. Canahuati are much better places to work. No wonder: They're among the few factories in San Pedro Sula with air-conditioning. At Inter Fashions, a plant run by a Canahuati associate in his Choloma park, workers paid by the piece to sew Levi's Dockers and Nike shorts average about $5.40 a day, twice the minimum wage.

More U.S. companies are seeking out relationships with operations such as Canahuati's, looking for some assurance of consistent quality and above-board labor conditions. Most forbid farming out work to any factory they haven't inspected, although unions and monitoring groups say unauthorized sub-contracting persists throughout Central America. The more progressive American importers—Levi's, Gap, and Reebok among them—maintain a regular presence at their contractors' sites, assessing both product quality and labor conditions. "Thirteen people came to check us from Levi's," says Roberto Palomo, a lawyer for Seolim, a joint Korean-Honduran venture that is attempting to pass muster to win a Levi's contract. "You can't fool these people."

Monitoring has its limitations, of course. Who's to know if a contractor cranks up the air-conditioning the day an inspector from Gap shows up? Other U.S. importers such as J. C. Penney, moreover, have done little to improve enforcement at their contractors, relying instead on quality-control inspectors who tend to be more concerned with buttonholes and delivery times than with fire exits. Despite the new flurry to fix sweatshops, plenty of holes remain in the system. Will Kathie Lee make a difference in the long run? Honduras is waiting.

By Elisabeth Malkin in San Pedro Sula

Leader of the PACK

One way for a small company to grow in a cutthroat market is to pick one of the countless competitive strategies available and ride it for everything it's worth. Another way is to pick them all

D O N N A   F E N N

CHRIS ZANE'S COMPETITORS DON'T like him much.

Though his business is still small ($1.2 million in 1995 sales), 30-year-old Zane is already the largest independent bicycle dealer in the New Haven, Conn., market. He's confident. ("Let Wal-Mart come—I'm ready," he boasts.) He's combative. ("I'll put you out of business," he's said to other dealers.) And, most important, he'll do almost anything to attract and keep customers. ("I'll give you lifetime service, guarantee you the lowest price, fix you a cappuccino.")

He'd better. Like similar retail businesses all over America, Zane's Cycles is under siege. Superstores and chains have taken over, leaving specialty bike retailers with only one out of every four sales; in Zane's market, three independent bike shops went out of business last year alone. "The smaller guys are fading away because they won't get into the game and compete at a higher level," says Craig Seeger, a Trek sales representative serving Zane's.

Far from fading, however, Zane has *gained* market share—growing his business 25% a year by putting into practice every customer-winning tactic he can think up, adapt, or steal. He has read the management tomes, sought out gurus, picked his suppliers' brains, conducted focus groups, and studied customer behavior in his own store and elsewhere. He aims, he says, not to sell to customers but to *own* them.

To be sure, Zane's kitchen-sink-included competitive strategy can appear scattershot. His story contains half a dozen fashionable management ideas: continual learning, the lifetime value of a customer, guerrilla marketing, bootstrapping, community-relations marketing, cost-controlled customer service. And his success begs a handful of questions: How did Zane's Cycles, an ordinary business in an extraordinarily competitive industry, create a service standard that has become his market's price of entry? How has it become the region's most visible bike shop? How has it turned intimacy and ingenuity into competitive advantages that not even the hyper-professionalized chains can match?

But what Zane's story is really all about, what binds those ideas and questions together, is a mentality that Zane insists no business—even the smallest—can do without. Call it nonstop, no-limits, no-scheme-is-too-small competitiveness.

Even better, Chris Zane would tell you, call it fun.

ZANE LAUNCHED HIS FIRST SERIOUS assault on his competitors 10 years ago, by offering one-year service guarantees (covering parts and labor on all routine service) when everyone else was promising 30 days.

"It took them two years to realize we were taking market share away from them, and then when they started offering a year, we offered two," recalls Zane. In 1986 he learned at a Manhattan trade show that some dealers were offering five-year service guarantees. "I figured that for most people, five years is the life of the bike," says Zane. "If they've had it for longer, they're probably not riding it that much, so your liability on service would not be that great." Why not, he mulled, offer lifetime free service?

"The core of my comfort is percentages. Everyone uses the free service the first year they have the bike, but I saw only 20% to 30% come back the second year. I figured my liability for lifetime free service would be minuscule." So in 1987 Zane raised the bar to the last notch, announcing free lifetime service on all bikes and making the offer retroactive. "We wanted to make our existing customers our apostles," he says.

His competitors balked. "Free service for as long as you own the bike is ludicrous," says John Budd, general manager of Action Sports. "But we've matched Zane tooth and nail." His shop now offers lifetime free service, as do most other bike retailers in Zane's market. Many feel they have no choice, and they're resentful that Zane has forced their hands. One dealer called him last year with a proposition: "I'll drop the lifetime service guarantee if you will." Zane just laughed. He had come to regard the guarantee as the foundation of his business and had extended it to everything he sold. "A guy once came in with a six-year-old pump that had worn out," recalls Zane. "I just gave him a new one."

Why? Because of Zane's bet on what that customer's lifetime of business would be worth to his store. "The guy had spent $60 on the best pump you can buy," he says. "So he's a premium purchaser, and here I have a chance to have him fall in love with us." Because Zane had a good relationship with the manufacturer, he knew he could send the broken pump back and get credit, no questions asked—so the cost of the return was zero. The potential payoff, however, was big enough that even if Zane had been forced to absorb the cost of the pump (about $30), it still would have made economic sense for him to take it back.

Consider this: "The guy has been in twice since then," says Zane. "He's probably spent $200 on accessories [a $100 net to Zane]." And when it's time for a new bike, Zane's betting that he'll get first shot at the sale. At an average cost of $400 for a bike, with a 35% margin, he stands to make another $140. And let's not forget the intangibles. A customer who is, well, thrifty enough to have a pump repaired is likely to be so impressed with getting something for nothing that he'll spread the word. "I'll bet he's told everyone about it," surmises Zane. "Everyone" probably being other serious and heavy-spending biking enthusiasts like the pump purchaser himself. In other words, Zane's ideal prospects.

So, the total invested: $30 (assuming Zane hadn't been able to get a manufacturer's refund). Total to the bottom line: $240, *plus* the profit from referral business. The result: a minimum 700% return on investment.

CHRIS ZANE'S CONTINUAL BUSINESS EDUCATION had started long before he could imagine computing the lifetime value of a customer—and it always focused on service. "If you give good service, you'll stay in business," one of his first mentors told him. "If you don't, you won't."

"Thanks, Mom," said Chris to Patricia Zane.

That was when Chris Zane was a teenager, and his company-building career was already under way. It had started in a garage when he was 12 years old and fixing bikes for his middle-class East Haven neighbors. The mechanically gifted Zane learned that a kid who delivered what he promised and made his customers his first priority could make out pretty well. "If he told someone he would fix a bike, he would do it, even if something else came up," says Patricia Zane.

Friends told their parents, and parents told their friends, and Chris Zane was soon pulling in $300 to $400 a week. "I had a Connecticut state tax ID number when I was 12," he recalls. "My dad made me get it." When he turned 16, Zane thought it was "time to get a real job" and started knocking on bike shops' doors. He landed in a downtown Branford shop but was soon told by the owner that he had better start looking elsewhere—the shop was going out of business. Zane's wheels began to turn.

"I told my parents I wanted to buy the inventory and take over his lease," he recalls. Most parents would have dismissed the idea as a childish whim, but, says Zane's mother, "we knew if he was committed to something, he would follow through. He wasn't a quitter." And Patricia and John Zane were quick to recognize a negotiating opportunity. They agreed to let their son borrow $20,000 from his grandfather on three conditions: Chris would pay back the five-year loan with 15% interest; his mother would tend the shop in the morning, but Chris would come in every day after school and do his homework at night; and, most important, his parents and grandfather would hold all the stock until he completed college. "All through high school I told my parents I wasn't going to college," says Zane. "But they told me they wouldn't give me ownership until I had a degree." He agreed.

He racked up $56,000 in sales that first year and managed to increase revenues by 25% annually over the next two years, an accomplishment that gave him self-confidence—a bit too much, perhaps. When he turned 18, Zane began to think it was time he stopped doing gear adjustment and started sitting behind a desk, leaving the hands-on business of customer service to his two employees. It didn't last for long. "I started to hear from people that the store didn't have the same feel," says Zane. "Things would slide, and we saw that business was flat. Then I woke up and put all my eggs in the service basket.

"The attitude changed from 'The customer is inconveniencing you and preventing you from doing your job' to 'The customer *is* your job,'" says Zane.

OVER THE NEXT SEVERAL YEARS, HE WENT out of his way to forge relationships with customers that would tie them to him for life. Guided by gut instinct and the ability to assimilate and apply every bit of information that might be useful to his business, Zane differentiated himself in the marketplace with a number of innovative tactics. The real kicker: like the lifetime free-service guarantee, Zane's service and marketing gambits often look expensive but usually cost him very little. Some examples:

▶ **No More Nickel-and-Diming.** "We stopped charging for anything that cost less than $1," says Zane, who started that policy 10 years ago. A customer who wanted, say, a master link—an inexpensive part that holds the chain together on a child's bike—would be given one free. "The cost to me is virtually nothing," says Zane. "We're not going to chase the pennies—we're looking at the long-term effect of giving someone a master link. You should see the look on people's faces." The annual cost: less than $150.

▶ **Community-Service Marketing I.** Zane's parents raised him with the expectation that he would give something back to the community, and he has. But he's also discovered that being a good citizen pays off. In 1989 he started the Zane Foundation, which now awards five $1,000 college scholarships to Branford High School seniors. He has financed the scholarships with revenues generated by 50 candy machines, scattered throughout the Branford area. All are labeled with Zane Foundation placards. "We're doing something our competitors aren't and that the category killers aren't. If people see that we're taking care of the community, they're more likely to come to us." After an initial investment of $2,500, Zane says, the program has paid for itself.

▶ **Community-Service Marketing II.** Zane also never misses an opportunity to work with school-age kids. He's spoken to kindergarten classes about bike safety, helped the police register bikes, and, when Connecticut passed a bike-helmet law in 1992, persuaded Trek to help him offer $40 helmets to kids at cost ($20). "Indirectly, we profited because we did something for the community," says Zane. "We also got a lot of publicity, and that boosted sales." The cost of the helmet program: $0.

▶ **Playing As If You're Bigger Than You Are.** Five years ago Zane made a strategic decision to commit 25% of his then-$36,000 advertising budget to a glossy 32-page catalog filled with his merchandise, which also offered 24 generic biking tips. Though the catalog looks original, it's actually produced by a co-op company; 16 pages are customized for Zane's Cycles, while the rest might be exactly the same for another bike dealer. Zane has exclusivity with the company for New Haven and nearby Fairfield and Litchfield Counties, so there's little chance of customers' receiving a copycat in the mail. Zane says the cost—$9,000 a year—is justified by the long shelf life the catalog earns by including the tips (advice about things like how to track your heart rate or improve your off-road riding). "People will come in with things circled in the catalog several weeks after it comes out," he says. The catalog reinforces Zane's customer-service philosophy and also gives the impression that his business is much bigger

than it really is. The same goes for his 800 number (800-551-BIKE), which works nationwide but is used mostly in Connecticut, where a town 5 to 10 miles away might be a toll call. "It costs me a $24 yearly fee, plus a maximum of $200 a month for incoming calls in the summer. It's an inexpensive way to make the business look big," says Zane.

▶ **Free Cellular Phones.** In February 1993 Zane was talking to a customer who was in the cellular-phone business and learned that while distributors charged approximately $225 for a telephone, the phone company would actually pay a $250 commission for each activation. Zane called Bell Atlantic immediately, proposing that Zane's Cycles become a phone distributor. His plan was to give away a phone to anyone who bought a bike—a value added for customers that would actually earn him a net profit of $25. Bell Atlantic was less than enthusiastic, but the rep agreed to visit Zane's shop. "I showed her the catalog, and that really set us apart from other bike shops for her," says Zane. "She began to see us an alternative channel of distribution." Bell Atlantic signed Zane up—making him the first retailer in the area to offer free phones. He activated 500 phones the first year, which earned him $12,500, plus another $25 a phone in co-op–advertising allowances. His profits are larger now, since the cost of phones fell to about $165, but commissions have remained the same.

▶ **Coffee Bar and Toy Corner.** Two years ago Zane decided he was hitting the wall in his 900-square-foot store, so he decided to move. Planning for $500 per square foot in annual revenues and striving to build Zane's Cycles to a $2-million business over the next three years, he settled on a 4,000-square-foot space just outside the main business district. Making a personal loan of $100,000 to his business, he renovated his new store meticulously, installing the most up-to-date display racks and even including a play area for children. There was just one problem. Six months after opening the new store, he began to hear from customers that the new place wasn't intimate enough. The high ceilings and white walls were uninviting, making the store feel more like a chain than the homegrown business it was.

Zane thought back to a trip he had taken to Lucerne, Switzerland, where he visited a bicycle shop that had a coffee bar. "I knew what I had to do," he re-

calls. He commissioned a cabinetmaker to build him a 14-foot mahogany coffee bar, positioning it in front of the window that separates the repair room from the retail operation. Customers could relax over a cup of gourmet coffee (the coffee suppliers provided the equipment), mull over a purchase, or just watch the mechanics. Zane would also give kids a free Snapple and sit them in front of the Lego table or a video while Mom and Dad sipped and shopped. "People fell in love with it," he says. The bar, built for him by one of his former managers, cost about $3,000.

▶ **Former Competitors as a Marketing Channel.** Call two of Zane's former competitors—now out of business—and you'll get this message: "The number you are calling is no longer in service. If you are in need of a bicycle dealer, Zane's Cycles will be happy to serve you. To be directly connected toll-free, please press zero now." By offering to pay the local yellow pages a small fraction of the defunct dealers' remaining advertising costs, Zane arranged to have their out-of-service phone numbers ring at his shop. The total cost to him is about $200 a month, which he'll continue to pay until a new book is published. Because the yellow pages helped him track the transferred calls, Zane knows he received 260 inquiries from his former competitors' customers last July alone. "The first day the line was changed, we sold a bike to a guy who asked why we closed our New Haven store," recalls Zane. "So the program paid for itself for that month." It also reinforces Zane's stronger-than-the-competitors image.

▶ **Price Guarantee.** While Zane's lifetime service guarantee was one of his best selling tools, it sometimes made customers suspicious. "They'd say, 'Sure, you're giving me lifetime free service, but what are you charging me for the bike?'" recalls Zane. He knew his prices were competitive, but customers wanted to find that out for themselves. So two years ago he started a 90-day-price-guarantee program: find it in Connecticut for less, and he'll give you the difference plus 10%. "Now we can say, 'Buy the bike, ride it, and if you find it for less, we'll take care of it.' Our pricing gained credibility." Last year, says Zane, his sales were up 54%, compared with his normal 25% growth rate; he reckons the store now handles 20% more customers. And the sales are easier. "We make money through volume because we spend less time with each customer making the hard sell—we can focus on the product," he says. Cumulatively, he's had to rebate less than $1,000. But, he says, "half the people who receive a rebate will spend it in the store that day."

"CHRIS'S MAIN OBJECTIVE IS TO TAKE market share from everyone around him," says Trek's Seeger. "I've watched his numbers go straight up while sales at the New Haven shop I used to deal with have gone down. I could see that people were going to Chris." Ray Keener, executive director of the Bicycle Industry Organization, in Boulder, Colo., says that though many bike shops are run by biking enthusiasts who do a good job of appealing to passionate cyclists, "Chris is good at going out there and grabbing people who are marginally interested and getting them into the store." Once they're there, Zane makes it difficult for them to leave without buying. And once they've bought, he blitzes them with reasons to come back—a gift certificate, a reminder that a child might be ready for a larger bike, and so on.

But there is also a downside to his devotion to customer service. His service guarantee, for example, has limited his opportunity for growth. Shortly after he initiated the guarantee, he was forced to drop a line of bicycles because the warranties "were killing us." While the manufacturer covered the cost of parts, Zane was obliged to provide free labor, and the number of repairs was cutting into his already-thin margins. With a lifetime of free service on every bike sold looming ahead of him, he decided to cut his losses and drop the brand.

A foray into the world of exercise equipment has also been problematic. In the winter of 1994, Zane began carrying a high-end line of treadmills—an attempt to diversify his business and to generate more sales in the slow winter months. He learned quickly that it wasn't a good fit. "It was very different from the bike business," he says. "Treadmills need adjustment more often than bikes do—and they're too big for the customer to load up and bring into the shop. We were going out to do in-home servicing every six weeks, and it cut deeply into our profits." Again he quickly cut his losses and discontinued the line. Still, he's committed to servicing the machines he's already sold—for life. An expensive mistake? Zane shrugs. "Those customers will see that we're honoring our commitment to them even though we're not carrying the line anymore, and they'll speak well of us."

It's a phrase Zane uses a lot when he's referring to customers—"they'll speak well of us." Indeed, every marketing gimmick, every guarantee, every freebie is designed in light of Zane's belief that the most sophisticated marketing in the world won't serve him as well as customer referrals. And that all comes down to how people are treated in the store. Zane doesn't, for example, make a point of hiring cyclists as salespeople. "I can teach anyone about a bike," he says, "but I can't teach them to be helpful or courteous. I've had people who know the product cold but who just don't have the ability to work with customers. They don't last long."

The attention to detail is an integral part of Zane's basic business philosophy, but it's also critical to his survival. Wal-Mart is coming to town, as is Ski Market, a category-killer sporting-goods store. "When a category killer comes in, you have to have all your programs in place," says Zane. "You have to work to be as strong as they are and kill them where they're weak. And customer service is where they're weakest."

He is not, in fact, comfortable with merely serving his niche, as a good specialty retailer probably ought to be. He wants to lure customers from Wal-Mart and reckons that the giant's presence will actually help him because "there will be more inexpensive bikes out there that need to be fixed." Soon he'll have a better point-of-sale computer system that will help him track customers more effectively and do more targeted marketing. Down the line, once he's hit his 1997 goal of $2 million in sales, he'll cautiously explore other markets.

And how do his competitors fit into all this? Well, they don't.

"Our 100% goal is to be *the* bike shop in New Haven County," says Zane. "And we won't stop there."

One project, however, he did stop pursuing. For seven years he had juggled college and the demands of company building, completing three years of course work toward the degree he had promised his parents he'd earn. It was a struggle. Finally, Patricia and John Zane relented. They were satisfied their son was on the road to success and were convinced of his commitment to the community. Chris, relieved to be let off the hook but uncomfortable with the prospect of unfinished business, presented an alternative scenario. "I want to be so successful that I'll be asked to give a commencement speech, and that's how I'll earn my degree," he told them. "It's not the traditional way, but there's no right path," he philosophized. He was, in fact, living proof of that. So in 1990, his parents transferred to him 80% of the stock. He'd earned it.

THE DO'S & DONT'S
OF WRITING A WINNING BUSINESS PLAN

A well-crafted plan can help you raise much needed capital. But more important, it should be used as a living document to help manage your business.

Carolyn M. Brown

IT IS RARE FOR BUSINESS OWNERS to secure a bank loan for seed money. But that's exactly what Gilda and Amir Salmon did. They snagged a $30,000 small business loan from Bergen Commercial Bank in Paramus, N.J., and the Paterson Economic Development Corp. in Paterson, N.J., to help finance their namesake salon two years ago. A solid business plan helped seal the deal.

Through their well-honed plan, the couple showed financiers that their small coiffing operation could compete in the commercial downtown sector of Paterson, N.J., where mom-and-pop shops were increasingly being overshadowed by mini-malls.

"The business plan is the first thing bankers ask to see," says Amir, president of Gilda & Amir's Salon Inc. "They want to know how much of your own money is invested in the business and what you have to offer as collateral. For us, it was $5,000 in savings and our house."

The bank also scrutinized the management section of the company's plan as well as its financial projections. "We outlined our combined 15-year experience in the hair care field. We also showed that we had an established following, with an average clientele averaging about 200 customers per month," Amir adds.

Because he provided extended financial estimates, Salmon says the bank gave him an additional $5,000 (the maximum amount available through the Development Corp. was $25,000). He notes that the one-to-three-year projections were conservative, with estimated earnings of $100,000. In fact, the business has exceeded those expectations; Amir predicts that profits will double this year.

While enthusiasm alone may convince your friends and family members that your business is destined for greatness, investors and bankers want the facts. They want an objective, in-depth analysis of the business opportunity with all the attendant risks and obstacles laid out in your business plan.

Whether intended to attract a prospective financier or define a structure for management, your business plan is a blueprint for operating your business. Most entrepreneurs make the mistake of seeing a business plan as a start-up tool alone. In fact, it should be

viewed as a living document that is referred to and revised throughout the life of your business.

"A business plan is a road map that gives a business direction," says Joseph Mancuso, founder of the Center For Entrepreneurial Management Inc. and author of *How To Write A Winning Business Plan* (Simon & Schuster). "It gives you your destination, and that's tremendously important, not so much for you, but for everyone involved, from employees to investors," he explains. "They don't want to just blindly follow your short-term directions; they want to know where the company is headed."

Like many fledgling business owners, the Salmons now realize that a business plan is a work in progress. They're in the process of rewriting the plan for their seven-employee concern.

"We outgrew our plan in the first year of operation," explains Amir, 31. "We need to more clearly spell out the duties of our board of directors. We also failed to give our employees any real direction about the business and knowledge about our products."

The Salmons, who also serve as platform

artists for Joico International, a worldwide hair care products manufacturer, will include in their revised plan how that relationship with Joico will impact their revenues and market presence.

Some business owners write several different versions of a plan, tailoring them to specific players, (i.e., bankers, investors, distributors, suppliers and customers). Whatever its goal, the basic format of a business plan is essentially the same.

WRITING A WINNING BUSINESS PLAN

Experts agree that there is just no substitute for thinking your business through and taking the time to put it down on paper. Mancuso explains that doing so will expose the bugs of your business, adding, "If you can work them out on paper, you will save yourself some serious time and money."

If you're writing just one to start, it should serve several purposes: It should be a development tool for the company's founders; a planning and evaluation tool for managers and other key people; a mission statement for customers; and a sales document for raising capital.

It should be as long as is needed to tell your company's story. Most experts agree that 25 pages is an ideal length, and that a start-up plan shouldn't exceed 50 pages. A good one, they say, will take at least six months to write. And remember to adhere to a basic format.

The Executive Summary. Just as the term implies, you should summarize the company's objectives, history, management and financials in this opening section. Discuss the nature of the business, location and state of operation. Provide clear descriptions of your product, customers, suppliers and address obvious concerns. You need to identify your niche and state any specific advantages you hold over your competition.

Lay out your primary goals and achievements. If you envision turning a profit in three years, say so, and refer to financial projections to back it up. Also, describe current milestones reached and their results. The summary should give the feeling that your venture can be profitable.

If you're requesting money, state how much money is needed and for what purpose. Discuss the potential return on the investment and the payback period.

Aim to be concise and comprehensive, and remember that first impressions count: Your one-to-three-page opener should ag-

gressively sell your business. It should entice the reader to "read on."

Market Analysis. Many experts who review business plans say that too often the marketing section is one of the weakest parts.

They advise that you must begin by sizing up your market. Who are your customers, and will they be attracted to your product or service? What is your price structure and how did you arrive at it based on standard markup, production costs and perceived value? A market overview should include the demographics of your target market, industry trends, the competition and future outlook.

For assistance, you can hire a professional market research firm, but bear in mind that most charge upwards of $2,000 per analysis. Don't despair: Most sources you'll need are easily accessible.

A good place to start is trade associations. Many are happy to provide data on their respective industries. Check the Encyclopedia of Associations. In addition to the U.S. Census Bureau's divisions of population and housing, you can get demographic and competitive information from the *Rand McNally Commercial Atlas and Marketing Guide, Thomas Register of Manufacturers* and back issues of *American Demographics* magazine.

Once, you've analyzed the market and

demand for your product or service, you need to define marketing strategies. Your plan must spell out the best ways to reach potential customers (i.e., direct marketing, advertising or special promotions).

Management Team. A plan is as good as the people who implement it. Investors often put more stock in the management of the company than in the product. Include biographies of yourself and other managers in the company. Treat these bios as expanded resumes, spelling out each person's role and financial stake in the company. Also, note relevant skills, degrees, certifications and prior experience.

"Entrepreneurs bring their own work history with them. Though most are very good at what they have done, they aren't necessarily skilled in all the details necessary to support a successful venture," says Annette C. Darnes, vice president and manager of the woman and minority assistance program at Union Bank in San Francisco. "One of the biggest downfalls of start-up companies is not developing in advance the internal plans for managing the business."

If there are more than five players on board, you should include an organizational chart. If you haven't hired everyone

---

BUSINESS PLANNING RESOURCES

There's no magic formula for a good business plan. However, bookstores and libraries are filled with guides and small business books with sample plans.

One good read is *Writing Business Plans That Get Results: A Step-by-Step Guide* by Michael O'Donnell (Contemporary Books; $12.95). This workbook is ideal for business start-ups. There are worksheets for every component of a plan.

Another good read is *Writing A Convincing Business Plan* by Arthur R. De-Thomas and William B. Fredenberger (Barron's; $16.95). Particularly helpful are the sections dealing with market analysis and operations.

Business guru Joseph Mancuso has a series of small business handbooks, including *How To Write A Winning Business Plan* (Simon & Schuster; $14.95) and *How to Start, Finance and Manage Your Own Small Business* (Random House; $17.95).

There are also a number of business planning software programs out there:
- Business Plan Toolkit by Palo Alto Software ($14.95);
- Plan Write For Business from Business Resource Software Inc. ($129.95);
- Microsoft Small Business Pack ($99).

Yet another resource is the 1996 **BLACK ENTERPRISE**/Nations Bank Entrepreneur's Conference, May 1–5, at Disney's Grand Floridian Beach Resort in Lake Buena Vista, Fla. For more information, phone: 800–543–6786; fax: 212–886–9600; mail: **BLACK ENTERPRISE**, Conference Department, 130 Fifth Ave., New York, NY 10011; or e-mail: bebusin@aol.com.

yet, describe each post and its required qualifications.

Financial Statements. Financial data and calculations are the make-or-break component of any business plan. After all, the goal is to be profitable. Whether you are a start-up or an existing business, provide projections for three to five years out. Indicate the expected highs and lows of the business. If your company is already in operation, you'll need to provide a profit-and-loss statement and a balance sheet. Other basic elements of the financial section are the cash-flow forecast and break-even analysis.

A balance sheet shows the status of the company's assets, liabilities and equity ownership. You should have a current financial snapshot of the business as well as a projected balance sheet showing how these figures are likely to change over time. A balance sheet should be updated yearly.

The profit-and-loss (or income) statement shows the results of operations over a period of time. It compares total revenues against all operating costs and expenses (i.e., salaries, supplies, insurance, marketing, overhead). Organized by fiscal year, these tables are used to determine net income and should be updated annually.

Cash-flow forecasts chart the movement of funds in (receipts) and out (disbursements) of the company. By monitoring the sources and uses of cash, you will have an idea of how much money or credit you'll need to carry out planned operations, and you'll be alerted when cash runs short. Forecast three to five years out.

The break-even analysis shows how long it will take for the business to make a profit. This figure is arrived at by calculating the business' fixed and variable costs and measuring them against projected revenue. You break even when sales revenues equal total cost.

"Few business plans have realistic financial projections," says Richard Magary, senior vice president of administration and former chief financial officer of American Shared Hospital Services, a publicly traded medical services company. Too often, entrepreneurs get caught up in wishful thinking. "Wring all the optimism out of your projections," Magary urges. "Realism is more convincing than naive enthusiasm." An alternative is to provide two scenarios, one that lists conservative projections based on weak market performance and the other, aggressive projections based on robust demand.

> Financial data and calculations are the make-or-break component of any business plan. After all, the goal is to be profitable. Whether you are a start-up or an existing business, provide projections for three to five years out.

While a good business plan is one that raises money, it's important that you tailor your plan to the type of financing you need. There are two major categories of financing: debt (loan) and equity (ownership interest).

Bankers will be interested primarily in the company's fixed assets, such as building, equipment, etc., and the collateral the business owner can offer. The bank's main concern is how and if you are going to pay back the loan at the going interest rate.

On the other hand, venture capitalists and other investment groups will want a chunk of your company and its profits. Usually, they want to earn at least a 30% to 35% risk-adjusted annual return on investment. In other words, they want to get back six times their money in three to five years.

A common mistake entrepreneurs make is inadequately addressing the return on the investment, says Liz Harris, vice president of Boston-based UNC Partners, a venture capital investment management firm. She says that venture capitalists want to know what they are getting into and when can they get out and how. So, provide an exit strategy that has timetables plus projected returns.

TAILORING AND UPDATING YOUR PLAN

When Harry Davis started Real-to-Reel Pictures Entertainment Inc. in February of 1992, he needed to raise about $20,000 in a private placement stock offering to produce two short films. Davis and his partners in this New York-based production company, Cornelius Pitts and Percy Davis (no relation), went to work on a business plan that took three months to complete.

By November, some 40 shares were sold to 12 people. The firm then raised another $100,000 to finance a 30-minute television pilot, called *Street Games,* a sports show that features interviews with today's star athletes, their families and childhood neighbors. While Real-To-Reel's five-year business plan provided a market study of the targeted audience for *Street Games,* financial projections for production costs were more than the company had anticipated, says Davis, the company's 38-year-old vice president.

As a result, Davis decided to change the name of the company to the Reel Deal Inc. and to restructure the firm as a non-linear television and multimedia pre- and post-production house. "We had to change our business plan to accommodate changes in the company," says Davis. "It necessitated new subsections, namely staffing, and another layer of details, such as how we were going to rent out the studio to earn additional funds." Specifically, the Reel Deal needed an additional $300,000 for state-of-the-art equipment and training courses.

"The idea now is to do everything ourselves. To shoot the film [or video], edit it, add the graphics and record the sound or music," says Kymbali Craig, creative director. The Reel Deal expects to do $350,000 worth of business this year by securing sizable budgets to produce film, television and music video projects and by selling shows the company produces. It also plans to do licensing and merchandising under the brand name, A Raw Art Vibe.

Davis and his partners now know the one secret to the success of seasoned entrepreneurs: that it's essential to constantly update your business plan. "You should use your business plan as a guide for the fiscal year that you are working in," says Kenneth Shead, president of Drew Pearson Marketing Inc. in Addison, Texas. "We are constantly revising our plan to reflect changes in the industry as it affects our market share." The 11-year-old firm (No. 22 on the BE INDUSTRIAL/SERVICES 100 list with $65 million in revenues) is the world's largest black-owned licensed sports and character headwear manufacturer.

"Every year we add elements to the

plan's executive summary on what's happening politically, socially and economically as it pertains to our business," adds Shead, a former national account executive for Xerox. "Unless you monitor and record ongoing trends in your market, it's impossible to chart your company's future."

Don Sutton learned the hard way the value of a business plan in understanding one's market. Last year, Sutton, founder and president of the Just Chairs furniture dealership in San Francisco, decided to raise $1 million through a private placement stock offering for expansion capital.

Sutton's first mistake was to operate the 11-year-old firm, which regularly posts sales of about $3 million annually, without a business plan for expansion.

His second faux pas was to hire a writer to assist with the prose and an accountant to crunch the numbers. Sutton says he relied too heavily on both, allowing the writer to direct the content and the accountant to develop the ratios for the financial projections. "The business plan was too long and the numbers didn't pan out," Sutton says. In fact, the long-winded plan made his proposal less attractive to investors.

But writing it did force Sutton to scrutinize his customers and competition in a way he'd never done before. He realized that he was missing a big share of the firm's potential market by focusing on corporate customers and the high-end of home office businesses.

"We had been sitting on excess inventory that was crying out for an outlet," says Sutton. "Our customers didn't care if a fabric was discounted— they wanted top quality goods at a good price." Sutton opened a clearance outlet, offering discontinued products but at discounted prices. Now Just Chairs can compete with superstores like OfficeMax and Office Depot without having any detrimental impact on the company's core business. Just Chairs recently opened its fourth Bay area showroom. A prototype of the business plan, this Silicon Valley outlet is the firm's highest volume location thus far is the San Francisco store.

It's been close to a year since the plan was completed; Sutton still intends to do a private placement stock route. Instead, he's using the business plan as a guide for the ongoing operation of his business.

By writing a business plan in the later stages of your company's life cycle, you may find gaps or things you hadn't thought about, says Sutton. "Once you find holes, you have to spend a lot of time and hard work filling them up." That's OK, experts say. Better late than never.

WHAT'S YOUR STORY?

Changing a company's culture requires
a comprehensive approach—
and a heavy dose of leadership.
A good storyteller, says Charlie Jacobs,
can help "fill in the white spaces."

John H. Sheridan

IT HAS BEEN SAID THAT MANY BUSINESSES SUFFER from too much management and too little leadership. The difference is rather clearcut, observes Charlie Jacobs. "Management, to a large extent, is about control. Leadership is about commitment," he says. "Management is about managing behavior. Leadership is about dealing with the way that people perceive the world they are part of."

So where does a manager turn to develop a talent for real leadership? One good place, Jacobs recommends, is the world of literature—especially Shakespeare.

Now that might seem like odd advice coming from a management consultant. But Charles S. Jacobs, who heads the Boston-based Amherst Consulting Group, wasn't always a consultant. He started out as a college professor, lecturing on Shakespeare at a small New Hampshire college. "If you can teach Shakespeare to 18-year-olds, you can analyze what is going on in a business," he says glibly.

Jacobs still draws upon the Bard of Avon as a teaching resource, but for a different purpose. These days his pupils are business executives—primarily managers who want to advance their leadership skills and successfully implement change in the organizations they run. Occasionally, in sessions with management groups—and even when working with people on the shop floor—he will show a video clip from Shakespeare's *King Henry V*.

"*Henry V* has what a lot of people consider to be the greatest leadership speech ever given," he says. The scene is the eve of a historic battle, where Henry's English troops are greatly outnumbered by the French army. Morale among his soldiers is low. "They're tired. They're hungry. They're sick. It is raining. Their camp is full of rats. And from the other side of the battlefield, they can hear the French popping champagne corks. The French are arguing about who is going to lead the battle and get all the glory."

When one of Henry's lords laments the fact that the English need more troops, Henry takes a contrary position—saying, in effect: No. If we had more people and we lose the battle, we simply would lose more people. And if we win, then we'd have to share the glory with more people.

It is an example, Jacobs points out, of "changing the meaning of the situation."

Henry then spins a story for his troops—"about how they are going to fight this battle and what is going to happen when they return home as celebrated heroes. . . . Henry is creating the story—the myth of the battle—before they ever fight the battle. At the end, when asked if the troops are prepared for the battle, he replies, 'All things are ready if our minds be so.'"

Naturally, Henry and his men live up to the legend, prevailing over a vastly superior force, in what historians regard as "one of the most fantastic battles ever fought."

What the English king did—and what good corporate leaders learn to do—was to subtly "change the perception that people have of the organization and the work they are doing," Jacobs says. But this requires skills—and a grasp of what makes people tick—that are seldom detailed in business-school texts.

"An understanding of literature and the humanities helps you to understand people—why they do the things they do," asserts the one-time professor.

Moreover, a smidgen of literary skill can help managers and executives become good corporate storytellers, able to create the necessary "myths" about their organizations and the roles that people must learn to play.

Too often, he says, company strategies—including corporate makeovers loosely classified as reengineering—fail because the implementation is fragmented and things are out of alignment. Simply put, there too many "holes" in the story describing how organizations and people get from here to there.

Jacobs cites two reasons reengineering efforts fail. "The first is that you don't reengineer something in isolation. If you have a lousy strategy, but a great process to get it implemented, it doesn't do you any good. The second is that all the pieces need to be in place, and they must be aligned with one another—the structure, systems, processes, culture, leadership, and strategy."

Think of a car with a six-cylinder engine. If one spark plug is misfiring, the whole vehicle shakes and sputters.

To an outsider, it is often readily apparent when things are out of synch—such as reward systems based on individual achievement when the company is trying to encourage teamwork. "It is amazing that people inside the company don't see it," Jacobs says. "And once you've alerted management of a company to the fact that elements of their organization are working at cross-purposes, that doesn't necessarily mean they will do anything about it. They may just go on and fight the next fire—'Yes, we agree with you. But I've got a problem making my numbers for this quarter.'"

When a new corporate thrust calls for a change in culture, businesses that are thin on leadership are particularly vulnerable. Part of the problem is that "corporate culture" is an elusive concept. "People talk about culture as something they need to deal with," Jacobs says. "But they don't know what levers to pull. They don't know how to change the culture. One reason is that culture is really an abstract concept—the sum of all the individual behaviors in the organization. If you think about changing culture as changing all the individual behaviors, you begin to get a better handle on what it really takes."

Moreover, people have a tendency to forget what drives behavior. And to a large extent, behavior is driven by how people think and how they feel about what is going on in the organization. "The idea of changing the organization, or changing the individual behaviors in the organization, requires that—in some way—you disconfirm what people are currently doing." For example, if managers perceive themselves as supportive of a participative, empowered environment, but their intimidating behavior projects something else, then they have to be made aware of the incongruity—and shown how they need to change. The key to be-

A READING LIST FOR LEADERS

IF LITERATURE CAN HELP MANAGERS UNDERSTAND PEOPLE better—why they do the things they do—what should the reading list include? After a moment's reflection, Charlie Jacobs ticks off the following titles:

1. *King Henry V*, by William Shakespeare, which has a masterful leadership speech.

2. *No Ordinary Time*, a biography of Franklin and Eleanor Roosevelt, by Doris Kearns Goodwin—"an absolutely brilliant study in leadership."

3. *Middlemarch*, a novel by George Eliot written in the 1800s. "It is incredibly comprehensive in helping to understand people."

4. *Competitive Advantage*, by Michael E. Porter—the only business book among his top six. Both this one and Porter's *Competitive Strategy* are "boring as hell, but solid books," says Jacobs. The latter has been called "the book of lists for strategists."

5. *Certain Trumpets*, by Garry Wills—"a study of 16 leaders, everybody from Martin Luther King to FDR and Madonna." (Actually, Madonna is portrayed as an "anti-leader.")

6. *An Anthropologist on Mars*, by Oliver Sacks. The author is a neurophysiologist who writes about people with neurological disorders. "The book tells you a lot about how people really operate when they are at peak efficiency."

coming an empowering manager, he says, is to learn to *ask* people what should be done rather than *tell* them. "That's not to say that you *never* tell people. But you start out by asking."

IN AN ASSIGNMENT AT BETHLEHEM STEEL Corp.'s Sparrows Point complex, Jacobs took a participative approach to cultivating a participative style. In a series of sessions, top managers met with groups of 60 subordinate managers in which they were instructed to ask their subordinates what it would take to achieve the key elements of a new vision. "Not only was the message they received about participation, but the structure of the session was one in which we systematized the participation. The process reinforced the message."

But employee participation is only one piece of the culture-change puzzle. In an old-line manufacturing industry, Jacobs says, it isn't enough to simply "empower" people. "You have to begin to change every way that they think about what they are doing. It is not just a question of changing the reward system. It is a question of changing every message, every cue that people get in the organization about the meaning that they ought to ascribe to their work.

"And that is where a good story can have tremendous power."

To change culture, a leader—in the mold of Henry V—will create a myth. "If the leader is really in touch with people and understands what is going on in the organization, the myth or the story that he or she creates will be powerful enough that people will want to buy into it."

Jacobs raises an important distinction between a myth and the company vision: "A vision is a snapshot. A myth is the snapshot as it plays out over time. Most visions really are the end of the story. The hard part of the story to create is the middle—how do I go from where I am today to where I need to be."

And that takes more than a consultant with a shrink-wrapped cure-all, Jacobs asserts. "A popular line is that a consultant is someone who borrows your watch to tell you what time it is—and then keeps the watch. It's unfortunate what consultants have done to their image. But it has a lot to do with the fact that there is a big market out there for the simple, one-shot panacea.

"To me, the most depressing thing about most management literature—and what most consultants are practicing—is the idea that there is an easy answer. Five years ago, it was Total Quality Management. Everybody is looking for *the* answer. But *nothing* solves all your problems."

That's why Jacobs' Amherst Consulting Group encourages taking a holistic approach—one it terms Transformational Integration—to major change efforts. And the most important elements, he asserts, are the people issues, including culture and the things that drive behavior. "If you have the wrong structure, or the wrong processes, or the wrong systems, but you have people who really care a whole lot, they will make things work. But if, on the other hand, you have the best system, the best structure, and the best processes, but people don't give a damn, they'll figure out how to make those things *not* work."

That's true at the upper echelons, too. At one client company, where senior executives were at odds over the implementation of new reengineering strategy, the CEO asked Jacobs to help secure agreement. "We put these five people off-site at a resort for three days. And guess what the real issues were? They weren't strategic issues or what markets to go into. The issues were that the CEO wasn't getting along with the CFO. The president was having a fight with the vice chairman. So when they tried to get things implemented, the divisions at the senior level just filtered down through the organization."

It's Not Too Late To Find the Ethical Answer

PRIVACY
Entitlement or Illusion?

n all the glowing talk about how voicemail, e-mail, the Internet and networked PCs are revolutionizing the corporate landscape, Laura Pincus believes there's another more troublesome side to the technology gold rush. Today's electronic systems also provide the tools to collect data and monitor the workplace with dazzling efficiency. "At the touch of a button, it's possible to view e-mail messages employees send to one another, listen to voicemail or telephone conversations, and actually see what's on their monitors while they're sitting at their computer terminals," says the director of DePaul University's Institute for Business and Professional Ethics. "It's also possible to view a dressing room or break area using a hidden video camera, and use surveillance devices to hear what's going on in various parts of an office or building."

By Samuel Greengard

Mind boggling capabilities, to be sure. But that's just part of the overall equation. Vast databases provide entree into a world of personal information about an applicant or employee—his or her driving record, credit history, medical records and much more. Find-

Employers have a right to information about their workers. Indeed, checking backgrounds secures safety, and monitoring activity promotes productivity. But workers, too, have a right and that's to privacy. Here's how you can achieve your need for information without sacrificing their dignity.

ing out who a person is and whether he or she might represent a future problem based on past information is as easy as a phone call or an online session. Not surprisingly, an entire industry has sprung up to conduct background checks on applicants and dig into existing employees' histories. And now, companies are developing badges with electronic sensors that let a boss know where a worker is at any given minute of the workday.

Orwellian? Perhaps. Scary? That depends on which side of the eavesdropping device you're sitting. These days, mention the word privacy in the same breath as the workplace and you're likely to stir a hornets' nest of emotions. Al-though the U.S. Constitution carries no specific guarantee of personal privacy, a 1992 Louis Harris poll found that 78% of all Americans express concern about their personal privacy—up from approximately one-third in 1970. A 1991 poll by Time/CNN found that 93% of all respondents believed companies selling personal data should be required to gain permission from the individual in advance. Yet, as Pincus puts it: "There's no simple method for determining what's right and what's wrong in the workplace. Neither Congress nor the courts have decided, and companies haven't come to a consensus." And, Evan Hendrix, publisher of the Washington D.C.-based newsletter *Privacy Times* adds: "There's a greater capability to snoop into people's lives now more than ever before."

Of course, employers argue that monitoring and surveillance are essential for a safe and secure workplace. Companies say this is to protect people and assets and limit legal liability. Some also believe that monitoring workers for speed or accuracy allows companies to boost productivity, improve customer service and weed out problem employees. There's plenty of evidence to support what these employers say. And there's a solid legal framework to bolster this position. Federal law backs the employer's right to monitor workers, and the laws of individ-

---

Making Privacy a Priority

Protecting confidential data and employee records isn't easy. But Atmel Corp., a San Jose, California-based company that manufactures specialized semiconductors, proves that it's possible. The firm, with $634 million in 1995 sales and 3,000 employees in the United States and Europe, has established elaborate procedures to ensure that human resources data doesn't fall into the wrong hands or leak to the wrong person. "There are inherent risks of doing business, but there are many ways to minimize those risks," says Bobbi LaPlante, the firm's corporate manager of human resources.

To begin with, employees files—still kept in paper-based folders—are locked away in file cabinets and can't be pulled by anyone other than an approved clerk in HR. If a manager needs to view an employee's file, human resources doesn't allow the file to go outside the HR department. Ditto for medical records, which HR keeps in a separate set of file cabinets that are off-limits to anyone outside the department. Not only does that ensure confidentiality about a disability or medical condition, it keeps highly sensitive medical information from becoming public if a court issues a subpoena to view an employee's records. Although all companies are supposed to separate health records from employee files, that's not always the case.

The firm also takes great care in the way it maintains information and how it uses data. Atmel avoids using Social Security numbers and instead generates a unique employee number—something only approximately 30% of firms do. That alone eliminates many of the concerns employees have over privacy. But it also makes it far more difficult for someone to misuse or commit fraud with an employee's Social Security number. In fact, the employee number is used only as a means of identification and nothing more.

Next year, Atmel will likely migrate to a computerized record-keeping system. But it's already mapping out the transition and working with its management information systems (MIS) department to create strong security protection, including a fire wall of sorts that will keep unauthorized users out. "Security and privacy are two areas that can't be overlooked when you're talking about electronic systems," LaPlante says. "HRIS data is as valuable and important as anything a company has."

In fact, that thinking permeates the way Atmel conducts its internal business. Privacy and confidentiality are stressed throughout the interview process—and many questions focus on issues relating to the topic. Existing employees not only receive a handbook that carefully spells out policy, they also receive ongoing training and briefings on privacy issues. And because Atmel's HR director is an attorney, it makes it far easier to follow the latest rulings and trends, passing the information onto employees. "It's something we drill into employees: a breach of privacy or confidentiality can cost you your job. Even something that's seemingly innocuous is an offense worthy of firing," says LaPlante.

Finally, the company is no less vigilant when it comes to the use of equipment and property. It has a strict policy covering what kind of information employees can have on their computers and how they use electronic media, such as e-mail and voicemail. It informs workers that desks, lockers, and file cabinets are company property, and that Atmel reserves the right to search them, if necessary. In reality, that rarely happens. Likewise, telephones, e-mail and voicemail aren't monitored—unless the company discovers that an individual is misusing the system or stealing. Concludes LaPlante: "You have to strike a balance. As an employer, it's necessary to create a secure environment and avoid liability, but it's also important to create a positive atmosphere and one in which creativity and innovation can flourish. It's a constant balancing act, but you can create an environment that works for everyone."

—SG

Policy Matters

Electronic mail has changed the workplace in more ways than almost anyone could have imagined just a decade ago. Today, information is zapped from one computer terminal to another instantaneously—creating a digital trail of conversations, thoughts and ideas. As with any technological revolution, society's ability to adapt to this new tool has lagged. Although 80% of all organizations communicate and share business information via e-mail, only 36% have policies addressing proper e-mail usage. More disturbing is the fact that only 34% have written workplace privacy policies. That's the finding of a recently released survey conducted by the Society for Human Resource Management (SHRM).

"Many organizations are unsure how to address privacy and technology concerns without interfering with the tremendous benefits of a tool such as e-mail—incrased efficiency, teamwork and flexibility," says Michael R. Losey, president of SHRM. But this laissez-faire approach can land an organization in serious trouble. In many cases, workers are confused about what is acceptable behavior and what isn't, as well as what their boss considers acceptable for requesting information and carrying on business. Is informal networking with an associate through e-mail deemed personal or professional? Is an occasional message to a friend or family member verboten?

"While employers believe they have the right to access e-mail messages, employees tend to believe their communications are private," writes Jeffrey A. Van Doren, a Pittsburgh-based labor and employment law attorney in a recent issue of *HR News*. "Implementing an e-mail policy can go a long way toward clarifying who legally owns and has the right to access and review e-mail system messages in the workplace." Indeed, a growing number of employees who feel their rights have been violated are taking such cases to court. And although the overwhelming majority of decisions have come down in favor of the company, the cost of defending such actions can be expensive, he asserts.

That's why DHL Systems, a Burlingame, California-based technology service company that's part of DHL Worldwide Express, decided to formulate a policy nearly one year ago. "We felt it was important that everyone knows exactly what the rules are. The idea was to be upfront and honest about what behavior is acceptable and what isn't," says Linda Giusti, human resources manager for the company. So, she and the firm's HR director and legal counsel, Margaret Phillips, began scanning articles, case law, legal memos and other companies' policies to glean ideas and ensure they weren't missing anything.

After several weeks of research, they created a draft policy. Then they asked staffers for feedback and additional ideas on creating a policy that would be realistic and fair. "That was a crucial step," says Phillips. "Having everyone's comments up front meant we could act proactively rather than reactively. It helped us deal with issues before they became problems." At the same time, the company had internal experts in HR, finance, legal and technology review the document to ensure it was accurate and would work. The final result? A single-page document that concisely spells out the organization's policies governing e-mail and online access—a policy that borrowed on other companies' experience but meshed with DHL Systems' own culture.

DHL Systems is an example of how a company can generate a policy so that everyone wins. It spells out that the company's e-mail isn't to be used for "communications of a discriminatory or harassing nature, or for obscene" messages or chain letters. It notes that occasional nonbusiness use is acceptable, but "employees may not abuse the privilege for any significant amount of personal business or pleasure." And it clearly states that information created on company computers is generally considered private, although the company reserves the right to review electronic files and messages "to ensure that these media are being used in compliance with the law and with company policy." Other parts of the document cover hacking into other employee's files and protecting confidential information when sending e-mail to outsiders or posting it online.

That's a good start. But as Don Harris, manager of HR systems for the New York Times Co., and chair of the International Human Resources Information Management Association puts it: "Companies get into problems not only because of a lack of policy, but also due to poor policy implementation. It's crucial to follow the guidelines." His committee is working to develop a set of professional guidelines for the use and protection of HR information in computers and other forms of electronic media. But, "ultimately, it's people who protect information, not policies. That's why people must understand policies and take responsibility for them," he says.

Amid all the discussion about respecting employees rights, it's important to remember that e-mail and other forms of online communication can pose a serious security risk. Even ardent privacy advocates agree that electronic communication provides an easy way for a disgruntled worker to zap information to himself or a friend outside of the company. The bottom line? "It's important to strike a balance. If you suspect there's a problem, it's a good idea to monitor an employee. But randomly monitoring e-mail just to see what's going on can lead to enormous problems," says Laura Pincus, director of the Institute for Business and Professional Ethics at DePaul University.—SG

To see DHL Systems' full policy regarding e-mail and electronic media, please go to http://www.hrhq.com/ and click on "Hot Topic."

ual states follow that lead. Indeed, the courts consistently rule that employers can do—without authorization—what government officials and police officers are forbidden from doing without a court order: bug phones, install cameras, scan e-mail and browse through desks, lockers and file cabinets. The workplace, after all, is a privately owned enterprise.

Naturally, workers feel their rights to privacy are being trampled. Sitting under the watchful eye of Big Brother isn't good for morale or overall productivity, they insist. Fearing that every move is being scrutinized isn't conducive to building an environment of trust, and can sometimes lead to physical and mental ailments from the stress. "When you worry that you can't have a private conversation with your spouse or send an important e-mail message to a friend without someone knowing about it and possibly reprimanding you, it affects your attitude and feelings about the company," says a manager for a large East Coast-based food manufacturer.

As always, human resources is caught in the crossfire—because it's the department charged with developing policies and dealing with labor issues. "It's an issue you have to take seriously. There are ethical reasons, legal reasons and practical reasons for devising a plan," says Bobbi LaPlante, corporate manager of human resources at Atmel Corp., a San Jose, California-based semiconductor manufacturer.

Society constantly changes the definition of privacy. In many respects, the battle over privacy is nothing new. For decades, civil libertarians and corporations have feuded over what's an acceptable policy and what data can be used to make a hiring or firing decision. In the early 1900s, Henry Ford was known to send investigative teams into the community to check on the morals and hygiene of assembly-line workers. Company towns, popular in the late 1800s and early 1900s, provided a highly

effective way for a boss to monitor virtually every aspect of an employee's life: their sexual orientation, political and religious affiliations, and what activities they engaged in after hours.

Over the years, general standards and legal principles have emerged. Today, it's clear that employers face liability for employees' actions. In fact, the "negligent hiring" tort mandates that an employer can be sued for failing to check adequately the background of a worker. But sudden and rapid advancements in technology have ratcheted up the stakes—pushing the debate squarely into the boardrooms and courtrooms of America. Says David Szwak, a Shreveport, Louisiana-based attorney who specializes in privacy infringement cases: "Unfortunately, in the attempt to improve efficiency and reduce risk, people lose sight of the fact that privacy isn't an abstract principle. When it's abused, people's lives are affected. Inaccurate information, leaked medical records and other breaches can create lifelong problems."

Steering Clear of Data Minefields

In recent years, the data-mining gold rush has reached frenzied proportions. Hundreds of companies now collect data on individuals, and then pass that information on to other database companies and employers interested in finding out who they might be hiring. Problem is, it's often fool's gold, because a lot of data is old, inaccurate or just plain wrong. And that takes an onerous tone if you consider that a report might include information on everything from liens to criminal convictions.

It's not difficult to understand why nearly half of all credit reports contain mistakes, and why the Federal Trade Commission reports more complaints about the accuracy of credit reports than any other consumer issue. Although information is distributed digitally, someone must manually type the information into the system. That is where the majority of the problems lie. A clerk who inverts two digits on a Social Security number or enters the wrong middle initial can unwittingly merge the records of two different people and generate a trail of misinformation. "A person's life can easily be ruined. They may not be able to get a job," says Evan Hendrix, publisher of *Privacy Times* newsletter.

How can an HR department ensure data is accurate and that it isn't opening the door for a lawsuit? First of all, Hendrix suggests that a human resources department obtain as much information as possible directly from the applicant and then let that individual know the company conducts background checks. "Be open and upfront about what you need

and what you're going to check," he suggests. "If someone chooses not to participate in the process, he or she can say so and not have to feel as though his or her privacy has been invaded."

Another option, says Hendrix, is to let an applicant obtain a credit report on his or her own, and then forward it to the company. That way, if there's an error, the applicant can attach a note of explanation and the matter can be investigated further. As an alternative, a growing number of companies are showing credit reports and background checks to applicants who are turned down. Again, if there's an error that might sway the hiring manager to reconsider, the issue can be resolved without conflict. "The main thing," says Shreveport, Louisiana-based privacy infringement attorney David Szwak, "is to be honest and upfront about what you're checking and make sure the applicant has an opportunity to correct mistakes."

Finally, it's crucial to use only the information that's relevant. That sounds simple enough, but many companies don't follow the rule. That means turning to a motor vehicle check or credit report only if it applies to the position an applicant is seeking. That means avoiding other data—perhaps on a tax lien or a divorce settlement—that has no bearing on the position. Says Szwak: "It's important to think about whether you're solving a problem or creating a bigger one by gathering information about a potential hire."

—SG

And there are plenty of horror stories to support his claim. Consider the case of James Russell Wiggins, who took a job with District Cablevision in Washington, D.C. a couple of years back. Six weeks into the new job, which paid nearly twice his previous position at Philip Morris, his boss promptly fired him because a background check from Atlanta-based Equifax noted that a James Wiggins had been previously convicted of cocaine possession. Wiggins protested that the information was wrong, but to no avail. Only later was it discovered that his identity had been confused with a James Ray Wiggins. By the time the dust had settled, the unemployed Wiggins had slapped a $10 million lawsuit against Equifax and Cablevision. The case currently is tied up in the courts. And it's only one of hundreds of such cases.

The widespread availability of such personal information presents vexing challenges—particularly within the human resources field. Dozens of companies provide detailed information—information you think is private—in database form, including motor vehicle records, credit reports, criminal records, telephone usage patterns and insurance coverage. That alone can raise questions about privacy and confidentiality, says Szwak. Factor in the sobering reality that nearly half of all credit reports and background checks include errors, according to a recent Congressional study, and it's easy to see why the James Russell Wiggins of the world are seething mad.

As database companies such as TRW, Equifax and Trans Union clamor to offer ever greater capabilities and one-stop shopping, the stakes inevitably become higher. "There's nothing intrinsically wrong with a company conducting a background check," says Szwak. "If an applicant is informed that the company conducts a check, and the company gathers only applicable information, that takes care of the privacy issue." But, he adds, "Too often, private information is publicly available. There's little or no consideration for what is private and what isn't."

Part of the problem is that no clear guidelines exist as to what should remain private. Is it a good idea for a company to use a credit report as a basis for hiring an accountant or money handler? Most HR professionals would say yes. But some also would argue the report is useful for making value judgments about an applicant's character. That gets trickier. "Using information that doesn't directly relate to the position can open the door to legal challenges," explains Claudia Terrazas, an attorney at the Privacy Right Clearinghouse, part of the University of California, San Diego's Center for Public Interest Law. Ditto the concerns over how motor vehicle records are used.

Now, some are rejecting the idea of credit checks entirely. "It's a gray area," says Sandra Penney, director of team member services for HR at Sovereign Bank, an $8.5 billion, 120-branch institu-

Safeguarding Privacy

Many breaches in privacy and confidentiality occur because companies haven't established adequate security measures or they're simply careless. A formal policy that outlines practices and expectations is a good start, but according to experts, such as Claudia Terrazas, an attorney at the Privacy Right Clearinghouse at the University of California, San Diego's Center for Public Interest Law, "It's important to think through all sorts of situations and realize how easy it is for information to leak out."

One of the most common ways highly confidential information winds up in the wrong hands is that key documents aren't shredded when they're thrown away. Attorneys, insurance companies and others routinely hire "dumpster divers" to sift through mountains of paperwork and find key documents about employees whose cases they're involved with. Thieves also comb through trash to find Social Security numbers and financial records that can be used to fraudulently obtain credit cards and loans in someone else's name. And it isn't just paper-based documents that are a threat. Diskettes, data storage tapes and other forms of magnetic and optical media are just as big a threat. In many instances, it's necessary to completely demagnetize or reformat a disk to expunge the data.

Faxes, telephones and voicemail also pose a threat. If the recipient doesn't have private access to messages, it's possible that others will see or hear them. The Privacy Rights Clearinghouse suggests that anyone sending sensitive data determine if it's acceptable to leave a message on a person's answering machine or fax, verify the accuracy of the phone number and then check transmission reports—or better yet check with the recipient—to ensure the information was received. Cellular and cordless telephones require extra care because anyone with a radio scanner can listen in.

Record keeping is another troublesome area. Two-thirds of all companies use Social Security numbers to identify employees. All too often, the number is also displayed on time cards, parking permits, employee rosters and even mailing labels. But, "Social Security numbers are extremely sensitive, because they can be used for financial fraud and other invasions of privacy," says Don Harris, manager of HR Systems for the New York Times Co. and chair of the International Human Resources Information Management Association.

Harris also points out that employees sometimes pass out private information unwittingly. "If there's an illness or a holiday card list, home addresses and phone numbers may be circulated without checking with the individuals involved. The intent is positive, but someone might perceive it as an invasion of his or her privacy. There's also the possibility that someone outside the organization could get their hands on the information. In many cases, if someone perceives it's an invasion of privacy then their privacy has been invaded."

—SG

"A Checklist of Responsible Information-Handling Practices" can be ordered from the Privacy Rights Clearinghouse, Center for Public Interest Law, 619/298–3396. E-mail: pc@pwa.acusd.edu. Internet Gopher site: gopher.acusd.edu.

tion headquartered in the suburbs of Redding, Pennsylvania. "It can become a quagmire because you wind up with inaccuracies, spouses who are at fault for financial problems, and people who may have had one episode in their lives in which they had a financial problem. So, where do you draw the line on what's acceptable and what isn't?"

Added to the fact that no clear guidelines about what should be private exist, society's definition of privacy itself changes over time. In the 1980s, the idea of testing for illegal drugs met fierce resistance. Civil libertarians attacked the effort and cases streamed into the courts. A decade later, with legality no longer in question thanks to a 1989 Supreme Court ruling, drug testing is used by thousands of companies, and many employees expect—even welcome—testing as a way to keep the workplace free of crime and

problems. Some companies even hire undercover investigators to ferret out drug dealers.

Likewise, as recently as 1992, an employer could use an online databank legally to determine whether or not a job-seeker had ever filed a workers' compensation claim. Not surprisingly, many companies simply had refused to offer a job to anyone who had ever filed a claim. The Americans with Disabilities Act changed that. It limited the use of electronic database searches until after a job offer is made. If an employer then discovers a history of claims, the company can shift that individual into another position that's deemed less risky or—if no safe job is available—rescind the offer.

The debate over legal boundaries continues to escalate. And, increasingly, the battle is spilling out of the

workplace and into the home—as a growing number of companies examine aspects of an individual's life formerly considered private. Indeed, employer advocates argue that a company has the right to hire the best qualified individual for the job. They also insist that companies have a responsibility to find employees who can adhere to quality-control, safety and health-care cost-containment standards. In fact, a 1994 survey by the Society of Human Resource Management found that 77% of human resources professionals endorse a company's right to establish differentials in insurance premiums for employees who smoke.

Critics contend that such thinking raises serious questions about where the line between work and private activities should be drawn. Diet, exercise, hypertension and genetic abnormalities could

Nothing Personal

Not surprisingly, emotions and opinions run high when it comes to employer monitoring practices. Employers generally agree on the basic premises for such oversight activity. Here are the percentages of respondents concurring with the following statements:

EMPLOYEE FAIR-MONITORING PRACTICE	GENERAL PUBLIC	EMPLOYEES	UNION MEMBERS
Procedures for listening-in and standards used to evaluate employee call-handling should be fully explained to employees.	89%	93%	92%
Employees should be told when they are hired for these jobs that supervisors will sometimes listen-in on business calls, so that employees can agree or not agree to work under these procedures.	88%	92%	95%
Employees whose performance is criticized should have access to any notes or recordings made of their calls, and given the opportunity to challenge the supervisor's evaluation.	86%	90%	96%
Problems with employee performance found from listening-in should lead to additional employee training, and only when performance fails to improve should disciplinary action be taken.	82%	87%	90%
Listening-in should be done only on business calls, with separate and unmonitored telephone facilities for employees to make personal calls.	73%	78%	83%
Management should involve employees in setting up standards and procedures for listening-in on business calls.	73%	77%	84%

Source: Privacy & American Business/Harris Survey, 1994.

For More Information

Here are some useful resources for gathering additional information on privacy issues:

Privacy and American Business, Center for Social and Legal Research. Two University Plaza, Suite 414, Hackensack, N.J. 07601. 201/996–1154. Fax: 201/996–1883. Publishes a newsletter examining privacy and business.

The Conference Board. 845 Third Avenue., New York, N.Y. 10022. 212/759–0900. Has various materials relating to privacy in the workplace.

The Privacy Rights Clearinghouse, Center for Public Interest Law, University of California, San Diego. 5998 Alcala Park, San Diego, Calif. 92110. 619/298–3396. E-mail: prc@pwa.acusd.edu. Gopher: gopher.acusd.edu. Offers fact sheets on a wide array of topics relating to privacy and work, including employment background checks and responsible information-handling practices.

Institute for Business and Professional Ethics, DePaul University. 1 East Jackson, Chicago, Ill. 60604. 312/362-6569. E-mail: lpincus@wppost.depaul.edu. Serves as a clearinghouse for information and news on privacy issues.

Privacy Times. P.O. Box 21501, Washington, D.C. 20009. 202/829–3660. A biweekly newsletter that tracks court cases and news on all privacy related topics.   —SG

easily become factors in hiring, they say. Hobbies, such as scuba diving or hang gliding, could disqualify job applicants. Already, some companies have opted to ban the consumption of alcohol after hours, even an occasional glass of wine with dinner. And government is getting into the act too. In 1993, the City of Athens, Georgia, proposed mandatory cholesterol testing for all job applicants—automatically eliminating those who tested in the highest 20%. After a chorus of protests, the idea was scrapped.

The emergence of electronic eyes and ears. Technology and electronic equipment have also transformed the workplace itself. A 1993 study conducted by *Macworld* magazine found that at companies with 1,000 or more employees, 30% of the firms have searched employees' computer files, electronic mail and voicemail. Altogether, it estimated that at least 20 million Americans may be subject to electronic monitoring through their computers. Of course, that doesn't include the use of telephones and video cameras, which could boost the number to 50 million

or more. In addition, data-entry clerks, word-processing clerks and customer-support specialists often work on terminals that allow monitoring for speed, accuracy and time spent working.

It's an issue that's attracting plenty of attention. And no topic seems to be as widely discussed as electronic mail, which has exploded in popularity in recent years. In fact, many workers simply aren't aware their e-mail can be monitored and examined by managers. "They believe it's private and that by deleting a message there's no longer any chance that anyone can see it," says DePaul University's Pincus. "They don't understand that deleted messages can be retrieved; they aren't aware that what they write can be used against them or cost them their jobs—particularly if they have made disparaging remarks against the company or a boss."

Of course any misuse of the e-mail system can be cause for discipline. Penney describes a situation that happened at Sovereign Bank. A year-and-a-half ago, two employees began zapping racy messages to each other over the bank's e-mail system. The notes con-

tained long and often graphic descriptions of various sexual acts. All this came to the company's attention only after the woman sent one of the messages to the bank's top executives by mistake. Ultimately, both were fired for misusing company time and resources, and Sovereign Bank immediately drafted an e-mail policy spelling out that private use of the network wasn't allowed. It also added a brief warning, which pops up anytime an employee composes a new message, that e-mail must be job- or work-related. And the company scans the mail system randomly to ensure compliance. Yet, even with such rules, Sovereign Bank does allow workers to send "brief and expedient" messages of a personal nature. "You certainly don't want to create a Gestapo-type organization," Penney says. "You have to use some common sense."

Voicemail is another hotbed of controversy. Many workers believe the messages they receive are private, and that they alone have access to their voicemail boxes. But that's simply not the case. In many instances, managers have access codes that allow them to listen to messages anywhere on the system. And, depending on how they monitor voicemail, it can lead to enormous problems. In fact, in what appears to be the first voicemail privacy case to hit U.S. courts, the manager of a McDonald's in Elmira, New York, Michael Huffcut, is currently suing the owner of the franchise, Fred Remillard,

> Privacy advocates rarely argue for eliminating all monitoring. The problem, they say, is that many employers approach the issue from the basic viewpoint that workers can't be trusted.

over invasion of privacy. The manager, who had been an employee of McDonald's for more than 20 years, began a romantic relationship with an assistant manager of another McDonald's in a neighboring town. The couple left racy messages on each other's voicemail—part of a system that linked a dozen franchises. At some point, Remillard and another employee retrieved the couple's messages and eventually played them to Huffcut's wife. The $2 million lawsuit is winding through the courts.

Then there's the Internet and the online world—which are supposed to help workers find information and stay up-to-date with news and trends. Unfortunately, unauthorized use of the Internet has forced many companies—such as Unocal Corp. and Rockwell International Corp.—to crack down on a new breed of cyberloafers who surf the World Wide Web, newsgroups and commercial services looking for sports scores, stock quotes and sexually explicit materials. In some cases, companies have found it necessary to track online usage and even monitor what appears on an employee's computer screen at any given moment.

Rules and regulations balance security and privacy. Privacy advocates seldom argue that all monitoring should be eliminated. The problem, they say, is that many employers approach the issue from the basic viewpoint that workers can't be trusted. "The fact is, there are valid reasons

for monitoring the workplace. Quality control, crime and misuse of company resources are all legitimate concerns. But too many companies apply blanket policies without considering the consequences. When you have an environment in which there's a lack of trust on all sides, you wind up in a downward spiral that has negative consequences for everyone," says Pincus.

Attempts to create laws that deal with the emerging technology have largely failed. Retiring U.S. Senator Paul Simon of Illinois continually has pushed for tighter standards that would require companies to alert workers about electronic monitoring, forcing an explanation about how the data is used. His most recent attempt, the Privacy for Consumers and Workers Act, has never been able to gain the necessary support. Although some states also have attempted to deal with the issue, the verdict is still out on how successful these attempts have been. Last December, Illinois Governor Jim Edgar signed a measure that allows an employer to listen in for "educational, training or research purposes." Although the law states that employers must gain permission before eavesdropping, it's unclear whether a one-time warning would suffice or if notice must be given each time listening is planned. And that has unions and worker advocacy groups howling mad.

Law or no law, part of the solution for employers is to develop clear policies and guidelines so that workers know what to expect, says Terrazas. That

means outlining how e-mail and voice-mail should be used, as well as when and how telephones and computers are monitored. "An employer can legally monitor e-mail without notifying employees," she says. "But that doesn't make it right." It's also important to "honor an employee's reasonable expectation to privacy. Videotaping a dressing room or using surveillance devices in a break room can constitute a violation of an employee's rights and create potential legal problems. Providing an employee with a locker and then searching without reasonable cause is damaging," Farrazas adds.

Some companies have gotten the message loud and clear. "It's far better to be proactive and upfront about your policy," says Margaret Phillips, director of human resources, contracts and legal for DHL Systems, the Burlingame, California-based technology services company of DHL Worldwide Express. "It's important to remember that you're dealing with human beings and not ants." Last year, with input from employees, DHL Systems developed a concise but comprehensive policy to deal with privacy issues related to computers and e-mail (see "Policy Matters"). Says Phillips: "You can't have a totalitarian state, but you also can't allow total freedom. The key is striking a balance that's fair for everyone."

Samuel Greengard is a contributing editor to PERSONNEL JOURNAL.

ETHICS FOR HIRE

Laundering images of soiled companies is turning into big business

It's a familiar routine. A scandal erupts at a large corporation. Bowing to public pressure, the board vows to get to the bottom of the mess, hiring a retired government big shot or blue-chip law firm to conduct an "independent" investigation.

Name a major company that's been in trouble recently, and it has probably gone through the drill. On July 1, Bankers Trust Co. released the results of an 18-month investigation into its wayward derivatives group, in which the New York law firm Cadwalader, Wickersham & Taft sharply criticized Bankers for lax internal controls. Mitsubishi Motor Manufacturing of America Ltd. in May asked former Labor Secretary Lynn M. Martin to examine its workplace policies. Her preliminary prescription for combating sexual harassment is due in mid-July. Swedish drug-maker Astra responded to its own sexual harassment scandal two months ago by commissioning a probe by New York law firm Winthrop, Stimson, Putnam & Roberts. On June 26, Astra announced it had fired Chief Executive Lars Bildman and another executive partially as a result of the findings.

A BILLION-DOLLAR INDUSTRY. Not surprisingly, the business of helping companies clean up their acts—a sort of Ethics Inc.—is booming. In June, KPMG Peat Marwick hired Winthrop M. Swenson, a former deputy general counsel at the U.S. Sentencing Commission, to join its new ethics consulting business. Arthur Andersen & Co. started a similar unit last October, choosing author and ex-Harvard University business school professor Barbara Ley Toffler to head its ethics unit. Competitors range from management consultants to law firms and private eye outfits to nonprofits such as the Center for Business Ethics in Waltham, Mass. "When you add it all together, you've probably got a billion-dollar industry," says Carole Basri, a Deloitte & Touche ethics consultant.

One reason: Ethics overhauls can be hugely expensive. Orange & Rockland Utilities in Pearl River, N.Y., found that out. In 1993, after running afoul of regulators for widespread financial improprieties, the small utility hired Price Waterhouse and the New Jersey law firm Stier, Anderson & Malone to do an independent investigation. A team of nearly 50 produced a 1,200-page report at a cost of some $7 million. Consultants charged more than $200,000 to design an internal watchdog program. They recommended opening a two-person ethics office at a cost of $175,000 annually. But Orange & Rockland President Larry S. Brodsky says the investment has paid off: "There's no question that we have regained the confidence of the regulators."

The drill that ethics mavens put companies through varies little. First, the investigation. Then a new corporate code of ethics is generally drafted. Ethics training is beefed up, and a toll-free whistle-blower hot line installed. Then ethics officers are frequently brought aboard to manage the training programs and investigate whistle-blower complaints. That's the template followed by disgraced companies since the defense-industry billing scandals of the 1980s, and there are signs that some recent victims of notoriety are following it. Martin says she plans to advise Mitsubishi to increase anti–sexual harassment training, install a monitoring system to track complaints, and hire consultants to review the new programs. Astra has declared it has "zero tolerance" for sexual harassment, slated training for September, and plans to put in an 800 number for ethics complaints.

But does the typical paint-by-numbers corporate ethical overhaul really wipe out malfeasance? Critics contend

---

HOW TO CONDUCT AN ETHICS OVERHAUL

Here's the step-by-step approach the pros usually advise

STEP ONE Hire an "independent" investigator to issue a report on the misconduct. Credible former government officials are preferred.

STEP TWO Write a new ethics policy. Deliver the document to all company employees with memo from CEO instructing them not to ignore it.

STEP THREE Expand training. Hire consultants, buy more videotapes, start scheduling regular informational sessions on subjects such as sexual harassment, bribery, etc.

STEP FOUR Install a whistle-blowers' hotline. Publicize the phone number to employees and establish and detail fully a systematic complaint procedure.

STEP FIVE Hire a full-time ethics officer. It's this person's job to investigate whistle-blower complaints, supervise training programs, and update the ethics policy.

that many companies are simply looking for window dressing. "They'll have a code of ethics, but there's no effort by senior management to assure middle management that they really mean it," says Swenson of KPMG Peat Marwick. "They'll do enough training to say that they do training, but they won't really analyze their training techniques to see if they are reaching people. They'll have a hot line, but there's no effort to assure people that there won't be retaliation."

A major problem is that many companies install off-the-shelf ethics programs modeled on federal law, rather than one designed to fix specific problems. In 1991, the U.S. Sentencing Commission defined seven elements of "an effective [corporate] program to prevent and detect violations of law." The idea was to ensure that companies with strong compliance programs are not unduly fined because of a lone wrongdoer. But companies now often use the law as a rigid map to design their ethics programs. "The federal sentencing guidelines have taken on a life of their own," worries Arthur Andersen's Toffler.

BUYING TIME. Another frequent source of shortcomings in a probe is the "independent" investigator. Some companies have less than honorable motives in mounting an outside investigation, notes Gerald C. Meyers, former CEO of American Motors Corp. First, the probe instantly produces good publicity. It also buys time with regulators, whose chronic understaffing often makes them willing to consider cutting back their own probe if the company's looks reasonably thorough. And doing even a cursory investigation on its own helps the company's legal position. The reason: An outside attorney's findings are generally privileged. Consequently, a company can get a grip on how badly employees behave and begin assembling its defenses with little risk of disclosure.

But independent investigators have a built-in conflict of interest because they are paid by the company they are supposed to be scrutinizing. And as suppliers of lucrative services to Corporate America, the law and accounting firms that usually run the probes are well aware a reward may be in store if they put the best face on the bad news. "All the biases are to come back with something the company wants to hear," says Meyers. Stanford University Law School professor Ronald J. Gilson contends the success of an independent probe "all depends on the board." . . .

The final dilemma: Even a sincere ethics revamp won't necessarily improve a company's behavior. In a 1995 study, the nonprofit Ethics Resource Center in Washington found that employees at companies with "comprehensive ethics programs" know the law better than workers elsewhere and are more likely to report violations. But they also felt just as much pressure to compromise standards in order to meet business objectives and said they witnessed just as much misconduct.

The lesson: Assuring ethical corporate behavior may be a big business. But it's one that has some maturing to do before it proves its full worth.

By Mike France in New York, with Peter Elstrom in Chicago and Mark Maremont in Boston

If you sit on any nonprofit boards, better read this article.

No more sweetheart deals

Edited by Laura Saunders

DO YOU SIT on the board of a tax-exempt organization such as a charity, a college, a museum or a church? Pay attention.

Congress has just enacted rules that could cost you and your fellow board members up to $10,000 combined if the IRS finds hanky-panky at the nonprofit. They also might bolster private lawsuits holding you responsible for the misdeeds, says Harvey Berger, a tax expert with Grant Thornton in Washington, D.C.

The new rules are in the innocently labeled Taxpayer Bill of Rights II, signed at the end of July. They give the IRS a tactical weapon with which to enforce the long-standing tax law declaring that no one is permitted to get rich off a charity. Until now, the only way the IRS could punish misdeeds at charities was to yank the charity's tax exemption. But doing so punished those the charity was supposed to help more than it did the miscreants.

Under the new rules, trouble starts if the IRS determines that there has been a misdeed with an "excess benefit." It could be a fat salary, a sweetheart contract or an embezzlement. If someone got an excess benefit, the IRS can both fine the recipient 25% of the benefit and demand that the benefit be given back to the charity. If the guilty party doesn't pay the money back, he or she owes twice the excess benefit to Uncle Sam.

Say a board member convinces the president of a college to let the school's insurance contracts to her firm, even though going with a rival would save the school $150,000. In turn, the board member is influential in voting the president a lavish salary, perhaps $200,000 higher than the norm at comparable universities. The IRS could force the repayment of both the $150,000 and the $200,000.

There are allegations, recently aired at hearings conducted by New York State authorities, that just such logrolling infected the management of Adelphi University in Garden City. The university insists that all the arrangements were proper. Maybe they were, but there's no question that the new rules, had they been in place, would have given the board far more reason to be circumspect.

What if a charity helped out a board member or an officer via a fringe benefit—for example, by picking up $750 of the officer's personal parking tickets? The IRS could call the payment an excess benefit, force repayment and levy a $188 fine. Once caught, the charity would not have the option of retroactively including the $750 in the officer's salary. To protect him from the penalty, it would have to have included the reimbursement on his original W-2.

What about directors who sit still for this kind of mischief? They can be fined a collective $10,000, even if they didn't profit. "This is a wake-up call to board members," says Berger.

So wake up, and make sure your nonprofit is behaving itself. The law is retroactive to Sept. 13, 1995.

—L.S.

Tapping Your Hidden Assets

If knowledge is power, it's hard to overestimate the value of the data buried in a company's operational systems. With a data warehouse, managers can extract that ore and refine it.

Edward Teach

Edward Teach is a senior editor at CFO.

The data gathering resumes every night shortly after 9:00 EST, when Sears, Roebuck and Co. retail stores on the East Coast start locking their doors. During the next six hours, from Sears stores across the country, the record of every point-of-sale transaction on that day—every Craftsman hammer sold, every Diehard battery, every Kenmore vacuum cleaner—will flow over leased network lines into three mainframe computers in Ohio, Illinois, and Texas. From there, the data will be dispatched to an NCR 3600 massively parallel processing computer in Columbus, Ohio. The machine's 250 processors and 864 disks power one of the world's largest commercial data warehouses: a Teradata database containing 1.8 trillion bytes, or terabytes, of sales information. Since May 1995, Sears has posted to the warehouse every sales transaction going back to December 1, 1993—currently averaging 1.5 million a day—from its more than 3,000 domestic retail locations.

"By 6:00 A.M. the next day, we've captured every sales transaction from every retail location," says Steven Junk, vice president for retail systems. Soon, sales data will begin flowing out—this time in small, highly selective bursts—to PCs on a local area network in Sears's Hoffman Estates, Illinois, store support office, where about 1,500 buyers, merchandisers, replenishers, inventory managers, and marketing analysts can begin poring over the numbers. Each PC is equipped with a custom-built software application that enables users to extract data from the warehouse and analyze it in any number of ways. If it's Monday, for instance, a merchandiser can ascertain in seconds not just how many of the

Trader Bay polo shirts advertised in Sunday's newspaper circular were sold, but where they were sold, in what color, and in what size. Were knit shirts a hit in the Northeast? Fresh shipments can be dispatched immediately to regional stores.

"User access to the data is real-time," says Junk. "For more complex queries, the terminal isn't tied up; you can launch the query and do other things until [the answer] comes back in three or four minutes."

Sears supplies a spectacular example of a significant trend in information management: skyrocketing demand for data warehouses. Surveys by Meta Group Inc., based in Stamford, Connecticut, indicate that 80 percent of *Fortune* 2,000 companies are building data warehouses. Another Stamford-based information technology advisory firm, Gartner Group, put the size of the market at year-end 1994 (exclusive of business intelligence software) at $1.5 billion, and expects it to approach $7 billion by 1999.

A horde of data warehouse vendors, from niche players to industry giants, is competing fiercely for clients. They offer a constellation of open-system technologies: software that siphons and transforms data from legacy systems, portable relational database management systems, increasingly powerful computers, sophisticated business intelligence software.

Why are companies flocking to data warehouses? Because data, stored in various operational and transaction-processing systems, is one of a company's most valuable assets—but only if it can be tapped and analyzed. That used to be a big *if*. Typically, ad hoc requests

"The average $1 billion company has 10 A/P systems, 13 billing systems, 12 payroll systems," says David Axson. A data warehouse is a step toward integrating legacy systems, and can provide common data across business processes.

for information were sent to an IS middleman, one of the few who had the programming skills to extract data from relevant data stores. After a week or so, the information would come back, usually printed on reams of green-bar paper. The data, which were old to begin with, then had to be rekeyed into spreadsheets for analysis. In this environment, says Junk, fulfilling complex requests "wasn't totally impossible—just unrealistic."

No longer. When up-to-date information about a company's products, customers, and suppliers is stored in a data warehouse, business users have immediate, direct access to the numbers they want when they want, not on some preestablished schedule. Thanks to powerful, intuitive analytic software, users don't need technical expertise—or IS middlemen, who retreat to administrative chores and maintenance. Because they are designed exclusively for decision support, warehouses are robust: like Sears's, they can support many concurrent users without noticeable loss of performance, At the same time, demand to access OLTP (on-line transaction processing) data stores is greatly reduced.

While the market phenomenon is new, data warehousing isn't. In the late 1980s, a few companies built large repositories of historical data for decision support. But the technologies available then were expensive, proprietary, and limited; warehousing was reserved for companies that could afford to spend $30 million on a project. Since then, costs have come down enormously, thanks to the ever-diminishing price of computer processing power and digital storage. According to Meta Group, the bill for a typical warehouse containing hundreds of gigabytes of data now ranges anywhere from $1 million to $3 million, including software, hardware, and consulting fees.

Key Benefits

A data warehouse enables cross-marketing on a previously unimaginable scale, which is why the biggest users have been financial services firms, insurers, telecommunications companies, and retailers. *How many New Yorkers buy homeowners' insurance from us? Let's offer them auto policies, priced cheap.*

But a data warehouse can provide at least four kinds of benefits to any type of company:

OPERATIONAL. Sales managers can better understand customer profiles; marketers can gain insight into product mix; financial analysts can dissect contribution margin.

TACTICAL. By centralizing records of what a company buys, a warehouse can give purchasing managers the needed leverage to negotiate better prices.

STRATEGIC. A data warehouse enables managers to

respond quickly to changes in a market or customer base. Should a retailer open a new store in a certain suburb, or a utility build a new generation facility? What will a university's freshman class look like in five years?

STANDARDIZATION. "The average $1 billion company has 10 A/P systems, 13 billing systems, 12 payroll systems," says David Axson, vice president of The Hackett Group, in Hudson, Ohio. "There are old computers and inconsistent data definitions—the systems don't talk to each other." Acquisitions and mergers may complicate the picture. A data warehouse, says Axson, is a step toward integrating and updating legacy systems, and can provide a semblance of common data across business processes.

"Since we populate our warehouse [with data] from old systems—some of them over 30 years old—the mere fact that we can integrate information from disparate systems is in itself a big step forward," says Pete Welbrock, senior business analyst in the IS group at Purina Mills Inc., a $1 billion–plus animal feed company based in St. Louis. In contrast to Sears's terabyte behemoth, Purina Mills's warehouse contains just 10 gigabytes of manufacturing, marketing, sales, and financial information. That's enough, however, for 140 users at 56 plants to forecast production to month-end, analyze sales and marketing data, and play out what-if pricing and product-mix scenarios.

What Goes In, Comes Out

The heart of the data warehouse is the database management system, from vendors such as IBM, Informix, NCR, Oracle, Red Brick, Software AG, and Sybase. The larger the database, the more computing power is needed. So-called symmetric multiprocessing servers are the usual platform for large warehouses. North of 500 gigabytes, the computing technology of choice is massively parallel processing (MPP). MPP machines divvy up queries among hundreds of processors, enabling terabyte databases to be scanned quickly. These computers aren't cheap; the price of the NCR 3600 that Sears uses begins at $1 million.

Two of the biggest headaches in building a data warehouse are deciding what information to put in it and how to get it there. One approach is simply to dump in as much data as possible. But that brute-force method can be costly and inefficient; experts generally recommend a selective approach. "Look at the key drivers of your business," says AXSON. "If your goals are to be the best in your market, to have the best product at the lowest price, then define information to measure your performance against those objectives. Then ask: Where in your business processes are those data?"

Simply identifying the sources of data can be a difficult,

The sheer volume of mistakes and inconsistencies in a company's operational data—for example, 100 versions of a customer name—may come as a shock to warehouse builders.

time-consuming task, says Nancy Mullen, associate partner, technology core competence, at Andersen Consulting LLP in Northbrook, Illinois. For one thing, it's commonly estimated that more than 70 percent of corporate data reside in legacy systems' nonrelational databases. Also, "the data in operational systems is not well documented," adds Mullen. "It may be 15 years old, and the people who built those systems may have left the company years ago."

Once the information sources have been located, data must be extracted, cleansed, and transformed. This is by far the most time-consuming phase in building a warehouse—and the most critical phase, too. Unless information is physically structured in consistent fashion, with certified sources and standardized definitions, a warehouse will simply propagate corrupt data more efficiently.

(Experts recommend data hygiene not just at the warehouse level, but at the source. However, it can take *years* for a large company to cleanse its operational systems.)

The sheer volume of mistakes and inconsistencies in a company's operational data—for example, 100 different versions of a customer name—may come as a shock. But semantic confusion must be addressed as well. How, exactly, should the various units of a company define total sales, or a price elasticity algorithm? "Distribution might say we had a great quarter," says Steve Cranford, partner in charge of the data warehousing practice at KPMG Peat Marwick LLP in Radnor, Pennsylvania. "Sales might say the opposite. If you look at their data, both might be right. The true answer might be that the company broke even for the quarter. That's why you have

Plumbing the Data

Moen Inc., a $700 million maker of faucets and plumbing supplies based in North Olmsted, Ohio, uses its data warehouse to plumb the depths of contribution margin. Updated on a daily basis, the warehouse contains 20 gigabytes of detailed sales information dating from 1993, according to Mark Zozulia, manager of information resource management. About 60 users from sales, finance, and marketing have access to the warehouse.

"We can now look at our variable selling expenses," says Zozulia. "Before, you'd see just customer profitability down to a standard margin line. Now, you can drill down and see true contribution margin by product, by customer, by channel."

Moen's data warehouse is entirely home grown, designed and built by a 15-person cross-functional team that included one database administrator and two senior programmers. Started in January 1995, the warehouse was in production six months later. Costs to date: $400,000 for the Oracle 7.1 database, HP 9000 Unix box, communications software,

and business intelligence software (Moen wrote its own extraction software); $350,000 to date for personnel costs.

"There was never a stated ROI on this project," comments Gary T. Gajewski, vice president of finance. "This was not a hard-cost project, but more of an infrastructure step." The project goals were to help Moen understand the market better, enhance the quality of its data, and improve access to information. "We did not want to expose ourselves to undue risk," says Gajewski. "We started small with nonsensitive information—sales history first. We're not going to close our books with [the warehouse]."

Analysts access Moen's warehouse with two Cognos front-end tools. One, Impromptu, is an ad hoc query tool that enables users to point and click through an interface and get direct access to detail-level information. The other, PowerPlay, is OLAP software, working with summarized data on a multidimensional database that is populated from the warehouse. "We create aggregate-style tables—people like to look at

information in spread-sheet style," comments Zozulia. "We take monthly data and roll it up by part number to populate PowePlay." For Moen executives like Gajewski, the Power-Play tool provides a summary-information briefing book.

Currently in progress is a financial modeling project. By this fall, Moen should be drawing data from the general ledger and other sources to support budgeting and forecasting on the warehouse. "At a lot of companies, finance gets the budgets in, puts them in PCs, rolls them up, and manages [the result]," says Bill Heitman, director of financial planning and analysis. "We want to let the various areas responsible for managing the costs input that information. Then, at budget time, they can change it to their heart's content. We also want to include our entire price waterfall information on this system—from list price all the way down to what the customer pays."

Heitman says the warehouse pays off in two ways: "Not only do we have information we didn't have before, we now have access we didn't have before."—E.T.

to define total sales, source the information from the appropriate systems, and put business rules around it."

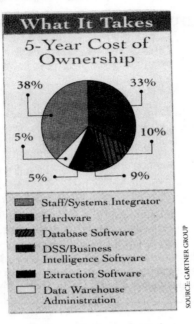

What It Takes

5-Year Cost of Ownership

38%   33%

5%   10%

5%   9%

SOURCE: GARTNER GROUP

- Staff/Systems Integrator
- Hardware
- Database Software
- DSS/Business Intelligence Software
- Extraction Software
- Data Warehouse Administration

Budget profile for an initial 50GB data warehouse serving two business areas, growing to 250GB and used by many areas after five years.

Minding the Metadata

Defining what constitutes a trade was paramount in establishing Fidelity Investments's financial data warehouse, says Paul A. Burmeister, vice president, financial systems and processing, at parent FMR Corp. in Boston. "At the retail level, if a customer wants to buy 1,000 shares of ABC Co., that may count as one trade, but it may be more than one trade for the unit [Fidelity Capital Markets] that actually has to execute the trade," he says. "You have to be very specific about what kinds of trades you're talking about." Definitions must be given not only in narrative terms, but in system terms—"which lines of code, which source systems."

Fidelity's 6 gigabyte financial warehouse was built to provide consistent internal reporting statistics for the company's many business units. To ensure the information is general-ledger quality, Fidelity established a data certification process, "by which you know where the data comes from, that it meets criteria for definition and accuracy, that it is verifiable from another source," says Burmeister. That process resulted in creation of a metadata layer, a fully automated system that updates which data are in the warehouse, where it came from (by file name and type), how it is calculated, and who uses the data. "We are preoccupied with certification and metadata," Burmeister says. "If someone isn't, God help them."

Basically an online information catalog, metadata is "the most important, and most difficult, thing you can possibly build when you're building a data warehouse," says Karen Rubenstrunk, director, application delivery

services, at Meta Group. Imagine a million-volume research library without a card catalog, and you've grasped the significance of metadata.

The data in a warehouse are usually a blend of atomic and summarized data. Warehouse consultants like to see an emphasis on the former, since summarized data limit depth of analysis. "Most departmental or functional warehouses have a high level of aggregation [in their data]," says Rubenstrunk. "It's easier to deal with." The problem is, at some point a business user may want to know, say, exactly which stores sold how many red Extralite shoes, and when they sold them.

How much data a warehouse should contain depends on user need. "We keep a whole lot of history, but only in the sense that we can help decisions going forward," says Sears's Junk. "The warehouse isn't a report card." Five years of sales history allows analysts to identify longer-term trends, but 10 years' worth might contain a great deal of irrelevant information. User need also dictates how often data are updated: monthly, weekly, daily—even, in the case of one fast-food chain, hourly.

Hot Links, OLAP, and Data Mining

The component of a data warehouse that matters most to end users is business intelligence software (BIS)—report writers, ad hoc query tools, multidimensional-analysis software. Installed on PCs or servers and generally priced from $500 to $1,000 a seat, such software enables users to tap data from the warehouse, format it, and analyze it. All BIS tools offer intuitive, easy-to-use interfaces, ranging from multidimensional databases accessed through spreadsheets to point-and-click tools with Windows-like screens, 3-D graphics, and "hot links" that invite users to drill further down into the data. A partial list of vendors includes Arbor Software, Business Objects, Cognos, Comshare, Dimensional Insight, Hyperion, MicroStrategy, Oracle, Pilot, Platinum Technology, and SAS Institute.

Currently the rage are so-called on-line analytical processing, or OLAP, tools (see "Spreadsheets on Steroids," November 1995). Unlike simple query and reporting tools, OLAP software allows users to analyze data in multiple dimensions: *How many lawn mowers did we sell in the Midwest in the third quarters of 1993, 1994, and 1995, and which sales reps sold the most?*

BIS tools are user-driven: a query is defined and launched. By contrast, another type of software, data mining tools, employs outer-limits techniques such as neural nets, decision trees, and "smart agents" to automatically search raw data for significant patterns and relationships. Data mining has obvious marketing applications—experts like to cite the case of the supermarket chain that discovered an unexpected affinity between diapers and beer—but it has a variety of other potential uses, such as detecting fraud or product defects.

All Hype Aside

Any company planning a data warehouse needs to consider this possibility: What if we spend $1 million on a warehouse—and no one uses it? The surest road to fiasco is to build a warehouse that isn't driven by an immediate, **identifiable business need. Who will the end-users be? What questions will they ask?**

"The 'Battlestar Galactica' model is fundamentally flawed," charges Donald DePalma of Forrester Research. "By the time you get there, the enterprise has changed."

Constantly augmented and updated, a data warehouse is always a work in progress; a process, not a finished product. The guiding principles are *flexibility* and *scalability*. Start small, say experts, with a pilot project—a "data mart" that serves a specific business unit or application. According to Karen Rubenstrunk of Meta Group, pilot projects generally cost between $50,000 and $200,000, depending on size (usually up to 15 gigabytes).

"Build the first data mart in a way that the second will be easy," says Andersen's Mullen. "Make sure the elements are sturdy enough to support increases in size and demand. I could use Microsoft Access to build my first one, if I wanted to have just six users. But then if I wanted to roll that out to regional sales managers—now I wish I had used Oracle."

Kevin Strange, research director at Gartner Group, advises against building multiple stand-alone data marts, as opposed to data marts that feed from a central warehouse. His favorite cautionary tale concerns an insurer that built separate data marts for its six lines of business—thus replicating the long-discredited "stovepipe" information model. The marts meet the insurer's tactical day-to-day needs, but because they aren't integrated, the insurer misses opportunities for cross-marketing.

True data warehousing "is like high-school sex—lots of people are talking about it, but few people are really doing it," asserts Strange. Even when starting small, Strange says, companies should build their warehouses with an architecture capable of serving a cross-functional, enterprise rollout. "Model the subject area thoroughly, so that you have all the data elements that all the business areas who will be plugging in will need," he advises.

Not every company is interested in the sort of cathedral-building an enterprise data warehouse requires.

Banking on the Warehouse

When Fleet Financial Group Inc.'s data warehouse for consumer assets came on line in 1992, it contained barely 2 gigabytes of data. "It was a current snapshot only, with no trended information," recalls Douglas Jacomine, systems officer, Fleet Services Corp. Four years later, the warehouse bursts with 330 gigabytes of account-level information on all Fleet consumer assets portfolios—credit cards, installment loans, first mortgages, equity loans. "We have 4 million account records in the current snapshot, and 90 million account records in three-year trended information," says Jacomine.

The nation's 11th-largest commercial bank uses the warehouse to support both day-to-day portfolio analysis and longer-term risk analysis and corporate strategizing. From 12 sites in New England, about 50 work stations equipped with Business Objects analytic software connect to the warehouse's Oracle Rdb database, which resides on a symmetric multi-processing DEC Alpha 8200 server. Eight full-time IS employees support the warehouse, with the part-time help of two or three consultants. Jacomine won't say how much it cost to put the warehouse together, but says Fleet is more than satisfied with its return on investment.

For example, when the Boston-based bank undertook a massive reorganization effort three years ago, "it was important to turn retrospectively on our business and get detailed reports," says Jacomine. Since trend analysis wasn't supported by the bank's legacy systems, five man-months of developer time were required to supply the deposits side of Fleet's business with the information it needed for the reorganization. "In the consumer assets world, we spent zero hours of developer time," says Jacomine. "[Analysts] were able to determine all the information they needed from the warehouse."

The data warehouse saves money in other areas as well. "We were spending over $300,000 a year on a third-party service to inquire on our credit card portfolios," says Jacomine. The warehouse has since replaced that service, and eventually will save Fleet about $750,000 a year by eliminating the need for such third-party providers.

To would-be warehousers, Jacomine recommends starting small. "Avoid the Big Bang," he warns. The concept should first be tested and proved on the business-unit level, addressing specific problems. And the warehouse better be scalable. Users will quickly demand more data as they learn what the warehouse enables them to do—such as, in Fleet's case, segregating portfolios by delinquencies and tracking them over time—while other units will want in on the action. "Every 18 months we're in crisis mode," jokes Jacomine.

Meanwhile, Fleet's deposits side will have its day; its warehouse should be in production sometime in 1997.—E.T.

Sara Lee Corp., the Chicago-based food and consumer goods giant, is content to let its more than 20 major divisions pursue data warehousing independently, says Jerry Matsumoto, executive director of information technology. "We are a very diverse, autonomously managed group of companies," he points out. "Our major divisions are all involved in different levels of information warehousing."

Nor does everyone think building an enterprise warehouse is the best solution. "The 'Battlestar Galactica' model is fundamentally flawed," avers Donald A. DePalma, senior analyst at Forrester Research Inc., in Cambridge, Massachusetts. "By the time you get there, the enterprise has changed." He thinks companies should concentrate on building targeted data marts for the specific informational needs of specific user groups. A data mart is still a warehouse, DePalma says; "it's just taken that three-year Rebuild The Universe part out of it."

What does the future hold for data warehousing? Both the very large—Gartner Group foresees 100 terabyte warehouses by the year 2000—and the relatively small, as vendors introduce low-cost warehouse solutions designed especially for data marts. Companies will routinely give suppliers and even customers access to their warehouses to track inventories, shipments, and order status. The Internet should accelerate this trend, as BIS vendors develop browser-friendly versions of their software.

Perhaps most intriguing is the possibility that companies will use data warehouses to drive operational systems. That's already on the drawing board at Sears.

"Our vision is to use this warehouse as the back end of our key operational systems," says Steve Junk. "In a couple of years, our price management system will be running against the same data elements in the warehouse. If someone's on the warehouse and wants to change a price, he'll be able to hit one key—and the change will flow to 28,000 registers." In five years, says Junk, all of Sears's transaction-processing systems will be based on the data structure established for the warehouse.

At that point, the company might consider updating the old slogan: Sears Really Does Have Everything.

How Job Seekers Should Approach The New Job Market

From three sets of annual surveys, data emerge about a real gap between the skills job seekers present and those that employers want—a gap career counselors can close.

William T. Mangum

William T. Mangum *is president of the Thomas Mangum Company, an executive search company founded in 1964. He has had extensive experience in executive search at all levels of the organization structure, as well as in work-force planning and organization development.*

Mr. Mangum is author of two books on job hunting and the job market, both published in 1995. They are 99 Minutes to Your Ideal Job *(John Wiley & Sons) and* The Job Search Work Book, A companion to 99 Minutes *(TMI Publications).*

Career counselors and job seekers share a substantial common need to learn about and adapt to a dramatically changed job market. It is a job market that over recent years has shifted from a job hunters' market to an employers' market, with a substantial tilt in the employers' favor. Equally important, the common goal of both career counselors and job seekers today includes two new factors: how to 1) develop and gain employer interest (obtain an interview) and 2) outshine the competition to obtain an offer in a difficult and competitive job market that shows few signs of changing. For some job hunters, this market—which they often describe as "lean and mean"—requires that they enhance both their job skills and job-hunting skills to conclude a successful job search. It is a demanding challenge for both job hunter and job counselor.

The 1996 job market continues to limp along, five years after the end of the 1990/91 recession, at nearly half the pace of previous recoveries. It has been especially difficult for new college graduates competing for fewer positions in an environment with an abundance of experienced talent available from continual downsizing. Major layoffs and reductions continue to rock a job market that seems unable to gather steam. The year 1996 began with the biggest one-month (January) binge of layoffs in two years, indicating the market continues to be tight and highly competitive for job seekers.

Data provided by a series of job market surveys since 1993 indicate job hunters today face greater changes and challenges than most have ever experienced in their careers (see Three Survey Series). The 1995 surveys indicate that 82 percent of job seekers find their job-search efforts have been "more difficult" or "substantially more difficult" than they had anticipated. Although the search has become somewhat easier than it was three years ago, it still takes a good deal of effort and time to get an offer (Figure 1).

Perception Gaps

More importantly, the job market surveys show a major disparity (candidate/employers skills gap) between what employers seek today versus what job seekers think employers want. In addition, employers are also seeking broader and greater skill levels from job hunters who often are unaccustomed to extensive competition and greater skill-level demands. In fact, today's job market provides many hiring employers with an abundance of talent to choose from, a situation that often allows them the luxury of seeking individuals with advanced skill levels not sought in prior years.

Not only are employers seeking top-notch basic skills, but extra skills as well, often with little relationship to

From *Journal of Career Planning & Employment*, Summer 1996, pp. 33-35, 60-61. © 1996 by the National Association of Colleges and Employers. Reprinted by permission.

Figure 1

Average Time to Find a Job and Difficulty of Job Search

Time/Difficulty	Job Hunters' Survey		
	1995	1994	1993
Number of months to find a new job	6.3	6.3	7.7
Number of contacts to obtain an interview	47.0	24.0	89.0
Number of contacts to obtain an offer	62.0	121.0	192.0
Number of interviews per month	4.0	4.4	3.1
Number of interviews required to obtain an offer	8.0	8.6	12.6

any academic program. For recent college graduates, as with all job seekers, the increased emphasis by employers on additional skill demands, such as presentation skills and being a team player, adds a new dimension of concern. Thus, career counselors have a big task ahead in advising job hunters of what is required today to be successful in a highly competitive job market offering fewer opportunities.

A close review of the 1995 survey results provides information for counselors and job seekers on the conditions with which they must deal in the 1996/97 job market. These current results show little difference from earlier ones that highlighted two significant facts in particular: one, that employers are placing an increased emphasis on broader and keener skills (e.g. cross-functional, presentation, communication, and personal computer); and two, that many job-hunting techniques used prior to 1991 no longer work (e.g. unsolicited resumes, unfocused resumes, and unprepared presentations). The data in Figures 2 and 3 provide a comparison of what employers (hiring managers and human resources professionals) cite as the greatest shortcomings of job hunters, versus what job hunters describe as the reasons for their job-search difficulties.

Note that the hiring managers and human relations personnel agree as to the three most prevalent shortcomings of job hunters, although they rank them in different orders. These three items—presentation skills, communications skills, and unrealistic expectations—have remained in the top three rankings for three years in four separate surveys conducted by the author.

Seldom do job hunters show in their survey responses, in telephone conversations, in interviews, or in group discussions, that skills (or the lack of skills) or unrealistic expectations are the reasons for their job-search difficulties. The absence of those specific responses by job seekers clearly show they have not gotten the message from employers *even though these skills have been in demand for years.* When this message goes unacknowledged and is combined with the current trend of employers using more stringent screening procedures—including placing greater emphases on cross-functional skills and presentation/communication skills—the candidate/employer skills gap appears even wider than it really is.

Who's to Tell Them?

With the current popular fix on "lean and mean" operations by American business management, it becomes understandable that job seekers are not getting the message about the candidate/employer skills gap that exists.[1] Most employers are operating at minimum staff levels and often at maximum working hours, and so, management is overloaded with work. Thus, hiring managers—and particularly human resource personnel—working with smaller or nonexistent staff, today have little time to advise or educate job seekers on their shortcomings. Such time is often just not available where the luxuries of providing even preliminary skill/job guidance have vanished into an overloaded, overworked job environment where many managers struggle just to keep pace with their major responsibilities.

As an end result, employers pay dearly for the large number of job hunters they must sift through who are "out of sync" or struggling in today's dramatically changed job market. The cost for employers involves the time to deal with an increasingly larger base of marginal candidates in their selection process with the procedures strained to the maximum in screening excessive numbers of unqualified candidates. In this process most employers find they do not have even the brief time required to help make their task easier by briefing candidates on the skills required. Thus, the ongoing cycle of inadequately advised or ill-equipped job hunters feeds on itself, resulting in tremendous unproductivity for both employers and job hunters.

Survey results from all three surveys and for all three sequential years have been very consistent. For the last three years, responses to questions asking about the most wanted skills and experience have placed personal computer skills in the top ranking twice and in the number two spot once (Figure 4). The item "being a team player" ranked as number three for the last two years.

Since most companies in the 1996 job market enjoy an employer's hiring market with an abundance of quality candidates, it is not difficult to understand why an added emphasis on presentation skills, communication skills, and realistic expectations exists. The fact that these three key areas have been identified for three consecutive years by the surveys quoted here, indicates the extent the job market has shifted since the 1990/91 recession. Prior to 1990, these items were not singled out in a market where job seekers often called the shots. However, the recent surveys found but few job seekers who express the concern that their expectations are often viewed by employers as unrealistic, and fewer still who see it as a rejection factor.

A Common Goal

Ultimately the responsibility for closing the candidate/employer skills gap falls to the job hunter with the assistance of a knowledgeable career counselor, external recruiter, search company, or other career or placement agent. Today, these professionals find themselves advising or counseling job hunters on a dramatically changed job market and the need for the broader

Figure 2 _____

Job Hunters' Greatest Shortcomings

Per Hiring Managers*

1. Poor communication skills
2. Poor presentation skills
3. Unrealistic expectations
4. Weak leadership skills
5. Lack of assertiveness

6. Poor management competency
7. Lack of cross functional skills
8. Negative attitude
9. Poor job knowledge
10. Spotty job history

Per Human Resources Personnel**

1. Unrealistic expectations
2. Poor communications skills
3. Poor presentation skills
4. Spotty job history
5. Inadequate job knowledge

6. Unexplained gaps in work history
7. Inadequate management competence
8. Poor leadership
9. Lack social skills
10. Negative attitude

  * Hiring Managers' Survey, 1995
 ** Employers' Survey of HR Personnel, 1994

Figure 4 _____

Skills and Experience in Demand

Per Hiring Managers*

1. Computer skills (PC)
2. Cross-functional skills
3. Being a team player
4. Leadership
5. Communication skills
6. Sales ability
7. Presentation skills
8. Being a risk taker

Per Human Resources Personnel*

1. Personal computer skills
2. Industry specific skills
3. Participative management style
4. Hands-on experience
5. Visionary thinking
6. Innovative/risk taking
7. Strategic planning
8. Cross-functional skills

  * Hiring Managers' Survey, 1995
 ** Employers' Survey of HR Personnel, 1994

and greater skills employers now seek. This is a tough challenge for those who advise discouraged job hunters.

These job market conditions have existed since at least 1991 and may well continue into the 21st century. It's a far cry from the "easy-to-find" job era of the 1960s, '70s, and '80s, and many job hunters haven't recognized the conceptual change to the "hard-to-find" era of the '90s. Many feel disheartened as they deal with the results of corporate restructuring and the unprecedented layoff carnage in the midst of a real economic recovery. In effect, they share a unique and difficult common goal with job counselors—that of learning how to effectively and successfully work today's unique job market, the most highly competitive and demanding of the 20th century.

Downsizing emerged in the late 1980s, and the surveys confirm that this activity continues today as a major operational method by which companies cut costs to become more competitive. Its effect on the job market has been critical. As shown in Figure 5, downsizing and layoffs were cited by job seekers as the major causes of their unemployment, causes that were cited as prominent in the 1993 and 1994 surveys as well.

Employers Need...

Today, the message for job and career counselors and job seekers is that employers are seeking a broader skills base than ever before, one that includes not only basic industry-specific skills and hands-on experience, but one with an added emphasis on four "extra" skills:

1. Personal computer skills
2. Cross-functional skills
3. Communication skills
4. Presentation skills.

Employers are also seeking "multi-dimensional" skills that today are often mandatory for many positions. These types of skills, such as being a team player and having a participative management style, are often essential now for being considered for many positions, from entry- level to experienced professional. The most important of these, as shown by the surveys, are:

- Team player
- Participative management style
- Being a risk taker
- Being innovative

Figure 3 _____

Reasons for Job-Search Difficulties

1. Lack of response
2. Limited number of jobs available
3. Negative employer attitude
4. Overqualified
5. Waiting for employer decision
6. Difficult to gain employer interest, even though qualified
7. No jobs available
8. Many candidates applying for same position

  —From Job Hunters' Survey, 1995

□ Visionary thinking
□ Sales ability
□ Strategic planning
□ Leadership.

Employers Suggest..

Job counselors and job hunters will also find most useful the guidelines employers and, more specifically, hiring managers have provided for job hunters in answer to the surveys' question: What suggestions would you provide for job hunters to better prepare for the increasingly competitive and challenging job market?[2] The 10 most frequently cited are:

□ Do research and homework on company.
□ Improve and increase skills.
□ Know the job market and keep current with it.
□ Develop good communication and presentation skills.
□ Be prepared for the interview.
□ Be computer literate.
□ Have realistic expectations.
□ Network, and find and nourish a mentor.
□ Maintain a positive attitude, demonstrate initiative, be persistent.
□ Focus your approach on specific employer needs.

Problem/Solution

Multiple sources of job market data gathered from around the country through telephone conversations and interviews with various job-concerned individuals and groups and from the

Figure 5. _____

Job Seekers' Most Frequently Cited Reason For Leaving Last Job

1. Downsizing
2. Layoffs
3. Merger/Acquisition
4. Retirement
5. Restructuring
6. Plant moved

—From Job Hunters' Surveys, 1993 to 1995.

surveys' responses indicate persuasively that the prime problem of job hunters today is with their adjustment to today's competitive, difficult, and dramatically changed job market. To find their proper places in the work force, they must first be aware of these changes, and then acquire the basic up-to-date skills required plus the additional skills now needed to compete effectively for selected job openings. They then should prepare as follows: 1) Develop a comprehensive job-search plan tailored to their skills, experience, and today's job market needs; 2) do their research and homework on the companies they're interested in; 3) focus on how their job skills relate to the specific employer by citing relevant experience; and 4) prepare well for their interviews.

The candidate/employer skills gap of what many job hunters perceive employers seek today, versus the reality of what employers now require, is

real. Thus, a major challenge exists for job counselors, advisers, and agents to assist their job-hunting clients on how to be winners in today's lean job market. These "teachers" now have a good start in this process, knowing about the significant and reliable time-sensitive information taken from the three surveys reported on here. The next step, of course, is to act upon it, making sure their clients, whether experienced, entry-level, or most particularly, freshmen who are just beginning to work toward postgraduate employment—making sure they move into the job search well prepared in the skills and attitudes the employers are buying.

References

[1] Mangum, William T. *99 Minutes to Your Ideal Job.* New York, NY: John Wiley & Sons, 1995.
[2] Mangum. Chapter 3.

Sample Survey Topics*

1. Average time to find a job and difficulty of job search.
   a. Number of months to find a job.
   b. Number of contacts to obtain an interview and offer.
2. Reasons for job-search difficulty.
3. Job market conditions.
4. New trends in salary and responsibility levels.
5. Most and least effective sources of job leads/interviews.
6. Effective company contact sources.
7. Personal traits for job-search success.
8. Hiring manager interview/selection criteria skills list.
9. Extent and form of discrimination experienced.
10. Employer hiring activity and business strategy.
11. Areas employers are having the greatest difficulty recruiting qualified candidates.
12. The most effective recruiting sources for experienced hires.
13. How employers have modified their selection procedures to adapt to the changing work force and business conditions.
14. Resume comments and suggestions.
15. Effectiveness of unsolicited resumes.

*Excerpted from the complete list of 70 survey questions and answers in *99 Minutes to Your Ideal Job.*

Three Survey Series, 1993 to 1995

For all the surveys reported on here, the majority of the answers to the questions were stated subjectively in narrative form rather than checked from a preselected list of items, giving great credence to the importance these points play in the employers' selection processes. Also, the fact that the surveys were conducted among three different groups of job-concerned personnel, and that the groups all show similar top 10 items in response to similar questions, with the same top three items recurring consistently, go a long way to substantiating both the validity and value of the information gathered.

- **Job Hunters' Surveys**
  Job Hunter's Questionnaire for executive, management, professional, and technical personnel, 1993, 1994, and 1995. Thomas Mangum Company.
  Conducted nationwide of some 6,000 active job hunters; response rates for successive years were 27, 20, and 22 percent, respectively.

- **Hiring Manager Surveys**
  Hiring Managers Questionnaire, 1994 and 1995. Thomas Mangum Company.
  Conducted nationwide of some 4,000 hiring managers; response rates for the two years were 16 and 14 percent, respectively.

- **Employment Market Survey**
  Employer Assessment of Current/Future Employment Market for executive, middle management, and professional staff, 1993 and 1994. A joint project of Employment Management Association (EMA) and Thomas Mangum Company (TMI).
  Conducted nationwide of human resources personnel of some 4,000 companies; response rates were 16 and 14 percent for the respective years.

For summaries of these surveys' data, see *99 Minutes to Your Ideal Job*, by William T. Mangum, copyright 1995 by John Wiley & Sons, Inc., ISBN 0-471-11126-0; and "Job Hunters' Survey" and "Hiring Managers' Survey," available from Thomas Mangum Company, 500 E. Del Mar Blvd., No. 19, Pasadena, CA 91101.

Case VII: *What to Do?*

You are the administrator, chief operating officer of a large medical school. You have been informed by your board chair that he has been able to gain major funding from a single giver, a major distiller and brewer, for a center to study and treat alcohol and drug abuse. This would enable the medical school to become far and away the leader for such issues in your geographical region.

- What do you do?
- What are your reasons for doing that?
- What values do those reasons reflect?

Using the Case of *What to Do?*

This is obviously the Faustian bargain, the chance to do good with the powers of evil. This case would be particularly interesting after a discussion of ethics and morality in industry. Try to get a discussion going on the merits of each position. It will be hard to tell where it may lead, but it could be very interesting.

Exercise VII: *Career Strategy*

What is your career goal?
Have you developed a plan to achieve your goal?

The concepts of business strategy can be adapted to help you formulate, implement, and fulfill your own "mission" in life. Your personal strategy should be designed to assess and utilize strengths (and overcome weaknesses), to accurately assess the opportunities and threats in the external environment, to develop, assess, and select from available alternatives, and to establish objectives for implementing your career plan. Finally, you will set milestones to provide evaluative feedback on your strategies for a successful and fulfilling career. Remember, strategic planning is a *process*—you can use this plan as a beginning point to review, renew, or adapt your career strategy during your entire work life. Think of this as a beginning rather than an end product.

Although the specific steps in developing a career strategy may vary, the process usually involves these steps: (1) prepare a personal profile, (2) develop professional goals in the form of a mission statement, (3) analyze the external and internal environment, (4) develop strategic career alternatives based on your analyses, (5) evaluate alternatives; select and defend the one most attractive to you now, (6) develop specific short-range career objectives and action plans, and (7) prepare a set of guidelines and milestones for evaluating your strategic plan as you set it into action.

Use these seven steps as major headings for your written career plan; follow directions and suggestions provided under each heading to follow.

1. Prepare a Professional Profile

The personal profile includes two steps, and the first is the most difficult because it asks you to examine yourself. This self-examination is an essential first step in developing a career strategy. Use the "Personal Goals/Values" to establish a set of priorities for yourself; begin by understanding what you value and what you hope to achieve with your life.

Second, examine those constituencies that shape your values and contribute to your life. What effect will home, church, or friends have on your career plans? For example, if you do not wish to move away from your geographic home, this represents a constraint that will be reflected both in your mission and the alternatives available to you.

2. Develop Professional Goals in the Form of a Mission Statement

Mission statements for organizations usually answer these questions: what business(es) are we in, and what business(es) do we want to be in for the future? Analogous individual questions may be: how am I positioned now, and where do I want these skills/interests to lead me? Answer these questions by focusing on the three aspects of mission development: what service/product do we offer the marketplace? who is our constituency? what is our distinctive competence in the marketplace? In other words, what do you have to offer or hope to offer that distinguishes you from all others? Your mission statement should be broad enough to encompass the activities you anticipate for your life and work, but not so broad as to be applicable to every other person. Begin to focus your interests on products, markets, and competencies you have.

3. Environmental Analysis

External Environment Many factors are beyond organizational control; these same factors are outside your control, but they nevertheless affect your career opportunities. Assess each aspect of the external environment as follows: competition (see *Occupational Outlook Handbook* or similar sources to assess the labor market; see *Industry Surveys* to assess a particular industry of *U.S. Industrial Outlook* for future prospects); economy; geography; technology; demographics (see *American Demographics* or similar sources for information); government rules and regulations.

Analyze these external factors to identify the threats and opportunities for achievement of your mission. If your mission statement focuses on a particular industry, then evaluate the external factors for the industry in this section. Otherwise, evaluate general conditions as they can apply to the general environment for business. Consider how situational conditions may shape opportunities. For example, joining an expanding company usually provides more career opportunities than working for a mature company that is not expected to grow. Similarly, working for a mobile manager means an increased probability that the position of the superior will become vacant; or one might progress along with a competent mobile manager.

While these external factors are listed separately here, we know that they have interactive effects on businesses and they will interact with one another in shaping your career opportunities. Thorough career plans will acknowledge these links. Successful career planning requires a systematic scanning of the environment for opportunities and threats. One has to be concerned about the present as well as forecast the future. Since there are a great many factors that need to be analyzed, planning one's career necessitates being selective and concentrating on those factors critical to personal success.

Internal Environment What are your strengths and weaknesses, given the external environment you face? If the market is competitive, what will make you most attractive? What weaknesses must you address to compete well in a compact market? Assess these strengths and weaknesses on internal dimensions of the firm as follows: marketing; management (including values); production; accounting and finance. Make a list of your strengths and weaknesses in each functional area. The relative importance of these skills differs for the various positions in the organizational hierarchy, with technical skills being very important on the supervisory level and conceptual skills being critical for top managers.

By assessing your weaknesses and strengths, now you are preparing to address them in the objectives and implementation phases of your career plan.

Conclude this section by making an overall assessment of your competencies. Do they match the market you face, and if not, what must you do to fill those gaps?

4. Develop Strategic Alternatives for Your Career

In developing career strategies, several alternatives are available. The most successful strategy would be to build on one's strengths to take advantage of opportunities. For example, if you have an excellent knowledge of computers and many companies are looking for computer programmers, you should find many opportunities for a satisfying career. On the other hand, if you are interested in programming but lack the necessary skills, the proper approach would be a developmental strategy to overcome the weakness and develop these skills in order to take advantage of the opportunities.

Your strategic plan thus far indicates that the market offers specific opportunities and presents threats. In addition, you bring identifiable strengths and weaknesses to that market. A person may have excellent managerial and technical skills but work in a declining company or industry. If this individual wishes to advance, he or she should find employment in an expanding firm or in a growing industry.

Use your environmental analyses to develop two or three viable alternatives for your career. State these alternatives in sentence form, then follow each with a list of the strengths and weaknesses for each alternative. In other words, what makes each attractive or problematic? Be sure that all are viable alternatives, given the market forecast as well as your goals, strengths, and weaknesses.

5. Select an Alternative

This is the part of career planning that most people like least—now you have to decide! Many people do not like making this commitment, fearing that it may limit them. That is true to some extent because every choice eliminates competing alternatives. Moreover, by setting goals we provide a measure by which success or failure can be judged. Sometimes we would rather have things "happen" than acknowledge failure to achieve objectives.

Factors that inhibit goal setting can be used to your advantage. First, as occurs in organizations, performance goals become a part of your personal appraisal process. If you know where you are going and how to get there, then you will be able to recognize and evaluate new opportunities that arise. Second, strategic planning for your career is a process just as it is for organizations. One does not set career goals all at once. Rather, goal setting is a continuing process that allows flexibility; professional goals can be revised in the light of changing circumstances. Another factor that reduces resistance to goal setting is the integration of long-term aims with the more immediate requirement for action. For example, the aim of becoming a doctor makes it easier to study difficult subjects that are necessary for the medical degree.

Strategic choices require tradeoffs. Some alternatives involve high risks, others low risks. Some choices demand action now; other choices can wait. Careers that were glamorous in the past may have an uncertain future. Rational and systematic analysis is just one step in the career-planning process, for a choice also involves personal preferences, personal ambitions, and personal values.

Do your alternatives all pass a consistency test? Are they in line with your preferences, ambitions, and values? Why or why not? Adapt strategies that do not meet the consistency tests.

6. Set Objectives; Action Plan for Implementation

How far in advance should you plan? The answer depends on your goals. Planning should cover a period of time necessary to fulfill the commitments involved in the decision made. Thus, the time frame of your career plan will differ with the circumstances. For instance, if you want to become a university professor, it is necessary to plan for university studies and preparation of seven to nine years. Regardless of your career, your long-term aim has to be translated into short-term objectives.

What are your long-range professional goals? Where do you want to be next year? In five years? In ten years? At retirement, what do you want to have accomplished? How far do you want to advance? How do you want to be remembered? (see Five-Year Projection below for direction).

So far your concern has been with the career direction. But the strategy has to be supported by short-term objectives and action plans that can be a part of the performance appraisal process. Thus, if the aim is to achieve a certain management position that requires a master of business administration degree, the short-term objective may be to complete a number of courses. Here is an example of a short-term verifiable objective: to complete the Business Policy course this semester with a grade of A. This objective is measurable, as it states what will be done, by what time, and the quality of performance (the grade).

How will you implement your career plan? What steps must you take? How much time will it take to implement your career plan? What are your short-term objectives? What detailed action plans will help you reach these objectives? Objectives must be supported by action plans. Continuing with our example, the completion of the management course may require a schedule for attending classes, doing the homework, and obtaining the support of friends and family, whose time with you is interrupted by university responsibilities. As you can see, the long-term strategic career plan needs to be supported by short-term objectives and action plans.

Develop Contingency Plans

Career plans are developed in an environment of uncertainty, and the future cannot be predicted with great accuracy. Therefore, contingency plans based on alternative assumptions should be prepared. While one may enjoy working for a small, fast-growing venture company, it may be wise to prepare an alternative career plan based on the assumption that the venture may not succeed.

If your top career choice is not attainable, what are your other options (given your education, preferences, etc.)? What other career plans do you have?

7. Evaluation of the Career Plan

Once you have articulated career goals, then you can monitor and evaluate your progress toward reaching them. Assuming that you work for a company that has formal evaluation, an opportune time for assessing yearly objectives is at the performance appraisal. This is the time not only to review performance against objectives in the operating area, but also to review the achievement of milestones in the career plan. In addition, progress should be monitored at other times, such as the completion of an important task or project.

Moreover, a career is more than the work you do, but includes other goals important to you. You need to supplement annual performance appraisals with your own schedule of evaluation. How will you monitor your career progress? What factors will you examine? What standards will you use to measure your own performance? How will you know if you are successful? If your interests or other opportunities take you in new directions, when will you revise your career goals?

A career plan doesn't guarantee that you will achieve your goals, any more than a strategic plan guarantees organizational success. What it does provide is a clear set of goals and objectives against which you can assess new opportunities, new challenges, and new directions for fulfilling your mission in life.

CASE VII; EXERCISE VII

Five-Year Projection

Project yourself into the future five (or ten) years. How old will you be in five years? What will your life be like then? How will your personal, family, and career circumstances have changed by that date? Of course, this is a highly imaginative projection, but attempt to be as realistic and objective as possible.

In completing this projection, you will be bothered by two questions repeatedly: (1) Should I describe my future the way I want it to be? or (2) Should I describe my future the way I really think it is going to be?

You will probably allow both factors to enter into your answers. Such a solution is both natural and desirable. This projection is for your benefit.

1. In five (ten) years my age is _____.

2. My occupation is (be as specific as possible) _____.
3. My specific responsibilities are _____.
4. My approximate annual income (or my family's is) _____.
5. My most important personal possessions are _____.
6. My family responsibilities are _____.
7. Of my experiences in the last few years, the most pleasant were _____.
8. Of my experiences in the last few years, the ones that gave me the greatest sense of accomplishment were _____.
9. In the last few years, several dramatic things have happened in my business and/or community that have interested me. Below is a summary of the highlights, including a description of how I was involved in these events _____.
10. In reviewing my "Five-Year Projection," the most important observations I made were _____.

Index

Answers to Exercise Questions on Page 163:

1. Yes, it follows July 3rd; 2. The man is not dead so he cannot be buried; 3. Light the match first; 4. All months have 28 days; 5. One hour. Take one immediately, followed by a second a half-hour later, and the third one hour after the first; 6. Two quarters and a nickel (the question says *one* is not a nickel); 7. No, the man is dead; 8. Twelve; 9. None—Noah was aboard the Ark, not Moses; 10. No, since at the time the coin was made, there was no way for someone to know it was 46 years before Christ was born; Alternate Question A: You don't bury survivors; Alternate Question B: One birthdate; Alternate Question C: Nine; Alternate Question D: Half way (because then it is on the way out).

Answers to Exercise Questions on Page 76:

15—Box of matches; 4—Food concentrate; 6—50 feet of nylon rope; 8—Parachute silk; 13—Portable heating unit; 11—Two .45 caliber pistols; 12—One case dehydrated Pet milk; 1—Two 100 lb. tanks of oxygen; 3—Stellar map of the moon's constellation; 9—Rubber life raft; 14—Magnetic compass; 2—Five gallons of water; 10—Signal flares; 7—First-Aid kit containing injection needles; 5—Solar-powered FM receiver-transmitter.

Credits/Acknowledgments

Cover design by Charles Vitelli

1. Managers, Performance, and the Environment
Facing overview—PhotoDisc, Inc.

2. Planning
Facing overview—TWR photo. 62—Courtesy of Michael Gelb, High Performance Learning.

3. Organizing
Facing overview—IBM Corporation photo.

4. Directing
Facing overview—IBM Microelectronics, photo by Tom Way.

5. Controlling
Facing overview—Digital Stock.

6. Staffing and Human Resources
Facing overview—PhotoDisc, Inc.

7. Perspectives and Trends
Facing overview—United Nations photo.

PHOTOCOPY THIS PAGE!!!*

ANNUAL EDITIONS ARTICLE REVIEW FORM

■ NAME: _____ DATE: _____

■ TITLE AND NUMBER OF ARTICLE: _____

■ BRIEFLY STATE THE MAIN IDEA OF THIS ARTICLE: _____

_____

■ LIST THREE IMPORTANT FACTS THAT THE AUTHOR USES TO SUPPORT THE MAIN IDEA:

_____

_____

_____

_____

■ WHAT INFORMATION OR IDEAS DISCUSSED IN THIS ARTICLE ARE ALSO DISCUSSED IN YOUR TEXTBOOK OR OTHER READINGS THAT YOU HAVE DONE? LIST THE TEXTBOOK CHAPTERS AND PAGE NUMBERS:

_____

_____

_____

_____

■ LIST ANY EXAMPLES OF BIAS OR FAULTY REASONING THAT YOU FOUND IN THE ARTICLE:

_____

_____

_____

_____

■ LIST ANY NEW TERMS/CONCEPTS THAT WERE DISCUSSED IN THE ARTICLE, AND WRITE A SHORT DEFINITION:

_____

_____

_____

_____

*Your instructor may require you to use this ANNUAL EDITIONS Article Review Form in any number of ways: for articles that are assigned, for extra credit, as a tool to assist in developing assigned papers, or simply for your own reference. Even if it is not required, we encourage you to photocopy and use this page; you will find that reflecting on the articles will greatly enhance the information from your text.